FOUNDERS AND FELLOWSHIP

Palmer's Tower, built in 1432: the only surviving part of the medieval College.

FOUNDERS AND FELLOWSHIP

The Early History of Exeter College Oxford, 1314–1592

JOHN MADDICOTT

OXFORD
UNIVERSITY PRESS

OXFORD
UNIVERSITY PRESS

Great Clarendon Street, Oxford, OX2 6DP,
United Kingdom

Oxford University Press is a department of the University of Oxford.
It furthers the University's objective of excellence in research, scholarship,
and education by publishing worldwide. Oxford is a registered trade mark of
Oxford University Press in the UK and in certain other countries

First Edition published in 2014

Impression: 1

Published in the United States of America by Oxford University Press
198 Madison Avenue, New York, NY 10016, United States of America

British Library Cataloguing in Publication Data
Data available

Library of Congress Control Number: 2013948400

ISBN 978-0-19-968951-4

Printed in Great Britain by
Clays Ltd, St Ives plc

Everything passes and vanishes;
Everything leaves its trace;
And often you see in a footstep
What you could not see in a face.

William Allingham (1882)

Preface and Acknowledgements

Founded in 1314, Exeter is the fourth oldest college in the university. Only University College, Balliol, and Merton are older. It is also the only one of these four to have hitherto lacked a modern account of its history. In the past thirty-five years histories of individual Oxford and Cambridge colleges have multiplied, so that they now comprise almost a genre. Oxford has produced some notable exemplars, most of them intended to appeal especially to a mixed readership of old members and professional historians as well as to general readers, and often published to coincide with an anniversary. Besides books on the three oldest colleges, we have had others on Brasenose, Christ Church, Lincoln, Magdalen, and Trinity; and more are in the offing. The present book on Exeter shares the same intended readership and the same celebratory aim, the year of its publication marking the College's 700th anniversary. But it differs in one central and obvious respect from all those mentioned above: it covers just the early part of the College's history, from the foundation to 1592. Here it resembles only one other Oxford history, A. B. Emden's *An Oxford Hall in Medieval Times*, dealing with the early history of St Edmund Hall and published in 1927; though it would be presumptuous to claim kinship with that pioneering work of scholarship, the forerunner of its kind, in any other way.

Some readers will be disappointed (but others perhaps relieved) that the book ends where it does, well before the roots of modern developments in the nineteenth century and before the age of College personalities, famous men, and anecdotes. For this premature termination there are two reasons, one practical, the other more intellectually defensible. First, the sources for medieval and Tudor Exeter are voluminous, probably more so than those for any other college of comparable age with the exception of Merton. More than 250 manuscript account rolls provide information, often entertaining information, on almost every aspect of College life up to the 1560s; and thereafter a further unbroken run of accounts continues into modern times. From these accounts can be extracted the names of the great majority of the fellows—a labour undertaken by Exeter's first historian, C. W. Boase. His groundbreaking if erratic *Register of Exeter College, Oxford*, published in two editions in 1879 and 1894, provides the basis for any prosopographical analysis and has been indispensable for the present work. In addition to the accounts, the manuscript College register supplies an annual record of College business from 1539 onwards, while the archives also contain the large collection of charters and deeds which we might expect to find for any ancient foundation. A further, external, source, the Petre papers in the Essex Record Office, hitherto barely used for Exeter's history, illuminate the relations between the College and its greatest benefactor in an unusually intimate way. To have digested this mass of manuscript material, along with the great quantity of sources already in print, and then to have taken the story up to the present, would have taken more years of work than I have felt able to give to the project. If modern times were to have been surveyed in the same depth as the preceding centuries, the result would have been an inordinately long, and almost certainly unpublishable, book. As it is, I think it may reasonably be said that the present book provides a fuller and more analytical account of one college's history in the medieval and early modern period than any hitherto available.

But the period from 1314 to 1592 also has an internal coherence, justifying its treatment as a single complete span in a larger overarching bridge which remains to be completed. It runs from the time of the College's foundation in 1314 to that of its refoundation by Sir William Petre and of the subsequent working out of the consequences of Petre's intervention. For almost the whole of this period the College took its bearings from Walter de Stapeldon's statutes, which were largely maintained in their integrity until they were superseded by Petre's statutes in 1566. The College's pre-existing catholicism, and its endorsement by Petre in his appointments to fellowships, eventually provoked a protestant and governmental reaction, bringing in a succession of new-broom protestant Rectors who transformed Exeter's fortunes. The book thus covers the years of what might be called catholic (and Stapeldonian) Exeter, until Petre's work brought Exeter's middle ages to an end. Given the salience of both men in the College's history, I have chosen to top and tail the book with fairly full studies of their work. Some parts of these studies—on Stapeldon's political activities, for example, and Petre's religion—may seem like digressions from the College's history *per se*. But the careers, interests, and mentalities of both men had a direct bearing on the sort of college which they wished to create and shape, and for this reason their lives are very much part of its story.

Although that story has had to remain incomplete, the intensive exploitation of a large body of material over a limited period has had some beneficial effects, which I hope may be evident to the reader. In particular, it has allowed me to exploit with reasonable thoroughness some themes which, in the histories of other colleges, have either been more cursorily surveyed or else omitted altogether for want of sources: for example, the College's finances, its responses to economic change, its relations with tenants, visitors, benefactors, and well-wishers, and its coherence as a community. My treatment of these and other themes would have been much the poorer had I not been able to draw on two great works of scholarship which have appeared in the past sixty years: Emden's *Biographical Register of the University of Oxford*, the initial port of call for anyone interested in the careers of the university's members;

and the first three volumes of *The History of the University of Oxford*, initiated by T. H. Aston, and an essential guide to the history of studies, faculties, college life, and much else. My footnotes will make plain my debts to these two authorities, and my bibliography my debts to others. My particular dependence on the published researches of a few earlier historians also deserves a special mention. Besides C. W. Boase, they include among the ancients Anthony Wood and H. E. Salter, and among the moderns Mark Buck, Jeremy Catto, Alan Cobban, and Nicholas Orme. I have been fortunate indeed to have had their work to guide me.

I have also accumulated some more personal and immediate debts. In the first place both the College and I owe a large and particular debt of gratitude to the anonymous benefactor whose generosity has made possible the publication of this book. Frances Cairncross, the College's current Rector, persuaded me to write, overcame my initial diffidence, and has been a source of encouragement throughout. The Governing Body greatly facilitated my use of the College archives. Without its benevolent cooperation the book would have taken twice as long to complete. James Willoughby read and commented on my pages concerning books and libraries, and both he and Richard Sharpe have kindly allowed me to draw on the draft text of the Exeter section from the forthcoming Oxford volume in the Corpus of British Medieval Library Catalogues. Michael Reeve gave invaluable assistance with the translation of a particularly knotty piece of the founder's Latin. Terry Hardaker made his cartographical skills available to me for the production of the book's two maps. Simon Bailey, Paul Brand, Peregrine Hordern, Nicholas Schofield, Richard Sharpe, Peter Spufford, and Paul Slack provided useful information and good advice on particular points. My path through the archives was smoothed by the courteous and helpful staffs of the Devon Record Office, the Essex Record Office, and the Exeter Cathedral archives, and especially by Ellie Jones, the current cathedral archivist. Pursuing possible illustrations has been a particularly daunting task, and here I am very grateful to the Revd Patrick Sherring, vicar of Ingatestone, to Max Carter, chairman of the Ingatestone Camera Club, and to Hugh Palmer, photographer for Exeter College. Others within the College gave me every assistance. Matt Baldwin, in the Development Office, has done sterling service in mastering the publisher's arcane instructions concerning 'artwork', and in preparing the illustrations for transmission to the press: a task beyond me. I am most especially obliged to Alison Dight, bursary officer and Tudor historian, who provided an English summary of a large part of the College register, photographed its pages for my use, and was unfailingly ready to answer a medievalist's questions about Tudor problems. She has greatly speeded the book's progress. Finally, the staff and associates of the Oxford University Press have been models of efficiency and helpfulness: Jenni Crosskey, production editor, Sarah Holmes, commissioning editor, Dorothy McCarthy, proof-reader, and Jackie Pritchard, copy-editor. To each and every one of these, humble and hearty thanks. It goes without saying that for all mistakes I take sole responsibility.

To Hilary, as always, I owe more than I can say.

For kind permission to make use of photographs and other material, I am greatly indebted to the following:

To Lord Petre, for the photograph of the letter signed by the seven Petrean fellows.

To John Blair, for the photograph of the brass of Thomas Plymiswood.

To The Bodleian Libraries, The University of Oxford, for the photograph of Bereblock's drawing of the College, MS Bodl. 13, fo. 12^v.

To Max Carter, for the photograph of Sir William Petre's tomb.

To William Watt, for the photograph of Bishop Stapeldon's tomb.

The quotation from the Thynne Papers, Vol. IV, on page 305 is included by permission of the Marquess of Bath, Longleat House, Warminster, Wiltshire.

John Maddicott

Contents

Colour Plates

Plate 9. The medieval College seal, attached to the deed appropriating the church of Menheniot to the College, 1478. In the upper panel are the Virgin and Child; below them, the kneeling figure of Bishop Stapeldon, flanked by two keys to his left (associated with St Peter, to whom Exeter cathedral is dedicated), and a sword (associated with St Paul) to his right; below again are the College arms, two bendlets wavy, originally borne by Sir Richard de Stapeldon, the founder's brother. The legend reads: 'S. RECTORIS ET SCOLARIUM DE STAPELDON HALL OXON'. This seal was in use from the College's earliest years.

Plate 10. The Rector's account for summer term, 'terminus estivalis', 1375. The first complete section lists receipts, the second, expenditure on the fellows' commons, with their absences from the College, and the third, incomplete, section, expenses (RA, 57).

Plate 11. The building account for the library, 1383. The opening section records the sources of funds. This is followed by expenditure on the purchase of timber, carpenters' wages, stone from Taynton, etc. (RA, 76).

Plate 12. John Bereblock's drawing of the College, 1566. The drawing shows Palmer's Tower, the range of buildings along Somenor's Lane, the chapel (with its cross), and the hall (projecting southwards). The drawing illustrates the very close proximity of the chapel to the residential block along the Lane (Bodleian Library, MS Bodl. 13, part 1, fo. 12ᵛ).

Plate 13. Exeter College, 1578—redrawn from Ralph Agas's map of Oxford. The drawing shows Palmer's Tower, the chapel to its east, and the parallel library and hall (with similarly tiled roofs) to its south. The buildings on the south-west corner of the site are the former Checker Hall, fronting Turl Street, and Peter Hall, fronting Brasenose Lane. Note the city wall, to the north of Somenor's Lane, and the College's relatively new western entrance, opening onto Turl Street.

Plate 14. Loggan's engraved view of the College, 1675. The building opposite the main entrance, with its six lancet windows, is the former medieval library, built in 1383 and by 1675 made into undergraduate rooms. To its left is the medieval chapel, with a large three-lancet west window. Almost opposite the west end of the chapel is Palmer's Tower, and, running eastward from the Tower, 'Rector's Row', occupying the original site of the College.

Plate 15. Portrait of Sir William Petre, aged 61, painted in 1567. The College's purchase of this portrait for £3 6s. 8d., a substantial sum for a painting at this date, is recorded in the accounts: see below, 293. It hangs in the College hall. The artist is unknown.

Plate 16. The master copy of Sir William Petre's statutes, 1566, signed on its final page by William Alley, bishop of Exeter, and by Petre himself, with Petre's seal attached. On the opposite page are various queries arising from the statutes submitted by the Rector and fellows and answered by Petre. The statutes are depicted against the original wooden box, with its metal clasp, in which they have always been housed (ECA, A. I. 2).

Plate 17. The concluding section of the Rector's accounts for 1567–8, signed by John Neale, the Rector, and five other fellows. The signatories include William Paynter, the sub-rector. Account rolls have finally been abandoned and the accounts have now moved into book form, as required by the Petrean statutes, which also called for the accounts to be signed by the Rector, the sub-rector, the dean, and the three senior fellows. The final signatory here is Edmund Lewknor, one of the new Petrean fellows. The novel need for signatures on the accounts emphasizes Petre's concern for probity and good order in financial matters (ECA, A. II. 9, fo. 12ᵛ).

Plate 18. Letter of thanks to Petre from his seven new fellows, 4 July 1566. Bereblock, whose drawing of the College appears as Plate 12, is the second signatory. Of the other signatories, Lewknor, Carter, Howlett, and Rainolds, all proved to be stout catholics (ERO, Petre Papers, D/DP Q13/1/1).

Plate 19. Title page of the works of Eusebius, edited by Erasmus, recording the book's gift from Petre. This is one of a number of books given to the College by Petre. The inscription records the book as the gift of 'Sir William Petre, knight, chancellor of the most noble Order of the Garter, and in the privy counsels of the most illustrious Queen Elizabeth. Anno Domini 1567, in the month of May' (Exeter College Library 9K 1549).

Plate 20. The remains of the College sundial on the south face of Palmer's Tower. This is almost certainly the same sundial which once bore Petre's arms and commendatory verses, maliciously defaced by the College's protestants, c.1583: see below, 314.

Plate 21. The first depiction of the College arms, 1574. The text records the ratification of the arms by Richard Lee, Portcullis herald, during his visitation of Oxford. The arms appear in the first benefactors' book, compiled in that year, and in part intended to record the College's history: see below, 320 (ECA, C. II. 11).

Plate 22. The tomb of Sir William Petre and Lady Anne Petre, Ingatestone church, Essex. Lady Anne was Petre's second wife. The effigies may have been the work of Cornelius Cure, later Queen Elizabeth's master mason, and sculptor of the Westminster abbey monument to Mary Queen of Scots. The College paid for the painting of the Petre effigies in 1591–2: see below, 314.

Maps

Abbreviations

Agrarian History, iii	*The Agrarian History of England and Wales*. Vol. III: *1348–1500*, ed. E. Miller (Cambridge, 1991)
Agrarian History, iv	*The Agrarian History of England and Wales*. Vol. IV: *1500–1640*, ed. J. Thirsk (Cambridge, 1967)
Anstruther	G. Anstruther, *The Seminary Priests*. Vol. I: *Elizabethan* (Durham, 1968)
Boase (1)	C. W. Boase, *Register of the Rectors and Fellows, Scholars, Exhibitioners and Bible Clerks of Exeter College, Oxford* (Oxford, 1879)
Boase (2)	C. W. Boase, *Registrum Collegii Exoniensis: Register of the Rectors, Fellows and other Members on the Foundation of Exeter College, Oxford*, new edn., OHS, xxvii (1894)
BRUO	A. B. Emden, *A Biographical Register of the University of Oxford to A. D. 1500*, 3 vols. (Oxford, 1957–9)
BRUO, 1501–40	A. B. Emden, *A Biographical Register of the University of Oxford, A. D. 1501 to 1540* (Oxford, 1974)
Buck	M. Buck, *Politics, Finance and the Church in the Reign of Edward II: Walter Stapeldon, Treasurer of England* (Cambridge, 1983)
Butcher	A. Butcher, 'The Economy of Exeter College, 1400–1500', *Oxoniensia*, 44 (1979)
CChR	*Calendar of Charter Rolls*
CIPM	*Calendar of Inquisitions Post Mortem*
CPR	*Calendar of Patent Rolls*
CRO	Cornwall Record Office
CRS	Catholic Record Society
D. and C.	Exeter cathedral, Dean and Chapter Archives
Darwall-Smith	R. Darwall-Smith, *A History of University College, Oxford* (Oxford, 2008)
DCRS	Devon and Cornwall Record Society
DRO	Devon Record Office
ECA	Exeter College Archives
EHR	*English Historical Review*
Emmison	F. G. Emmison, *Tudor Secretary: Sir William Petre at Court and Home* (London, 1961)

ERO	Essex Record Office
Green	V. H. H. Green, *The Commonwealth of Lincoln College, 1427–1977* (Oxford, 1979)
HUO, i	*The History of the University of Oxford.* Vol. I: *The Early Oxford Schools*, ed. J. I. Catto (Oxford, 1984)
HUO, ii	*The History of the University of Oxford.* Vol. II: *Late Medieval Oxford*, ed. J. I. Catto and T. A. R. Evans (Oxford, 1992)
HUO, iii	*The History of the University of Oxford.* Vol. III: *The Collegiate University*, ed. J. McConica (Oxford, 1986)
Jones	J. Jones, *Balliol College: A History*, 2nd edn. (Oxford, 1997)
JRIC	*Journal of the Royal Institution of Cornwall*
L. and P.	*Letters and Papers, Foreign and Domestic, of the Reign of Henry VIII*, ed. J. S. Brewer, J. Gairdner, and R. H. Brodie (London, 1862–1932)
Martin and Highfield	G. H. Martin and J. R. L. Highfield, *A History of Merton College* (Oxford, 1997)
ODNB	*Oxford Dictionary of National Biography*
OHS	Oxford Historical Society
PP	Petre Papers, Essex Record Office, D/DP Q13/1/1
Reg.	Exeter College Archives, College Register, 1539–1619
Reg. Brantingham	*The Register of Thomas de Brantyngham, Bishop of Exeter (AD. 1370–1394)*, ed. F. C. Hingeston-Randolph, 2 vols. (London, 1901–6)
Reg. Bronescombe	*The Register of Walter Bronescombe (AD. 1257–80) and Peter Quivil (AD. 1280–91)*, ed. F. C. Hingeston-Randolph (London, 1889)
Reg. Grandisson	*The Register of John de Grandisson, Bishop of Exeter (AD. 1327–1369)*, ed. F. C. Hingeston-Randolph, 3 vols. (London, 1894–9)
Register, ed. Boase	*Register of the University of Oxford.* Vol. I: *1449–63, 1505–71*, ed. C. W. Boase, OHS, i (1885)
Register, ed. Clark	*Register of the University of Oxford.* Vol. II, parts 1–4, ed. A. Clark, OHS, x–xii, xiv (1887–9)
Reg. Lacy	*The Register of Edmund Lacy, Bishop of Exeter, 1420–1455*, ed. G. R. Dunstan, 5 vols., DCRS, new ser., 7, 10, 13, 16, 18 (1963–72)
Reg. Stafford	*The Register of Edmund Stafford (AD. 1395–1419): An Index and Abstract of its Contents*, ed. F. C. Hingeston-Randolph (London, 1886)

Reg. Stapeldon	*The Register of Walter de Stapeldon, Bishop of Exeter (AD. 1307–26)*, ed. F. C. Hingeston-Randolph (London, 1892)
RS	Rolls Series
SA	*Statuta Antiqua Universitatis Oxoniensis*, ed. S. Gibson (Oxford, 1931)
Salter, *Survey*	H. E. Salter and W. A. Pantin, *Survey of Oxford*, 2 vols., OHS, new ser., xiv, xx (Oxford, 1960–9)
SCO	*Statutes of the Colleges of Oxford*, 3 vols. (London, 1853)
Statutes	*The Statutes of Exeter College, Oxford* (London, 1855)
TNA	The National Archives
VCH Oxfordshire, iii	*Victoria County History of Oxfordshire*. Vol. III: The University of Oxford, ed. H. E. Salter and M. D. Lobel (Oxford, 1954)
VCH Oxfordshire, iv	*Victoria County History of Oxfordshire*. Vol. IV: *The City of Oxford*, ed. A. Crossley (Oxford, 1979)
Watson	A. G. Watson, *A Descriptive Catalogue of the Medieval Manuscripts of Exeter College, Oxford* (Oxford, 2000)
Wood, *Athenae*	A. Wood, *Athenae Oxonienses*, 3rd edn., with additions by P. Bliss, 4 vols. (London, 1813–20)
Wood, *Colleges*	A. Wood, *The History and Antiquities of the Colleges and Halls in the University of Oxford*, ed. J. Gutch, 2 vols. (Oxford, 1786–90)
Wood, *History*	A. Wood, *The History and Antiquities of the University of Oxford now first published in English by John Gutch*, 3 vols. (Oxford, 1792–6)

A Note on Money

The monetary unit of a mark is frequently referred to in the text below. One mark is two-thirds of a pound, that is, 13s. 4d.

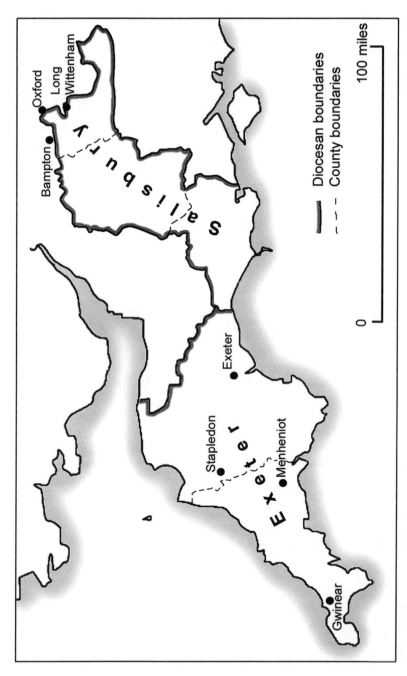

MAP 1. The hinterland of Exeter College

I

Walter de Stapeldon and his College, c. 1260–1326

1. FROM BACKWOODS TO BISHOPRIC VIA OXFORD

The hamlet of Stapledon, where the founder of Exeter College was almost certainly born and brought up, lies in the remote countryside of north-west Devon, about 40 miles north-west of Exeter and about 8 miles from the border with Cornwall.[1] In the middle ages it was a part of the parish of Milton Damerel, whose church stands about 4 miles to the north. Today Stapledon is not much more than a farm and a few houses lying in a hollow at the end of a lane leading off the road from Holsworthy to Okehampton. The land is poor. Heavy clay soils, the product of the notoriously refractory Culm Measures, allow for little besides rough grazing for beef cattle and some low-grade arable cultivation, and much of the local landscape is nowadays given over to the conifers of the Forestry Commission. Barring the conifers, the general economy was not so very different in the middle ages. What arable there was grew oats and rye, suitable for a damp climate and ill-drained soils, but with little value as cash crops and greatly inferior to the wheat and barley cultivated in the lusher climate of south Devon. After the Black Death, when population fell and demand slackened, much of the land was abandoned—a sure sign of its marginal quality. Cattle there always were, but the region's distance from large urban markets must have limited the profitability of all types of farming, arable and pastoral. Far from the booming corn and sheep country of the midlands, East Anglia, and the south-east, it was not a locality where any farmer could expect to make a fortune.[2]

---

[1] 'Stapledon' is the modern spelling of the place-name; 'Stapeldon' is the medieval and generally used spelling of the family name: for example, in Buck's biography and in all literature connected with the College. At the risk of inconsistency I have therefore retained these two different spellings for place and person.

[2] For the agriculture of this region, see H. Fox, 'Medieval Farming and Rural Settlement', in R. Kain and W. Ravenhill (eds.), *Historical Atlas of South-West England* (Exeter, 1999), 273–6; H. Fox, 'The Occupation of the Land: Devon and Cornwall', in *Agrarian History*, iii. 157–8; H. Fox, 'Taxation and Settlement in Rural Devon', *Thirteenth Century England*, 10 (2005), 167, 178–9.

From this unpromising part of the world came a future bishop of Exeter, treasurer of England, and founder of an Oxford college. We do not know when Walter de Stapeldon was born, but we can make a reasonable guess from his first appearance in the records. This came in 1286, when, as a party to a lawsuit, he was described as *magister*, a title rarely borne except by those who had graduated as masters of arts. In Stapeldon's case we know that he had graduated at Oxford, for he tells us so himself, in a document intimately connected with his College's foundation and to which we shall return.[3] The clerk who recorded the plea interlineated his title as though it were an afterthought and not familiarly known, so at this time he may have been a *magister* of no long standing. Since the course leading to the MA stretched over nine years, Stapeldon's début as an Oxford undergraduate must have come about 1277 or perhaps a little earlier; and if he went up at what seems to have been the usual age of 16 or 17 we can place his birth about 1260, in the later years of Henry III's reign.[4]

How Stapeldon got to Oxford is an insoluble mystery. An Oxford education was expensive, and it seems highly unlikely that Walter's parents would have been able to fund his schooling, still less the years of university study necessary for his master's degree. Nothing in the family background suggests wealth. Walter's father, William de Stapeldon, played some part in the social and administrative life of his neighbourhood, but he was never more than an inconspicuous figure, rarely featuring in the sources. He was not a knight and makes only one certain appearance in the records of government—in 1281, when he appeared before the justices at Exeter as one of the jurors for Black Torrington hundred, where his home at Stapeldon lay.[5] This shows only that he was a freeman rather than a villein and that he enjoyed a certain local prominence. More revealing are his other appearances as a witness in local deeds. There are sixteen of these, to all of which members of the Dinham family are parties; and in thirteen of them a leading role is played by Sir Oliver Dinham, head of his family until his death in 1299.[6] Dinham was the most powerful lord in this part of Devon: a loyal supporter of the crown, resident at his great manor of Hartland on the north Devon coast, and in national terms a minor baron, who fought beside Edward I in Wales in 1277 and 1282, and was summoned to parliament in the 1290s.[7] It seems fairly clear from William de

    [3] TNA, JUST 1/1273, m. 11; Buck, 12, 225; below, 35–6.
    [4] For the age of entry to Oxford, see J. I. Catto, 'Citizens, Scholars and Masters', *HUO*, i. 170, and A. Cobban, *English University Life in the Middle Ages* (London, 1999), 19–21.
    [5] TNA, JUST 1/181, m. 47, JUST 1/184, m. 1; Buck, 10 n. 4.
    [6] CRO, Arundell of Lanherne and Trenrice, AR/1/609–12, 614, 615/1 and 2, 617, 623–6, 962/2, 1032, 1053–4. These deeds were formerly at Wardour Castle and are cited by Buck, 12 n. 8, with their Wardour call numbers.
    [7] For the Dinhams, see R. P. Chope, *The Book of Hartland* (Torquay, 1940), 26–37; M. Jones, *The Family of Dinan in England in the Middle Ages* (Dinan, 1987), esp. 26, 32–4; and *The Complete Peerage*, Vol. IV, ed. V. Gibbs and H. A. Doubleday (London, 1916), 369–72.

Stapeldon's witnessing of his charters that Stapeldon *père* filled some minis-
terial role in his entourage, perhaps as a bailiff or other local agent; an
impression strengthened by his once appearing as an attorney for the delivery
of land to Dinham.[8] None of this suggests that William was of much more
than local importance. We should probably place him somewhere between
the upper peasantry and the lower gentry, the sort of man who would later be
called a yeoman or franklin, of some consequence in his parish and hundred,
but of none at all in his county, let alone the wider nation.

We know nothing about William's lands, but it is probably safe to assume
that they did not extend beyond Stapeldon itself. Almost all the woods and
fields featuring in the deeds which he witnessed lay in nearby parishes—
Sheepwash, and Peters Marland in the neighbouring hundred of Shebbear,
and Bradworthy in his own hundred of Black Torrington. The improbability
of a man with such limited horizons having the means to pay his son's way
through Oxford is strengthened by the size of the family which he had to
support. William Stapeldon and his wife Mabel, so named in later provisions
for masses for their souls,[9] had four sons and three daughters. Walter was
almost certainly the eldest of the family. Two of his brothers, Robert and
Richard, were, like Walter himself, especially notable for their subsequent
careers. Robert, like Walter, graduated at Oxford, where by 1305 he was
professor of civil law and principal of Checker Hall, standing near the site of
Exeter's present Turl Street entrance and later to be absorbed by the College.[10] That Robert as well as Walter should have had a distinguished Oxford
record only deepens the mystery of what made this initially possible. Richard,
the third brother, appears to have risen far and fast on Walter's coat-tails and
was often associated with him, not least in the founding of his College. He
was a knight by 1314, when he represented Devon and Cornwall in parliament; lord of the manor of Stapeldon in 1316, by which time he had built up a
considerable estate not only in the neighbourhood of Stapeldon but also in
Cornwall; and a man intermittently involved in the administration of his
county. The two brothers often acted together to acquire property, and
Walter's high position at court and in the county probably did much to secure
his brother's promotion. When he died about 1332 he was buried beneath a
grand tomb in Exeter cathedral famous for its sculptured carving of his
esquire holding his master's horse.[11]

The remaining members of the family were of less consequence. Thomas,
the fourth brother, entered the church, held a series of livings in Devon and
Cornwall, amassed property, became a canon of Exeter, and was buried in the

---

[8] CRO, AR/1/626.   [9] *Reg. Stapeldon*, 339; Buck, 10.
[10] Buck, 27; Salter, *Survey*, i. 52–3; below, 141–2.
[11] Buck, 19–27; M. Swanton (ed.), *Exeter Cathedral: A Celebration* (Exeter, 1991), 162 (where
Richard is misnamed Robert).

cathedral in 1342. His career too probably owed much to his eldest brother. The three sisters, Douce, Mabel, and Joan, all made local marriages, presenting Walter with some eleven nephews and nieces, whose interests again he helped to foster. Two of his nephews, Thomas and Richard, sons of Douce, were given prebends in Stapeldon's cathedral.[12] It is rarely possible to say much about emotional ties in the middle ages, but the Stapeldon family looks to have been an especially close-knit one, with Walter, its oldest and most illustrious member, at its head and centre. But Walter himself looked upwards and backwards to his parents. The one morsel of solid information which we have about their relationship comes from the arrangements made by Stapeldon in 1322 for the celebration of a posthumous anniversary mass on 11 February each year, on which day, so his parents had told him, he had been born (but in what year he frustratingly fails to tell us).[13] When he founded his College he made provision in his statutes of 1316 for the College chaplain to say regular masses for his soul and for those of his parents and benefactors.[14] That his affection for his parents was unusually strong, and more than a matter of conventional *pietas*, is suggested by their burial at Exeter, either outside or more probably inside the cathedral: Mabel, his mother, in 1307 and William, his father, in 1309.[15] This was an exceptional honour for two very ordinary lay people, only vicariously distinguished as the parents of the current bishop, who might have been expected to lie together in Milton Damerel churchyard rather than in the shadow of the cathedral.

Though Stapeldon may have owed much to his parents and acknowledged his debt to them, it seems unlikely that he also owed them anything for his education. But if family help was not available, support must have come from a patron, for these were the only two resources open to boys and young men aspiring to a university education. Who might such a patron have been? There are some indications that we should look in the direction of the Dinham family, towards whom Stapeldon's early preferment in the church is the most significant pointer. In September 1294, and again in 1297, he is named as rector of Aveton Giffard, a village in the fertile country of the South Hams between Plymouth and the Dart estuary in south Devon.[16] This was the first ecclesiastical appointment which we know him to have held, perhaps some eight or nine years after his coming down from Oxford. The then lord of the manor, who must have presented Stapeldon to the living, was Sir Robert Dinham.[17] Robert's relationship to the head of the family, Sir Oliver Dinham,

---

[12] Buck, 28–35; *Death and Memory in Medieval Exeter*, ed. D. Lepine and N. Orme, DCRS, 47 (2003), 108.

[13] *Reg. Stapeldon*, 375, 377; Buck, 12.   [14] *Reg. Stapeldon*, 305.

[15] *Death and Memory*, ed. Lepine and Orme, 107–8.

[16] *CPR, 1292–1301*, 93, 271; Buck, 13.

[17] *CChR, 1257–1300*, 341; *CIPM*, ii, nos. 177, 205; C. C. Shaw, *A History of the Parish of Aveton Giffard* (Kingsbridge, c.1966), 29–30.

is nowhere stated. But the two men were often in each other's company, serving together in Wales in 1277, for example,[18] and the likelihood is that Robert was Oliver's younger brother. At this time presentation to a first living often provides a vital clue to the presentee's main benefactor, a patron in all senses, and we may take it that this was the case with Sir Robert Dinham. Here we might both recall the links between Walter's father, William, and Sir Oliver Dinham, and go on to note another connection. Before he became bishop, Stapeldon had already struck up a close relationship with Hartland abbey, as the abbey's advocate or legal representative, and after his death his services were gratefully acknowledged by the abbey. The abbey's patron was Oliver Dinham, lord of Hartland, whose position allowed him to approve abbatial elections among other things, and it is not too speculative to see him commending the family's protégé to the canons of Hartland, thus equipping them with an able legal defender and at the same time putting some lucrative business in Stapeldon's direction.[19] It is no more than a further straw in the wind that after Stapeldon's death two valuable silver jugs bearing the arms of Dinham were found among his many possessions.[20]

This is all regrettably inconclusive. There is no evidence that either Robert or Oliver Dinham had any interest in education, still less that their patronage took Stapeldon first to school and then to Oxford. Yet the links between the Stapeldons and the Dinhams were seemingly close, despite their social distance. Robert Dinham certainly did Walter de Stapeldon a good turn in presenting him to Aveton Giffard, and no other potential patrons are in sight. We might construct a scenario in which the Dinhams spotted the precocious abilities of the two Stapeldon boys—for Robert as well as Walter went to Oxford—from a family in their service and pushed them forward; yet it would remain no more than a construction. In other similar cases the local priest, or possibly the local bishop, might take a hand in giving clever boys their opportunities, but in the case of the Stapeldons there is nothing to show this. All we can know for certain is that, somehow, Walter de Stapeldon got to Oxford.

To have done so he must already have had a good prior education. Teaching in thirteenth-century Oxford was conducted wholly in Latin, and fluency in the language was a necessity for all those starting out as undergraduates. It would be all the better for them if they had some grounding in logic, since logic underlay the whole syllabus. Teaching in both could be had at a grammar school, where instruction in Latin grammar covered not only genders and declensions of nouns, conjugation of verbs, and so on, but also, by

---

[18] *CPR, 1272–81*, 189. Cf. *Reg. Bronescombe*, 362; CRO, AR/1/611, 614, 615/1 and 2, 625.
[19] Buck, 34–5 and n. 211; S. Wood, *English Monasteries and their Patrons in the Thirteenth Century* (Oxford, 1955), 31, 48, 165.
[20] *Reg. Stapeldon*, 569.

Stapeldon's time, the signification of words, the so-called 'modistic grammar'.[21] It seems likely that Stapeldon acquired this basic training in Devon, possibly at Exeter, where a grammar school had existed since the twelfth century, if the money could have been found to allow him to board there.[22] But there may have been other more local schools, at Holsworthy or Barnstaple or Okehampton, about which we know nothing. Oxford itself remains a more remote possibility, for there too grammar schools were to be found.[23]

When Stapeldon went up to Oxford about 1277 he entered a university which, it goes without saying, was almost unimaginably different from its modern successor. By providing a higher education for the talented young they resemble each other only in the broadest of ways. Since Stapeldon's Oxford training shaped his whole subsequent career and did much to determine the nature of the College which he founded in 1314, nearly forty years after his own matriculation, it is worth saying a little about the sort of university which he entered as a young man. Late thirteenth-century Oxford probably had about 1,500 to 2,000 students. Many of them, perhaps most, would have received the first tonsure (one reason why there were so many university barbers), giving them access to the privileges which minor clerical orders conferred and putting them on the road to priestly ordination.[24] There were no formal procedures for admission. The aspiring undergraduate simply had to find a resident master of arts who would accept him and enter him on the master's roll or *matricula* (hence 'matriculation'); though no doubt acceptance would depend on the would-be student showing that he had the qualifications for study.[25] He might then move into lodgings as a rent-paying boarder, but he would be more likely to find a place in a hall. The number of Oxford halls at this time is unknown, but there were probably at least a hundred, each under the direction of a *magister*, who supervised the teaching and general welfare of his charges. Robert de Stapeldon, Walter's brother and principal of Checker Hall in 1305, was one such. The master was generally a tenant, often renting his property from a local monastic house, and paying his way from the fees that he received from his students. The hall, essentially a large town house, provided eating facilities and accommodation, with three or four students usually sharing a room. Some halls had a further room for the master's lectures. In all these ways the hall resembled a college. The essential difference was that the hall, unlike the college, had no endowment; it was

[21] N. Orme, *Medieval Schools from Roman Britain to Renaissance England* (New Haven, 2006), 86–127. For 'modistic grammar', see Orme, *Medieval Schools*, 96. Cf. J. M. Fletcher, 'The Faculty of Arts', *HUO*, i. 373.

[22] N. Orme, *Education in the West of England, 1066–1548* (Exeter, 1976), 42–8.

[23] *VCH Oxfordshire*, iii. 40–3; Orme, *Medieval Schools*, 245; Catto, 'Citizens, Scholars', *HUO*, i. 170.

[24] Catto, 'Citizens, Scholars', *HUO*, i. 155–6; Cobban, *English University Life*, 3.

[25] Catto, 'Citizens, Scholars', *HUO*, i. 188; Cobban, *English University Life*, 7.

hardly more than a hall of residence. A college, on the other hand, had an endowment provided by its founder, which gave its students a modest income and other material support.[26] But college students were in a tiny minority. At the time of Stapeldon's arrival there were only three colleges, Merton, University College, and Balliol, the latter two barely beyond the inchoate stage of early beginnings, and as yet negligible in their impact on the wider university. It was as a member of a hall, its name and location unknown, that Stapeldon almost certainly spent his student years.

As far as can be seen, which is not very far, Oxford students came from relatively unexalted backgrounds—sons of the gentry, minor landholders, and the professional classes.[27] Stapeldon would have been in good company. For all such men, the costs of study would have been quite large, and in some cases intolerably so. Money had to be found for lecture fees (lecturers were paid directly by their students), hall fees, books, maintenance, and eventually for degree fees, which were particularly heavy.[28] This was one reason why so many undergraduates dropped out before completing their degrees: perhaps as many as half those who came up. But a further reason lay in the difficulties posed by the course of study, which was long, onerous, and intellectually taxing. Students would normally start out in the faculty of arts, from which a very few graduates would go on to higher degrees in canon and civil law, theology, and medicine.[29] The arts course, followed by Stapeldon, was divided into two parts, with the BA degree taking four years and the MA a further three, with a further two years to be spent lecturing as a 'regent master'. For the BA the undergraduate studied the trivium—logic, grammar, and rhetoric—and for the MA the quadrivium, comprising arithmetic, geometry, astronomy, and music. The basis of the whole course was a firm grounding in Aristotelian logic, for which the key texts were the *Prior* and *Posterior Analytics*, supplemented by Aristotelian philosophy in general. The sort of problem to which the novice was exposed might be that of equivocation, 'the fallacy committed when a word has different senses in the different numbers of a syllogism': *Whatever runs has legs; the Seine runs; therefore the Seine has legs.*[30] The teaching largely took the form of lectures on the set texts and of oral disputations, all, of course, in Latin; and since books were in short

[26] C. H. Lawrence, 'The University in Church and State', *HUO*, i. 121–2; Catto, 'Citizens, Scholars', *HUO*, i. 175–83; J. R. L. Highfield, 'The Early Colleges', *HUO*, i. 225–31.
[27] Catto, 'Citizens, Scholars', *HUO*, i. 168–9; Cobban, *English University Life*, 6.
[28] Catto, 'Citizens, Scholars', *HUO*, i. 170–3; J. Dunbabin, 'Careers and Vocations', *HUO*, i. 568–70; Cobban, *English University Life*, 35–42.
[29] The best outline of the arts course will be found in Fletcher, 'Faculty of Arts', *HUO*, i. 372–92, from which the remainder of this paragraph and the following paragraph largely derive.
[30] Fletcher, 'Faculty of Arts', *HUO*, i. 376; P. O. Lewry, 'Grammar, Logic and Rhetoric, 1220–1320', *HUO*, i. 407. The definition of 'equivocation' is that of the *OED*.

supply and there was no university library, the system placed a premium upon a quick understanding and an accurate memory.

It seems to have been assumed that most students, having qualified for the BA by residence, attendance at lectures, and participation in disputations, would proceed to the MA course. For this the aspiring *magister* was expected to offer lectures in order to supplement his qualification for the BA, to attend further lectures given by masters, and to dispute effectively both with fellow students and with a senior scholar, who, having taken his MA, was now obliged to teach. The student would be obliged to defend propositions of his own against opponents and, on other occasions, to attack his opponents' propositions. Qualification for the MA depended on completing the course, securing the commendation of the student's master, and gaining the broader backing of fourteen other masters, who were expected to testify to the student's knowledge and religious beliefs. The new *magister*, having incepted—that is, entered formally upon his mastership—at the end of his third year, was then obliged to lecture and dispute as a regent master for a further two years. At that point he would have to decide on a career: either to remain in the arts faculty and to continue to teach, or to proceed to a higher degree, or to leave the university and seek a benefice. The last of these was the course followed by most new *magistri*—Stapeldon among them.

These dry details describe an academic programme that was arduous in the extreme. No wonder that so many students dropped out or that inception as a master was regarded as a high achievement, often celebrated by a great and expensive feast.[31] To style this education 'a process of mind-sharpening rather than mind-broadening' is perhaps to depreciate its intellectual outcomes.[32] Anyone graduating as a *magister*, like Stapeldon, would have learnt to think logically and precisely, to argue rationally, to detect and rebut errors in the arguments of others, and to make those fine distinctions which were and are a mark of intellectual ability. He would also have shown determination and commitment in striving for so long towards what must often have seemed a distant goal on what must often have been barely adequate resources. The graduate *magistri* who emerged from this gruelling process were members of a small intellectual elite, thought, in the words of the university's later bidding prayer, to be 'duly qualified for the service of God in church and state'.

Stapeldon venerated Oxford and was sharply aware of how much he owed to the university. From his earliest youth, he later said in the endowment charter for his College, the university had 'brought me on in the study of letters, nurtured me...and when she had finished nurturing me secured, albeit undeservedly, my advancement'.[33] Yet after his coming down from Oxford about 1286 that advancement was hardly rapid, at least in the church.

[31] Catto, 'Citizens, Scholars', *HUO*, i. 190.
[32] Dunbabin, 'Careers and Vocations', *HUO*, i. 565; cf. 573.   [33] Buck, 225; below, 35.

The rectory of Aveton Giffard, worth some £9 a year and held from 1294 or earlier until Stapeldon resigned the living some time after his election as bishop in 1307, provided one source of income.[34] But Stapeldon is unlikely to have resided there for long, if at all, and it is probable that the parish work was undertaken by a deputed vicar. His main base was Exeter; and there is just enough information to show something of his progress in the affairs of the cathedral, the see, and the city, but not enough to throw light on the mechanism of his ascent. What information there is comes late. By 1300 he was acting as official (a formal title) to the bishop, Thomas Bitton: in effect, the bishop's right-hand man, deputizing for him in the work of the diocese whenever necessary. A year later he is first mentioned in the records as a canon, though his prior appearance in the senior role of Bitton's official suggests that he was securely established in the cathedral, probably as a canon, well before this. And in 1305 he was chosen as cathedral precentor, the leading cathedral dignitary after the dean, charged with the oversight of the choir.[35]

By this time, however, he had returned to Oxford to study for a higher degree in civil law (that is, Roman law). His second period at the university forms a mysterious interlude in his life, whose importance for his subsequent career was out of all proportion to our slight knowledge of it. That knowledge derives from one source: the record, preserved in an Exeter cathedral manuscript, of a longstanding quarrel between Stapeldon and the Dominican friars of Exeter. The quarrel was terminated in April 1306, when we are told that Stapeldon, already a professor of civil law, was residing in Oxford 'for the purpose of study' and about to incept in both canon and civil law: two subjects closely related and normally studied together.[36] The course in civil law usually took four to six years to complete, and Stapeldon may therefore have been absent from Exeter since about 1300, though we know of long periods of absence only from 1305.[37] He was evidently well set up in Oxford by then, for the location of his peace-making with the Dominicans was 'the hall of the said Master Walter at La Oriole of Oxford'. Stapeldon was thus seemingly the principal of an Oxford hall and presumably drawing an income from its students. The hall's character is especially interesting. 'La Oriole' was a large house, expensive to rent and probably one of the most desirable local properties, standing on the present site of the south-east corner of Oriel College.[38] Its landlord was James of Spain, himself an Oxford *magister*, the illegitimate son of King Alfonso X of Castile, nephew of Edward I's former

[34] Buck, 13, 31; *Reg. Bronescombe*, 412.   [35] Buck, 14–15, 17.
[36] A. G. Little and R. C. Easterling, *The Franciscans and Dominicans of Exeter* (Exeter, 1927), 45, 76–9; L. E. Boyle, 'Canon Law before 1380', *HUO*, i. 538–9. For the substance of the quarrel with the Dominicans, see Buck, 15–17.
[37] J. L. Barton, 'The Study of Civil Law before 1380', *HUO*, i. 525; Buck, 17–18.
[38] C. L. Shadwell and H. E. Salter, *Oriel College Records* (Oxford, 1926), 114–15.

queen Eleanor, a pluralist on a large scale, and possibly an old acquaintance of Stapeldon's, for among his many ecclesiastical offices was a canonry of Exeter, held from 1283 to 1300.[39] In Stapeldon's tenancy of this grand house, rented from such a conspicuous figure, we catch a glimpse of his rising prosperity and of the web of connections with the wider world, beyond his diocese and his university, with which he was beginning to be caught up.

Stapeldon's doctorate in Roman law was more than another academic trophy. Founded upon the Justinianic *Code* and *Digest*, the study of Roman law, entailing as it did 'the application of theoretical principles to practical situations', gave its practitioners the entrée to royal service and so potentially to considerable wealth.[40] Knowledge of Roman law was what would nowadays be called a transferable skill. Edward I had used civil lawyers to argue the case for his sovereignty over Scotland, and from the 1290s they were regularly employed, as Stapeldon would be, to represent the king's interests on embassies and at the papal curia. For matters such as the negotiation of treaties and the settlement of international disputes, their technical expertise was essential, especially in dealings with the *parlement* of Paris, the French central court, which used civil law procedure.[41] To judge by his subsequent career in Edward II's service, Stapeldon's own expertise, deriving from his Oxford degree, was exceptional. It comes as no surprise that the large collection of books found in his palace at Exeter after his death was dominated by works on civil and canon law, including a copy of the *Digest*, 'bought at Oxford', and worth the very large sum of 6 marks.[42]

There is a piquant contrast between the broad horizons opened up by Stapeldon's doctorate in civil law and his concurrent activities on a more local stage. From the early 1290s he began to emerge as a man of property in Devon. He acquired a number of houses and rents in Exeter, and his admission as a freeman in 1300, at the instance of the mayor and community, implies that he already cut a figure in the city and may have done it some notable service. More surprising was his rising status as a rural landholder, on a fairly modest scale, it is true, but on one much larger than that of his father. His first known acquisition of land, in the hundred of Shebbear, came in 1291. At some point he had taken a lease on the manor of Milton Damerel, which included the family home at Stapledon, before giving up his tenancy in 1300; while in 1306, at just the time when he was incepting in civil law at Oxford, he acquired a valuable property in Cornwall from his brother Richard and Richard's wife Joan, perhaps paying as much as 200 marks for it. In 1304 he

[39] *BRUO*, iii. 1736–8; Catto, 'Citizens, Scholars', *HUO*, i. 175; Highfield, 'Early Colleges', *HUO*, i. 238.

[40] Dunbabin, 'Careers and Vocations', *HUO*, i. 573–4.

[41] Dunbabin, 'Careers and Vocations', *HUO*, i. 582–7; G. P. Cuttino, *English Diplomatic Administration, 1259–1339*, 2nd edn. (Oxford, 1971), 141–4.

[42] *Reg. Stapeldon*, 563–5.

had been litigating over other property in south Devon. The impression of growing wealth is confirmed by his purchase of a valuable north Devon wardship, that of Richard Merton, in 1300. He was a man on the make.[43]

Where did his money come from? His rectory at Aveton Giffard, by no means a rich living, was worth only about £9 a year, as we have seen, and his canonry at Exeter only £4.[44] But he clearly possessed some marketable talents which may have proved more lucrative. His service as advocate for Hartland abbey, both before and after he became bishop, will not have gone unrewarded: the canons of the house subsequently wrote of his acting 'with foresight, prudence and judiciousness' and providing them with counsel and aid in their affairs.[45] He may have filled a similar role for Torre abbey in south Devon, whose monks appointed him as their proctor to attend a church council at St Paul's in December 1302. The proximity of Stapeldon's home to some north Devon parishes in which Torre had extensive interests—Bradworthy, Shebbear, and Sheepwash—and the consequent possibility that Stapeldon might act as their local protector, may have been one factor which drew them together.[46] Perhaps his legal expertise also lay behind the favour shown to him by the city fathers at Exeter. We begin to get our first intimations that Stapeldon was a good man of business, and one whose abilities were enabling him to weave a network of useful local associations. The same deductions might also be drawn from his dealings in property. But there is other evidence to suggest that he may also have strengthened his position in more questionable ways. In 1305 one William Prodhomme complained that Walter and his brother Richard had imprisoned him until he had agreed to grant them all his lands in two places in the neighbourhood of Exeter.[47] Neither the truth of the complaint nor its outcome is known. But intimidation and disregard for the law were to feature prominently in Stapeldon's later career, and his local rise may have owed something, perhaps much, to the same methods.

The contrast between the large opportunities opened to Stapeldon by his degree in civil law, and his more mundane wheelings and dealings with friends, neighbours, and possibly enemies in Devon may now seem more apparent than real.[48] Both his decision to return to Oxford to read for a higher degree, and his west country activities, marked him out as a man of ambition,

[43] Buck, 13–14; *Exeter Freemen, 1266–1967*, ed. M. M. Rowe and A. M. Jackson, DCRS, Extra Ser., I (1973), 6.

[44] Buck, 13, 48, 53; N. Orme, *Exeter Cathedral: The First Thousand Years, 400–1500* (Exeter, 2009), 94–5.

[45] Buck, 35 n. 11.

[46] Buck, 13; *Councils and Synods*, II. ii, ed. F. M. Powicke and C. R. Cheney (Oxford 1964), 1222, 1224–5; D. Seymour, *Torre Abbey* (Exeter, 1977), 171–92.

[47] *CPR, 1301–7*, 355; Buck, 22; below, 25–6.

[48] One of his enemies may have been William Martin, a leading Devon landholder and a powerful local magnate. Martin backed the Exeter Dominicans in their quarrel with Stapeldon in

aware of his capabilities, of where they might lead, and of the influence which he could wield for others' advantage and his own. The new possibilities now opening before him were shown by the first peak in his upward progress, which came with his election to the bishopric of Exeter on the death of Bishop Bitton in 1307. He was elected on 13 November 1307 by a large majority of the cathedral chapter: fifteen of the twenty-one canons voted for him, while none of the other candidates attracted more than three votes. Although the election was challenged by a local and litigious clerical malcontent, Richard Plympstoke, the challenge was fought off. Stapeldon was enthroned in December 1307 and received the temporalities of his see from the king in March 1308.[49] He was to remain as bishop for nearly twenty years.

It is not hard to see why Stapeldon's candidature for the bishopric should have been so favoured. His qualifications were manifold. Unlike many thirteenth-century bishops, he was no outsider in his see, but a local man, already a member of the chapter, and with diocesan experience as Bitton's official which had familiarized him with the bishop's role. His academic prowess was proof enough of his intelligence and of his capacity for work, and made him an ornament of his cathedral, of whom any electing body could be proud. He was described in the contemporary record of his election as 'a man of great merit, as one who after long studies in letters ... was found worthy to deserve a doctorate in canon law'.[50] Nor can it have come amiss that Stapeldon had already attracted the attention of the king. In June 1306, within two months of his receiving his Oxford doctorate, Edward I had appointed him as a member of an embassy to France, possibly dispatched in connection with Prince Edward's investiture with Aquitaine.[51] Although it is not known whether he took part, the appointment itself was a mark both of the immediate rewards to be gained from his Oxford studies in civil law and of his having come to the king's notice. After Edward I's death in November 1307 the new king, Edward II, maintained his father's regard for Stapeldon by backing him strongly against his antagonist, Plympstoke. Cathedral chapters were often subject to royal interference, usually in the interests of clerks and ministers for whom the king wanted canonries and other offices, and any bishop who could deflect and deter such interference would have been seen as an asset.

These were all good reasons for Stapeldon's election. But, above all perhaps, the chapter saw him as a potentially able and energetic pastor and leader, possessing the personal, professional, and academic qualities needed to defend the see's rights, administer its property vigorously, and represent it effectively in the king's counsels—no saint but, more usefully, a practical man of business.

1301; Stapeldon lost a land plea against Martin in 1304; and Martin supported Prodhomme's complaint alleging false imprisonment by the Stapeldon brothers in 1305: Buck, 14–15, 22.

[49] Buck, 38–47.   [50] Buck, 47.   [51] Buck, 18.

2. THE SERVICE OF STATE AND CHURCH, 1307–22

When Stapeldon became bishop of Exeter in 1307 he was about 47 years old, well into middle age and, as it turned out, more than two-thirds of the way through his life. Yet it is only at this comparatively late stage in his career that we can begin to chart his doings with any fullness. We have seen how fragmentary is our information on his early life. We do not know how he got to Oxford or when he was ordained or when he became a canon of Exeter. Between his first appearance as a *magister* in 1286 and his first recorded acquisition of land in 1291 nothing at all is known about him. But with his election to the see came a much more public role, creating a correspondingly larger body of sources. Stapeldon's episcopal register now provides a full account of his ecclesiastical activities, while the records of royal government show something of his new career as a politician and royal minister. If we cannot always discern the springs of his actions, we can at least say what his actions were.

Stapeldon's period as bishop coincided almost precisely with the reign of Edward II: Edward came to the throne some four months before Stapeldon's election in November 1307 and was deposed some four months after his murder in October 1326. The reign was marked by political upheavals, violent conflict, and disasters both natural and man-made hard to parallel in the history of medieval England. Much yet by no means all of this was the fault of the king. Edward inherited from his father a failing and expensive Scottish war, but his abilities were no match for his difficult legacy. His patronage of favourites, first the parvenu Piers Gaveston and then, later in the reign, the two Hugh Despensers, father and son, alienated his magnates and produced a demand for political change which resulted in the reforming code known as the Ordinances, drafted by a party of bishops and barons in 1310–11. Gaveston was finally executed by a magnate faction in 1312, producing a feud between the king and his cousin Thomas, earl of Lancaster, judged by Edward to have been responsible for Gaveston's death, which lasted until Lancaster's own execution after a brief civil war in 1321–2. The ongoing war with Scotland culminated, but did not end, with the utter humiliation of defeat at Bannockburn in 1314. This was followed by a three-year period of harvest failure and famine which resulted in many thousands of deaths. As the famine eased, open political conflict returned with the rise of the younger Despenser, the supreme influence at court from 1322 until the revolution which overthrew both men (and Stapeldon) in 1326. Although factional conflict was not continuous, since Edward's patronage allowed him to buy support and supremacy, it provided the reign's dominant note. It was the product of a king lacking the political nous and managerial skills needed to create consensus, dogged by repeated and expensive failure in war, and personally incapable of either efficient government or effective military leadership. The violence which had resulted in Gaveston's execution and then in Lancaster's reached its climax in 1326, when an invasion from France, led by Edward II's queen Isabella and her lover Roger Mortimer, and a popular rising in London, brought the whole regime to a bloody end.

In the years before he became treasurer in 1320, Stapeldon's role in the disturbed politics of Edward II's reign is not easy to judge.[52] His election drew him unavoidably into public life, for as bishop he now received a summons to every parliament and so had to spend time outside his diocese, usually in London. He was always a royalist, but in his early years as bishop he appears to have stood on the sidelines of politics. He did not always attend parliament, sending his brother Robert as his proctor in 1308 and 1309 (and his general use and promotion of his family was still more marked after he became bishop than it had been previously).[53] He nevertheless benefited from Edward's patronage, receiving a grant of markets and fairs on four of his episcopal manors in 1309 and a second royal favour, at the instance of Gaveston, in 1310. He took part in the election of the Ordainers in 1310, but his good relations with the king, and perhaps with the favourite, may help to explain why he himself was not among the reformers. From about 1311 there is growing evidence of his political weight and of his importance to Edward. He first witnessed a royal charter in September 1311—a new mark of his presence and standing at court. He received further favours about this time; he attended every parliament from 1313 onwards; and in September 1314, shortly after Bannockburn, he was one of three men chosen to open parliament in the king's absence. By 1315 he was active on the council, and he became a sworn member of the new council established at the Lincoln parliament of January 1316. He was a regular attender at court and at three royal assemblies in 1317, along with a group of magnates who stood particularly close to the king and at a time when Edward's relations with Thomas of Lancaster were deteriorating rapidly. All the signs point to his increasingly royalist alignment. But to keep these activities in perspective we should remember that it was towards the end of this phase of his career that he established his new college: in April 1314 Stapeldon Hall received its first endowment; in October 1315 Stapeldon bought the first buildings on the present site for its scholars' accommodation; and in April 1316 he drew up its statutes.[54] Politics was only one of the several different worlds in which he moved.

The bare record of Stapeldon's activities shows his rising influence, but does little to explain it. As usual with medieval politicians who do not feature in contemporary chronicles, the roots of place and power may seem to be

[52] Unless otherwise stated, all the information in this paragraph derives from Buck, 121–2, 127–9.
[53] *Reg. Stapeldon*, 311, 416.   [54] Below, 32–6.

obscure. Yet in Stapeldon's case we can do something to uncover them. Apart from his general willingness to work for a king who was in need of friends rather than favourites, Stapeldon's usefulness lay in his diplomatic expertise, and this in turn rested on his Oxford training in civil law. The main problems which diplomacy might solve, or at least ameliorate, lay in relations with France.[55] England and France had been at war between 1294 and 1303, and the war had left a legacy of uncertainty and dispute. One issue lay in the claims of both sides for losses incurred during the conflict. Another, more long term and more serious, grew from the feudal status of Gascony, held since 1259 by the king of England, as duke of Aquitaine, from the king of France. That this allowed Gascons with grievances to appeal over the head of the king-duke to the Paris *parlement* was a constant source of friction. Add to this volatile combination the particular succession of a run of short-lived French kings, Louis X (1314–16), Philip V (1316–22), and Charles IV (1322–8), which occasioned, at each accession, a demand for homage from Edward II for his Gascon territories and in recognition of French lordship, and it becomes easy to see why Edward stood in need of all that diplomacy might offer.

Stapeldon was peculiarly well equipped to serve him here. It was not only that the issues of diplomacy, especially the question of reparations and the dealings with the Paris *parlement* occasioned by the Gascon problem, demanded the ability to ground arguments on civil law; the rules for arbitration too, for example, were borrowed from this source.[56] Stapeldon also had useful personal contacts, their origins obscure, with the French royal house, invoking the help of the French king Philip IV in his rebuttal of Plympstoke's challenge to his election in 1307–8.[57] We have seen that his initiation into royal diplomacy may have come as early as 1306, when he was appointed to serve on a mission to Gascony, but it was not for several more years that his services were called on again.[58] In 1310 and 1311 he was appointed to act on embassies overseas, to Gascony and to the church council at Vienne, but on neither occasion did he go. In 1312 he and other legal experts were called on to prepare the case for the defence of the king's Gascon interests in the *parlement*, and in the next six years he took part in six diplomatic missions, five of them to France. The most notable was that of 1315, when Stapeldon and the earl of Pembroke were sent to the French court on business arising from the Anglo-French treaty of 1303 and from the interminable question of Gascon appeals. It is interesting to find that Stapeldon, and not his high-ranking

[55] On Anglo-French relations, see Cuttino, *English Diplomatic Administration*, 62–100; and M. Prestwich, *Plantagenet England, 1225–1360* (Oxford, 2005), 302–3.

[56] Cuttino, *English Diplomatic Administration*, 82–3.

[57] *Reg. Stapeldon*, 12; Buck, 40.

[58] Unless otherwise stated, all the information in the remainder of this paragraph is drawn from Buck, 122–7.

aristocratic colleague, acted as spokesman for the English party, and that the negotiations culminated in a 'business dinner', when bishop and earl were entertained by the new French king, Louis X.[59] He had travelled a long way, and in more than miles alone, from his family home in remote north Devon. Possibly in 1316, and more certainly in 1319, his missions were concerned with the arrangements to be made for Edward's homage to the French kings, first Louis X and then, after his death in 1317, to the new king, Philip V. His only journey outside France took him to the Low Countries in 1318, where he was asked to report on the suitability of the 8-year-old Philippa of Hainault as a future bride for the king's son, the young Edward. Her physical description provides a welcome, if incongruous, interlude among the often desiccated contents of his register: 'hair fine enough, between blonde and brown ... neat head ... looks very much like her father ... not too tall nor too short for her age.'[60]

The value which Edward set on Stapeldon's services, both in domestic policy and in diplomacy, did not stem only from his legal expertise, and still less from his descriptive powers, but from his personal qualities. In 1317 the king told Pope John XXII that he had found Stapeldon to be 'mature in counsels, and prudent and farsighted in his actions (*in consiliis maturum et agendis circumspectum et providum*)'. The language is remarkably similar to that used later, and quite independently, by the canons of Hartland, who had found their advocate to have acted 'with foresight, prudence and judiciousness (*provide, prudenter et sapienter egerit*)' in their business.[61] These concordant testimonials point to a minister distinguished not solely by his intelligence and learning, but by a practical sagacity hard to identify in any of Edward's other advisers. This was a quality which Edward himself signally lacked. Given too the advantages stemming from age and experience—Stapeldon was some twenty-five years older than Edward—it is hardly surprising that Edward should have set such store by his advice.

Nor is it surprising, in view of all this, that Stapeldon should have been appointed treasurer in February 1320. It is true that he had hitherto shown no particular financial aptitude; though no bishop could manage a bishopric and its estates without acquiring some adeptness with money and figures. His promotion was both a tribute to his general administrative skills and a token of Edward's confidence in him, and it marked his coming of age as a civil-servant bishop, member of a group familiar throughout the middle ages. It is at this point that he first appears in the chronicles, two of which note his

[59] Buck, 125; J. R. S. Phillips, *Aymer de Valence, Earl of Pembroke, 1307–1324* (Oxford, 1972), 87; P. Chaplais, *English Diplomatic Practice in the Middle Ages* (London, 2003), 237.
[60] *Reg. Stapeldon*, 169; Buck, 126; Prestwich, *Plantagenet England*, 215.
[61] Buck, 35, 129; above, 11.

appointment.[62] His time as treasurer was marked by growing political tensions. The rapid ascent of the younger Despenser at Edward's court, and his aggrandizement in the Welsh marches, produced a baronial reaction which led to the devastation of the lands of both Despensers in May 1321 and the sentences of exile passed on them in the parliament which followed in July and August. But the younger Despenser soon rejoined Edward and after a brief civil war the rebels were defeated at Boroughbridge in Yorkshire in March 1322. Their leader, Thomas of Lancaster, was beheaded, his followers executed, disinherited, or forced into exile, and power effectively delivered into the hands of a narrow court faction. Stapeldon was to be one of its most prominent members.

Until then his role in these dramatic events had been marked by a characteristic wariness, a facet of the prudence gratefully acknowledged by the king and the canons of Hartland. He received minor favours from Edward and acted for him in the parliament of October 1320 and in other unspecified ways. But he identified closely with neither side and was absent in his diocese, prudently again, when the opposition magnates were devastating the Despenser lands in the spring of 1321. Although he was among the episcopal mediators who later negotiated a temporary settlement between king and barons in the summer parliament, he retired from the treasurership at his own request almost immediately after parliament had ended, and he remained in his diocese throughout the rebellion which ended at Boroughbridge.[63] His only political intervention came in January 1322, when, in response to a royal letter sent to ten bishops asking for an opinion on the legality of the Despensers' exile and whether it could lawfully be revoked, he offered an exculpatory and hesitant reply: he had not been present when sentence had been passed, but it was his opinion that any revocation should take place in parliament, since the original sentence had been imposed there.[64] The tone of his letter was less that of a man taking a stand on constitutional propriety than of one showing caution, even timidity, in the face of a demand for political commitment which, once given, might jeopardize his whole future. It is difficult to avoid the impression that he was waiting to see which side might win. But after Boroughbridge, with the king's opponents scattered and his allies triumphant, that commitment could be given without risk (or so it must have seemed) and caution thrown to the winds.

It may do Stapeldon an injustice, however, to regard his resignation of the treasurership and his return to his diocese during the political crisis of 1321–2 as no more than the avoidance of trouble. From the start of his episcopate,

---

[62] 'Annales Paulini', in *Chronicles of the Reigns of Edward I and Edward II*, ed. W. Stubbs, 2 vols., RS (London, 1882–3), i. 287; *Flores Historiarum*, ed. H. R. Luard, 3 vols., RS (London, 1890), iii. 191.

[63] Buck, 133–40.   [64] *Reg. Stapeldon*, 441–2; Buck, 138–9.

politics and government had competed for his time and energy with the
management of his diocese; and if his increasing involvement in national
affairs took him more frequently to court and parliament, his diocese was
by no means set to one side. More than most dioceses, Exeter stood in need of
careful supervision, active pastoral engagement, and episcopal nourishment.
In the early fourteenth century it was remote, dispersed, difficult to peram-
bulate, and poor. Of all the English dioceses only Rochester was poorer.
Comprising the whole of Devon and Cornwall, it contained on its western
margin a semi-alien population speaking a different language and posing a
particular problem for pastoral care.[65] Priests appointed to some Cornish
livings were expected to speak Cornish, a language which Stapeldon admitted
he did not know.[66] Exeter, the bishop's home, situated as it was in the south-
east corner of the diocese, was in some ways an inconvenient base. More than
most bishops, a successful bishop here would need an uncompromising
willingness to travel.

In managing this difficult diocese Stapeldon showed some of the same
characteristics which marked his involvement in national politics: energy,
efficiency, and sound judgement. Until he was appointed treasurer in 1320
he spent about 40 per cent of his time in his diocese. The proportion was
higher before 1316, when he became a leading member of the king's council,
and a good deal lower, only about 9 per cent, during his first period as
treasurer from February 1320 to August 1321.[67] Summoned to parliament
in January 1309, he had pleaded the pressure of diocesan business as a
reason for his absence.[68] The diocese was divided into four archdeaconries,
Cornwall, and, for Devon, Exeter, Totnes, and Barnstaple. Stapeldon made
six formal visitations to Cornwall and Totnes, and four to Barnstaple,
besides making three other journeys to Cornwall.[69] His main business
was that of any bishop: ordinations, confirmations, the dedication of
churches, and the visitation of parishes and religious houses. In his work
here he showed himself to be the opposite of negligent: a strict disciplinar-
ian, who promoted the need for reformation, moral improvement, and good
order. Visiting the south Devon parish of Ashburton in 1314, for example,
Stapeldon found a deplorable state of affairs. The church service-books were
insufficient and decayed; the pyx for the eucharist was made of wood and
had no lock; some of the altars had no frontals; some of the priestly
vestments were lacking; the chancel was badly roofed, and the north aisle
ruinous. All this must be put right before Michaelmas, under penalty of a
£20 payment to the cathedral fabric fund; though Stapeldon made a

[65] Buck, 47–8. For the linguistic boundary between English and Cornish in Cornwall, see
N. Orme, 'The Cornish at Oxford', *JRIC* (2010), 51.
[66] *Reg. Stapeldon*, 219.   [67] Buck, 60.   [68] *Reg. Stapeldon*, 416.   [69] Buck, 61.

characteristically precise and thoughtful exception for the repair of the north aisle, which would clearly take longer.[70]

The same vigorous attention to detail was shown in his visitation of religious houses, though here the record is sparser than for parochial visitations. If his relations with Hartland abbey were close and congenial, as we have seen, he nevertheless pulled no punches when, after his visitation, he compiled ordinances for the house's reform in February 1320. Much that was wrong at Hartland may be deduced from them. The abbot was to be present with the canons in the choir for church services. At least once a month he should eat with the brothers in the refectory. The ill-maintained dormitory and the badly roofed bell tower should be repaired. The lack of books was to be made good within a year, under penalty of a £10 payment to the cathedral fabric fund. It was disgraceful that pigs were running loose within the monastic enclosure; they were to be shut up within a suitable place.[71] That these and other ordinances (there was a good deal else that was unsatisfactory) were drafted a few days before Stapeldon became treasurer emphasizes the sharply contrasting worlds in which he moved and the attention to detail which does something to account for his success in both. The provision of pigsties at Hartland abbey had more in common than might at first be supposed with the minute interest which Stapeldon the treasurer was later to take in the collection of the king's debts.

He could on occasion show a deep and kindly concern not only for the spiritual welfare of his charges but for their material welfare as well. When the prior of Bodmin resigned from his office in 1310 on the grounds of age and infirmity, Stapeldon made careful provision for his retirement, ordering that he should have a private chapel for his use, a generous allowance of food and income, a companion chosen from among the canons for his honourable and peace-loving qualities, and two servants, whose wages were to be paid by the priory. In addition, he was to be freed from all conventual duties.[72] Another entry in his register again illuminates Stapeldon's character through his pastoral work, but from a different angle. Thomas Crey, a fuller by trade, from Keynsham in Somerset, was suddenly struck blind one night while he slept. He later dreamt that if he visited the church of the Holy Cross at Crediton in Devon his sight would be restored. He did as his dream had directed, and on 1 August 1315, while he was praying before the altar of St Nicholas in the church, and while Stapeldon happened to be celebrating mass in the same church for the feast of St Peter ad Vincula, he received his sight. This was reported to Stapeldon, who was sceptical 'because such things ought not to be believed too easily'. Thomas was ordered to appear before the bishop, to

[70] *Reg. Stapeldon*, 64.
[71] *Reg. Stapeldon*, 171–3; Chope, *Book of Hartland*, 63, 67–72; Buck, 62–3.
[72] *Reg. Stapeldon*, 49–50.

whom he told his story on oath. Stapeldon asked him if he could now see, to which Thomas replied 'yes'. Still sceptical, Stapeldon asked him on what finger and on what hand he wore his episcopal ring, with many other questions, to all of which Thomas gave satisfactory answers. His wife and neighbours, who had come with him to Crediton, then attested on oath that he had indeed been blind when he arrived there. At last convinced that this was a true miracle, Stapeldon ordered the bells to be rung and solemn thanksgiving offered to God, the Virgin Mary, the Holy Cross, and all saints.[73]

This little story is worth telling for the light which it throws on Stapeldon's qualities: his hard-headedness, his good sense, his critical acumen, and his piety. The more practical of these qualities were seen in some of Stapeldon's other diocesan activities. As early as 1314, for example, he was handsomely praised by the dean and chapter for what he had done to enlarge and improve the episcopal estate, putting up new buildings, repairing old ones, acquiring new property, and enriching the see more than any of his predecessors.[74] But beyond the see's material welfare, two other causes stood still closer to Stapeldon's heart, both of them in different ways relevant to the foundation of his Oxford college. They were the rebuilding of his cathedral, and the provision of a trained and educated parish clergy for his diocese.

The rebuilding of Exeter cathedral had begun in the 1270s, with the partial demolition of the Norman cathedral and its replacement by one in the Gothic style. The new work had made good progress before Stapeldon's accession, by which time most of the east end, with its presbytery and choir, had been completed. Stapeldon presided over the furnishing of the choir, including its high altar, reredos, stalls, rood screen, and bishop's throne, and over the building of the crossing and early work on the new nave.[75] He was, however, much more than a passive spectator. He threw his weight behind both fund-raising and patronage. His predecessor, Bishop Bitton, had made an annual contribution of £124 18s. 8d. to the building fund, and this Stapeldon continued. But he also set about raising money vigorously throughout the diocese, levying an annual tax on clerical stipends for three years from 1310, setting aside fines and penalties for the fund, as we have seen at Ashburton and Hartland, and encouraging gifts and legacies. All these sources of revenue were put in the shade by his own munificent gift of 1,000 marks in 1324 to facilitate the building of the nave.[76] Some of the aesthetic choices behind the new work were almost certainly his. This was most true of the huge bishop's

---

[73] *Reg. Stapeldon*, 126–7; G. Oliver, *Monasticon Diocesis Exoniensis* (Exeter, 1856), 75–6.
[74] Buck, 69 n. 234.
[75] Buck, 52; Orme, *Exeter Cathedral*, 46–7; B. Cherry and N. Pevsner, *The Buildings of England: Devon*, 2nd edn. (London, 1989), 368.
[76] Buck, 51–3; Orme, *Exeter Cathedral*, 47–8.

throne, built in 1313–16 with oak from the episcopal estates and described by Pevsner as 'the most exquisite piece of woodwork of its date in England and perhaps in Europe'.[77] His purchase, during one of his visits to London in 1320–1, of azure, gold foil, and white lead for decorative embellishment points to a similarly close personal interest in the progress of the rebuilding.[78] The choir of the cathedral as it stands today, with its rood screen, sedilia, and throne all dating from his time (the reredos and the stalls have gone), is, along with his College, Stapeldon's greatest surviving monument. It was perhaps only a little inappropriate that he should have been buried close to the high altar, in a place normally reserved for a cathedral's founder and perhaps set aside for him by his own hand (see Plate 1).[79]

It is hard to doubt that Stapeldon saw the emergent cathedral, not only as an offering to the glory of God, but also as a lasting memorial to himself and a celebration of the high status of his office. His interest in the education of the parish clergy, on the other hand, lacked any similar trace of self-advertisement. His concerns here were shared by many bishops in the thirteenth and fourteenth centuries, but in Stapeldon's case we can go some way towards measuring them qualitatively and comparatively. Since 1298 the pope had allowed priests to keep the income from their benefices for their support while they took time off to study at a university. But to secure leave of absence for this purpose they needed a licence from the bishop. It was a testimony to the overriding importance which Stapeldon attached to an educated clergy that he granted more of these licences than any other bishop for whom figures have been computed: 439 altogether, or about 24 a year.[80] The licences recorded in his register show that the system was far from being standardized and suggest that Stapeldon took a close interest in each case. Often the licence was for one or two years' study only. This was sufficient for a basic grounding in the arts syllabus but quite insufficient for the completion of a university degree, and we must assume that such students swelled the ranks of the numerous others who came to university with no intention of carrying their course through to a conclusion.[81]

During the priest's absence the spiritual needs of parishioners remained an important consideration for the bishop. When Stapeldon granted study leave to the priest of St Mawgan-in-Pyder in Cornwall, for example, he stipulated

---

[77] Cherry and Pevsner, *Devon*, 377.

[78] *The Accounts of the Fabric of Exeter Cathedral, 1279–1353*. Part I: *1279–1326*, ed. A. M. Erskine, DCRS, 24 (1981), 126, 134.

[79] Cherry and Pevsner, *Devon*, 376–8; Buck, 53.

[80] K. Edwards, 'Bishops and Learning in the Reign of Edward II', *Church Quarterly Review*, 138 (1944), 79; Buck, 59; Cf. L. E. Boyle, 'The Constitution "Cum ex eo" of Boniface VIII', in his *Pastoral Care, Clerical Education and Canon Law, 1200–1400* (London, 1981), viii. 263–302, esp. 297.

[81] e.g. *Reg. Stapeldon*, 156, 160, 165; Dunbabin, 'Careers and Vocations', *HUO*, i. 568–9.

that he must return to his parish for the sacred season of Lent in order to attend to the cure of souls.[82] In some cases, perhaps when the priest's intellectual abilities were obviously more limited, he might be told to study at a grammar school rather than a university. So it was with Robert Umfraville, priest of Lapford, who was additionally ordered to come to the bishop annually to report on his progress.[83] In other cases formal educational arrangements might be dispensed with altogether. John Resueydon, the 'inadequately educated (*in literatura minus sufficiens*)' priest of Filleigh, was enjoined to take an 'adequately educated' chaplain as his companion to instruct him in the cure of souls.[84] The more able might be given a choice of universities—'to study at Paris or Oxford as he chooses'; 'at Paris or elsewhere'.[85] The most able might be licensed to study theology or canon law, though this was unusual.[86] Any survey of these and other cases leaves the impression that the initiative for study leave invariably came from the bishop, that each candidate was scrutinized carefully, and that the resulting prescription was designed to match both the talents and the needs of the potential student. Here was another example of Stapeldon's practical and scrupulous approach to the requirements of his office and his diocese, and of his conscientiousness. It comes as no surprise to find that he was second only to Simon of Ghent, bishop of Salisbury, in the number of graduates whom he collated to benefices.[87]

The purpose behind this whole enterprise was to create priests who would be intellectually capable of instructing their parishioners in the doctrinal and moral teachings of Christianity, and perhaps too of refuting their doubts and answering their questions. One firm pointer in this general direction lies in Stapeldon's instructions to at least four of his priests that they should learn by heart the *Summula* of Peter Quinel, Stapeldon's predecessor in the see from 1280 to 1291. Quinel's *Summula* was a basic guide to Christian belief and practice, containing short commentaries on the Ten Commandments and the Seven Deadly Sins, instructions about penance and confession, and directions to the parish priest to teach his flock the basic minimum of the Lord's Prayer, the Creed, and the Ave Maria—three texts which, interestingly enough, Stapeldon was himself to translate into French, presumably for pastoral purposes. The *Summula* was in effect a teaching handbook, and Quinel himself had laid down that every priest should possess a copy and seek to understand it.[88] Since it ran to some 5,000 words of Latin, Stapeldon's instruction that it should be learnt by heart was a tall order; but since he set

---

[82] *Reg. Stapeldon*, 338; see 344 for a similar case.
[83] *Reg. Stapeldon*, 229; see 225 for another priest told to attend *scholas grammaticales*.
[84] *Reg. Stapeldon*, 242.   [85] *Reg. Stapeldon*, 46, 47.
[86] *Reg. Stapeldon*, 83, 182, 278, 294.   [87] Edwards, 'Bishops and Learning', 78.
[88] *Reg. Stapeldon*, 204, 242, 243, 256, 565; Buck, 60. The *Summula* is printed in *Councils and Synods*, II. ii, ed. Powicke and Cheney, 1060–77.

time limits for the task of learning it, and in one case named a penalty for failure, he clearly expected the order to be followed. Only a priest with good Latin and a modicum of education would be able to comply; and only a priest with some training in grammar—that is to say, logic and rational argument— would be able to expound Christian teaching to his parishioners. The ideal, probably rarely attained, was stated by the parishioners of Dawlish when the bishop's representatives visited them in 1301. Their vicar, they said, did not reside in person, but his deputy lived a good and decent life 'and instructs them very well in spiritual matters'.[89]

Stapeldon's drive for an educated priesthood was thus a central feature of his episcopate. He was a bishop in some ways dauntingly secular and worldly, but one who also showed a deep concern with the essentials of the Christian life at the ground level of the parish and who saw the education of parish priests as essential for the Christianizing of the laity. Beyond that lay the hope of salvation, for which living the Christian life was a prerequisite. All these considerations were in Stapeldon's mind when he came to found his College. It is entirely appropriate that his cathedral tomb shows him clasping, not the crozier usual for a bishop, but instead a book.[90] Books and learning were fundamental to his whole scheme of things.

Stapeldon's life between 1307 and 1322 was thus divided between his service to the king, as 'parliamentarian', counsellor, and diplomat, and his administration of his diocese. We can obtain some idea of his many preoccupations, and of how he partitioned his time between them, by following his itinerary for two typical years, 1313 and 1314: years which, in national affairs, saw the battle of Bannockburn, in Exeter College's history, the initial endowment of Stapeldon Hall, and in Stapeldon's own career, the first of his journeys to France that we can be sure of.

The opening of the year 1313 found Stapeldon on his episcopal manor of Faringdon in Hampshire, always a favourite resort.[91] In late January he moved on to Stockwell, in Lambeth, on the south bank of the Thames, before leaving London for France on 10 February, in company with the earl of Pembroke.[92] He remained in France until early May, returning to London by 9 May, but crossing back to France, this time with the king, at the end of the month and staying there until mid July. He was thus absent from the two parliaments which met in March and early July. He was in London and at Stockwell or Faringdon for most of the next three months, returning to his

[89] *Reg. Stapeldon*, 132–3. For this visitation, see Orme, *Exeter Cathedral*, 85–7.
[90] Swanton (ed.), *Exeter Cathedral: A Celebration*.
[91] Stapeldon's itinerary is set out in *Reg. Stapeldon*, 551–3. Unless otherwise stated, all that follows is taken from this source.
[92] Buck, 124.

diocese only in early December, having been absent since August 1312. He then immediately set out on a long visitation, leaving Exeter about 7 December and conducting ordinations at Crediton on 12 December and on a much larger scale at Totnes on 22 December, when some 160 men received the first tonsure and some 50 were ordained priests.[93] This tour took Stapeldon to the far west of Cornwall and terminated at St Buryan, near Land's End, on 13 February 1314. He returned through his home country of north Devon, ordaining at Holsworthy, Hartland, and Barnstaple, and reaching Exeter again on 24 March, after an absence of nearly four months. There he remained, with a brief excursion to Staverton and Ashburton in south Devon, until about 8 April. It was at Exeter on 4 April 1314 that he sealed the deed establishing the endowment for his Oxford college.[94] He moved to London in May and then had a long break at Faringdon for most of June before returning to his diocese in late July. He was at Faringdon when the battle of Bannockburn was fought on 24 June. He remained in Exeter or its vicinity for most of August, with a journey to his south Devon manor of Chudleigh in the middle of the month, and then travelled north, via Tewkesbury, to York, where the post-Bannockburn parliament met in September. He left York in early October and was back in his diocese by the end of the month, visiting the family home at Stapledon on 1 November, no doubt to see his brother Richard, who resided there,[95] before striking westwards into Cornwall for most of that month. He returned through south Devon, spending Christmas at his episcopal manor of Paignton.

In the course of two years he had paid some five visits to London, spent about five months in France, journeyed as far west as St Buryan and as far north as York, and interspersed periods of frenetic activity with what look like long holiday breaks on his manors. Yet with our eyes fixed on these broadening horizons, it would be easy to overlook the degree to which he remained a man of Devon, firmly rooted in a locality to which he was bound by ancestral, familial, and personal ties. He was the last bishop of Exeter for some 170 years to be born and bred in the county,[96] and his travels must have made him intimately familiar with its landscape and people. His itinerary shows him to have visited some seventy-three places in Devon during his episcopate, most frequently perhaps his episcopal manors of Bishop's Nympton, Bishop's Tawton, Chudleigh, Clyst Honiton, and Paignton, but also such small and remote villages as Cookbury and Down St Mary in north Devon. His large family, enlarged still further by numerous nephews and

---

[93] *Reg. Stapeldon*, 490–3.   [94] Buck, 224–7; below, 28.
[95] For Richard's residence at Stapledon, see *Reg. Stapeldon*, 301.
[96] Four of his thirteenth-century predecessors (Brewer, Blund, Bronescombe, and Quinel) had been Devonian, but the next after Stapeldon was Peter Courtenay, 1478–87.

nieces after the marriages of his sisters, remained almost wholly Devonian in its members' lands, livings, and interests.[97]

That Stapeldon himself identified closely with the Devon community and had a stake in its politics is suggested by two small incidents. In 1318 the county saw a disputed parliamentary election. Matthew Crowthorn alleged that he had been chosen as one of the two county members by the bishop of Exeter and Sir William Martin, with the assent of the other good men of the county, but that the sheriff had duplicitously returned another man in his place. It was clearly assumed that the bishop and one of the county's leading landholders should have a decisive voice in parliamentary elections. Knowing this, we might reasonably wonder whether Sir Richard de Stapeldon's return as one of the members for both Devon and Cornwall in 1314—a very unusual double election—and for Devon alone in 1319 did not owe something to Walter's influence.[98] The second incident occurred in October 1320, when Stapeldon, then in London, came across King John's charter for Devon in the hands of the abbot of Tavistock. This charter, granted in 1204 and confirmed by Henry III in 1252, freed the whole county, with the exception of Dart-moor and Exmoor, from the oppressive forest law and placed restraints on the similarly oppressive powers of the sheriff. Having seen it, Stapeldon thought it sufficiently important to order its transcription into his register under the heading *Carta de libertatibus Devonie*, 'the charter of the liberties of Devon'.[99] Stapeldon had no obvious personal interest in this charter and he presumably judged it worth preserving for the benefit of the whole county. Far travelled though he may have been, he continued to have strong local loyalties.

The locality too provided the setting for Stapeldon's more questionable activities, most of them directed towards the promotion of his family. His elevation of his brother Thomas to prebends at Exeter and in the bishop's chapel at Bosham in Sussex, and to various other west country livings; of his nephew, another Thomas, to his own former living of Aveton Giffard in 1309, to another prebend at Bosham, and to the archdeaconry of Exeter in 1318; and of Thomas's brother Robert to yet another prebend at Bosham and a canonry at Exeter, were all perhaps unremarkable.[100] Although the scale of Stapeldon's patronage may have been exceptional, any great man might have done as much for his kinsmen. Other doings were more disreputable. In 1317 Stapeldon had acted illicitly and in collusion with his brother Richard and Richard's childless wife, Joan, to break an entail established by Joan's grandfather. The effect was to divert property to Richard and the childless Joan which should

---

[97] Buck, 11, 18–35.
[98] *Parliamentary Writs and Writs of Military Summons*, ed. F. Palgrave, 2 vols. in 4 (Record Comm., London, 1827–34), II. ii. 133–4, 210, Appendix, 138; Buck, 74–5.
[99] *Reg. Stapeldon*, 139–40.   [100] Buck, 28–9, 31.

have gone to Joan's sister Thomasina and her heirs.[101] In another episode, dating from the previous year, he had put pressure on his ward John Arundell to marry Stapeldon's niece Joan. There had been a confrontation in the hall of Sir William Martin at Combe Martin in north Devon, and in the presence of Martin and of the two Stapeldon brothers (both venue and company another mark of Stapeldon's local weight), in which Arundell had at first refused to comply with his guardian's wishes. Two months later, however, in the bishop's house at Horsley in Surrey, he gave in, but only on condition that he should not be disparaged by the marriage. Evidently Stapeldon's niece was reckoned socially inferior to the heir to a modest estate of five manors in Devon and Cornwall.[102] More revealing still of Stapeldon's lack of scruple in such matters was the accusation made against him by the widow of a Cornish knight in 1315. She alleged that she had rented a manor to a local parson, William Milburn, for 40 marks a year; but Milburn had paid her nothing for six years and had then sold the manor to a stranger, all 'by the maintenance of the bishop of Exeter and Richard of Stapeldon, his brother'.[103] There is nothing to substantiate the accusation, but it would have been temerarious to complain against such powerful local figures if the complaint lacked all substance; and Stapeldon's rampant acquisitiveness after 1322, some signs of which had indeed appeared even before he became bishop, make it seem entirely plausible. There were many other property transactions in which the two brothers participated as partners,[104] and we may reasonably wonder what machinations lay behind their bland recording in the sources. The locality was valuable to Stapeldon partly because it was where coercive power could be most effectively exercised.

3. THE FOUNDATION OF STAPELDON HALL

Like the foundation of a religious house, which it resembled, the foundation of an Oxford college in the middle ages was a long, complicated, and expensive business. This was particularly true of the foundation of Stapeldon Hall, as Exeter College was first known. An endowment had to be put together, a site found for the new body of scholars, and rules worked out for their governance. In the case of Stapeldon Hall the main complication, in what would become a standard process for collegiate foundation, lay in the nature of the endowment. The Hall's initial endowment comprised only the tithes attached to a Cornish parish church. The income from this source was not passed on directly, however, but was paid through the chapter of Exeter

---

[101] Buck, 22–3.
[102] *Reg. Stapeldon*, 34; Buck, 34; *The Cornish Lands of the Arundells of Lanherne, Fourteenth to Sixteenth Centuries*, ed. H. S. A. Fox and O. J. Padel, DCRS, 41 (2000), xiv–xv.
[103] *The Parliament Rolls of Medieval England, 1275–1504*. Vol. III: *Edward II, 1307–1327*, ed. S. Phillips (Woodbridge, 2005), 60; Buck, 22.
[104] Buck, 21–2.

cathedral, who held the endowment and acted as its trustees. The working out of these arrangements entailed some intricate negotiations, and they took a long time. Stapeldon's intentions became plain as early as 1311, but they did not come fully to fruition until he gave his new foundation its statutes in April 1316.

Surviving documents, mainly held in the archives of the cathedral and the College, make the order of events clear enough, and only a few pieces of the puzzle seem to be missing. At Westminster on 24 May 1311, Gilbert de Clare, earl of Gloucester, acting at Stapeldon's request, agreed to allow the dean and chapter of Exeter to acquire and retain in perpetuity an acre of land in the Cornish manor of Drannack and the advowson of Gwinear, the manorial church. Gwinear lay (and lies) in the Penwith district of west Cornwall, about 3 miles south-west of the modern Camborne, and not far from the coast. The proceeds of the land and the appropriated church were to be used 'to sustain and maintain in perpetuity poor scholars studying the knowledge of letters in the university of Oxford'.[105] This is the first intimation that we have of Stapeldon's plans. But prior to this grant there must have been some negotiations with the holder of the manor of Drannack and its church at Gwinear, through which his assent to the future deal had been secured. This was Sir Reginald Beville, a prominent Cornish knight, five times MP for his county between 1295 and 1306, and a man closely involved in the county's administration.[106] Since he also held land in Stapeldon and neighbouring places in north Devon, it seems certain that he had long been known to both the Stapeldon brothers.[107] Gilbert de Clare was involved in the transaction as Beville's immediate lord for the Drannack property, so that any alienation of that property affected his rights.

Clare's assent having been secured, the next step followed on 2 December 1311, when Beville, at his manor of Woolston, near Poundstock, in north-east Cornwall, granted away all his rights in the acre and the advowson—not, however, either to the dean and chapter or to Walter de Stapeldon, but to Walter's brother, Sir Richard de Stapeldon. On the same day Beville appointed an attorney to deliver seisin (that is, possession).[108] Shortly afterwards Laurence Beville, son of Ralph Beville, and perhaps Reginald's nephew, released all his rights in the property, first to Reginald and then to Sir Richard de Stapeldon.[109] Nine months later, on 21 October 1312, the king granted Richard licence to alienate acre and advowson to the dean and chapter 'for the

---

[105] D. and C., 2142, 2922; Buck, 101; Boase (2), vi, where Clare's grant is misdated to 1312.

[106] For Beville's career, see *Parliamentary Writs*, I. 489. For Beville, Gwinear, and Drannack, see C. Henderson, 'The 109 Ancient Parishes of the Western Hundreds of Cornwall', *JRIC*, new ser., ii, pt. 4 (1956), 201, and T. Taylor, 'Bevile of Drennick and Woolston', *JRIC*, 17 (1907–8), 236–9.

[107] *Feudal Aids*, Vol. I (London, 1899), 356.   [108] D. and C., 1487, 1497, 1498, 2922.

[109] D. and C., 1488, 1489, 2422.

sustenance of twelve scholars in the university of Oxford...for them to receive the same, and to appropriate the church for that purpose'.[110] This is the first we hear of a specific number of scholars for the new foundation. The way had thus been cleared for Sir Richard de Stapeldon to transfer the property to the dean and chapter. But it was only after another long interval that the transfer was finally made, at Crediton and in Walter's presence, on 22 March 1314.[111]

With the Drannack land and the Gwinear advowson now securely in the possession of the dean and chapter, Stapeldon Hall could at last be legally established. The key document, in effect the foundation charter of the College, was drawn up in chapter at Exeter on 4 April 1314. Now preserved in the College archives, it takes the form of a preliminary statement by Stapeldon as to his intentions in founding the Hall, followed by a further statement of the terms for its financial support, to which both bishop and chapter set their seals.[112] The preliminary statement will be discussed later; here we will summarize only the 'business' section of what is a lengthy document.

By his endowment charter Stapeldon grants the revenues of the church of Gwinear to the chapter of Exeter cathedral, which is already in possession of the advowson. He does so after due consultation with the chapter, with John le Deneys, rector of Gwinear, and with Adam, archdeacon of Cornwall, and with their consent. The revenues are to be used for the maintenance of the twelve scholars of Stapeldon Hall in Oxford studying 'philosophy', and are to be handed over to the Hall's proctor in two annual instalments at Easter and Michaelmas. The chapter may enter into possession of the church's revenues on the resignation or death of the current rector, John le Deneys, but a portion of the revenue is to be set aside for the establishment of a vicarage. If the chapter fails to pay over the monies at the due dates, causing hardship to the scholars, it is to pay a fine of £4, half of which is to go to the bishop's alms and half to the Holy Land. All matters relating to the election and governance of the scholars and to the appropriation of the church are to be reserved to Stapeldon and his episcopal successors, and to the archdeacon and his successors.

At this point we may draw breath and survey more reflectively the arrangements made by Stapeldon between May 1311 and April 1314 for the maintenance of his projected college. The essence of his scheme drew on a device used by many pious laymen to endow or enrich a religious house: that is to say, the appropriation of a parish church. The revenues of a church consisted principally of tithes, the tenth part of the parishioners' produce, divided between the greater tithes (all varieties of corn) and the lesser (hay, calves, lambs, etc.). Normally both sorts of tithes were in the hands of a rector who

---

[110] *CPR, 1307–13*, 504.   [111] D. and C., 1500, 2922; Buck, 101; Boase (2), viii.
[112] ECA, M. III. 3, printed in Buck, 224–6. For comment, see Buck, 102.

was the parish priest. But the more valuable greater tithes might be alienated by the holder of the living who had the right of advowson (presentation to the living) to an external body, usually a monastery but in our case the chapter of Exeter. To provide for the continuing care of the parish and the services of its church, the appropriator now in possession of the greater tithes would agree to the appointment of a vicar, who would be paid a relatively small annual stipend and permitted to collect the lesser tithes.[113]

Stapeldon's establishment of the College in this way is likely to have involved considerable expense. Whether the advowson and the acre of land had originally been sold by Beville to Richard de Stapeldon, and thence to Walter, is nowhere directly stated. The sale of advowsons was usually forbidden and had indeed been condemned as simony in Bishop Quinel's *Summula*, commended by Stapeldon to his parish clergy. But it was common enough in thirteenth-century Cornwall; and some inducement is likely to have been offered to Beville to persuade him to part with what was an important piece of property.[114] Stapeldon himself in his deed of endowment wrote that the Exeter chapter now stood as patron of the church *ex nostro perquisito*, 'by our acquisition', seemingly meaning 'by purchase'.[115] If Beville had no male issue, as the renunciation of rights only by Laurence Beville, probably his nephew, and not by any son and heir, would appear to indicate,[116] then his willingness to part with family property, presumably for a good price, becomes more understandable. The rights of John le Deneys, the current rector, would certainly have had to have been bought out, since it was his tithe income that was being diverted to the chapter for the ultimate benefit of Stapeldon Hall. Hence the careful record in the deed of endowment that le Deneys had consented to its terms. Since a vicar, Andrew Tregiliou, was appointed for Gwinear shortly afterwards, on 8 November 1314, it seems likely that le Deneys had resigned the rectory when the deed was drawn up, so allowing the tithe income to go to the chapter.[117]

The terms on which the vicarage was eventually established in September 1319 throw some further light on the whole arrangement. The vicar was to have the houses formerly attached to the rectory, together with one acre of glebe, for which he was to pay the dean and chapter an annual rent of 2s. It is very probable that this glebe acre is the single acre of land in Drannack which

---

[113] For these arrangements, see e.g. J. R. H. Moorman, *Church Life in England in the 13th Century* (Cambridge, 1946), 5–6, 114–25.

[114] *Councils and Synods*, II. ii, ed. Powicke and Cheney, 1068; C. R. Cheney, *From Becket to Langton: English Church Government, 1170–1213* (Manchester, 1956), 124; M. Page, 'The Ownership of Advowsons in Thirteenth-Century Cornwall', *Devon and Cornwall Notes and Queries*, 37 (1992–6), 336–41.

[115] Buck, 226. For 'perquisitio' as meaning 'acquisition by purchase', see *Dictionary of Medieval Latin from British Sources*, Fasc. X (Oxford, 2006), 2231.

[116] Cf. Taylor, 'Bevile of Drennick', 226 n. 1.   [117] *Reg. Stapeldon*, 252.

had figured in all these transactions since the first of the series in May 1311 and which, as it happens, disappears completely from the record after its grant to the dean and chapter by Richard de Stapeldon, along with the advowson, in March 1314. If so, it would indicate that the eventual need to establish a vicarage had been in Stapeldon's mind from the start. The remaining terms for the vicarage list the lesser tithes (hay, flax, hemp, etc.) and other revenues which the vicar is to receive, stipulate that he is also to have an annual stipend of £2 from the dean and chapter, and lay down that he is to provide hospitality for the chapter's agents when they come each year to harvest and sell the tithe corn.[118]

It has been worth setting out these arrangements in some detail, for they gave Stapeldon's foundation its primary source of income for the rest of the middle ages. They were in some ways peculiar and perhaps reflected the position both of Stapeldon and of his diocese. There was great variety in the ways in which the early Oxford colleges were endowed, and no common pattern had underlain the financing of Stapeldon Hall's three predecessors, University College, Balliol, and Merton.[119] It was usual for a college to accumulate an endowment in land; the founder might also supply cash, by gift or legacy; and the revenues of appropriated churches might also make a useful contribution. Stapeldon Hall, however, was unique in its initial dependence solely on the revenues from a single appropriated church. In part, this reflected Stapeldon's own lack of land. As far as can be seen, he had no family inheritance, and although in the course of his life he put together a considerable estate, it mainly comprised small parcels of land, sometimes acquired by dubious means. These factors made Stapeldon's holdings unsuitable for an endowment. He certainly lacked the cornucopia of manors which another founder, Walter de Merton, was able to accumulate and pass on to his foundation.[120]

The further reasons for the role chosen by Stapeldon for the chapter of Exeter are nowhere made plain, but are not beyond explanation. When the Hall itself was not yet in being and its future was still uncertain, it made sense to nominate a third party, with guaranteed permanence, as trustees for its endowment. Walter de Merton had followed a precisely similar course in 1262, when he had given property to Merton priory to hold in trust for his intended college.[121] Convenience was also a factor. Oxford was some 250 miles from Gwinear, and the levying of the tithe income by the members of the new foundation would have been laborious, time-consuming, and expensive. As it was, the responsibility for selling the tithe corn and getting in the

[118] *Reg. Stapeldon*, 332–3; Buck, 102 n. 23.
[119] For the endowments of the early colleges, see T. H. Aston and R. Faith, 'The Endowments of the University and Colleges', *HUO*, i. 287–309.
[120] Aston and Faith, 'Endowments', *HUO*, i. 297–8.   [121] Martin and Highfield, 11.

money lay with the Exeter chapter, and the role of the Hall's agents was limited to no more than the 150-mile journey to Exeter to collect the income: arduous enough, but much less so than a trek from Oxford into the wilds of west Cornwall. It was left to the chapter, too, to deal with recalcitrant tithe-payers and with any other problems that might arise; while the sanctions set out in the deed of endowment were intended to ensure that its members took their responsibilities seriously. In exchange, the chapter gained the Gwinear advowson, the right of presentation to the living, which at no point lay with the Hall or the later College. These arrangements would also enable Stapeldon and his successors, through their position and residence in Exeter, to keep a continuing eye on the levying and disbursement of the Gwinear revenues. The Hall enjoyed its independence, yet it was to remain closely linked to its founder, his successors, and the Exeter chapter. No other early Oxford college rested on quite this basis.

The transactions needed to establish Stapeldon Hall were diverse and numerous. From the initial permission given by Gilbert de Clare for the grant of the Gwinear advowson to the dean and chapter in 1311, to the deed of endowment in 1314, at least seven charters and grants went to the Hall's foundation. Many parties were involved: Gilbert de Clare, the king, Reginald Beville, Laurence Beville, Richard de Stapeldon, the archdeacon of Cornwall, the rector of Gwinear, and the chapter of Exeter. There must have been many oral negotiations behind the scenes which the written sources fail to reveal, and these, as well as Stapeldon's involvement in national politics and diocesan administration, do much to explain the protracted and episodic nature of the foundation process. Stapeldon's hand lay behind all this activity. It was he who had sought Clare's permission for the acquisition of Gwinear and he who, three years later, drew up the deed of endowment which brought Stapeldon Hall into being. The whole process reflected both the businesslike and methodical qualities, as well as the foresight, which characterized his more public activities. The deed of endowment was a particularly careful piece of planning and drafting. With its record of the consultation of the interested parties, its provision for the establishment of the vicarage, its arrangements for the biannual payment of the Gwinear revenues to Stapeldon Hall, and its definition of the future rights of bishop and chapter, it covered all eventualities. In 1325 Stapeldon was to speak of the 'heavy labours and expenses' which he had incurred in founding his Hall,[122] and even by 1314 there was much to justify his words.

The most mysterious aspect of these transactions was the leading role played in them by Sir Richard de Stapeldon. The two brothers had always been exceptionally close, as we have seen,[123] but in the founding of the

---

[122] Boase (1), xlii.   [123] Above, 10–11, 25–6.

College Richard seems to have acted almost as Walter's *alter ego*. He journeyed to Westminster to witness Clare's initial grant made there in May 1311; it was to him, and not to Walter or to the Exeter chapter, that Reginald Beville granted acre and advowson, that Laurence Beville quitclaimed his rights in the same property, and that the king issued his licence to alienate in 1312; and it was he who made the final grant of the property to the dean and chapter. His leading role persisted through all the subsequent steps in the College's foundation, as we shall see. Walter's initiative, however, was transparent throughout, and there can be no question of his concealing his own role or intentions behind a fraternal 'front man'. Expediency provides one possible solution to the mystery. The bishop's increasing involvement in politics, diplomacy, and administration may have simply made it convenient for him to leave the mechanics of the transfer of the Gwinear property in the hands of a local man whom he trusted more than any other, while reserving for himself the all-important terms of the endowment set out in the deed of April 1314.

Even before the drafting of the deed of endowment Stapeldon had begun to acquire property in Oxford for his projected foundation. The first acquisition came in April 1312, when John of Ducklington, a wealthy Oxford clothier and later mayor of the town, sold two tenements jointly to Stapeldon and Richard of Widslade, another Oxford *magister* and precentor of the church of Crediton, for 80 marks.[124] The two tenements comprised Hart Hall, on the site of the present Hertford College, and Arthur Hall, behind the church of St Peter-in-the-East.[125] Later, on 7 April 1314, within days of the establishment of the endowment, Widslade remitted his share in both Hart Hall, now called 'Stapeldon Hall', and Arthur Hall. His charter was drawn up at Oxford and witnessed by a little group of the bishop's associates, including his brother Richard and John de Treiagu, his steward.[126] Shortly afterwards, in May 1314, Stapeldon was licensed by the king to grant the tenements to his twelve scholars (see Plate 3).[127] But the two sites must rapidly have proved unsatisfactory, perhaps because they were small and unadjacent. Although they were probably occupied for a time by the new scholars, they were soon abandoned, though kept in hand for their rental value; and within eighteen months Stapeldon Hall had migrated to the present site of Exeter College.

The move was made possible by three property acquisitions in October 1315. All came from another cleric, Peter de Skelton. On 6 October Skelton granted to Stapeldon a messuage called St Stephen's Hall, precisely located as

---

[124] Boase (2), 286. For the acquisition of all these properties, see Buck, 102–3. For Ducklington, *VCH Oxfordshire*, iv. 38. For Widslade, Buck, 58. Widslade probably came from the place of that name in Lamerton, west Devon.

[125] Salter, *Survey*, i. 148, 156, maps NE III, NE V.

[126] Boase (2), 286–7. For Treiagu, see Buck, 75.   [127] ECA, L. I. 4; *CPR, 1313–17*, 115.

lying opposite to the north wall of the city between Northgate and Smithgate, the latter situated near the north-east corner of the present Clarendon Building. Two further grants followed. On 7 October Skelton gave Stapeldon another tenement comprising two chambers and a backyard and known as 'La Lavandrie', lying east of St Stephen's Hall; and on 8 October, the reversion of a third tenement lying east of La Lavandrie, up against the schools of the arts faculty (see Plate 4). St Stephen's Hall was given as a freehold, while the remaining two tenements were held from the abbess and convent of Godstow.[128] These three tenements fronted the lane which lay just inside the city wall, both wall and lane now buried beneath the College's Margary quadrangle and the Rector's lodgings and garden.[129] The three grants were all made far from Oxford, at the bishop's Devon manor of Chudleigh, where Stapeldon was himself almost certainly staying,[130] and all three were witnessed by Richard de Stapeldon. The precaution was taken to have Skelton's grant of St Stephen's Hall confirmed by the king on 4 November 1315 and, three days later in London, to secure a quitclaim from Skelton's brother John of any rights which he might have in the property.[131] Stapeldon's title was now as watertight as it could be.

Behind these grants, so fundamental to the College's history, lay an intricate pattern of relationships and aspirations. Like almost everyone else involved in this story, Peter de Skelton was an Oxford *magister* and west country priest. Rector of St Stephen's-by-Saltash in Cornwall since 1302, he must have been well known to Stapeldon, who had given him leave of absence for study in 1309 and would do so again in October 1315, immediately after his grants of Oxford property.[132] From 1296 he had been building up a holding on the site which became St Stephen's Hall, though it was not until his grant of 6 October 1315 that the site was so named. Skelton's acquisitions had begun with a grant from yet another Oxford *magister*, William de Coudray, whose clerk he was,[133] and his aim was almost certainly to set himself up as the principal of his own hall, named after his Cornish parish. But Stapeldon must have persuaded him to change his mind in favour of the fledgling College, for his grant was made at the bishop's request. There were inducements. Stapeldon paid him the considerable sum of £40 for the tenement and may have promised him the period of study leave which followed almost immediately after the grant. But Skelton also made the grant 'for the salvation of my soul and of my benefactors' and was promised that the priest serving the twelve scholars of Stapeldon Hall would bear him in mind both before and after his death and would say a special collect for him among the

---

[128] ECA, L. V. 7; A. II. 1, fos. 96ᵛ–97ʳ; Boase (2), xii; Buck, 103.

[129] Salter, *Survey*, i. 55, map NE II. For a more detailed discussion of the College site, see below, 139–45.

[130] *Reg. Stapeldon*, 553. [131] *CPR, 1313–17*, 367; ECA, L. V. 7.

[132] *BRUO*, iii. 1706. [133] Boase (2), xi–xii.

Hall's benefactors.[134] Here Stapeldon was as good as his word, for this provision was later included in the list of duties laid down for the Hall chaplain in Stapeldon's statutes.[135] Skelton may have been old and ailing at this time, and the hope of salvation more than usually urgent; for he died in September 1316, within a year of his grant. He was buried in Exeter cathedral—appropriately enough for one who had done so much to forward its bishop's plans.[136]

It was Stapeldon who provided the endowment of Stapeldon Hall; but the Hall was brought into being by what was both a friendly and a business arrangement between these two men, both united by their roots in the west country and in Oxford, and by their concern for learning and its promotion at their university. If Skelton was anxious about the fate of his soul, Stapeldon wished to see his foundation, already provided for by the Gwinear tithes, firmly grounded in property. These aspirations, partly the same, partly different, but always compatible, underlay their bargain.

The mundane processes which created Stapeldon Hall tell us little about its creator's motives and intentions. For these we have to go to two sources: the deed of endowment issued in April 1314, and the statutes which Stapeldon issued for the Hall two years later in April 1316. The first of these, the endowment deed, is a remarkable piece of work. Surviving only in the College archives, it takes the form of letters patent issued by Stapeldon to 'all the faithful in Christ' (see Plate 2). Its 'business' part, setting out the Gwinear arrangements, we have already looked at. But this is prefaced by a lengthy reflective statement in which Stapeldon sets out what amounts to both a philosophy of education and a hymn of praise and affection for Oxford as a seat of learning.[137] Since this was certainly drafted by Stapeldon himself and takes us closer to his innermost thoughts about the value of education and learning than any other source, it deserves summary and comment.

Stapeldon begins his discourse with some theological ruminations. Man's intellect, free before the Fall to penetrate the mysteries of the heavens and to acquire knowledge, has been clouded by the Fall's consequences and has been darkened further with the passage of time. But God in his beneficence has decreed the teaching of the liberal arts to restore to helpless man the perfection of judgement which he could not achieve through natural reason. Through this gift the diverse languages of many nations are brought together in Latin as a common tongue, and the deeds of the fathers and of princes are set down in books. Having introduced the liberal arts into his discourse, Stapeldon now proceeds to the subjects of the trivium and the quadrivium,

---

[134] ECA, L. V. 7; CPR, 1313–17, 367.   [135] Reg. Stapeldon, 305.
[136] Death and Memory, ed. Lepine and Orme, 105.
[137] ECA, M. III. 3, printed in Buck, 224–7. I am very grateful to Professor Michael Reeve for his help with the translation of this difficult text.

beginning with logic. Through the same gift of God, the conflicts between truth and falsehood are settled by reason and argument; the causes of the generation and decay of all bodies, and of how earthly things are governed by the course of the heavens, are apprehended and understood (an allusion to Aristotle's natural philosophy and in particular perhaps to his treatise *De generatione et corruptione*). Voices are blended in harmony to produce a hymn of joy and to show how the Lord may be worshipped in music; scholastic teaching marks out furthest boundaries through the computation of length, breadth, height, and depth; and philosophical enquiry strives to acquire knowledge of heavenly bodies. (Here he has successively surveyed music, arithmetic, geometry, and astronomy, the four quadrivial subjects.) From the same gift of God comes knowledge of the two laws (civil and canon law), through which quarrels are settled and each is given his due. Finally, learning rises to the height of the holy scriptures, and the spirit which gives life is brought forth from the letter which kills. In these concluding sentences Stapeldon has moved away from the quadrivium and on to the value of higher degrees in civil and canon law and in theology.

After having surveyed the origins of knowledge and learning, their uses, and their embodiment in the arts course and in the higher degrees available at the university, Stapeldon turns to Oxford. In the branches of knowledge and learning already enumerated, the venerable and glorious assembly of the masters and scholars of the university of Oxford shines like the sun in the firmament of the church militant, illuminating the whole earth with the brilliance of its radiance. From this well-head flow streams of knowledge (mixed metaphors had not yet been invented), which irrigate and fertilize with blessed virtues the soil of the church. In this garden grow flowers which fill the hearts of all faithful Christians with a wonderful fragrance. Then Stapeldon moves on to practicalities. It is necessary for the prelates of the church and the princes and nobles of the kingdom, and it adds to the glory of their role, to have for the benefit of their governance men of dedication and dignity conspicuous for their learning and virtue, so that by their wise counsels they may rule felicitously over the flock entrusted to them. By the grace of heaven the study of letters produces such men, suckling them as children with sweet milk and feeding them with solid fare and the enjoyment of greater richness when they reach maturity.

Stapeldon then turns to the contemporary university, to his own education, and to his current purposes. The university of Oxford, he writes, has always been accustomed to produce men eminent in learning, wise in counsel, and outstanding in their merits and virtues, as is evident through many testimonials at the present day. 'She it was that from the early years of my life brought me on in the study of letters, nurtured me when she had brought me on, and when she had finished nurturing me, secured, albeit undeservedly, my advancement.' With the foregoing considerations in mind, and in order to enlarge and exalt the university to the glory of God and the church, to nourish the patrimony of Christ committed to his charge (surely an allusion to the needs of his bishopric), and to nurture from the riches of the church those who, with a marvellous desire for goodness, seek the incomparable pearl of learning, he has given the church of Gwinear to the chapter of Exeter. Then follow the detailed arrangements for the bestowal of the Gwinear revenues on the scholars of Stapeldon Hall.

For all its apparent verbiage this is an exceptionally interesting text, remarkable for its imaginative breadth and for the qualities of mind which it displays. Beginning with a theological account of the consequences of the Fall, it moves on through a discussion of the benefits to be derived from Latin learning and from the university's arts course and its higher degrees, and culminates in a rapturous but reasoned laudation of the university of Oxford and its *magistri*, of whom Stapeldon himself, as he tells us, was one. It enshrines a philosophy of education which in some ways anticipates elements of those of Newman and Jowett. The purpose of the arts course is to foster humane learning and an understanding of God's world and his universe through the study of natural philosophy. But its application is also practical. Logic enables men to distinguish between truth and falsehood; arithmetic and geometry nourish the practical art of mensuration; the study of the two laws facilitates the settlement of disputes. Most valuably of all perhaps, a university education produces wise and skilled men for the service of church and state. Stapeldon publishes here what is in effect a manifesto, but one intended, despite its universal address, for no wider public than the chapter of Exeter and the scholars of his new foundation, where the document was deposited and where it remains. It encouraged both these parties to look beyond the practical arrangements for the Gwinear tithes, set out in the second part of the text, to the mental qualities, Christian virtues, and ethos of service which the endowment was intended to foster. No other Oxford founder in the middle ages stated his credo so comprehensively or so eloquently.

How far was that credo reflected in the statutes drafted by Stapeldon for his Oxford hall? In his deed of endowment Stapeldon clearly had in mind the need for statutes to regulate the affairs of his foundation, for he had there reserved to himself and his successors the right to determine the means by which his scholars were to be elected and governed. But it was not until 26 April 1316, just over two years later, that he published his statutes. The long delay between endowment and statute-making probably resulted from Stapeldon's other preoccupations. He had travelled to York for parliament in the autumn of 1314, conducted a diocesan visitation into Cornwall, journeyed to France for two months and then to Cornwall again in the summer of 1315, and was appointed to the king's council in January 1316.[138] His Oxford plans

---

[138] Buck, 62, 127–8; *Reg. Stapeldon*, 553; above, 14–15, 18.

had to be fitted into the interstices of a busy public life, and isolating them may lead us to forget that they were interwoven with many other activities.

Rather surprisingly the statutes survive only in a fifteenth-century transcript preserved in the Exeter cathedral archives, and not at the College.[139] Since they provide a key to understanding much of the subsequent history of the College, it is worth spending a little time on their content. They comprise a relatively brief and simple text divided into sixteen headed sections. Stapeldon begins with the most basic matter: the number and choice of the scholars (later to be called 'fellows'). At Stapeldon Hall there are to be thirteen scholars, twelve of them studying 'philosophy' (that is, the arts course comprising the trivium and quadrivium) and the thirteenth a priest-chaplain reading for a higher degree in theology or canon law. The first scholars are to be chosen by the bishop. Thereafter the scholars themselves are to elect, choosing those the more fit to make progress, the more virtuous in character, and the more impoverished in their means. They are to be 'sufficient sophists at least', meaning that they are already engaged on the arts course, well advanced in the study of logic, and probably at the end of their second year;[140] and they are to be selected from those born or resident in the diocese of Exeter, eight from the three archdeaconries of Devon and four from the archdeaconry of Cornwall. The priest-chaplain is to be nominated by the Exeter chapter and accepted by the other scholars without demur. If any subsequent benefactor augments the Hall's resources, then other scholars may be chosen from the diocese where the new resources lie or as the benefactor wishes. New scholars are to be elected by a two-thirds majority of the existing scholars; and if any candidate fails to achieve a sufficient majority an appeal may be made to the chancellor of Oxford, provided that the leading candidate has at least six votes.

The scholars are to be supervised by one of their number with the title of Rector. He is to allocate rooms in order of seniority, to appoint servants, and to administer the Hall's finances. The first Rector is to be appointed by the bishop, and thereafter he is to be chosen by the scholars or by the chancellor if they cannot agree. He is to account each term for all his receipts and expenses, to pay all outstanding debts, to put any surplus in the scholars' common chest, and to hold office for one year. An election is to be held annually on the

---

[139] D. and C., 3625, printed in *Reg. Stapeldon*, 30–8, but not part of Stapeldon's manuscript register. The statutes were also printed for the 1855 Commission: *Statutes*, 3–10.

[140] Professor Orme has argued that 'sufficient sophists' may have been no more than exschoolboys, who had already begun the study of logic, and that it was perhaps Stapeldon's intention to support twelve such students from the start of their time at Oxford: Orme, 'The Cornish at Oxford', 55. But it is clear from Stapeldon's later ordinance of 1322 that the 'sufficient sophists' are already 'of the faculty of arts', and the *sophismata* from which they took their title were logical exercises undertaken for the BA degree: see Boase (1), lv, and Fletcher, 'Faculty of Arts', *HUO*, i. 379–80. A 'sufficient sophist' can only have been a student who was already well advanced on the BA course.

eighth day after Michaelmas and the outgoing Rector is to be eligible for re-election, provided that he has rendered his accounts and paid off any arrears. No one can refuse to accept election as Rector, on pain of permanent expulsion from the Hall. Finally, the Rector is empowered, with two senior scholars, to settle disputes and to punish those in breach of the statutes.

Stapeldon then turns to the priest-chaplain, setting out his liturgical duties and his further obligation to celebrate mass for the souls of the bishop, his successors and predecessors, his parents and benefactors, and for a certain John Toller and *magister* Peter de Skelton. Stapeldon himself was also to be commemorated in another way, through the name of his foundation. This was to be called Stapeldon Hall for as long as the scholars should remain, even if the Hall's location should change.

Next come detailed regulations for the scholars' maintenance, discipline, and studies. Each is to receive 10*d.* a week for commons (that is, food and drink), with an additional 20*s.* a year for the Rector and the Chaplain, and 10*s.* a year for each scholar. These allowances are to be paid a year in arrears, at the start of Michaelmas term, and anyone in residence for only a part of the year is to be paid pro rata. The income from Hart Hall is to be used for the maintenance of the Stapeldon Hall buildings, after the needs of Hart Hall itself have been met. Each scholar is to have four weeks' vacation every year to visit his friends and relations and to conduct business, but if he is absent for more than four weeks the allowance is to be stopped and applied instead to the Hall's common fund. Any scholar absent for five months in a year, for any reason except serious illness, is to lose all his rights—but he may be re-elected if the other scholars see fit. Any Rector dying or leaving office within the academic year is to be replaced within eight days. If the Rector dies in the summer vacation, then a new election is to be held after Michaelmas in the usual way, and in the meantime the scholar senior by date of election is to act as Rector. Every scholar, once admitted, is to hold his scholarship for a probationary year, at the end of which he may be ejected from the Hall if two-thirds of the scholars so decide. The scholars are to take care not to act out of malice against anyone who ought to be retained. Once past the probationary year, no scholar can be removed without legitimate cause, proved verbally before the Rector. A negligent Rector can be removed only by the chancellor, but the power to appoint a replacement still remains with the scholars.

Rules are then laid down for the course and syllabus to be followed by the scholars during their time at the Hall. Every scholar is to follow the arts course, to determine (that is, qualify as a bachelor) within six years, and to incept (that is, to qualify as a *magister*) within a further four years. The new *magister* is then to lecture for another two to three years (as a regent master), after which he is to leave the Hall, allowing another scholar to be elected in his place. If a scholar obtains an income of £3 a year from another source, or accepts a benefice of any value whatever, then he is to vacate his scholarship. The scholars are to dispute twice a week. Natural philosophy is to be the subject of every third disputation, and logic of the other two. All the masters and other scholars of the hall are to be present at each disputation unless dispensed from attendance by the Rector. The regent masters (that is, the senior *magistri* now lecturing) may be the more easily dispensed from attending at the disputations of the sophists (meaning here the undergraduates reading for the BA).

The statutes' final sections cover a miscellany of matters. Gifts and legacies to the scholars are to be used for the benefit of the community, either to add to the number of scholars or to purchase books or for other communal purposes. The same is to be done with any surplus monies remaining once commons and allowances have been paid. There is to be a common chest for the Hall's muniments, the keys for its three locks being kept by the Rector, the senior scholar, and the chaplain. Stapeldon empowers himself to add to, subtract from, amend, and interpret the statutes. Every scholar on the day of his admission is to take an oath before the Rector and at least three scholars to observe the statutes and any further regulations established by the bishop, and to preserve the rights, liberties, and possessions of the Hall (an oath still taken by incoming fellows in almost identical terms today). Stapeldon further reserves the right, for himself and his successors or their deputies, to visit the Hall annually in order to see that the statutes are being observed and the scholars properly maintained, and to inspect the accounts of the previous year, which should be presented in summary form. In this way negligence might be punished, errors amended, things needing to be supplemented might be so supplemented, and those needing correction might be corrected, according to God and justice.

Stapeldon's statutes reveal much about his qualities, his intentions, and the future direction of his foundation. They were a masterpiece of concision, which covered every aspect of the Hall's corporate life and almost every conceivable eventuality. Although time would reveal their limitations,[141] which could hardly have been foreseen in 1316, they were to last in essentials until superseded by Sir William Petre's statutes in 1566. Like Stapeldon's detailed arrangements for the appropriation of Gwinear, they point to a particularly orderly mind, capable of surveying and anticipating a range of possible contingencies and of providing succinct solutions to likely problems. They remind us of Stapeldon's probable skill as a chess player, suggested by the three chess sets found in his room at Exeter after his death.[142]

The statutes provided Stapeldon Hall with a simple administrative structure. It comprised a small body of young men, all enjoying formal parity, with

---

[141] For some of these limitations, see below, 94–7, 113, 244.   [142] *Reg. Stapeldon*, 565–6.

the exception of the Rector and the chaplain; and even the Rector held office for only a year before returning to the ranks or standing again for re-election. Although the statutes distinguished between the Hall's members in terms of their academic advancement, placing *magistri* above bachelors and bachelors above sophists, who were mere undergraduates,[143] all enjoyed the same commons and allowances (again with the exceptions of the Rector and the chaplain) and all were referred to as *scolares*, 'scholars'. The *magistri* might lecture to the sophists and attend their disputations, but the later division between 'dons' and undergraduates did not exist: all were *scolares*, sharing in the endowment, engaged on the arts course, and sworn to observe the statutes. Equality and democracy ruled in other ways too. The authority to elect both new scholars and the annual Rector, as well as to dismiss or re-elect probationers at the end of their probationary year, lay with the scholars themselves. True, the senior were given some privileges—for example, in the choice of rooms[144]—and no doubt quality often carried more weight than quantity in the Hall's affairs, according to Aristotelian principles with which all would have been familiar. Yet this division may have been partly bridged by the relative youthfulness of the whole body. Since the statutes allowed no one to remain a scholar for more than about thirteen years, no scholar can have been more than about 30 years old.

The academic ranking at the Hall, and the progression which its members followed, from sophists to regent masters, was largely common to all members of the university—or at least to those who stayed the course, for, as we have seen, many did not. The democratic election of the head of the house, too, was a practice followed at other Oxford and Cambridge colleges.[145] But some features of the new foundation were more unusual. The selection of scholars from one tightly defined part of the country, the diocese of Exeter, was unique. Though two scholars were later added from the diocese of Salisbury, in accordance with Stapeldon's wish that later benefactors might nominate scholars from other dioceses, the early roots of Hall and College in the far west largely determined its membership into the seventeenth century. 'None of the colleges before 1379 was so closely associated with a particular region as Exeter was with Devon and Cornwall.'[146] Given Stapeldon's own local affiliations, by birth and office, this was perhaps less surprising than another feature of the statutes: their omission of any privileges for founder's kin. An earlier founder, Walter de Merton, had established his College primarily for his kinsmen, and the same principle was later followed at Queen's, New College, and All Souls.[147] Stapeldon, who had three sisters

[143] *Reg. Stapeldon*, 304.   [144] *Reg. Stapeldon*, 304.   [145] Buck, 107.
[146] Highfield, 'Early Colleges', *HUO*, i. 236. For scholars from Salisbury diocese, see below, 74–5.
[147] Highfield, 'Early Colleges', *HUO*, i. 246; *The Early Rolls of Merton College*, ed. J. R. L. Highfield (Oxford, 1964), 7.

to Merton's seven, and whose closeness to his relatives and concern for their promotion is everywhere apparent, might have been expected to follow suit. But Merton's provision was founded on an equitable principle which did not apply in Stapeldon's case. By alienating his lands to his College, Merton deprived his kinsmen of their inheritances, for which College places offered some compensation. Stapeldon, with no similarly rich inheritance to pass on to his foundation, may have felt no similar obligation. His relatives could afford to be indifferent to the Gwinear tithes which were the basis of the Hall's endowment.

Two further features of the Hall's statutes were peculiar, the one highly unusual, the other unique. The scholars of Stapeldon Hall were expected to take only the arts course, the chaplain alone being permitted to study for a higher degree; and the Hall's Rector was to hold office for only one year, with the possibility of re-election but with no possibility of permanent or life tenure. The arts-only nature of the Hall had been intended from the start, for Stapeldon's deed of endowment, drafted two years before the statutes, had envisaged his scholars studying 'philosophy', a shorthand word for the basic arts course. Stapeldon Hall was not entirely alone in this respect, since the scholars of Balliol were also initially restricted to arts. But even Balliol made provision for six graduates in theology by its new statutes of 1340, and the two colleges which preceded Stapeldon Hall, University College and Merton, had a large graduate component from the start. University College indeed was reserved exclusively for graduates, as were Oriel and Queen's, the next foundations after Stapeldon Hall.[148] It is not difficult, however, to see the reasons for this anomalous restriction. As we shall see, Stapeldon's intention in founding his Hall was to provide graduate priests for the parishes of his diocese. Any training beyond the arts course would keep men away from their parishes, where there was work to be done, and in any case was hardly necessary for parochial tasks. Although he had spoken with glowing respect of higher degrees in civil and canon law and in theology in the preface to his deed of endowment, and had commended the service to church and state for which such degrees supplied a qualification, they were more for those employed in the higher echelons of royal and ecclesiastical administration than for humbler parish priests.[149] Nor would the meagre income from the Gwinear tithes have been sufficient to support men through the long years of further study necessary for higher degrees. Very unusual though an all-arts foundation was, it tallied well enough with Stapeldon's aspirations and resources.

Stapeldon's insistence on annual rectorships is more difficult to explain. Among the medieval Oxford colleges only Stapeldon Hall followed this rule for its head of house, and, like the barring of access to higher degrees, it was to

---

[148] Jones, 6, 16; Highfield, 'Early Colleges', *HUO*, i. 245; *VCH Oxfordshire*, iii. 118, 132.
[149] Cf. T. H. Aston, 'Oxford's Medieval Alumni', *Past and Present*, 74 (1977), 29–30.

cause problems and resentments in the centuries which followed.[150] Buck has suggested, plausibly enough, that Stapeldon may have had in mind the annual election of the university's proctors, who also rendered annual accounts.[151] But it is possible too that annual elections were intended to prevent the potentially dangerous consequences of a permanent accretion of power in the hands of a single scholar. One possible analogy here may lie in the reforming pressure applied at various points in the thirteenth and fourteenth centuries for the annual election of sheriffs, the crown's leading local officials, whose annual replacement was demanded by reformers in 1258 and again in 1340. On the first of these occasions, and almost certainly the second too, the intention was to prevent the sheriffs 'becoming arrogant in their offices and the readier to inflict injury', and to encourage them 'the more strictly to refrain from excesses', since they knew that they would have to account for themselves at the end of the year.[152] It may seem farfetched to envisage parallels between academic rectors and oppressive sheriffs. But Stapeldon's experience in government must have familiarized him with the many ways in which office might be misused, and it would not be surprising if he used his statutes to guard against even power's mildest tendency to corrupt.

Stapeldon's broad intention in founding his Hall was to augment the academic resources of the university, for whose masters and their learning he showed an almost passionate admiration. The statutes complement the preface to the deed of endowment by showing that the Hall was intended to provide for those who wanted to learn and who possessed the necessary mental and moral qualities, but who lacked the necessary means. Stapeldon's own interest in learning is strikingly brought out in the statutes, where he went so far as to name some of the technical exercises in logic which his scholars were to follow.[153] The academic lessons of Stapeldon's youth had evidently not been forgotten, and the statutes of no other college were so precise or so prescriptive. But these studies, though of value in themselves, were a means to an end. The enlargement of the university, to which the Hall made its own contribution, was 'to the honour of God and of holy mother church'. Both might be honoured through the provision of educated men; and although Stapeldon may have had it in mind that the highest positions in church and state were likely to be filled by those possessing higher degrees— men like himself—there were plenty of opportunities for the lesser elite of *magistri* also to serve. The practical end of a university education was the

[150] Below, 79–83, 116–17, 266.   [151] Buck, 107.
[152] R. Gorski, *The Fourteenth-Century Sheriff* (Woodbridge, 2003), 37–8; *Documents of the Baronial Movement of Reform and Rebellion, 1258–1267*, ed. R. F. Treharne and I. J. Sanders (Oxford, 1973), 262–3.
[153] *Reg. Stapeldon*, 304, 307: 'Abstracciones, Obligaciones, Cynthategrammeta, Circasigna...'. For the meaning of some of these terms, see Lewry, 'Grammar, Logic and Rhetoric', *HUO*, i. 407, 409–10, and J. A. Weisheipl, 'Ockham and the Mertonians', *HUO*, i. 619–20.

PLATE 1. The tomb of Walter de Stapeldon, c.1330, in the quire of Exeter cathedral.

PLATE 2. Stapeldon's grant of the church of Gwinear to the chapter of Exeter cathedral for the benefit of Stapeldon Hall, 4 April 1314.

PLATE 3. Letters patent from Edward II permitting Stapeldon to grant two messages to twelve scholars studying in the University of Oxford, 10 May 1314.

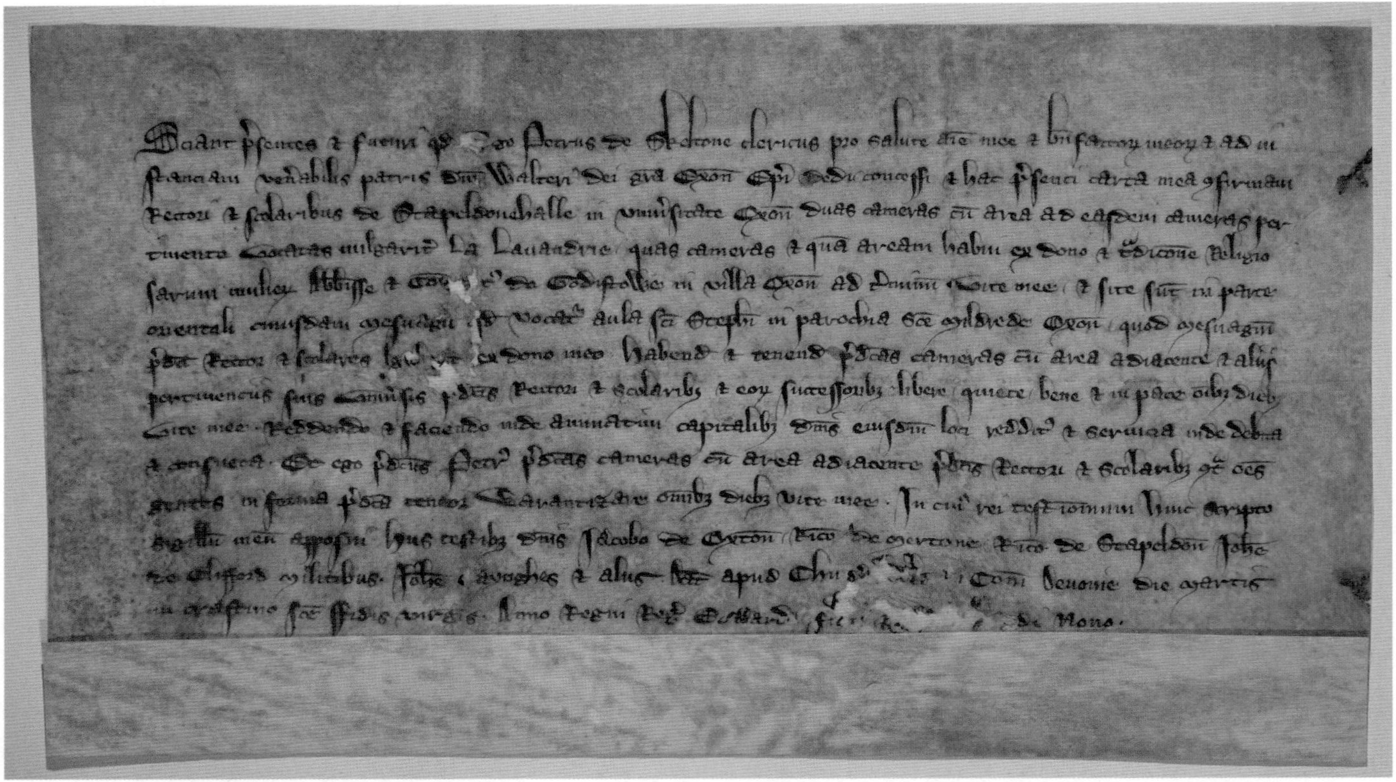

PLATE 4. Grant from Peter de Skelton to the Rector and scholars of Stapeldon Hall, at Stapeldon's instance, of two chambers and a yard called 'La Lavandrie', 7 October 1315.

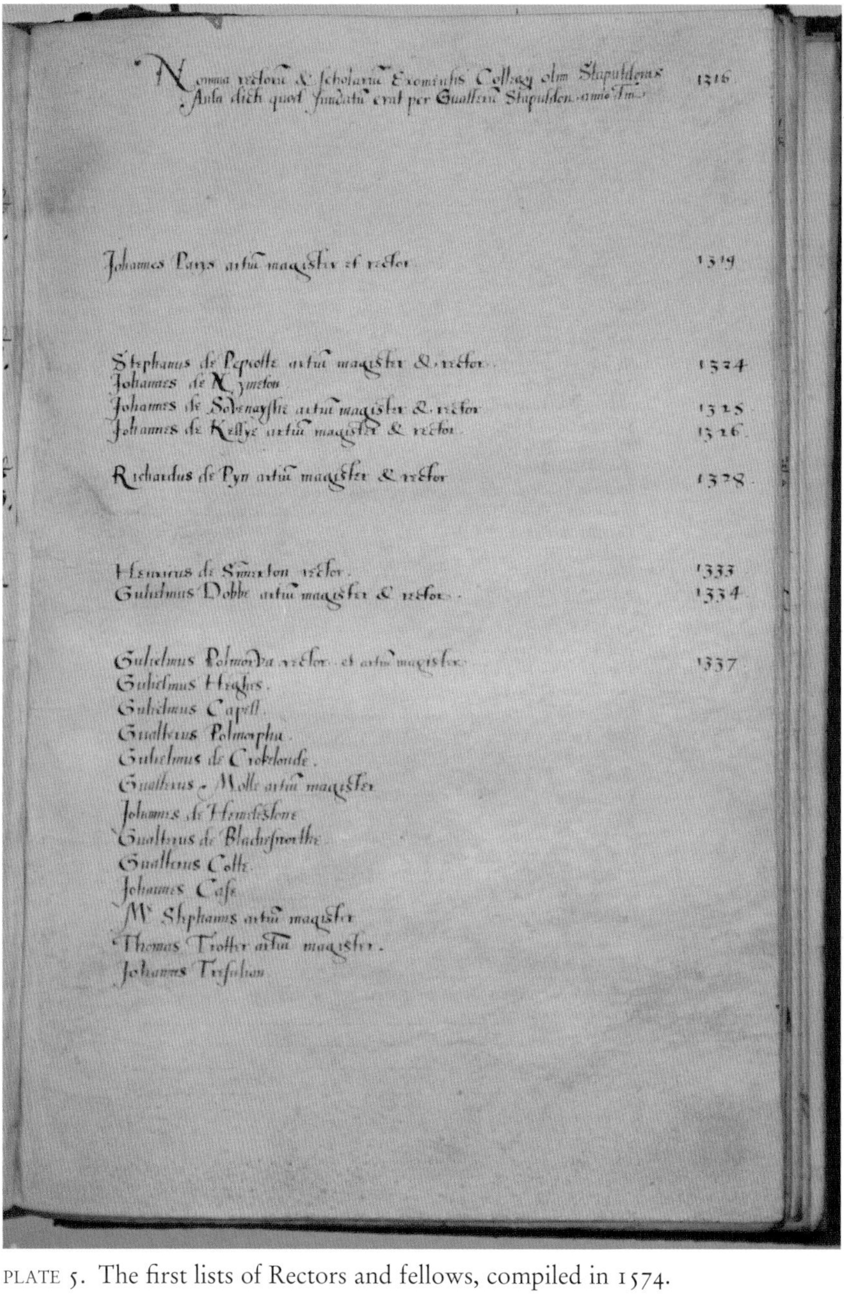

Nomina rectorū & scholariū Exoniensis Collegij olim Stapuldenas 1316
Aula dicti quod fundatū erat per Gualtrū Stapuldon annie Tm.

Johannes Parys artiū magister et rector   1319

Stephanus de Peprotte artiū magister & rector.   1324
Johannes de Kyneton
Johannes de Sokenayshe artiū magister & rector   1325
Johannes de Kellye artiū magister & rector.   1326.

Richardus de Pyn artiū magister & rector   1328.

Henricus de Smarton rector.   1333
Gulielmus Dobbe artiū magister & rector.   1334

Gulielmus Polmorva rector. et artiū magister.   1337
Gulielmus Hughes.
Gulielmus Capell.
Gualterus Polmorpha.
Gulielmus de Crokeloude.
Gualterus Molle artiū magister
Johannes de Hemelestone
Gualterus de Blachesnorthe
Gualterus Colle.
Johannes Cafe
Mr Stephanus artiū magister
Thomas Trotter artiū magister.
Johannes Trefulion

PLATE 5. The first lists of Rectors and fellows, compiled in 1574.

PLATE 6. Brass of Thomas Plymiswood, fellow, 1384–96, in Bampton church, Oxfordshire.

PLATE 7. The original College chapel, built 1319–26.

PLATE 8. The medieval College chest.

PLATE 9. The medieval College seal, attached to the deed appropriating the church of Menheniot to the College, 1478.

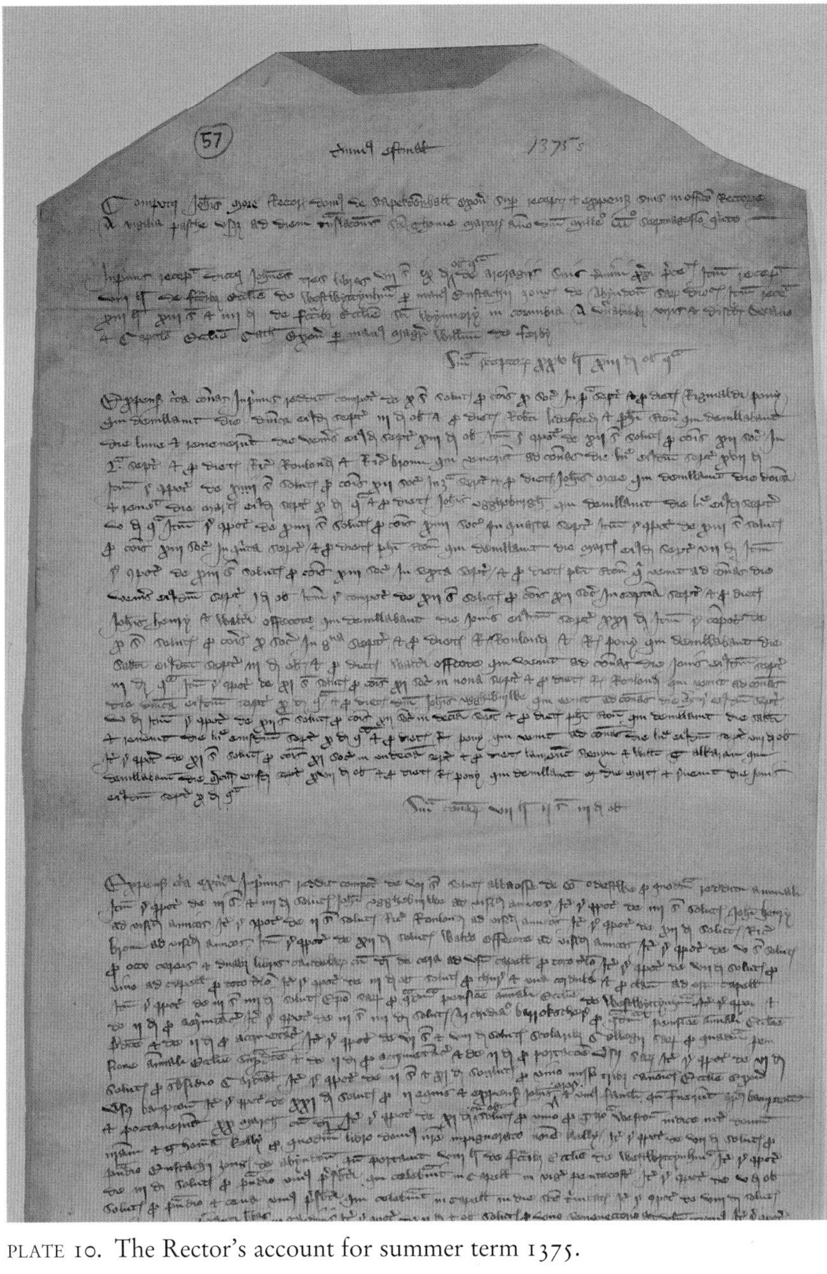

PLATE 10. The Rector's account for summer term 1375.

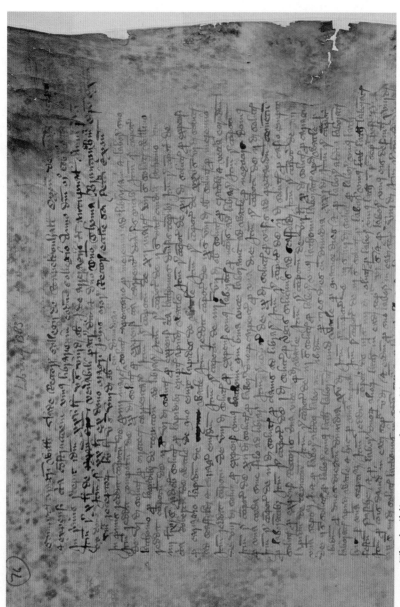

PLATE 11. The building account for the library, 1383.

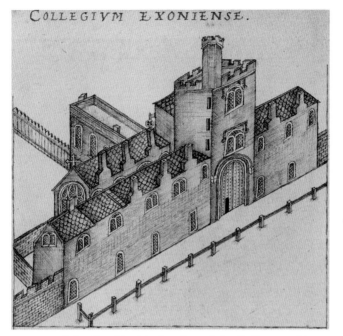

PLATE 12. John Bereblock's drawing of the College, 1566.

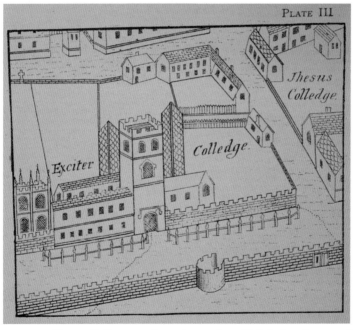

PLATE 13. Exeter College, 1578—redrawn from Ralph Agas's map of Oxford.

PLATE 14. Loggan's engraved view of the College, 1675.

return of Stapeldon's scholars either to the parishes of Devon and Cornwall, there to instruct their flocks in Christian teaching and Christian living, or to the administrative and pastoral service of the diocese, where, for example, most of the senior cathedral clergy were *magistri* in Stapeldon's day.[154] This is nowhere stated in so many words. But Stapeldon's stipulation that a scholar obtaining a benefice must forfeit his place at the Hall, his refusal to support scholars beyond their allotted thirteen years or so, and the numerous licences for study leave which, as bishop, he issued to local clergy, all point strongly to an assumed connection between the life of the Hall and the life of the diocese.

There was no common pattern behind the foundations and early histories of the first Oxford colleges: all came into being in different ways and with different constitutions, reflecting the aspirations and resources of their founders. Certain features nevertheless recur in their statutes. All had religious objectives, which the statutes usually state;[155] all were intended to relieve the material needs of those who might otherwise struggle through impoverished years of study at unendowed halls; and the founders of most stressed that the beneficiaries of their generosity were to be able, upright, and poor. Stapeldon's injunctions on this last point followed those of the University College statutes and were in turn to be followed by those of Balliol, Oriel, and Queen's.[156] Yet if Stapeldon Hall shared in a set of common principles it was in other ways distinctive. Its relative poverty, its members' exclusive origins in Devon and Cornwall, and their exclusive study of arts, as well as the democratic weighting which gave the same voting rights to an undergraduate sophist as to a regent master, all gave Stapeldon Hall a concentrated and unified character which may have been less in evidence at grander and more diversified establishments such as Merton.

The years between the making of the statutes in 1316 and Stapeldon's death in 1326 saw the Hall firmly established. It built up a full complement of scholars, acquired a good deal of additional property, and maintained a fruitful relationship with its founder which saw Stapeldon continue to give both guidance and money. Although its resources remained slender, it began to fulfil its purpose, and even the obloquy which descended on Stapeldon in his later years, followed by his sudden and violent death, did not threaten his foundation.[157] By the late 1320s, at the start of Edward III's reign, it had the statutes, the site, the endowments, the membership, and the continuing oversight of the bishops of Exeter needed to give it permanence.

---

[154] See, e.g., the lists of Exeter deans, precentors, and chancellors in Le Neve, *Fasti Ecclesiae Anglicanae, 1300–1541*. IX: *Exeter Diocese*, comp. J. M. Horn (London, 1964), 3–4, 7–9.

[155] Highfield, 'Early Colleges', *HUO*, i. 244.

[156] F. de Paravicini, *Early History of Balliol College* (London, 1891), 186. Oriel: Statutes of Oriel College, *SCO*, i. 8. Queen's: Statutes of Queen's College, *SCO*, i. 12. University College: *Munimenta Academica*, ed. H. Anstey, 2 vols., RS (London, 1868), ii. 781.

[157] Below, 57, 68–9.

After its investment with the Gwinear tithe income, the new society could begin to acquire its first scholars. In his statutes Stapeldon speaks as though this process has not yet been completed ('on the first occasion the number should be made up by Walter, bishop of Exeter...or if he dies before the number is completed...'[158]), and it is not until 1319 that we have any names (see Plate 5). In July of that year John Paris, 'Rector of the hall which is called Stapeldon Hall at Oxford', gave an undertaking that the building of a chapel for the Hall would not be to the detriment of the Hall's parish church of St Mildred (which stood on the present Lincoln College corner of Brasenose Lane and Turl Street). His undertaking was witnessed by four men whom we can safely assume to have been among the Hall's scholars: Richard Norreys, Henry Bloyou, Stephen Pippecote, and John de Sevenaysshe. To these early names we can add one occurring slightly later: Philip of Chalvedone, named in Stapeldon's register as a *magister* of Stapeldon Hall in 1321.[159] Coming into view so close to the foundation, all six are likely to have been chosen by Stapeldon himself, and this, as well as their standing as the Hall's earliest known members, gives them a peculiar interest.

Three of the new scholars were almost certainly from Devon: Pippecote from Pippacott in Braunton, north Devon; Sevenaysshe from Seven Ash in Kentisbury, also north Devon; and Chalvedone from Chaldon in Cullompton, mid Devon.[160] Norreys, in 1317 rector of Inwardleigh, in Stapeldon's native hundred of Black Torrington, was very probably a Devonian too. Bloyou was a member of a Cornish family. Two, Pippecote and Bloyou, had been ordained acolytes by Stapeldon in 1311 and 1314 respectively, while Sevenaysshe had received the first tonsure from him in 1311. Norreys had been granted leave of absence from his parish to study in 1317, and was granted three further periods of study leave between 1321 and 1324, during which time he presumably remained at the Hall. Norreys, Paris, and Sevenaysshe were already *magistri* in 1319 and must have been veteran university men when Stapeldon chose them. Only Norreys, as rector of Inwardleigh, is known to have had prior parochial experience, but most went back to parishes when their time at Stapeldon Hall was over: Paris to become vicar of St Kea in Cornwall, Bloyou to be rector of Ruan Lanihorne, Cornwall, from 1320 (and later to be a canon of Exeter), and Norreys to be rector of Ugborough in south Devon, from 1329. Pippecote must have been a rising figure at the time of his first appearance, for he was elected Rector of the Hall in three successive

[158] *Reg. Stapeldon*, 304.
[159] ECA, E. V. 5; Boase (2), 288–9; *Reg. Stapeldon*, 537. Unless otherwise stated the biographical information which follows on these men is taken from Boase (2), 1–2, and *BRUO*, i. 205 (Bloyou), 384 (Chalvedone), ii. 1366 (Norreys), iii. 1424 (Paris), 1484 (Pippecote), 1672 (Sevenaysshe).
[160] For these places, all farms and hamlets, see J. E. B. Gover, A. Mawer, and F. M. Stenton, *Place Names of Devon*, 2 vols. (Cambridge, 1931–2), i. 34, 50, ii. 562.

years from 1322 to 1325. He ended his days as vicar of Braunton in 1348, probably dying during the Black Death of the following year, when the living fell vacant. This little group, all of them known to Stapeldon, had thus established a *cursus honorum* of study at the Hall and subsequent return to a west country parish, which Stapeldon himself had intended and which was to be followed by generations of Exeter men until the nineteenth century.

If the filling of the scholars' places was one mark of the Hall's establishment, the expansion of its property portfolio was another. In the early 1320s its collection of Oxford holdings was augmented in order to extend its main site and to build up an income from rents.[161] The only acquisition in the first category was Fragon Hall, once tenanted by Peter de Skelton and purchased by the Rector and scholars in 1323. Lying immediately east of the main block of Skelton tenements acquired by Stapeldon in 1315, and so adjacent to the Hall's existing buildings, it made a useful addition to its purchasers' residential space.[162] All the remaining properties were acquired for rent and were recognized as *aule extrinsece*, 'out halls'. First came Batayl Hall, granted by Gilbert de Bedeford in August 1320, and lying in the suburbs, just west of St Mary Magdalene church, near the site of the present Randolph Hotel.[163] Next was Ledenporch, bought by Stapeldon for £60 in August 1323, granted to the Hall two weeks later, and standing halfway along the modern Ship Street, on land now occupied by Jesus College.[164] Finally came two other halls later to be incorporated within the College boundaries. Sheld Hall, fronting Turl Street and standing on the site of the present chapel, was granted by William Siward, a London fishmonger, in 1325; and Scot Hall, fronting St Mildred's Lane, now Brasenose Lane, came into the Hall's possession about the same time.[165]

The early Oxford colleges all tended to enlarge their domains through the acquisition of local properties, some to retain in hand, some to let out. University College, for example, built up its holdings in ways very similar to Stapeldon Hall.[166] But particularly noticeable at Stapeldon's foundation was the role of the founder himself. Although Stapeldon's hand is clearly visible only in the purchase of Ledenporch, it almost certainly lay behind other transactions. Gilbert de Bedeford, the grantor of Batayl Hall, is sometimes named as 'Bideford', suggesting a connection with Stapeldon country in north Devon, and it was Stapeldon's seal that was used to authenticate his

---

[161] Buck, 104–5, for a brief account.
[162] ECA, L. V. 4; Boase (2), xiv, xvi, 293–4; Salter, *Survey*, i. 55–6, map NE II.
[163] ECA, L. V. 3; A. II. 1, fos. 105ᵛ–106ʳ; Boase (2), xiv; Salter, *Survey*, ii. 218, map N IV.
[164] ECA, L. V. 7; A. II. 1, fos. 80ʳ–81ʳ; Boase (2), xiv–xv; Salter, *Survey*, i. 123, map NE I.
[165] ECA, L. V. 7; A. II. 1, fos. 87ᵛ–88ʳ; Boase (2), xvii, xxiii; Salter, *Survey*, i. 53–4, 58, map NE II.
[166] Darwall-Smith, 12, 26.

grant, since, as Bedeford noted, his own seal was unknown. The grant was witnessed by a group drawn from Stapeldon's circle, including, predictably, his brother Richard.[167] William Siward, the grantor of Sheld Hall, appointed two men to deliver seisin to the Rector and scholars, one of whom was Robert Hereward, the bishop's nephew and close associate, who had played the same role in the delivery of Batayl Hall.[168] Scot Hall had been granted initially by William Brabazon to Stapeldon and to William Prodhomme, possibly Stapeldon's grand-nephew, in 1325, and the grant had been witnessed by John de Treiagu, the bishop's steward. Since it was in the hands of the Rector and scholars in the same year, it must have been passed directly on to them, though no grant is extant.[169] It is a fair assumption that all these grants either came from Stapeldon or were initiated by him. One other benefaction, outside the general run of Oxford properties, was more certainly his. In July 1320 he bought the advowson of the church of West Wittenham in Berkshire, now Long Wittenham, some 10 miles from Oxford and in the diocese of Salisbury, from the prior of Longueville Giffard in Normandy for 100 marks. Two years later he gave it to the Hall, though it was not until 1355 that it was finally and fully appropriated and began to yield an income.[170]

In the additional statutes for his Hall which he drafted in 1325, Stapeldon was to speak feelingly of the 'heavy labours and expenses' which he had sustained in its foundation. His expenses are impossible to calculate but they must have been considerable. At a minimum they comprised the £5 paid to the crown for a licence to alienate Gwinear in 1312,[171] the 80 marks paid for Hart Hall and Arthur Hall in 1314, the £40 paid for St Stephen's Hall in 1315, the 100 marks paid for the Long Wittenham advowson in 1320, and the £60 paid for Ledenporch in 1323. But this expenditure, totalling £225, takes no account of the initial purchase of the Gwinear advowson, the buying out of Gwinear's rector, the acquisition of the other Oxford properties, and the administrative and legal costs occasioned by all these transactions, for which we have no figures. The total cost to Stapeldon is likely to have amounted to many hundreds of pounds.

Yet Stapeldon's spending did not at first bring the Hall much profit beyond the basic income from Gwinear; rather the reverse. Even with the additional Oxford properties, the Hall's revenues by the mid 1320s were still exiguous. The first surviving College accounts, the earliest for any college except Merton, give us an idea of the situation.[172] The Gwinear tithes were worth

[167] ECA, L. V. 3; Boase (2), xiv; *BRUO*, i. 185; Buck, 104.
[168] ECA, L. V. 7; Boase (2), xvii.   [169] Boase (2), xxiii; Buck, 104–5.
[170] Buck, 103–5, 110; below, 73–5.   [171] *CPR, 1307–13*, 504.
[172] Boase published accounts for October 1324–October 1325, December 1325–March 1326, March–June 1326, and December 1326–April 1327 (and for some later years): Boase (1), 170–3. These survive in the College archives: ECA, RA, A–D. But many parts of the accounts which Boase was able to read are now illegible, and his edition must therefore be regarded as a primary

some £20 to £23 a year, while income from Oxford properties added another
£5 or £6, to make an annual total of about £25 to £30. By comparison with
Merton's annual income of about £340, this was pitiful, and it was slight too
compared with University College's rather later income of £40 to £50.[173] The
'out halls' were as yet far from being the profitable investment that might have
been expected, chiefly because they were run down, needed money spending
on them, and could not be fully let. The first account, for 1324–5, shows that
£10 4s. 8d. had been spent on building a new kitchen and stable for Ledenporch and on repairs to Arthur Hall, Hart Hall, Sheld Hall, and Batayl Hall,
while the recorded income from these properties amounted to only £6 11s. 2d.
The account for 1325–6 marks down rents from Scot Hall, Batayl Hall, and
Sheld Hall as 'not received'. A similar mark-down for Arthur Hall is
explained by the property's being 'not fully occupied'. The account for
summer term 1326 notes that 6d. has been lost because a study at Scot Hall
has been left unoccupied for a term, and a further 6d. lost for the same reason
at Ledenporch. These rare facts about the cost of student accommodation
suggest that demand was slack for property that had to be maintained but
could not always be let.[174]

In these difficult circumstances expenditure often exceeded income. The
upkeep of the Hall and its community, chiefly spending on commons and
allowances for Rector, chaplain, and scholars, cost a maximum of about £36 a
year. This may have been reduced by the occasional lack of a full complement
of scholars and by savings when some were out of residence, but it was
augmented by servants' wages and the cost of maintaining buildings, leaving
the hall frequently in deficit.[175] There was one source of relief. In 1316 a loan
chest had been established by Ralph Germeyn, another Oxford *magister*,
Stapeldon's successor as precentor of Exeter, and no doubt his friend. Probably created under the terms of Germeyn's will (for he died in that year), and
with a capital of 20 marks, it existed to make loans to the Hall as a corporate
body or to its individual scholars.[176] But it did little to increase the Hall's
endowments, which remained perilously slim. In 1326–7 the Hall had to
borrow £1 16s. from the Germeyn chest to pay the scholars their commons
and to meet other expenses. Had income not been supplemented by generous
cash gifts from Stapeldon himself—two of £22 15s. 6d. and £18 10s. in 1324–5,

source. All the figures cited below are taken from it. The College's early finances are discussed
in Aston and Faith, 'Endowments', *HUO*, i. 300–2.

[173] Martin and Highfield, 68; Darwall-Smith, 25 and n. 18.

[174] Catto, 'Citizens, Scholars', *HUO*, i. 171, records a student rent for a shared room of ½ d. a
week in 1324—apparently the same as that charged by Stapeldon Hall in the 1320s.

[175] Aston and Faith, 'Endowments', *HUO*, i. 301; cf. Buck, 105–6.

[176] Boase (1), xliii; Boase (2), xxxv; *BRUO*, ii. 756; Aston and Faith, 'Endowments', *HUO*, i.
301–2; Boyle, 'Canon Law', *HUO*, i. 550.

and two of 10 marks in 1325-6—it would have been impossible for the Hall to pay its way.[177]

Stapeldon's purchases and gifts were not the only mark of his continuing care for his foundation. That some of the most prominent members of his family were consistently involved with the arrangements for its endowment and enrichment points in the same direction. His brother Richard witnessed nine of the various deeds of endowment, his nephew John Caignes, son of his sister Joan, eight, William Hereward, either his brother-in-law or his nephew, three, and John Prodhomme, his nephew, three.[178] By associating those close to him with his projects and plans at Oxford, Stapeldon may have hoped to bind them to his purposes in a sort of compact and so to ensure the Hall's nurturing and continuance beyond his own demise.

But more directly revealing were his own interventions in its governance during his final years. In 1322 the members of the Hall wrote to him to ask for his rulings on various points arising from the statutes. Their questions are summarized, and his responses set out, in a letter addressed to 'the Rector and scholars of Stapeldon Hall at Oxford' and written from Exeter on 22 April 1322.[179] It throws an interesting light on the sorts of issues which preoccupied Stapeldon's scholars and on his own pragmatic cast of mind. First came the question of elections. The scholars said that they were bound to elect eight men from the three Devon archdeaconries, choosing the more able, the more upright, and the more impoverished. But what if a place was vacated from one of the archdeaconries and the candidate best qualified to fill it came from another archdeaconry? Back came the commonsense answer: the best candidate should be elected, regardless of the archdeaconry, for the intention must always be to elect the most suitable person. Again, the statutes provided that the Rector should settle disputes between scholars. But they said nothing about a dispute between a Rector and a scholar (a point suggesting the internal tensions which may well have been present in such a small and close-knit community). What then? Stapeldon replied that in such a case the chancellor of the university should adjudicate, but it would be altogether better if the dispute could be settled by arbitration or else composed amicably by the other scholars. Again, the statute laid down that four scholars should be elected from the archdeaconry of Cornwall. But parts of the county lay under the bishop's peculiar jurisdiction and not the archdeacon's. Were men from these parts to be eligible? The answer was: yes, they were, the bishop's

[177] Aston and Faith, 'Endowments', *HUO*, i. 301, state that it is not clear whether these payments in the accounts are donations from Stapeldon or whether Stapeldon was simply forwarding the Cornish revenues to the College. But the accounts distinguish between monies paid 'from the goods of our lord bishop' and others from 'the lords dean and chapter of Exeter', the one Stapeldon gifts, the other Gwinear income.

[178] Buck, 11, 113-14 and n. 100.

[179] For both documents, see ECA, F. IV. 1, published in Boase (1), xl–xliii. Cf. Buck, 111-12.

jurisdiction being deemed to be part of the archdeaconry. Again, the statutes stipulated that scholars should continue to receive their commons during the four-week period of allowed vacation. But what about the annual 10s. allowance? Was that also to cover the vacation or was it to be docked pro rata? No reduction was to be made, replied Stapeldon, unless absence extended beyond the statutory four weeks. Finally, the statutes stated that every scholar must determine in arts within six years and incept within a further four years. But what if illness prevented a scholar from qualifying within the allotted time? The reply was judicious. An illness lasting less than four weeks in any one year should call for no extension of time. But if the illness lasted for longer than four weeks, cutting into the time available for scholastic exercises, then the periods for determination and inception should be extended pro rata by dispensation from the Rector and the majority of the scholars.

These exchanges show the absolute centrality of the statutes to the Hall's existence, the scrupulous wish of the Rector and scholars to follow them, and Stapeldon's humane, eirenic, and practical way of interpreting them. Like his acquisitions of property, his responses to the Hall's questions show that his was still very much the guiding hand behind its progress. Some of the same qualities, though presented in a more prescriptive way, come through in the additional statutes which he sent to the Hall in July 1325. These were of his own devising and, unlike his earlier interpretations, did not rest on initiatives from below. They were designed to provide for new circumstances and to impose firmer discipline on the Hall's members, while at the same time making allowances for human frailty. If a Rector died or left office during the long vacation, then all the scholars were to be present at the election of his successor after Michaelmas, on pain of two weeks' loss of commons, unless duly excused by the Rector and at least two scholars—in which case the absentee's commons should be restored. At disputations, the scholastic exercises which marked essential steps towards determination and inception, all the regent masters and scholars of the Hall were to be present from start to finish (had some been sloping off, weary or bored?), unless absent on the Hall's business or possessing another reasonable excuse acceptable to the Rector. No member of the Hall was to spend the night elsewhere while at the university, nor were strangers to be admitted save by general consent. An exception was to be made for the admission of the bishop's relatives and household, since—and we have noticed this passage before—he had laboured so hard and at such expense on the Hall's foundation. The *magistri* and scholars were to be present in chapel for the celebration of mass on Sundays and feast days. Finally, Stapeldon advised, 'not by the force of statute but only by that of admonition and precept', that when the scholars gathered at table or elsewhere they should speak only French or Latin, so as to become proficient in these tongues, to their long-term reputation and benefit.

If these additional statutes had a theme, it was one designed to enhance what would nowadays be called 'collegiality'. The requirement that all should be present at rectorial elections, at disputations, and in chapel, as well as that demanding night-time residence, was in part disciplinary, in part religious, and in part intended to assert the need for association and a common presence in the affairs of the Hall. The statutes also suggest that Stapeldon had the scholars' future welfare very much in mind. This was the explicit motive behind his injunctions concerning languages, but it also underlay his demand for general attendance at disputations: the disputants would benefit from the superior presence of the *magistri* and from their criticisms, while the wits of all would be sharpened by the propositions and responses batted to and fro. The hall was an egalitarian and largely self-governing society, where every member had a voice and a vote which must be used, but it was first and foremost an academic community whose *raison d'être* was learning.

One of Stapeldon's last acts in relation to his Hall may have been to consecrate its chapel in the spring or summer of 1326 (see Plate 7). He had been given permission to do so by the bishop of Lincoln, in whose diocese Oxford lay, on 3 April 1326, but he was heavily engaged in political and financial business at this time and we cannot know if he was able to take advantage of his colleague's licence.[180] In any case by this time he had another educational project in mind. In January 1325 he had been licensed by the king to alienate the advowson of the church of Yarnscombe in north Devon, together with three acres of land there, to the local priory of Frithelstock in order to found and fund a chantry for his soul and the souls of his ancestors. In April 1326, however, he changed his mind. The recipients were now to be the master and brothers of St John's Hospital, Exeter, and the beneficiaries to include Stapeldon's ancestors and all the faithful departed.[181] But according to his successor, Bishop Grandisson, writing in 1332, his ultimate intentions had been more ambitious and public-spirited. He had wanted to use the Yarnscombe revenues to found a school where boys should be taught grammar and educated in virtuous living; and Grandisson had linked this aspiration with his other foundation at Oxford for the study of logic. His aim was the same in both cases: to provide an education for priests and especially for those with pastoral responsibilities in the parishes.[182] By the time of his death, said Grandisson, he had already obtained the consent of the Exeter chapter to this scheme, and we know from another source that by December 1329 the school was a going concern, with a master, John de Sevenaysshe, who had recently been a *magister* at Stapeldon Hall and its Rector in 1325–6. It was Grandisson who went on to provide the school with statutes, though how far these were derived from plans bequeathed by Stapeldon is not clear. The school was to

[180] Boase (2), 289–90; Buck, 106, 160.   [181] *CPR, 1324–7*, 77, 257; Buck, 112.
[182] *Reg. Grandisson*, ii. 666–9; Orme, *Education in the West of England*, 48–9; Buck, 112–13.

have ten or twelve pupils drawn from the archdeaconries of Devon and
Cornwall and from the cathedral choristers, while the lord of Yarnscombe
was to nominate another. They were to be chosen for their ability and relative
poverty, to receive commons of 5*d*. a week, and to hold their scholarships for
no more than five years. The master was to receive the same commons and an
additional allowance of 26*s*. 8*d*. a year.[183]

There were some close similarities here between the school's method of
funding and its constitution and those of the Hall: both were supported
through the appropriation of a church, used similar criteria for selecting
their members, provided commons for those members and additional allowances for their heads, and applied strict time-limits to their members' entitle-
ment to funding. In view of all this, and of Stapeldon's role as founder of both,
it is possible that Hall and school were intended as a double foundation, with
the school sending its pupils to the Hall, as would later be the case with
Winchester and New College. But if this was what Stapeldon had planned, his
plans never came to fruition, though the school survived until 1540. Although
his project demonstrates once again Stapeldon's powerful and philanthropic
bent towards education and learning, there is no proof that he had anticipated
William of Wykeham or Henry VI.[184]

4. NEMESIS, 1322–6

On 9 May 1322 Stapeldon was appointed as the king's treasurer for a second
time. He was to hold office until 3 July 1325, and even after his replacement he
was to remain high in the king's counsels and one of his most trusted
lieutenants.[185] At the time of his appointment Edward II appeared to be
supreme. The short civil war of 1321–2 had resulted in the defeat of the
rebellious barons at Boroughbridge in March 1322, the execution of their
leader (and Edward's cousin), Thomas of Lancaster, and the confiscation of
the lands of the contrariants, as the rebels were known. This brought the king
a huge accession of landed wealth. Most of Edward's enemies were either
dead, in exile, or too cowed and enfeebled to offer resistance. But events were
to prove, though only after some time, that Edward's position was much less
secure than it may have seemed on the morrow of Boroughbridge. It rested on
the support of a narrow, self-interested, and increasingly detested clique. Both
court and government were dominated by the younger Hugh Despenser,
seconded by his father. The younger Despenser's greed for land and riches,
his influence over the king, and his use of brutal and extra-legal tactics to
achieve his ends made him deeply hated. Nor were there any compensating

---

[183] *Reg. Grandisson*, i. 240, iii. 666–9; *BRUO*, iii. 1672.

[184] Orme, *Education in the West of England*, 49.

[185] Buck, 140, 154–5. The best short account of this period is Prestwich, *Plantagenet England*,
205–16, 243–4, 303.

national gains to offset the oppressiveness of Edward's government. In 1322, during the last Scottish campaign of the reign, Edward was almost captured, and the humiliating truce which followed in 1323 left Robert Bruce as de facto king of Scotland. In 1324 the recurrent problem of Gascony led to war with France and the loss of most of the province. Edward had flouted some of the most basic rules of medieval kingship: to govern justly and in accordance with law, to distribute patronage equitably, and to provide effective military leadership. The revolution which swept him from power in 1326, instigated by his queen Isabella, was the consequence.

Stapeldon was a leading member of this predatory but ineffectual regime. So too was his counterpart, the chancellor, Robert Baldock, but Stapeldon's financial role made him the more prominent of the two. 'There are indeed four greater persons among the men of England', wrote the author of the *Vita Edwardi Secundi* in 1325, 'the bishop of Exeter lately treasurer, Robert Baldock now chancellor, the Despensers, father and son.'[186] His activities at the centre of government increasingly took him away from his diocese, where he spent only about 9 per cent of his time during his years as treasurer.[187] A member of the king's council, he was also energetically if intermittently engaged in the more public side of Edward's government.[188] He was one of a commission appointed to negotiate peace with the Scots in 1322, he and a fellow bishop were deputed to open parliament in November 1322, and he spoke for the king at the later parliament of November 1325. He was heavily involved in preparations for an English expedition to Gascony in 1324, and accompanied the queen and Prince Edward to France in 1325. If he was less conspicuous than he might have been, it was probably because he was more continuously occupied with office work at the exchequer.

It was here, as treasurer, that Stapeldon put his own considerable administrative and business expertise at the king's service, to his own eventual cost. Thanks to the work of Dr Mark Buck, we can now see that the fiscal policy implemented and to some extent shaped by Stapeldon was among the leading factors which did most to undermine Edward's regime. It aim was simple: to enrich the king and the Despensers, and to enable Edward to amass a fortune. 'Serve us in such a way that we should become rich', Edward wrote with unashamed frankness to Stapeldon and his colleagues at the exchequer in September 1323. Despenser's objectives were the same: 'that we may be rich and may attain our ends'.[189] In this both men were remarkably successful. When Stapeldon left office in July 1325 over £69,000 in cash was left in the treasury at the Tower, while by September 1324 the younger Despenser had

[186] *Vita Edwardi Secundi*, ed. and trans. W. R. Childs (Oxford, 2005), 240–3.
[187] Buck, 60.   [188] Buck, 140–62, for a full survey of Stapeldon's political work.
[189] N. Fryde, *The Tyranny and Fall of Edward II, 1321–26* (Cambridge, 1979), 94; Prestwich, *Plantagenet England*, 208.

nearly £5,900 on deposit with Italian bankers.[190] To put these figures in perspective we might note that the annual income of Thomas of Lancaster, by far the richest of Edward II's earls, was some £11,000, the income of other earls perhaps £5,000–6,000, a baron's income perhaps £600, and a knight's perhaps £40. When one chronicler wrote that Edward was 'the richest king that ever was in England after William Bastard of Normandy', he almost certainly spoke the truth.[191]

Most of Edward's money did not come from taxation. Indeed after the grant of a tax in the parliament of November 1322 the king received no more, and was twice refused taxes by the commons, in acts of conspicuous courage, in the parliaments of February 1324 and November 1325.[192] Instead, Edward's wealth largely derived both from the lands of the contrariants, the dispossessed rebels of 1322, worth some £12,600 a year,[193] and, still more contentiously, from relentless pressure on the king's ordinary subjects, whose routine obligations to the crown were now fiercely exploited. Pressure was applied in two particular and connected ways: through the rigorous auditing of all accounts presented at the exchequer by the king's officials, in order to reveal debts owing to the crown, and then through the unsparing collection of those debts. Though the initiative for these policies may have come from Edward, or more probably from the younger Despenser, Stapeldon was the driving force behind both. His was the main responsibility for the sorting and arrangement of the voluminous records of the exchequer which began in 1320 and whose chief purpose was to reveal monies owing to the crown. His too was the hand behind the three great exchequer ordinances of 1323, 1324, and 1326, the last promulgated after Stapeldon had left the treasurership but a mark of his continuing influence even out of office.[194] These were long and complex documents, designed to simplify and enforce accounting at the exchequer, to define precisely the duties of the various exchequer officials concerned with accounting, and to separate desperate debts from those which might still be collected. The ordinances showed all Stapeldon's customary practicality, command of detail, and astute business sense. In the first ordinance, for example it was laid down that because the hearing of accounts needed 'great diligence and perfect quiet'—in what was mainly an oral procedure in which the senior exchequer officials confronted the accountant—no judicial plea should be heard at the exchequer while accounting was taking

---

[190] Buck, 170; Fryde, *Tyranny and Fall*, 94; E. B. Fryde, 'The Deposits of Hugh Despenser the Younger with Italian Bankers', in his *Studies in Medieval Trade and Finance* (London, 1983), chapter III, 348.

[191] *The Brut*, ed. F. Brie, Vol. I, Early English Text Soc., 131 (1906), 225; Buck, 193.

[192] Buck, 145–6, 157–8. For Stapeldon's role at the exchequer during his treasurership, see Buck, 163–96, and M. C. Buck, 'The Reform of the Exchequer, 1316–1326', *EHR*, 98 (1983), 241–60.

[193] Buck, 190.   [194] Buck, 160, 168–9, 173; Buck, 'Reform of the Exchequer', 245–6.

place. Another section of the ordinance decreed that itinerant justices should deliver their estreats—copies of the lists of amercements and fines imposed at their sessions—as soon as the sessions had ended, in order to avoid the long delays of the past, whereby 'the king has received . . . great damages'.[195] The clarification of responsibilities, and the provision of accurate information concerning obligations to the crown, were to be among the pillars of the new financial order.

Behind most of this activity lay the drive to levy debts: a policy which, in the ways in which it was enforced, was bound to be deeply resented. In the thirteenth and fourteenth centuries the crown had a multitude of debtors, frequently men and women who had struck some financial bargain with the king or had been amerced in the courts for some judicial offence. But debts had often been payable in instalments, allowed to run on for years, or else entirely overlooked in the great muddle of the records. Under Stapeldon, however, this laxity was countered by a new rigour. Debts outstanding for decades, in some cases as far back as Henry III's reign, were now called in; payment by instalments was conceded much less readily; exceptional pressure was put on sheriffs to collect debts owing to the crown in the counties; claims for allowances submitted by royal officials were often refused.[196] The net of royal demands was spread still more widely when, in January 1324, the king ordered the collection of all debts owing to the contrariants, again often extending many years back into the past.[197] This policy soon became a public issue. In the parliament of February 1324 the commons complained that debts incurred under Henry III were now being levied, even though some had been paid and others pardoned; and in the following parliament too there were further complaints about the levying of debts already pardoned, 'to the very great oppression and impoverishment of the people'.[198]

The growing hostility towards Stapeldon, however, owed almost as much to his avaricious pursuit of his own interests as to his role as the ultra-efficient executor of the crown's fiscal policy. For the first time in his career, his character and ambitions became the subject of comment in the chronicles. The author of the *Vita Edwardi Secundi* wrote that he was 'greedy beyond measure, and during his term of office he had become extremely rich'. Another wrote that he was 'fumische [irascible] and without pity', 'a covetous man and had with him no mercy'. The Rochester chronicle adds more generally that he was 'widely hated in the kingdom'. But perhaps most telling of all is a comment made privately by Stapeldon's successor, Bishop Grandisson, in a letter written to Pope John XXII in 1328. Explaining the poverty of his see, Grandisson told the pope that his episcopal manors had been 'through

---

[195] *The Red Book of the Exchequer*, ed. H. Hall, 3 vols., RS (London, 1896), iii. 851, 901.
[196] Buck, 173–5, 178.   [197] Fryde, *Tyranny of Edward II*, 102–3.
[198] Buck, 176; W. M. Ormrod, 'Agenda for Legislation, 1322–c.1340', *EHR*, 105 (1990), 32–3.

hatred of my predecessor...utterly destroyed and laid waste'.[199] In the countryside as elsewhere, Stapeldon's fall had evidently been celebrated by an orgy of destruction and looting.

Even before he became treasurer, Stapeldon had been a wealthy man, able, for example, to offer the crown the huge sum of £400 for the purchase of a wardship in 1315.[200] The chroniclers' verdicts—greedy beyond measure, irascible, a covetous man without mercy—are backed by a number of particular complaints against Stapeldon which show something of his methods and the resentment which they provoked. Two examples may stand for about half a dozen others. Isabella Crok, the widow of a Gloucestershire knight, had received dower in two of her former husband's manors after his death. She married again, but her second husband was a rebel in the war of 1321–2, and as a consequence Isabella's dower manors, which were rightfully hers, were confiscated. Isabella then sued in parliament for their return. But Stapeldon coveted both manors, so Isabella said, and falsely told the king that both she and her second husband had been among the rebels. Edward had then granted both manors to Stapeldon, who, 'by his power and under colour of his office', had kept Isabella out of her lands for three years. In the second case Roger atte Watere and his wife Cecily alleged that Stapeldon, 'by the power of his office', had forced Cecily to surrender part of her inheritance, comprising land in Sussex, and that in consequence the couple had been so impoverished that they could not afford to sue at law for its return.[201] These are partisan allegations. But for both there is some documentary support, and they tally so closely with the broader charges of the chronicles and with other cases discussed by Buck that they have to be taken as a factual record. When we come to consider how Stapeldon, bishop of a relatively poor see, was able to give 1,000 marks to his cathedral in 1325–6, paying £285 in a single dona-tion,[202] and how he was able to build up the property of his Hall in the same period, we should bear in mind that he was never more prosperous (nor more detested) than in the years of his treasurership. Always wealthy, 'by the power of his office' he grew wealthier still.

The odium in which Stapeldon was held was particularly marked in London, where, according to the Rochester chronicle, he was 'especially hateful' to the people.[203] The reasons are not far to seek. Within the capital Stapeldon's wealth

---

[199] *Vita Edwardi Secundi*, ed. Childs, 336–7; *Brut*, ed. Brie, 238; Buck, 210, 214; *Reg. Grand-isson*, i. 95–6.

[200] *Calendar of Fine Rolls, 1307–19*, 244–5.

[201] Buck, 198–200, and for other complaints against Stapeldon, Buck, 197–216. Buck seems to me to go too far in his defence of Stapeldon: see esp. Buck, 155, 215. For other complaints which Buck does not consider, see TNA, SC 8/14/664, SC 8/37/1811, SC 8/73/3624, SC 8/81/4001.

[202] *Accounts of the Fabric of Exeter Cathedral*, ed. Erskine, i. 164; above, 20.

[203] Buck, 210.

was flaunted in a grand new house standing just outside Temple Bar, its grounds running down to the Thames. His customary highhandedness had gone to its building, which, according to one chronicle, had made use of stone robbed from the nearby Carmelite friary and, according to an inquest in 1327, had illicitly taken in land formerly held by Thomas of Lancaster. It was a storehouse for Stapeldon's treasure, in jewels, silver, and books, and it was apparently not his only London house, for another in Old Dean's Lane, just north of St Paul's, is mentioned in one account of his last hours.[204] His own riches stood in contrast to the burdens which he had imposed on the city, from which he had been 'an excessively harsh exactor'.[205] He was blamed by the Londoners for the judicial eyre of 1321, the London visitation of the king's justices, which had resulted in fines on the citizens, a legal challenge to the city's liberties, heavy expenses, and the replacement of the elected mayor by a royal nominee. In addition, at some point in these years, the farm of the city paid annually to the crown was raised from £300 to £400.[206] Nor were the Londoners immune from the treasurer's debt-collecting activities, their vulnerability increased by the exchequer's proximity at Westminster and by the role of the Tower as the command centre for the king's fiscal accumulation.[207]

It was in London that Stapeldon was to meet his end. The beginning of that end, which was also the end of Edward's regime, came with the confiscation of Queen Isabella's lands in September 1324, shortly after the outbreak of war with France in June. This was both a pre-emptive counter to any possible sympathies which Isabella might display for the cause of France, where her brother Charles IV was now king, and yet another measure intended to raise money. Stapeldon was widely blamed for this provocation, and not only, we may suspect, because the bulk of the confiscated lands lay in Devon and Cornwall, within his diocese.[208] Just a year later, in September 1325, Isabella's mission to France set the seal on the queen's enmity towards the bishop. Isabella had gone to France with the young Prince Edward, so that Edward could perform homage for Gascony in place of his father. The king's own absence from the country was reckoned by the younger Despenser to present too great a danger to the regime, given the rising popular anger against it. The queen was accompanied on her mission by Stapeldon and two other dignitaries, but Stapeldon spent only about two weeks in France before fleeing back to London, apparently to escape a plot against him at the French court, where Isabella and Edward remained. Some months later, in December 1325, Isabella charged Stapeldon by letter with having failed to provide her with

[204] *Brut*, ed. Brie, 238; Thomas of Walsingham, *Historia Anglicana*, ed. H. T. Riley, 2 vols., RS (London, 1863–4), i. 182; *Reg. Grandisson*, i. 4; C. L. Kingsford, 'Historical Notes on Medieval London Houses', *London Topographical Record*, 10 (1916), 117; *Croniques de London*, ed. G. J. Aungier, Camden Soc. (London, 1844), 52; Buck, 220.
[205] *Chronicon de Lanercost*, ed. J. Stevenson (Edinburgh, 1839), 255; Buck, 212.
[206] Buck, 188, 211.   [207] Buck, 170.   [208] Buck, 151–2.

protection, allying with the younger Despenser against her, and neglecting to pay her household expenses.[209] She refused to return to England until Despenser was removed. The queen's long sojourn in France, in company with the heir to the throne and with a party of disaffected exiles around her, played on growing English fears of an invasion. These fears dominated the early months of 1326, when Stapeldon was heavily engaged in attempting to organize the coastal defence of the south-western counties.[210]

Invasion finally came on 24 September 1326, when the queen, the prince, the exiles, and a mercenary army drawn from Gascony and the Low Countries landed in Suffolk.[211] Isabella's forces gathered strength as they marched on London. On 2 October the king left the city, fleeing westwards with the Despensers and Baldock. Stapeldon meanwhile had been in his diocese, but he reached London in the first days of October, summoned thither to attend an ecclesiastical council called by the archbishop of Canterbury in the vain hope of making peace. The bishops sought to negotiate with the queen, but nothing came of this. Isabella had appealed for help to the Londoners, who now rose for her. Order rapidly broke down as the London mob took to the streets. Stapeldon was denounced as the queen's enemy, ambushes were laid for him, and his house outside Temple Bar was looted and burnt. Evidently unaware of all this, Stapeldon then made the fatal mistake of riding into the city from his Middlesex manor of Enfield to have lunch at his other house in Old Dean's Lane. When he heard that his Temple Bar house had been pillaged and realized his acute danger, he first headed for the Tower, but then, hearing the crowd, rode to seek sanctuary in St Paul's. But outside the north door of the cathedral he was caught, dragged from his horse into Cheapside, stripped of his armour, and beheaded with a bread knife by one Robert of Hatfield. His head was sent to the queen. After various indignities his body, presumably reunited with his head, was eventually buried in Exeter cathedral on 28 March 1327. As was fitting for one of the cathedral's greatest benefactors, his tomb was given a place of honour just north of the high altar (see Plate 1). By the time of his burial both Despensers had been executed, Edward II deposed, and a new king crowned in Westminster abbey.[212]

5. EPILOGUE

Some considerable time after Stapeldon's death, probably in 1328, an inventory and valuation was made of the dead bishop's possessions remaining in his palace at Exeter.[213] We do not know what may have been removed, but

---

[209] Buck, 156–8.   [210] Buck, 159.

[211] The following account of Stapeldon's last days derives entirely from Buck, 217–23.

[212] *Reg. Stapeldon*, xxxi–xxxii; *Death and Memory*, ed. Lepine and Orme, 108.

[213] The inventory is printed in *Reg. Stapeldon*, 562–70, and is abstracted with comments in G. Oliver, *Lives of the Bishops of Exeter* (Exeter, 1861), 438–42. It deserves more attention than it has received.

certainly a good deal was left, as those making the inventory found when they went round room by room. The chapel, for example, was packed with rich vestments and liturgical vessels, more than sixty items in all, including the bishop's mitre, valued at the extraordinary sum of 260 marks or nearly £175. This was the single most valuable item in the entire palace. The wardrobe, a general storeroom used mainly for cloth and clothes, was equally well supplied with robes, table linen, towels, and a variety of rich hangings, but also including, more mundanely, a branding iron for horses and a canvas device for trapping partridges. The silver plate, kept in an unspecified place, was listed separately: some ninety-one items, the most valuable a jasper cup with a foot and cover of gold, worth 20 marks, but also including cups and basins embossed with the arms of England and France and of the local families of Dinham and Martin. The total value was nearly £170. Little was missed by the inventory makers, even down to the two wash-basins in the hall, the pots and pans in the kitchen, and the five old tankards and the half-full barrel of German wine in the cellar.

But more interesting than any of this were the books and the contents of the bishop's chamber. We do not know the full extent of Stapeldon's library, since some of his books were stored in his Temple Bar house, destroyed in 1326. But what remained at Exeter was impressive enough: ninety-one volumes valued altogether at £201 10s. 6d. The library was especially rich in works on canon and civil law, including his copy of the *Digest*, 'bought at Oxford'. The books, however, ranged well beyond those reflecting Stapeldon's academic studies and professional interests. Also present were works on pastoral theology, including Gregory the Great's *Dialogues* and *Pastoral Care*, some seven volumes of sermons, including some of St Bernard's, three complete bibles, and glossed copies of the Gospels. There were altogether thirty-four theological and devotional works, suggesting an interest in theology and the Bible as deep as that of a professional theologian. Some of these books are noted as having been acquired from the local clergy, presumably by gift or purchase. Other contemporary bishops possessed large collections of books, but we may suspect that Stapeldon's collection was unique in its size and range.[214]

The contents of Stapeldon's chamber revealed a more quotidian and human side to his character, the possessions of the domestic man rather than the scholar. They included a great hunting horn tipped with silver gilt, and several other horns; one large magnifying glass, two smaller ones, and a pair of spectacles; leashes for dogs and hawks, one made of green silk for a hawk; half a pound of azure, perhaps acquired for decorative work in the cathedral; three chess sets, one of them worn out; and three sugar loaves, two of them worth £1 5s. 1d., but the third, almost consumed by mice, worth only 7s. Yet before we conjure up too pathetic a vision of this elderly man, with his weak eyes, his sweet tooth, his penchant for chess, and his outdoor days with his hawks and hounds, surely long past in his later years, we might note what else was found in his chamber: £801 0s. 8d. in English money, 1,006 gold French florins ('agnels d'or'), worth about £200, and 4,000 gold Florentine florins, worth about £650—a hoard worth altogether about £1,650.[215] In addition, the chamber housed silver plate, beyond that already listed, with an estimated value of £515, and some eighty rings, three of them described as 'beautiful'. Whatever else Stapeldon may have been, we can be sure that he was inordinately rich.[216]

Stapeldon's library and his treasure brought into sharp juxtaposition two of the most prominent features of his character and career: his dual interests in learning and education, and in wealth and self-advancement. Preceding as it must have done any opportunities for financial gain, his Oxford training had been the making of him, as he himself recognized in the preface to his Hall's deed of endowment.[217] His return to Oxford in middle age, as a canon of Exeter and after about twenty years away, was an unusual career move, perhaps referred to in his autobiographical statement (Oxford 'nurtured me when she had brought me on') and perhaps too a consequence of his having previously lacked the resources to move directly from the arts course to further years of study for a higher degree. Even when he had left the university, he retained a close interest in its institutions and in its syllabus of studies, commenting in his prefatory statement on the value of the liberal arts, and later prescribing in the Hall's statutes details of the exercises in logic which his scholars were to follow. Equally striking was his insistence, both in the 1316 statutes and in his additions of 1325, that all his scholars should be present at academic disputations. His reflections on the consequences of the Fall, again in his prefatory statement, suggests that he may too have been conversant with current debates in the theology faculty. Though his career as bishop, diplomat, and royal minister took him into worlds removed from that of the university, he remained in some ways a don *manqué avant la lettre*.

---

[215] I am very grateful to Dr Peter Spufford for help in identifying the parcels of foreign coins from their descriptions in the inventory. Of the 4,000 Florentine coins, 3,000 had come from the crown as a loan in 1325 and were later repaid by Stapeldon's executors: *Calendar of Memoranda Rolls, 1326–1327* (London, 1968), no. 841; cf. Buck, 194 n. 243. But even if these monies are discounted, the hoard remained huge.

[216] But note that Thomas Bitton, Stapeldon's predecessor, had left an even larger hoard: his moveable goods were valued at nearly £5,400 on his death: *Accounts of the Executors of Richard Bishop of London 1303, and of the Executors of Thomas Bitton Bishop of Exeter 1310*, ed. W. H. Hale and H. T. Ellacombe, Camden Soc. (London, 1874), 1–12; N. Orme, 'Thomas Bitton', *ODNB*.

[217] Buck, 225; above, 35–6.

Stapeldon was not only learned but clever. Of the forty-five bishops active under Edward II, seven were doctors of theology and nine doctors of law, either canon or civil, but of the nine only Stapeldon and Archbishop Greenfield of York had degrees in both laws.[218] To follow these arduous courses through to completion demanded unusual intellectual powers. Yet even if we take account of these too we shall still not quite get the measure of Stapeldon's mind. William of Dene, the Rochester chronicler, while noting that Stapeldon came to be hated, acknowledged that he was a man 'particularly loyal, farsighted and discerning'—*fidelis, providus, et discretus*.[219] The word 'providus', also applied to him by Edward II in 1317 and posthumously by the canons of Hartland, and meaning 'circumspect, prudent, provident, exercising foresight', encapsulates the quality of practical wisdom which some of his contemporaries saw in Stapeldon, the canons of Exeter in 1307 as much as King Edward II. He himself had written of 'providencia', the noun to the adjective 'providus', as one of the attributes needed by decision-makers in church and state.[220]

In many ways the foundation of Stapeldon Hall exemplified precisely these qualities. In seeking to provide an educated clergy for the diocese of Exeter, Stapeldon saw the Hall as a practical means to a practical end; and in both his deed of endowment and his statutes he supplied the practical mechanisms to allow it to perform this function effectively and into the indefinite future. 'Providencia' was much in evidence. Yet the Hall's ultimate end was spiritual, for in training priests Stapeldon intended to provide the laity with the means to redemption through the medium of priestly learning and teaching. Difficult though it may be for us to appreciate the connection, his narrow and apparently pedantic directions about such matters as attendance at disputations and particular exercises in logic concealed a much broader and more elevated ambition. Behind the façade of the arts syllabus lay a spiritual endeavour: like any good pastor, Stapeldon aimed at the salvation of his flock.

And not theirs alone, but his too. Stapeldon's role in his last years, as one of the leading members of a detested regime and a man set on manipulating power for his own advantage, is enough to explain his violent end. It was his close association with the king, *regia familiaritas*, Bishop Grandisson was later to say, that had made his predecessor so hateful to many; and Stapeldon himself stated, in a more local and limited context, that his troubles had begun

---

[218] Edwards, 'Bishops and Learning', 58–9. Edwards has Greenfield alone as a doctor of both laws, but a contemporary source tells us that in 1306 Stapeldon had licence to incept in both: Little and Easterling, *Franciscans and Dominicans of Exeter*, 78–9. This is accepted by Emden: *BRUO*, iii. 1764.

[219] Buck, 210.

[220] Buck, 225; above, 16. The definitions of 'providus' are taken from the standard Latin dictionaries.

when he became a royal minister.[221] He had flown too near the sun. But there was no sudden moral transformation here: merely the accentuation of a facet of his character which had always been in evidence but which now had wider opportunities for its expression. He had been accumulating wealth, probably by dubious means, even before he became bishop, and the complaints of his highhanded and self-seeking dealings during his middle years in the see linked both back to his early life and forward to his time as the king's treasurer.[222]

Condemned as 'greedy beyond measure', Stapeldon did not need his skills as a canonist and biblical scholar to remind him of the fate ultimately reserved for the rich and the oppressor. His uneasy awareness of the growing dangers, spiritual rather than political, to which his activities exposed him is suggested by the precautions which he put in place to guard against them. In the form which they took they bespeak an uneasy conscience. In March 1322, between his two stints as treasurer, he endowed a chantry in his cathedral's adjacent charnel chapel, where intercession was to be made for him in his lifetime and, after his death, for his soul and for the souls of his predecessors and successors and of all the faithful departed. Five of his predecessors had already endowed chantries in the cathedral, so there was nothing unusual about this. But in two ways Stapeldon's chantry was out of the ordinary. First, the deed of foundation began with a preamble which spoke of 'the terrible day' when all should stand trembling before the judgement seat to receive what was due to them for their conduct in life. The language is heartfelt and by no means conventional. Second, the bulk of the deed took the form of 'an elaborate ordinance'. It not only set out the financial arrangements for the chantry's support, but also, and in great detail, the form which the various services and masses were to take, and the times and seasons when they were to be celebrated.[223] It is as though these precise stipulations were essential if the chantry's salvific purpose was to be achieved. In February of the following year, during his time as treasurer, he made similar arrangements for the celebration of masses on his birthday in the collegiate church of Crediton, writing, as he had also written in founding his chantry, of the need to perform such works as might intercede for him, in life as in death.[224] Stapeldon had always been anxious to secure prayers for himself and his circle, and had taken a share in some half a dozen other obits (that is, anniversary services) and chantries.[225] But in his last years the spiritual concerns which his actions suggest may have become more pressing.

One further example, already mentioned, is particularly telling. In January 1324 he received licence to alienate land and advowson to the prior and canons of Frithelstock, the nearest monastic house to his family home at

---

[221] *Reg. Grandisson*, i. 96; Buck, 214, 228.   [222] Above, 11, 25–6.
[223] *Reg. Stapeldon*, 374–6; N. Orme, 'The Charnel Chapel of Exeter Cathedral', in F. Kelly (ed.), *Medieval Art and Architecture at Exeter Cathedral* (London, 1991), 165; Buck, 69–70.
[224] *Reg. Stapeldon*, 377–8.   [225] Buck, 70–1.

Stapledon, to found 'certain chantries and maintain certain alms for the souls of the bishop and his successors'. But in April 1326, as we have seen, this arrangement was superseded, and the endowment transferred to St John's Hospital, Exeter, with the object of providing grammar scholarships for boys.[226] We cannot know why Stapledon changed his mind. But he may well have thought that the provision of scholarships was more useful to religion, and therefore more spiritually beneficial to him, than the mere establishment of a chantry in a monastic church for his own private benefit.

It is in this context, as well as in that of diocesan needs, that we should place the foundation of Stapeldon Hall. The clause in the Hall's statutes enjoining its chaplain to pray daily for the well-being of Bishop Walter and his associates while they lived, and for the souls of the bishop, his predecessors and successors, when they had 'migrated from this light', was central to the Hall's purpose. Its foundation came well before the end of his career, and before he had achieved notoriety as the king's minister, but already he had much to burden his conscience. The Hall was another sort of chantry chapel, an engine of perpetual and regular prayer for the salvation of the founder and a few other beneficiaries, where the consequences of 'of things ill done and done to others' harm' might be mitigated. But as a training ground for priests, founded by Stapledon's labours and at his expense for the promotion of religion, it was also the supreme example in his life of the good works which he must have hoped would weigh the balance of judgement in his favour on that 'terrible day' which all must eventually face.

Its later history must now be set out.

---

[226] *CPR, 1324–27*, 77, 257.

Anatomy of a College, 1327–1500

1. TRENDS AND SOURCES

At the outset of this chapter we must note some changes in terminology. The first concerns the name of Stapeldon's foundation. Known to Stapeldon and his contemporaries as 'Stapeldon Hall', from the mid fourteenth century it became intermittently known as 'Exeter Hall' and then eventually as 'Exeter College'.[1] To avoid confusion we shall from now onwards abandon its original name and use instead what was to become its permanent one. A second change concerns the word used for the College's members, which underwent a similar semantic shift. In the statutes and other early documents the members are 'scolares', 'scholars', but this word soon gives way to 'socii', though the former term often survived in legal documents such as deeds. Both 'scolaris' and 'socius' (to use the singular forms) are conventionally translated, and will be henceforth, as 'fellow'—the normal modern term for a senior member of a college.

At the time of Stapeldon's death in 1326 his foundation was one of only five secular colleges—University, Balliol, Merton, Exeter, and Oriel—in a university where by far the greater number of students still lived in unendowed halls or, to a lesser extent, in lodgings. By 1500 this situation had changed, though not yet radically. The earlier colleges had been joined by five others—Queen's, New College, Lincoln, All Souls, and Magdalen—two of which, New College and Magdalen, towered over all the rest in wealth and numbers.[2] Of the older colleges, only Merton could compete with these two. During the same period the number of halls had declined sharply, from at least 123 in 1313 to 62 in 1505. Many, however, had not disappeared completely, but instead had been absorbed by the colleges, continuing to exist as dependent establishments, often under principals who were fellows of the governing

---

[1] Below, 147–8.
[2] For wealth and numbers, see A. B. Cobban, 'Colleges and Halls, 1380–1500', *HUO*, ii. 622–3, and T. A. R. Evans and R. J. Faith, 'College Estates and University Finances, 1350–1500', *HUO*, ii. 654–5.

college.[3] Simultaneously, from about the early fifteenth century, the colleges and halls began to provide tutorial-style teaching for some of their members, in addition to the university lectures and disputations which had traditionally supplied both the foundation and the superstructure of a university educa-tion. In the case of the colleges, these pupils often formed a new category of undergraduate boarders who were not fellows and had no share in the endowment but who lived in college rooms.[4] The majority of students were almost certainly still accommodated within halls, whether independent (though regulated by the university) or composites of college 'empires'. Nevertheless, Oxford was on the way to becoming the collegiate university which would emerge more fully in the sixteenth century.

Both colleges and halls existed within a university which underwent few fundamental changes in the later middle ages. Its constitution had been estab-lished much earlier, in the thirteenth century. At its head was the chancellor, 'the chief officer of the university', invariably a doctor in theology or canon law, elected by representatives of the faculties, and holding office for two years. But by the end of the fifteenth century the post had evolved into one filled by a non-resident grandee, almost always a bishop, while the commissary, or vice-chancellor, oversaw the routine management of the university. Below the chancellor were the two proctors, responsible for supervising degree exercises, enforcing discipline, and accounting for the university's meagre income and expenditure. The governing body of the university was the 'great congregation' or convocation of resident masters and doctors, which controlled all major legislation; though hardly inferior was the congregation of regent masters, those *magistri*, mainly young men, who had completed the MA course and now for two years took on the university's teaching as the next stage in their careers.[5] Within the university the dominant academic body was the faculty of arts, the portal to higher degrees, through which all wanting to go on to theology, civil or canon law, or medicine had to pass. Some restricted exemp-tions were made for some members of religious orders and, by the end of the period, for lawyers. The arts syllabus continued to be dominated, as it had always been, by Aristotelian learning, beginning with Aristotle's works on logic and going on to cover his writings on ethics, metaphysics, moral philoso-phy, and natural sciences.[6] It is true that by the mid fifteenth century individual

  [3] J. Catto, 'The Triumph of the Hall in Fifteenth-Century Oxford', in R. Evans (ed.), *Lordship and Learning: Studies in Memory of Trevor Aston* (Woodbridge, 2004), 209–23. Numbers in halls: Catto, 'Triumph of the Hall', 209 n. 2.
  [4] Below, 159–63.
  [5] *SA*, xxi–xxii, lxx–lxxvii; W. A. Pantin, *Oxford Life in Oxford Archives* (Oxford, 1972), 20–4, 76–81, 85–6.
  [6] J. M. Fletcher, 'Developments in the Faculty of Arts', *HUO*, ii. 320, 323–4; T. A. R. Evans, 'The Numbers, Origins and Careers of Scholars', *HUO*, ii. 535–6; J. A. Weisheipl, OP, 'Cur-riculum of the Faculty of Arts at Oxford in the Early Fourteenth Century', *Mediaeval Studies*, 25 (1964), 167–76.

scholars were beginning to take an interest in new classical texts in Greek and Latin literature brought in from Italy, most notably by the university's great benefactor, Duke Humfrey of Gloucester; and these humanist concerns had some influence on the arts syllabus.[7] But in general a student of Stapeldon's generation would not have felt much out of place two hundred years later in Renaissance Oxford.

Perhaps the most important changes to the university resulted from external events rather than from internal reorganization or mere evolution. The leading role here was played by the Black Death and subsequent plagues. The most salient effect of these repeated epidemics was to bring about a significant decline in the university's numbers. There are, of course, no certain figures. But it seems likely that Oxford's student population was at its height around 1315, about the time of Exeter's foundation, when there may have been at least 2,000 in residence. That numbers shrank after the Black Death is clear from the evidence of falling rents and the disappearance of halls, and from contemporary comments and modern work on the numbers at Merton.[8] Those colleges heavily dependent on Oxford property for their income suffered disproportionately, while the gainers were college founders such as William of Wykeham, for whom city land was now cheaply available.[9]

Exeter was immune from none of these developments, but, like all colleges, it had some anomalous features which took its history in particular directions. These we have already looked at: its narrowly defined local affiliations; the restriction of its students to the arts course; its overwhelming dependence on revenues from appropriated churches; and the limitation of its head, the Rector, to a one-year term of office. This last peculiarity means that we cannot write the history of the College in terms of rectorships, as we might write national history in terms of reigns or as the history of other colleges, such as University College, with heads who served for long periods, can be written. All these factors weighed against Exeter's achieving the kind of distinction which accrued to colleges with more liberal statutes and more open-handed founders, such as Merton. Yet not all were to the College's disadvantage. Its regional connections, stronger than those of any other college, gave Exeter a large group of friends, counsellors, and benefactors, most of them former members concentrated in the churches of the west country—an uncovenanted but beneficial part of Stapeldon's legacy. All these themes will emerge in the course of this chapter.

The history of Walter de Stapeldon can be traced through the chronicles and records of his time. The history of his foundation is much more difficult

---

[7] Fletcher, 'Developments', *HUO*, ii. 342–4; J. I. Catto, 'Scholars and Studies in Renaissance Oxford', *HUO*, ii. 768–83.

[8] The best discussion is Evans, 'Numbers, Origins', *HUO*, ii. 485–97.

[9] Darwall-Smith, 82–3.

to write. Unlike Stapeldon, none of Exeter's medieval Rectors was a public figure and none elicited any recorded comment from contemporaries. Only a few letters to and from the bishops of Exeter throw some light on character and circumstances. Nor for this period do we have any record of college meetings, of the sort which occasionally survive for Merton. Such meetings were certainly held, but the issues raised and the decisions taken are almost always unknown.[10]

We do, however, have one invaluable source, without which this book could not have been written: the Rectors' accounts. Under Stapeldon's statutes the Rector was obliged to keep annual accounts, to be presented each term to the fellows and at the end of the year, in summary form, to the bishop at his visitation. Many of these survive: some 205 between 1324 and 1500. Before 1354 the survivors are few, occasional, and fragmentary, but from then on they proliferate. Of the 167 years between 1354 and 1500, full annual accounts survive for 104 years (62 per cent). Of the 668 terms in the same period, accounts survive—adding isolated term-survivors to full years—for 465 terms (70 per cent). A fair number of accounts, particularly in the years up to 1393, are for single terms only. But long runs of accounts cover much of the fifteenth century—from 1437 to 1448, 1449 to 1459, and so on—and short runs of two or three years are common throughout. Though outdated accounts must soon have ceased to be of much practical value, they were always of interest to later generations, and most were endorsed in the sixteenth century with the appropriate Rector's name.

Exeter's accounts are a remarkable resource, outstripping those of most other early colleges in their number and informativeness. Balliol has no surviving accounts before 1544; those of Oriel, a college almost contemporary with Exeter, cover only 1409 to 1415 and 1450 to 1525; while none survives for University College before 1381–2, and the numerous later accounts are much less full than those for Exeter in what they choose to record.[11] The Exeter accounting year began in October and was divided into four terms: winter (from early October to mid December), Lent (from mid December to just before Easter), summer (from just before Easter to early July), and autumn (from early July to early October).[12] For each term the account recorded the Rector's name and the term dates; itemized receipts; weekly

<hr>

[10] Martin and Highfield, 72–3; below, 118–19.

[11] R. H. Darwall-Smith, *Account Rolls of University College, Oxford*. Vol. I: *1381/2–1470/1*, OHS, new ser., xxxix (1999), xxxiv, xlviii–xlix. Mr Darwall-Smith's survey of early college accounts overlooks those of Exeter.

[12] The terms are so titled in the accounts for 1367–8: RA, 44–7. In what follows the accounts are cited by ECA roll number, and, within the roll, by the four annual terms into which most rolls are divided. So, for example, RA, 220/2, indicates that the material will be found on the section of the roll dealing with the year's second, Lent, term. Some accounts cover only one term and these are cited by one roll number only: e.g. RA, 19.

expenditure on commons; other expenses, always itemized, often in great detail; and payments to the main College servants. At the end of each term a balance was struck, showing whether the College was in surplus or in deficit. The account for the year's final term has an additional record of the annual allowances paid to fellows under the statutes, and was followed by a balance for the year. Since the primary purpose of the accounts was to record the Rector's financial liabilities under the statutes, some payments going directly into the College chest which was the repository for the College's money went unrecorded. These occasionally included major benefactions and may also have included payments from undergraduates. But for the most part the accounts provide a comprehensive overview of the College's getting and spending, in a form which barely changed between Stapeldon's lifetime and the late sixteenth century.

The accounts' primary value lies in their providing the names of the College's fellows, usually supplied in the record of their weekly commons and yearly allowances. But they also enable us not only to trace the ups and downs of the College's finances through the decades but also to gather information on such matters as building expenses, the travels of the Rector and fellows, the furnishing of College rooms, and the laying out of the College garden. They are augmented by other internal records, though none so useful. As we would expect, deeds recording accessions of property have been carefully preserved and are sometimes complemented in the accounts by details of the preceding transactions. Of external sources, the most helpful are the registers of the bishops of Exeter, the College's visitors and patrons, whose intervention in its affairs sometimes takes us beyond the formalities of accounts and deeds to illuminate the conflicts and human problems which sometimes arose in this small community. The records of the Exeter dean and chapter are similarly helpful in charting the College's relations with the Cornish churches of Gwinear and Menheniot, main sources of income but ones held in trust by the cathedral authorities for the College's use.

Two modern works are so fundamental to the writing of the College's history, and so full of information from the sources, as to count as sources themselves. C. W. Boase's *Register of the Rectors and Fellows of Exeter College, Oxford* was first published in 1879 and appeared in a revised second edition in 1894. Boase was an Open Scholar at Exeter from 1847 to 1850 and a fellow from 1850 until his death in 1895. For most of that time he was history tutor and librarian.[13] He had an intense interest in the College's history and a close knowledge of its archives, and in the first edition of his *Register* he published from the archives the earliest surviving account rolls to 1337, together with some later ones and a selection of other documents. But the

---

[13] W. P. Courtney, rev. J. R. Maddicott, 'Charles William Boase', *ODNB*.

primary value of both editions of the *Register* lies in the terse, note-form biographies which it was their main purpose to provide. These are often supplemented by verbatim extracts from the manuscript accounts. The biographies are prefaced by a lengthy history of the College, discursive, allusive, rambling, full of interesting details, and again containing many extracts from the records. Boase's origins in Cornwall—he came from Penzance—gave him local knowledge which he put to especially good use in identifying the home hamlets and villages of the fellows. He was an infuriatingly wayward historian, preoccupied by detail, careless with references, and unreflective in his cast of mind. Although he had read all the accounts, for example, one looks in vain for any ruminations on the College's finances. But if his *Register* is more of a compendium than anything else, it is indispensable for anyone working on the College history at any period.

A more wide-ranging and obvious source is A. B. Emden's three-volume *Biographical Register of the University of Oxford to A.D. 1500*, published between 1957 and 1959, with a fourth volume terminating in 1540 and published in 1974. Emden adds greatly to, and sometimes corrects, what Boase has to say about Exeter fellows. His work is especially helpful in tracing their careers after they left the College, drawing on the whole run of bishops' registers, printed and unprinted, and a variety of university records only partly known to Boase. Although he sometimes passes over *magistri* who are very likely to have had an Oxford training, his work remains a mighty achievement and one which makes it possible to reconstruct the outlines of many lost lives.

2. BEFORE AND AFTER THE BLACK DEATH, 1327–80

The history of the College does not generally lend itself to a narrative approach. The record is too flat, and largely devoid of the peaks, troughs, and personalities needed to carry the story forward. That is why this chapter has for the most part a thematic structure. But the thirty years after the Black Death are an exception. Full of incident, they both contributed to the permanent shaping of the College and brought forward some of the main themes underlying its development during the remainder of the middle ages; and they can be seen as a continuous set of linked episodes.

In the earlier period between Stapeldon's death in 1326 and the coming of the Black Death in 1348 such episodes are rare. The sources are sparse. Too few and incomplete for us to be able to deduce much from them, the accounts nevertheless suggest a well-ordered and moderately prosperous College. Perhaps surprisingly, the murder of the founder and the change of government which followed had no discernible effects. The College's place in the university, its character as a religious institution, and its founder's favourable reputation within Oxford, all gave it immunity from the sort of violent retribution which fell on Stapeldon's lands in Devon. In the months after the murder the accounts show the fellows continuing to draw rents from their 'out halls', to take funds from the Germeyn chest to pay for their commons, and to spend money on building repairs.[14] The old routines remained the order of the day.

The last of the early accounts, covering the two terms from December 1336 to July 1337, shows that the College then had the full complement of thirteen fellows envisaged in the statutes.[15] At their head was the Cornish rector, William de Polmorva. He was a living link with Stapeldon, having received half a mark as a 'poor scholar' from Stapeldon's executors towards his education in 1331. But he soon moved on from Exeter to become a fellow of University College in 1340 and then one of the founding fellows of Queen's in 1341. His nomination there by the founder, Robert de Eglesfield, his later doctorate in theology, and his position as chancellor of the university in 1350–2, all point to personal qualities which may have been recognized early on by his election as Rector of Exeter.[16] The College's income for these two terms amounted to just over £24, suggesting a total annual income of perhaps £40 to £50. The greater part of this, nearly £17, came from the College's original endowment of Gwinear, with the Oxford properties of Hart Hall, Arthur Hall, Ledenporch, and probably Batayl Hall and Sheld Hall, contributing a further few pounds. New properties continued to accumulate. In 1333 William Dobbe, a fellow, gave the College two schools (or lecture halls), valuable for their rent income, and two years later the College acquired Bedford Hall, one of several halls fronting St Mildred's Lane (now Brasenose Lane), whose line was soon to help define the College site.[17] It is perhaps not going too far to read a certain self-confidence into the few records of these few years.

After 1337 the accounts fail us until 1354. These years are the darkest in Exeter's history. We know the names of only one Rector, John Blatcheswall, and three fellows, and then only because they were parties to a deed in 1344.[18] When our sources resume, with accounts covering the winter term of 1354 and the first three terms of 1355, the Black Death has passed through, and much has changed in consequence. At a national level the plague which struck England in 1348 probably killed a third to a half of the population. It reached Oxford in November 1348 and raged until July 1349, carrying off two heads of religious houses, two chancellors of the university, and two provosts of Oriel. Merton lost a number of fellows[19] and Exeter enjoyed no immunity. The first post-plague accounts suggest that the College had only seven fellows

---

[14] Boase (1), 172–3.   [15] Boase (1), 177–8.
[16] Boase (1), 177; *BRUO*, iii. 1492; J. R. Magrath, *The Queen's College*, 2 vols. (Oxford, 1921), i. 95–6. For migration to other colleges, see below, 80–1.
[17] Boase (2), xx, 3, 294; Salter, *Survey*, i. 59, 70.   [18] Boase (2), xvii.
[19] *VCH Oxfordshire*, iv. 18–19; Evans, 'Numbers, Origins', *HUO*, ii. 492–3.

in 1354, compared with the thirteen of 1337, and some of the seven were almost certainly elected after the plague. In 1357 numbers apparently dropped to five, rising to thirteen again only in 1360.[20] Devastating in a different way was the plague's impact on the College's property. Throughout Oxford the plague left many properties vacant, causing a sharp loss of rental income to colleges and religious houses, and establishing a pattern to which Exeter conformed. Receipts sections are missing from the accounts until 1357, but when they begin again income from the College's off-site properties is conspicuously absent. Between 1357 and 1364 Hart Hall alone yielded rent, and then only intermittently.[21] Arthur Hall, Sheld Hall, Ledenporch, and Batayl Hall, all yielding in the 1320s and 1330s, have disappeared from the record. Particularly telling is the later evidence for Batayl Hall and Ledenporch. Batayl Hall had paid one pound in rent for two combined terms in 1334. When it reappeared in 1365, it was rented out for 3s. 4d., and a workman was employed in collecting stones 'from the garden of Batayl Hall'. The hall appears to have fallen into ruin and to have become the garden which it was to remain for many years. A little more light is thrown on its history by the further statement in the account that the rent had been in arrears for eighteen years, taking us back to the year before the plague struck.[22] Ledenporch, standing on the south side of the present Ship Street, had gone the same way. There too stones were being cleared from the site in 1365, but no income is recorded until 1376, when it was let as 'the garden by the north gate'.[23] Here and elsewhere the plague had left Oxford a city of green and empty spaces.

This process had its most visible and permanent effect on the main College site, for all the signs are that it was in these years, and largely as a consequence of the Black Death, that the present College garden came into being. In the early fourteenth century the site of today's garden was occupied by halls and their attached yards and gardens, tenements with a narrow frontage on Brasenose Lane, or St Mildred's Lane as it then was (we have to think away the present high wall), and running back towards and beyond the line of the present library. All are shown on the accompanying site plan (below, 140). Some were academic halls for students and some private houses. It is instructive to follow their fortunes, as far as we can, in the pre- and post-Black Death years. At the east end of the present garden, under and just to the west of the present mound, lay St Patrick's Hall. Some halls, like colleges, had particular regional affiliations, and this one may have been associated with Irish students. It was apparently still functioning as a hall in 1324, when it served to define the

---

[20] RA, 1, 7, 18.
[21] 6s. 8d. in 1357; £2 in 1360–1; 15s. in 1361–2; 3s. 4d. in 1363: RA, 7, 18, 19, 23, 28. There may, of course, have been further income in terms for which the accounts are missing.
[22] Boase (1), 174, 176; RA, 33; Salter, *Survey*, ii. 218.
[23] RA, 33, 62; Salter, *Survey*, i. 33.

eastern boundary of Scot Hall, the next hall to the west. But in 1360 College workmen were paid for repairing the wall 'between our chapel and the Irishmens' garden'—'desportum hybernicorum', 'desportum' meaning a garden for recreation rather than for the kitchen. Much later, in the 1480s, we are told specifically that a garden had replaced the old St Patrick's Hall.[24]

Next to the west came Scot Hall, an academic hall once occupying the middle part of the present garden. It had come into the College's possession about 1325 and was paying rent in the following year. But after that year it is never heard of again, and it is a fair assumption that it too had become part of the College garden, most probably after the Black Death and as the demand for student accommodation fell away.[25] Scot Hall's neighbour, again to the west, was Castell Hall, another academic hall. This was bought by the College in 1358 for £15, presumably to link Scot Hall and Bedford Hall, lying to east and west respectively, which were already in College hands. By 1360 we know for certain that its site had become a garden, for men were paid for working 'in the *disportum* where Castell Hall was situated', and in 1362 for building a wall 'in the *disportum* where Castell Hall formerly lay'.[26] Last in the line of halls came Bedford Hall itself, lying at the far west end of the present garden and on the site of the present Senior Common Room and the east end of the hall. As we have seen, Bedford Hall had come into the College's possession in 1335. Exeter paid a small ground rent for this hall to the priory of St Frideswide's, as it did for several of its halls, but in 1348—a significant year—this was remitted and the hall disappears from the records.[27] Was the remission of rent a consequence of the plague's having rendered the site valueless? Had any of these halls continued as going concerns, they would almost certainly have featured in the accounts, either as paying rent or, if managed directly by the College, as subjects for expenditure on building repairs. That they do neither leaves no room for doubt that by 1360 all four had gone.

The clinching evidence for their replacement by a garden is provided once again by the accounts. The earliest accounts from the post-plague period, for 1354–6, contain no mention of any garden. Then, in March 1357, come sudden signs of intense activity. One man is paid for a day's work, and another, 'Peter', for nine days' work 'in sowing and making the gardens (*ad seminand' et ad faciend' disportorum*)'. The plural 'gardens' may suggest work on the site of more than one former hall. There were two purchases of seed and 'Peter' was paid additionally for pruning trees. Further payments followed in 1358 to labourers planting, repairing, and digging in the garden.

---

[24] Boase (2), xxi (from RA, 16); xxiii and n. 1; Salter, *Survey*, i. 57–8, map NE II.
[25] Buck, 104–5; Boase (1), 172; *HUO*, i, map 3; Salter, *Survey*, i. 58.
[26] RA, 12, 18, 23; Boase (2), xxi; Salter, *Survey*, i. 58–9.
[27] Above, 69; Salter, *Survey*, i. 59–60.

At the same time another group was paid for work on 'the little garden next to the kitchen', suggesting a distinction between this small garden and the larger *disportum* on the site once occupied by the halls.[28] From this point onwards garden expenses—for building work, purchasing and sowing seed, and planting trees—become a frequent feature of the accounts.

We can therefore say with some certainty that the laying out of the garden as we know it today was begun in the spring of 1357, and that the drop in the number of fellows, the sharp fall off in rental income from Oxford properties, and the creation of the College garden were all in their different ways consequences of the Black Death. But the plague also set its mark, if less directly, on College government, bringing in a short period of disorder, dissension, and general upheaval in the College's affairs. At the centre of these troubles was the first post-plague Rector whom we know of, Robert Trethewey. Rector when the accounts begin again in 1354, Trethewey was a Cornishman, probably from one of the two Tretheweys in the far west of the county. His election as Rector, whenever it happened, is likely to have been a result of the very limited choice open to the electing fellows after the plague had drastically thinned their numbers—for, most unusually, Trethewey seems to have been only a bachelor rather than the *magister* who usually headed the college. Eight of his nine predecessors had been so styled, but Trethewey is merely termed 'dominus', the usual word for a bachelor of arts, both in his own accounts and in other contemporary records.[29] Those accounts indicate that this fairly junior figure was no man of business. They are in a state of confusion. All six surviving for his rectorship are for expenses only. There is no record of receipts, and the layout of the accounts suggests that none was kept. Nor, consequently, is there any striking of balances at the end of each term. Some accounting periods overlap in a thoroughly muddled way, while that for autumn 1355 fails to provide any total for the fellows' commons and ends abruptly in mid sentence: 'Item, he renders account of . . .'. The auditors would have despaired.

Under the statutes, however, the auditors were the fellows, and the evidence of misgovernment which the accounts reveal may explain their next move. In March 1357 Trethewey was ejected from the rectorship in what appears to have been a coup. His accounts for the first eleven weeks of the Lent term proceed in the usual way, but for the last four weeks of term he was superseded by one of the fellows, William Fatte, who accounts for these final weeks. Since the first garden expenses are recorded in Fatte's section of the

---

[28] RA, 6, 9, 10. The gardens are further discussed below, 141, 145–6.

[29] For Trethewey, see Boase (2), 5–6; *BRUO*, iii. 1897; RA, 1–6; Orme, 'The Cornish at Oxford', 79. The only other early Rector who may not have been a *magister* is William de Polmorva; but since the accounts give him no title of any kind when we know that he was at least *dominus*, this proves little: Boase (1), 177; *BRUO*, iii. 1492.

account, he may well have been the garden's initiator. The accounts for the next term are missing, but when the series resumes in autumn 1357 a new Rector, John Hall, has taken over, though Trethewey remains a fellow, drawing his commons until 1358.[30]

Trethewey's removal from the rectorship in mid term has no parallels in the history of the medieval college. Behind it almost certainly lay more than his unbusinesslike ways. Hall's first account as Rector records a payment of £4 11s. 4d. from Trethewey to the College 'from the goods of the house (*de bonis domus*)'. Later, in the summer term of 1358, his last term as fellow, he paid over a further £4 in two instalments 'for money in which Robert was held to the house by a certain obligatory writing'. These were not negligible sums; the first was nearly a quarter of that term's revenues.[31] It looks as if Trethewey may have been guilty of peculation, using his rectorial control of the College's finances to appropriate its funds, and so provoking his dismissal. His subsequent career does nothing to allay these suspicions. After vacating his fellowship he went on to study canon law, but shortly afterwards, in 1364, he was accused with others of assaulting a man in London who was coming to Westminster at the king's summons, and—a separate accusation—of successfully plotting to secure the release of a felon from Exeter castle. Later, in 1372, when he was rector of East Allington in south Devon, he was excommunicated by Bishop Brantingham of Exeter for unspecified 'contumacies and offences': a sentence which, 'in hardness of spirit', he defied for a year before submitting. He died in 1391 as rector of St Phillack in his native Cornwall.[32]

Robert Trethewey was a bad lot, whose elevation to the headship of his College was probably an indirect result of the limitations of choice imposed on the electors by the plague's culling of the fellowship. But his rectorship saw one large and permanent achievement, though it owed as much to circumstance as to Trethewey's own initiative. It was during his time, in 1355, that the College finally secured possession of the church of West Wittenham (now Long Wittenham), which was to remain one of its main financial resources for many centuries. This marked the end of a long story. We have seen that the advowson of Wittenham had originally been bought in 1320 by Stapeldon from its French holder, the prior of Longueville Giffard in Normandy, and granted to the College in 1322.[33] Stapeldon's primary intention was to enhance the College's endowment. Its appropriation of the church would place it in the position of rector, allowing it to take the greater part of the tithe revenues and to appoint a vicar to see to the pastoral care of the parish and to subsist on a portion of the remaining revenues. The planned arrangement paralleled that already made for Gwinear, appropriated to the

---

[30] RA, 6, 10.   [31] RA, 7, 10.
[32] *CPR, 1361–4*, 535, 542; *Reg. Brantingham*, i. 190, 301; *BRUO*, iii. 1897.
[33] Buck, 103–4; Boase (2), xxix–xxxi; above, 46.

dean and chapter of Exeter with the revenues going to the college. But while Gwinear was in Stapeldon's own diocese, and so subject to his direction, Wittenham was in the diocese of Salisbury. Lying just south of the Thames in Berkshire, near Abingdon and only about ten miles from Oxford, its proximity to the College must have been one of its attractions and its subjection to the bishop of Salisbury one of its drawbacks. The need to secure the bishop's consent to the terms of the appropriation, and in particular to the share of the revenues to be assigned to the vicar, caused difficulties which were still unresolved at Stapeldon's death.[34] New problems soon arose when the College's title was disputed by three or four claimants, including Thomas de Stapeldon, Walter's brother, leading to a lawsuit in the court of common pleas. But eventually the College's right to the advowson was recognized by the court, and in February 1330 the first Exeter rector, Richard Pyn, was presented to the living by the College.[35]

Pyn was an eminently suitable choice. A *magister* and former Rector,[36] he answered to Stapeldon's ambition to provide educated clerics for parish work, and his appointment further exemplified the bishop's intention of enhancing the patronage of his foundation. But although Exeter now had the advowson, the terms of the appropriation remained to be settled. A series of tedious negotiations ensued, during which Pope John XXII intervened to confirm the appropriation but also to stipulate that a suitable income should be reserved for the vicar and that the appropriation could go ahead only when the current holder of the living had either resigned or died.[37] This last was the real stumbling block. Pyn survived as rector until 1355, or shortly before, and his inconvenient longevity deprived the College of the Wittenham revenues for some twenty-five years. It was only in April 1355, following on from Pyn's death, that Exeter finally took possession of the church. This was marked by a great ceremony in which Robert Trethewey had a central role, solemnly entering the church, going to the bell tower, ringing the bell, and then proclaiming the College's possession to a great crowd of people assembled in the church and the adjacent rectory. Later in the year the terms of the appropriation were at last settled by Robert Wyvil, bishop of Salisbury. The College was to pay small annual pensions to the bishop, the archdeacon of Berkshire, in whose immediate jurisdiction the church lay, and the dean and chapter of Salisbury. More crucially, within two years two new fellows were to be elected from the diocese of Salisbury and the two fellowships were to become a permanent part of the College establishment. The enlargement of

---

[34] *Reg. Grandisson*, i. 181–2, 200, 387–8.

[35] *The Registers of Roger Martival, Bishop of Salisbury, 1315–1330*, ed. K. Edwards, C. R. Elrington and S. Reynolds, 4 vols., Canterbury and York Soc. (1959–72), i. 405–6, iii. 235–6.

[36] *BRUO*, iii. 1535. Emden errs in giving Pyn's parish as Little Wittenham rather than Long Wittenham.

[37] ECA, N. II. 4. Some of these documents are briefly summarized in Boase (2), xxix–xxxi.

the fellowship in this way had been envisaged from the start and was probably intended by Stapeldon. In return, the College was to receive the greater tithes of corn and hay from the parish, leaving the vicar with the lesser tithes of wool, lambs, etc., and with the rectory house for his residence.

The full and final acquisition of the church of Wittenham was one of the great events in the College's medieval history. It both raised its income by some 40 per cent and somewhat broadened the area of its recruitment.[38] The diocese of Salisbury was coterminous with the three counties of Dorset, Wiltshire, and Berkshire, but the addition of two new fellows from this large tract of country did little to dilute the College's original west country stock. It was a curious incidental result of the new arrangement that Somerset was now left as the only south-western county outside the College's purview. To judge by their surnames, the first two Salisbury fellows were Walter Ramsbury (in Wiltshire), a fellow in 1358, and Thomas Hanney (in Berkshire), elected in 1360.[39] Their election naturally had financial consequences, but the few pounds a year needed for their commons and allowances took only a small proportion of the new revenues. These had started to come in almost immediately. They are first recorded in autumn 1356, when 'our chaplain of West Wittenham...carried money to us', and by 1357–8, when we have the first figures, they amounted to at least £23.[40] The achievement of this gratifying result had consumed the time and energies of two rectors, Trethewey and Hall, and several of the fellows for much of the mid 1350s. The accounts show them paying frequent visits to Wittenham, seeking legal counsel about the appropriation, riding into Wiltshire to confer with the bishop, taking advice about the sale of crops, and, on one occasion in 1357, meeting in the new College garden to discuss with the vicar the terms for the endowment of his vicarage.[41] Trethewey's role in all this does something to offset the impression of his incompetence which the accounts otherwise suggest. More clearly than in any of the earlier sources, the College emerges as a business community, actively managing and promoting its own affairs.

If the acquisition of Wittenham held out the prospect of a new prosperity for the College, it was one soon overshadowed by a new danger: the return of the plague in 1361. The second plague was predictably less virulent than the first, but perhaps not by much. It struck in the summer of 1361 and persisted through to the autumn. Children, adolescents, and men proved particularly vulnerable.[42] Oxford and its colleges may have escaped more lightly than some communities, but Queen's College for one is known to have been devastated, losing at least three of its very few members, and leaving the

[38] For the financial value of Wittenham, see further below, 130–2, 135–6, 192–3, 197.
[39] *BRUO*, ii. 867, iii. 1544; Boase (2), 8, 9. [40] RA, 4, 7, 8, 9. [41] RA, 3/2, 4, 5, 6, 7.
[42] *The Black Death*, trans. and ed. R. Horrox (Manchester, 1994), 85–8; W. M. Ormrod and P. G. Lindley (eds.), *The Black Death in England* (Stamford, 1996), 4–5, 152.

Provost and the two remaining fellows to make provision against the college's complete extinction.[43] Although there is no direct reference to the plague in the Exeter accounts, its impact may be traced through the disappearance of some fellows from the record of weekly commons and annual allowances, and the subsequent election of replacements. In the Lent term of 1361 there were thirteen fellows intermittently in residence, two short of the full complement of fifteen resulting from the new Salisbury fellowships.[44] Within a few months the advent of the plague had caused a general dispersal of the fellows. Numbers in the autumn, long vacation, term always fell away, but in 1361 they did so to an exceptional degree. There were never more than four fellows in residence, and in mid July only one. Even in the following term, October to December, during the university's working year, numbers in the first six weeks of term never rose above five. As always in plague outbreaks, fear and flight are in evidence here. Of the twelve fellows active in the first three terms of the year, four—John the Chaplain, Roger Dounhed, John Wyseburgh, and William Aleyn—had disappeared by December 1361 and are never heard of again. One or two may, of course, have moved off into benefices, but Emden's comprehensive search of episcopal registers is likely to have revealed this. That they had certainly vacated their fellowships is suggested by the number of newcomers who appear among the fellows. Between October 1361 and July 1362 some six new men were elected: Robert Blakedon, John Foxleigh, William Middleworth, Robert Rygge, Thomas Swyndon, and John Trevisa.[45] We could reasonably conclude that at least four fellows had succumbed to the plague—nearly a third of the total fellowship.

To a small and close community the plague of 1361, like the Black Death itself, must have been deeply unsettling. It arrived in the form of sudden death, brought in a crop of new men who were ignorant of the College's practices and traditions, and weakened links with the past. To anyone who took a providential view of events, as all would have done, what followed within months of the plague must have seemed like a second act of God, though one less serious in its consequences. On 15 January 1362 the country was swept by a great storm. It was noticed by most contemporary chroniclers, and with reason, for its violent passage demolished towers, steeples, and belfries, flattened mills, felled trees, and wrecked houses. It was the greatest storm known to the sources before that of November 1703 made famous by Defoe.[46] Not surprisingly, it set its mark on Exeter too, uprooting trees in the garden of Hart Hall, tearing the tiles from the roofs of the College, bringing

---

[43] *VCH Oxfordshire*, iv. 19; Magrath, *The Queen's College*, i. 102–4.

[44] RA, 19.   [45] RA, 20, 21, 22, 23; Boase (2), 10–12.

[46] The main chronicle accounts are brought together in C. E. Britton, *A Meteorological Chronology to A.D. 1450* (London, 1937), 144–5. Cf. *The Black Death*, trans. and ed. Horrox, 86; W. M. Ormrod, *Edward III* (New Haven, 2011), 473.

down chimneys, and stripping the lead from the chancel roof at Wittenham, where eight fellows went shortly afterwards to survey the damage. At £1 10s. the total repair bill for what the account for Lent term 1362 calls 'the great wind (*magnus ventus*)' came to more than 10 per cent of the term's expenses; though something was recouped by selling the fallen timber from Hart Hall.[47]

The second plague of 1361 and the 'great wind' of 1362 were only two of the natural disasters, major and minor, which followed within a generation of the Black Death. A third, still more threatening to Exeter's survival than the plague, was the great famine of 1369–70 and its aftermath. This produced a crisis in the College's affairs which lasted for some five years. It was set off by the nationwide failure of the harvest in 1369 and by another outbreak of plague, which combined to raise corn prices to between two and three times their normal level, and one never exceeded between 1350 and 1500.[48] Unfortunately the famine's early effects on the College are impossible to assess, since the accounts are missing between autumn 1369 and summer 1372. But evidence from the register of Thomas Brantingham, the current bishop of Exeter, and from subsequent accounts suggests that the cumulative effects were almost ruinous. Harvest failure is likely to have depressed the College's tithe revenues from Gwinear and Wittenham, while raising the price of its food supplies. A letter from Brantingham to the Rector and fellows, written on 20 June 1370 at the height of the famine, probably in response to an appeal from them, suggests exactly this. It provides the first indication of the College's plight. As a consequence of the dearth, prevalent now for a long time, wrote Brantingham, they were burdened with insupportable debts and unable to sustain themselves from their statutory commons. For this reason, and setting aside the statutes, he gave each of them permission to take 10s. from the College chest in order to pay their debts.[49] A few months later, in November 1370, Brantingham again came to the rescue by allowing each fellow to take an extra 4d. a week in commons. The allowances for commons had already gone up from the 10d. a week prescribed by Stapeldon to 1s., probably in 1365. Now this was raised to 1s. 4d. What resulted from this alleviation is concealed by the absence of accounts. But when these resume, in summer term 1372, they show that the fellows' commons, plainly still inadequate, were now being supplemented by additional payments termed 'excesses (*in excessibus*)'.[50]

[47] RA, 23.
[48] J. E. Thorold Rogers, *A History of Agriculture and Prices in England*. Vol. I: *1259–1400* (Oxford, 1866), 213; D. L. Farmer, 'Prices and Wages, 1350–1500', *Agrarian History*, iii. 434, 445–7, 449, 502; Ormrod, *Edward III*, 474.
[49] *Reg. Brantingham*, i. 223; Boase (1), xliv; Boase (2), lv. The texts of these and subsequent letters in the edition of Brantingham's register are in all cases to be preferred to those printed in Boase (1).
[50] *Reg. Brantingham*, i. 234; Boase (1), xlv; Boase (2), lv; RA, 36, 51.

All this is consistent with a crisis caused by dearth and by corn prices which, after peaking in 1369–70, nevertheless remained generally high until 1376.[51] Raising the allowance for commons offered no real solution to these problems, since it assumed that the money could be found to pay for any increase. Yet as far as can be seen from the accounts, income remained roughly static from 1372–3 to 1376–7. The plea of the Rector, John Dagenet, to Brantingham in September 1372, 'considering the dearth', to do what he could to expedite payment of the Gwinear revenues by the dean and chapter of Exeter, 'without which we cannot live', suggests the urgent need to boost income in the face of rising costs.[52] It was under Dagenet, known to have been Rector from March to October 1372 but probably in office for longer,[53] that the desperate situation of the College emerged most clearly. Arrears accumulated and loans were sought in all quarters. The wages of the College's main servants, manciple, cook, barber, and laundress, all fell into arrears for one or two terms before being finally made up in the summer of 1372.[54] The annual allowances and weekly commons for the fellows similarly slipped into arrears, and some remained unpaid until 1374.[55] The humiliating loan to the College of 4 marks from its barber, made against the pledge of a bible redeemed in 1374, was another mark of these extraordinary circumstances.[56]

Nor did the situation improve under the next Rector, Robert Lydford, 1373 (or possibly 1372) to 1374. Brantingham's permission, given to the Rector and fellows in September 1374, to raise the commons allowance by a further 2d. a week, since the previous allowance was insufficient 'on account of the present dearth', was an indication that the substance of the College's difficulties had not changed.[57] Debts continued to accumulate. Two of the university loan chests were drawn on for loans, in return for pledges of books; a silver censer was pledged in return for another loan; and schedules of debts were drawn up showing, inter alia, that the farmer of the Wittenham tithes had had to bear the cost of repairing the barn, properly payable by the College. In these circumstances the College must have found the gift of 10 marks from Brantingham, given in the summer of 1374, especially welcome.[58] Still more indicative of the College's troubles was the fate of another gift, made for a specific purpose but used for a different one. In October 1374 Bishop Rede of Chichester generously presented twenty-five books to the College. The gift was complemented by a further one of £20 specifically allocated for the repair of the library. But within a few months most of this

[51] Thorold Rogers, *Agriculture and Prices*, 213–14; Farmer, 'Prices and Wages', *Agrarian History*, iii. 434, 502–3; Ormrod, *Edward III*, 474.

[52] *Reg. Brantingham*, i. 284; Boase (1), xlv–xlvi; Boase (2), lvi.

[53] The accounts on either side of Dagenet's two recorded terms as Rector are missing, so we cannot tell for how long he held office.

[54] RA, 51.   [55] RA, 53, 54.   [56] RA, 54; Boase (2), xlviii.

[57] *Reg. Brantingham*, i. 345; Boase (1), li; Boase (2), lix.   [58] RA, 54, 55.

money had been spent 'on other business of our house'. Some was subsequently repaid, but there is no sign in the accounts that the bulk of it was ever used for its designated purpose.[59] Penury had driven the College to break trust with a generous benefactor.

It was only from 1375 that the marks of crisis disappeared from the accounts, as corn prices dropped,[60] debts were paid off, and stability restored. Though there were to be other periods of acute financial difficulty in the mid fifteenth century, that lasting from 1370 to 1375 was more intense than any other. It showed how vulnerable the College was to the pressures of external forces and how inadequate were its resources to withstand violent fluctuations in the economic cycle. The sense of impending dissolution, carried over even into better times, may be reflected in the mysterious mission of one of the fellows to the papal curia in 1377 'for the perpetuation of our house'.[61] Had it not been for the Wittenham tithes, secured in 1355, the College might indeed have gone under.

Yet there were almost certainly other factors in play which exacerbated these problems. They were revealed by dissensions within the College, and central to those dissensions was the divisive figure of William Frank. A fellow from 1368, and probably Rector for some period from 1369 to 1371,[62] Frank was akin to Trethewey in his capacity for mischief. Apart from the record of his commons in 1368–9, the first we hear of Frank is in October 1371, when Brantingham appointed two episcopal deputies to deal with his offences.[63] He had heard, Brantingham wrote, that *magister* William Frank and the senior fellow of the college had unjustly impeded the election of a Rector, to the College's prejudice and to the detriment of its standing. The bishop's two deputies, one of them, Thomas Carey, a former fellow, and the other, Henry Whitfield, possibly one, and certainly closely associated with Exeter,[64] were to visit the College, compel the fellows to elect, and punish those resisting. The senior fellow, Frank's co-obstructor, may well have been Robert Lydford, fellow since 1365, soon to be Rector himself, and later one of Frank's

[59] Watson, 138; RA, 56; Boase (2), xlviii. For Rede's gift of books, see below, 102–4.

[60] Farmer, 'Prices and Wages', *Agrarian History*, iii. 434, 502–3; Ormrod, *Edward III*, 474.

[61] RA, 63.

[62] Boase (2), 14, followed by *BRUO*, ii. 721, states that Frank was Rector in 1370–1. But in the absence of any account for this year there is no proof; though a reference of 1373 to expenditure 'in the time of William Frank' (RA, 53) shows that he was Rector at some stage.

[63] *Reg. Brantingham*, i. 246; Boase (1), xlv; Boase (2), lv.

[64] For these two see *BRUO*, i. 355, iii. 2037–8. Emden denies the claim of Boase (2), 7, that Whitfield was a fellow of Exeter. But since he was admitted to Queen's in 1351–2 he may well have previously been a fellow of Exeter in a period, 1337–54, when the accounts are missing and the names of the fellows largely unknown; in which case he would have been an early migrant from Exeter to Queen's. Whitfield's close involvement with Exeter, acting for the College at the papal curia, serving as the bishop's visitor to the College, and giving books to the library, all suggest that he was more than a mere well-wisher.

colleagues as a fellow of Queen's.[65] When the case next surfaces, in January 1372, Brantingham is writing to Edward III to say that he has excommunicated William Frank, 'who pretends to be the warden of Stapeldon Hall', for contumacy, and now seeks the help of the secular arm against him.[66] Shortly afterwards, in March 1372, Frank was apparently expelled from his fellowship,[67] but almost immediately he was elected to another at Queen's.

We cannot be sure of what was at issue here. But it may well be that Frank, having been Rector for a year or two, divided the College, or played on existing divisions, by seeking re-election at the end of his term in October 1371. That he had a faction behind him is evident from Brantingham's revelation that he had the senior fellow of the College as his partner and from the bishop's injunction to punish those resisting. These divisions arose in the midst of the financial crisis which we have just examined—and to which Frank himself may have contributed. In March 1372 Rector Dagenet received £1 5s. 10d. 'from money remaining in the hands of William Frank', which hints at peculation, as in the earlier case of Trethewey, and suggests that Frank may have absconded with some of the College's cash.[68] It was a comparatively minor offence, though perhaps symptomatic of more major ones, that he also took with him one of the College's library books. The account for summer 1376 records that the College paid 6s. 8d. for a copy of Aristotle's *Metheora*, one of the set books for the arts course, 'which book has been missing for a long time and was out to (*de electione*) William Frank when it first went missing'.[69] He is the first known fellow (though by no means the last) to make off with a College library book.

Frank's departure for Queen's exemplifies a more extensive trend in the years around 1370, and one suggestive of deeper divisions within the College than those occasioned merely by his own misconduct. Between 1365 and 1375 four Exeter fellows departed to fellowships at Queen's, five to Merton, and one to Merton and then Queen's.[70] Migration from one college to another

---

[65] Boase (2), 14, assumes that Frank was the senior fellow to whom Brantingham refers. But Frank was not the senior fellow at this time; and the better edition of Brantingham's letter reads '...magister Willelmum Fraunke, ac senior socius collegii nostri Stapildonehalle...injuste impediunt...'. Note the plural verb. Boase (1), xlv, has 'impediit'. For Lydford, see *BRUO*, ii. 1185.

[66] *Reg. Brantingham*, i. 143; Boase (2), lv–lvi.

[67] So *BRUO*, ii. 721. There is no proof of Frank's expulsion. But his departure from the College in the first week of summer term 1372 was certainly precipitate: see RA, 51, where the 'commons' section notes Frank's departure in that week—William Frank 'who left the community on Saturday of the same week'. Since Frank was later expelled from Queen's, he may have enjoyed the distinction of expulsion from fellowships at two Oxford colleges.

[68] RA, 51.

[69] RA, 61. For the *electio* system, see below, 105–6.

[70] Exeter to Queen's: William Frank (Ex., 1368–72; Qu. from 1372), *BRUO*, ii. 721; Robert Blakedon (Ex., 1361/2–67; Qu. by 1372), *BRUO*, i. 198; Robert Lydford (Ex., 1365–75; Qu., from 1375), *BRUO*, ii. 1185, RA, 59; John Trevisa (Ex., 1361/2–69; Qu. from 1369), *BRUO*, iii.

was a routine feature of the medieval university. But such a concentration of departures from one College in such a short period was exceptional, and without parallel in Exeter's medieval history. The migrations may have owed something to the shortages brought about by the famine (though conditions are hardly likely to have been much better elsewhere); and the ability of migrants to pursue at other colleges the higher degrees from which they were barred by Exeter's statutes was a special cause of Exeter's position as an 'exporting' college, as we shall see.[71] But it is difficult to believe that some of these migrations were not also symptomatic of other dissensions within the College, impossible now to identify and visible to the historian only in the records of the Frank affair. The migration to Queen's had important consequences, for the former Exeter fellows, under the leadership of a Devonian (and probably Exonian) Provost, Henry Whitfield, came to form the core of a factional grouping opposed to the College's native northerners. This eventually led to the election of William Frank as an 'anti-provost', against the claims of the northerners' candidate, and to the secession of Frank's party from the college, probably in 1377, taking with them a large collection of the college's moveable property.[72] It looks as if dissent as well as dissenters may have been one of Exeter's exports to Queen's. After this heady career Frank's eventual billet as the rector of a rural parish in Wiltshire may have seemed something of a come-down.

These difficulties did not disappear with Frank's departure. The 1370s proved to be an altogether disturbed and disturbing decade. In June 1372, while the financial crisis continued, there was yet again a disputed election to the rectorship. Two fellows, neither of them named in the sources, received equal numbers of votes. In such cases the statutes put the final decision in the hands of the chancellor of the university, who chose one of the two. The backers of the disappointed candidate, 'sons of iniquity', as the chancellor called them, then appealed to Bishop Brantingham; but they had no right to do this, and the commissary, the chancellor's deputy, quashed the appeal.[73] The College was soon in trouble on another front in 1373, when one of the fellows, Henry Beaumond, was unjustly deprived of his 'status and degree', meaning presumably his fellowship, only to be restored by Brantingham's

1903. Exeter to Merton: Thomas Brightwell (Ex., 1364–8; Mer. from 1368), *BRUO*, i. 266–7, Boase (2), 122; Robert Rygge (Ex., 1361–64/5; Mer. by 1365), *BRUO*, iii. 1616; John Park (Ex., 1364–9; Mer. by 1372), *BRUO*, iii. 1425; Richard Pester (Ex., 1367–72; Mer. from c.1375), *BRUO*, iii. 1469; Thomas Swyndon (Ex., 1362–5; Mer. from 1365), *BRUO*, iii. 1635. Exeter to Merton, then Queen's: William Middleworth (Ex., 1361–5; Mer. from 1365; Qu., 1369–81/82), *BRUO*, ii. 1279–81.

[71] Below, 95.
[72] The best account is D. C. Fowler, 'John Trevisa and the English Bible', *Modern Philology*, 58 (1960), 88–93; see also Magrath, *The Queen's College*, i. 104–11.
[73] *Reg. Brantingham*, i. 265; Boase (1), xlvii; Boase (2), lvi–lvii. This document is misdated by Boase to 1373.

order after the chancellor had vouched for his character. Beaumond may not have been an entirely innocent party, for by 1379 he had again been deprived of his fellowship 'on account of his demerits', this time by the bishop's deputed visitors. He was restored, for a second time, only in June 1379, when he had sworn to mend his ways.[74]

More surprising in its ramifications was another dispute involving John Dedemore, College chaplain in the early 1370s. In 1373 or 1374 the Rector, Robert Lydford, had deprived him of his post, his room, and his commons, with the consent of the whole fellowship. We do not know the nature of his offence, but the Rector later cited in his own defence the statute permitting the fellows to dismiss a chaplain found to be unsuitable or, as the Rector put it in Dedemore's case, 'rebellious, incorrigible, or otherwise unfit'. Dedemore had then appealed to the chancellor, contrary to the statutes, which allowed no appeal. When the Rector had protested, the chancellor had responded with amazing ferocity, excommunicating Lydford, barring him and another fellow from all university teaching for three years, and prohibiting on pain of imprisonment any lawyer from pleading the case of the Rector or the bishop, equally an aggrieved party. The Rector and fellows had countered with an appeal to the court of Canterbury, the highest ecclesiastical tribunal, and the case had eventually come before an extraordinary panel of judges, presided over by the bishop of London, and including two other bishops, the chancellor of England, and the keeper of the privy seal. The verdict, an uneasy compromise, was that Dedemore's dismissal should stand but that he should be restored to the first vacant place at the College. A later accusation against him, of threatening violence to a London carter, suggests that the fellows may have been correct in judging him unsuitable for the chaplaincy.[75]

There must have been hidden currents in the Dedemore case. That the dismissal of an obscure Oxford college chaplain should eventually be considered by some of the highest in the land suggests that Dedemore had powerful backers, perhaps among the aristocracy. Since Dedemore had presumably been nominated by the dean and chapter of Exeter, as he should have been under the statutes, he may have been regarded as an outsider, for whose misjudged appointment the College bore no responsibility. In the matter of the disputed election to the rectorship and of Beaumond's first dismissal, the fellows appear to have been more at fault. But, taken in conjunction with William Frank's earlier defiance of authority, all these cases from the 1370s point to a disorderly and unruly College. In part this resulted from the founder's statutes, which had unwittingly encouraged dissension by imposing

---

[74] *Reg. Brantingham*, i. 316, 401; Boase (1), xlvii–xlviii, lii; Boase (2), lvii, lx.
[75] *Reg. Brantingham*, i. 327–30; Boase (1), xlviii–li; Boase (2), lvii–lix, 17; *BRUO*, i. 555; *BRUO*, ii. 1185, under 'Lydford, Martin', makes an important correction to Boase (2).

annual elections to the rectorship.[76] In part too it resulted from the tensions inherent in the daily working of a small, closed, residential community at a time when money was in short supply and living conditions difficult. Bishop Brantingham, arbitrator, judge, and benefactor, must often have felt exasperated by the repeated need to intervene in the affairs of Exeter College.

Until the 1360s the College's links to its founder did not depend only on the role of Stapeldon's episcopal successors as patrons and visitors. If the statutes were followed, prayers should have been said daily in college for Stapeldon's soul, and the celebration of masses for the founder was sometimes noticed in the accounts.[77] But there were also living links with the past. At this time they were most evident in the person and career of James Multon, Stapeldon's great-nephew. Multon was the son of Stapeldon's niece Margaret, daughter of his sister Douce, by Margaret's marriage to Thomas Multon, a man with a substantial landed estate in Devon and Somerset.[78] James followed in his great-uncle's footsteps to Oxford: Stapeldon's executors paid £20 for his maintenance in 1334, probably as an Oxford student, and contributed to the costs of his inception as master of arts in the same year. He had lodgings in Oxford in 1349, by which time he was a bachelor of civil law.[79] If he had matriculated at the usual age of about 17, he would have been born about 1310. It is very likely, therefore, that in his boyhood and youth he would have known his great-uncle, the bishop, and it is possible that his generous treatment by Stapeldon's executors marked him out as a favourite member of the family. When the accounts begin again in 1354, Multon can be seen to be playing a prominent part in the life of Stapeldon's foundation. A canon of Exeter cathedral from 1350, he frequently delivered the Gwinear revenues to the College on behalf of the dean and chapter.[80] In the summer of 1359 he was treated to wine and beer when he came 'to enquire about the state of the house', probably as the bishop's deputy.[81] He was entertained on other occasions too, once staying the night while returning from London, and he seems to have spent a good deal of time at nearby Abingdon, where he was several times consulted about the College's business.[82] We can sense that he was a useful contact, valued for his advice and practical help, and enjoying in return the hospitality of the College.

Sometimes in Multon's company was a more mysterious figure, but one who may also have had links with the founder's family. John de Stapeldon was a monk of Abingdon and prior there by 1361. He too was entertained by the College, on at least one occasion quite lavishly: in 1355 10d. was spent on wine and spices for him when he called on matters connected with the appropriation of Wittenham, and he was regularly involved in the College's

---

[76] As Brantingham later noted: *Reg. Brantingham*, i. 543–4.   [77] RA, 27, 33.
[78] Buck, 11, 32.   [79] *Reg. Stapeldon*, 577; *BRUO*, ii. 1328.
[80] RA, 9, 14, 16, 20, 22, 23, 24, 31.   [81] RA, 14.   [82] RA, 10, 16, 17, 19, 21.

relations with the church there in the 1350s.[83] He came again in 1362 'to discuss the business of the house'. In the same year the Gwinear money was handed over to him by Multon for delivery to the College,[84] and Multon's sojourns at Abingdon suggest that the two men were well known to each other. Who exactly Stapeldon was is less clear. Walter de Stapeldon had no married brothers besides Sir Richard de Stapeldon, and no collateral male descendants besides Sir Richard's bastard son, another Richard.[85] It is conceivable that John was another such bastard or possibly a descendant of an unknown cousin of the bishop. But, given both the coincidence of name and John's close association with the College, a family connection of some sort with the founder seems highly likely. John certainly had links with Devon, not only by association with Multon, perhaps his relative, but through his friendship with John Lydford, Devonian, canon lawyer, and canon of Exeter, who left money in his will for masses for John de Stapeldon's soul.[86]

The disappearance of John de Stapeldon—he is last heard of in 1362—may have marked the severance of one of the College's last direct ties with its founder. More certainly, the death of James Multon in 1366 marked another. By the late 1360s it is unlikely that any of Exeter's associates could remember Bishop Stapeldon, separated as they were by at least forty years. But the interest of both men in the College exemplified more than continuities with the past and the sense of obligation which Stapeldon's distant kinsmen may have felt towards his foundation. It also showed the external help and support which the College was able to attract and which was to be a recurrent feature of its corporate life.

The thirty years after the Black Death constituted the most turbulent period in the College's early history. Natural disasters—recurrent plagues, harvest failures, dearth—interacted with a sometimes divided and badly governed fellowship to cause troubles which could only be settled by the intervention of the College's visitor, the bishop of Exeter. In twice wiping out a high proportion of a very small collegiate body, the two plagues of 1348–9 and 1361 served to disrupt continuity, to weaken the corporate fabric of the College, and perhaps to facilitate the election of such an unsuitable Rector as Robert Trethewey. By encouraging migration to other Colleges the dearth of 1369–70 and the financial difficulties it brought may have had comparable effects. For all these disabilities the appropriation of the church of Wittenham in 1355 offered some compensation, both in the corporate effort which it necessitated and more especially in its enhancement of the College's revenues. Yet in the short term it did little to solve Exeter's problems. Even without the external inflictions of plague and dearth, the sudden removal of Trethewey

---

[83] RA, 3/2, 4, 22; Boase (2), xxix, n. 2(j).   [84] RA, 23, 25.   [85] Buck, 26.
[86] Reg. Stafford, 390; John Lydford's Book, ed. D. M. Owen, DCRS, 20 (1975), 6.

from office in 1357, the extrusion of Henry Beaumond from office in 1372, followed by the humiliation of having to restore him on the bishop's orders, and the two disputed elections of the same decade, all suggest unsettling disharmonies among the fellowship. Stapeldon, wise in the sometimes rancorous ways of small communities, had made provision at several points in his statutes for the peaceful resolution of disputes. But he had perhaps not foreseen the extent to which such difficulties might involve the person and office of the Rector.

After Beaumond's second restoration in 1379 calm seems to have descended. Brantingham remained as bishop until 1394, but there is nothing either in his register or in the College accounts to suggest that he again had to intervene in the College's affairs in anything other than a routine way. Meanwhile, the building of the new library in 1383, discussed below, signified the restoration of both the College's self-confidence and its finances. In illuminating the College's strengths and weaknesses, the events of the preceding period had also adumbrated most of the themes of its subsequent history: the character of the fellowship, the uncertainties of its financial position, the central role of its Rector, the development of its site, the roles of the bishop of Exeter and the Exeter dean and chapter, and the important part played in its affairs by external friends and benefactors. Nothing, however, has yet been seen of the origins, studies, and intellectual life of the College's members. These are the topics which, in a more analytical way, will now be addressed.

3. FELLOWS: ORIGINS

We know the names of some 330 men who were fellows of Exeter between 1318 and 1500. They come almost exclusively from the accounts, where fellows appear by name as the recipients of weekly commons and annual allowances and as participants in College business. For years in which no accounts survive, names are almost always lacking; so that, for example, we are ignorant of the identity of almost all fellows in the accountless years between 1337 and 1354. Even so, our 330 probably comprise something like three-quarters of all fellows active in this long period. Few other early colleges are so well placed. From University College, the names of 99 fellows are known from the fourteenth and fifteenth centuries; from Queen's, 110; and from Balliol perhaps 80 before 1400. Only the much larger Merton, with some 700 to 800 names, has a more numerous corps of known fellows.[87]

The geographical origins of this multitude are much easier to assess than their social origins. The most distinctive feature of Exeter, already much referred to, was its intensely regional bias towards the two south-western

[87] Darwall-Smith, 29; Magrath, *The Queen's College*, ii. 284–91; Jones, 21; G. C. Brodrick, *Memorials of Merton College*, OHS, iv (1885), 154–245.

counties. Under Stapeldon's statutes eight fellows were to come from the three archdeaconries of Devon and four from Cornwall, to whom were added the two Salisbury fellows after the appropriation of Wittenham in 1355. Of the 289 fellows to whom Boase assigned a county or diocese of origin, 171 (59 per cent) came from Devon, 75 (26 per cent) from Cornwall, and 43 (15 per cent) from Salisbury diocese. Although Boase's particular attributions are not always reliable,[88] these proportions seem about right, mirroring as they do the 8:4:2 proportions of fellows statutorily assigned to the three areas. Similarly, and again using Boase's attributions, Devon supplies 40 Rectors (58 per cent), Cornwall, 23 (33 per cent), and Salisbury diocese 6 (9 per cent). Devon was thus the clear focus of the College's external links, its prominence magnified by the role of the dean and chapter of Exeter as trustees for the Gwinear revenues and by that of the bishop of Exeter as the College's visitor. The accounts show the Rector and fellows travelling more frequently to Exeter than to anywhere else, and when the College was short of funds in 1457 it was to Devon that the Rector went 'to solicit money from the friends of the College'.[89] There were other more distinctive marks of the College's identification with Devon. That some, probably many, of the fellows spoke with a broad Devon accent is verifiable from spellings in the accounts, where the surname 'Fatte' becomes 'Vatte', 'Foxlegh' becomes 'Voxlegh', and 'focalia' (fuel) becomes 'vocalia': the standard English 'F' giving way to the Devonian 'V'.[90] Fellows from the west of Cornwall, on the other hand, may have had not only local accents, but also a different mother tongue, since Cornish was the native language.[91] If this was so, they would have been trilingual, not only in Cornish but in English and Latin as well.

If the College was thus in some ways a provincial society transplanted to Oxford, it is more difficult to say how far it was also a social microcosm. The family origins of all but a tiny proportion of Oxford students in the later middle ages are unknown. There is a general consensus, however, that many came from the prosperous free peasantry and rural yeomanry, some from merchant families, the urban bourgeoisie, and the ranks of the lawyers, some, perhaps more, from the gentry, and a very few from the nobility.[92] As far as can be seen, the fellows of Exeter fell into the same broad categories. The numbers whose origins are known with anything approaching certainty are pitifully small. Martin Lercedekne (fellow, c.1372–4) was the seventh son of Sir John Lercedekne, a Cornish knight;[93] Walter Lyhert (c.1420–5), later

[88] Orme, 'The Cornish at Oxford', 56.   [89] RA, 156/3; below, 137.
[90] RA, 6, 24, 25; Boase (2), 38; D. Postles, The Surnames of Devon (Oxford, 1995), 19–20.
[91] Orme, 'The Cornish at Oxford', 51.
[92] Catto, 'Citizens, Scholars', HUO, i. 569–70; Evans, 'Numbers, Origins', HUO, ii. 511–15; Cobban, English University Life, 5–7.
[93] BRUO, ii. 1133.

bishop of Norwich, was the son of a miller from Lanteglos-by-Fowey;[94] William Palmer (c.1420–34), perhaps the greatest of Exeter's medieval Rectors, was the kinsman and possibly the son of John Palmer, mayor of and MP for Launceston in Cornwall;[95] John Rowe (c.1426–41), Palmer's successor as Rector, left money in his will to two namesakes, one a smith and the other a dyer, suggesting a fairly humble set of relations;[96] and John Halse (1423–7), later bishop of Coventry and Lichfield, was the second son of Sir John Halse, of Kendon, near Kingsbridge in Devon, justice of king's bench under Henry V.[97] These few fellows, with fathers and kinsfolk who were artisans, townsmen, gentry, and lawyers, were probably representative of the larger whole. The only conspicuously missing group is the upper peasantry; but Walter de Stapeldon himself may be invoked to fill that gap.

Two of these groups deserve a word more: gentry and townsmen. As Orme has shown, Cornish gentry families are quite well represented among the fellows of Exeter. For example, John Cergeaux (fellow, 1353–5), John Burwyke (1420–30), Michael Trewynard (1429–38), and Walter Kyngdon (1456–68) all shared this background.[98] The Devon gentry, by contrast, seem to have provided few if any fellows, and the families who supplied the county's sheriffs, members of parliament, and justices of the peace—Chudleighs, Pomeroys, Bonvilles, Champernouns, and others—are noticeably absent. So it was too with the nobility. The greatest families in the county, the Courtenay earls of Devon and their collateral branch, the Courtenays of Powderham, were intermittently involved in the affairs of the College and sent some of their younger sons to Oxford, but none was elected to a fellowship at Exeter; though Peter Courtenay, from the Powderham branch, later bishop of Exeter, was an undergraduate in the mid fifteenth century.[99] As for townsmen, possible names are few and far between. But small towns were spread more thickly in Devon and Cornwall than in most parts of England, and fellows who shared an urban background with William Palmer may have been quite numerous. Much must have depended on the presence of local schools, and here Exeter, the provincial capital, may have scored especially highly. Not only was it the largest town in the diocese, but it had three schools, the cathedral song school, the grammar school, and the school attached to the hospital of St John initiated by Stapeldon.[100] The last two in

[94] William of Worcester, *Itineraries*, ed. J. H. Harvey (Oxford, 1969), 106–7; *BRUO*, ii. 1187–8.

[95] Boase (2), 33; J. S. Roskell, L. Clark, and C. Rawcliffe, *The History of Parliament: The House of Commons, 1386–1421*, 4 vols. (Stroud, 1992), iv. 5.

[96] *BRUO*, iii. 1598–9; D. N. Lepine, 'The Origins and Careers of the Canons of Exeter Cathedral, 1300–1455', in C. Harper-Bill (ed.), *Religious Belief and Ecclesiastical Careers in Later Medieval England* (Woodbridge, 1991), 98.

[97] *BRUO*, ii. 856; R. C. E. Hayes, 'John Hals', *ODNB*.

[98] Orme, 'The Cornish at Oxford', 48, 64, 65, 70, 81.   [99] Below, 160, 166–7.

[100] Orme, *Education in the West of England*, 47–53.

particular were potential recruiting grounds for the College. One schoolboy, John Rowe, named as a 'poor clerk' of the hospital school in 1406 and bequeathed clothing and a small sum of money by one of the Exeter canons, with directions that he should later be sent on to a grammar school, was almost certainly the same John Rowe who had a smith and a dyer for relatives and who went on to become Rector of the College and then himself a canon of Exeter.[101] He is the only one of our 330 or so fellows whose schooling we can be reasonably sure about.

Entry to the College through election could be gained at any time of the year. It often happened in mid term and was sometimes marked in the accounts by a note that the new fellow had 'entered into commons'. How candidates for election came forward we cannot easily tell. But since potential fellows had to be 'at least sufficient sophists', according to the statutes, and therefore well advanced on the arts course, they must already have had a record and a local reputation on which they could be judged by the electing fellows, who had to guide them Stapeldon's injunction that his scholars should be those 'the more fit to learn, the more virtuous in character, and the more impoverished in means'. And since every matriculating student had to be under a master who was responsible for his academic progress, references of a kind could no doubt be sought. Evidence from 1420 and 1439 suggests that candidates might be nominated by a group of fellows, that elections to fellowships, sometimes fiercely contested, might divide the College, and that the bishop might keep a sharp eye on proceedings.[102] It is quite likely that the bishop himself, the College's patron, nominated candidates from time to time, and that others were put forward by members of the Exeter chapter, who frequently included former fellows of the college, or by the heads of other ecclesiastical institutions in Devon, such as the prior of the hospital of St John. There were different routes to a fellowship but almost all of them led back to the west country and perhaps on occasion to the region's senior churchmen.

4. FELLOWS: STUDIES AND ACADEMIC CAREERS

Like almost all other Oxford students, those who would later become fellows of Exeter entered the university as members of the faculty of arts in order to follow the arts course. An outline of the normal progression has already been given and need not be repeated in any detail.[103] The student studied the seven liberal arts of the trivium and quadrivium, was nurtured on Aristotle's logic and natural philosophy, normally determined as a bachelor after four years,

[101] Reg. Stafford, 395; Orme, Education in the West of England, 49 n. 2.
[102] Reg. Lacy, i. 60–4, ii. 152–3; below, 122–4.
[103] Above, 7–8. The best accounts of the arts course are Weisheipl, 'Curriculum of the Faculty of Arts', and Fletcher, 'Developments', HUO, ii. 315–45.

incepted as a *magister* after a further three years, and then went on to lecture as a regent master for a further two years. The system had three special characteristics. First, many of those participating were both teachers and taught. This especially applied to the bachelors, who were expected to give 'cursory' lectures on the set texts to undergraduates while at the same time engaging in disputations and attending lectures as they themselves moved towards inception as *magistri*. Second, all were comparatively young. Even regent masters, after nine years or so of study, are likely to have been no older than about 30. And, third, the method of teaching was primarily oral, through lectures and disputations. Knowledge of the set texts was derived mainly from lectures, and books, though necessary, played a secondary role.

Exeter's arrangements, determined by its statutes, were generally consistent with this scheme, but differed in some important ways. As we have seen, Stapeldon had laid down that those aspiring to fellowships should be 'sufficient sophists at least', so ruling that when elected they were to have made some two years' progress towards determining as bachelors. But more advanced entrants were not specifically ruled out, and in the fifteenth century Bishop Lacy assumed that those elected might already be bachelors. We shall see later that this was sometimes the case.[104] All scholars except the chaplain were to study 'philosophy' (i.e. the arts course). They were to determine within six years and spend no more than another four years on the MA course. After a further two years' necessary regency they might lecture for one more year while retaining their fellowships, but they must then leave. The maximum period for which a fellowship might be held was thus some thirteen to fourteen years. Stapeldon's statutes had also made provision for teaching within the College. There were to be twice-weekly disputations, two on logic to one on natural philosophy, which all were to attend, including the regent masters unless they were excused by the Rector. This provision was later reinforced in the face of what was evidently reluctance on the part of senior fellows to sit through elementary and what might no doubt be tedious proceedings: masters and fellows, Stapeldon ruled, were to be present at the start of disputations and to stay until the end. In disputations on *sophismata*, however, conducted by the College's most junior members, regent masters might excuse themselves more easily than others.[105]

These statutes were in some ways restrictive, in others liberal. In confining the fellows' studies to the arts course they ruled out by implication any progression to higher degrees (except on the part of the chaplain). Yet they also allowed incoming fellows the extraordinarily long period of six years to work for the BA. It is not easy to explain this very curious provision. But it is perhaps likely that Stapeldon envisaged a long period of broken study in

---

[104] *Reg. Lacy*, i. 61; below, 91–2, 98.
[105] *Reg. Stapeldon*, 304, 307, 309; Buck, 111–12; above, 38–9, 49.

which parochial service or some other opportunity to earn money might temporarily suspend attendance at the College. It was, after all, not at all unusual for parish priests to be granted periods of leave, sometimes repeatedly, to study at Oxford. Stapeldon himself had been exceptionally prolific in making such grants, and when he spoke in his statutes of his scholars' pursuit of the arts course for six years 'continuously or interruptedly (*continue vel interpollatim*)' this is surely what he had in mind.[106] Equally unusual was his explicit provision for teaching, via disputations, within the College, in which all should participate. The statutes of most of the early colleges made no such provision. Like the university itself, Exeter was from the start a community of instruction in which seniors and juniors were to work together.

How far did the statutes govern the composition and academic practices of the college? Beyond recording rent income from schools which the fellows used for their lectures or, in one case from 1398, 'where [John] Jakys (*c*.1394–*c*.1401) determined',[107] the accounts have almost nothing to say about the academic work which was at the centre of College life. From their evidence alone we might imagine that the fellows spent most of their time on entertaining visitors, riding to Wittenham, supervising the garden, or consenting to the spending of money.[108] But from the accounts a good deal of statistical information can be extracted to reconstruct the academic *cursus honorum* across the long period covered by this chapter. A few opening snapshots of the fellowship at different dates will set the scene. In 1369, the year of famine, it comprised three *magistri*, including the Rector, four bachelors (termed 'domini'), and four untitled men who were presumably undergraduate sophists.[109] In 1376 six out of fifteen fellows were *magistri*.[110] In 1420 there were six *magistri*, four bachelors, and three sophists;[111] and in 1454 eight *magistri*, three probable bachelors, and three sophists.[112] If the mix was predictable, the apparently higher proportion of *magistri* in the fifteenth century was perhaps less so. This is a point to which we shall return.[113]

It was an assumption of the statutes that all incoming fellows would eventually qualify as *magistri*, but this was not true of Oxford students in general nor of Exeter's in particular.[114] Between 1350 and 1400 we have the names of 133 fellows, of whom 62 (47 per cent) are known to have become MAs; from 1400 to 1450 the figures are 64 and 55 (86 per cent), and from 1450

---

[106] *Reg. Stapeldon*, 307; Buck, 59.   [107] RA, 95/4.
[108] For these aspects of the fellows' activities, see below, 118, 131–2, 144–5, 151–2.
[109] RA, 50.   [110] RA, 62.   [111] *Reg. Lacy*, i. 63; Boase (1), 235; Boase (2), lxi.
[112] Figures compiled from the list of those receiving annual allowances in RA, 153/4 and from details of their careers in *BRUO*.
[113] Below, 92–3.
[114] Cf. Catto, 'Citizens, Scholars', *HUO*, i. 189–90; Fletcher, 'Developments', *HUO*, ii. 327. All statistical information between this point and the end of the section derives from analyses of the biographies given in *BRUO* and in Boase (2).

to 1500, 79 and 55 (70 per cent). While these statistics indicate a fluctuating but rising proportion of *magistri*, they also point to the better sources for the fifteenth century, when the first surviving register of congregation provides an admittedly patchy record of degrees awarded.[115] Allowing for the still remaining lacunae in the sources, we might guess that perhaps 20 per cent of those entering the College dropped out at some stage. The costs of determining as bachelor were heavy and may have deterred some from going even this far; inception as *magister* was also expensive and may have discouraged others from proceeding beyond the BA.[116] Though the College could provide continuing support to its fellows through their commons and allowances, this may not always have been a sufficient inducement to continue. To reach the summit as a *magister* was by no means the inevitable result of election to an Exeter fellowship.

We can chart in more detail the progress of some fellows towards the BA. Between 1360 and 1500 we have dates for the election to their fellowships and subsequent determination as bachelors for fifty-three fellows, about 19 per cent of the total of known fellows; though all but two of these names come from the fifteenth century. Only one of the fifty-three took more than four years to determine. Six took approximately four years—presumably, if coming in as two-year sophists, taking advantage of the six years which the statutes allowed for the BA course. Thirty-one of the fifty-three took less than four years, and of these nine determined in eighteen months or less from admission. Some even did so within a few months of arriving in College. Richard Palmer, admitted on 30 May 1478, determined later that summer.[117] It is still more surprising to find that fifteen of the fifty-three (28 per cent) were already bachelors, and probably therefore in their early twenties, at the time of their admission. The statutes did not preclude this—those who were 'at least sufficient sophists' might indeed be bachelors—but it surely cannot have been what Stapeldon had intended. The most extreme example is that of John Tharsher, already a BA by 1462 but admitted to a fellowship only in July 1465, by which time he had probably been principal of a hall for some years.[118]

While a majority of Exeter's incoming fellows were thus well advanced towards the BA at the time of their election, a substantial majority were already bachelors. Some may have been still more senior. In one apparently

---

[115] *The Register of Congregation, 1448–1463*, ed. W. A. Pantin and W. T. Mitchell, OHS, new ser., xxii (1972), xiv–xv.
[116] J. M. Fletcher and C. A. Upton, 'Expenses at Admission and Determination in Fifteenth-Century Oxford: New Evidence', *EHR*, 100 (1985), 331–7; Catto, 'Citizens, Scholars', *HUO*, i. 190; Fletcher, 'Faculty of Arts', *HUO*, i. 390.
[117] *BRUO*, iii. 1421. Emden gives 1479 as the year of Palmer's determination, but the accounts show that he determined in 1478: RA, 174/3; Boase (2), 46.
[118] *BRUO*, iii. 1859.

exceptional case from 1420 the College elected a man who was already a regent master and so necessarily in the final phase of his fellowship—to the indignation of Bishop Edmund Lacy, who accused the Rector and fellows of being in breach of their statutes.[119] And so they were, in terms of the spirit if not the letter of the statutes. This tendency to elect older men was paralleled by another trend, which can be followed through from the mid fourteenth century. Between 1350 and 1500 there was a steady rise in the length of time for which fellowships were held. It was at its shortest in the 1350s and 1360s, when the duration of a fellowship averaged 5.3 years in both decades. The brevity of tenure here, much less than the thirteen or fourteen years envisaged by Stapeldon, may reflect in part the mortality resulting from the plague of 1361.[120] But it probably also reflects another consequence of both plagues, the Black Death of 1348–9 as well as the second plague: the plenitude of benefices which plague mortalities had made available and which held out to fellows the prospect of an advantageous move from a modestly remunerated fellowship to a more lucrative parish or cathedral canonry. But by the 1380s and 1390s this phase was over, and the period of a fellowship had lengthened to some 7.7 years. Thereafter it rose still more markedly. Between 1420 and 1500 the average duration was 10 years. Within this eighty-year span there were three decades in which the average was between 9 and 10 years; two between 10 and 11 years; and two—in the 1430s and 1480s—between 11 and 12 years. By comparison with the mid fourteenth century, the period for which a fellowship was held had almost doubled.

The trend becomes still more conspicuous if we isolate the number of fellows who remained in their fellowships for the statutory maximum of fourteen years or who exceeded that maximum. Before 1390 it is impossible to find any fellow who fell into either category. The first to do so was John Gynne, a fellow in 1390 and Rector from 1395 to 1399, who finally vacated his fellowship in 1407 for the Devon living of Brent.[121] From this point until the end of the century 5 fellows held their fellowships for 14 years, 7 for 15 years, 5 for 16 years, 4 for 17 years, and 2 for 18 years. At the outer limit of this trend was John Trott, elected in 1488 to a fellowship which he held until his death twenty-four years later in 1512.[122]

What forces underlay this tendency to extend the tenure of fellowships, sometimes to the maximum and, in clear breach of the statutes, even beyond? In part, the extension of tenure was a consequence of another fifteenth-century development: the progression of some fellows to higher degrees, again in breach of the statutes. To this we shall return. But more generally it probably reflected the same factor which had determined the much shorter tenures of the mid fourteenth century—the availability of benefices or, in the

[119] *Reg. Lacy*, i. 61.   [120] Above, 75–6.   [121] *BRUO*, ii. 843.
[122] *BRUO*, iii. 1909.

later period, the lack of it. In the later middle ages the number of benefices accessible to university graduates was in sharp decline. For this there were many reasons. Papal provision, the direct appointment to a benefice by the pope, often in response to graduates' names submitted by the universities, effectively ceased in the early fifteenth century.[123] Monasteries, facing new financial problems, met that challenge by appropriating more churches and creating modestly endowed vicarages, which few graduates would want.[124] Other benefices were combined as the population stagnated or fell, while new collegiate foundations at both Oxford and Cambridge increased the competition among graduates for those benefices that were available.[125] The result was 'a net decline in the possibilities for promotion to benefices after spending some time at a university', leading to what the universities saw as 'a crisis of patronage'.[126] In these circumstances there was every inducement to prolong the tenure of a fellowship: to wait longer for a suitable benefice while continuing to enjoy the modest livelihood that a fellowship afforded. Since so many fellows must now have been regent masters and above, taking teaching fees and in some cases enjoying the perquisites of university office, the wait need not have been excessively painful. The inducement to move must have been much less marked than had been the case a century earlier.

The extension of tenure up to and beyond the maximum period of fourteen years, and the increase in the number of senior figures among the fellowship, had two important effects. First, it considerably reduced the intake of new fellows, as the figures in Table 1 show. The decade of the 1360s was exceptional, with a high turnover of fellows resulting from mortality (the 1361 plague) and migration (to other colleges). But throughout the late fourteenth century the numbers elected were considerably higher than those for the fifteenth century, particularly for its last two decades. The number of elections in the 1490s was just one-third that for the 1360s. Since the number of elective fellowships was fixed at fourteen (plus the unelected chaplain), the presence of long-stay fellows meant that opportunities for election arose less frequently. Older men gained at the expense of the aspiring young.

The second effect of the extension of tenure was arguably more beneficial. It allowed the fellows of Exeter to contribute more to the running of the university. In the fourteenth century the College's participation in university government had been minimal. It had, for example, supplied only two proctors, compared with eleven each from Merton and Oriel.[127] But in the fifteenth century there was a remarkable change. From 1420 to 1479 New

[123] R. N. Swanson, 'Universities, Graduates and Benefices in Later Medieval England', *Past and Present*, 106 (1985), 45.

[124] Swanson, 'Universities', 35–6.   [125] Swanson, 'Universities', 37, 53–5.

[126] Swanson, 'Universities', 45, 60.

[127] See the list of proctors to 1434 in *Snappe's Formulary and Other Records*, ed. H. E. Salter, OHS, lxxx (1924), 319–34.

TABLE 1. Number of admissions to fellowships by decade

1360s	1370s	1380s	1390s	1400s	1410s	1420s	1430s	1440s	1450s	1460s	1470s	1480s	1490s
36*	26	24	23	20	13	18	17	16	18	18	18	13	12

College and Merton supplied most university officers, but they were closely followed by Exeter, which preceded six other colleges.[128] If we look to particular offices we might note that the College supplied fifteen proctors between 1403 and 1498 and seven keepers of university chests in the 1450s. This must reflect to some extent the more senior standing of Exeter's fellows by comparison with their fourteenth-century predecessors; the proctors, for example, were invariably regent masters in arts. Since a proctor's remuneration might be as much as £5 to £10 a year, or ten to twenty times the annual allowance due to a fellow, we can also gain an idea of the inducements which may have persuaded some fellows to retain their fellowships for as long as possible.[129]

These important changes in the academic constitution of the College did not happen insensibly. In the election of more senior figures, in the lengthier tenure of fellowships, in the progression of some fellows to higher degrees which we shall now discuss, and in the overriding of the statutes needed to make these developments possible, there was a strong element of intention and conscious planning. This is revealed most clearly in relation to higher degrees. As we have seen, in the fourteenth century Exeter's position as an arts-only College, determined by its statutes, made it unique among the Oxford colleges. Even Balliol, founded on the same basis, was allowed by its new statutes of 1340 to elect six graduates to study theology.[130] The restrictiveness of Exeter's statutes had serious consequences, particularly for the future careers of the fellows. It limited the prospects of the most able. The highest offices in church and state usually went to those with higher degrees. Of Oxford men appointed to the episcopate between 1216 and 1499, for example, 45 per cent had graduated in law, 28 per cent in theology, and a mere 8 per cent in arts alone. For royal and episcopal service, too, those from the higher faculties were preferred over the artists.[131] The story was the same with the highest university office, the chancellorship, which was invariably held by a doctor in theology or, as time went on, of canon law; mere artists were ruled

[128] A. B. Cobban, 'Colleges and Halls, 1380–1500', *HUO*, ii. 623.
[129] A. B. Emden, 'The Remuneration of the Medieval Proctors of the University of Oxford', *Oxoniensia*, 26–7 (1961–2), 204.
[130] Jones, 16.   [131] Aston, 'Oxford's Medieval Alumni', 28–9.

out by statute.[132] Between 1350 and 1460 five chancellors had begun their academic careers at Exeter—William de Polmorva, Robert Rygge, Thomas Brightwell, Thomas Hendyman, and Walter Trengoff—but all five had been elected to the chancellorship after leaving the College and gaining doctorates in theology.

For fellows wanting to go on to higher degrees, one solution to the problem posed by the restrictiveness of the statutes was migration to another college. As we have seen in our earlier discussion of the concentrated migrations of 1365–75, migration between colleges was commonplace in the medieval university.[133] It cannot always be specifically related to the advantages denied by one college and offered by another. But it is surely significant that of the twenty Exeter fellows who migrated to other colleges between 1337 and 1400, mainly to Merton or Queen's, eight are known to have proceeded to a degree in theology, either as bachelor or doctor. Others almost certainly left Exeter with this intention but failed to fulfil it. Since both Merton and Queen's were primarily established for those taking higher degrees in theology and law, any migrant to either college is likely to have had that motive.

There is little doubt that by the late fourteenth century the restrictions imposed by Stapeldon's statutes were causing discontent within the College, and on a wider front than that relating to higher degrees. Other colleges were able to revise their statutes in response to changing circumstances and novel aspirations. Balliol's new statute of 1340 permitting some graduates to study theology had been in part a response to pressure from the fellows, who wished to be given this opportunity and who had seen their younger colleagues move off to Merton for higher studies beyond the arts course. Balliol's statutes were further revised in 1433 and 1470, and completely rewritten in 1507.[134] University College followed the same path, with four new sets of statutes between the foundation statute of 1280/1 and the late fifteenth century.[135] Exeter's statutes, however, remained formally unchanged until they were superseded by the Petrean statutes of 1566.[136] Though the bishops of Exeter were sometimes prepared to dispense from the statutes in minor matters, as when Bishop Brantingham permitted temporary increases in commons during the difficult times of the early 1370s,[137] it may well be that, as Stapeldon's successors and guardians of his legacy, they set their face against any more wholesale updating of what the founder had decreed.

By the turn of the fourteenth century opinion within the College was moving strongly in favour of fundamental changes to the statutes. The

[132] Boyle, 'Canon Law', HUO, i. 540; W. J. Courtenay, 'Theology and Theologians from Ockham to Wyclif', HUO, ii. 3; Pantin, Oxford Life, 85.
[133] Above, 80–1.   [134] Jones, 12, 16, 21–2, 39–46.
[135] Darwall-Smith, 7–8, 13–15, 18–21, 23–5, 64–6.   [136] Below, 270–83.
[137] Above, 77–8.

pressures for change are revealed by one of the most remarkable texts in the College's early history, and one that comes from an improbable source. In the papal register for 1405 is a letter from Pope Innocent VII to the Rector and fellows, written in response to their petition to him for changes to the statutes.[138] The petition itself does not survive, but its terms are given in the pope's reply. The Rector and fellows had begun by summarizing the main clauses in Stapeldon's statutes before going on to request their amendment in eight particular respects. The most important were these. They asked that their commons should be raised from 10d. to 12d. a week, with a further rise to 18d. in five festal weeks, justifying their request by pointing to the recent increase in the College's resources. They asked that, after incepting as MA, any fellow who wished to do so should be able to stay on for 'several years' beyond the year of his inception and to receive his commons throughout. They asked that after a possible four years as teaching regents they should resign their regency, be dispensed from compulsory attendance at disputations in logic and natural philosophy (the basis of the early part of the arts course), and instead study theology and dispute in that faculty. They asked that the College should no longer be called 'Stapeldon Hall' but rather 'the college of Exeter'. And they asked that the level of new income, whether from a benefice, an inheritance, or another source, whose acquisition should compel a fellow to leave the College should be set at 10 marks, or £6 13s. 4d. (rather than the £3 of annual income or benefice of any value prescribed in Stapeldon's statutes). All this the pope conceded. In one respect he went beyond what had been asked for, allowing the fellows to retain their fellowships for ten years beyond the year of their inception as MA. Those wanting to do so could thus serve their time as regent masters, normally for two years, go on to enjoy the further year permitted in the original statutes, and then proceed to the theology course, which took a further seven years.[139]

The procedure exemplified in this letter, a College petition to the pope followed by the papal response, was highly unusual. Like all dealings with the papal curia, the promotion of the College's cause must have been expensive; but, unlike some of the College's other rare missions to the papacy, it has left no trace in the accounts, which survive in full for 1404 and 1405.[140] The petition was apparently forwarded by three men, the bishop of Piacenza, the abbot of Osney, and Thomas Polton, archdeacon of Taunton and English representative at the curia,[141] none of them known to have had connections

---

[138] *Calendar of Entries in the Papal Registers relating to Great Britain and Ireland: Papal Letters*, Vol. VI: *1404–15*, ed. J. A. Twemlow (London, 1904), 47–9.

[139] For the length of the theology course, see *Register of Congregation, 1505–17*, ed. W. T. Mitchell, 2 vols., OHS, new ser., xxxvii (1998), i. 305.

[140] RA, 101, 102, 103. For an instance of payment for a mission to the curia in the accounts, see RA, 63 (1377).

[141] *Cal. Papal Registers*, vi. 49. For Polton, see *BRUO*, iii. 1494–5.

with the College, and it may be that the costs were borne privately by the Rector and fellows. Perhaps taking advantage of Innocent's reputation as 'easygoing and ineffective',[142] the College's *modus operandi* looks to have been a way of appealing directly to the highest authority in order to bypass the bishop, in this case Edmund Stafford, who would have been the normal authority to adjudicate on the statutes. It would hardly have been surprising if the College had wanted to avoid going to Stapeldon's successor, since its petition amounted to a partial rejection of its Stapeldonian inheritance. The requested change of name, from Stapeldon Hall to Exeter College, is particularly arresting, since Stapeldon had specifically decreed that as long as his foundation lasted it should be known as 'Stapeldon Hall'.[143] But more germane to the deeper discontents of the fellows (though equally contrary to Stapeldon's wishes) was the request to be allowed to study theology and to be given the additional fellowship years which alone would make this possible. The request for an increase in the level of wealth which would compel a fellow to leave the College was another way of extending the tenure of a fellowship. A fellow would now need an income more than twice that laid down in the statutes—£6 13s. 4d. compared with £3—before his novel access to such funds would cause him to leave.

Though Stapeldon's statutes were never formally abrogated, Innocent VII's concessions were tantamount to their wholesale revision. Corrected in one minor detail, they were reissued by Innocent's successor, Gregory XII, and the value set on this second definitive version was shown by its preservation in the College archives, where it remains with its leaden *bulla* still attached.[144] So far as we know, the bishop of Exeter made no objection to this fait accompli. Perhaps he was not told or, more likely, felt unable to challenge papal authority. We have already seen some of the effects which followed: in particular, the extension of the fellow's term, which led to the presence within the College of some very senior figures, fellows of some seventeen or eighteen years' standing. John Gynne, fellow from 1390 to 1407, was the first to take advantage of the new dispensation.[145] Other changes sanctioned by the papal bull came in more gradually. It was only in 1408–9 that fellows' commons were raised from 10d. to 1s., with higher allowances for festal weeks, and it was not until 1430 that the Rector began to style himself 'of Exeter College' rather than 'of Stapeldon Hall' in his accounts: the nearest we come to an official change of title. Even then, 'Stapeldon Hall' lingered on into the last quarter of the fifteenth century.[146]

---

[142] J. N. D. Kelly, *The Oxford Dictionary of Popes* (Oxford, 1986), 234.
[143] *Reg. Stapeldon*, 305–6.   [144] *Cal. Papal Registers*, vi. 13–16; ECA, L. II. 9.
[145] Above, 92.   [146] RA, 107, 108. For the change of name, see below, 147–8.

The progression to higher degrees in theology, which Innocent had also sanctioned and which was perhaps the main desideratum of the Rector and fellows, came in more rapidly. Its introduction coincides in an interesting way with the career of John Shute, fellow since 1396 or before, and Rector in 1404–5, at just the time of the College's petition to the pope.[147] When he ceased to be Rector, Shute also vacated his fellowship, leaving the College for the Devon living of Bishop's Nympton. At some stage he graduated as a bachelor in theology; and since there is nothing in his subsequent activities as holder of various benefices in Devon and Cornwall to suggest that he took time off to return to Oxford to study, it seems highly likely that he was engaged on theology during his time at Exeter. His may have been the initiative behind the petition, perhaps intended, *inter alia*, to legitimize his own course of studies. Thereafter a steady trickle of Exeter fellows progressed from the arts course to theology. Between 1405 and 1500 we know of some eleven who obtained qualifications in theology during the period of their fellowships and a further nine who obtained similar qualifications after leaving the College but whose theological studies may have begun during the period of their fellowships. Typical of the first group was John Evelyn, fellow from 1438 to 1451, who graduated as a bachelor of theology in 1449 and went on to hold various benefices in Devon and Cornwall before ending his career as a canon of Exeter.[148] The numbers of theologians may seem small, but higher degrees, entailing as they did years of further study, were never likely to be the choice of the majority. Nevertheless, the option was now available and the status of the College correspondingly raised. It had ceased to be the only College in the university whose fellows could not go beyond the arts course. One further consequence of this change was a decline in migration to other colleges. By contrast with the nineteen migrants who left Exeter for other colleges between 1340 and 1400, only ten left in the next sixty years, and after 1460 migration appears to have ceased altogether until the second half of the sixteenth century, when it resumed on a very limited scale. The possibility of progression to higher degrees in theology was one factor which, by the mid fifteenth century, had helped to create a more self-sufficient College.

These changes in the constitution of the College were perhaps the most important between the time of Stapeldon and that of Petre. Not only did it move from being an arts-only college to one where it was now possible to read for higher degrees in theology, but its age balance also changed. Senior men were elected, most of them already beyond the level of the sophists envisaged by Stapeldon, and some of them already bachelors or even *magistri*; the tenure of fellowships was extended, and in consequence the number

[147] *BRUO*, iii. 1699. Emden fails to note Shute's rectorship, vouched for in the accounts: RA, 102.
[148] *BRUO*, i. 653.

of junior fellows, still some years away from determination as bachelors, contracted. The scale of these changes should not be exaggerated. As we have seen, those who chose to stay on beyond the thirteen and fourteen years of the original statutes were never very numerous, nor were those choosing to proceed to theology. Yet Stapeldon's statutes had been breached. The petition of the Rector and fellows to Innocent VII suggests that the statutes were seen as shackles on the College's progressive development, while the request for a change in the College's name, in direct repudiation of Stapeldon's express wish, suggests a degree almost of resentment at the founder's legacy. The quasi-covert nature of the College's approach to the pope, so going behind the back of the bishop, points to a sense of uneasiness about the radical nature of the changes that were being sought.

It would be easy to see the spirit behind these changes as being essentially one of self-interest: a higher income bar for the termination of fellowships facilitated longer tenure, extended fellowships could be supported through the perpetuation of weekly commons, now raised to a higher sum, while access to higher degrees potentially opened the way to lucrative posts, both inside and outside the university. Yet it is striking that the pressure for higher degrees never extended beyond theology, and that theology alone was the subject undertaken by those fellows who went on to further study. There was no suggestion that fellows should be allowed to read canon or civil law, subjects which led to the best rewarded places in church and state and which could be pursued at other colleges such as Merton and Queen's. The probability is that the desire for higher study in theology was motivated as much by religious commitment, by the wish for a fuller training for the work of the church, and even by intellectual curiosity as by any mere appetite for self-advancement. This is a point of view supported by a survey of the College's intellectual life, to which we now turn.

5. FELLOWS: INTELLECTUAL LIFE

Some Oxford colleges in the later middle ages enjoyed either an extended period of intellectual experiment and innovation which went far to create a college reputation and tradition, or else a more short-lived flowering of particular skills and interests, often centred on a particular generation of fellows. Merton in the first half of the fourteenth century was home to a brilliant school of logicians, mathematicians, and scientists;[149] Queen's in the years around 1400 did much to promote and energize the study of theology and philosophy;[150] while in the fifteenth century New College and Magdalen began to be associated with a new style of clear and elegant Latin writing,

[149] Weisheipl, 'Ockham and the Mertonians', *HUO*, i. 615–58; Martin and Highfield, 46–62.
[150] Catto, 'Wyclif and Wycliffism at Oxford, 1356–1430', *HUO*, ii. 228, 238; Catto, 'Scholars and Studies', *HUO*, ii. 782.

developed under the influence of humanist models from Italy.[151] Possessing
the permanence and the endowed fellowships which the halls lacked, these
colleges at least were well placed to foster intellectual enterprise.

So far as can be seen, Exeter had nothing comparable to show for itself.
A few fellows went on to achieve fame after they had left the College, and no
doubt the grounding in the arts syllabus which they had received at Exeter
helped on their way. John Trevisa (fellow, c.1361–9), pioneer translator
of Latin works into English, and possibly associated with the Wycliffite
translation of the Bible, did much of his work after he had left a second
fellowship at Queen's for the service of the baronial family of Berkeley.[152]
Another distinguished old member, William Wey (c.1430–41), achieved fame
as a pilgrim, traveller to Jerusalem, and travel writer only in the late 1450s and
early 1460s, when he was a fellow of Eton.[153] Four fellows went on to
bishoprics, though long after they had vacated their fellowships. Walter
Lyhert (fellow, c.1420–5) was bishop of Norwich from 1446 to 1472; John
Arundel (c.1420–31), bishop of Chichester from 1459 to 1477; Michael
Tregury (1422–7), archbishop of Dublin from 1449 to 1471; and John Halse
(1423–7), bishop of Coventry and Lichfield from 1459 to 1490.[154] Others
who were never fellows gave the College a kind of distinction by association.
Among the boarders whom the College took in increasing numbers during
the fifteenth century, for example, was Thomas Gascoigne, who rented a
room in Exeter in 1429 and went on to become one of the leading reformist
critics of the contemporary church.[155] Another was William Grocyn, one of
the founding fathers of Greek learning in England, who boarded in College
from 1491 to 1493.[156] These men mingled with the fellows and ate with them
in hall; but any influence which they may have exercised on them has gone
unrecorded. Of the fellows themselves it is impossible to point to any, still less
to a group, who made a mark on contemporary culture and learning during
the period of their fellowships.

There were some obvious reasons for Exeter's failure to stand out. The
restriction of fellowships to the arts course, at least until 1405, must have
inhibited ambition and the opportunities for independent thought. The size of
the fellowship, fifteen at most, was too small to create the sort of critical mass
which favoured intellectual exchange and exploration. The most productive
colleges tended to be the largest: Merton, with up to fifty fellows before the
Black Death, New College with a statutory forty.[157] The College's Rectors,

[151] Catto, 'Scholars and Studies', *HUO*, ii. 769–70, 778–9.
[152] *BRUO*, iii. 1903; A. Hudson, *The Premature Reformation* (Oxford, 1988), 394–7.
[153] *BRUO*, iii. 2028–9.   [154] *BRUO*, i. 49–50, ii. 856, 1187–8, iii. 1894–5.
[155] *BRUO*, ii. 745–8. For boarders, see below, 157–9.
[156] *BRUO*, ii. 827. There is no evidence, *pace* Boase (2), lxxii, that Grocyn 'taught Greek in the
College Hall'.
[157] Martin and Highfield, 62; Cobban, 'Colleges and Halls', *HUO*, ii. 612.

holding office for only a short period, and heavily involved in finance and administration, were not well placed to give an intellectual lead.[158] There was no figure like Thomas Chaundler, Warden of New College from 1454 to 1475, who 'devoted himself to instructing his charges in Ciceronian prose and civility in the tradition of Bruni'.[159] Exeter's ethos was entirely different.

But it was not necessarily inferior. The object of the College, as Stapeldon had seen it and as it continued to be throughout the later middle ages, was not to advance learning but to train the future clergy of the diocese of Exeter (and later of Salisbury). Achievement was to be measured not by intellectual originality but by the influence of college-trained clergy on local congregations, on the efficient management of local churches, and, in many cases, on the work of the cathedral at Exeter. Success here is necessarily unknowable. Yet the fellows were not devoid of larger ambitions, as they showed by their request of 1405 to the pope to be allowed to study theology—perhaps high-mindedly eschewing the advanced degrees in canon and civil law which were likely to lead to greater worldly success. One way to gauge those ambitions, and to assess the interests and intellectual capital of Exeter's fellows, is to look at the College's resources in books and libraries.

The acquisition of books had from the start formed part of Stapeldon's plans for his College. According to the statutes, gifts and legacies might be used for their purchase, and it would have been surprising if Stapeldon's will, which does not survive, had not left some part of his own very large collection to the College.[160] If it did, there is nothing to show this. Some of the earliest surviving accounts, for summer term 1326 and winter 1329, record the purchase of unspecified books (perhaps choir books rather than library books),[161] but for the next few decades there is little evidence for acquisitions. In 1357 three books, including a bible, a book 'concerning the prophets', and parts of the works of Aquinas, were redeemed from one of the university loan chests, while two further unidentified books were brought up from Devon in 1366 and another from Exeter in 1368.[162] More informative are entries in the accounts recording the College's commissioning in 1366 of 'a book called Dumbleton' and the purchase of another described as 'Heytesbury'; for John Dumbleton and William Heytesbury were both eminent Mertonian logicians and natural philosophers, active in the 1330s and 1340s, and their works would have been some of the most up-to-date commentaries available for Exeter's bachelors and regent masters lecturing on the arts course.[163] The later acquisition, in 1390–1, of three commentaries on different works of Aristotle

[158] Below, 113–16.   [159] Catto, 'Scholars and Studies', *HUO*, ii. 779.
[160] *Reg. Stapeldon*, 307, 563–5; above, 39.
[161] Boase (1), 172, 174; Watson, xviii. I am grateful to Dr James Willoughby for pointing out to me that unspecified 'books' mentioned in accounts often denote choir books.
[162] RA, 8, 40, 44.   [163] RA, 39; Watson, xviii–xix; *BRUO*, i. 603, ii. 927–8.

by the earlier and still more eminent Mertonian Walter Burley, one purchased and the other two probably so, would have been equally useful.[164] Unlike gifts of books, which might not always suit the requirements of readers, those commissioned or purchased represented the College's real needs. 'A bought book was a wanted book.'[165] These books confirmed Exeter's reputation as an arts college, its syllabus dominated by Aristotelian learning.

If the build-up of books for much of the fourteenth century appears to have been slow and shallow by comparison with what we shall see to have been the more numerous and wide-ranging acquisitions of the fifteenth century, this may be in part illusory. The sources for the early period are relatively poor. Not only are there long gaps in the accounts, but the wills which often record later gifts of books are almost non-existent before 1400. No bequests of books are known to have been received by the College before 1410,[166] other than Bishop Rede's, discussed below; but it is hard to think that none was made. Yet this initial impression of fourteenth-century dearth and fifteenth-century fecundity is unlikely to be entirely false. That only two of the College's books now surviving are known to have been acquired in the fourteenth century, while some twenty-seven survivors came in the fifteenth century, suggests a real contrast rather than one merely apparent.[167]

One large exception breaks into the generally meagre story of Exeter's early book collection: the lavish gifts of books made to the College by William Rede, bishop of Chichester. Among the greatest book collectors of his age, Rede may well have been at Exeter as a young man. He first appears as a fellow of Merton in 1344, but it is quite possible that he had followed the arts course at Exeter during the College's dark period between 1337 and 1354, when the absence of accounts has deprived us of almost all the fellows' names.[168] Certainly Exeter was second only to Merton in Rede's affections. He had strong ties with the College's home territory of Devon and mentioned his Devon kinsmen in his will. One of them, Richard Pester, fellow of Exeter from c.1367 to c.1372 and of Merton from 1375 to

---

[164] RA, 85, 86/1, 87; Watson, xix.

[165] N. R. Ker, 'Oxford College Libraries before 1500', in his *Books, Collectors and Libraries: Studies in the Medieval Heritage*, ed. A. G. Watson (London, 1964), 309.

[166] When payment was made for chaining books left by Robert Rygge (fellow, 1361–c.1364) and John Lydford: RA, 113.

[167] Fourteenth-century survivors: MSS 28, 35 (Watson, 39–42, 52–9). Fifteenth-century survivors: MSS 3, 6, 14, 21, 23, 25, 31, 43, 45, 51–68 (Watson, 6–7, 10–11, 16–17, 27–30, 32–5, 36–7, 46–50, 73–4, 75–6, 88–108). I have omitted the few survivors from Rede's gifts: see below, 105, for these. It may be, of course, that some of the fourteenth-century books were discarded from the library in the fifteenth century as outdated or fit only for lending.

[168] *BRUO*, iii. 1556–60; R. Thomson, 'William Reed, Bishop of Chichester (d.1385)—Bibliophile?', in G. H. Brown and L. E. Voigts (eds.), *The Study of Medieval Manuscripts in England: Festschrift in Honor of Richard W. Pfaff* (Tempe, Ariz., 2010), 281–93. I have followed the conventional spelling of the bishop's name rather than Thomson's variant.

1381, became his executor.[169] In 1374 Rede embarked on a first distribution of his books, giving a hundred to Merton, twenty-five to Exeter, and others to Queen's.[170] Later, under the terms of the will which he made in 1382, Pester was given a further hundred books, reserved for his own use during his lifetime, then for the use of the bishop's kin at Merton and Exeter, and afterwards for the use of the fellows of the two colleges. In fact, the legacy was more or less split in half, with Pester and the bishop's other executor delivering forty-five books to Exeter in 1400. In an indenture made with the Rector and fellows, the books were listed by title, and conditions were set out for their use.[171]

Because we know so little about Exeter's books prior to 1374 it is difficult to be sure about the extent to which Rede's gifts transformed the collection. But it is likely that they greatly increased both its size and its range. They were far from being the standard fodder for the arts course. Those given in 1374 were divided into four categories under the headings philosophy, medicine, mathematics, and theology. Although they included four basic Aristotelian texts, by far the largest group comprised ten works of theology. Among them was a copy of Book IV of Peter Lombard's *Sentences*, the standard textbook of systematic theology, and the only one among the first batch of books now remaining in the College.[172] The forty-five books which came in 1400 were still more varied, with few academic textbooks, a number of patristic authors (Augustine, Isidore, Gregory the Great), some works of pastoral theology, and even some books of poetry and music. In a general way all these books may have been intended by Rede to service the university curriculum, to enhance the education of the clergy, and to serve their needs as future priests.[173] Book IV of the *Sentences*, for example, was concerned with the sacraments, and its coverage of such topics as baptism, marriage, and penance would have been particularly helpful for the parish clergy. But the new collections went beyond those aims in broadening the whole scope of the reading material now easily accessible to the fellows of Exeter. We might reasonably wonder whether the request made by the Rector and fellows to the

[169] *BRUO*, iii. 1469; Rede's will: F. M. Powicke, *The Medieval Books of Merton College* (Oxford, 1931), 87–91.

[170] R. M. Thomson, *A Descriptive Catalogue of the Medieval Manuscripts of Merton College, Oxford* (Woodbridge, 2009), xxiv–xxv; Thomson, 'William Reed', 284–5. The indenture listing the books given in 1374 is printed in Watson, 138–9, from ECA, E. V. 2. 1374. The gift of twenty books to Exeter mentioned in Rede's will (Powicke, *Medieval Books*, 88) subsumes this earlier gift and is not a separate bequest.

[171] Thomson, *Descriptive Catalogue*, xxv–xxvi; Thomson, 'William Reed', 285–6. The indenture, badly damaged, is ECA, E. V. 2. 1400 and will be printed in the Oxford volume of the *Corpus of British Medieval Library Catalogues*. I am very grateful to Professor Richard Sharpe for allowing me to use the transcript prepared for this volume.

[172] Watson, 138–9; Thomson, 'William Reed', 291–2. Peter Lombard's *Sentences* is now MS 32: Watson, 50–1.

[173] Thomson, *Descriptive Catalogue*, xxiv, xxviii; Thomson, 'William Reed', 292–3.

pope in 1405 to be allowed to study theology did not owe something to the stimulus and widening of horizons provided by Rede's recent additions to the College's books.

We can be more certain that Rede's gift of 1374 acted as a stimulus to something else: the building of a new library. In the College's earliest days its few books had probably been kept in a locked chest, as was the common practice.[174] Only in the 1370s can we be sure that there was a library, for in 1372 comes the first mention in the accounts of the chaining of a book, and this must signify the existence of a reference collection housed in a building.[175] Rede's gift two years later included £20 for repairing the library (which we have already seen was partly diverted to other purposes) and a further £25 for chaining the donated books. The repair work may have included the thatching of the library, carried through in 1375.[176]

But in 1383 the accommodation of the College's books was put on a new footing by the decision to construct a new library. This was a mark of the return both of economic stability and of the College's self-confidence after the financially disastrous years of the 1370s; at the time of Rede's gift no such expensive project could have been contemplated. As it was, by 1383 the fellows not only had Rede's twenty-five books in their possession but they may already have known of the additional books which they were to receive under the terms of his will, made in 1382. And if it hardly seems necessary to us to build a new library to house some seventy books we should remember that in medieval libraries chained books such as Rede's were laid flat on rows of desk-lecterns and not stored upright on horizontal shelves in the modern (and most space-effective) way.[177] The building account for the new library survives in the College archives (see Plate 11).[178] It shows that the work took some six months, through the spring, summer, and early autumn of 1383. Superior stone was brought in from the famous Taynton quarries, near Burford, and other stone from Wheatley, closer to home.[179] Gone was the thatch; not only was the new library stone-built, but it was roofed with lead and whitewashed. The total cost came to nearly £58, about a year's income for the College. It was met by a generous grant of £20 from John More, Rector at the time of Rede's gift and by 1383 rector of St Petrock's, Exeter;[180] by a further donation of £10 from Bishop Brantingham; and by a subvention of just under £25 from College funds, leaving a deficit of just over

---

[174] M. B. Parkes, 'The Provision of Books', *HUO*, ii. 459.

[175] RA, 51; Boase (1), xi; Watson, xvii n. 2. The chained book was a copy of Hrabanus Maurus, *de naturis rerum*.

[176] Watson, xvii, 138; RA, 58; above, 78–9.

[177] Cf. N. R. Ker, 'Chaining from a Staple on the Back Cover', in his *Books, Collectors and Libraries*, 326; Thomson, *Descriptive Catalogue*, xxix.

[178] RA, 76, printed in Boase (1), 178–9, summarized in English in Boase (2), 344–5.

[179] Cf. W. J. Arkell, *Oxford Stone* (London, 1947), 38, 62.   [180] *BRUO*, ii. 1303.

£2. At some time during the episcopate of Bishop Stafford, 1395 to 1419, the library was widened and extended through the bishop's generosity, possibly to house the second tranche of Rede's books which arrived in 1400.[181] But in essence it was the same as that shown in Loggan's 1675 view of the College: a substantial first-floor building, aligned north–south and situated along the line of the present quadrangle's north range (see Plate 14). It survived until replaced by that range in 1708.[182]

Exeter's library very probably had a prototype in the much grander and more famous library at Merton, which still survives. Merton's library was largely built between 1373 and 1378, and its building, like Exeter's, seems to have been in part a response to Rede's gifts, more generous to Merton than to Exeter. Like Exeter, Merton drew for its stone on the Taynton quarries owned by William Humberville, who was the master mason and probably the designer responsible for Merton's library.[183] Exeter too bought its stone from 'William the mason' and may also have relied on him for the library's design. The 'simple cusped' lancet windows found at Merton, for example, are very similar to those shown on Loggan's view of Exeter's library.[184] Merton's links with Exeter at this time were close. Several Exeter fellows, like Richard Pester, Rede's kinsman, had recently gone on to fellowships at Merton, and Exeter's fellows visited Merton for the latter's annual feast.[185] It would not have been surprising if Rede's generosity had sparked a common response in, or even collaboration between, colleges which were already *en rapport*.

Very few of the seventy books given by Rede to Exeter now survive. Of the twenty-five listed on the 1374 indenture only three remain: the copy of the *Sentences* already mentioned and retained in the College, a Life and Miracles of Becket, now at Douai, and a medical work by Avicenna, now at Merton (MS 224).[186] Of the forty-five listed on the 1400 indenture, only two survive, one at Exeter (MS 19, a canon law work by William of Pagula) and another at Merton (MS 257, a mixed collection of proverbs, theology, etc.).[187] It is a telling comment on the fate of Exeter's medieval books in general that we now have only five items, 7 per cent of the total benefaction, from these two great collections.

Perhaps less surprising than this low survival rate is the almost complete disappearance of another category of book once much more numerous than the chained books, like those given by Rede, which were retained for

---

[181] *Reg. Lacy*, iv. 299–300; below, 121.   [182] Boase (2), 358; *VCH Oxfordshire*, iii. 117.
[183] Thomson, *Descriptive Catalogue*, xxix–xxx; Martin and Highfield, 88–91; E. A. Gee, 'Oxford Masons, 1370–1530', *Archaeological Jnl.*, 109 (1952), 60–1.
[184] Boase (1), 178; Gee, 'Oxford Masons', 61.   [185] Above, 80–1; below, 151.
[186] Watson, 50–1, 133–4; Thomson, *Descriptive Catalogue*, 162.
[187] Watson, 25, 134; Thomson, *Descriptive Catalogue*, 198 (where the Exeter origin of this book is overlooked).

reference. In all colleges books reserved for lending stood in contrast to the reference library of chained books. By the so-called 'electio' system, fellows were allowed to make a 'choice' of books which they wished to borrow. The terms of the loan varied from college to college—Oriel's books, for example, were redistributed annually—but we do not know those which applied at Exeter.[188] Our first Exeter reference to an 'electio' book comes from the 1370s, when so much information begins to accumulate about the College's books. In 1376 the College replaced a copy of Aristotle's *Metheora* which had been 'from the *electio* of master William Frank' and had now been missing for a long time. Since Frank had vacated his fellowship in 1372, the 'electio' system must have been in place by then, and it had probably been established much earlier.[189] The fortunate survival of the title of Frank's 'electio' book, a set text for the arts course, suggests that 'electio' items were mainly text books for the use of the more junior fellows who had not yet incepted for the MA. Payment for the binding of a 'textus philosophie' 'from the *electio* of John Mattecote', another fellow, in 1383 points in the same direction, for this too is likely to have been an Aristotelian work.[190] The borrowing of 'electio' books was recorded in a register, new copies of which were bought in 1405 and 1410. There must have been a substantial number of these books, since it took John More, one of the university's stationers, two days to value them in 1457.[191] At Merton it has been estimated that as many as nine-tenths of the College's books, perhaps 450 volumes, may have been 'for the *electio* of the fellows'.[192] That with one exception all Exeter's 'electio' books have disappeared, as have those of almost all other colleges, is partly to be explained by the wear-and-tear to which frequent borrowing subjected them, but more particularly by the ending of the 'electio' system in the sixteenth century and the probable mass discarding of the manuscript books in favour of cheaper printed versions.[193]

From the early fifteenth century onwards the books acquired by the College took on a distinctive complexion. They were mainly theological works, and primarily aids to the biblical studies which formed the basis of the theology course. This was another of the several important consequences of the papal permission of 1405 enabling fellows to proceed to theology after graduating in arts. Using the accounts, wills, and notices of gifts, we can make a rough classification of these acquisitions. Of the fifty-six books known by title or author which came to the College in the fifteenth century, thirty could

[188] Parkes, 'Provision of Books', *HUO*, ii. 456–8.   [189] RA, 61; above, 80.
[190] RA, 74.
[191] RA, 105, 111, 157/1. For More, see Parkes, 'Provision of Books', *HUO*, ii. 419–20.
[192] Ker, 'Oxford College Libraries before 1500', 304.
[193] N. R. Ker, 'The Provision of Books', *HUO*, iii. 455–7; Watson, xix–xx. The two probable survivors are Bodleian Library, MSS Auct. D. 4. 9, and Bodley 42: see *HUO*, iii. 456 and Watson, 133–4.

be classified as biblical commentaries or aids to biblical study, three as pastoral theology, three as patristics, and thirteen as other theological works; though there is inevitably a certain arbitrariness about these divisions. Of the biblical commentaries, the most splendid and complete was the College's set of the works of Hugh of St Cher, the French Dominican scholar of the thirteenth century. Written in Oxford over a long period, from 1452 to 1484, and almost entirely at the expense of Roger Keys—a Devon man, Warden of All Souls from 1443 to 1445, precentor of Exeter cathedral from 1459 until his death in 1477, and friend of the College—it survives in seventeen volumes, with a supplementary volume of sermons, as one of the treasures of the College library, its borders beautifully illuminated with floral decorations.[194] The work of Nicholas of Lyra, the fourteenth-century French Franciscan scholar and author of the standard exegesis of the Bible, and of his indexer, William Norton, was also represented.[195] There was at least one other copy of Book IV of Peter Lombard's *Sentences*, in addition to that given by Bishop Rede.[196] Other biblical commentaries included Haimo of Auxerre on the Pauline Epistles,[197] Stephen Langton on the book of Tobit,[198] and Nicholas Gorran on Luke.[199] Of theology more generally, the College possessed two selections from the works of Robert Grosseteste, scholar-bishop of Lincoln in the thirteenth century,[200] and a number of theological handbooks.[201] Altogether outside the usual range of its books were Thomas Hanney's fourteenth-century grammatical treatise for boys, *Memoriale juniorum*, and the Latin poem *The Distichs of Cato*, a work of moral instruction widely used in grammar schools. Both were bequeathed to the College in 1483 by William Elyot, a Devon cleric formerly in the service of Bishop Lacy.[202] We might think that the fellows would have had little use for such elementary works. If there was a choral foundation at Exeter, bringing young boys into the College, their presence might be explained. But this does not seem to have been the case.

The total number of books in the College's possession by 1500 is impossible to assess with any accuracy. Exeter now holds some sixty-five books which were or may have been in its hands during the middle ages, though this total is distorted by the eighteen volumes of Hugh of St Cher.[203] If these are

---

[194] Watson, 84–108 and plate 4. For Keys, see *BRUO*, ii. 1045–6.

[195] RA, 144/1; Boase (2), 37; *BRUO*, ii. 1191 (bequest of John Lyndon). William Norton: MS 16, Watson, 18.

[196] Watson, 27.   [197] RA, 144/1.   [198] MS 23, Watson, 33–5.   [199] RA, 145/4.

[200] MS 21, Watson, 27–30; TNA, PROB/11/10 (will of James Babbe, fellow, 1476–84); *BRUO*, i. 85.

[201] RA, 180/1; Boase (2), xxxvii n. 2; *BRUO*, ii. 688 (bequest of Edmund Fitchet), 1288 (bequest of William Moggys).

[202] MS 14, Watson, 16–17; N. Orme, 'William Elyot, a Fifteenth-Century Registrar, and his Books', *Archives*, 26 (2001), 112–13, 116.

[203] Watson, xxii–xxiii.

counted as a unit, the figure drops to circa forty-seven. We have seen that of the seventy books given by Rede only five now survive and only two of these still belong to Exeter. If the forty-seven or so survivors in the present collection reflect the same survival rate of about 7 per cent, the library may originally have possessed some 670 books. But other calculations suggest that this figure is a good deal too high. A tally of all the books likely to have been in the library by the end of the fifteenth century, compiled from Professor Watson's catalogue of surviving books, from the lists of those given by Rede, from those mentioned by author or title in the accounts, and from recorded gifts and bequests, produces a more realistic total of some 230 to 240 books. Allowing for the many items likely to have gone unrecorded, we would perhaps not be far wrong in reckoning that Exeter may have possessed some 300 to 400 books by 1500. By comparison with Merton, which may already have possessed some 500 books by 1375,[204] this was a relatively modest collection—but for a college of Exeter's size and limited resources it was a highly respectable one.

Partial and incomplete though the evidence is, it points convincingly towards Exeter's possession of a well-stocked library by the end of our period. It catered not only for the great majority of fellows who did not proceed beyond the arts course, and who may have made particular use of the 'electio' books, but also for the small minority who went on to read theology. We should not assume, however, that the theology books would interest only the College's theologians. The sort of books coming into the library in the fifteenth century widened the intellectual opportunities open to all its members. If most came by bequest or gift (and this was true of all college libraries), others might be actively sought. The accounts for winter term 1485 provide a rare personal detail in recording the costs of carriage for 'two great volumes of a theological work called Panthilogion [a theological encyclopedia] given to us by Mr Gwille, canon in the chapel royal of St Stephen's Westminster, by the sole exertions of the Rector'.[205] Since the Rector compiled the accounts, he at least thought that he had worked hard and done a good deed in acquiring these particular books for the College. To lay hands on useful books was worth an effort.

Exeter's book collection was that of a small, conservative community, lacking any visible sign of the humanist influences from Italy which created a new university library from the generosity of Duke Humfrey of Gloucester and which were beginning to percolate into other and newer colleges, such

---

[204] Ker, 'Oxford College Libraries before 1500', 304.
[205] RA, 180/1; Boase (1), 26; Boase (2), xxxvii n. 2. 'Mr Gwille' was John Gurlle, B.Cn.L: *BRUO*, ii. 838. The Rector in 1485, John Smyth, was senior proctor of the university, but had no degree in theology: *BRUO*, iii. 1717. The work in question may be a printed copy of Rainerius Iordanis de Pisis, *Pantheologia*.

as New College and All Souls.[206] But Rede's gifts, the investment in the new library in 1383, its physical enlargement made possible by Bishop Stafford's benefaction, the steady inflow of gifts and bequests during the fifteenth century, and the increasing proportion of theological works, all suggest a community with intellectual interests and a strong sense of purpose, and one faithful to the spirit of its founder's ideals. It was in its books and its library that the life of the mind in the late medieval College was best represented.

There was one episode in the intellectual life of the late medieval university which might have been expected to touch Exeter: the career of John Wyclif, Oxford master, logician, and theologian, and, in the final phase of his career, heretic and enemy of the church. In his time Wyclif was associated with four Oxford colleges, none of them Exeter. He was a fellow of Merton in 1356, Master of Balliol in 1360, Warden of Canterbury College from 1365 to 1367, and resident in Queen's in the early 1360s, in 1374–5 and 1380–1, and possibly in other years during the 1370s.[207] It was when he moved from arts to theology, gaining his doctorate in 1372 or 1373, that he began to acquire the reputation of a radical and subversive thinker, whose arguments had dramatic implication for the world beyond the Oxford schools. In the 1370s his lectures in the theology faculty and his writings led him onto dangerous ground. The true church, he asserted, was not a priestly institution, but the body of the elect; only the elect, in a state of grace, were entitled to lordship (a powerful blow at the basis of papal authority); the temporal claims and wealth of the church could not be justified; the Bible represented eternal truth and should be made available to all. Still more deeply shocking was Wyclif's denial of transubstantiation: even after its consecration by the priest, the eucharistic bread remained bread, though Christ was spiritually present in it. It was hardly surprising that his teachings turned the greater part of the university against him. In 1381 his views on the eucharist were formally condemned by a committee appointed by the chancellor, William Barton, and Wyclif then withdrew to his rectory at Lutterworth in Leicestershire. External condemnation followed in 1382, when the Blackfriars council convened by William Courtenay, the new archbishop of Canterbury, anathematized a selection of Wyclif's opinions on theological matters ranging well beyond the eucharist. But Wycliffite sympathies within the university were far from a spent force. It was only with Archbishop Arundel's *Constitutions*

---

[206] But note that Ker recognized humanistic script in the Rector's accounts for the late 1470s, which Southern failed to detect: Ker, 'Oxford College Libraries before 1500', 314 n. 63; *VCH Oxfordshire*, iii. 108.

[207] *BRUO*, iii. 2103–6. The fullest account of Wyclif's Oxford career will be found in J. I. Catto, 'Wyclif and Wycliffism at Oxford, 1356–1430', *HUO*, ii. 175–261. For a summary account of Wyclif's thinking, see e.g. M. Keen, *England in the Later Middle Ages*, 2nd edn. (London, 2003), 184–8.

of 1409, which set strict limits to free theological discussion, and, to a lesser extent, with the archbishop's visitation of 1411, that Wyclif's teachings were finally deprived of an Oxford outlet.[208]

Although we know the names of relatively few of Wyclif's Oxford followers, particularly in the movement's earliest stages, by 1382 there was clearly a Wycliffite party within the university.[209] Wyclif was no longer, if he had ever been, an isolated figure. The Wycliffites had some affiliations with particular colleges. It is likely to have been Wyclif's residence in Queen's that brought him into contact with Nicholas Hereford, fellow there from 1369 to 1375, and subsequently Wyclif's leading Oxford disciple. Another Queen's Wycliffite and colleague of Hereford, at least for a short time, was Robert Alington, fellow from 1379 to 1386 or later.[210] Mertonians were still more prominent: 'from the 1380s to the 1420s many Merton men evidently took a passionate interest in Wyclif's ideas.' John Aston, fellow of Merton from 1362 to 1372 and again in the 1390s, was as conspicuous as Hereford in the early days of the movement and seems to have remained a recalcitrant Wycliffite to the end of his life; while in the mid 1390s a group of Mertonians, led by William James, were vigorously pursued for their heretical views by the secular authorities.[211] Finally, two successive principals of St Edmund Hall, William Taylor (1405–6) and Peter Payne (1411–c. 1413), were both late converts to Wyclif's doctrines.[212]

Altogether absent from the record are the names of any Exonian Wycliffites. No fellow of Exeter is known to have been implicated in the various condemnations of Wyclif and his followers. There is a certain irony in the fact that Exeter stood closer than any other college to the schools situated in Schools Street, lying along the line of the present proscholium of the Divinity School, where Wyclif's extremist views were expounded in his lectures of the 1370s; it is even possible that he may from time to time have lectured in one of the four schools belonging to the College. There may conceivably have been sympathizers among the fellows. Occasional hints suggest as much. William Serche, fellow from 1381 and sometime chaplain, was removed from his chaplaincy by Archbishop Arundel in 1384: an intervention from above which suggests a particularly serious offence.[213] John Alward, fellow in

---

[208] A. Hudson, *The Premature Reformation* (Oxford, 1988), 82–4. For Arundel's visitation, see Catto, 'Wyclif', *HUO*, ii. 248–52.

[209] Hudson, *The Premature Reformation*, 69–73; Hudson, 'Wycliffites (active c.1370–1420)', *ODNB*.

[210] *BRUO*, i. 30–1, ii. 913–15; Hudson, *The Premature Reformation*, 70, 93.

[211] A. Hudson, 'Wyclif's Books', in L. Clark, M. Jurkowski, and C. Richmond, *Image, Text and Church, 1380–1600: Essays for Margaret Aston* (Toronto, 2009), 24; *BRUO*, i. 67; Hudson, *The Premature Reformation*, 88–9.

[212] *BRUO*, iii. 1441–3, 1852; A. B. Emden, *An Oxford Hall in Medieval Times* (Oxford, 1927), 125–61.

[213] *BRUO*, iii. 1670; Boase (2), lxiv, 20, 290–1. Boase (2), 20, states that Serche was removed 'for Wiclifism', but we cannot be sure of this.

1408 and later Rector, bequeathed to the College a still surviving manuscript containing two of Wyclif's sermons preached in 1376 and 1377.[214] Yet these are slender foundations for any suggestion of Wycliffism at Exeter. There is no evidence that Exeter ever possessed any of Wyclif's main works, as, for example, did Balliol and Queen's; nor can any case be made for Wyclif's having access to Exeter's library, as he may just possibly have had access to those of Queen's, Balliol, and Merton.[215]

If the College played no obvious part in Oxford Wycliffism it may be because its members lacked the qualifications to contribute to, and perhaps even to appreciate, the theological debates and disputations of the 1370s. As an arts-only College, Exeter can never have provided fertile soil for Wyclif's views. It is noticeable that Wyclif's leading followers, most conspicuously Nicholas Hereford and John Aston, were drawn from the theology faculty, like Wyclif himself. Nor could the College contribute much to the movement's second Oxford phase, when, from about 1390 onwards, the master's works were excerpted, summarized, indexed, and drawn upon for the compilation of voluminous theological handbooks: work which demanded a deep knowledge of scriptural exegesis and patristics as well as skill in handling biblical language.[216] These qualities were much more likely to be found in a college specializing in theology, such as Merton, than at Exeter.

But this is not quite the whole story. It is a striking fact that several notorious Wycliffites had, at an earlier stage in their careers, been fellows of Exeter. Most prominent among them was Robert Rygge, a Devonian, fellow from 1361 to about 1365, and then a fellow of Merton from 1365 to 1380. Qualified by virtue of the doctorate in theology which he obtained during his Merton years, Rygge was a member of Chancellor Barton's committee set up in 1380 to enquire into Wyclif's views on the eucharist, and he was almost certainly one of the committee's dissenting minority who refused to condemn Wyclif. As Barton's successor as chancellor—a remarkable election of a known Wyclif sympathizer—he continued to support Wyclif's Oxford associates before being induced to submit shortly after the Blackfriars council in 1382. He remained close to his first College, acting as visitor for Bishop Brantingham in 1378 and leaving money and books to the College in his will. One of those books, now MS 31, survives at the College. By the time of his death in 1410 his respectability as a canon of Exeter from 1392 and chancellor from 1400 was beyond question.[217] Accompanying Rygge when he submitted in 1382 was Thomas Brightwell, fellow of Exeter from 1364 to

---

[214] MS 6, Watson, 10–11.
[215] Hudson, *The Premature Reformation*, 85; Hudson, 'Wyclif's Books', 15–24.
[216] Hudson, *The Premature Reformation*, 103–10, esp. 109.
[217] *BRUO*, iii. 1616–17; J. Catto, 'Robert Rygge', *ODNB*. The book which Rygge bequeathed to the College is now MS 31: Watson, 46–50.

1369 and of Merton from 1368 to 1382. At the Blackfriars council he was charged with partiality towards the Wycliffites, but his initial sympathies with Wyclif lasted hardly longer than those of Rygge.[218] A third erstwhile Wycliffite, more closely linked with Exeter at the time of his association with Wyclif, was Laurence Stephen, sometimes known as Laurence Bedeman, fellow of Exeter from 1372 to 1380, and Rector for part of his final year. His precipitate departure from the rectorship on 16 April 1380, in mid year, may well have had some connection with his Wycliffite views, for by 1381 he was believed to be 'one of Wyclif's more notorious followers'. He joined Wyclif's other disciples, Hereford, Aston, and Alington, on a preaching tour through Winchester diocese in that year, and later in the year preached in his native Cornwall. Summoned to answer before Bishop Brantingham, he was acquitted of preaching error and shortly afterwards took up the west Devon living of Lifton, which he held until his death in 1422 or 1423. He had probably never been more than a radical preacher who shared Wyclif's antagonism towards the friars and whose evangelical fervour had led him temporarily into the Wycliffite camp.[219]

Exeter's Wycliffite record, therefore, is almost wholly negative. A few former fellows may have temporarily inclined towards Wyclif's views, but their sympathies said nothing about those of the current fellows of the College. If Stephen was removed from the rectorship as a dangerous man, which is entirely possible, the College's wish to conform would be manifest. Those who were fellows at the height of the Wycliffite furore, in the years around 1380, were none of them exposed to prosecution; nor is there any evidence for an Exonian role in the long underground movement by which Wycliffism was perpetuated in Oxford after the master's death in 1384. For every college and hall Wycliffism was brought firmly into the foreground again by Arundel's *Constitutions* of 1409, which ordered all heads of houses to 'enquire into the doctrinal views of all students once a month and report offenders'.[220] Here was another task for the Rector of Exeter. But there is nothing to show how this order was enforced in any house, if indeed it was. As far as can be seen, the fellows of Exeter were, with the possible exception of Laurence Stephen, at all points orthodox. Their intellectual interests are better demonstrated by their library and their books than by their engagement, or the lack of it, with the great theological and political issues which sprang from Wyclif's teaching.

[218] *BRUO*, i. 266–7; Hudson, *The Premature Reformation*, 77–8.

[219] *BRUO*, iii. 1772; Boase (1), 270–1; Boase (2), lxv–lxvii, 17; J. I. Catto, 'A Radical Preacher's Handbook, *c.*1383', *EHR*, 115 (2000), 900–4. Stephen's replacement as Exeter's Rector by William Talkarn may be significant, for it was Talkarn whom Archbishop Arundel imposed on the college as chaplain in 1384, in place of the errant William Serche: Boase (2), 20, 290–1. It rather looks as if, in 1380, one Rector of dubious sympathies was replaced by another of impeccable orthodoxy.

[220] Hudson, *The Premature Reformation*, 82.

6. THE COLLEGE: GOVERNMENT AND ADMINISTRATION

Throughout the later middle ages Exeter's administrative structure was simpler than that of any other college. Responsibility for the College's affairs, particularly its finances, lay solely with the Rector. Although he might need to seek the consent of the fellows for exceptional decisions, there was no bursar or sub-rector or dean to assist him. In the Rector's absence the senior fellow normally took charge. The absence of a bursar was particularly remarkable. Even a house as small as University College had a bursar, chosen annually from among the fellows and responsible for keeping the accounts. Even Queen's, with fewer fellows than Exeter, had a clerk of the treasury and two fellows elected annually as chamberlain (effectively bursar) and treasurer to assist the provost.[221] Exeter's organization, by comparison, was primitive. No structure of offices had been provided for in Stapeldon's statutes, and it was not until the Petrean statutes of 1566 that one was devised. We can see once again how the permanence of the founder's statutes hampered the possibilities of change. For some 250 years the College was effectively managed by the Rector alone.

The Rector's primary task was to supervise the College's finances and to keep the accounts. Under the statutes he had to account each term before the fellows for monies received and spent, and to present his accounts in summary form before the bishop at his annual visitation.[222] Keeping the accounts involved the mastery of quite complicated sets of arithmetical calculations. Especially complicated were those for the College's expenditure on fellows' commons and allowances, where pro rata deductions had to be made for each day's absence beyond the statutory absences allowed by Stapeldon. This was not child's play, and to be exposed to the termly scrutiny of the fellows or, still worse, the annual inspection of the bishop must have been daunting. It is understandable that John Rygge, Rector in 1440–1, should have headed his roll of accounts 'Jesus have mercy (*Jhesu Miserere*)' and that his successor John Lyndon should have followed suit with a similar heading, 'O God, make haste to help me (*Deus in adiutorium meum intende*)'.[223] Understandably too, the annual signing-off of the accounts was sometimes an occasion for minor celebrations, and from 1397 to 1419 small payments for beer at the College's expense on the days when the Rector accounted were themselves a regular feature of the accounts.[224] Any cash surplus remaining at the end of the accounting process was placed in the College chest, to be carried forward as a receipt on the next term's account. But any deficit had to be temporarily met by the Rector from his own pocket. Only in the following term could he

---

[221] *Account Rolls of University College*, ed. Darwall-Smith, i. xvii; *HUO*, ii. 670; R. H. Hodgkin, *Six Centuries of an Oxford College: A History of the Queen's College, 1340–1940* (Oxford, 1949), 11.

[222] *Reg. Stapeldon*, 305, 308.   [223] RA, 140, 142.   [224] RA, 94–122 *passim*.

expect repayment from the College, when the sum repaid was entered as an expense on the account.

The variety of hands which sometimes appear in the accounts for a single rectorship suggests that the Rector did not always write the accounts himself. He may have employed an amanuensis, perhaps drawn from the fellows, as certainly happened on occasion in the sixteenth century.[225] Yet the clerk clearly wrote at the Rector's dictation or from notes compiled by him, since the Rector's personal responsibilities are often emphasized by his speaking in the first person. In 1356 Rector Trethewey claimed 3s. 9d. in expenses for riding boots 'which the rector had when I went to Sherborne on the business of the house'.[226] In 1389 Rector Thomas Dyer claimed 2d. for beer 'when I was at Wheatley for stone' (presumably selecting stone from the Wheatley quarries for College building works).[227] In 1400 Rector John Jakys claimed 4d. for his expenses 'in the house of Nigel Cotyngham when I received money from him'. (Cotyngham was vicar of Bampton, in south-west Oxfordshire, where the Gwinear tithe money sent up from Exeter was often collected.)[228] In 1417 Rector John Alward—the possessor of some of Wyclif's sermons and later donor of books to the College—claimed 2d. for money given 'to labourers in our property outside the north gate when Mr William Fylham [another fellow] and I were there to see to the proper positioning of the new wall'.[229] All these entries point to the Rector's personal engagement with a very diverse range of College business.

They also hint at the amount of travelling which the Rector's office entailed. Any Rector must have expected to spend a large part of his time on horseback. Often it was the need to secure the College's income from its two main sources, Gwinear and Wittenham, that took him away from Oxford. Robert Clyst, Rector for an unusually long period from 1359 to 1365, was especially active. In winter term 1361 he rode to Exeter to collect the Gwinear money from the cathedral's steward, hiring a horse and taking a servant with him. A few months later he rode to Harwell and Sutton Courtenay in Berkshire 'on divers occasions on the business of the house', again hiring a horse; and he also visited Abingdon. All these journeys are likely to have been connected with the College's nearby church at Wittenham. In summer term 1362 he was again at Harwell and Wittenham, where he went to view the season's corn, and also at Abingdon, travelling there to see about the money owed to the College by the executors of the recently deceased farmer of the Wittenham tithes. In the autumn he was in Exeter again to collect a portion of the Gwinear money, and he several times visited Abingdon, Harwell, and Wittenham. Finally, in the summer of 1363 he travelled to Sherborne in Dorset, one of the bishop of Salisbury's manors, to discuss with

[225] Boase (2), 71 (1560).   [226] RA, 5.   [227] RA, 82. Cf. above, 104.
[228] RA, 97/3; below, 128–9.   [229] RA, 120/4.

the bishop the taxes payable for the church at Wittenham.[230] Since Clyst was very probably a regent master with lecturing duties—he had obtained his BA by 1355—he cannot have found it easy, any more than any other Rector, to reconcile his university obligations with his responsibilities to the College. He had to be equally at home in the schools and in the saddle.

This pattern was typical of the working lives of the late medieval Rectors. After the 'Berkshire circuit' of places around Wittenham, the Rector's most frequent destination was Exeter. Occasionally he had to travel further to distant Gwinear, as Rector John Evelyn did in the summer of 1444.[231] No doubt these trips sometimes provided opportunities to visit family and friends at the College's expense, but they cannot have been comfortable journeys. A visit to Exeter meant a ride of about six days, not always in safety: John Jakys was robbed on his way there in 1400 and claimed 5s. from the College for his losses.[232] An extension to Gwinear probably doubled the journey time. Occasionally the Rector's mission was a more delicate one than the routine collection of the Gwinear money. In 1457, at a time of financial crisis, the Rector put in a claim for his expenses while in Devon 'to solicit money from the friends of the College': the first known instance of rectorial fund-raising.[233] Had stress then been invented, the Rector would surely have suffered from it.

It is not surprising that the man who had to shoulder these responsibilities was almost invariably a *magister* and so, like Clyst, a senior member of the College. Only when the fellowship was much reduced in numbers might a mere bachelor be elected, as the bachelor Robert Trethewey was in the years after the Black Death.[234] The Rector required an unusual combination of qualities: proven academic expertise, a head for business and finance, the practical good sense to manage the fellowship, and a public-spirited willingness to work hard for the College. The compensations were largely, but not wholly, intangible: local prestige and respect, a certain amount of power and patronage (the statutes authorized the Rector to allocate rooms and appoint servants), and, more materially, an annual stipend of 20s. rather than the 10s. allowed by Stapeldon to each fellow. Responsibilities were thus balanced by rewards, and it is difficult to know whether election was welcomed or deplored. Stapeldon, with characteristic good sense, had laid down that no fellow, once elected as Rector, could decline to serve, on pain of exclusion from the house.[235] This suggests that resistance to election might be expected. On the other hand, the evidence for disputed elections, already discussed,

---

[230] RA, 21, 23, 24, 25, 27.   [231] RA, 144/4.
[232] The distance from Bampton to Exeter was reckoned to be a five-day journey: J. Blair, *The Medieval Clergy of Bampton*, Bampton Research Paper 4 (Oxford, 1991), 22. Bampton was about a day's journey from Oxford. For the robbery of Jakys, see RA, 97/2.
[233] RA, 156/3.   [234] Above, 72.   [235] *Reg. Stapeldon*, 305.

indicates that the office might be coveted, at least by some.[236] Re-election at the end of the year was not uncommon. Of the 73 known rectors between 1319 and 1500, a majority, 43, held office for one year only; but 9 held office for 2 years, 8 for 2 to 3 years, 8 for 4 years, 3 for 6 years, and 2, William Palmer (Rector, 1425–32) and John Rowe (1433–40), for 7 years.[237] Re-election must surely have rested on the willingness, even keenness, of the candidate to stand; for while a reluctant candidate might be pressed into a single year's service it is hardly likely to have been possible to press him to serve repeatedly against his will.

Most of the longer periods of office fell in the fifteenth century rather than the fourteenth. The later period saw not only the seven-year stints of Palmer and Rowe, but also two of the three six-year terms and five of the eight four-year terms. This was in part a natural consequence of the lengthening tenure of fellowships and of their extension to make it possible for some to read theology.[238] There had been, however, one earlier attempt to do away altogether with the annual elections which made Exeter's position so anomalous among the early colleges. In 1384 Bishop Brantingham had deplored the problems arising from his predecessor's statute requiring annual elections. They encouraged slothfulness in office and insufficient attention to business which needed to be quickly dispatched, while frequent elections also produced serious discord, to the College's loss. For these reasons Brantingham laid down that the current Rector, William Slade, and his successors should remain permanently in office unless they proved to be negligent or otherwise unsuitable.[239] Brantingham's injunction provides us with useful insights into some possible drawbacks of the contemporary practice—inefficiency, a tendency to leave business over to the next Rector, jockeying for office, and the general neglect of the College's interests. But it was disregarded. Slade continued in office for only one more year, and life Rectors were not instituted until the Petrean reforms of the sixteenth century. At the end of each year the fellows evidently preferred to retain the choice between re-election and new election.

His period of office over, the Rector generally stepped back into the ranks of the fellows for a year or two before vacating his fellowship, either to engage in further study outside the College or to take up a benefice. John Rowe, for example, after relinquishing his seven-year rectorship in 1440, held his fellowship for a further year, studying theology, before he moved on to become sub-dean of Exeter cathedral.[240] Most Rectors, therefore, would have had

---

[236] Above, 79, 81.
[237] For a list of rectors, with their periods of office, see *VCH Oxfordshire*, iii. 113–14. This list needs correction in some minor points.
[238] Above, 91–4, 98–9.   [239] *Reg. Brantingham*, i. 543–4; Boase (1), lii–liii; Boase (2), lx.
[240] *BRUO*, iii. 1598–9.

their predecessors present in College and at their side: a situation, one imagines, that would have had both advantages and disadvantages. From the mid fifteenth century onwards there was a tendency for the retiring Rector to vacate his fellowship along with the rectorship, as a term at the College often much longer than comparable terms in the fourteenth century came to an end. Sometimes the retiring Rector would move directly to a benefice, as John Lyndon did when he became dean of Crediton in 1442 after vacating fellowship and rectorship. Sometimes he might continue to rent a room in College, as John Philipp did when he ceased to be fellow and Rector in 1470.[241] Even the lengthier rectorships of the fifteenth century were no more than brief intervals in what were often extended academic and clerical careers.

Almost all the College's medieval Rectors remain as no more than names with attached lists of degrees, offices, and benefices. We cannot know them as men. It is appropriate that the only Rector whose career throws some light on his character and attributes is the sole holder of the office whose name is familiar today: William Palmer, who gave his name to Palmer's Tower, the one surviving feature of the medieval College, and whose contribution to the College is still remembered in the College's bidding prayer. As we have seen, Palmer was the kinsman and possibly the son of John Palmer, onetime mayor of Launceston and MP for the town.[242] He was probably elected to his fellowship at Exeter in the winter term of 1420, by which time he was already a BA: one of those advanced students whose election became increasingly common in the fifteenth century.[243] When he was elected to the rectorship in 1425, he had additionally incepted as MA and was now likely to be lecturing as a regent master. His reputation as Rector rests on two achievements. First, coming into office during a period of acute financial difficulty for the College, he restored its fortunes, moving it from deficit to surplus by instituting a policy of strict economy and by taking in undergraduates and others as rent-paying boarders.[244] Second, he was a great builder, giving the College the very large sum of £100 for building, and putting in hand various new works, mainly in 1432, his last year as Rector. Besides his eponymous tower, which gave the College a grand new entrance from the street, these included four chambers to the west of the tower, a lodging for the Rector, and an eastward extension to the chapel.[245] It is not surprising that such an enterprising and generous fellow, and one possessing such obvious business acumen, should have been elected and then re-elected for seven successive years. Not exactly an achievement but still worth noting is the change in the College's name

[241] *BRUO*, ii. 1191, iii. 1476.   [242] Above, 87.

[243] *Reg. Lacy*, i. 63; *BRUO*, iii. 1422, from which all unreferenced information in this and the following paragraph is taken.

[244] Below, 134–5, 159–60.

[245] Boase (2), 269; RA, 133/4 (accounts for chapel extension), printed in Boase (1), 179–80.

which he instituted. In 1430 he titled himself in his accounts, not 'Rector of Stapeldon Hall', like all his predecessors in their accounts, but 'Rector of Exeter College': the nearest we come to an official renaming of the College.[246]

After vacating the rectorship in 1432, Palmer remained a fellow for a further two years before moving to the Devon living of Ringmore, and then in 1438 to the precentorship of the church of Crediton: a prestigious and well-remunerated post.[247] But he did not forget his old College. He thrice served as Bishop Lacy's visitor, in 1439, 1442, and 1453; he gave the College two sets of vestments in 1446; and in 1460, when he was still at Crediton but nearing the end of his life, he made arrangements with the then Rector, John Philipp, for the celebration of his obit (an annual anniversary service) after his death.[248] He was later commemorated in the east window of the chapel by a stained-glass depiction, seen and recorded by Anthony Wood in the seventeenth century, showing him gowned and kneeling above a Latin inscription which read 'Pray for the soul of master William Palmer, fellow of this place, who caused this chapel to be lengthened'.[249] Well did he deserve the prayers of his College.

Although Exeter had no formal administrative structure, neither Palmer nor any other Rector governed as an autocrat. The fellows too had a part to play. One or two fellows often accompanied the Rector on his travels, while the sanction of the whole body was usually invoked to warrant any exceptional transactions, especially financial transactions. There are many entries in the accounts where the Rector has carefully noted that a particular decision was taken 'with the unanimous consent of the fellows'. The phrase was used to authorize a large loan of 16 marks to the vicar of Wittenham in 1361; a loan to a fellow, Thomas Kelly, in 1363; an advance of 5s. on another fellow's annual allowance in 1364; an allowance made to the farmers of the Wittenham tithes in 1438–9; a loan of £4 to the College from the reserves in the College chest; and so on.[250] In these cases the fellows were drawn into the government of the College by the Rector's need to show that he had not acted *ultra vires* and to justify himself when his accounts came to be presented. There must have been College meetings where these and other decisions were taken, as there were, for example, at Merton.[251] But the only meetings that we know of are those convened annually in the first few days of the new winter term to elect the Rector, and others held more irregularly to elect fellows. They almost certainly took place in the chapel, where one such election was

---

[246] Below, 148.
[247] Cf. N. Orme, 'The Church of Crediton from St Boniface to the Reformation', in T. Reuter (ed.), *The Greatest Englishman: Essays on St Boniface and the Church at Crediton* (Exeter, 1980), 102, 110.
[248] Boase (2), 33; *Reg. Lacy*, ii. 164, 266, iii. 170; ECA, L. III. 10.
[249] Wood, *Colleges*, 116; Boase (2), xlvii–xlviii.   [250] RA, 20, 27, 30, 138, 139/1.
[251] Martin and Highfield, 72–3. Meetings were held three times a year.

discussed in 1357, but no records of attendance or business for these or other meetings were kept until the late 1530s.[252]

There was one figure whose work was essential to the smooth running of the College, but who stood outside and below the fellowship. That was the manciple, later known (from 1408) as the *pincerna* or steward.[253] Of the four permanent College servants—manciple, cook, barber, and laundress—the manciple was by far the most important. His superiority was reflected in his salary of one pound a year in the 1350s, rising to £1 6s. 8d. in 1374, compared with the cook's 8s., rising to 13s. 4d., the barber's 4s., rising to 6s. 8d., and the laundress's 5s., rising to 10s. (reflecting the general post-Black Death rise in wages).[254] If his primary job was to see to the provisioning of the College— buying in food and drink for the annual feast, for example[255]—he also acted as a general factotum, combining the roles of domestic bursar, steward, and land agent. In 1355 we find him hiring a horse for the College; in 1358, supervising workers repairing the barn at Wittenham; in 1396, selling firewood from the garden; in 1409, travelling to Devon to collect money; and in 1454 journeying to Gwinear to arrange for the farming of the tithes and to bring back the tithe money.[256] These last two examples emphasize the degree to which his work overlapped with that of the Rector, in a period when the manciple's responsibilities in general were increasing. The manciples of the late fifteenth century, no longer mainly anonymous figures, like their fourteenth-century predecessors, were often substantial men in their own right. One, William Brystow, had his obit celebrated annually in the college.[257] Still more conspicuous was John Bradeston, who served the College for at least twenty years from the 1470s to the 1490s and rented a College house in the town.[258] His multifarious activities recur throughout the accounts—riding to Bampton to collect the Gwinear money sent up from Exeter,[259] negotiating on the College's behalf for the acquisition of property,[260] and getting in supplies for the fellows' commons.[261] Beneath the Rector, the manciple acted as the College's junior executive officer and maid-of-all-work.

The one major external constraint on the government of the college and the freedom of action of its Rector and fellows lay in the authority vested by the statutes in the bishop of Exeter. Stapeldon had laid down that he and his successors should have the power to alter and amend the statutes; and the unavailing exercise of this power had been shown when Bishop Brantingham attempted to do away with annual elections to the rectorship. But more

[252] RA, 8; below, 180–1, 183–4.   [253] RA, 107 records the new title for the first time.
[254] RA, 1, 53.
[255] RA, 23, 178/2, 179/2, etc. The manciple's work is better recorded in the sixteenth century: see below, 204–6.
[256] RA, 2, 12, 93/1, 110, 153/4.   [257] Boase (2), 268, 309–10.
[258] RA, 186/4; Salter, *Survey*, ii. 116.   [259] RA, 175/1, 180/2, 186/1.
[260] RA, 179/3, 187/1.   [261] RA, 177/4.

important, because more regularly invoked, were the powers exercised through the bishop's annual visitation. The statutes had authorized the bishop or his deputies to conduct such visitations and to use them to examine the state of the College, to inspect the accounts, and to set right any failings.[262] In assessing the ways in which the bishops fulfilled this role we are hampered by the patchiness of the evidence in the episcopal registers: evidently some registrars regarded their bishop's dealings with the College as extra-diocesan business not worth recording. Fortunately, however, the accounts often mention visitations, largely because they entailed expenditure on food and drink for the visitors; and they can therefore be used to supplement the information in the registers, though they rarely throw light on the outcome of the visitation. Brantingham's register, for example, shows the bishop commissioning six visitations, in October 1371, October 1372, May 1374, September 1378, May 1384, and November 1387, while the accounts record others in 1376 and 1382.[263] The register of Bishop Stafford records no visitations, but the accounts show the bishop visiting the College in 1396, 1397, 1398, and 1399.[264] It is a fair assumption that visitations took place in most years. Those which brought the bishop himself to the College were in a minority. More usually, the visitation was conducted by his appointed deputies, often former fellows now resident elsewhere in Oxford or holding canonries or other posts in west country churches. William Palmer's three visitations were of this sort. To judge by the one visitation recorded in any detail, that for 1420, the proceedings took place in the College chapel and involved the Rector's presentation of the accounts, which were inspected and discussed by the visitors, followed by the examination of the fellows under oath, first collectively and then individually, as to the state and government of the College.[265] The prospect of having sympathetic visitors, familiar with the College and its ways, must have mitigated, though not perhaps removed, any apprehensions which the Rector and fellows may have had about an approaching visitation. After it was over conversation and reminiscence over welcome food and drink no doubt followed.

There was a marked pattern in the relations of Stapeldon's various successors with the College. The next four bishops—John Grandisson (1327–69), Thomas Brantingham (1370–94), Edmund Stafford (1395–1419), and Edmund Lacy (1420–55)[266]—all took their responsibilities seriously and were benefactors and good friends of the College. The arms of two of them, Grandisson, 'benefactor to this house', and Stafford, 'benefactor', were later

---

[262] Reg. Stapeldon, 308; above, 39.
[263] Reg. Brantingham, i. 146, 147, 155, 161, 177, 246; RA, 62, 74.
[264] RA, 94/1, 94/4, 95/2, 96.   [265] Reg. Lacy, i. 63.
[266] I omit the very brief episcopates of James Berkeley (1326–7) and John Catterick (1419), which had no effects on the College.

displayed in the College.[267] All four gave or bequeathed books to the College library,[268] and some were generous donors of money. Brantingham, the only one of the four who was not a graduate, gave 10 marks in 1374, at the height of the College's financial crisis, a further £10 towards the new library, and money for a new window, presumably for the chapel, in 1387.[269] Lacy, more parsimonious, gave £5 in 1450; but he was a graduate of University College and it was there that his gifts mainly went.[270] The most generous of the four was Edmund Stafford. Not only did he extend and re-roof the library, as we have seen, but he paid for the construction of new rooms beneath it, for a portico to the chapel, with a room beneath, for the part re-roofing of the hall, and for the building of a new western gate to the College, at a total cost of more than 200 marks. He was the most munificent single donor between Stapeldon and Petre; and it is a cautionary indication of the lacunae in the accounts that we know of his munificence only because his successor, Edmund Lacy, listed his building projects when he enjoined the College to pray for his soul in their daily masses and to keep his obit annually.[271] There were in addition other less obvious ways in which the bishops could help the College. All controlled extensive ecclesiastical patronage in Devon and Cornwall, particularly in the cathedral and in collegiate churches such as Crediton, which was often used for the benefit of former fellows; and on at least two occasions the bishop's help was invoked by the College to speed the payment of the Gwinear tithe money, held back at Exeter by a dilatory dean and chapter.[272]

Yet the bishops were also Stapeldon's heirs, and this made their role partly a disciplinary one. They saw themselves as standing in the founder's shoes, conservators of his statutes and defenders of his legacy, and they often adopted a strongly proprietorial tone in their dealings with the College. To Brantingham, Stapeldon Hall was 'our hall' and he was its 'founder and patron (*fundator ac patronus*)'.[273] Lacy spoke of himself even more grandiosely as 'sole patron, founder and ordinary of [i.e. having ecclesiastical jurisdiction over] the College'.[274] If Brantingham was sometimes prepared to dispense the Rector and fellows from the restrictions of the statutes, allowing them to draw extra commons, for example, in times of dearth and

[267] *The Visitations of the County of Oxford, 1566, 1574, 1634*, ed. W. H. Turner, Harleian Soc., 5 (London, 1871), 100.
[268] *Reg. Grandisson*, iii. 1553; *Reg. Brantingham*, ii. 745; RA, 125/2, 157/3; Boase (2), l–li; *BRUO*, iii. 1750.
[269] RA, 54, 78; Boase (2), lvi, n. 1; Boase (1), 178; above, 78, 104.
[270] RA, 149/4; Darwall-Smith, 60, 85.   [271] *Reg. Lacy*, iv. 299–304.
[272] Highfield, 'Early Colleges', *HUO*, i. 242; *Reg. Grandisson*, i. 524–5; *Reg. Brantingham*, i. 284.
[273] *Reg. Brantingham*, i. 345, 543.   [274] *Reg. Lacy*, ii. 152.

difficulty,[275] Lacy was more insistent on the statutes' full observance, often to the point of highhandedness.

Two episodes from his episcopate illuminate this whole question of the bishop's disciplinary relationship with the College. The first dates from 1420.[276] In that year Lacy conducted his first visitation of the College, acting through a deputy, Walter Trengoff, then chancellor of the university but also a former fellow and Rector. The visitation was set in train by what Lacy regarded as two serious breaches of the statutes. In the first, the College had elected a new fellow from the diocese of Salisbury in the place of an outgoing fellow from Devon, although, Lacy said, there were plenty of well-qualified scholars from his own diocese (and we need to remember that, under the statutes, and after the appropriation of Wittenham in 1355, there was a strict apportioning of fellowships between Devon, Cornwall, and Salisbury diocese). In the second, in place of an outgoing fellow from Cornwall, the fellows had elected one who was already a regent master, although the statutes stipulated that fellows should be at least sophists and at most bachelors. Since the statutes had in fact set no upper limit for election, this last statement was Lacy's invention. This second election had again been carried through at the expense of men from the bishop's own diocese, who had no other college open to them in the university. The implication, never clearly stated, was that the second incoming fellow should also have come from Cornwall, like the man whom he replaced, but that his origins lay elsewhere. The outcome was that the six fellows who had nominated the two supposedly disqualified candidates were sentenced by Trengoff to lose their commons for five weeks: in effect a substantial fine of 5s. each. The possibility of further penalties was reserved for the bishop's decision.

This case is particularly instructive. Lacy intervened directly in the affairs of the College, in defence of the statutes and as the statutes entitled him to do. Yet it is clear that behind his desire to enforce the statutes lay his further concern to preserve the College as a training ground for the clergy of his diocese, whose claims were overridden when men from another diocese or very senior figures were elected in their place. If the relationship between Exeter and its visitor was closer and sometimes more uncomfortable than that between other colleges and their visitors, it was because the College had an ancestral and almost umbilical attachment to the diocese of its visitor, and one founded not only on the statutes but on the interests of both parties. The diocese of Exeter provided not only a large part of the College's income, from Gwinear, but also the major source of employment for the fellows when their days at the College were over. The College provided the diocese with a steady supply of educated clergy, which it was in the bishop's interests to maintain.

---

[275] Above, 77–8.   [276] *Reg. Lacy*, i. 60–4; Boase (2), lx–lxi.

As the link between diocese and College, he played a role hard to parallel among the other colleges of the university.

The second episode came later, in 1439. Its main elements are set out in a letter from Lacy to John Rowe, then Rector.[277] The bishop had heard from many reports, he said, that one Richard French, a well-qualified scholar from the diocese of Exeter, had been elected to a fellowship 'by the wiser and more senior part of the fellows'. But a rival candidate, Richard Bokeler, had attracted an equal number of votes (in fact almost certainly more), and the case had been referred to the chancellor of the university for a decision. Lacy here alluded to the authority which the statutes gave to the chancellor to settle election disputes when neither candidate had the two-thirds majority required for election but each candidate had six or more votes.[278] The chancellor had come down in favour of French. But eight fellows had refused to accept this verdict and had prevented French from entering into his fellowship. If the College was at its full strength of fifteen, the 'wiser and more senior party' must have numbered seven against the dissenting majority of eight—which explains why Lacy should have been concerned to stress the quality rather than the quantity of the minority party. The chancellor had nevertheless acted entirely within his rights in preferring the minority candidate. The upshot in this case was that the contumacious eight were summoned to appear before the bishop at his Devon manor of Chudleigh: the only occasion known to us when a group of fellows were cited to distant Devon for disciplinary reasons. In the event, French entered into his fellowship in the same year, vacating it only in 1456, while the disappointed candidate, Bokeler, was elected in the following year, 1440, and remained until 1448.[279]

Like the first episode, this intricate little dispute has its own lessons. If the bishop's statement can be believed, it shows a College fiercely divided, and one where the majority of the fellows were not prepared to accept the provision in the statutes intended to govern divisions of just this sort. Since Bokeler's party were in the majority, they had an understandable grievance; but they were not in the right. The bishop, for his part, stood foursquare behind the statutes, but, as in the first case from 1420, his diocesan interests were also directly involved. He went out of his way to stress French's origins in the diocese of Exeter and his qualifications for a fellowship under the statutes. Bokeler, on the other hand, was very probably from Dorset, in the diocese of Salisbury.[280] Although Lacy did not make this point, his stand shows that once again it was rights of a man from his own diocese that he judged to have been impugned by the refusal of the fellows to admit French. The statutes were in danger of being breached at the expense of the future clergy of the diocese, and ultimately at the expense of the wider church and

---

[277] *Reg. Lacy*, ii. 152–3; Boase (2), lxi–lxii.   [278] *Reg. Stapeldon*, 304.
[279] *BRUO*, i. 210, ii. 727.   [280] Boase (2), 38.

the lay congregations whom an educated clergy existed to lead to salvation. The smallest issues could have the largest implications.

In his drive to enforce Stapeldon's statutes Lacy was the zealot among our four bishops, and the tone in which he addressed the College was sometimes almost unbalanced. Commissioning William Palmer to visit Exeter in 1453, he wrote of 'the many crimes and outrageous offences (*plura crimina et delicta enormia*)' perpetrated in the College by some of the fellows, contrary to the statutes and the College's good customs. If left unchecked, they would bring total ruin on the College.[281] It is hard to know what could have caused this episcopal outburst; certainly nothing which disturbed the even tenor of the accounts. But Lacy was the last bishop of the period to take such a probing interest in the College's affairs. After his death in 1455 the pattern of Exeter's relationships with its bishop-visitors changed markedly. Exchanges dwindled and episcopal intervention declined. Most of the seven bishops who ruled the see between 1456 and 1502 stayed for no more than a few years; at least one, Oliver King (1492–5), was non-resident; and only Peter Courtenay (1478–87) had roots in the west country. Courtenay indeed, a member of one of the most powerful families in Devon, and formerly an undergraduate boarder at the college, was the one bishop with whom the College maintained regular and beneficial contacts, as we shall see.[282] The registers of all these bishops are mainly thin and incomplete,[283] but their silence on relations with the College is echoed in the accounts. They provide no firm evidence for visitations, though the small gifts of gloves which were regularly presented to the bishops may mark social visits.[284] It may be significant that no gifts, either of books or of money, appear to have moved in the other direction, by contrast with the days of Grandisson et al. The College was now a more independent institution, still constitutionally bound to the bishops of Exeter, but effectively free from their disciplinary intervention and largely deprived of their beneficent patronage.

In its government, as in so many other ways. Exeter differed from other colleges in the late medieval university. Its system of annual rectorships, its rudimentary administrative structure, with no subordinate College officials besides the manciple, and, until 1455, its exceptionally close relationship with its visitor, the bishop of Exeter, all set it apart from other colleges. Some of these peculiarities hampered its development. Brantingham had marked down the disadvantages of annual rectorships; while the duty-bound determination of the bishops to maintain Stapeldon's statutes probably lay behind the

---

[281] *Reg. Lacy*, iii. 170; Boase (2), lxii.   [282] Below, 166–7, 171–2.
[283] DRO, Chanter Catalogue 12, Parts 1 and 2; D. M. Smith, *Guide to Bishops' Registers of England and Wales* (London, 1981), 82–3.
[284] e.g. RA, 183/1, 184/1, 184/2, 190/2.

College's appeal to the pope when, in 1405, it wished to break out of the rigid framework of duties and studies which Stapeldon had erected. Of course, the statutes could always be surreptitiously relaxed by the College's own practices, and we have seen several cases in which this happened. But such an insouciant attitude might always provoke a sharp episcopal riposte, as the fellows found when Bishop Lacy came down on them in 1420 and 1439. And, besides, every fellow at his election had taken a solemn oath on the Gospels to observe the statutes, and some may have had conscientious scruples about mitigating their rigours. Wholesale changes in the organization of the College, even supposing that they were wanted (and the failure of Brantingham's plan for permanent rectorships suggests that they were not), could hardly be introduced in such a way. Created and restricted by the statutes, the governance of the College was to remain unchanged in essentials from Stapeldon's day to Petre's. Exeter's existence owed everything to Stapeldon; but so too did its relative lack of distinction.

7. THE COLLEGE: FINANCES, c.1375–c.1475

The 150 years after the Black Death were unfavourable to all middling landowners, whether minor gentry, minor monastic houses, or minor Oxford colleges. The immense fall in population in 1348–9, and its failure to recover, tipped the balance of economic power away from landlords and towards wage labourers, peasants, and small farmers. The wages of skilled craftsmen doubled from 3d. to 6d. a day between 1350 and 1415, and those for an unskilled labourer from 2d. to 4d. Although wages stabilized thereafter, their initial rise was bound to present problems for any institution with buildings in constant need of repair. Corn prices did not respond quite so dramatically to population decline, but respond they did, with the years after 1376–7 bringing in 'a remarkable period of low prices'.[285] For those dependent on the tithe revenues from appropriated churches, consisting chiefly of money raised from grain sales, this again made for adverse circumstances. The financial history of Exeter College was shaped not only, or even mainly, by internal factors, but by these prevailing economic trends.

Exeter was never a rich college, and in the prevailing environment it sometimes had to struggle hard to stay afloat. We have already seen how the combination of plague, dearth, rising food prices, and mounting debts worked together to threaten its existence in the late 1360s and early 1370s; and not until a hundred years later, with the acquisition of new property in the late 1470s, discussed below, was its future anything like assured.[286] Between

---

[285] E. H. Phelps Brown and S. V. Hopkins, 'Seven Centuries of Building Wages', in E. M. Carus-Wilson (ed.), *Essays in Economic History*, Vol. II (London, 1962), 172; Farmer, 'Prices and Wages', *Agrarian History*, iii. 434.
[286] Below, 165–73.

1357–8, the first year for which a calculation becomes possible, and 1477–8, just before the new revenues arrived, the College's average annual income was between £60 and £70, though this average concealed large fluctuations. The maximum was £87 in 1365–6 and the minimum £42 in 1470–1.[287] In terms of secular society, an income of this size put the College roughly on a par with a moderately wealthy knight. It was small by comparison with those of the larger Oxford colleges—New College and Magdalen, c. £500–600, All Souls and Merton, c. £400[288]—and small even by comparison with that of a College with fewer fellows, such as Queen's, whose income has been estimated at £150 to £200. For some of the time it was rather larger than that of University College, which averaged £40 to £50 for the two decades after 1390 but rose to about £80 for much of the fifteenth century, and it was perhaps a little larger than that of Oriel.[289] If Exeter was thus not quite the poorest of the Oxford colleges it certainly lay towards the bottom of any 'league table' of wealth.

Until the acquisition of a second Cornish church, Menheniot, in 1478, by far the greater part of the College's income came from its two appropriated churches, Gwinear in Cornwall and Wittenham in Berkshire. Until about 1440, when, as we shall see, their yield fell away, these two churches usually produced about £50 to £60 a year, or about 80 to 90 per cent of the College's income. Both churches generated comparable revenues and neither was consistently more valuable than the other. Other regular sources of revenue raised comparatively trivial amounts. A few pounds came in from the renting out of halls, such as Hart Hall, let for £2 a year for much of the fifteenth century; from the schools which the College possessed in Schools Street, along the eastern boundary of the College site; and from other Oxford property. But unlike University College, which in the early fifteenth century drew about two-thirds of its income from its Oxford property,[290] Exeter had little besides its own site within the town walls, and so was less at the mercy of the economic decline which affected the city in the later middle ages. The College did build up a small portfolio of Oxford properties in addition to those acquired in or shortly after Stapeldon's time, notably Karol Hall, in the little bailey of the castle, near St Ebbe's Street, given by Roger Ford, vicar of Bampton, in 1388;[291] a tenement in the great bailey, now Queen Street, given by John Harris, bedel of theology, in 1460;[292] and Peyntour's Hall, often known as Culverd Hall, in St Giles on the present site of St John's College,

---

[287] RA, 36, 37, 38, 39, 168. My figures include only 'new money' generated within the year and discount surpluses carried forward from one year to the next. All figures in this section derive from my analysis of the accounts.

[288] Evans and Faith, 'College Estates', *HUO*, ii. 654–5.

[289] Evans and Faith, 'College Estates', *HUO*, ii. 654–5; Darwall-Smith, 44, 86; *VCH Oxfordshire*, iii. 121.

[290] Darwall-Smith, 82.   [291] Boase (2), 268, 307; Salter, *Survey*, ii. 129.

[292] Boase (2), 268; Salter, *Survey*, ii. 117.

which was purchased in 1478.[293] But the cost of repairs to these properties largely offset, and sometimes wiped out, what little income they produced, and their financial value was small. Much more valuable, because more directly useful to the College, were the various halls acquired on the central site, discussed in a later section.[294] Although these likewise produced only a small rent income, their acquisition represented a series of well-planned moves towards the expansion of the site and the provision of further College accommodation. All these revenues might occasionally be supplemented by gifts of money, mainly from former fellows.

In most years the College's expenses totalled £60 to £70: dangerously close to the level of its receipts. The best year was 1386–7, with expenses of only £45, and the worst 1421–2, when they rose to an enormous £162.[295] Much expenditure was unavoidable. The largest single item in almost every year was the cost of fellows' commons, set at 10d. a week until 1408 and generally 1s. a week thereafter. Expenditure on commons usually accounted for some £40 to £50 of annual income, or well over half the total received. To this sum had to be added the annual allowances paid to the Rector and fellows under the statutes and the further payments made to them, again statutorily, for absences while 'visiting friends'. Taken together, these might amount to another £9 or £10, or about 15 per cent of receipts. Almost as onerous, and more difficult to cope with because less predictable, were expenses for the maintenance of buildings, exacerbated as they were by high wage rates. The College's medley of wood and stone buildings was in constant need of repair: tiles had to be replaced, chimneys rebuilt, windows and stairs renewed. Costs for these works loom large in the accounts. Besides the expenses of commons and building repairs, other sources of expenditure were numerous but minor in cost. Almost every account mentions the purchase of plates, dishes, and utensils for the kitchen, cloths and towels for the hall, wine and incense for the chapel, candles in exuberant varieties for hall and chapel, and parchment for the accounts themselves. Rather more weighty, and again unpredictable, were the business expenses of the Rector and fellows as they travelled into Berkshire or to Exeter to secure the College's income. On a more positive note, the costs of litigation and lawyers, prominent in the accounts of some other colleges (University College spent one-third of its income on legal expenses in 1384–5),[296] were only an occasional expense and generally a small one. Exeter's limited property also set limits to the possibilities for litigation.

The bedrock of the College's resources was the tithe income from Gwinear and Wittenham. Revenues from appropriated churches played an important part in the finances of most Oxford colleges, but no college was so exclusively

---

[293] Boase (2), 268, 297; Salter, *Survey*, ii. 201–2; RA, 174/3; below, 168.
[294] Below, 141–3.   [295] RA, 78, 79, 125.
[296] Darwall-Smith, 142. Cf. Evans and Faith, 'College Estates', *HUO*, ii. 639–40.

dependent on them as Exeter. Without the Gwinear revenues, wrote Rector Dagenet in 1372, the life of the College could not be sustained.[297] But the money from the Gwinear tithes alone, Exeter's original endowment, would have been quite insufficient for the College's maintenance had it not been augmented from 1355 by the income from Wittenham. Without this addition to its holdings, almost doubling their value, the College might well have foundered. Securing and protecting the income from the two churches was a constant preoccupation of the Rector and fellows throughout the period, necessitating much travel, frequent negotiations in the localities, and occasional resort to law. For these reasons the College's management of these two resources, and its relationship with the people and places which produced them, are worth exploring in a little detail.

The College's relations with Gwinear were more problematic than those with Wittenham. This was partly an effect of distance. While Wittenham was only about 10 miles from Oxford, just across the Thames in Berkshire, Gwinear was some 250 miles away in remote west Cornwall. But there was also a striking contrast in the methods by which the two resources had come to be managed. The church at Gwinear had been appropriated to the dean and chapter of Exeter, and not to the College, and it was the dean and chapter who were responsible, under the arrangements made by Stapeldon, for managing the tithes, appointing a vicar for the parish, and handing on the revenues to the College. But in the case of Wittenham, the church had been appropriated by the College and was fully in its hands. The College could thus make what arrangements it wanted for collecting the income and could appoint whom it wanted as vicar.

Difficulties often arose in obtaining the money from Gwinear, and different methods were tried at different times. As we have seen, the dean and chapter were sometimes slow in passing on the money and may have regarded their obligations as irksome. Theirs was the task of seeing to the sale of the tithe crops, collecting the money, taking it to Exeter, and arranging for its transmission to Oxford. The Exeter chapter accounts show that the tithes might sometimes be sold to the vicar of the parish or given over for sale to a commission of Exeter canons, occasionally including a former fellow of the College.[298] Either way of raising the proceeds (and there may have been others) involved exertion. Those proceeds reached the College in a variety of ways, some of which we have already glanced at. Often, particularly in the 1360s and 1370s, the money was collected from Exeter by the Rector or one of the fellows. This was perhaps the quickest and most certain way of laying hands on it. Sometimes it was brought directly to the College by a friend or

---

[297] *Reg. Brantingham*, i. 284; above, 78.
[298] Sale to vicar in 1377: D. and C., 3777, fo. 40. Sale via a commission, including William Slade, former fellow, in 1382: D. and C., 3777, fo. 33.

other visitor: by James Multon, Stapeldon's grand-nephew, for example, in 1364, by a passing canon of Exeter in 1389.[299] Perhaps most frequently it was transmitted via Bampton, about 13 miles south-west of Oxford, where the manor and church were held by the dean and chapter of Exeter and whence the money, sent up from Exeter by the chapter's carrier or a returning vicar, could conveniently be collected by the Rector or by a fellow.[300] There was thus no single way of delivering the money, nor apparently was it delivered at fixed terms. The means of exploiting what was a vital source of revenue were often haphazard.

In the late 1370s yields from Gwinear declined sharply. This was noted in the chapter accounts, which in 1379 recorded that the tithes in that year sold for only £29 6s. 8d., when in previous years they had been sold for £31, £38, or even £40. The College accounts tell a similar story. In 1360–1 the Gwinear tithes had realized £40; in 1378–9, only £22.[301] Underlying this decline was the national trend towards falling corn prices from the mid 1370s onwards. Both falling yields and the mutual interests of the two parties, College and dean and chapter, help to explain an important change in the management of the Gwinear revenues which took place shortly afterwards. The chapter accounts for 1385, explaining a nil return from Gwinear, state that in that year the tithes 'were sold by the agents (*procuratores*) of the fellows of Stapeldon Hall, Oxford, for the use of the fellows, and therefore nothing here'.[302] At this point the Gwinear tithes disappeared permanently from the chapter's reckoning. Although the cathedral authorities never relinquished their formal position as appropriators of Gwinear, in practice the management of the Gwinear tithe income now lay in the hands of the College. It became normal for the College either to appoint an agent in Cornwall to sell the tithes on the College's behalf and to receive a salary in exchange for his work, or to nominate a farmer who would pass on the farm, a fixed annual sum, in payment for the tithes, while keeping for himself any surplus beyond the farm. Both these methods were tried at different times from 1385 onwards. The means of transmitting the money remained much the same, with the *procurator* or farmer normally sending the cash to Exeter cathedral, thence to be either collected by the College or forwarded to Bampton.

The direct links now established between the College and Gwinear did not always make it easier to secure the College's money. Supervision at such a distance was difficult. When, about 1545, the Rector and fellows petitioned chancery against the negligence of the vicar of Gwinear, who had allowed the church and barn there to fall into decay, they spoke of their own impotence to correct him, being 'of very small ability and power, and dwelling far from the

[299] RA, 31, 84/1.
[300] Blair, *The Medieval Clergy of Bampton*, 12–19; RA, 82, 83, 85, etc.; above, 114.
[301] D. and C., 3777, fo. 41; RA, 18, 19, 20, 21, 67, 68, 69, 70.   [302] D. and C., 3777, fo. 50.

said county of Cornwall, and being very strangers and having very small friendship there'.[303] Though there may be an element of exaggeration here, this had no doubt been largely true from the start. The Rector occasionally had to make long journeys to Cornwall to negotiate terms with a new farmer or agent, as Rector William Grene did in 1409.[304] Payments often fell into arrears, as happened in 1445, when the local farmer, Peter Trevuwyth, still owed money from 1438 and had to be pursued at law for payment.[305] Potentially much more serious was the long campaign waged between 1402 and 1404 by John Beville to regain the Gwinear advowson which his ancestor Sir Reginald Beville had alienated in 1311 to Stapeldon's brother, for onward transmission to the dean and chapter. Beville, a former sheriff of Cornwall, was a powerful enemy, and the case which he brought over Gwinear, heard in the court of common pleas, represented a threat to the College's whole position. Joining forces with the dean and chapter to defend the case, the College spent heavily on lawyers both in London and in Devon: one of those rare occasions when legal expenses bulked large in the accounts. Eventually the dispute seems to have been settled by arbitration, with no visible loss to the College beyond its expenses.[306] But it had shown the precarious position in which the Rector and fellows were placed by their dependence on a very few major resources. The loss of Gwinear would have moved the College towards extinction.

Exeter's relationship with Gwinear was distant in other senses besides the geographical. The College was too far away to build up close bonds with the parishioners who, as tithe payers (and no doubt reluctant ones), provided so much of its income. When opportunity offered the Rector and fellows did what they could to reciprocate for the very large benefits which they derived from Gwinear. In 1362 they entertained a party of Gwinear parishioners to dinner when they were passing through Oxford, perhaps on pilgrimage.[307] In 1407 9d. was spent on 'a scholar from our parish in Cornwall', presumably an Oxford student.[308] And in 1445 the College contributed 40s. towards the building of a new bell tower at Gwinear.[309] Its contribution must have been an ex gratia one, since responsibility for the repair and maintenance of the church would have lain with the parishioners and with the dean and chapter as holders of the advowson. This was another factor which set some distance between the College and the providers of its Cornish income.

Exeter's position with regard to Wittenham was both similar and different. The Wittenham tithes were normally farmed, as they often were at Gwinear, usually to a local merchant or to the vicar of the parish. With these men, as with the parish generally, proximity allowed the College to establish the close

---

[303] TNA, C 1/1217/62.   [304] RA, 109.   [305] RA, 145/2.
[306] RA, 100/2/4, 101/1/2/4; D. and C., 1496, 1946, 3498/4; above, 27.
[307] RA, 24.   [308] RA, 106/3.   [309] RA, 145/4.

and harmonious relationships which were inevitably lacking at Gwinear. Eustace Young, for example, or Eustace of Abingdon, as he was sometimes called, farmed the Wittenham tithes almost continuously from 1369 to 1388. Often referred to familiarly as 'Staci' in the accounts, he was frequently given dinner in the College when he brought over the Wittenham money and was clearly regarded as a good friend.[310] Similar long-lasting associations were formed in the fifteenth century. John Shepherd, vicar of Wittenham, farmed the tithes, either by himself or with a partner, from 1437 to 1462, and proved to be so well disposed towards the College that on at least one occasion he paid over an instalment of the tithe income in advance of the due date, as the Rector noted with gratified surprise in the accounts.[311] The College regularly sent small presents, often a hat or gown, to its Wittenham tithe-farmers.[312] When the farmer was also vicar of the parish he might have a third identity as a former fellow of the College. Thomas Symon, fellow from c.1475 to c.1483, for example, was presented to the living by the College, probably on resigning his fellowship, and held it until 1487.[313] This too must have favoured harmony. These relationships were replicated, at least for a time, with the Wittenham parishioners. For the first forty years or so after the church's appropriation the parishioners were sometimes hospitably entertained by the College, on occasion in company with their vicar. In 1358 the vicar and others were given wine and beer in hall; in 1376 the parishioners were entertained to dinner and drink; and in 1392 four visiting parishioners were again dined at the College's expense.[314] Whether the need to economize or mere parsimoniousness explains the disappearance of these entertainments after the 1390s is unclear.

Problems generally arose only in the intervals between the resignation or death of one farmer and the appointment of another. At these times the College was faced with the direct management of the Wittenham lands— supervising the harvest, gathering the tithes, and selling the produce. The Rector and fellows then had to be prepared to stand in as agricultural entrepreneurs. In the late summer of 1487 John Mayne, one of the College's senior fellows and an ordained priest, spent seven weeks at Wittenham overseeing the harvest and the carriage of the tithe sheaves. The accounts records receipts from sales of wheat, malt, and hay, the wheat and malt sold at Oxford and at Wittenham, the hay at Southampton.[315] Similar direct sales by the College occur at other points in the fifteenth century.[316] But these were relatively infrequent, and when a new farmer had been found the fellows must have been relieved to return from their labours as harvest supervisors and corn

---

[310] RA, 47, 53, 57, 65, etc.   [311] RA, 139/1 (1439).   [312] RA, 146/1, 178/3, etc.
[313] BRUO, iii. 1840.   [314] RA, 10, 61, 88/3.   [315] RA, 182/1/2/3/4.
[316] e.g. in 1421, when barley, chaff, straw, peas and beans, and rye, all from Wittenham, were sold by the College: RA, 124/3.

merchants to their more normal academic routines. Or, *per contra*, did they perhaps welcome these bucolic interludes in the Berkshire countryside?

On at least one occasion there was a legal challenge to the College's position at Wittenham, though not one remotely so serious as Beville's challenge over Gwinear. In 1466 New College claimed a £5 annual allowance from the Wittenham revenues, a claim not finally seen off until 1486.[317] More regularly vexatious were the overhead costs associated with the possession of Wittenham. Responsibility for repairs to the church, which at Gwinear fell on the Exeter chapter and on the parishioners, at Wittenham lay with the College. The church was already under repair in 1366, when a fellow accompanied a plumber there to see to work on the roof.[318] But a much more frequent cause of expense was the great timbered barn, whose sixteenth-century successor still stands close by the church at Long Wittenham. The first major outlay on the barn came in 1358, three years after the church's acquisition,[319] and spending continued throughout the period. The Rector himself was frequently drawn into the minutiae of repair work, discussing the barn's repair with a carpenter in 1364 and having to borrow just over £3 from the College chest for further repairs more than a century later in 1489.[320] The barn was essential for the storage of the College's tithe corn, which would normally be released on to the market only gradually through the year. But if its maintenance was a necessity, it was also a bothersome and expensive nuisance.

We are now in a position to trace the general financial fortunes of the College from the last quarter of the fourteenth century until a new era begins with the acquisition of additional properties in the late 1470s; and here we partly follow, but to some extent deviate from, Dr Andrew Butcher's pioneering study of the College's finances.[321] After the period of intermittent crises in the twenty-five years following the Black Death, Exeter's financial position stabilized. Between 1375 and 1416 only one year, 1406–7, showed a deficit, and in most years surpluses varied between a few shillings and £11. A surplus remaining at the end of the year was carried forward to the next year's receipts, so reinforcing any upward trend in income. New buildings and new purchases suggest a mood of financial confidence. We have already noted the building of the new library in 1383, a substantial share of the costs of which were met by the College from its own funds.[322] A new room was added in 1401–2 at a cost of about £24, partly met by donations from fellows and former fellows.[323] The purchase of Checker Hall for £20 in 1405–6 was a further mark of buoyancy. This was a particularly valuable

[317] *Newington Longeville Charters*, ed. H. E. Salter, Oxfordshire Record Soc. (1921), xxix–xxx; RA, 180/1, 181/1.
[318] RA, 40.   [319] RA, 11.   [320] RA, 31, 183/4.
[321] A. F. Butcher, 'The Economy of Exeter College, 1400–1500', *Oxoniensia*, 44 (1979), 38–54.
[322] Above, 104–5.   [323] RA, 95/1/3, 98/2; Butcher, 46.

acquisition, since it adjoined the College's main site and fronted Turl Street; though the outlay necessitated by its purchase may have contributed to the brief one-year deficit in 1406–7.[324] The cost of the College's annual feast on the day of St Thomas the Martyr, always a good barometer of Exeter's economic health, held steady at £1 to £2 until 1408, after which it rose above £2 in several years, suggesting that the College saw no great need for economies.[325] With the revenues from Gwinear also on a temporarily rising trend, reaching £47 in 1403–4, the largest known figure to date,[326] the opening years of the fifteenth century were some of the most prosperous in the College's early history. When the Rector and fellows petitioned Innocent VII in 1405 for a revision of the statutes there was merit in their argument that the recent increase in the College's means justified both a rise in the fellows' commons from 10*d*. to 1*s*. a week (implemented in 1408) and an extension of the period for which fellows might remain at the College.[327] Only the return of the plague in 1407 temporarily disrupted these halcyon years. In the summer and autumn of that year the fellows spent a good deal of their time attending funerals: the accounts record at least fourteen, among them, those of parishioners at Wittenham, fellows of New College and Queen's, a canon of Osney, and the sons of Nicholas Norton, Oxford's town clerk.[328] But there is no sign that the plague had any direct or long-term consequences.

Running counter to the national economic trends, Exeter's good fortune in these years perhaps owed most to a relatively low level of routine expenses and a partial recovery in the revenues from Gwinear, which rested in turn on the exceptional buoyancy of Cornish grain prices.[329] Fortune's wheel, however, was the proper symbol for Exeter's financial history. From 1416 or a little earlier (the accounts are missing for 1415–16) the situation began to deteriorate, and deficits were recorded in every year between 1416–17 and 1426–7. This ten-year run of deficits was unprecedented. It was partly caused by falling receipts, which averaged £64 a year between 1401 and 1415, but only £60 between 1416 and 1427. Revenues from both Gwinear and Wittenham fell away by a few pounds. But the main problem lay in soaring expenditure. Expenses averaged £68 a year between 1401 and 1415, but £110 a year between 1416 and 1427. In 1421–2 they reached the huge sum of £162, larger by far than any other figure for annual expenses in the medieval period.[330]

[324] RA, 105/1; Boase (2), xxi–xxiii; Salter, *Survey*, i. 52–3; Butcher, 42.

[325] Butcher, 52.   [326] RA, 101.   [327] *Cal. Papal Letters*, vi. 47–8; above, 96.

[328] RA, 106/4. The plague of 1407 is noticed in the Queen's College account rolls, which also record other outbreaks in 1401 and 1414: Magrath, *The Queen's College*, i. 133. The latter two plagues made no mark on the Exeter accounts, but the College is unlikely to have been immune from their effects. The accounts for 1407–8, from which it might have been possible to deduce mortality among the fellows, are missing.

[329] For Cornish grain prices, see J. Hatcher, *Rural Economy and Society in the Duchy of Cornwall, 1300–1500* (Cambridge, 1970), 146–7.

[330] RA, 125; above, 127.

Some of the forces behind this extraordinary inflation are perceptible from the accounts. Every account was burdened by accumulating deficits, for just as surpluses helped to create a 'virtuous circle' by adding to the following year's income, so deficits were also carried forward and had to be eliminated, at least temporarily, by an appropriate payment to the Rector who had borne the initial loss. This was then entered as an expense on the account. In winter term 1421, for example, miscellaneous expenses (excluding fellows' commons and servants' wages) amounted to nearly £35, but just over £31 of this total was accounted for by a payment to the Rector to meet the cost of the previous year's deficit.[331]

Three other more material factors were also in play. First, this was a period of exceptionally heavy building expenses. There was a large repair bill for Hart Hall in 1418, for example,[332] while repairs to Karol Hall cost £2 7s. 9d. in autumn term 1420, a substantial proportion of the £12 total for that term's miscellaneous expenses.[333] Secondly, expenditure on commons had increased, largely as a result of the increase in weekly allowances introduced in 1408. The cost of commons averaged about £28 a year in the 1390s, but about £32 a year in the 1420s. Finally, the College was not immune to the external pressures resulting from the policies of the government. These were the years of Henry V's conquests in France and of England's subsequent wars to defend them. Heavy taxation was one consequence. Between 1416 and 1420 the College paid more in taxes than in any comparable period, including one exceptionally large payment of £2 7s. 5d. in 1420.[334]

It was William Palmer, Rector from 1425 to 1432, who restored the College to solvency after this decade of financial debility. We have already looked at Palmer's general achievement and at the seven-year rectorship, a record at the time, by which the College's appreciation of his work was measured.[335] By 1428–9 Palmer had put an end to the College's deficit financing and restored it to surplus: a favourable situation which was to outlast his time in office. Although the accounts throw only a limited light on how this improvement was brought about, one of Palmer's policies in particular stands out: that of strict economy. Between 1428 and 1432 expenses averaged only about £58 a year compared with the annual average of £110 for the previous decade. Extraordinary expenses were pared to a minimum: those for Lent term 1426 covered little more than necessities for chapel and kitchen, those for winter term 1428, amounting to a mere £1 11s. 7d., little more than linen for hall and table.[336] The costs of the annual feast also fell, reaching what was almost a record low of 17s. 6d. in 1431.[337] At the same time receipts rose, and rents from the letting of rooms to undergraduates and senior boarders became a

---

[331] RA, 124/4, 125/1.   [332] RA, 121/4.
[333] RA, 123/4; Boase (2), xiv–xv n. 2. Boase's 'White Hall' is Karol Hall.
[334] RA, 123/2.   [335] Above, 117–18.   [336] RA, 128/2, 130/1.   [337] RA, 133/2.

conspicuous feature of the accounts, pointing to what was clearly an attempt to increase income.[338] Palmer's major building campaign, including the construction of his great stone entrance tower, marked a justifiable return to the confident and positive mood which the College had last experienced a quarter of a century earlier.

But this was not to last. Between about 1440 and the late 1470s Exeter experienced a long period of financial difficulties. They were almost as serious as, and certainly more protracted than, those of the previous period of financial crisis, in the early 1370s. The downturn began slowly and reached its trough during the 1460s, when every year between 1463 and 1470 returned a deficit. Unlike the shorter period of stress between 1416 and 1425, the causes were almost entirely external, lying in a national depression from whose effects the College could do little to protect itself. 'The great slump of the mid-fifteenth century', as it has been called, was rooted in a lack of demand. Across western Europe the supply of coin fell steeply, curtailing market and monetary transactions; the level of population in England, already stagnant, may actually have declined; and the price of grain, a vital factor in the calculations of all landlords and tenants, and already low, fell further. The price of barley was some 30 per cent lower in the 1450s than in 1400, and in the 1440s 'the average prices of wheat, rye, barley and peas . . . were lower than they had been for a century'.[339]

These depressive trends were mirrored with some precision in the fortunes of the College. Most noticeable, and most damaging, was the drop in income from both Gwinear and Wittenham. This reflected the nationwide fall in grain prices, possibly exacerbated by the dangers and difficulties of transport during the civil disorders of the 1450s and early 1460s. The Wars of the Roses may not have left the College unscathed. The Gwinear revenues suffered most. Between 1410 and 1430 they had averaged an annual £30, but this dropped to £19 in the 1440s, to £20 in the 1450s, to £16 in the 1460s, and to £15 in the 1470s. The tendency at Wittenham, though less pronounced, was similar. Between 1400 and 1420 the annual yield of the Wittenham tithes averaged £25, but this dropped to £21 between 1440 and 1460 and in the 1470s, and to £20 in the 1460s.[340] The proximity of markets along the Thames valley—Oxford, Abingdon, Wallingford, Henley—may have meant that

---

[338] Below, 159–60.

[339] J. Hatcher, 'The Great Slump of the Mid-Fifteenth Century', in R. Britnell and J. Hatcher (eds.), *Progress and Problems in Medieval England: Essays in Honour of Edward Miller* (Cambridge, 1996), 240, 243–5, 248; J. L Bolton, *Money in the Medieval English Economy, 973–1489* (Manchester, 2012), 232–3, 243–4, 263.

[340] Compare these figures with the graph of receipts and expenditure in Butcher, 51. They roughly correspond. The accounts for the 1430s are too incomplete to provide useful figures for comparison with those for the subsequent period.

demand in this region was better sustained than in Cornwall; but the same downward trend was evident in both places.

How did the Rector and fellows respond to the challenges which the slump posed to their existence? In part, they economized. Although in most years the College usually had a full or nearly full complement of thirteen to fifteen fellows, non-residence became frequent in this period and may have been encouraged in order to reduce expenditure on commons. In the summer term of 1458, for example, the College had fourteen fellows, but on average no more than six drew their weekly commons. The others must have been absent.[341] Annual expenditure on commons averaged £30 from 1430 to 1460, but dropped to £27 in the 1460s. Building activity similarly declined almost to nothing, and there was no repetition of the building programme which Rector Palmer had initiated some years earlier. Between 1440 and 1469 'the most expensive building for which record survives is the construction of a new privy in Hart Hall (£4. 12s)'.[342] The annual feast was another obvious target for economies. By contrast with the £1 to £2 spent on the feast in the early years of the century, annual costs averaged 14s. in the 1450s and just over 11s. in the 1460s and 1470s. The feast of 1475 cost a mere 8s. 5½d. and that of 1479 only 8s. 2d., the lowest figures ever recorded.[343] These economies were complemented by some unusual ways of raising money. On four occasions between 1446 and 1451 the College sold horses, including one described as the (or a) 'college horse',[344] and on four occasions between 1456 and 1458 the small proceeds from the sale of pigs appear among the receipts.[345] No similar sales feature elsewhere in the accounts, and it seems likely to have been economic necessity which forced the fellows to turn their collective hand towards trading in livestock. And was it the same necessity that in 1457 drove the College to pay a university stationer for his work in valuing the College's 'electio' books from the library, perhaps with a view to selling or pledging the whole collection?[346]

Much more important, however, at least as a short-term solution to the College's problems (though no path to salvation), was the resort to loans.[347] They came from three sources: from the College chests, including both the common chest, the College's 'treasury', which received any cash surpluses remaining at the end of the year, and also the Grevyll and Germeyn chests, endowed by past benefactors to create a reserve to be drawn on in difficult times;[348] from the university loan chests, used rather less frequently, perhaps

---

[341] RA, 157/3/4. See also Butcher, 40, 46.   [342] Butcher, 46–7.

[343] Butcher, 52; RA, 172/2, 176/2.   [344] RA, 146/4, 149/1/2, 151/1.

[345] RA, 155/2/3/4, 157/2.   [346] RA, 157/1; above, 105–6. for the 'electio' system.

[347] See especially Butcher, 42–5, and his table of loans on p. 50. All unreferenced information in this paragraph derives from Butcher.

[348] For the Grevyll and the Germeyn chests, see Boase (2), xxxv. Both were founded in Stapeldon's time.

because cautions in the form of books or plate had to be deposited in return for loans; and from private individuals, often fellows or former fellows of the College. For the first forty years of the fifteenth century loans had played a very minor and infrequent part in the financing of the college, but between 1440 and 1479 they multiplied as the College's financial position deteriorated. During this period some 61 loans were taken out by the college.[349] The peak year was 1460–1, when a total of £34 12s. 8d. was raised in eight separate loans, mainly from the College's own Grevyll and Germeyn chests. This was considerably more than the year's revenues from Gwinear and Wittenham, which came to only £26 6s. 8d.[350] At other times friends, associates, and fellows were particularly generous. John Philipp, for example, Rector from 1464 to 1470, lent a total of £19 6s. 8d. during the period of his rectorship, without, of course, any expectation of profit, since loans bore no interest. The largest loan, and one of the largest in the College's history, was one of £20 made in 1444 by Walter Lyhert, fellow from c.1420 to 1425, Provost of Oriel at the time of the loan, and soon to be bishop of Norwich.[351] There is nothing in the accounts to suggest that he was repaid, and perhaps he did not expect repayment. Here and in other instances, payments from individuals recorded as loans may in fact have been gifts, put at the College's disposal out of a sense of obligation and affection. At the worst of times the College could call on fellows past and present to sustain it.

Had it not been for the availability of credit, the College would have moved into deficit long before it did. From 1456–7 until deficits began in 1463–4, and in several earlier years from 1440–1 onwards, the surplus showing on the accounts resulted from loans. Even then, surpluses were often achieved only by a narrow margin. Despite loans of £13 5s. in 1450–1, for example, the accounts showed a surplus of only 10s. 1d. at the end of the year.[352] But in any case, neither loans nor gifts could provide more than a stopgap remedy for the College's difficulties. The Rector and fellows had no means of knowing whether the good times would ever return, and there was only one way to secure the College permanently against financial distress. That was to increase its slender endowment and to acquire property which could be made to yield an income. From 1457 comes evidence that the College intended to pursue this course of action. The Rector's fund-raising visit to Devon in the summer of that year 'to solicit money from the friends of the College' was intended to produce the cash needed to acquire a royal licence to alienate land into mortmain: that is, into the hands of an undying corporation, the College, whose permanence would permanently deprive the

---

[349] To Butcher's table of loans should be added £9 5s. 4d. from William Baron, then Rector, in 1463: RA, 161/1.
[350] RA, 159.   [351] RA, 144/3; *BRUO*, ii. 1187–8; Butcher, 45, 50.
[352] Butcher, 52; RA, 150/4.

king and other intermediate lords of their rights over the alienated land. The
Rector's efforts were successful. At least £16 came in as gifts and loans at the
time of his visit, making a substantial contribution to the very large cost—just
over £23—of the licence granted by the king in the same year. John Colyford,
fellow and Rector years before in the 1420s and now prior of St John's
Hospital, Exeter, was one major donor.[353] Though the licence applied only
to the acquisition of land within Oxford, it pointed clearly in the direction
from which salvation seemed likely to come—and did come in the final
quarter of the century, as we shall see.

The College's financial history was thus one of sharp fluctuations. The
difficulties brought by mortality and dearth which characterized a large part
of the twenty-five-year period following the Black Death were followed by
some forty years of stability and relative prosperity, lasting until about 1416.
Then followed a ten-year period of deficits, caused mainly by high expenditure unmatched by any attempt to economize, which lasted until the recovery overseen by Rector Palmer between 1427 and 1432. But its effects were
short-lived, and from about 1440 a thirty-year depression set in which
reached its nadir in the 1460s. These oscillations in the College's position
were typical of all Oxford colleges, though not all followed the same pattern
as Exeter. At University College, for example, the fifteenth century was a time
of growth, when the College's income, having lagged behind that of Exeter,
moved ahead. In Exeter's case the College's ups and downs resulted from both
internal and external factors, though the latter were the more significant. The
fall in population brought by plague, and its failure to recover, brought in a
regime of low corn prices and high wages. This was inimical to the interests of a
small society such as Exeter, whose income came mainly from the sale of corn
and whose position meant that it could not avoid regular outlays on buildings
and repairs. These unfavourable circumstances were magnified during the
slump of the mid fifteenth century, when the College faced problems beyond
its control brought about by a contraction of the whole national economy.
    The College responded to these periods of difficulty in various ways: in the
1370s by seeking help from its patron, the bishop of Exeter; under Rector
Palmer, by imposing economies; and in the mid century period by raising
loans and by a wide range of minor initiatives. Expenditure was cut back,
applications for money made to friends and well-wishers, and goods sold.
Much depended on the enterprise of individual rectors. Rector Palmer
redeemed the situation which he inherited, while the long rectorship of
John Philipp from 1464 to 1470, in the trough of the depression, suggests
that he was seen by the fellows as the pilot to weather the storm. But the

---

[353] RA, 156/3; *BRUO*, i. 471; *CPR, 1452–61*, 366; Butcher, 52; above, 115.

College's primary problem, whose consequences even the most competent Rector could do little to ameliorate, lay in the nature and exiguity of its endowment, which left its income exposed to fluctuations in the price of corn and vulnerable to every turn of the economic cycle. How this problem was overcome will be described in the chapter's final section.

8. THE COLLEGE: SITE

In the beginning Exeter College occupied a very small part of its present site. But during the next 175 years, between Stapeldon's death and the start of the sixteenth century, the site's history was one of continuous expansion, so that by the end of the period its boundaries were similar to, though by no means identical with, those of the modern College. The main difference lay along its northern edge. The northern boundary of the medieval College paralleled the present Broad Street, but lay about a hundred feet to its south. From west to east, across the middle of the present Margary quad, ran the town wall, and just inside the wall was a narrow lane called Somenor's Lane in the fourteenth century, later Exeter Lane, and sometimes Cornwall Lane, perhaps in recognition of Exeter's Cornish connections. At its west end this lane joined Turl Street and continued across the Turl along the line of the present Ship Street. At its east end, behind the present Sheldonian Theatre, the lane joined Schools Street, lined on both sides with the university's schools or lecture rooms. Schools Street ran roughly north–south, through the present proscholium of the Divinity School, and then past the present front of Brasenose College towards St Mary's church. Joining Schools Street from the west was St Mildred's Lane, now Brasenose Lane, and both this thoroughfare and Turl Street followed their present courses.[354]

Somenor's Lane ran directly in front of Palmer's Tower, the College's main gate from about 1430. The College thus faced north, towards the wall, and not west, as it does now. The relationship between tower, lane, and wall can be clearly seen on Ralph Agas's view of the College from the north, drawn in 1578 (see Plate 13).[355] The three original tenements secured by Stapeldon for his College—St Stephen's Hall and La Lavandrie, comprising the two Godstow tenements—ran west–east, with the most westerly, St Stephen's Hall, probably situated a little to the west of the present Palmer's Tower. These three tenements were soon to be joined by Fragon Hall, acquired in 1323 and lying east again. All four holdings occupied an area comprising part of the present Margary quad, the Rector's lodgings, and the northern part of the

---

[354] The College site and its boundaries are shown on Map 2. They can also be reconstructed from the map in Salter, *Survey*, ii, map NE II, and from the plan in Boase (2), Plate IV. For the streets and their names, see Anthony Wood, *Survey of the Antiquities of the City of Oxford*. Vol. I: *The City and Suburbs*, ed. A. Clark, OHS, xv (1889), 111–13, and J. Cooper, 'Street Names', *VCH Oxfordshire*, iv. 475, 477.

[355] L. Durning (ed.), *Queen Elizabeth's Book of Oxford* (Oxford, 2006), 27, 124.

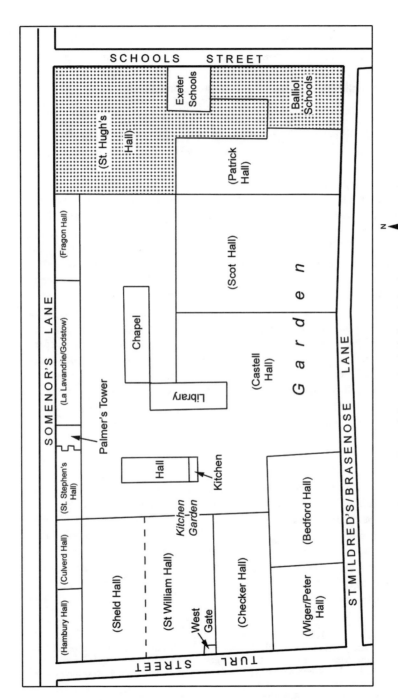

SCHOOLS STREET

(St. Hugh's Hall)

Exeter Schools

Balliol Schools

(Patrick Hall)

SOMENOR'S LANE

(Fragon Hall)

(La Lavandrie/Godstow)

(St. Stephen's Hall)

(Culverd Hall)

(Hambury Hall)

Palmer's Tower

Chapel

Library

Hall

Kitchen

(Scot Hall)

(Castell Hall)

G a r d e n

Kitchen Garden

(Sheld Hall)

(St William Hall)

West Gate

(Checker Hall)

(Bedford Hall)

(Wiger/Peter Hall)

TURL STREET

ST MILDRED'S/BRASENOSE LANE

N

Former Halls, now absorbed, shown in brackets
Non-Exeter properties stippled

MAP 2. The Exeter College site, c.1450

Rector's garden. They covered perhaps a quarter of the area of the present College.

This small site, little more than a short row of houses along Somenor's Lane, was tightly constricted by adjacent properties. To the east of Fragon Hall, on the corner of the lane and Schools Street, was St Hugh's Hall, belonging to Balliol. Probably another hall extinguished by the Black Death, it was a garden by 1370 and was later taken over for the building of the Divinity School.[356] To the south of the Stapeldon block were two large halls, Castell Hall and Scot Hall, both opening onto St Mildred's Lane. To the west, along Somenor's Lane and then turning south into Turl Street, were six other halls, mainly private houses. The lack of room for expansion on the south side of Stapeldon's original properties, blocked in as they were by the halls along St Mildred's Lane and their long back extensions, explains the peculiar siting of the first College chapel, which ran parallel to the two tenements of La Lavandrie and probably no more than about twenty-five feet from their rear quarters—roughly along the middle of the present rectorial garden (see Plate 7). It is likely that the chapel was constructed across the back yards of these tenements and that its two-storey height deprived them of a good deal of southerly light, as was noted in the eighteenth century.[357] This situation would surely not have been tolerated had there been space to site the chapel further to the south, on the land occupied mainly by Castell Hall at the time of the chapel's building in the 1320s.[358]

Much was to change over the next 175 years. By 1500 all the properties bounding or near to the original site, and initially restricting its expansion, had been incorporated into the College. The only exceptions were the properties along Schools Street, mainly lecture rooms, which remained in various hands and gave the College an irregular eastern boundary. There was clearly a policy, pursued over the years, of extending the site towards its natural boundaries: westwards along Somenor's Lane, southwards along Turl Street, and eastwards along St Mildred's Lane. We have already seen how most of the halls along St Mildred's Lane, notably Scot Hall, Castell Hall, and Bedford Hall, were acquired between 1325 and 1358, disappearing as halls and re-emerging to provide open land for the College garden as demand for urban property fell after the Black Death.[359] Expansion in other directions took place over a more extended period. Culverd Hall, to the west of the original Stapeldon block, together with its neighbour to the west, Hambury Hall, standing on the corner of Somenor's Lane and Turl Street, came to the

---

[356] Salter, *Survey*, i. 56.

[357] Rector Stinton's addition to Prideaux's survey of the College *c*. 1790: Boase (2), 316–17.

[358] In 1358 Castell Hall was described as being opposite to the chapel on the south side: Boase (2), xx.

[359] Above, 70–2. For what follows, see Salter, *Survey*, i. 54–5; RA, 40.

College in 1366, though they were not legally made over until 1380. Sheld Hall, adjacent to Hambury Hall in Turl Street, had been in College hands since 1325. St William Hall, south of Sheld Hall, had been acquired on lease from the Hospital of St John the Baptist (on the site of the present Magdalen College) by 1393 and probably much earlier. Checker Hall, south again, was incorporated into the college in 1405. Finally, Wiger Hall, known from c. 1400 as Peter Hall, which lay south again, on the corner of Turl Street and St Mildred's Lane, where the College kitchen has been since the seventeenth century, was rented by the College from Osney abbey in the early fifteenth century and purchased in 1470. Its takeover completed the medieval phase of the College's expansion. These five, from Hambury Hall to Peter Hall, have to be fitted into the 190 feet or so of Turl Street frontage between Somenor's Lane and St Mildred's Lane; so we should imagine each of them as having a narrow front to the street and a long back section. Only two areas remained to be brought into the College to take it to its present boundaries: the south-east corner of the present garden, under the mound, acquired from Balliol in 1572; and Somenor's Lane and the area lying to its north, towards Broad Street, acquired mainly from the seventeenth century onwards.[360]

These halls all came to the College by grant or purchase. Occasionally what appears to be a grant may in fact be a purchase. This was the case with Culverd Hall and Hambury Hall, granted to a group of four men, including three fellows of the College, in 1366, and later given by them to the College. The accounts, however, show that the College paid £8 in 1366 for 'a *placea* [an empty piece of land] annexed to our hall on its western side', which must indicate the double purchase.[361] The halls were put to a variety of uses. Most appear to have been absorbed by the College, vanishing as separate entities and leaving no trace on the records after their initial acquisition. This was the fate of the halls along St Mildred's Lane, whose sites largely became the College garden, and also of Culverd, Hambury, St William, and Sheld Hall. Culverd and Hambury, situated somewhere near the west end of the present chapel, had probably fallen into ruin after the Black Death and were open land at the time of their acquisition. Agas's view, which shows no building at the College's north-western corner, suggests that their former sites remained in this state in the late sixteenth century. The site of St William Hall formed part of the College's kitchen garden by the late fourteenth century.[362] Sheld Hall, an early acquisition, was yielding rent in 1330.[363] After the Black Death it may have remained standing, to provide the College with additional rooms, or more probably it too vanished. Certainly it yielded no rent.

---

[360] Salter, *Survey*, i. 69; Wood, *City of Oxford*, i. 113.
[361] Boase (2), xvii–xix; Salter, *Survey*, i. 52–5.   [362] Salter, *Survey*, i. 53; below, 145.
[363] Boase (1), 174.

As far as we can tell, all these halls had been private houses prior to the acquisition by the College. But Peter Hall and Checker Hall had always been academic halls (Stapeldon's brother Robert had been principal of Checker Hall in 1305) and they were maintained as such after their acquisition.[364] Each had a principal who was usually a fellow of the College and who normally rented the hall from the College. Checker Hall in particular provided a home for the College's senior boarders, ex-fellows and others, and possibly for undergraduates: two groups whose members became prominent in the fifteenth-century College.[365] It seems fairly clear from the general pattern of these acquisitions that they served a number of purposes: to carry the College towards the edges of its street-bound site, to enhance its standing, to provide money and accommodation, and—an easily overlooked purpose—to make available space for future building. The new library of 1383, for example, projecting well to the south of the College's original site, appears to have been built on land vacated by the College's appropriation of Castell Hall.

The disposition of buildings on the College site is not always easy to plot. Loggan's view of 1675, shown in Plate 14, allows us to place the new library (occupying a site along the north side of the present main quadrangle) and the original chapel (lying at right angles to the library, with its west end roughly opposite the inner face of Palmer's Tower). More difficult to situate is the hall. It seems to have been aligned north–south, partly parallel to but also slightly north and west of the library, on ground now occupied by part of the main quadrangle. The survey of the College made by Rector Prideaux in 1631 states that it 'stood in the midst of the quadrangle',[366] perhaps on land once belonging to Sheld Hall and St William Hall. There is no reference in the accounts to enable us to date its building, but this may well have fallen in the period between 1337 and 1354, for which no accounts survive. In the College's earliest days the fellows presumably made use of the hall in St Stephen's Hall, a former academic hall and Stapeldon's earliest acquisition, for their meals. Adjacent to the purpose-built hall, and almost certainly immediately to its south, stood the kitchen, which, like the remains of the hall itself, survived until Prideaux's rectorship. It was linked to the hall by a pentice, probably a covered way which may have served as a screens passage.[367] And adjacent too was the buttery (*promptuarium*), used for the storage of supplies, including table linen.[368]

---

[364] Salter, *Survey*, i. 52–3; Wood, *City of Oxford*, i. 598–9; Catto, 'The Triumph of the Hall', 214 n. 16.

[365] Below, 157–61. Note e.g. the payment of 9s. in 1454 by Richard Bokeler, fellow, 1440–8, for his 'great room' in Checker Hall: Boase (2), 38.

[366] Boase (2), 318 and Plate IV; Wood, *Colleges*, 112.   [367] Boase (2), 319; RA, 152/1.

[368] RA, 118/4.

Various other buildings were accommodated on the medieval site. By 1361 there was a 'great gate', with a room or rooms to its west.[369] This was the main entrance to the College from Somenor's Lane, and it probably stood somewhere near, if not actually on, the site of Palmer's Tower, which replaced it. In the early fifteenth century Bishop Stafford paid for a new west gate opening onto Turl Street.[370] It stood roughly on the site of the present main gate, and the palisaded entrance to the College which it provided can be seen on Agas's view (see Plate 13). Useful though this no doubt was to a College which had now acquired most of its modern Turl Street frontage, the north gate—first the 'great gate', then Palmer's Tower—continued to provide the main, and more imposing, entry to the College until the early seventeenth century.[371] Somewhere on the site there was also a thatched stable for the College horse,[372] a latrine or latrines, expensively rebuilt in 1393,[373] and several wells, whose ropes, buckets, and winding gear needed constant attention.[374]

Changes to the stock of College buildings came mainly by way of piece-meal additions and extensions. We have already noted the main changes in the fifteenth century: Bishop Stafford's payment for the enlargement of the library, a room beneath the library, and a portico for the chapel, besides the building of the west gate; and Rector Palmer's construction of the gateway tower and four chambers to its west, and his extension to the east end of the chapel.[375] After the completion of all this work in the early fifteenth century, the number and disposition of the buildings was to remain much the same until Prideaux rebuilt a large part of the College in the early seventeenth century. After his time there was left of the medieval college only Palmer's Tower and some adjacent rooms, the old chapel, which had become the library, and the old library, now turned into rooms. To the eye of an observer before Prideaux's time the most striking feature of the College would have been its lack of an orderly plan. In particular, Exeter lacked the quadrangle which by 1500 almost every Oxford college possessed: Balliol, University College, Merton, New College, All Souls, and Magdalen all had their quadrangles.[376] What came, by the sixteenth century, to be called the quadrangle seems to have been merely the narrow oblong of land lying between the chapel and the backs of the properties along Somenor's Lane or, perhaps more probably, the similar oblong lying between the chapel and the hall.[377] But Exeter was characterized, not by quadrangles in our sense, but by right

---

[369] RA, 19.   [370] Reg. Lacy, iv. 299–300; above, 121.
[371] The west tower gateway was first built in 1605: Boase (2), 358.
[372] RA, 28, 39, 68.   [373] RA, 91/2.   [374] RA, 12, 42, 44, etc.
[375] Above, 117–21. For building in the late fifteenth century, see below, 168–9.
[376] Darwall-Smith, 56–9; J. H. Harvey, 'Architecture in Oxford, 1350–1500', HUO, ii. 754, 766.
[377] Boase (2), 316–17; below, 222.

angles and parallel lines: hall parallel to the library, chapel parallel to the original line of tenements along the lane, library and chapel meeting at a right angle. 'The whole College was but a confused number of blind streets', wrote Prideaux, the energetic wielder of the new broom.[378] If the material shape of the College thus lacked any overall coherence, it was because the site had grown by sporadic accretion, and buildings had been constructed and extended over a long period, as space and funds permitted. Only under Prideaux did money and rectorial enterprise come together to create a new Exeter.

A large part of the site was given over, not to buildings, but to gardens. The accounts speak of at least two gardens. The *disportum*, the garden for recreation created in the years after the Black Death and occupying much of the site of the present garden, has already been mentioned several times. In addition, however, there was a kitchen garden, *ortum coci*, variously referred to as 'the little garden next to the kitchen', 'our little garden', and 'the little garden at the end of our kitchen'. It filled a large part of the area once occupied by St William Hall, off Turl Street, and may have extended towards the north-west corner of the College, where Hambury Hall and Culverd Hall had once stood.[379] It was provided with its own well.[380] Money was regularly spent on both gardens: on labourers, often women, sowing, planting, and weeding, on the destruction of moles, the lopping of trees, and the repair of walls. Labour costs were considerable. Occasionally we can see signs of the replanning and change which must have taken place more than once over the years: in 1402, for example, when payments for cutting down trees, receipts from the sale of an ash tree, and the subsequent purchase of grass seed all suggest that a grove was being replaced by a lawn.[381]

Naturally the more productive of the two gardens was the kitchen garden. An asset possessed by most colleges,[382] at Exeter as elsewhere the kitchen garden was primarily intended to provide for the culinary needs of the fellows. Exeter's produced leeks, onions, apples, nuts, and probably much else.[383] Hazel trees were planted in 1375 (for their nuts?), and saffron, a more unusual and valuable plant, was grown, harvested, and sold in 1477, probably

[378] Boase (2), 319.

[379] RA, 80, 104, 116. The payment of a ground rent for the kitchen garden to the Hospital of St John the Baptist, the corporate landlord of the former St William Hall, proves the identity of the garden with the site of the former hall.

[380] RA, 154/4.   [381] RA, 99/2/3.

[382] For college kitchen gardens, see J. M. Fletcher, 'The Organisation of the Supply of Food and Drink to the Medieval Oxford Colleges', in A. Romano (ed.), *Università in Europa: Le istitutioni universitarie dal Medio Evo ai nostri giorni: strutture, organizzazione, funzionamento* (Rubbettino, 1995), 209–10.

[383] RA, 46, 49, 52, etc. (leeks); RA, 55, 156/4 (onions); RA, 95/4 (apples); RA, 142/4 (nuts). Boase (2), xxix n. 2, prints many extracts from the accounts relating to garden produce.

for medicinal purposes.[384] Most of these relatively few commodities appear in the accounts only because the surplus was marketed. Vegetables and fruit grown exclusively for home consumption, probably in more variety, do not usually feature; but the strawberries seemingly given to the visiting Dr Edgcombe in the summer of 1484 may well have been home grown.[385] Within the garden there must also have been room for pigs, sold on several occasions in the financially difficult years of the 1450s,[386] and for hens: a hen house was bought in 1403 and another repaired in 1430.[387] The College had many facets, but it was among other things a miniature horticultural enterprise, a rural smallholding in the middle of a large town. The sight of labourers planting leeks, of pigs and hens turning over the ground, and of water being drawn from the well for the garden must all have been part of the familiar backdrop to the fellows' lives.

If an aerial observer had been able to compare the College block, bounded by Somenor's Lane, Turl Street, St Mildred's Lane, and, on the east, by Schools Street, with the same block in 1500, he would have been struck by the change from a site crowded with buildings to one where open space was much more prominent. In 1320 the perimeters of the site were lined on both sides with halls, most of them private houses but some academic halls, and on the eastern side with lecture rooms. In 1500 the lecture rooms largely remained, now grandly augmented by the new Divinity School. But most of the halls had gone, their sites now gardens or open land, while those that remained had been incorporated into the College. Agas's view shows a College where vacant land seems to predominate over buildings and where street frontages are bounded by bare walls as much as by houses and halls. The primary cause of these changes was the decline in the demand for property and in the size of the university resulting from a catastrophic fall in population in 1348–9 and its failure to recover thereafter. Yet they also represented, not only the opportunities now available for an acquisitive drive by the College to take its site to its natural boundaries, but also an aesthetic outlook which valued gardens for the pleasure and recreation that they could provide and an economic sensibility which looked to a degree of self-sufficiency in food supplies. The Rector and fellows may seem to have been preoccupied with their academic affairs and with getting and spending on their institution's behalf. But the evidence of the site provides a different view of their common mentality.

---

[384] RA, 56, 173/3. Compare Fletcher, 'The Organisation of the Supply of Food and Drink', 209–10, for saffron at Queen's.
[385] RA, 179/3; Boase (2), xxxix n. 2.   [386] RA, 155/2/3/4; above, 136.
[387] RA, 101/1, 131/3.

9. THE COMMUNITY OF EXETER COLLEGE
AND ITS WAY OF LIFE

Exeter College in the later middle ages comprised a body of men living together in a particular place and united by common purposes: the pursuit of learning, the practice of teaching, the acquisition of qualifications, and the promotion of the general welfare of the house. A community in the true sense of that overused word, it was sometimes referred to as such. In 1440 money was taken from the common chest 'for the benefit of the *communitas*', and in 1489 a gift was noted as given 'to the *communitas* of the College'.[388] The most powerful reinforcement of the College's basic credentials here came from its regional affiliations. The Devon origins of most of Exeter's fellows, with a strong minority from Cornwall and a much smaller minority from the diocese of Salisbury, is likely to have made for an unselfconscious cohesion and a shared sense of belonging which are hardly susceptible to historical analysis. At all times the great majority of the fellows will have been familiar with some of the same people, places, and ecclesiastical institutions—the cathedral, the bishop, parish churches, and local families. There was an abundance of common topics here for conversation and reminiscence; while the frequent visits of the Rector and fellows to the west country, and the frequent return of former fellows to the College from their west country livings, perpetuated the material links between the College and its region. This was a community nourished by its roots.

Such a body might be expected to have had a single recognized name as a mark of its identity, but this for a long time the College lacked. Its official designation, insofar as it had one, can be traced through the Rector's headings to his accounts. In the earliest days he described himself as Rector 'of the scholars of Stapeldon Hall'; in 1356, 'of the house of Stapeldon Hall'; in 1365, 'of the hall of Stapeldon Hall'; in 1375, 'of the house of scholars or college of Stapeldon Hall'; and in 1391, 'of the college of Stapeldon'.[389] But there was already a parallel though weaker tradition associating the college with Exeter. As early as 1332 a deed granting St Hugh's Hall to Balliol could refer to the neighbouring property as being held by 'the Rector of the house of scholars of Exeter Hall'.[390] The College is styled in the same way in the will of Simon de Bredon, former fellow of Merton, made in 1368.[391] In the 1370s Bishop Brantingham used the titles 'Stapeldon Hall' and 'Exeter Hall' apparently interchangeably, and so too at the same time did Bishop Rede of Chichester, whose indenture recording his gift of books to the College speaks of 'the hall

---

[388] RA, 139/3, 183/2.   [389] Boase (1), 171–7; RA, 10, 36, 59, 86/2.
[390] *The Oxford Deeds of Balliol College*, ed. H. E. Salter (Oxford, 1913), 148.
[391] Powicke, *Medieval Books of Merton College*, 84. Bredon's will is the unnamed source referred to as 'Lyte' in Boase (2), iii n. 1.

of Stapeldon or Exeter'.[392] That there was a growing reluctance to continue with the old name of Stapeldon Hall, despite Stapeldon's injunction in the statutes that the name should endure as long as his foundation lasted, is suggested by the request of the Rector and fellows to Pope Innocent VII in 1405 that the College should in future be known as 'the college of Exeter'.[393] The early Oxford colleges had often been known indifferently as colleges or halls—'Balliol Hall' and 'Merton Hall' were common usages—so eliding the distinction, at least in terms of title, between the endowed college, governed by its statutes, and the unendowed hall, governed by its principal. The general change in nomenclature, from hall to college, seems to have followed from William of Wykeham's foundation of 'St Mary's college of Winchester in Oxford', or New College, in 1379.[394] The fellows of Stapeldon Hall may have felt that they were behind the times in continuing to call their College a 'hall'. As for the proposal to drop Stapeldon's name, they perhaps judged that few besides themselves now kept Stapeldon in mind and that 'Exeter College' gave a clearer indication of their institution's origins and identity.

But the pope's agreement to the requested change of name made no immediate difference, and the confusion of titles continued for some time. Bishop Lacy in 1420 (and in most of his subsequent dealings with the College) wrote of 'Stapeldon Hall', but Edmund Fitchet, former fellow, making his will in 1427, left a book to 'Exeter College'.[395] It was only in 1430 that the College itself began to take a firm line on its proper designation. In that year William Palmer, until then 'Rector of the hall or college of Stapeldon Hall', like all his immediate predecessors, began to head his accounts as 'Rector of Exeter College',[396] and the accounts always followed this usage thereafter. By the 1450s other sources were referring to 'Stapeldon Hall' only rarely. In 1462 Roger Keys, handing over to the College another volume in his splendid set of the works of Hugh of St Cher, could refer to 'the Rector and fellows of Exeter College in Oxford called Stapeldon Hall'; while the deed granting Menheniot to the College in 1478 showed the process of transition particularly well by speaking of 'Stapeldon Hall, now commonly called Exeter College'. True, as late as 1488 the writer of a deed could speak of 'Stapeldon Hall elsewhere called Exeter College'.[397] This was, however, the last gasp of a dying tradition. The emergence of Exeter College, at least in a literal and official sense, was one more aspect of the many-sided work of Rector Palmer, but it was another fifty years or so before the name became fully established.

[392] *Reg. Brantingham*, i. 223, 234, 284; Watson, 138.
[393] *Cal. Papal Registers*, vi. 48; above, 96.
[394] Emden, *An Oxford Hall*, 45; Highfield, 'Early Colleges', *HUO*, i. 228.
[395] *Reg. Lacy*, i. 60, iv. 9.   [396] RA, 132; above, 118.
[397] Watson, 92; ECA, M. IV. 5; L. V. 4.

The lack of any fixed name for the College before 1430 can have done little more than mildly impair (if that) the fellows' sense of their own standing as a community. Any detraction from that sense was more than counterbalanced by a number of powerful factors. Foremost among these was residence. Broadly speaking, most fellows resided within the College, and so kept company with each other, for most of the time, but all were absent for some of the time. Throughout the period the pattern of residence during the year was consistent and predictable. Stapeldon had laid down that every fellow should be present at the start of the year for the election of the new Rector, which took place eight days after Michaelmas on 6 October, immediately before the opening of the university term on 10 October. Those absent from the election were to lose two weeks' commons: a rule whose occasional enforcement suggests that it was generally observed.[398] The accounts of the outgoing Rector would have been presented to the fellows a few days before the election. For most of the College's winter term—the university's Michaelmas term—the great majority of the fellows were present, though in any week one or two might be absent. During Christmas week and the week after numbers fell off somewhat: a drop from eleven or twelve at the end of the winter term to eight or nine over Christmas would have been typical. By the start of the university's Hilary term on 14 January, or shortly afterwards, most fellows had returned into residence. At Easter some left Oxford for a short while, returning for the start of the Easter term about ten days after the feast. Numbers usually remained high through May and June, but began to drop again towards the end of the university term and the approach of the long vacation in early July. They were at their lowest in August and September, when numbers fell to two or three, and very occasionally to one, before rising again in the weeks around Michaelmas as the new year loomed.

1409–10 was as typical a year as any. Fourteen fellows were in residence at the start of the year in October, and the full complement of fifteen for most of the following term. For Christmas week numbers dropped to nine and then to six in the week following, before building up again to thirteen by mid January and to fourteen for most of the term. In Holy Week, after the end of term, they dropped to seven and then to four for Easter week: an unusually large fall-off. They held steady at thirteen or fourteen for most of the midsummer period, but declined to nine at the start of July. By mid August only two fellows were in residence, and numbers never rose above five until the end of September.[399] Occasional crises might disturb this pattern. In 1407, when plague struck Oxford during the summer, there was a precipitate exodus from

---

[398] Boase (1), xlii; *Reg. Stapeldon*, 309. For the dates of university terms, see *SA*, lxxx–lxxxi. For the enforcement of the election rule, see e.g. RA, 144/2 (1443): Mr Baleham 'lost 2s. because he was not present at the election of the Rector'.

[399] RA, 110, 111, 112, 113.

the College which brought numbers down to six by mid June and to three by early July.[400] Again, during the financially desperate years of the 1460s fellows tended to stay away from the College, and the numbers in residence were often well below the norm. But for the most part the College's residential year followed the same course in 1500 as it had done nearly 150 years earlier.

The accounts also enable us to see what this general pattern meant for individual fellows. Stapeldon's statutes allowed each fellow four weeks' absence during the year, taken either continuously or piecemeal, so that he could visit relatives and friends. He could take this vacation without any deduction from his annual allowance of 10s., payable at the year's end, but longer absences, except for reasons of illness or College business, were to be penalized by a pro rata deduction from the allowance.[401] The account for the year's fourth and final term lists the names of all fellows receiving allowances and the amount received by each, thus permitting the calculation of the number of days absent. Most fellows in most years appear to have taken rather more vacation than the basic four weeks. In 1429–30, for example, thirteen fellows, including the Rector, received allowances. The recently elected (and later to be famous) William Wey received money only for the portion of the year between his election and the year's end. Of the eleven others (excluding the chaplain), only two received the full 10s. allowance, indicating that they had been away for no more than the statutory four weeks. Three received allowances suggesting that they had been absent for approximately six extra days; one for nine days; one for twenty-seven days; two for forty-eight days; and one, John Hancock, for fifty-four days.[402]

We should thus envisage a College where there was a good deal of coming and going, where fellows might take a few days off at Christmas and Easter and a longer break in the summer, and where a very few might be absent for two to three months (but none for as long as the five months beyond the statutory month which Stapeldon had deemed to warrant expulsion from the house[403]). For most fellows, therefore, and for much the greater part of the year, the College was home.

Within it, potentially the strongest communal bond was that forged by eating and drinking at the common table. As in most comparable societies, commensality is likely to have strengthened sociability and to have deepened the esprit de corps of this compact little body of men: fellowship bred fellowship. In this connection, one high point in the College year was the feast of St Thomas the Martyr (Thomas Becket), to whom, together with the Virgin Mary and St Peter, the College chapel had been dedicated in 1326.[404] The feast was held annually on St Thomas's day, 29 December. Our first

[400] RA, 106/3/4.   [401] Reg. Stapeldon, 306.   [402] RA, 131/4.
[403] Reg. Stapeldon, 306.   [404] Boase (2), xxvii–xxviii.

record of it comes from 1333, when it seems to have been celebrated only by wine-drinking.[405] It remained a drinks-only occasion in the mid 1350s—wine in 1354, spiced beer in 1356—before emerging as a full-blown feast in 1357, when wine, fruits, figs, almonds, and 'tartes' were all served.[406] The menu in 1360 was still more lavish and included spiced beer, three gallons of wine, ducks, capons, rabbits, piglets, venison, eggs, cheese, honey, and ginger.[407] Soon afterwards the accounts cease to provide an itemized menu, recording only the total spent, but showing that it was a rare year indeed when there was no feast. Rather surprisingly, the feast did not swell the numbers of those present in College during the Christmas vacation when the feast was held. There were only five fellows to enjoy the gourmet junketings of 1357; the rest may have preferred home comforts in Devon or Cornwall to the midwinter company of their festive colleagues. Numbers were made up, however, by invitations extended to outsiders. Four guests were entertained at the College's expense in 1354, and the accounts note the festal expenses of the fellows 'and other friends' in 1400.[408] In return, the fellows visited other colleges on their patronal feast days, going to Balliol on St Katherine's day, to Merton on the feast of St John the Baptist, to New College on the Annunciation, and, very occasionally in the fifteenth century, to Lincoln on St Mildred's day (but never apparently to Queen's, Oriel, or University College).[409] Convivial dining already extended beyond the walls of any single college.

But the festivities on 'the gaudy of St Thomas', as it was sometimes called, were only the most splendid of many more routine occasions for eating, drinking, and entertaining. Exeter's hospitality was generous in its frequency and extensive in its social breadth. We have already noticed the food and drink given to the parishioners of Gwinear and, more often in the late fourteenth century, to those of Wittenham. Visiting members of the Devon aristocracy and gentry called by from time to time and were predictably well received. The son of Hugh Courtenay, earl of Devon, coming to hear mass on the feast of St Laurence in 1355, was entertained to breakfast; Sir Peter Courtenay and his brother, sons of a later earl, were given wine in 1392; and Sir Richard Courtenay and Sir Edward Courtenay, the latter then heir to the earldom of Devon, were entertained in 1401.[410] Some might have a particular reason to visit the College. When Sir John Halse, justice of king's bench and another Devonian, called in 1424, it was perhaps to see his second son, another John, the future bishop of Coventry and Lichfield, who had been elected to a fellowship in the previous year. Since he gave the College 6s. 8d. during his

[405] Boase (1), 175.   [406] RA, 3/1, 6, 9.   [407] RA, 19; Butcher, 47 n. 44.
[408] RA, 3, 97/2.
[409] e.g. RA, 90 (Balliol, 1392), 91/3 (Merton, 1393), 97/2 (New College, 1400), 145/4 (Lincoln, 1445).
[410] RA, 2, 88/3, 98/3.

stay, but cost only 1s. 9½d. to entertain, the College came off well from his visit.[411] Former fellows were particularly frequent visitors, coming back to their old College to keep in touch, to enjoy the company of their friends and successors, and to be wined and dined. In 1391, for example, Reginald Povy, who had vacated his fellowship as long ago as 1376 and was now rector of Colerne in Wiltshire, was entertained to drink. Canons of Exeter, sometimes themselves old members, were also regular guests, occasionally bringing with them the money due for the Gwinear tithes.[412]

We might be more surprised to find two other categories of guest: women and townspeople. It was not uncommon for women to be communally entertained in College by the fellows (who proved here to be more enlightened than their successors for most of the twentieth century). Lady Eleanor Hill (or Hull), probably a member of one of the several Devon and Somerset gentry families of that name, was entertained to wine and spices in 1420, when she gave the College 20s. She came again in 1431, this time with her son (prospecting for a place perhaps?).[413] Sometimes wives accompanied their burgess husbands to a dinner held to conclude some piece of business. So, for example, Thomas Pedyngton and Alice his wife, important people in the town, were dined in 1388, when they made over to the College the rent from Karol Hall.[414] Another transaction in 1396 saw wine and beer given to John Salven and other burgesses 'on divers occasions when there was discussion about our tenement in the parish of St Peter le bailey'.[415] Finally, a generous contribution of 6s. 8d. to the College building fund for a new room, given by Agnes, wife of Roger Chiddesley, one of the university bedels, may explain why both Agnes and Roger were invited to dinner in the summer term of 1401.[416]

Windows open here on a busy social world. Those whom the College treated were almost as diverse as Chaucer's pilgrims: a royal justice and a university official, sons of the nobility, country parishioners, a well-born lady, cathedral canons, former fellows, Oxford burgesses and their wives. The material gains that might accrue, like the gifts of money from Sir John Halse and Lady Eleanor Hill, were only the smallest and most visible part of the benefits which the entertainment of guests must often have brought in less tangible ways. Food and drink for visitors maintained links with potential patrons and protectors such as the Courtenays, harmonized relationships with the parishes from which the College drew its wealth, kept the College in touch with its old members, on whose goodwill and generosity as donors

[411] RA, 126/4; BRUO, ii. 856.
[412] RA, 87/2; Boase (2), 17; BRUO, iii. 1509–10; above, 129.
[413] RA, 124/1, 132/3.   [414] RA, 81; Salter, Survey, ii. 130.   [415] RA, 93.
[416] RA, 98/2; Salter, Survey, i. 194; BRUO, i. 414. For the role of the bedels, see esp. M. B. Hackett, 'The University as a Corporate Body', HUO, i. 85–7.

and testators it was greatly dependent, and oiled the wheels of friendship with the town and townspeople, whose cooperation the College needed in its property transactions (and there is no sign in the records of town-and-gown hostility—rather the reverse). The nexus of relationships with west country families was strengthened, and the College's regional links reasserted. The shillings and pennies scattered liberally through the accounts for spending on entertainment were bread on the waters, to be found again after not so many days.

College entertainment centred on the hall. Like other colleges, Exeter had no common room before the late seventeenth century. Though the fellows no doubt gathered from time to time in each other's rooms—on the day after the St Thomas's feast in 1406 they met to drink beer in the Rector's room[417]—the hall remained the focus of the College's social life, to a greater degree than in more modern times. We know a good deal about its internal appearance and furnishing. It was strewn with rushes or rush matting, frequently renewed, provided with a sideboard and a washbasin, and its whitewashed walls were hung with draperies or possibly tapestries.[418] John Colyford, former fellow, gave the College a 'pictured cloth (*pannus depictus*)' for the hall in 1460.[419] By 1405, and probably much earlier, there was a high table, approached by steps, and provided in 1418 with its own towels and table cloth.[420] We do not know the identity of the privileged who sat there, but it may well have been reserved for the *magistri* and their guests, with the bachelors and sophists sitting below them in the body of the hall. Stapeldon had recommended that the fellows should speak only French or Latin at table, to gain practice in those languages.[421] But the life of the hall need not always have been quite so austere as his recommendation might suggest. It was perhaps there that the fellows played on the *citola*, a zither-like instrument for whose repair the College paid in 1372.[422] And was it in the hall that they also hung the bird cage given to them by Roger Chiddesley in 1414?[423] Their mental world cannot have been entirely dominated by the round of academic and business concerns—Aristotle, determination and inception, Gwinear and Wittenham. They had their recreations too.

Still more central than the hall to the communal life of the College was the chapel (see Plate 7). Like the hall, the first-floor building, with rooms beneath, which served as the chapel from the 1320s to the 1620s, can be imaginatively visualized from the accounts. It had a paved floor which, like the floor of the hall, was covered with rush matting.[424] Its interior was adorned with images,

---

[417] RA, 106/2.   [418] RA, 6, 37, 54, 94/2/4. Boase (2), xli–xlii, supplies further details.
[419] Boase (1), xiii; RA, 158/4.   [420] RA, 105, 122/1, 125/3, 144/1.
[421] *Reg. Stapeldon*, 309–10.   [422] RA, 52, 53.   [423] RA, 118/4.
[424] RA, 29, 110, 132/1. Boase (2), xlv–xlvii, supplies further details.

and by 1424 it had an organ.[425] In earlier times music may also have been made on a *fiola*, a viola-type instrument bought for the chapel in 1377.[426] The chapel had its own set of liturgical books, some of them chained and laid out on desks, as in the library.[427] These were often augmented by gifts from fellows and former fellows. When the fellows were present in chapel they sat next to the door, at the west end, where hooks were placed by their seats in 1372, perhaps for their gowns and cloaks.[428]

More significant than these small material details was the liturgical life of the chapel. Chapel services would have filled a large part of the day, though it was very probably the chaplain alone who was present at most of them. Stapeldon had been very precise in the regime which he set out for the chapel, stipulating that the chaplain should each day observe the canonical hours and say the seven penitential psalms, the litany for the living, and the office for the dead.[429] The chaplain charged with these duties may have been a rather isolated figure in College, since he was not elected by the fellows, but chosen by the dean and chapter of Exeter, and was the only fellow allowed by the statutes to read for a degree in theology or canon law.[430] During the quite frequent periods when there was no chaplain it was usual for any fellow in priest's orders to take the services. How many services the fellows normally attended is impossible to say. In 1396 the accounts record wine drunk 'in the presence of the kinsmen of the lord bishop of Exeter after vespers', and daily attendance at matins and vespers, with further services on Sundays and feast days, may have been the norm. The fellows of University College had to attend five services on feast days, and those of Exeter may have followed a similar programme.[431]

The chapel served not only as a sanctum for daily prayers, but as a site of memory: a place where the dead were remembered, commemorated, and prayed for. To some extent this function was maintained by material means. In the winter term of 1374 the College paid for the making of a *tabula*, a board, for the chapel 'on which are inscribed the names of the benefactors of the house, living and dead'. The stimulus here was almost certainly Bishop Rede's munificent gift of books, made in the same term.[432] In 1448 8*d*. was paid for the making of three similar boards 'of the names of benefactors' (who must have been numerous), perhaps in response this time to the handsome legacy of 50 marks handed over by Cardinal Beaufort's executors in the same year, soon to be established as a separate loan chest. The model may have been the *tabulae* which sometimes hung from the pillars of parish and monastic

---

[425] RA, 42, 126/2, 167/1.   [426] RA, 63.   [427] RA, 55.   [428] RA, 51.
[429] *Reg. Stapeldon*, 305.
[430] For the presentation of Robert Stonard as chaplain by the dean and chapter in 1419, see D. and C., 3625, fo. 177.
[431] RA, 93; Darwall-Smith, 80.
[432] RA, 55. For similar displays in Merton chapel, see Highfield and Martin, 150.

churches to record and preserve the names of local families.[433] In a College context they may have resembled the honours boards which hang in many school halls or the war memorials in many of today's college chapels.

But more permanent (at least as it seemed then) and more prominent, increasingly so as time went on, were the obits or anniversary masses, 'annual commemorations for the souls of the deceased',[434] celebrated in the College chapel. In all churches, from parish church to cathedral and college chapel, the corporate commemoration of the dead grew in significance in the later middle ages, becoming a characteristic feature of religious life. Stapeldon had initiated the practice in his College by requiring the regular celebration of masses, in the presence of the fellows, for his own salvation, for that of his predecessors and successors, his relatives and benefactors, and certain other named men.[435] One of those successors, Bishop Edmund Stafford, among the most generous of the College's benefactors, was prayed for in the fellows' daily masses and commemorated in an annual obit from 1430 onwards.[436] But it was only in the half century after 1450 that obits and other forms of commemorative service proliferated in the College chapel, often as the result of an endowment made by a former fellow for his own benefit and for that of his friends and benefactors. The current fellows would normally receive a small payment for attendance at these services. One of the earliest of such arrangements was made in 1450, when former fellow John Colyford, then a brother at the hospital of St John in Exeter, had given the College 20s. to pay for prayers for two otherwise unknown ladies, Elizabeth Cheseldon and Margaret Hedon, following this up in 1451 with a further gift of £5 for prayers for the souls of a Devon knight, Sir Thomas Carew, and Elizabeth his wife.[437] In 1460 William Palmer, the former Rector, made a similar arrangement with the College, securing agreement to the annual celebration of his obit, at which each fellow present was to receive 2d.[438] By the 1490s there were weekly masses 'for benefactors' throughout the term, which those fellows in orders took in rotation for a fee of a shilling.[439] In addition there were annual obits for some eight or nine named benefactors,[440] including Edmund Stafford, Fulk Bourgchier, Lord Fitzwarin (a Devon magnate whom we shall meet again as a benefactor instrumental in obtaining the living of Menheniot for the College),[441] William Palmer, Robert Lydford (fellow from 1365 to 1375 and

---

[433] RA, 148/3; Boase (2), lxx and n. 1; N. Saul, *English Church Monuments in the Middle Ages* (Oxford, 2009), 340–1.

[434] D. Lepine, 'Cathedrals and Charity: Almsgiving at English Secular Cathedrals in the Later Middle Ages', *EHR*, 126 (2011), 1071. For a valuable account of obits at Exeter cathedral, see *Death and Memory*, ed. Lepine and Orme, 239–48.

[435] *Reg. Stapeldon*, 305; above, 38, 62.   [436] *Reg. Lacy*, iv. 299–304.

[437] RA, 149/4, 150/4; Boase (2), 31, 268; *BRUO*, i. 471.

[438] ECA, L. III. 10; Boase (2), 33; above, 118.   [439] e.g. RA, 194/2.

[440] RA, 176/1, 178/1, etc.   [441] Below, 166, 168.

in his time a great friend to the College),[442] John Polyng (an Exeter cleric who bequeathed the College some property within the city),[443] and Roger Keys, whose magnificent donation of the works of Hugh of St Cher to the College library in 1470 had been given on condition that the Rector or one of the fellows celebrated an annual obit and mass for him.[444] All these obits, and a few others, continued to be celebrated until the Edwardian Reformation of the 1540s.[445]

The multiplication of obits and commemorative masses was not peculiar to Exeter, but was common to all colleges in the later middle ages.[446] Their primary purpose was salvific: they were intended to shorten the beneficiary's stay in purgatory. Here, in form and function, developments within the College mirrored those within the English church at large. But in a more tangential way obits and masses strengthened the ties of continuity both with deceased benefactors in general and with a few leading benefactors in particular. Already rooted in place, the College community was extended in time through these commemorative services. Since it was not the chaplain alone, but the whole body of the fellowship, which participated in them (and had a financial inducement to do so), it was that whole body which kept in mind past fellows, friends, and benefactors. What was ostensibly an act of intercession was also a kind of communal act of remembrance and of thanksgiving for past favours received. And just as commemorative services proliferated in the second half of the fifteenth century, so too, in a related development, did gifts to the College chapel. Often these were relatively small gifts, sometimes with no restrictions as to their use, sometimes reserved for a special purpose: 7s. 9½d. in 1474, for example, from John Lyndon, Rector nearly forty years earlier and now dean of Crediton, for the chapel pavement.[447] One such gift in 1498 moved the Rector, John Atwell, to an emotional outburst almost unprecedented in the accounts. Recording among his receipts a donation of 6s. 8d. from Thomas Laury, fellow from 1476 to 1484 and now vicar of Modbury in south Devon, Atwell noted that the money was 'for the use of the chapel, and this is noble (hoc est nobile)'.[448] It is a pity that medieval scribes knew nothing of the exclamation mark.

If the hall and chapel were Exeter's two communal centres, as they would have been in any college, fellows must also have spent much of their time in their rooms. Though two fellows might occasionally share a room, as did John Heale and his colleague Yeate in 1414,[449] it was more usual for them to have individual rooms, sometimes with an additional *studium*, an inner

[442] BRUO, ii. 1185.   [443] BRUO, iii. 1495.   [444] Watson, 92.
[445] Below, 233–4.
[446] See e.g. Darwall-Smith, 60, 64; Green, 41, 55, 75, 95, 104–6.
[447] RA, 171/4; BRUO, ii. 1191. For a biography of Lyndon, see Orme, 'The Church in Crediton', 116–17.
[448] RA, 192/4; BRUO, ii. 1109.   [449] RA, 119/2.

cubicle which could be locked.[450] The wooden construction of these rooms, with spaces under floorboards and behind wainscots, made them a prey to vermin, and a payment of 8*d*. in 1364 to a rat-catcher 'for destroying rats in the rooms' reminds us of the vulnerability of this densely packed community to the rat-borne plague.[451] Structural alterations to rooms, often involving the making of new hearths and chimneys, were the responsibility of the College, which also, from the late fifteenth century, employed a carpenter to make beds and clothes presses for the fellows.[452] In general, however, furnishings were the business of the occupant. An adjunct to many rooms, first recorded in the accounts for the 1460s, was the fuel-house, a separate small room rented to a fellow or other College tenant for the storage of firewood.[453] Probably not an innovation but an old feature now yielding rent, the fuel-house of the accounts may perhaps mark a new determination to exact every penny of income from College property in that most difficult of decades.

By the fifteenth century Stapeldon's foundation was beginning to acquire far more rooms than were needed for its fifteen fellows. The College's original thirteen fellows may have filled its three original tenements with no space to spare, but later expansion substantially enlarged the accommodation available. The building of a new room in 1397, the creation of two further rooms under the library and under the chapel portico as a result of Stafford's benefaction, the construction of four new rooms to the west of the tower by Rector Palmer, and, above all perhaps, the acquisition of Checker Hall in 1405 and of Peter Hall in 1470, all greatly increased the College's stock of rooms. This gave Exeter the capacity to share in a development common to other colleges at both Oxford and Cambridge in the late fourteenth and fifteenth centuries: the letting of rooms to men who were not on the fellowship.

This marked an important change. If it did not reorder the College in essentials, it certainly modified its complexion and its academic and generational mix. The new men, the College's tenants, fell into two categories: mature scholars, and undergraduates. By the sixteenth century both groups might be known, collectively and confusingly, as 'commoners', *commensales* (literally 'co-tablers'), but the senior boarders, as we may call the first group, were more commonly known as 'sojourners', *suggenarii*, while the undergraduates were initially known merely as 'scholars', *scolares*.[454] The senior boarders were of several sorts. Some were former fellows of other colleges. In 1403, for example, *magister* Robert Gilbert took up a room at Exeter shortly

[450] e.g. RA, 192/3. For the *studium*, see Catto, 'Citizens, Scholars', *HUO*, i. 180.
[451] RA, 28.   [452] Alterations: e.g. RA, 55, 95/1. Carpenter's work: e.g. RA, 178/1, 190/2.
[453] Entries for fuel-houses first appear in 1461: RA, 159/2.
[454] Cobban, *English University Life*, 95–120, provides the most comprehensive account. See also Darwall-Smith, 20, 75–7, and below, 212–14, 216.

after vacating his fellowship at Merton.[455] Others were former fellows of Exeter, renting rooms in their old College while staying on in Oxford for further study or in expectation of a benefice. William Holcomb, fellow from 1466 to 1476, rented a room in this way in 1476, after vacating his fellowship, and again in 1483–4 before moving on to a succession of livings in Devon and Cornwall.[456] Others again might have no prior connection with Exeter or any other College but simply wanted a room in Oxford while they continued with their studies. The early humanist Cornelio Vitelli, who moved to Oxford from Paris in 1490 and rented a room in 1491–2, was perhaps the most eminent tenant in this category. He was a contemporary of the better-known William Grocyn, former fellow of New College, another leading humanist, and Exeter's tenant from 1491 to 1493.[457] A small but significant sub-group comprised heads of monastic houses or the scholars nominated by them for study at Oxford. The abbot of Torre in Devon rented 'the small room adjoining the kitchen' for his canon, Richard Cade, in 1457, while the prior of Barnstaple, another Devon house, rented a room in 1464.[458] A more distinguished monastic tenant was Henry Deane, prior of Llanthony by Gloucester, who had a room in most years between 1473 and 1488 and went on to become bishop of Bangor and eventually archbishop of Canterbury.[459]

These sojourners or senior boarders may be regarded as peripheral members of the College community. They enjoyed few of the privileges of the fellows, and there were not many of them: never more than six in a single year, and usually only three or four, far fewer than the sixteen who might sometimes be found at University College, the most receptive of all the colleges to sojourners.[460] They nonetheless made a contribution to the College out of proportion to their numbers. The College's primary purpose in taking them in was financial. They paid for their meals and most paid a relatively high rent for their rooms—usually 13s. 4d. a year or rather more (William Holcomb paid 16s. for his room in 1476), closely comparable to the rates charged by other colleges.[461] Some might become benefactors or even develop a long-standing and advantageous attachment to the College. Nicholas Gosse, a onetime resident in College and principal of Checker Hall in 1451 and

---

[455] RA, 101/1; *BRUO*, ii. 766.   [456] RA, 173/1, *BRUO*, ii. 945.

[457] RA, 186/2/3, 187/1; *BRUO*, ii. 827, iii. 1950.

[458] RA, 157/2, 162/1; *BRUO*, ii. 377. For monastic commoners in general, see Cobban, *English University Life*, 116–19.

[459] RA, 172/3, 173/2, 182/3, etc.; *BRUO*, i. 554; *A Calendar of the Registers of the Priory of Llanthony by Gloucester, 1457–66, 1501–25*, ed. J. Rhodes, Gloucestershire Record Ser., 15 (2002), xviii–xix.

[460] H. E. Salter, *Medieval Oxford*, OHS, c (1936), 100; Darwall-Smith, 75.

[461] RA, 73/2; Cobban, *English University Life*, 96, 102–3.

1464, became perhaps the College's third largest benefactor of the fifteenth century, behind Bishop Stafford and Rector Palmer.[462] As diners at the common table,[463] they may have provided a valuable supplement to the social and intellectual life of the College. In terms of regional origins, experience, and intellectual range, they were often more distinguished and drawn from a broader spectrum than the fellows and, over dinner in hall, may have opened the fellows' eyes to a world rather wider than their own. We might at least expect the company of Grocyn and Vitelli to have brought a whiff of Renaissance Italy to mealtime conversations.

The senior boarders, mainly mature scholars, who formed one category of commoner, proved to be a long-lived though ultimately transient group, who made no permanent mark on the College's history. Much more important in the long term was the second category, the undergraduate commoners who began to appear in the fifteenth century. The College had always had some undergraduate members, sophist fellows below bachelor status, but these later undergraduates were different. Like their older counterparts, the senior boarders, they were not on the foundation, but were merely tenants of College rooms. The progenitors of the much larger undergraduate body of the sixteenth and later centuries, they emerge in most Oxford and Cambridge colleges about this time.[464] Their origins may have owed something to a university statute of about 1411 which had laid down that, for disciplinary reasons, all scholars had to be members of halls or colleges; though the halls rather than the colleges would have continued to be the normal home for most students.[465] The Exeter records, however, suggest that undergraduates began to appear rather later and quite suddenly, in the middle years of Rector Palmer from 1428 onwards, and that the admission of these rent-payers was a step towards the restoration of the College's solvency after a decade of financial difficulty. In the winter term of 1429, for example, the receipts section of the accounts shows 16*d*. paid 'for Richard's room', 20*d*. 'for Holdethe's room', 20*d*. 'for little Russell's room', and 3*s*. 4*d*. 'for the room of Plesaunte and Martyn for last year'.[466] That these men are given neither title nor full names points to their inferior status, below the level of those dignified with both, the mainly *magistri* who feature in the accounts as fellows or senior boarders. They were also distinguished from their superiors by their very modest room rents, rarely more than 3*s*. 4*d*. a year, though an otherwise unidentified 'lord John (*dompnus*, i.e. *dominus Johannes*)' paid 13*s*. 4*d*. for his

[462] Boase (2), 268 n. 2; below, 166–7, 172.
[463] Salter, *Medieval Oxford*, 100; Cobban, *English University Life*, 96.
[464] Cobban, *Medieval English Universities*, 193–6, 326; Cobban, *English University Life*, 96–7, 119–20; Green, 52–6.
[465] *SA*, 208; Fletcher, 'Developments', *HUO*, ii. 317; Catto, 'Triumph of the Hall', 220.
[466] RA, 131/1.

room from 1429 to 1434.[467] Was he perhaps a nobleman's son, with a claim to better-class accommodation?

For Palmer's last four years as Rector there were between six and eight of these undergraduate boarders. But after his time they are recorded in the accounts in no systematic way, and, mysteriously, when they do appear it is not as rent-payers but as the possessors of rooms on whose repair the College has spent money, recorded on the expenses side of the accounts. In 1447, for example, the College spent 1d. on repairing the door to 'Ayschcombe's' room, and in 1448, 2d. on whitewashing the same room; but Ayschcombe appears nowhere else on the accounts and no rent is recorded for his room. He may well have been the John Ashcomb who obtained his BA in 1450 and who would therefore have been an undergraduate in 1447–8.[468] Similarly, in 1447 3d. was spent on the door of 'Vady's' room: again, an otherwise unknown name.[469] Occasionally these terse entries yield valuable nuggets of information about College residents. In 1450 1d. was spent on repairing the lock 'in Courtenay's room'. This almost certainly refers to Peter Courtenay, then about 18 years old, the third son of Sir Philip Courtenay of Powderham, Devon, an Oxford BCL by 1457, and a future bishop of Exeter and prominent friend of his former college. But again Courtenay does not appear to have been paying rent for his room.[470] It is interesting, if not surprising, to find one of the College's few aristocratic undergraduates coming from the county which provided the majority of its fellows.

Exeter's admission of undergraduates from the late 1420s placed it among the first colleges at either Oxford or Cambridge to make this move.[471] But because of the peculiarities of the records numbers are impossible to assess. After the systematic listings of Rector Palmer's day, an undergraduate in a room needing no repairs might go completely unrecorded. The reasons for the failure of the accounts to note rent payments from undergraduate rooms are difficult to fathom. One possibility is that at least some undergraduates may have been boarded out at Hart Hall, Exeter's dependency, paying rent to the Hall's principal, who was usually a fellow of Exeter. The College would then make its profit from the rent which the principal in turn paid to Exeter, fixed at 40s. a year from the 1440s.[472] Others may have had rooms in Checker Hall or Peter Hall, on the main site, and again paid rent to the Halls'

---

[467] RA, 131/3, 132/3, 133/4, 135/1. Boase (2), 31, suggests that this may be John Colyford, fellow, 1419–27, and Rector, 1424–5. But he gives no reason for this guess, which seems unlikely to be right.

[468] RA, 147/3, 148/3; *BRUO*, i. 55.   [469] RA, 148/1.

[470] RA, 149/4; BRUO, i. 499–500; R. Horrox, 'Peter Courtenay', *ODNB*. Emden asserts that there is no evidence for Courtenay's membership of Exeter College.

[471] Cobban, *English University Life*, 119.

[472] N. Saul, 'The Pre-history of an Oxford College: Hart Hall and its Neighbours in the Middle Ages', *Oxoniensia*, 54 (1989), 334, 336.

principals. Or it may be (perhaps the likeliest possibility) that some rents, like some benefactions,[473] failed to pass through the Rector's hands and went, unaccounted for, directly into the College chest, by contrast with the room rents regularly recorded for senior boarders.

An alternative if equally uncertain answer may be related to another and connected development: the beginnings of tutorial teaching, traceable first in subsidiary halls and then within the College itself. This was an important innovation in its own right, and one which brought the undergraduate onto the College stage not only as a resident but as a pupil. It was not entirely unprecedented. Stapeldon had made provision for regular disputations within the college, and throughout the university 'hall lectures', given by a hall principal or graduate, and intended to supplement the formal university lectures, had been laid on since the fourteenth century.[474] In the first half of the fifteenth century, however, these began to be supplemented by a different type of instruction, the individual teaching provided by a tutor for his pupils. The earliest evidence for this is closely related to Exeter's history. In 1424 John Arundel, fellow from 1420 to 1431 and later bishop of Chichester, was principal of an unnamed hall, possibly Black Hall (adjoining Hart Hall), which was often governed either by fellows of the College or by men closely connected with it.[475] Like most of the principals of Hart Hall, he therefore held his principalship in tandem with his fellowship. Arundel kept a notebook which illuminates both the teaching and the domestic arrangements within his hall.[476] It shows him acting as tutor to a group of undergraduate commoners. He received money from one pupil's father to cover the cost of the pupil's commons, and he employed three tutors, two of them, John Burwyke and John Beaucomb, also fellows of Exeter, to assist with the teaching. Burwyke was to receive 10s. for each of three terms, provided that the number to be taught did not exceed twenty-two; so this was an operation on some scale. We might also note that Burwyke's teaching fees would triple the 10s. annual allowance which he received as a fellow of Exeter. The expense account for one pupil, W. Clavyle, shows him paying Arundel for his commons (6s. 10d. for Michaelmas term), for his share of a room (6d.), for lecture fees (1s. 8d.), for books and clogs (10d.), and for much else. Although Clavyle and his fellow undergraduates would be expected to attend university lectures and disputations, their hall was more than a hall of residence, since it was partly there that they were taught. Checker Hall and Peter Hall, resembling Hart

---

[473] Butcher, 40.

[474] *Reg. Stapeldon*, 307; Pantin, *Oxford Life*, 36; A. B. Cobban, 'Decentralized Teaching in the Medieval English Universities', *History of Education*, 5 (1976), 199–200.

[475] Catto, 'The Triumph of the Hall', 214 n. 16.

[476] A. B. Cobban, 'John Arundel, the Tutorial System, and the Cost of Undergraduate Living in the Medieval English Universities', *Bulletin of the John Rylands University Library*, 77 (1995), 143–59, for what follows.

Hall in usually drawing their principals from among the fellows, are likely to have functioned in a similar way. And to the names of the fellow-tutors employed by Arundel at his hall we might add the comparable name of Robert Takell, fellow of Exeter from 1442 to 1450, who, in 1448 or shortly before, was acting as tutor (*creditor*) to John Broughton of Hart Hall, for whose debts to the Hall's manciple he stood as guarantor.[477]

The example of Arundel and his hall raises a question more directly pertinent to the history of the College: were undergraduates resident within the College also being taught by the fellows? To judge by the stipend which Burwyke received for his teaching, there would certainly have been some financial inducement to teach; and if fellows such as Burwyke, Beaucomb, and Takell were teaching undergraduates outside the College, it seems highly likely that others were also doing so within, and that an undergraduate such as Peter Courtenay was receiving some of his tuition from men who were in effect College tutors. Since any teaching fees would go directly to the fellow-tutor, the College accounts provide no way of confirming this guess. For the last years of the century, however, they begin to provide some solid evidence of another sort. They show that in the autumn term of 1496 *magister* William Forde, a fellow since 1484, paid 8*d*. 'for a room for his scholars (*pro cubiculo scolariis suis*)', and that in the Lent term of 1497 he paid 16*d*. for the same.[478] Similarly, *magister* Sandeleroy, otherwise unknown, paid 12*d*. for a room for his *scolarii* in 1498.[479] These entries are particularly significant, since 'scolaris' in this context normally signifies a pupil.[480] Finally, in 1498 and 1499, *magister* John Goldyng, a fellow from Cornwall, paid rent for a room for 'Trethin', whose lack of a Christian name or title identifies him as another undergraduate: a nice case of a Cornish tutor taking on a Cornish pupil.[481]

This little clutch of references shows that by 1500 some fellows of the College had their own pupils, for whose rooms they were paying. Presumably they then recovered the money from those same pupils, together with additional tuition fees. We might wonder whether this was the case earlier and whether our apparently freeloading undergraduates were in fact renting their rooms from their tutors and not from the College; or whether perhaps fellow-tutors were paying for their pupils' rooms without expectation of future repayment. At University College in the late fourteenth century two 'portionists', seemingly undergraduates, fail to appear in the College accounts and

---

[477] *Registrum Cancellarii Oxoniensis, 1434–1469*, ed. H. E. Salter, OHS, xciii–xciv (1932), i. 157–8; Saul, 'Pre-History of an Oxford College', 337; *BRUO*, iii. 1844.

[478] RA, 190/4, 191/2; *BRUO*, ii. 705.   [479] RA, 192/4.

[480] A. B. Cobban, *The King's Hall within the University of Cambridge in the Later Middle Ages* (Cambridge, 1969), 69 n. 3, 73; Cobban, 'John Arundel', 150.

[481] RA, 192/4, 193/4; *BRUO*, ii. 788, iii. 1898, *s.v.* 'Trethurf'; Orme, 'The Cornish at Oxford', 79, 83. In the manuscript the pupil's name is clearly 'Trethin' and not 'Trethurf', as given by Emden and followed by Orme.

may have been supported by the fellows.[482] On balance these possible explanations in Exeter's case seem unconvincing; but so do all possible solutions to the conundrum of the undergraduate who apparently pays no rent. Even without an answer to this particular problem, however, we have clarified the main lines of a story with a future. By the late 1420s the College was taking in undergraduate boarders, who, initially, at least, were paying rent for their rooms, and whose introduction was linked with the College's concurrent financial difficulties. Before this time there is no sign of their presence, either as payers of rent or as otherwise unknown men whose rooms the College repaired. We can only conclude that their introduction came suddenly and that it was the work of the Rector, William Palmer, who once again stands out as the most enterprising and innovative of the College's late medieval Rectors. Given the slightly earlier teaching arrangements existing in John Arundel's unnamed hall, it is highly likely that some of Palmer's undergraduates were receiving tuition within the College. By the late 1490s, when the records begin to associate particular fellows with their own *scolares*, this was certainly the case. It was in some such way, and at a date earlier than most Oxford colleges, that Exeter acquired its first undergraduates and its fellows their first pupils.

As far as can be seen, undergraduates were no more than fringe members of the College community. While they shared in its academic purposes, they remained birds of passage. Unlike the young sophists among the fellows, whom they resembled in age and in similarity of studies, they had no part to play in College business. Still further towards the fringe of the community, though perhaps more necessary to the College's well-being than its undergraduates, were the members of another group: the College servants. We have already seen that there were four of these: the manciple, a key figure in the College organization, whose work has already been discussed, the cook, the barber, and the laundress. This was the usual establishment in all colleges.[483] Of the last three, the cook was the most highly paid, receiving 8s. a year in the 1350s, rising to 13s. 4d. by 1495.[484] Like the manciple, he served under contract, and in 1492, and probably in earlier years, he had his own room in College.[485] The laundress was paid 5s. a year in the 1350s, rising to 13s. 4d. by 1495. She sometimes turned her hand to needlework, repairing the chapel vestments on two occasions in the 1480s for extra pay.[486] The barber, the least well paid of the quartet, received 4s. a year in the 1350s, rising to 8s. by 1495. An essential figure in a university world where all scholars were normally tonsured (and where barbers were sufficiently important to have their own

[482] Darwall-Smith, 52.   [483] Above, 119; Darwall-Smith, 77.
[484] Butcher, 41, and RA, 190/2 for all the comparative wage rates.   [485] RA, 127/2, 186/2.
[486] RA, 179/1, 181/2.

university guild[487]), Exeter's barber, like the laundress, may have been employed by several colleges. These wage rates were towards the lower end of the range paid across the colleges: at New College the laundress received a munificent 40s. a year in the fifteenth century, and at Merton 20s. a year, while at the other end of the scale the University College laundress received a mere 8s. All these servants, however, were probably able to profit from tips: W. Clayvyle, John Arundel's undergraduate pupil in 1424, certainly reckoned on tipping the cook and the maniciple.[488] One perhaps surprising feature of the domestic scene is the absence of reference to more menial servants. It is only when the accounts note in 1494 that tunics were purchased for 'the poor people of the kitchen (*pauperculi coquine*)' that we are made to realize that there were hewers of wood and drawers of water who have gone unrecorded.[489] How they were paid remains a mystery.

On just one occasion the College servants appear as part of the wider College community. In 1478 Nicholas Gosse, that proven friend and benefactor of the college, made arrangements with the Rector, John Orell, for the annual celebration of his obit in the College chapel after his death.[490] He ordained that each year the College should set aside 13s. 4d. for this purpose. From this money small sums were to be paid to those present at the obit. The celebrant was to receive 12d.; each fellow, 6d.; the clerk of the chapel, the maniciple, the cook, the barber, and the laundress, 3d. each; and the kitchen boy (*puer coquine*) 2d. Any residue was to be spent on that day's food or on that for the Sunday following the service, at the discretion of the Rector or senior fellow. Gosse thus envisaged a full chapel, where the servants would keep company with the fellows, sharing in his bounty and in return joining in prayers for his salvation. It was not the prayers of the fellows alone that were valued, but those of the servants too; and the celebration of his obit must have been one of the very rare moments when fellows and servants came together as members of a single body. The service was still being held, and the same amount of money disbursed, in 1535.[491]

To speak of the College as a community is thus not to speak imprecisely or anachronistically. Its small size, the common origins of most of its fellows in the west country, and their common pursuits, all created powerful if intangible bonds. Like all communities, the College was from time to time divided by dissent. We can see this most clearly in the case of disputed elections,[492] but no doubt there were other occasions, unrecorded in the accounts or in

---

[487] Catto, 'Citizens, Scholars', *HUO*, i. 155.
[488] Cobban, *The King's Hall*, 235; Cobban, 'John Arundel', 153; Darwall-Smith, 77–8.
[489] RA, 189/2.
[490] ECA, L. V. 4, summarized in Boase (2), 297, but without the details as to attendance.
[491] Boase (2), lxxvi, n. 1.   [492] Above, 79–82, 122–3.

bishops' registers, when fellows fell out. Close proximity did not always breed amity. Yet beneath these temporary divisions we can sense a strong affection for the College and a common willingness to work for its interests. As with a great medieval Benedictine abbey or a modern Oxford college, 'loyalty to the corporation' was a guiding principle.[493]

It was sometimes shown by a willingness to place personal resources at the College's disposal. The building of a new room in 1397, the construction of new windows for the hall in 1409–10, and the building of a new kitchen in 1483, were all supported by the contributions of past and present fellows.[494] It was 'because he was once a fellow here' that Henry Gardyner gave 20s. to the College in 1463.[495] Nor was it only the College itself that attracted the fellows' support, but also the needs of its individual members. When John Otery, fellow from c. 1367 to c. 1369, broke his arm while engaged on college business (a fall from a horse?) the fellows all agreed that the College should meet his substantial medical expenses of 13s. 4d.[496] More long-term commitments were entered into in the fifteenth century. When John Burwyke, one of John Arundel's teaching team in 1424, was incapacitated in some way in 1428, he continued to receive his commons 'out of piety and from the alms of the fellows', as the account states. As 'a sort of pensioner on the college', Burwyke remained on the books and drawing his commons for some time after he had vacated his fellowship.[497] A similar case arose in 1442, when John Bulsey, then Rector-elect, was struck down by an illness which evidently affected his mental state. Though seemingly unable to carry out the duties of his position, he too was maintained at the College's expense, receiving both his commons and his annual allowance for three years after vacating his fellowship.[498] If one prop of the community was a powerful impulse to promote the interests of the house, another was a more humane concern for the welfare of its individual members.

10. RECOVERY AND EXPANSION, 1475–1500

After the stresses and strains of the mid century depression, the quarter-century from 1475 to 1500 marked a period of recovery and expanding self-confidence for the College. In the first place, the recovery was financial. Receipts began to rise again from 1475–6. Income in that year, at £78, was 50 per cent up on the £52 of 1473–4, the nearest year for which figures survive.[499] The £155 received in 1482–3 was the highest annual revenue in the fifteenth century,[500] and income exceeded £100 for ten of the eighteen

[493] Cf. C. R. Cheney, *Hubert Walter* (London, 1967), 14–15, for some reflections on this theme.
[494] RA, 95/1, 109/1, 112, 178/3/4.   [495] RA, 161/1; Boase (2), 20.
[496] RA, 41.   [497] RA, 130/2, 131/1, 133/1; Boase (2), 32.
[498] *Reg. Lacy*, ii. 266–7; RA, 143/2, 144/4, 145/2; *BRUO*, ii. 305.   [499] RA, 171, 172.
[500] RA, 178.

years for which full accounts survive between 1481–2 and 1499–1500. If we were to consider income alone, and not expenditure (to which we shall return), we would count this period as one of the most prosperous in the College's early history.

The recovery, like the slump which had preceded it, partly reflected trends in the national economy. Just as the slump had been largely caused by a shortage of silver, and a consequent decline in prices and market transactions, so the recovery seems to have mirrored an expansion in the silver supply from the early 1470s, as overseas trade grew and German silver mining resumed.[501] At no point did the pulses of the national economy leave Exeter unaffected. But the new money now entering the College came only to a limited extent from the traditional sources which would have been responsive to this sort of change. Income from Gwinear rose, but not dramatically. Averaging £24 a year for the 1480s and £19 for the 1490s, it was a good deal higher than it had been in the depths of the slump, but a good deal lower than it had been in the first twenty years of the century.[502] Income from Wittenham hardly rose at all. The College's salvation lay not in rising customary revenues but rather in new acquisitions, and in one in particular: the church of Menheniot.

The process which led to the College's establishment here was tortuous but revealing. Menheniot lies a few miles from Liskeard in east Cornwall. In 1478 the glebe and advowson of the church were held by a group of four patrons, comprising three men and a woman: Fulk Bourgchier, Lord Fitzwarin; Edward Courtenay, a distant relative of the Courtenay earls of Devon and later to be created earl himself by Henry VII in 1485; and one Halnaetheus Mauleverer and Joan his wife. The current rector of the church was Peter Courtenay, former undergraduate of the College, now dean of Exeter, and soon to be Exeter's bishop.[503] Though there must have been preliminary discussions about which we know nothing, the records show the four joint patrons making the first moves in the College's favour. By two transactions in January and April 1478 they granted their titles to glebe and advowson to a group of three men closely associated with the College: Nicholas Gosse, then chancellor of Exeter; Walter Wyndesore, fellow from c.1444 to c.1458, Rector from c.1453 to 1457, and currently sub-dean of Exeter; and John Lyndon, fellow from c.1434 to 1442, Rector in 1441–2, and currently dean of Crediton.[504] After obtaining a royal licence to alienate the advowson,[505] Gosse and his two colleagues granted it to the dean and chapter of Exeter. Once the church had been appropriated by the dean and chapter, a vicar was to be appointed on a fixed stipend and the bulk of the tithe revenues passed on to

[501] Hatcher, 'The Great Slump', 270–1; P. Spufford, *Money and its Use in Medieval Europe* (Cambridge, 1988), 363–4.
[502] Cf. Butcher, 39.   [503] Above, 160.
[504] ECA, M. IV. 5; *BRUO*, ii. 795, 1191, iii. 2123.   [505] D. and C., 1176.

the College.[506] The Menheniot arrangements thus replicated almost precisely those made by Stapeldon for the church of Gwinear. The only difference lay in the stipulation that the vicar of Menheniot was to be a fellow or former fellow of the College. The College was thus provided with a useful piece of patronage in the form of a benefice which was more valuable than Gwinear and so more likely to be attractive to a potential fellow-vicar.[507] For the scheme to take effect the current rector, Peter Courtenay, had to resign the living, and this he did, probably on his election to the see of Exeter in June 1478.

This plan, however, did not quite work out. In 1479 the College appointed as its first vicar William Baron, fellow from 1453 to 1464, Rector from 1460 to 1464, and currently a resident senior boarder.[508] But there were immediate disputes about the amount to be set aside for the vicar's portion, partly due to the ambiguous drafting of the original division of the revenues, and in June 1479 both parties, Baron and the Rector and fellows, submitted their differences to Peter Courtenay, the new bishop. Courtenay's ruling was simple and was accepted by both sides. Baron was to pay the college £20 a year in two instalments and—it is implied but not directly stated—to retain the remainder of the tithe income.[509] In other words it was the College and not the vicar, as originally intended, which was to draw a fixed sum from the living. This settlement was to govern relations between the College and the vicar of Menheniot for the remainder of our period, and indeed well into the seventeenth century.[510]

This involved story has been worth telling, not only because it shows how the College gained an important source of revenue, but because it illustrates some of its strengths at this time. It had started from a position of weakness. The document which permitted the appropriation of the living had spoken of a petition from the Rector and fellows for relief from their poverty, which, they said, was preventing them from fulfilling the religious purposes of their founder. It looks therefore as if the original initiative leading to the acquisition of Menheniot had come from the College in the aftermath of the depression. But the securing of an income from the church there depended upon the cooperation of many interested parties: the four joint holders of the advowson; Peter Courtenay, first rector, then bishop; the three intermediaries, led by Gosse; and the dean and chapter of Exeter, who may not have welcomed the gift of an advowson which brought them no gains and some possible inconvenience. The inducement offered to the four existing patrons to surrender their rights was probably not financial but spiritual: the deed of

---

[506] D. and C., 1177; Boase (2), vii n. 1, liii n. 1 (the document cited by Boase is in ECA, M. IV. 5); Historical Manuscripts Commission, *Various Collections*, iv (1907), 87.

[507] In the *Taxatio* of 1292 Menheniot was valued at £8 and Gwinear at £5 13s. 4d.: *Taxatio Ecclesiastica Papae Nicholai IV* (London, 1802), 147–8.

[508] *BRUO*, i. 115.   [509] D. and C., 1190.   [510] Cf. Boase (2), 346.

appropriation stated that prayers were to be said by the College chaplain for the four, and also for Elizabeth, wife of Fulk Bourgchier, during their lifetimes, and that they were to be remembered in annual obits after their deaths.[511] The rise in the value set on salvific prayers and masses during the fifteenth century meant that the College possessed an increasingly desirable currency which it could easily pay out. The actions of the three intermediaries were more directly altruistic. They wanted to do their best for the College; and since two of them, Gosse and Wyndesore, were leading members of the Exeter chapter they were well placed to do so. The huge cost of the royal licence to alienate—at least £120—was again met by former fellows and associates. These included two of the three intermediaries—Gosse, who lent £5, and Lyndon, who gave £20. In addition, John Colyford, who we have met before as a former fellow and Rector, gave £50, and Thomas Copleston, a senior boarder, lent £5. The largest contribution came from the executors of Henry Webber, former dean of Exeter and an old friend of the College, who gave £60.[512] As we have seen repeatedly, the College's friends and former members were one of its greatest resources. To one of them, Nicholas Gosse, we shall return.

The acquisition of Menheniot raised the College's income by about a quarter. But it was only the most important of a series of acquisitions which were made in these years and which marked a return of confidence after the retrenchments of the slump. In 1478 the College paid £20 for a new property in St Giles known as Peyntour's Hall, an inn and brewhouse, which stood where St John's College now stands. The adjacent property, a tenement with barn and arable, was given to the College in 1488.[513] Further afield, the College in 1486 paid some £24 for a farm of about 60 acres at Benson in south Oxfordshire.[514] Finally, in 1493 Exeter was apparently granted (but was this a concealed purchase?) Clifton Ferry, which provided a crossing over the Thames near the present village of Clifton Hampden.[515] Since the ferry crossing formed part of the direct route from Oxford to Wittenham, which lay only about a mile beyond the southern landing-stage, the Rector and fellows must have had in mind the convenience of having this important transit point under their own control.

The acquisition of new properties was matched by substantial spending on the old. This was a boom period for College building. The major project was the construction of a new kitchen in 1483, at a total cost of £60, nearly half

[511] ECA, M. IV. 5; Boase (2), liii n. 1, whose excerpt omits some of these details.
[512] ECA, C. II. 11 (benefactors' book); M. IV. 5; Boase (2), liii n. 1, 268 and n. 2. For Webber, see BRUO, iii. 2005. He had been given wine, beer, and a pair of gloves on a visit to the College in 1456: RA, 155/3.
[513] Boase (2), 297; Salter, Survey, ii. 201–2; RA, 174/3 (for the cost of Peyntour's Hall), 185/4, 190/1 (adjacent tenement); ECA, L. V. 4.
[514] ECA, M. II. 3; Boase (2), 369–70.   [515] ECA, M. II. 7; Boase (2), liii, 329.

that year's revenues. This was a substantial work, for which the College bought in oak beams, other oak fitments, and at least twenty cartloads of stone.[516] But the total building costs of c. £73 in 1483–4 were exceeded in 1485–6, when they rose to c. £81, much of it spent on the refurbishment of the hall.[517] The following year saw a large outlay on the property in St Giles.[518] How far all this was necessary is impossible to judge; but such lavish spending on building projects could be as easily viewed as a mark of imprudence as of confidence.

In the short term it may have looked increasingly like imprudence. Though College income rose, it did not keep pace with expenditure, and between 1481 and 1492, years which saw the height of the building boom, the accounts slipped back into deficit. It must have been hoped that the new properties would yield a good income, but, with the exception of Menheniot, they hardly did so. Peyntour's Hall brought in £3 in some years[519] and in others apparently nothing. The adjacent tenement was usually worth 8s. to 10s. a year.[520] The farm at Benson was rented out for about 31s. a year,[521] while a little later the ferryman at Clifton Ferry paid the College about 16s. a year, some of which was frequently offset by the cost of repairing his boats.[522] In a good year these new acquisitions thus brought in some £5 to £6. They may have raised the standing of a College which had always lacked much property, and have been regarded as a sensible long-term investment, but at the time they made only a small contribution to income.

A much more important resource, as always, lay in the generosity of friends and former fellows. The most munificent gift of the period, large by any standard, was the £40 received in 1485 from Dr Dennis Orleigh, prior of the hospital of St John at Exeter.[523] Orleigh, a mystery man with no discernible connection with the College or indeed with Oxford (though his doctorate points to an Oxford training), was admiringly described by the Rector as 'a most special benefactor to us', and on several occasions he was presented with gifts of gloves, a customary way of honouring friends, benefactors, and superiors.[524] Nicholas Gosse, generous as ever, gave £15 towards the cost of Peyntour's Hall—three-quarters of its cost.[525] John Philipp, former fellow and Rector, and in 1483 rector of St Olave's church in Exeter, contributed £20 to the building of the new kitchen.[526] These were only the largest of a number of gifts which came in during the period. But very helpful though they were, gifts were irregular and not to be relied on, and the College often got by in the

[516] RA, 178/2/4, 179/1. Butcher, 47, usefully surveys buildings costs at this time, but mistakenly gives £64 as the cost of the kitchen.
[517] RA, 180/3; Butcher, 47.   [518] RA, 182/1.   [519] e.g. RA, 178/1 (1482).
[520] e.g. 183/1 (1488), 185/4 (1491).   [521] e.g. 186/1/3, 187/1/2.
[522] e.g. RA, 188/3, 190/1.   [523] RA, 180/2; Boase (2), 269.
[524] RA, 180/2, 181/2.   [525] RA, 175/1; Boase (2), 268.
[526] RA, 178/3/4, 179/1. Boase (2), 42, greatly underestimates Philipp's contribution.

1480s and early 1490s only by withdrawing cash from the common chest—surplus money which had accumulated during good years—and, occasionally, by borrowing from the various university chests.[527]

Financial stability was restored from 1492 onwards. Income continued at a high level, while expenditure fell sharply, largely as a result of a fall in building costs. Expenditure had averaged £107 a year in the 1480s, but then declined to £86 in the next decade. One sign of this reviving prosperity was the rise in spending on the annual feast. In the 1480s this had, if anything, been even lower than in the frugal years of the 1460s, but in the 1490s it rose sharply. We have to go back to 1414 to find a sum larger than the £1 15s. 6d. spent on the feast in 1499.[528] Yet throughout this period, and not just in the 1490s, the College was coming to be characterized by a confident expansiveness which went beyond the indulgence of a bigger and better feast. It found something of a keynote in ostentation and artistic display. One small sign of this was the construction of battlements, recorded in the accounts for 1485–6 and part of the building boom of these years—perhaps the battlements depicted on Palmer's Tower and along the College's northern wall in Agas's view of 1578 (see Plate 13). They may have been erected in emulation of Magdalen's battlements, of about a decade earlier, and have been designed to show that a small and relatively insignificant College could rival a much larger and grander one.[529] Another mark of the same spirit was the completion, between 1480 and 1484, of the final volumes in the magnificent set of the works of Hugh of St Cher, most of the earlier volumes having been given by Roger Keys, who had died in 1477. The College provided the bulk of the money for the writing, illumination, and binding of these beautiful volumes, though some came by way of gift from John Combe, a canon of Exeter.[530] Both the battlements and the books were emblematic of an aesthetic sense which was also a signification of status.

There is one other aesthetic reminder of the College and its ethos during these years, still surviving, and then and now more publicly displayed than the library-locked volumes of Hugh of St Cher. For some sixty years, from about 1427 to 1488, the university had been engaged on the most ambitious and grandiose project in its medieval history: the building of the Divinity School and, above it, Duke Humfrey's library. In the decoration of the Divinity School Exeter makes a surprisingly prominent showing, as Mr Stanley Gillam was the first to point out.[531] It is on the vaults of the Divinity School,

---

[527] Butcher, 43–4, 50.   [528] RA, 119/2, 194/2; Butcher, 47, 52.

[529] RA, 180/1/2; Butcher, 47. For Magdalen's battlements, see Harvey, 'Architecture', *HUO*, ii. 766.

[530] Watson, 85, 97–8, 107–8; *BRUO*, i. 472–3. Extracts from the accounts relating to this work are printed in Boase (1), 26.

[531] S. Gillam, *The Divinity School and Duke Humfrey's Library at Oxford* (Oxford, 1988), 38–40.

completed between 1480 and 1483, and 'one of the marvels of Oxford',[532] that the College's standing is most vividly demonstrated. Exeter's shield of arms appears three times on the vaults—an honour given to no other college. More specifically interesting are the three names and five sets of initials which appear on the bosses of the vault. The three names (surnames only) are those of John Rowe, Thomas Ruer, and John Orell, fellows of Exeter respectively from c.1475 to c.1490, 1479 to 1491, and 1465 to 1481.[533] The initials include those of William Merifield, Rector from 1479 to 1480, and fellow until 1482, John Mayne, fellow from c.1477 to c.1489 (whom we have already met supervising the harvest at Wittenham), James Babbe, Rector from 1482 to 1484, the period of the vault's construction, and possibly those of Walter Coose, fellow from 1472 to 1478, and chaplain in 1478.[534]

The College's extraordinary salience, amid other bosses which commemorate assorted grandees—archbishops, bishops, magnates, chancellors of the university—is hard to explain. But although the Divinity School was built on former Balliol property, its west end abutted Exeter, just as its later extension, the Convocation House, does now, and Gillam has suggested that the College's honoured place on the vaults was perhaps intended as a thanks offering for the College's forbearance during the long period of disturbance caused by the building operations. This is possible. But it is perhaps more likely that those commemorated had contributed from their own pockets to the financing of the great project which lay on their doorstep and that this was their and their College's reward. Known benefactors figure conspicuously among others commemorated in the same place.[535] The vault is both the most visible surviving memorial to any group of Exeter fellows and also an advertisement for their College, its place in the university, and its rising pretensions during an unusually invigorating decade.

Underlying the College's aggrandizement may have lain an awareness of the support to be expected from some powerful and benevolent patrons and friends. The examples of two such men, Peter Courtenay and Nicholas Gosse, will bring this section to a close. As we have seen, Courtenay had been an undergraduate at Exeter in 1450, and he did not forget his College, nor it him, in later life. There was nothing very unusual in the gifts of expensive gloves several times sent to him by the College.[536] More suggestive was the College's more splendid gift of five yards of crimson cloth, costing a handsome £3 6s. 8d., given to celebrate his return from exile with Henry Tudor in 1485.[537] Close ties were equally evident in the letter sent to him in 1480 to tell him of

---

[532] J. Sherwood and N. Pevsner, *The Buildings of England: Oxfordshire* (Harmondsworth, 1974), 258.

[533] *BRUO*, ii. 1400, iii. 1599, 1604.

[534] *BRUO*, i. 85, 483, ii. 1250, 1263; Boase (2), 45; above, 131.

[535] Gillam, *The Divinity School*, 34–5, 38.   [536] RA, 181/2, 183/1.

[537] RA, 180/1; Boase (1), 26; Boase (2), lxx.

the supposed death of King Edward IV—a false rumour, as it turned out.[538]
On his side, Courtenay had promoted the process by which the College
gained its £20 a year from the church of Menheniot, and, more surprisingly,
had played a part in the acquisition of the land at Benson in 1486. He was one
of a number of feoffees, who included, equally surprisingly, Edward Courtenay, former patron of Menheniot and now earl of Devon, as well as the Rector
and several fellows of the College, to whom the current holders of the Benson
land surrendered their rights.[539] Presumably the presence of two such powerful men among the feoffees was intended to ensure that the grantors kept to
their side of the agreement. Courtenay's involvement in such a comparatively
minor transaction may be the mark of a relationship which ran deeper, and in
ways more beneficial to Exeter, than the records reveal.

The relationship of Nicholas Gosse with the College was more visible and
more protracted than that of Courtenay. We have already heard much of him.
Gosse was an Oxford graduate, and by 1447 a bachelor of theology, but never
a fellow of Exeter. In the 1450s, however, he was living on the site as principal
successively of Checker Hall and Peter Hall, Exeter's two academic halls, in
which role he paid rent to the College.[540] It was in that difficult decade that his
goodwill first became apparent in a series of loans which extended into the
1460s and which totalled some £13.[541] He played some part in securing a
tenement in Queen Street for the College in 1460,[542] but it was in relation to
the acquisition of Peyntour's Hall and the Menheniot advowson in 1478–9
that his regard for Exeter was at its most conspicuous, as we have seen. His
gift of £15 enabled the College to buy Peyntour's Hall; and if his was the
moving spirit behind the acquisition of Menheniot, as seems likely, he did the
College a service which made a permanent difference to its fortunes. In
another beneficial by-product of the Menheniot transaction Gosse made
over the surplus monies, amounting to nearly £21, remaining from the
funds raised to cover the cost of the church's appropriation.[543] He assisted
the College in a more routine way when on many occasions, as canon and
then chancellor of Exeter from 1459 onwards, he forwarded the Gwinear
revenues from Exeter to Oxford.[544] It was no wonder that such a friend was
well looked after by the College, especially during his fairly frequent appearances in Oxford. Breakfast was laid on for him in 1469, 8d. was spent on a
gallon of wine at his leave-taking in 1473, he was presented with a valuable
pair of furred gloves in 1476, and more gloves and wine followed when he
appeared in company with another canon of Exeter in 1481.[545]

[538] RA, 176/4.   [539] ECA, M. II. 3.   [540] RA, 151/2/3; BRUO, ii. 795; above, 143.
[541] Butcher, 50.   [542] Boase (2), 309; Salter, Survey, ii. 117.
[543] RA, 175/4; Boase (2), lii n. 1.   [544] RA, 160/2, 169/3, etc.
[545] RA, 167/2, 170/3, 173/1, 177/1.

Although Gosse was exceptionally generous, he was in some ways typical of the College's major benefactors in the second half of the fifteenth century. Like him, almost all were Oxford graduates and high-ranking clerics holding senior posts in the greater churches and ecclesiastical institutions of Devon: deans and chancellors of Exeter, deans and precentors of Crediton, priors of St John's Hospital in Exeter. Few were parish clergy and few from Cornwall. One or two were notable pluralists, whose surplus wealth from their benefices was diverted towards the College. Gosse himself had canonries in two dioceses and held two churches in Devon and one in Cornwall while he was also chancellor of Exeter. His motives in giving, like those of other donors, must have been mixed, but in his case, as in theirs, the desire for salvation was high among them. The arrangements which he made with the College in 1478 for the future celebration of his obit formed part of his agreement to make £15 available for the purchase of Peyntour's Hall. In effect the gift was conditional on the obit. It was his support and that of other churchmen like him—John Lyndon, John Philipp, Dennis Orleigh—that underpinned the College's revival in the last decades of the fifteenth century.

11. CONCLUSION: *PLUS ÇA CHANGE...*?

Walter de Stapeldon had a clear view of the purposes of a university education. He set it out in the deed by which he endowed his college in 1314:

The prelates of the church and the princes and nobles of this kingdom need to have for the benefit of their governance—and having them redounds to their glory—men of dedication and dignity conspicuous for their learning and virtue, so that strengthened in deliberation and taking every decision with shrewdness and foresight they may successfully govern, under the prince of peace, the flock entrusted to them. Such are the men that the study of letters produces by the grace poured into them from heaven.[546]

Some 164 years later, in 1477 or 1478, the Rector and fellows of the now long established College took a similar view of its purpose. It had been founded, they said, 'for the increase of learning, the strengthening of the faith, and the augmentation of divine worship', all of which were threatened by their current poverty.[547] Although Stapeldon had stressed the benefits which educated men brought to church and state, and the Rector and fellows the more general spiritual functions of the College, both parties had seen its role in essentially similar terms. It was a religious institution whose members were instilled with learning in order that God might be better served.

This was only the most obvious point of comparison between the College which Stapeldon had in mind and its late fifteenth-century projection. In other ways besides fundamental purpose, the College was still one that

---

[546] Buck, 225.   [547] Grant of advowson of Menheniot, 1478: ECA, M. IV. 5.

Stapeldon would have recognized. His name continued to cling precariously to it, though by the 1470s Stapeldon Hall had been largely superseded by what was 'now commonly called Exeter College'.[548] But much more important was the continuing authority of Stapeldon's statutes. Formally speaking, and to a large extent in practice, the statutes still governed the constitution and procedures of the College. The election of twelve fellows from the diocese of Exeter, the nomination of the chaplain by the chapter of Exeter, annual elections to the rectorship, the system of allowances, and the Rector's responsibility for compiling, and the fellows for auditing, the accounts, were all still in place. Of these features of the statutes, the College's regional affiliations were most central to its purpose. They followed Stapeldon's prescription almost precisely. The great majority of the fellows still came from Devon and Cornwall; and if, as a consequence of the appropriation of Wittenham in 1355, two fellows had since been drawn from the diocese of Salisbury, that too was in accordance with Stapeldon's wish that the augmentation of the College's resources from another diocese should lead to the augmentation of the fellowship from that diocese.[549] All this part of Stapeldon's legacy remained intact. If undergraduates were now also predominantly drawn from the west country, as the examples of Peter Courtenay and John Goldyng's pupil, Trethin, may suggest, that legacy would have been reinforced.

Behind these continuities lay the continuing role of the bishops of Exeter in the College's affairs, at least until Lacy's death in 1455. Stapeldon had bequeathed to his successors substantial powers of oversight. They were given the right to enquire into the maintenance of the statutes, to punish their neglect, to amend any deviation from them, and to supplement them when necessary.[550] In effect these powers made future bishops the guardians of the statutes, though there were naturally limits on the extent to which guardianship could be exercised at a distance. That Stapeldon's statutes were never fully revised or brought up to date, unlike the statutes of most of the early colleges, can only have been due to the conservative consciences of the bishops of Exeter. This too is likely to explain the appeal of the Rector and fellows to the pope in 1405 when they wanted to amend the statutes. The pope could give them what they almost certainly suspected that the bishop would be unwilling to concede.

But the bishops' conservatism was not unthinking, nor was their allegiance to Stapeldon's statutes only a matter of conscientious obligation, let alone mere sentiment. They viewed the college as a nursery of educated priests for their diocese (and here they were at one with Stapeldon himself) and as a guarantor of their regular supply. Changes to the statutes in the direction envisaged by the Rector and fellows might have impaired these functions.

---

[548] ECA, M. IV. 5; above, 148.   [549] *Reg. Stapeldon*, 304.   [550] *Reg. Stapeldon*, 308.

The progression to higher degrees in theology, the extension of the fellows' tenure of their fellowships, and the rise in the value of a benefice whose acceptance would necessitate departure from the College—desiderata set out in the College's petition to the pope—would all work together to prolong the holding of fellowships. Since the number of fellowships was fixed at fifteen, this was bound to reduce the number of priests returning to the diocese from the College. The anger of Bishop Lacy when the College apparently passed over fellowship candidates from his own diocese in favour of those from elsewhere exemplified the bishop's anxiety to maintain their number. His attitude was both principled and self-interested. Any alteration to, or over-riding of, the statutes might jeopardize the work of the church and its pastoral ministry within the diocese, for which the bishop was ultimately responsible and on which the salvation of so many souls was seen to depend.

Yet in the fifteenth century the changes desired by the fellows came about, gradually and undramatically, perhaps even surreptitiously, and certainly without any recorded reaction from the bishops, who in any case, and with the exception of Peter Courtenay, seem largely to have lost interest in the College after Lacy's death. By 1450 some fellows were proceeding to higher degrees in theology and some were holding their fellowships for more than the maximum of thirteen or fourteen years stipulated by Stapeldon. This was seemingly achieved by taking advantage of the concessions offered by the pope and without any explicit revision of the statutes. The new order was perhaps acceptable because the changes which it brought were on a small scale—only eleven fellows are known to have qualified in theology between 1405 and 1500—and did not fundamentally change the character of Exeter as an arts-only college. More significant was a related development: the election to fellowships of men who were already well advanced in their studies—in some cases bachelors or even *magistri* (if the word of Bishop Lacy can be relied on[551]), well beyond the level of those who were 'at least sufficient sophists' which Stapeldon had defined as the minimum qualification for election. All these developments had the effect of weighting the College towards a more senior body of rather older men, the sophists fewer and the *magistri* more numerous, and away from the young men's college of the fourteenth century.

Other changes would perhaps have been more obvious to a time-travelling fellow of Stapeldon's generation who came back in 1500. Most obvious would have been the expansion of the College site. On all sides except the north the College had expanded to reach virtually its modern boundaries, taking in two halls, Checker Hall and Peter Hall, which in Stapeldon's days had been independent institutions, and consigning others to the oblivion of garden

---

[551] *Reg. Lacy*, i. 61; above, 122.

and open space. Equally significant was another sort of expansion, but one linked to the first: the growth of the College's fringe membership of commoners, both senior boarders who were mature students, and undergraduates. The College now had the space to house these peripheral newcomers, whose presence both enlarged and diversified Stapeldon's foundation. In the long term, the gradual assumption of responsibility, by at least some of the fellows, for the teaching of the undergraduates would come to appear as perhaps the most portentous development of the period.

The roots of change were various and lay both outside and within the College. They were not, in the first place, political. Although Stapeldon himself had been at the heart of the country's political life in his generation, and Exeter owed much to the profits which he had accumulated in his political career, subsequent national events made almost no tangible impact on his foundation. If the dramatic political history of the later middle ages impinged, the College records fail to show it. The Hundred Years War, the Peasants' Revolt, the deposition of two kings, Richard II and Henry VI, and the Wars of the Roses, all appear to have passed the College by. Only in its regular payment of taxes to the king, frequently recorded in the accounts, did Exeter appear as part of the political community. Even the career of Wyclif, close to home and as much political as religious, left Exeter untouched in its wake. No doubt the affairs of the realm provided everyday subjects for conversation among the fellows; but it is hard to see how they affected the affairs of the College.

Much more pronounced as an external cause of change were the period's massive demographic and economic shifts. Occasional harvest crises, successive plagues, the waning of the population, the effects of population decline on prices and wages, and, in the mid fifteenth century, a shortage of currency formed the unpromising background to Exeter's late medieval history. Plague mortality in 1348–9 and in 1361 (and probably in other years) affected the fellowship directly, though empty places were soon filled, and the profusion of vacant benefices offered better prospects to the survivors, tempting some fellows in the 1350s and 1360s to exchange their fellowships for benefices after a relatively short tenure. But it was not only benefices that fell vacant. So too did Oxford properties, leading to the disappearance or reduction of rents, and, more positively, to the enlargement of the College site. The level of prices, whether for labour or for corn, was a greater cause for concern. In an era of high wages, the burden of payments to tilers, thatchers, building workers, and casual labour of all kinds, though difficult to measure statistically, is likely to have been heavy; while the price of corn was of vital interest to a College which drew some 80 to 90 per cent of its income from the sale of tithes. When the Rector and fellows petitioned for additional resources in 1477 or 1478, they blamed plague, 'the mortality of men', and the sterility of the land for their poverty.[552] The resulting acquisition of Menheniot was of special value because it gave them a fixed sum, £20 a year, leaving the vicar, and not the College, to make what profit he could from the sale of tithe corn on an uncertain market. The rents payable by commoners, particularly senior boarders, offered another, though minor, source of relief. In the case of undergraduates, the need for that relief in the 1420s may have been a prime motive for their introduction to the College.

Though Exeter enjoyed periods of relative affluence—the years around 1400 were one such period, the 1490s another—its resources were rarely sufficient to provide financial security. The Wittenham revenues gained in 1355 were soon eaten into by the harvest failure of 1369, the extended crisis of indebtedness which followed, and the long-terms trends in prices and wages already discussed. The Menheniot revenues gained in 1478, though they had a more visibly beneficial effect on the College's fortunes, were intended in the first place to ameliorate the desperate financial situation which had built up over the previous thirty years. When daily needs and inescapable expenses had been met, there was at no point much money left over for grand projects. Hence all the College's major building schemes and some of its property acquisitions depended heavily on donations from Rectors and fellows, former fellows, friends, and associates: the new stone-built library of 1383, the new room of 1397, Stafford's extension of the library and other works, Palmer's extension of the chapel and other works, the acquisition of Peyntour's Hall in 1478, and the building of the new kitchen in 1483, could none of them have been financed wholly, or even in most cases mainly, by the College. Exeter's physical transformation, an important aspect of the general changes of the period, owed almost everything to benefactors. They also stood behind the enormously expensive purchase of royal licences to alienate land in mortmain, the necessary preliminaries to new acquisitions, obtained from the crown in 1456 and 1478. The College was fortunate indeed in its friends.

If demographic and economic factors were among the main external drivers of change, the internal drive came mainly from the aspirations of the fellows themselves. These were manifested most clearly in the petition of 1405 to the pope—for a change in the College's name, fewer disputation exercises within the house, freedom to study theology, longer periods of fellowship residence beyond inception, and larger allowances for commons. Behind this petition lay not only narrow self-interest, but also a broader desire to bring the College into line with other colleges: to distinguish it more clearly from the unendowed halls, to end its anomalous position as an arts-only College, and to give those fellows who were so minded the chance to achieve the same sort of scholastic distinction and qualifications available to the fellows of other

[552] ECA, M. IV. 5.

colleges. Despite the changes which followed, the continuing predominance of the arts course, beyond which few fellows progressed, though they were now free to do so, meant that Exeter's alignment with other colleges was by no means complete. But the College nevertheless lost some of the singularity which had marked it out in earlier days. The admission of commoners, both senior boarders and undergraduates, and the declining role of the bishops of Exeter from the time of Lacy's death onwards, both contributed to this process; for the first was a change undergone by most colleges in the fifteenth century, while the second consigned the visitor to the peripheral position which he occupied, again, in most colleges. Closer integration with what was becoming a collegiate university was similarly fostered by the exceptionally high proportion of university offices which went to Exeter's fellows from 1420 onwards.[553] As time progressed, points of comparison with other colleges, rather than points of contrast, became the salient features of Exeter's corporate life.

Throughout the period, however, there was one constant which will have been evident at many points in the preceding pages. The tendency of the fellows of Exeter College to move back to benefices in the diocese of Exeter when their college days were over was even more marked in the fifteenth century than in the fourteenth. Between 1350 and 1400 the names of some 132 fellows are known. Of these, 3 became chancellors of Exeter cathedral, and 2 canons of Exeter; some 33 are known to have gone on to hold benefices in Devon and Cornwall, in some cases before or after service in other dioceses; and some 20 are known to have held benefices only in other dioceses. Between 1450 and 1500 the names of some 77 fellows are known (and the noticeable decline in numbers by comparison with the first fifty-year period was a mark of the rise in the number of years for which fellowships might now be held). Of the 77, one became sub-dean of Exeter and one a canon; 41 are known to have gone on to hold other benefices in Devon and Cornwall; and some 12 are known to have held benefices in other dioceses. The proportion of those holding west country benefices, either in the cathedral or in the diocese at large, amounted to 29 per cent of the total fellowship for the first period and 56 per cent for the second. But these are minimum figures only, and there are likely to have been some presentations to benefices which escaped the notice of the bishops' registrars in their compilation of the registers which are our main source. Through all the vicissitudes of the College's history between Stapeldon's death and the end of the fifteenth century, the Stapeldonian ideal of Oxford-educated west country men returning home to serve the churches of the west country was preserved intact.

---

[553] Cobban, 'Colleges and Halls', *HUO*, ii. 623; above, 93–4.

3

Prices and Princes

The Era of the Reformation, 1500–1560

I. TRENDS AND SOURCES

The sixteenth century saw changes in the dynamics of the university and the experiences of its members greater than those of any period since the formative years of the early thirteenth century.[1] They came from several directions. The most significant was the increased role of the state in the university's affairs, as, from Henry VIII's reign onwards, successive rulers sought to impose their contrasting religious programmes on a predominantly conservative and catholic body. For any college fellow the rapid shifts in religious policy were the most prominent and disconcerting feature of the local scene. But state intervention had a more positive role in encouraging a second change: the slow emergence of a humanist pattern of education, one beginning to move away from a formal syllabus still largely dominated by Aristotle and to give more weight to the literature of Greece and Rome. None of the Reformation monarchs lacked respect for learning and all saw virtue in the classics, whether as part of a broad education for the clergy or as a grounding in statecraft for the state's servants. This change interacted with another: the growth of the undergraduate body and of undergraduate teaching provided by the colleges. By the second half of the century that teaching was beginning to draw on classical literature, partly in response to a consumer demand which judged the classics at least as useful as the mental skills developed by Aristotelian learning for the careers in public life which many undergraduates were to follow.

State intervention, religious change, the growth of humanism, and the rise of the undergraduate were the points of departure in a landscape where much remained familiar. Neither the structure of the university nor the arts syllabus embodied in the statutes was radically changed in the sixteenth century. The

---

[1] This and the following paragraphs draw mainly on *HUO*, iii, chs. 1, 3, 4.1, and 10.

main structural change was incremental rather than innovatory. More colleges were founded (Brasenose, 1509; Corpus Christi, 1517; Cardinal College, later King Henry VIII's College, and later still, Christ Church, 1525, 1546; Trinity, 1555; St John's, 1557), and more halls disappeared, creating what has rightly been described as 'the collegiate university'.[2] At its foundation in 1314 Exeter was one of four colleges; at its refoundation by Sir William Petre in 1566 it was one of fifteen. For all these colleges the century which gave rise to a university of colleges was one of difficulty. The changes brought by the Reformation not only demanded a rapid internal response to external demands for the abandonment of familiar allegiances, but also at several points, most frighteningly in 1546, threatened the colleges with the fate of the monasteries: dissolution. The physical environment too was hostile. Plague and other epidemic diseases seem to have recurred more frequently than in the previous century, shutting down lectures and tutorials and causing fellows to scatter into the countryside, while rapid inflation, particularly in the 1540s, reduced the value of the fixed rents on which most colleges were dependent and raised the price of consumables.

If all colleges were affected by these changes, Exeter was especially vulnerable to their impact. Its endowment remained one of the smallest among the colleges and its constitution in some ways ill suited to meet new challenges. Annual rectorships disrupted continuity, weakened the Rector's authority, and risked internal division when unity was most necessary, while the College's traditional role as an arts-only college denied it the ballast and the counsel of the older and more experienced men reading for higher degrees who dominated other colleges such as Merton. Stapeldon's statutes, even though amended in 1405 to allow some graduates to read theology,[3] assumed a stable and static world which was far from the realities of the sixteenth century.

These are some of the themes to be pursued in this chapter. The basis for the study remains the accounts kept by the Rector, complete for the whole period save for a remarkably few missing years.[4] The accounts are slightly less detailed than their predecessors, but they continue to provide an invaluable record of fellows' names and activities and of the College economy. Then from about 1540 we have an equally valuable source in the College register, a book recording the business of the fellowship year by year which is in effect the first set of governing body minutes. Bought for 3s. 4d. as a blank book by Rector John French in 1541, but with a few retrospective entries going back to 1538, the register throws more light on the composition of the fellowship

---

[2] The sub-title of *HUO*, iii.   [3] Above, 95–7.
[4] The missing years are 1520–1, 1536–7, 1541–2, 1553–4, 1556–7, 1559–60, 1562–3.

and the organization and structure of the College than any earlier source.[5]
It records the annual election of the Rector every October; the fellows,
sojourners (i.e. senior boarders), and College officers for the year; the election
and admission of new fellows and the resignations of outgoing fellows; the
fellows' academic progress, whether determining as bachelors or incepting as
masters; and a miscellany of College business, including the leasing of property and the fellows' agreement to various rules and customs. The one College
group whom the register completely ignores are the undergraduates. And in
addition to accounts and register we can still draw on Boase's biographical
register of the College and a further volume of Emden's biographical register
for the university. When Emden terminates in 1540 we are much less well
informed about the careers of Oxford's and Exeter's graduates. Paradoxically
perhaps, as we move into the early modern period we begin to know less
about the formalities of these past lives than we already know about those of
the College's medieval fellows.

2. FELLOWS: ORIGINS, TENURE, AND CAREERS

Between 1501 and 1565, on the eve of the Petrean re-endowment of the
College, some 136 men were elected to fellowships at Exeter. The social origins
of almost all of them remain as obscure as those of their medieval predecessors.
Men from gentry families are perhaps more readily identifiable than in the
earlier period. Richard Tremayne (fellow, 1553, 1559–60), for example, was
the fourth of the eight sons of Thomas Tremayne, whose fine house still largely
survives at Collacombe, near Tavistock, and whose family is commemorated
with an elaborate monument in nearby Lamerton church.[6] Another from the
same background was Thomas Fortescue (1557–9, 1561–9), one of the six sons
of Lewis Fortescue of Fallapit, baron of the exchequer, and prominent member
of a landed family from East Allington, near Kingsbridge, in south Devon.[7]
Others from similar backgrounds include Richard Fountayne (1556–9),
Thomas Kempthorne (1557–60), William Pollard (1559–65), and Edward
Risdon (1561–4), three of them from Devon and the fourth from Cornwall.[8]
If there seem to be more such gentry sons among the sixteenth-century fellows
than among those of the previous two centuries, this may be partly due to an
expansion of the sources which record them, notably the heralds' visitations.[9]

---

[5] RA, 234/2. The register is ECA, A. I. 5, hereafter cited as 'Reg.'. It terminates in 1639.

[6] Boase (2), 67; J. Prince, *Danmonii Orientales Illustres: The Worthies of Devon*, new edn.
(London, 1810), 739–42; K. R. Bartlett, 'Edmund Tremayne', *ODNB*; Cherry and Pevsner,
Devon, 277–8, 530.

[7] Boase (2), 69–70; W. G. Hoskins, *Devon* (London, 1954), 318; M. Steggle, 'Thomas Fortescue', *ODNB*; Cherry and Pevsner, *Devon*, 346. Fortescue is the only fellow of Exeter whose
claim to fame is given in the *ODNB* as 'translator and alleged sorcerer'.

[8] Boase (2), 69, 70, 71.

[9] Cf. J. L. Vivian, *The Visitations of the County of Devon: Comprising the Heralds' Visitations
of 1531, 1564 and 1620* (Exeter, 1889–95).

Other fellows came from the leading burgess families of the city of Exeter. The father of William Peryam (1551) was a prominent Exeter merchant, twice mayor, while William's brother John, a later benefactor of the College, was also mayor of Exeter.[10] Hercules Ameridith (1551–3) was the second son of Griffith Ameridith, a Welsh émigré settled in Exeter, who became a leading draper in the city and later its MP.[11] Much more difficult to trace are the origins of fellows, perhaps the majority, who came from yeoman families in the countryside or from small-town society. If the surname of William Shepreve (1559–65, 1566–8) is indicative of his ancestry, at least one of his sheep-reeve forefathers may have been no more than a minor manorial official.[12] In general, it is hardly possible to go beyond the banal: a fairly large proportion of Exeter's fellows are likely to have come from gentry families, a larger proportion from lesser and middling families in town and country, and some from the leading families in the west country's largest town. No fellow is known to have come from the nobility. In all this the College's social composition probably did not differ much from that of its medieval precursor.

We know hardly more about how men came by their fellowships than we know about their social origins. Only one source throws any light on their education. In a letter written to Sir William Petre in 1565, John Neale, then Rector, appealed for Petre's help in restoring the former school at Week St Mary in north-east Cornwall. Not only had he been educated there, he said, but so had 'many hundreds of Devon and Cornish men and always a ready (and now a needful) nursery for Exeter College'. The school at Week, famous in its day, had been founded in 1506 by Lady Thomasine Percival, a native of the place and widow of a wealthy London merchant. A very popular establishment, providing boarding places and a free education in grammar both for the sons of the gentry and for others further down the social scale, it had lasted until the Edwardian Reformation of the 1540s and had evidently served as a feeder for the College—perhaps the school of many west country fellows besides Neale.[13] But all others come into view only after their schooldays. Some came to Exeter from other colleges or halls. John Babbe had been an undergraduate at Oriel and St Mary's Hall before he secured a fellowship at Exeter in 1559.[14] Occasionally one of Exeter's own sojourners, his qualities presumably well known to the College, might be promoted to a fellowship.

---

[10] Boase (2), 66; W. T. MacCaffrey, *Exeter, 1540–1640* (Cambridge, Mass., 1958), 80, 150, 214, 258.

[11] Boase (2), 67; MacCaffrey, *Exeter*, 212, 257–60; S. T. Bindoff, *The House of Commons, 1509–1558*, 3 vols. (London, 1982), i. 317–18.

[12] Boase (2), 70.

[13] ERO, D/DP Q13/1/1, letter of John Neale to Sir William Petre, 22 August 1565; Orme, *Education in the West of England*, 173–82; below, 268.

[14] Boase (2), 70.

Richard Tremayne, a sojourner in 1552, was elected to a fellowship in 1553, when he was already a bachelor.[15] Sometimes an influential outsider might put forward a candidate, not always successfully. Hugh Oldham, bishop of Exeter from 1505 to 1519, is said by John Hooker, historian of Exeter city, to have nominated one Simon Atkins for a fellowship, only to see him turned down by the College, to Oldham's chagrin (and Atkins's probable gain as a later fellow of the more distinguished and wealthy Corpus Christi College).[16] There was thus no single route to a fellowship, and qualified men came in from different directions.

We know much more about the formal steps by which a fellowship was secured, thanks to the existence of the register which records them. Progress towards a full fellowship came in three stages—election, admission, and confirmation after a probationary year. Elections might be held at any point in the year and usually took place soon after a fellowship had fallen vacant, either by resignation or, much more rarely, by death. Admission to commons, giving the new fellow the right to board and lodging, normally followed within a few days or, at most, weeks. When John Peter resigned on 6 March 1542, after having held his fellowship since 1538, the fellows waited only a day before electing his successor, John Whetcombe, on 7 March. Whetcombe was then admitted to commons on 8 April.[17] We have the impression that there was often someone waiting in the wings for a fellowship to fall vacant and that candidates had sometimes been lined up in advance of any vacancy. The fellow's oath, its terms laid down in Stapeldon's statutes, would be taken at the time of admission. About twelve months later, having completed his probationary year, the probationer fellow would normally be confirmed in his fellowship. Robert Taynter, for example, was elected on 4 December 1544, admitted to commons on 3 January 1545, and confirmed as a full fellow, with the assent of the majority of the fellows, on 5 January 1546.[18] It was at this final stage that the probationer was vulnerable to challenge. When William Shepreve was confirmed as fellow on 16 November 1560 it was 'because none of the fellows opposed him on the grounds of character or moral conduct': so it was clearly possible to be voted down on those grounds.[19] Resignations, usually to take up a living, were similarly hedged about with formalities, and entailed the explicit renunciation of all the rights vested in the former fellowship and the surrender of the fellow's keys.[20] All these ceremonies took place in the chapel and in the presence of the Rector and other fellows. The same procedures had almost certainly been followed since the early days of the

[15] Reg., 52, 55; Boase, 67.
[16] Prince, *Worthies of Devon*, 600; N. Orme, 'Hugh Oldham', *ODNB*; *BRUO, 1501–40*, 16–17.
[17] Reg., 26.   [18] Reg., 39, 41.   [19] Reg., 75.
[20] e.g. William Peryam, 1551 (Reg., 55), Reginald Daniel, 1556 (Reg., 61).

College, but it is only with the inauguration of the register in the mid sixteenth century that they become fully visible.

A more dynamic investigation of Exeter's fellowship must follow a trail whose course is set by numbers and by the issues arising from numbers: the fellows' length of tenure, the changing pattern of their careers, and the changing balance within the College between undergraduate fellows, bachelors, and *magistri*. Statistical though much of the evidence is, it illuminates in a more humane way some interesting developments in social and academic history. There is broad agreement among historians that the numbers attending the university in the sixteenth century were far from stable. They peaked in the 1520s, began to drop increasingly rapidly from the 1530s, and reached their nadir in the 1540s and early 1550s, before beginning to climb again from the mid 1550s and much more markedly from the 1560s.[21] As early as 1523 there were minor lamentations about falling numbers,[22] but it was only in the 1530s that the trend became noticeable. One cause was the dissolution of the monasteries. Not only did this bring about the disappearance of student monks and friars from Oxford (with consequences even for a secular college such as Exeter[23]), but it also discouraged laymen from coming forward for university places. Under the year 1539 Anthony Wood, the seventeenth-century historian of the university, wrote: 'Few there were, whether doctors, masters or bachelors, that commenced in these times, and fewer there were that now encouraged the taking of degrees. Those of a religious profession were accounted a scorn to most people...and the academians themselves, who expected also to be dissolved, laid under a scandalous censure.'[24] The subsequent progress of the Reformation worked to depress numbers still further, since it meant that the church 'no longer appeared to offer a safe and lucrative career to university graduates'.[25] In addition, the rise in prices, already given as an explanation of falling numbers in the 1520s but much more pronounced twenty years later, almost certainly acted as a deterrent by raising the cost of a university education. It was Wood again, writing under the years 1551–2, at the height of the country's religious upheavals, who remarked that 'the scholars were reduced to an inconsiderable number in respect of former times...Others would not go to the expense or charge of a degree, because all their hopes of preferment were blasted.'[26] The symbiotic relationship

[21] L. Stone, 'The Size and Composition of the Oxford Student Body, 1580–1910', in L. Stone (ed.), *The University and Society*. Vol. I: *Oxford and Cambridge from the 14th to the Early 19th Century* (London, 1974), 6, 16, 82, 91; C. Cross, 'Oxford and the Tudor State', *HUO*, iii. 148; J. McConica, 'Studies and Faculties: Introduction', *HUO*, iii. 152–5; J. M. Fletcher, 'The Faculty of Arts', *HUO*, iii. 162–3.
[22] *Epistolae academicae, 1508–1596*, ed. W. T. Mitchell, OHS, new ser., xxvi (1980), 148–51.
[23] Below, 229–30.   [24] Wood, *Annals*, ii. 68.
[25] Cross, 'Oxford and the Tudor State', *HUO*, iii. 141.
[26] Wood, *Annals*, ii. 110, 113–14. For the price rise, see below, 195–6.

between church and university, which had sustained both since the university's foundation, was in danger of falling apart.

The history of Exeter's fellowship exemplifies these general trends. Over the period as a whole the College generally retained a full house of fifteen fellows. But in the 1540s, and still more so in the early 1550s, fellowships became difficult to fill. The October roll-call of fellows set down annually in the register records only 14 fellows in 1542 and 1546, 13 in 1551, 11 in 1552, 13 in 1553, and 14 in 1554. Only in 1555 did numbers rise again to 15.[27] Occasional comments in the register show something of the problems underlying the figures. When Robert Taynter resigned his fellowship in 1546 'no one in the university was found capable of succeeding him'.[28] When another fellow, John Bonetto, died on 2 July 1551, 'no suitable scholar from Cornwall could be found to be elected in his place'.[29] The tight regional restrictions on the College's fellowships evidently created an additional hindrance to their filling. Even as late as 1563–4 the two fellowships vacated by Henry Chichester and Edward Risdon lay unfilled for some time.[30]

One symptom of declining numbers, and a cause of the difficulty in filling fellowships, was the rapid turnover among the College's fellows. They came and went with increasing rapidity. A crude pointer in this direction lies in the contrast between our 136 fellows elected between 1501 and 1565, and the mere 106 elected in the previous sixty-five-year period from 1435 to 1500.[31] The decade-by-decade figures for the duration of fellowships in the sixteenth century provide a more refined guide to trends, but one which points firmly in the same direction. As we have seen, the average duration of a fellowship for those elected between 1420 and 1500 had been 10 years,[32] and that for the new century's first decade from 1501 to 1510 hardly differed at 9.8 years. After a downward swing to 7.5 years between 1511 and 1520, it rose again to 8.9 years for those elected between 1521 and 1530. Thereafter it fell. The tenure of those elected in the 1530s averaged 7.2 years; in the 1540s, 5.9 years; and in the 1550s, 4.7 years. In a predictable and related way the last two decades saw exceptional numbers of elections to fellowships. Between 1501 and 1510 there had been only fourteen elections, but there were twenty between 1541 and 1550, and thirty-six between 1551 and 1560. The increasing rate of turnover in the 1540s and 1550s was remarkable. About 50 per cent of the fellows held their fellowships for four years or less. Some came and went within a year. John Fessarde, elected in December 1543 and admitted in January 1544, vacated his fellowship in the year of his admission. William

---

[27] Reg., 28, 41, 55, 57, 59, 60, 61.   [28] Reg., 41; Boase (2), 65.
[29] Reg., 54; Boase (2), 66.   [30] Reg., 80, 81, 82.
[31] The statistics in this and the following paragraphs are derived from information provided by Boase (2), *BRUO, 1501–40*, and Reg.
[32] Above, 92.

Peryam, later to make a name for himself as a judge and chief baron of Queen Elizabeth's exchequer, was elected in April 1551 but resigned in October. The record for brevity of tenure was held by George Fitz, who was elected on 10 June 1556 but resigned on the same day.[33] For these men and others like them the world evidently held out some more enticing prospect than the holding of a College fellowship.

For some, this might be the traditional prospect of a living. Fessarde, for example, left his fellowship in 1544 to become vicar of Tisbury in Wiltshire, a particularly rich living which he held for the next twenty-two years.[34] But another and still more interesting set of statistics points to the declining attractions of a clerical career, in exactly the way posited by Anthony Wood. Between 1501 and 1510 the great majority of the College's fellows—85.7 per cent—moved on to benefices. But thereafter a downward trend sets in. After a fall to 71 per cent between 1521 and 1530, the proportion dropped very sharply to 47 per cent in the 1530s, to 35 per cent in the 1540s, and to 33 per cent in the 1550s. These figures need to be treated with caution. Bishops' registers in the sixteenth century are notoriously thin and may not record all institutions to benefices; and when Emden's *Biographical Register* terminates in 1540 we are dependent on Boase for information on benefices, and his search of the registers was less thorough than Emden's. But it is Emden's data, not that of Boase, which already shows the decisive decline in the number of fellows taking up benefices in the 1530s. All in all, the trend seems clear enough.

These figures confirm the radical upset to career patterns brought by the Reformation. For this there were many particular causes, among them the limitations imposed by the Pluralities Act of 1529 on the holding of multiple benefices, the dissolution of many collegiate foundations under Edward VI, and the widespread and growing lay contempt for the clergy.[35] The possibilities for both social respect and standing and for material advancement within the church were diminishing. What then were the alternatives to clerical employment open to the departing fellows of Exeter? There are some pointers to help us answer this question. A handful of fellows left to follow a legal career, via a training at the Inns of Court. On resigning his fellowship, William Peryam went first to Clifford's Inn and then to the Middle Temple; George Fitz, the one-day fellow of 1556, may have gone to the Inner Temple; and William Pollard was already at the Inner Temple in 1565, when his prolonged absence from the College cost him his fellowship.[36] The numbers

[33] Boase (2), 64, 66, 68–9; *BRUO, 1501–40*, 204.   [34] *BRUO, 1501–40*, 204.
[35] R. O'Day, 'The Reformation of the Ministry, 1558–1642', in R. O'Day and F. Heal (eds.), *Continuity and Change: Personnel and Administration of the Church in England, 1500–1642* (Leicester, 1976), 56.
[36] Boase (2), 66, 69, 70; J. A. Hamilton, rev. D. Ibbetson, 'William Peryam', *ODNB*.

here are very small, but before the crisis years of the 1550s they are non-
existent; and the trend towards law was a general one, not confined to Exeter
alone.[37] A different sort of legal training was provided by the baccalaureate in
civil law. Four of those elected between 1551 and 1560 went on to read for the
BCL after graduating in arts—Richard Reede, Hercules Ameridith, Richard
Braye, and William Paynter.[38] As far as can be seen, no Exeter fellow had
previously taken this degree, which opened the way to a career in diplomacy,
the civil service, and the ecclesiastical courts.[39] A similarly practical choice
was made by those fellows who went on to read for higher degrees in
medicine. In the fifteenth century only three men had made that choice, but
between 1520 and 1550 six fellows followed the same course, though not all
did so during the period of their fellowships. A degree in medicine was
entirely compatible with a clerical career. John Dotyn, fellow from 1528 to
1539, Rector in his final two years, bachelor of medicine in 1534, doctor in
1559, and Exeter's most prominent medical man, ended his days as parish
priest of Kingsdon in Somerset. But for most of its possessors a medical
degree provided alternative openings to those available in the church.[40]

The decline in numbers attending the university, the rapid turnover of
fellows and the relative brevity of their time in College, and the waning
popularity of a clerical career, were all parts of a congeries of changes which
affected Exeter in the mid century decades and which sprang ultimately from
the demoralizing and switchback progress of the Reformation. Instability
within the church bred instability within the College, threatening the continuity and corporate life of the fellowship as elections and resignations
followed in quick succession. These developments had a marked effect on
the structure of the fellowship and the balance within it between undergraduates, bachelors, and *magistri*. Until about 1530 a remarkably high proportion
of those elected to fellowships went on to incept as masters: a minimum of
92.9 per cent of those elected between 1501 and 1510, 81.2 per cent from the
cohort of 1511 to 1520, and 90 per cent from that of 1521 to 1530. But in the
1530s and 1540s only about 70 per cent of those elected proceeded to
inception, and this figure dropped sharply to 41.7 per cent in the 1550s.
Given what we know about the high turnover of fellows from the 1530s
onwards, this is what we might expect: the paucity of *magistri* was an
inevitable consequence of the growing number of early departures from the
College. This was a general phenomenon, not confined to Exeter, as Wood
again noted when, under the year 1556, he recorded 'a great scarcity of

[37] O'Day, 'The Reformation of the Ministry', 57.   [38] Boase (2), 66, 67, 70, 71.
[39] J. Barton, 'The Faculty of Law', *HUO*, iii. 271, 281.
[40] Boase (2), 58; *BRUO, 1501–40*, 173; G. Lewis, 'The Faculty of Medicine', *HUO*, iii. 213,
250–2. For Dotyn's medical books, see below, 210–11.

masters in the university'.[41] But it had its own special impact on Exeter. In 1560, a year when only two of the College's fourteen fellows were *magistri*, a mere bachelor, John Neale, was elected Rector, 'such was the scarcity of masters'. We have to go back to the election of the bachelor Robert Trethewey in the years of demographic crisis after the Black Death to find a parallel.[42]

A second and related structural change became evident about the same time. In the early years of the century undergraduates, often still some way from BA status, were quite frequently elected to fellowships, sometimes in greater numbers than the bachelors who also came forward for election. This was as Stapeldon had intended. But from the 1520s a change is perceptible. Of the twenty-one fellows elected in that decade, three were already masters, ten were already bachelors, and of the eight undergraduates elected several were on the verge of determining as bachelors. William Cholwell, for example, was admitted to his fellowship on 15 February 1527 and admitted by the university as bachelor on 27 February, determining in the same term.[43] The same trend was still more evident in the 1530s, when the majority of those elected— ten out of seventeen—were already bachelors and almost all the seven undergraduates elected were only a few weeks, or at most months, away from achieving their bachelor's degree. It is impossible to account for this trend with any certainty. But one plausible conclusion might be that there was a dearth of early-stage undergraduates seeking election, reflecting the general decline in numbers coming to the university and causing the College to look to the ranks of advanced undergraduates and bachelors for its new fellows. Whatever the explanation may be for this pattern of elections, the effect was to increase the proportion of bachelors among the fellows. Of Exeter's fifteen fellows in 1535, one was an undergraduate, five were bachelors, and ten were masters. Of the fifteen in 1539, one was an undergraduate, seven were bachelors, and seven were masters. For the first thirty years of the century the masters among the fellows had consistently and substantially outnumbered the bachelors—by eleven to four, for example, in 1510, by nine to three in 1530. Now this was no longer the case.

This 'rise of the bachelors', temporary though it proved to be, caused tensions within the College which are revealed for us in a remarkable document drawn up on 21 December 1539 and later entered into the new College register.[44] Drafted by the Rector, John French, it drew on both the advice of the fellows and the recollections of former members of the College (*alumni*)— men now, so French said, 80 years old. It is set out as a statement of College

---

[41] Wood, *History*, ii. 133.   [42] Reg., 75; Boase (2), 68; above, 72.

[43] *BRUO, 1501–40*, 116.

[44] Reg., 31–5, printed in Boase (1), 182–4. Boase (2), lxxiii–lxxxi, provides a summary translation, and Southern, *VCH Oxfordshire*, iii. 109, a brief comment.

customs directed against 'the insolence of the bachelors (*bachalaureorum insolentia*)' and 'the affronts of the young (*iuventus contumelia*)' towards the Rector; and its preface suggests that it was intended to provide rules of conduct for the College's contumacious juniors in order to restore peace and good order to a society riven by disputes.

In signalling the tensions between the senior *magistri* and the junior bachelors, the text provides some lively glimpses of College life, especially in matters of dress and general conduct. Its directions are peremptory. All fellows are to wear black boots and to dress like priests, forswearing shirts parted down to the navel, dangling and protruding folds of cloth, and plaited collars, of the sort worn by courtiers. In chapel, the bachelors and *scolastici* (the undergraduate fellows) are to avoid noise, storytelling, profane literature, and indecorous manners, attending rather to their prayers, leaving their heads uncovered, and standing to join in the singing of the canticles. The bachelors are to come early to chapel, so as not to hold up the celebration of the mass. They are to frequent the College library, studying there every evening from 6 p.m. to 8 p.m. from early October until just before Lent, and they must attend lectures, disputations, and other academic exercises. They must respect the *magistri* and not be too familiar with them; and it was another point of division, and a mark of hierarchy noted in the text, that most of the *magistri* were in priests' orders, unlike the bachelors. Bachelors eating with the Rector must do so with heads uncovered, and until they had taken the master's degree they should wear gowns reaching to their knees. Other prescriptions applied more generally. No one should rise from the table before the Rector has said grace or take anything from the buttery without the permission of those in charge; and all must wear the dress appropriate to their degrees at university sermons and theological disputations.

The Rector's 'manifesto'[45] suggests that his position and that of the other *magistri* was under threat from the disrespectful behaviour of a group of young bloods. French had been Rector for less than two months when his manifesto was drafted, and his authority was weakened, like that of all the College's early Rectors, by his one-year term of office. He paints a picture of a College where the bachelors were not only at odds with those in authority but also with the seemly and decorous traditions of the College itself—dressing like courtiers, treating the chapel like a common room, neglecting their studies, and ignoring the customs of the dinner table. What lay behind all this is unclear. But the empowerment of the bachelors by their rise to numerical parity with the *magistri*, at seven a side in 1539, must have been one factor.

Yet there may well have been more to it than this. Four men in particular were the probable ringleaders among the bachelors: William More (admitted

---

[45] Southern's word: *VCH Oxfordshire*, iii. 109.

fellow, October 1537; BA, February 1538); John Tremayne (admitted, October 1537; BA, February 1538); Robert Yendall (BA, February 1538; admitted,
April 1538); and Thomas Nanconan (BA, May 1538; admitted, May 1538).[46]
All four were readmitted to commons in late September or early October
1538, evidently after a period of suspension, the usual punishment for some
delinquency; and this, together with their status as newly fledged bachelors in
1539, strongly suggests that they were the target of the Rector's outburst.
Behind their behaviour there may have lain more than a desire to taunt and
ridicule authority, for religion too may have been an issue. Both within and
without the university numbers of the rebellious young were taking up the
new cause of protestantism at this time, and Dr Susan Brigden has noted that
'it was usually the undergraduates and younger dons who were won to the
new faith, to the alarm of elder dons'.[47] There are some clear hints that this
was the case at Exeter. The bachelors' lack of respect for the mass and for the
general sanctity of the chapel is especially suggestive. So too is the much later
role of one of the four, William More, as a committed protestant, whose
continuance in office as Rector was to be imposed on the College by the royal
visitation of 1549 and who lost office at the accession of the catholic Queen
Mary.[48] The probable family connections of another of the four, John Tremayne, point in a similar direction. He was almost certainly the brother of
Richard Tremayne, elected fellow in 1553, who is known to have had a twin
brother of that name. Both were members of a strongly anti-catholic family
and Richard Tremayne in particular was a protestant zealot, who fled to
Germany at Mary's accession.[49] And was the argument of French's manifesto,
which cited at length from the Old Testament and the Pauline epistles, an
attempt to controvert the protestant young through the use of the scriptures
by which they might have been expected to set such store?

Yet the prominence and weight of the College's bachelors did not last much
beyond this episode. In place of the bachelors and the undergraduates on
the point of determining as bachelors who had dominated elections in the
late 1530s, the College was by the 1540s electing more junior figures. Of
the twenty elections of that decade, fifteen were of undergraduates and only
five of bachelors; and most of the undergraduates were elected at a relatively
early stage in their careers, well before they qualified as bachelors. This trend
became even more pronounced in the disturbed decade of the 1550s, when
undergraduates were elected in thirty out of thirty-six elections. We have

[46] RA, 231/4; Boase, 61. In commenting on those readmitted to commons Boase overlooks
More.
[47] S. Brigden, 'Youth and the English Reformation', Past and Present, 95 (1982), 41–2.
Cf. J. Loach, 'Reformation Controversies', HUO, iii. 366–7.
[48] Reg., 50; Boase (2), 61; below, 234–5, 238.
[49] Prince, Worthies of Devon, 740; Boase (2), 61, 67; C. H. Garrett, The Marian Exiles
(Cambridge, 1938), 309–12; below, 238.

already seen that in the 1550s fewer than half of the College's bachelors went on to incept as masters,[50] and it must also be the case that the pool of external bachelors from whom the College might normally have been expected to recruit fellows was also shrinking, forcing the College to elect undergraduates still in mid course and aggravating the shortage of *magistri*. It had always been the case that many students left the university after taking the BA; at least at Exeter, the early decades of the sixteenth century, when an unusually high proportion of bachelors stayed on to incept as masters, had been the exception. But in the century's middle decades the turmoil in the church, and—perhaps equally important—the rapidly rising costs of a university education as inflation took hold, meant that more graduates were content with the bachelor's degree and lacked the incentive to go further.

The first three decades of the sixteenth century, prior to the religious changes of the 1530s, had been times of relative stability for Exeter's fellows. The *magistri* had been preponderant among them, they had held their fellowships for moderately lengthy periods of eight or nine years, and most had gone on to take up benefices in the time-honoured way. But from the early 1530s stability began to give way to flux and change. Fellows came and went more rapidly, periods of tenure diminished, fewer fellows went on to benefices, fewer proceeded to the MA, the number of resident masters diminished, and the fellowship was increasingly drawn, not from existing bachelors, but from undergraduates. These developments were most pronounced in the 1550s, marked as that decade was by violent spasms of religious change. Behind them all lay a fall-off in the university's population. Its fundamental cause lay in the receding prospects of a settled clerical career which the possession of a university degree had formerly seemed to guarantee. That these were also years when prices were rising rapidly meant that for many men the investment of time and money needed for the protracted progress through the arts course no longer seemed worthwhile.

   In all these fields Exeter's experiences exemplified general trends. Changes in the crown's religious policies, the uncertain outlook for the clergy, and falling numbers posed problems which affected all colleges. But in Exeter's case these problems were exacerbated by the College's relative poverty: a subject to which we now turn.

3. THE COLLEGE: FINANCES

Despite its large accession of property in the late fifteenth century Exeter remained a poor college until it was rescued from penury by Sir William Petre

---

[50] Above, 187.

in the mid 1560s. For the first half of the sixteenth century we can compare the wealth of the colleges in four different years and in each of the four years Exeter is among the least wealthy. Table 2 shows this. All figures are in pounds, rounded to the nearest pound, except for those in the third column, which are given in pounds, shillings, and pence. 'K. H. VIII' is King Henry VIII's College, later Christ Church.

These figures consistently place Exeter among the three poorest colleges in Oxford, in three out of four years in company with Balliol and University College. The various valuations and assessments suggest that its income was about 9 per cent of that of the university's wealthiest college, either Magdalen or New College. Besides those skyscrapers of affluence Exeter's little tower hardly rose above the horizon. Almost all its income derived from sources which were already in place at the start of the century. Of these, the three churches of Gwinear, Wittenham, and Menheniot were by far the most important. According to the valuations of 1535 and 1546, both of which list and value individual revenue streams, they yielded £71 19s. 4d., or 87 per cent of total revenue, in the former year, and £71 11s. 4d. in 1546, again

TABLE 2. Comparative wealth of the colleges

1522		1535		1536		1546	
New Coll.	336	Magd.	1232	Magd.	3. 1. 10	Magd.	1068
Magd.	330	New Coll.	969	New Coll.	2. 11. 4	New Coll.	910
All Souls	200	K. H. VIII	812	K. H. VIII	2. 0. 10	All Souls	433
Merton	133	Corpus	453	All Souls	1. 2. 9	Corpus	429
Corpus	133	All Souls	432	Corpus	1. 2. 2	Merton	311
Lincoln	100	Merton	398	Merton	1. 0. 5	Queen's	185
Oriel	100	Queen's	339	Queen's	0. 17. 6	BNC	183
Univ.	50	Oriel	183	Oriel	0. 8. 9	Oriel	177
Exeter	40	BNC	131	BNC	0. 6. 5	Lincoln	161
Queen's	40	Lincoln	121	Lincoln	0. 5. 10	Balliol	87
		Balliol	86	Exeter	0. 4. 8	Exeter	82
		Univ.	86	Univ.	0. 4. 1	Univ.	77
		Exeter	83	Balliol	0. 4. 1		

Column 1: 1522. Grants made by colleges and other institutions for the recovery of the king's lands in France: *L. and P.*, III. ii. 1048.

Column 2: 1535. Income of monasteries and colleges. Figures for gross income, before deductions: *Valor*, ii. 243–86.

Column 3: 1536. Assessed college contributions towards the stipend of King Henry VIII's lecturer in theology: *SA*, 339; *HUO*, iii. 559.

Column 4: 1546. Valuation of college incomes made for the chantry commissioners: TNA, E 315/441, fos. 11^r, 15^v, 31^r, 44^v, 60^r, 73, 80^r, 86^v, 93^r, 100^v, 113^v, 106^r.

87 per cent, in 1546. The remaining income came largely from Oxford city properties, valued at £7 4s. 8d. net (including Hart Hall) in 1535 and £6 15s. net (excluding Hart Hall) in 1546. The annual rents of 40s. from Clifton Ferry and 31s. from the small estate at Benson made up most of the remainder.[51]

The two valuations of 1535 and 1546 provide no more than approximate guides to the College's income. They record only regular income from external properties, so omitting incidental and irregular profits from room rents, sales, and gifts and legacies. As a proportion of total income the percentage figures for the three churches just given are therefore too high, perhaps by about 5 to 10 per cent. The Rector's accounts provide a more, though not wholly, accurate guide. They show an average cash income of some £88 from 1501 to c.1540, rising from an average of £79 a year in the century's first decade to about £95 a year in the 1530s. The revenues from the three churches contributed just over 70 per cent of these totals, Oxford properties about 4 to 5 per cent, and room rents about 4 per cent. In many years income was boosted by substantial withdrawals from the reserves in the College chest.

On the expenses side, the greatest and most regular outlay was on the fellows' commons and allowances, as it had always been. The valor of 1535 estimated these at £53 15s. and that of 1546, at £53 4s. 2d., or about 65 per cent of total revenue in both years: a proportion roughly corroborated by the accounts. As inflation took hold from the 1520s onwards the amount spent on commons was supplemented by additional payments which raised College spending on food and drink by large sums.[52] Other expenses were very miscellaneous, again as always. Repairs to buildings formed their largest component, but they also included servants' wages, chapel costs, purchase of kitchen equipment, and the entertainment of visitors.

The College's general financial position fluctuated. Broadly speaking, it maintained a fair degree of financial stability until the early 1530s, after which it encountered a long stretch of rough, and sometimes extremely rough, water which lasted until the Petrean refoundation in 1566. Even at the century's opening, with revenues coming in from the new properties acquired in the 1470s and 1480s, and before the price rise, there were lean times. The accounts show deficits in six out of ten years between 1501 and 1510, and subventions from the common chest in five years. But there was a slow recovery between 1511 and 1520, and a more marked rise in the next decade. The receipts of £103 in 1521–2 were the largest since the turn of the century.[53] Expenditure on the College feast, always a gauge of prosperity, averaged an annual £1 11s. between 1501 and 1510, rising to £1 14s. between 1511 and 1520, and then rising again to £2 18s. in the 1520s. In 1529 it reached an unprecedented £3 12s.

---

[51] *Valor*, ii. 268–9; TNA, E 315/441, fos. 113ʳ–113ᵛ.   [52] Below, 196.   [53] RA, 215.

9d.[54] Even allowing for inflation, the figures for the feast suggest that, despite its relative poverty, the College could do more than keep up with rising prices.

Signs of difficulty became much more evident in the 1530s. Four years showed a deficit,[55] and, if the 'long' decade expands to take in 1540, in four years, too, monies were taken from the common chest, to the large total of £36 9s. 4d.[56] Expenditure on the feast reached a new peak of £3 18s. 2d. in 1530, then declined;[57] and in 1534 and 1535, both years in which money was withdrawn from the chest, there was no feast. This was hardship indeed. In the autumn term of 1536, College silver was sold for £16, the largest single item among that year's receipts.[58] Some of the immediate pressures behind these expedients are directly deducible from the accounts. To some extent they resulted from what might be regarded as prudent investments. Such, for example, were the purchase of a house in Cat Street for £8 in 1531 and the construction of new rooms in College costing just over £8 in 1533, both likely to bring in a future rent income.[59] Other causes point to weaknesses within the College. The account for winter term 1531, showing a deficit of £7 9s., is followed by a list of debts owing to the College and totalling £44 11s. 11d., about half a year's income. Substantial sums were owing from Gwinear (£13 6s. 8d.) and Menheniot (£10), and lesser ones from a number of named individuals, including the manciple (£37 9s. 1d.) and three of the College's sojourners.[60] It cannot have helped that in 1533 the Rector, John Pekyns, was accused in a marginal note on his account of having doctored the account to show the year's receipts as £12 1s. 6d. less than the money he had received, fraudulently and presumably to his own profit.[61] Contributing to the College's problems was management that was both inefficient and perhaps corrupt.

The 1540s showed a similar but perhaps more intense pattern of difficulties. Although no year produced a deficit, in four years surpluses were only achieved through withdrawals from the common chest. In 1543 these are said to have been made for the expenses of building and commons, and in 1544 for commons and other necessities, suggesting that reserves were now being used to subsidize routine expenditure.[62] Between 1542 and 1550 there were nine such withdrawals from the chest, totalling £83 13s. 2d: a depletion larger and more concentrated than any other in the century. As in the 1530s, the problem partly lay in the volume of unpaid debts owing to the College.

<hr/>

[54] RA, 223/2.
[55] 1531–2, 1532–3, 1536–7 (roll missing but deficit recorded in next roll), 1537–8: RA, 226, 227, 231.
[56] 1533, 1534, 1535, 1540: RA, 227/2, 228/2, 230/2, 232/2, 234/1.   [57] RA, 224/2.
[58] RA, 230/3.   [59] RA, 224/3, 227/3; below, 196–7, for Cat Street.
[60] RA, 225/1; Boase (2), 60.   [61] RA, 235/2, 237/1.   [62] RA, 235/2, 237/1.

A list of arrears and debts drawn up in October 1543 shows debts amounting to £33 5s. 4d., including £10 12s. owed by John Pekyns, the miscreant Rector of 1533. Arrears amounted to £16 7s. 3d., mainly owed by the College's sojourners for room rents, but including £10 for Menheniot, and £2 6s., until 1539 a year's rent, from Hart Hall.[63] Some of these debts, but by no means all, were partly paid off in the following term. Building expenses, particularly heavy in this decade, added to the College's financial troubles. In the winter term of 1542 they totalled £12 10s. 9d., nearly 12 per cent of the total expenditure for the year. £2 14s. 4d. was spent on repairs to the College's house in the town parish of St Peter le Bailey, equivalent to just over four years' rent from the property; while in 1549 repairs to Hart Hall cost £9 5s. 11d., again about four times the annual rent.[64] The portfolio of outlying properties built up by the College, surveyed in more detail below, could be a liability rather than an asset.

We are handicapped in providing any similar assessment for the 1550s by the disappearance of three account rolls for 1553–4, 1556–7, and 1559–60. But the incomplete evidence of the surviving rolls indicates a partial recovery, with no deficit years, full yields from the three main properties at Gwinear, Menheniot, and Wittenham, and tighter controls on spending. Nevertheless substantial withdrawals continued to be made from the common chest (a minimum figure of £50 13s. 4d. is given by the seven extant accounts), building expenses remained high, and allowances for commons had to be substantially increased by additional subventions from College funds. The events of the early 1560s were to show that whatever minor relief from financial stringency the College may have seemed to enjoy in this decade had been no more than a temporary respite.[65]

Behind all Exeter's financial problems lay the effects of soaring inflation on a very slender endowment income. The mid Tudor period saw the steepest and most prolonged price rise in England since the early thirteenth century. Its causes are controversial, but they included an increase in demand set off by population growth, an increase in the money supply resulting from a favourable balance of foreign trade, a decline in grain supplies as arable was converted to pasture, and—less controversially—a massive debasement of the currency between 1542 and 1551.[66] Its manifestations are plainer. Between 1500 and 1560 agricultural products, primarily grain, almost trebled in price, while in the same period the price of a basket of consumables comprising grain, meat, cheese, etc., rose by more than two and a half times.[67] Wages

---

[63] RA, 235/4.   [64] RA, 235/2, 239/4, 241/4.   [65] Below, 250–3.

[66] For differing explanations, see R. B. Outhwaite, *Inflation in Tudor and Stuart England* (London, 1969), *passim*, and P. Bowden, 'Agricultural Prices, Farm Profits and Rents', *Agrarian History*, iv. 594–8.

[67] Bowden, 'Agricultural Prices', *Agrarian History*, iv. 595, 847–8; E. H. Phelps Brown and S. V. Hopkins, 'Seven Centuries of the Prices of Consumables, compared with Builders' Wage Rates', in Carus-Wilson (ed.), *Essays in Economic History*, ii. 182, 194.

declined in real terms, but rose sharply in monetary terms: from 6*d.* to 10*d.*
a day for a skilled craftsman and from 4*d.* to about 7*d.* a day for a labourer.[68]
For all those living on or close to a fixed income, these changes were to prove
very hard to accommodate.

Exeter's endowment, adequate enough for the era of stable or gently rising
prices which lasted until the 1520s, proved quite inadequate to cope with the
effects of rampant inflation. Had it not been for the accession of new properties in the late fifteenth century, the College might well have failed to
survive. The accounts show that average annual income rose by about 41
per cent between 1501 and 1560, far less than the rise in prices. The difficulty
of feeding the College in these years provides one concrete illustration of its
plight. As we have seen, each fellow's allowance for commons had been fixed
since 1408 at 1*s.* a week, but at a time of rapidly rising prices this was entirely
insufficient, and if hunger was to be kept at bay means had to be found of
circumventing what was in effect a statutory requirement. The answer lay in
what were known as 'decrements', *decrementa*, lump sum payments made to
the manciple for the purchase of extra provisions, over and above those
chargeable to commons.[69] Payable by the College and normally appearing
on the expenses section of the accounts, decrements resembled the extra
payments termed 'excesses' which had been used to supplement commons
in the similarly difficult circumstances of the early 1370s.[70] They first began to
appear regularly on the accounts from 1522–3, just at the time when inflation
was taking hold, and thereafter they featured in every year's accounts. In that
first year they amounted to only £3 7*s.* 7*d.*,[71] but by the 1540s they averaged
£11 2*s.* a year and by the 1550s, £13 3*s.*—about 11 per cent of total average
spending for these decades. The most expensive year for decrements was
1545–6, when they cost the College £16 18*s.* 3*d.*[72] Here is one of the best
examples of the dire effects of the price rise, not only on the College's
finances, but on its way of life.

Any effective counter to inflation was crippled by the College's inability to
increase its revenues commensurately. The only addition to its properties in
these years was the house in Cat Street, on the west side of the street, just

---

[68] Phelps Brown and Hopkins, 'Seven Centuries of Building Wages', in Carus-Wilson (ed.),
Essays in Economic History, ii. 172.

[69] For the meaning of decrements, see Green, 194–5. That decrements were additions to
commons is conclusively shown by those few accounts in which they are added at the end of
the 'commons' section: e.g. RA, 226/1, 246/1. When, as normally, they appear under 'expenses'
they are usually followed by further and smaller sums *pro batellis domus* and *pro nota domus*: see
e.g. the account for 1566 printed in Boase (1), 181. These seem to represent other exceptional
outlays.

[70] Above, 77.

[71] RA, 216/1–4. Decrements are very occasionally recorded earlier, e.g. in 1500–1 and 1503–4:
RA, 195/2, 198/4.

[72] RA, 238/1–4.

south of the present Radcliffe Camera.[73] Bringing in a mere pound a year
from the time of its purchase in 1531, it hardly provided a road to financial
salvation. But more serious than the absence of new additions to the College's
estate was the tendency of rents and farms from the main properties either to
remain static or to rise only marginally during the period. The farm of £20 a
year paid by the vicar of Menheniot, fixed at the time of the church's
acquisition in 1479, remained the same in 1639.[74] The rent for the small
College holding at Benson, fixed at 31s. in the 1480s, remained the same in
1561.[75] The farms of the two oldest properties, the churches at Gwinear and
Wittenham, did rise, but by nothing like the rate of inflation—Gwinear from
£19 in 1510 to £28 13s. 4d. in 1560 (51 per cent), Wittenham from £23 in 1512
to £24 8s. in 1558 (6 per cent).[76] Those who reaped the profits were the
farmers or, in the case of Menheniot, the vicar, who were able to sell the
parochial tithes on a rapidly rising market. No wonder that Menheniot was
such a favoured billet for former fellows of the College. After years of relative
austerity in College they could enjoy the fat of the land.

    These deleterious arrangements had several causes. In the case of Menhen-
iot, the sum of £20 represented three-quarters of the tithe income in 1479 and
rested on a legally binding agreement made when the vicarage had been
established in that year, during an era of stable prices.[77] There was no easy
way in which it could be increased in a very different economic climate, which
had seen the real value of the £20 farm drop by more than a half. In the case of
its other properties, the College partly followed the contemporary conven-
tions for the leasing of land, applying them to the leasing of tithe income as
well as real property. Land was normally let on a long lease or for a term of
lives at a fixed rent; and when the lease was renewed the lessee or the new
tenant was expected to pay an entry fine, usually equivalent to one or two
years' rent.[78] At a time when prices were rising rapidly, long leases were
clearly disadvantageous to the College, as to any landowner, yet the College
continued to enter into them. In 1546, at the height of the inflationary spiral,
the College renewed the lease of Benson for a further twenty-one years at the
old rent of 31s. a year.[79] In 1547 the Wittenham tithes were leased to Thomas
Piers of Hinksey for five years, but in 1549 the lease was extended to twenty-
two years and in 1551 for a further forty-one years.[80] In a similar way the
Gwinear tithes were leased for eighteen years in 1549 and for a further
twenty-one years in 1565, at £28 13s. 4d., the rate fixed about 1540.[81] There

---

[73] Above, 194; Salter, *Survey*, i. 78–9, map NE III.   [74] Above, 167; Boase (2), 346.
[75] Above, 169; RA, 250/1/3.   [76] RA, 204, 207, 248, 250.
[77] For the three-quarters proportion, see Boase (2), 346.
[78] Bowden, 'Agricultural Prices', 675, 684–6; G. E. Aylmer, 'The Economics and Finances
of the Colleges and University, c.1530–1640', *HUO*, iii. 524–5.
[79] Reg., 41; RA, 241/1/3, etc.   [80] Reg., 48, 53; ECA, N. II. 5; Boase (2), 326.
[81] Reg., 53; ECA, M. III. 3; RA, 234.

is no indication in the accounts that fines were being levied when leases were renewed, but it may be that any fines imposed were divided between the head of the College and the fellows, as happened in most colleges, so failing to appear as corporate income. Exeter may have been following the common practice whereby 'the individual heads and fellows were profiting at the expense of their respective foundations'. Yet at most colleges—All Souls, Brasenose, etc.—at least a proportion of the fine went to the college; while at Exeter no part of any fine entered the accounts.[82]

All these leases had the consent of the whole fellowship, as the register is usually careful to state. Why did the fellows act in such an unbusinesslike way? Convention provides part of the answer. Originating in the fifteenth century, when land was plentiful and tenants scarce, long leases were perpetuating a tradition which offered a high degree of security to the lessee.[83] Exeter's lessees often had a longstanding relationship with the College, which the fellows may have been reluctant to jeopardize. Successive generations of the Barratt family, for example, had held the farm at Benson since its acquisition by the College in the 1480s (and would continue to do so until the late eighteenth century).[84] For many years in the mid sixteenth century the Piers family occupied a similar position at Wittenham, enjoying a friendly relationship with the College which was as much social as business.[85] Occasionally those who enjoyed these favourable terms were themselves Exeter fellows. William Shepreve, who took a forty-one-year lease of the Wittenham tithes in 1561, in succession to the Piers family, had been a fellow since 1559.[86] Underlying these arrangements there was a mixture of respect for convention and tradition, charitable inclination, and a human desire to show favour. It was only when Petre took the College in hand in the mid 1560s that both long leases and leases to fellows were prohibited, and the College compelled to adopt tighter and more efficient practices.[87]

There was not much to make up for the losses threatened by rising prices and declining income from property. Those valuing the Oxford colleges in 1546 had noted that, in Exeter's case as in that of some other colleges, the gap between income and expenditure was customarily met from legacies, gifts, and exhibitions (that is, donations for the support of scholars).[88] But this was hardly true. Before Petre's appearance, the sixteenth century was a very lean period for benefactions. Here it contrasted strongly with the late fifteenth century, when the College had been given the church of Menheniot and much else. The benefactors' book shows that at least eleven individuals gave money

[82] Aylmer, 'Economics and Finances', *HUO*, iii. 524–5, 527–8, 534.
[83] Cf. Bowden, 'Agricultural Prices', 675, 684–6.
[84] Above, 168–9; Boase (2), 369; Reg., 41; ECA, M. II. 4.
[85] Boase (2), 326. For College gifts to Thomas Piers and his wife, see e.g. RA, 238/1, 240/1.
[86] Boase (2), 70.   [87] Below, 278.   [88] TNA, E. 315/441, fo. 114.

to the College between 1450 and 1485, but thereafter no monetary benefaction of any kind is recorded until the Petrean refoundation; though there were three gifts of books and one of silver.[89] The accounts add a little to this, but note only slim pickings: eleven gifts and legacies of money between 1503 and 1566, amounting to a mere £18. The largest was a legacy of £6 from Edmund Fletcher, a former Rector, in 1541.[90] A few legacies may have gone unrecorded—Henry Laurence, another former Rector, left the College 40s. in 1545 which does not appear in the accounts[91]—but these are unlikely to have been either numerous or large.

To some extent the fall-off in benefactions at this time affected all colleges. The religious upheavals which began in the 1530s deterred conservative churchmen, always the most generous benefactors, from giving to institutions whose fortunes and futures seemed uncertain.[92] Yet this cannot be the whole story. Even during the thirty years prior to the Reformation Exeter received very few benefactions, in contrast, for example, to Lincoln, which added at least four to its endowment, worth some hundreds of pounds. Brasenose too profited similarly, with some twenty-eight significant benefactions in the century following its foundation in 1509. Both these colleges gained much from the particular generosity of one man: William Smith, bishop of Lincoln, founder of Brasenose and visitor of Lincoln College.[93] But notably absent from the short roll-call of Exeter's sixteenth-century benefactors were its visitors, the bishops of Exeter. If in the previous two centuries they had been among the College's most openhanded patrons, Grandisson, Brantingham, Stafford, Lacy, and Courtenay had no emulators among the later bishops. Hugh Oldham, bishop from 1505 to 1519, is said to have 'purposed to bestow large revenues on Exeter' until, thwarted by the College in his attempt to nominate to a fellowship, he decided instead to give his money to Corpus. This was a huge opportunity missed, for Oldham's gifts to Corpus were worth some £4,000, plus additional land: far more than the value of Petre's later donations to Exeter.[94] The multiplication of colleges between 1450 and 1550 offered such potential benefactors as Oldham a wider range of choices as to the destination of their wealth. Nor did Exeter produce any bishops from its own ranks who might have come to its aid; though John Holyman, sojourner in the 1520s and 1530s (but a former fellow of New College), became bishop of Bristol in 1554, and John Chardon, fellow from 1565 to 1568, became bishop of Down and Connor in 1596, beyond the end of our period.[95]

[89] ECA, C. II. 11.   [90] RA, 234/4; Boase (2), 55.   [91] BRUO, 1501–40, 344.
[92] Green, 80.
[93] Green, 70–80; J. M. Crook, Brasenose: The Biography of an Oxford College (Oxford, 2008), 10–14, 22–4.
[94] Prince, Worthies of Devon, 600; Orme, 'Oldham'; McConica, 'Rise of the Undergraduate College', HUO, iii. 18 n. 2; above, 183.
[95] BRUO, 1501–40, 295; Boase (2), 73–4.

In general, what money there was in benefactors' pockets flowed to the new colleges, especially perhaps Brasenose, Corpus Christi, and Christ Church, and it is striking that three of the university's oldest colleges, University College, Balliol, and Exeter, were among its poorest, in this period as in the later middle ages. The new colleges had a certain *réclame*, derived in some cases from their association with humanism and the new learning. This ancient one was different. Small, narrowly regional in its membership, closely identified with the basic arts course, with few men going on to higher degrees, and fewer, if any, with humanist interests,[96] Exeter had much less to commend it. If gifts and legacies did hardly anything to ameliorate its financial position, it was partly because Exeter lacked allure.

If benefactions were few and minor, what of loans? In the fifteenth century the College had relied extensively on loans, both from its own chests and from those of the university, to tide it over periods of particular financial stringency.[97] In the sixteenth century, however, loans from the university chests ceased to be available. As sources of funds the chests were in decline from the early years of the century, and the *coup de grâce* was delivered in 1544, when those kept in the university church were broken into and the university's cash stolen.[98] The running down and then the termination of this external resource doubtless explains why no loans from the university chests are recorded in the College accounts and why, as we have seen, the College drew so exclusively and extensively on its own common chest to meet exceptional needs. But in the fifteenth century the fairly frequent withdrawals from the common chest had usually been regarded as loans, to be repaid when funds permitted. In the next century, by contrast, such repayments are almost never recorded.[99] Both the ending of loans from the university chests and, partly in consequence, the College's forced reliance on its own cash reserves, can only have contributed to the sense of ongoing financial crisis which started in the 1530s and lasted until the College's re-endowment by Sir William Petre.

Since the time of its foundation Exeter has been at risk from the inadequacy of its endowment. In the fourteenth and fifteenth centuries, however, its poverty had been ameliorated by some very generous benefactions and by a multitude of smaller gifts and legacies. In the late fifteenth century these were capped by a large-scale accession of new property. It raised College income by about a third, and, in an era of stable prices, was sufficient to support an extensive building programme. But when prices began to rise, gradually in the 1520s,

---

[96] Below, 208, 212.   [97] Butcher, 42–4; above, 136–7.
[98] *The Register of Congregation, 1448–1463*, ed. Pantin and Mitchell, 428–31; McConica, 'The Collegiate Society', *HUO*, iii. 725–6.
[99] An isolated example occurs in 1540, when £22 was replaced in the common chest: RA, 234/1.

more steeply in the 1530s, and soaringly in the 1540s and 1550s, all the advantages conferred by the growth of the endowment were lost, and the College's position became one of extreme difficulty. The College's own practices contributed to its plight, most notably its tolerance of long leases and its failure or inability to pursue its debtors for their debts and arrears. But in the main the College was at the mercy of economic circumstances beyond its own control, and not for the first time. In the mid fifteenth century the threat had come from price deflation, which lowered income. A hundred years later it came from price inflation, which raised costs, particularly the costs of food and of the wage labour needed to keep buildings in repair. In both periods an inadequate endowment exposed the College to the chilling winds of economic change.

The consequences affected individual fellows as much as their College. Rising prices must have been in part responsible for the declining length of the fellows' tenure. Rapid inflation made College life increasingly uncomfortable as it ate into the standard of living determined by the fellows' allowances for weekly commons and annual stipends. Shaped as they had been by the Stapeldonian ideal of plain living and high thinking, these allowances at Exeter had never been particularly generous. Despite the price rise, the customary payment for commons remained at the 1s. a week fixed in the early fifteenth century, while the annual stipend was still set at the 10s. a year prescribed by the 1316 statutes. To make a trivial comparison, in 1316 10s. would have bought about 3,030 eggs, in 1560 about 490.[100] Any discontents provoked by such a fall in living standards are likely to have been heightened by the much more generous allowances paid by the new colleges, whose founders could take account of current economic conditions and prescribe sums for commons and allowances at a more realistic level. By contrast with Exeter's 1s. a week for commons and 10s. a year for stipends, for example, the respective figures for Trinity, founded in 1556, were 1s. 8d. and £2 13s. 4d., while St John's, founded in 1557, paid £8 a year for the commons, stipend, and clothing of a senior fellow, and £5 10s. for those of a bachelor. It was perhaps no wonder that in 1556 three fellows moved from Exeter to become founding fellows of Trinity.[101] The grass really was greener on the other side of the wall.

It is true that to concentrate solely on the fellows' fixed sums for commons and stipends may exaggerate the decline in their fortunes. We have seen how the money spent on commons was supplemented by substantial decrements (to the cost of the College); nor did their allowances provide the fellows' sole source of cash. An annual pound or two could be made from payments for the

[100] Thorold Rogers, *Agriculture and Prices*, ii. 452, iii. 217.
[101] C. Hopkins, *Trinity: 450 Years of an Oxford College Community* (Oxford, 2005), 22–3, 29; W. H. Stevenson and H. E. Salter, *The Early History of St John's College, Oxford*, OHS, new ser., i (1939), 152; below, 240.

celebration of weekly masses and annual obits for friends and benefactors—
the valuation of 1546 reckoned these to be worth just over £20 divided
between the Rector and fellows[102]—and some fellows will have augmented
their income further through the receipt of teaching fees from undergraduates. If any fines taken at the renewal of leases were also divided among the
fellowship, as seems possible, income will again have risen. Yet the value of all
these supplements to basic income, like that income itself, will have been
whittled away by relentless inflation. It is hard to doubt that in 1550 the
average fellow of Exeter was less well provided for than his counterpart half a
century earlier.

4. THE COLLEGE: GOVERNMENT AND ADMINISTRATION

The main features of Exeter's government and administration in the sixteenth
century were carried forward from the past and subsisted until the structure
of the College was radically altered by Petre's new statutes of 1566. The
annual election of the Rector, his responsibility for the accounts, the periodic
audit of the accounts, and the role of the bishop of Exeter as the College's
visitor, were all set out in Stapeldon's statutes and maintained well into the
Tudor age.

Of the twenty-two Rectors elected between 1501 and 1566, most held
office for two or three years. Only three ruled for a single year, none for
four years, only one, Philip Bale (1521–6), for five years, and only William
More (1546–53) equalled the seven-year tenures of his fifteenth-century
predecessors, William Palmer and John Rowe. Bale's prominence in university administration—he served as keeper of two university chests, collector of
university rents, junior proctor, and clerk of the market—and the large library
of books which he left to the College point to the unusual combination of
business abilities and scholarly interests which may explain his long reign.[103]
More's seven-year rectorship owed less to his abilities than to his protestant
sympathies, which led the Edwardian visitors to the College to order his
perpetual continuance in office: the first occasion on which the fellows' right
to elect had been overridden and a Rector effectively imposed on the College.[104] In general, the relatively short term of office enjoyed by most Rectors
was consistent with the shortening periods for the tenure of fellowships
which we have already noted.

The Rector had a commanding position within the College in more ways
than one. From 1511 comes the first evidence for his residence in the Tower
(that is, Palmer's Tower), when the accounts record the provision of a
cupboard for his room there; and it was probably there too that he stood
guard over the common chest containing the College's money. The residence

[102] TNA, E 315/441, fo. 114ʳ.   [103] Above, 116; *BRUO, 1501–40*, 22.
[104] Below, 234–5.

of the head of house in a gate tower, and beneath the treasury, was the usual arrangement in most colleges.[105] Exeter's Rector, however, may not have spent much time in his room. The accounts leave the impression that he perhaps travelled less extensively than his medieval predecessors, but College business still frequently took him away from Oxford—to London often, to Devon in 1516, to Canterbury in 1522, to Exeter in 1556 to consult the bishop about the College's statutes, and to the College properties at Benson and Wittenham on many occasions.[106] In 1524 he was at Benson 'to look over the lands'.[107] The horse which he bought from the College for 23s. in 1526 must have been a necessary tool of his trade.[108]

Beneath the Rector was a small corps of minor administrators. From c.1540 their roles and titles are revealed to us for the first time in the College register, which records their annual election every October, at the same time as the Rector's election. They comprised two bursars, two keepers and two auditors of the common chest, and sometimes two or three keepers and auditors of the Germeyn chest.[109] A fellow might hold more than one of these offices, and the total number of office holders was usually five or six, about a third of the fellowship. The institution of the bursars, apparently absent from the medieval College and first mentioned in 1518,[110] brought Exeter into line with other colleges, but their work was circumscribed by the general financial control exercised by the Rector, and their tasks seem to have been limited to collecting some rents, notably those for the hire of lecture rooms in Exeter's schools, and making occasional payments for repairs.[111] They presented no accounts and in no way usurped the Rector's position. Nor are the keepers and auditors of the chests likely to have had much to do. Payments into the common chest were largely confined to year-end cash surpluses (in years which produced a surplus rather than a deficit), while withdrawals, though much more frequent than in the past owing to the College's deteriorating financial position, normally took place only once or twice a year and had in any case to be authorized by the fellowship. This was not the fellows' only collective role. As we have seen, their consent had long been necessary for much College business,[112] and from the mid sixteenth century the register exists to give us a broader view of that business. All elections, admissions, and attendant oath-swearings, whether of Rectors, fellows, or sojourners, took place in meetings of the fellows in chapel. Similarly, all leases of College property had to be authorized by the fellows, as did any special payments: to the manciple, for example.[113] It was the wide range of

---

[105] RA, 206/1; J. Newman, 'The Physical Setting: New Building and Adaptation', *HUO*, iii. 623–4.
[106] RA, 206/3/4, 211/2/4, 214/4, 215/4, 226/1, 247/2, 251/3.   [107] RA, 217/2.
[108] RA, 220/3.   [109] e.g. Reg., 24 (1541), 61 (1355).   [110] RA, 213/1.
[111] e.g. RA, 219/2, 226/2.   [112] Above, 118–19.   [113] e.g. Reg., 48; RA, 210/3.

their collective responsibilities, not so very different *mutatis mutandis* from those of a modern governing body, which fortified the existence of the College as a community.

For a large part of the preceding period the chief external influence on the College and its government had been that of its visitor, the bishop of Exeter. As benefactor, counsellor, arbitrator, judge, and well-placed friend, the bishop had often played an important role in College affairs.[114] That role had declined after 1450; and the absence of benefactions from the sixteenth-century bishops, and the complete silence of their registers on any links with the College, may lead us to think that they continued to count for very little in the College's life.[115] But the silence of the registers may be more a mark of their decline as a full record of episcopal business than of the decline of links between bishop and College. Besides Hugh Oldham's commendation of a favoured fellowship candidate, we know of only a very few occasions when the bishop intervened or was called in aid. In 1547 the fellows appealed to Bishop John Veysey to rule on a point derived from the statutes regarding the value of a benefice taken by a fellow which might compel him to vacate his fellowship. The bishop's reply was copied into the College register. Later, during the drafting of Sir William Petre's statutes in 1565–6, Bishop William Alley was quite properly consulted about the terms of the new statutes.[116] But this very slim record is belied by the more extensive pattern of contacts revealed by the accounts. Presents of gloves were frequently sent to the bishop;[117] visits from him are recorded in 1523, 1547, and 1561 (and there were almost certainly others);[118] letters were sent to him in 1520 and 1542, taken by the Rector on the first occasion;[119] his injunctions, perhaps resulting from a visitation, were copied out for the College in 1543;[120] and the Rector went to Exeter to consult him about the statutes in 1556.[121] These scraps of information, no more than a minimum record, suggest rather more frequent contacts than those of the second half of the fifteenth century. The bishops may not have been generous benefactors, like some of their late medieval predecessors, but they were respected as successors of the founder and as guardians and interpreters of his statutes.

More essential than the bishop to the daily running of the College were its servants. The quartet present from the College's earliest days—maniciple, cook, laundress, and barber—were joined in the sixteenth century by a fifth member, the promus or butler, in charge of the buttery and hall. He first appears in the accounts in 1529, and his counterparts at Lincoln in 1541 and at

---

[114] Above, 119–24.
[115] The sixteenth-century registers exist only in manuscript: DRO, MSS Chanter Catalogue, 13–18.
[116] Reg., 44; below, 266–7, 274–5.   [117] e.g. RA, 197/3, 214/2.
[118] RA, 216/4, 239/2, 250/3.
[119] RA, 214/3, 235/expenses 1.   [120] RA, 235/expenses 3.   [121] RA, 247/2.

Balliol by Elizabeth's reign—so this may have been a development common
to most Oxford colleges in the sixteenth century.[122] By far the most important of these five was the manciple, variously and confusingly known as
mancipium, obsonator, dispensator, pincerna, and *oeconomus*. His status was
recognized by his annual salary of £1 6s. 8d., compared with 13s. 4d. for the
cook and laundress, and 8s. for the barber. All, in addition, took their
commons from the College.[123] Although the manciple's office was an old
one, it is only the more prolific records of the sixteenth century that allow us
to see the range of his activities. He was often a prominent figure in the
university or the town. Richard Pate, Exeter's manciple in the early years of
the century, was yeoman bedel of arts in the university, a potentially lucrative
post, while William Pawe, manciple for some twenty-five years from c.1532 to
1557, was also a freeman of the city and one of its bailiffs.[124] Although the
manciple was still employed on general business for the College, as he had
been earlier, going to London, for example, to represent the College in a
lawsuit in 1506,[125] his main task was to provision the College from funds
which the Rector and fellows made available to him. He received week by
week the 1s. per fellow allocated for the fellows' commons, together with any
decrements voted by the College,[126] buying food and drink in the town both
for the fellows and for the sojourners and undergraduates. The fellows paid
him directly for goods supplied over and above their commons, while
sojourners and undergraduates paid him for their actual commons, since
they received nothing freely. Any sojourners, and almost certainly any fellows, with undergraduate pupils were responsible for seeing that their charges
paid their debts to the manciple shortly after the end of each term.[127]

The responsibility of the manciple for the College's money and purchases
gave him many opportunities for profiteering: 'peculation was the occupa-
tional disorder of the manciple.'[128] Victuals might cost less than the sum
allocated by the College or charged to the individual (though in an era of
rapidly rising food prices this was perhaps a difficult trick to pull off), or the
leftovers might be privately sold, or backhanders taken from market traders in
return for the manciple's, and the College's, custom. Hence the oath imposed

[122] RA, 222/2; Green, 232 n. 3; Jones, 66.
[123] RA, 195/1. *Valor*, ii. 269, mistakenly gives the manciple's salary as £3 6s. 8d.
[124] C. I. Hammer, Jr., 'Oxford Town and Oxford University', *HUO*, iii. 75–6, 79–80;
Selections from the Records of the City of Oxford, 1509–1583, ed. W. H. Turner (Oxford,
1880), 154, 190.
[125] RA, 200/2.   [126] RA, 206/4, 215/1.
[127] *SA*, 372; DRO, MS Chanter 732 (unfoliated). This manuscript appears to be a stray from
the College archives which has found its way into the Exeter episcopal archive. It contains, *inter
alia*, the Petrean statutes and the oaths sworn by sojourners, undergraduates, and College
servants. For a debt owed by an undergraduate at Hart Hall to the Hall's manciple for commons
and battels, see Saul, 'Hart Hall', 337.
[128] Hammer, 'Oxford Town', *HUO*, iii. 79.

on the manciple—and manciple, promus, and cook all took oaths of office—not only to provide wholesome food (*edulia salubria*), but also to take no bribe or profit (*lucrum*) for his purchases.[129] But since the manciple usually received payment only in arrears for supplies provided to order for fellows, sojourners, and undergraduates, he had to set an element of risk against the possibilities of gain. It was illustrated by the claim made by William Pawe in 1557 that the College should settle all the unpaid debts for commons, decrements, and battels owed to him by departed fellows, sojourners, and undergraduates. The claim was contemptuously rejected by the Rector and fellows: 'to do this would lead to the ruin and destruction of all colleges.'[130] But there is no need to feel sorry for the manciple, who can rarely have left office out of pocket. The lucrative opportunities open to him were perhaps recognized in the curious practice of the College's taking an annual payment from him, usually between £2 and £5, 'for his office'. This is once described as a rent (*redditus*).[131] In effect, the office was farmed. Convention dictated that the manciple should be paid a respectable salary, but the money came back to the College with advantage in the manciple's farm.

5. STUDIES AND BOOKS

It was as true of the sixteenth century as it had been of the middle ages that, of all that went on at Exeter, we know least about the subject most central to the College's existence: the academic studies of the fellows. The foundation of those studies was, as it had always been, the syllabus of the faculty of arts, leading first to the bachelor's degree and then to the master's.[132] The syllabus changed surprisingly little in this period, and the influence of humanism and the new learning derived from Greece and Rome was very limited. The basis for study remained the seven liberal arts of the trivium and the quadrivium. The works of Aristotle still lay at the core of the syllabus, teaching and learning still primarily took the form of lectures and disputations, and successive revisions of the statutes, in 1549 under Edward VI and in 1565 under Elizabeth, did little more than tinker with the traditional curriculum.

Yet although the formal syllabus largely ignored 'modern' subjects—not only Greek and Latin literature but also geography, history, and modern languages—it was not entirely fossilized. Aristotelian logic, for example, was

---

[129] DRO, MS Chanter 732.

[130] Reg., 65; Boase (2), lxxvi–lxxvii. But the College in 1553 had settled the debts of John Fessarde, a former fellow, to the manciple, though Fessarde had left the College nine years earlier: Boase (2), 64.

[131] RA, 231/4. For other instances, see e.g. RA, 235/receipts 3 (1543: £3 11s. 7d. from Mr Pawe for his office, due at Easter); RA, 236/3 (1544: £4 7s. 8d. from the manciple for his office, due at Easter).

[132] Unreferenced statements in this and the following paragraph derive from Fletcher, 'Faculty of Arts', *HUO*, iii. 157–99.

partly cut loose from its medieval commentators, leaving its students free to concentrate on texts,[133] while Pliny and Quintilian, humanist favourites, were introduced into the Edwardian statutes. The main changes, however, came less in the subject matter of teaching than in its structure. Public lectures, given for all members of the university, multiplied and took on a new role. New public lectureships in Greek and Latin, supported financially by sub-ventions from the colleges and halls, were established in 1535 (and here at least was a major concession to the Renaissance); while the regius professorship of theology founded in 1540 was followed by others in Greek, Hebrew, civil law, and medicine.[134] At the same time the old system which compelled newly graduated *magistri* to lecture for two years as regent masters after receiving their degrees was beginning to break down, as masters simply failed to lecture or sought dispensations on the grounds of their teaching duties within the colleges. These duties pointed to a third development in the organization of teaching, in the long term the most important: the growth of college teaching, with particular fellows taking responsibility for particular pupils. This was not an innovation—we have seen its origins in the fifteenth century—but it became much more prominent from the mid sixteenth century onwards, as undergraduate numbers rose and the lectures of the regent masters declined. By Elizabeth's reign a teaching system based on a combination of the uni-versity's public lectures, given by salaried lecturers, and the colleges' tutorials was coming into being.

Exeter's part in this evolution is largely hidden. Only one source fleetingly reveals the place of the College's students in the traditional arts syllabus: Rector French's manifesto directed against 'the insolence of the bachelors' in 1539.[135] French was greatly concerned with the studies of the College's younger members. Both fellows following the scholastic life (that is, fellow undergraduates) and the battelers, the ordinary undergraduates, he stipulated, were to attend the public lectures in Hart Hall and the various disputations and exercises, *sophismata* and *variationes*, held there. By 'variations' he meant the arguments which a student was expected to present for and against a set thesis.[136] If they failed to appear they were to be punished by the Hall's principal or reported to the Rector for a more severe punishment. The College's senior members clearly took seriously their duty to oversee the academic progress and discipline of their juniors. Hart Hall, rather than the College itself, seems to have been Exeter's academic base, with its principal, almost always a fellow of the College, enjoying a supervisory role. Since by

[133] So Fletcher, *HUO*, iii. 176–7. But see J. McConica, 'Humanism and Aristotle in Tudor Oxford', *EHR*, 94 (1979), 293–8, for a different view.
[134] G. D. Duncan, 'Public Lectures and Professorial Chairs', *HUO*, iii. 335–61.
[135] Boase (1), 183–4; Boase (2), lxxiv; above, 188–90.
[136] Fletcher, 'Faculty of Arts', *HUO*, iii. 170.

1552 the Hall had some forty-two undergraduate members, while the College had only about thirteen, it was perhaps not surprising that it provided the main venue for teaching; though by 1553 at least some academic exercises, known as *correctiones*, took place on Saturdays in the College hall, apparently after an interlude under Edward VI when they had ceased.[137] French's statement shows too that teaching, whether by lectures or by disputations, was intended both for undergraduate fellows and for those other undergraduates not on the foundation. In academic terms, if not in terms of rank and prestige, both groups were on a par, though the fellow undergraduates, the product of competitive election, might perhaps have been expected to be the more able.

Within the College the academic relationship between tutor-fellows and their undergraduate pupils remains a dark subject. We have already seen that fellows sometimes paid the College for the rooms occupied by their pupils and that they were more generally responsible, in the last resort, for the clearance of the pupils' debts to the College. But no source tells us about the academic guidance which they provided. At some other colleges, certainly by the middle of Elizabeth's reign, college teaching went beyond the syllabus to include elements of humanistic thought and texts.[138] Some colleges had a strongly humanist bent from a much earlier date—notably Corpus Christi, where Greek and Latin literature was in the ascendant from the time of the College's foundation in 1517.[139] It was at the richer colleges, Magdalen, New College, and All Souls, and possibly at Queen's and Merton, that new public lectureships in Greek and Latin were established in 1535.[140] In common with other colleges, Exeter made small annual payments to support some of these lectureships, paying 2s. 4d. in 1557, for example, towards the salary of Robert Warde, fellow of Merton and the university's praelector in philosophy.[141] But these payments represented an obligation rather than a particular interest. If the humanist strengths of other colleges were reflected in teaching at Exeter, there is nothing to show it—and it seems unlikely.

How far is this picture altered or confirmed by what we know of Exeter's books and library? For almost all Oxford libraries the sixteenth century was, in varying degrees, a period of tribulation and loss.[142] The advent of printing

---

[137] *Register*, ed. Boase, xxiv–xxv; Reg., 59; Boase (1), 40; Wood, *History*, ii. 110–11; Saul, 'Hart Hall', 337.
[138] Fletcher, 'Faculty of Arts', *HUO*, iii. 179–80; McConica, 'The Collegiate Society', *HUO*, iii. 694–703.
[139] J. McConica, 'The Rise of the Undergraduate College', *HUO*, iii. 17–22.
[140] Duncan, 'Public Lectures', *HUO*, iii. 342.
[141] Duncan, 'Public Lectures', *HUO*, iii. 343–4; RA, 248/1. E. Russell, 'The Influx of Commoners into the University of Oxford before 1581: An Optical Illusion?', *EHR*, 92 (1977), 725 n. 1, 727 n. 3, is wrong to assume that these payments were made to Exeter's internal college lecturers: they were made to university lecturers.
[142] See in general N. R. Ker, 'Oxford College Libraries in the Sixteenth Century', in his *Books, Collectors and Libraries*, 379–436, and Ker, 'The Provision of Books', *HUO*, iii. 441–77.

seems to have led to the discarding of older manuscripts as they came to be superseded by the latest printed editions, while the religious changes of the 1530s and 1540s may have resulted in the destruction of older works seen as outdated, obscurantist, or opposed to the religious orthodoxy of the moment. There may be exaggeration in the traditional views which have seen the royal visitations of 1535 and 1549 as occasions for the wholesale purging of Oxford's libraries. But destruction there undoubtedly was, at Exeter as elsewhere.[143] The mid century period is as likely a time as any for the loss of much of the College's medieval collection and the reduction, for example, of Bishop Rede's munificent gift of seventy books to the five which now survive. Some categories of books were particularly vulnerable to the forces of change, notably saints' lives, scholastic philosophy, and theology. One book from Rede's collection containing the life and miracles of Becket, now at Douai, was found by its sixteenth-century translator 'among a chaos of cast books and waste paper', and Professor Andrew Watson has remarked that it is 'something of a miracle' that the College's magnificent fifteenth-century set of Hugh of St Cher's scriptural commentaries survived.[144] Exeter's 'electio' books, reserved for borrowing by the fellows, may have been discarded at the same time. Nicholas Smale, fellow from 1508 to 1516, is the last known fellow to have borrowed an 'electio' book; nor, in contrast with the preceding period, are there any references to these books in the accounts.[145]

To some extent new accessions made up for these losses; to what extent is unclear. The accounts record no purchases of books during the entire period; and the fact that in the college valuations of 1546 three of the four colleges failing to mention library spending in their returns—Exeter, Oriel, and University College—were among the university's poorest suggests that lack of money may have affected this activity as much as other branches of College expenditure. The richer colleges, notably Magdalen, New College, and All Souls, bought regularly enough, at least from 1535 onwards.[146] But purchase had never been the main method of acquiring books. Gifts and bequests had always been more important, and the accounts show that books continued to come to the College in these and other ways. In 1501 2s. was spent on the carriage of books from Devon, another 4s. 2d. on bringing money and books from the same county in 1503, and a further 8d. on the carriage of five books

[143] For differing views, see Wood, *History*, ii. 107 (1550: 'the libraries of Exeter, Queen's and Lincoln were with others purged'); Ker, 'Oxford College Libraries', 400, 409–10; Ker, 'The Provision of Books', *HUO*, iii. 365; A. Watson, 'The Post-Medieval Library', in *Unarmed Soldiery: Studies in the Early History of All Souls College, Oxford* (Oxford, 1996), 70–3.

[144] Watson, xxi, 133.

[145] Watson, xix–xx, 133–4; Ker, 'The Provision of Books', *HUO*, iii. 455–7.

[146] Ker, 'Oxford College Libraries', 388 n. 1, 400–5.

from Bampton in 1547.[147] Since Bampton was held by the cathedral church of Exeter we may guess that these books too came from Devon. Money continued to be spent fairly frequently on chaining books.[148] Occasional gifts from former fellows and well-wishers are also recorded; in 1508 three books came from John Philipp, who had vacated his fellowship as long ago as 1470;[149] and others came in 1539 from Richard Duke, fellow from 1501 to 1515, and from an unknown 'Pollard', perhaps the John Pollard who was a sojourner in 1539–40.[150]

Since Duke died in 1539, his gift probably came as a legacy; and such other few legacies as we know of are sometimes more informative about the sorts of books which came to the College in these years, all of them from former fellows. The benefactors' book records a legacy of a bible and 'many other books' in 1519 from Thomas Symon, fellow from 1475 to c.1483, and a former vicar of Wittenham.[151] In his will of 1534 Peter Carsley (1483–7), who ended his life as canon of two cathedral churches and chaplain to the king, left to the College a copy of Gregory the Great's *Moralia* and of Alexander Carpenter's *Destructorium viciorum*;[152] Philip Bale (1510–30), the works of Augustine, Ambrose, Jerome, Gregory, certain works of Bede, and other books to be chosen by his executors;[153] John Moreman (1510–22), by his first will of 1542, left to the Rector his ten-volume edition of Augustine printed by Froben at Basle in 1529–30 (the first certain evidence of printed books destined for Exeter);[154] while Henry Laurence (1530–43) bequeathed unspecified books at his death in 1545.[155] They were brought to the College from his vicarage at Kidlington in the autumn of that year. These gifts and legacies do something to offset the impression of a largely friendless College, passed over by potential benefactors, given by the paucity and meagreness of monetary benefactions. At least Exeter's former fellows remembered the College with affection and goodwill, and left it what they judged to be most useful for its work.

This was perhaps especially true of the College's greatest book-donor, John Dotyn, whose bequest to the library was the most valuable and interesting of the period. Dotyn, fellow from 1528 to 1539 and Rector for his final two years, was a specialist in medicine, who studied for the baccalaureate in medicine during his time as a fellow and supplicated for his doctorate in 1559, shortly before his death in 1561. He ended his life as parish priest of Kingsdon in Somerset, where his memorial brass describes him as *medicus ac astrologus insignis*, 'distinguished doctor and astrologer'. He left to the

---

[147] RA, 196/2, 198/1, 239/4.   [148] e.g. RA, 218/2, 238/2.
[149] RA, 202/3; Boase (2), 42; *BRUO*, iii. 1476–7.
[150] RA, 232/4; Boase (2), 50–1; *BRUO*, i. 602.   [151] ECA, C. II. 11; *BRUO*, iii. 1840.
[152] TNA, PROB 11/25, fo. 45ᵛ; *BRUO*, i. 363–4.   [153] *BRUO, 1501–40*, 22.
[154] *BRUO, 1501–40*, 400.   [155] *BRUO, 1501–40*, 344; RA, 237/4.

College 'all my books of physic and natural philosophy', twenty-two of which, probably the entire collection, still survive in the College library.[156] They comprise most of the standard medical works of the time, including a large collection of the works of Galen, and others on botany. Dotyn's was 'the only at all considerable collection of medical books acquired by an Oxford college library before the last years of the sixteenth century'.[157] In this field at least Exeter's library now excelled.

But in general what little we know about the library between 1501 and c.1560 suggests that this was a period of loss rather than gain. With the exception of Dotyn's books, probably in any case of limited practical use (only four other fellows went on to read for higher degrees in medicine in the period), no large collections came to the library. Those books acquired via legacies were mainly the classics of patristic theology (Augustine, Gregory, etc.) or the staples of pastoral theology (Carpenter's *Destructorium*), books of the sort known to have been in the medieval library. An earlier copy of the *Destructorium* had been given to the College in 1452.[158] Only Moreman's bequest of the works of Augustine printed by Froben, a famous edition with Erasmus as editor and commentator, suggests any humanist contribution; and in any case these books were left to the Rector and not to the College. How far the library's collections were supplemented or complemented by the private collections of the fellows is impossible to say. We might expect such collections to have become commoner as printing reduced the price of books and placed them within reach of those on a fellow's modest income.[159] But we have only one surviving inventory of a fellow's books to go by for this period: that made on the death of John Conner, fellow and chaplain from 1523 to 1549, and vicar of St Peter in the East, Oxford, from 1558. Conner was the longest serving fellow of the century. The fifty-six books which he possessed at his death were almost all biblical commentaries, sermons, and other theological works, including those of such favourite medieval authors as Nicholas of Lyra, appraised at 6s. 8d. and the most valuable book in Conner's collection. It was a small library 'with a distinctively conservative flavour...and a relative absence of reformed texts'—perhaps not surprising for one who had gained his baccalaureate in theology in 1524 and had been chaplain for so long.[160]

<hr>

[156] *BRUO, 1501–40*, 173, 718–19 (Emden lists Dotyn's books by title, with their current Exeter Library call-numbers); A. B. Connor, *Memorial Brasses in Somerset* (reprint, Bath, 1970), 313.
[157] Ker, 'Oxford College Libraries', 424. For further information on Dotyn, see G. Lewis, 'The Faculty of Medicine', *HUO*, iii. 224–5, 239, 248, 254, and below, 247–9.
[158] Above, 103–4, 106–7; Boase (1), 22.
[159] Cf. Ker, 'The Provision of Books', *HUO*, iii. 467–8.
[160] *BRUO, 1501–40*, 133–4, 718–19; R. J. Fehrenbach and E. S. Leedham-Green, *Private Libraries in Renaissance England*. Vol. III: *PLRE 67–86* (New York, 1994), 156–63.

As far as we can see, Exeter's academic standing from the start of the sixteenth century until the time of the Petrean reforms was very similar to its standing in the previous century. It remained a small College, its fellows almost all reading for degrees in arts and its intellectual milieu influenced hardly at all by the humanist learning which pervaded some of the newer and richer colleges, such as Magdalen and Corpus Christi. A few fellows—some sixteen between 1500 and 1566—went on to higher degrees in theology, but only about half of these began or completed their theological studies during their time at Exeter. The proportions among the fifteenth-century fellows had been about the same.[161] No fellow is known to have published a book during the period; though John Moreman, perhaps the most learned of them, wrote an unpublished commentary on Paul's epistle to the Romans.[162] The College was, of course, subject to the academic changes which affected all colleges: the revision of the statutes governing the arts faculty, the provision of public lectures and their subsidizing by the colleges, the growth of under-graduate teaching. But otherwise in its academic status and reputation Exeter marked time.

6. SOJOURNERS AND UNDERGRADUATES

Besides its fellows the College had two other categories of residents: sojourners and undergraduates, the latter distinct from those relatively few undergraduate fellows who were on the foundation. Both groups originated in the fifteenth century, as we have seen, but the proliferation of sources means that we know more about them in the later period.

This was particularly true of the sojourners, whose names were listed in the register at the start of every academic year from 1539 onwards. As in the fifteenth century, the sojourners were senior boarders, renting rooms in College, dining with the fellows in hall, and paying the manciple for their commons—unlike the fellows, whose commons were paid by the College. Like the fellows, they were formally admitted to commons, taking an oath on the occasion of their admission. Their numbers varied between two and twelve, but there were usually about seven in College, almost all of them *magistri*, and thus senior figures, but including a few bachelors. Some were resident for long periods, others came and went, often residing for a year or so of study. William fitz William, dean of Wells, admitted as a sojourner in 1545, was presumably one of these.[163] As in the fifteenth century again, a number were former fellows, either staying on as rent-payers beyond the termination of their fellowships or taking time off from their parishes for study and recreation among old friends. So, for example, John Bury, fellow from 1526 to 1536, returned as a sojourner from 1539 to 1543, when he was vicar of

[161] Above, 98.   [162] Prince, *Worthies of Devon*, 601.   [163] Reg., 40.

St Breocke in Cornwall and of Axmouth in Devon, and Richard Fountayne, fellow in the late 1550s, came back to reside for a year in 1564–5, when he was vicar of Loddiswell in Devon.[164] As was the case in other colleges, some sojourners might be more intellectually distinguished than any of the fellows. One such was Richard Croke, a sojourner in Exeter from 1535 to 1546, and an important figure in the history of English humanism: pupil of William Grocyn, once himself an Exeter sojourner, student and associate of Erasmus, lecturer in Greek at Cambridge, and a pioneer in the institutional teaching of Greek in England. But if the fellows' interest in the new learning was stimulated by the presence among them of this famous man—and one famously quarrelsome and disagreeable—there is nothing to show it.[165]

The sojourners' oath, which shared some of its terms with that of the fellows, suggests that the sojourners were closely integrated into College life and might sometimes presume on their privileged position.[166] They swore to be faithful to the College, to respect its good fame, to reveal nothing of the 'secrets and sayings uttered at table' or elsewhere in the College, to refrain from meddling in elections, to receive no stranger to live in the College without the permission of the Rector and fellows, and to settle their debts to the College within three weeks of the end of each quarter. But more interesting still is the sojourners' obligation also to settle other debts due from 'any scholar of yours', since this shows that the sojourners might have undergraduate pupils for whom they had to take financial responsibility. In 1562, when undergraduates living in the town—a group removed from college discipline and so always viewed suspiciously by the authorities—were told to appear before the vice-chancellor to state the names of their tutors, two undergraduates gave the names of Exeter sojourners: Thomas Casbrycke named Oliver Whiddon, a *magister*, and John Ford named Paul Amerson, a bachelor.[167] No doubt teaching fees from pupils helped to pay the rent.

The sojourners' relationship with the fellows was one of mutual advantage. They brought much needed money to the College, and if they had undergraduate pupils they brought more. In other ways too they were useful men to have around. That they were bound by their oath 'to defend and maintain with your counsel and other aid the good estate of this house' implies that they might be called on to advise or use their influence on the College's behalf. From the early 1560s the register sometimes notes that particular sojourners were *generosi*, 'gentlemen', a flourish which suggests that the fellows were glad to have such well-born and well-connected men among

[164] *BRUO, 1501–40*, 88–9; Reg., 82, 87; Boase (2), 69.
[165] *BRUO, 1501–40*, 151–2; J. Woolfson. 'Richard Croke', *ODNB*.
[166] DRO, MS Chanter 732. The form of the oath is given in both Latin and English and appears to date from c.1575.
[167] *Register*, ed. Clark, II. ii. 6. For the two sojourners, see Boase (2), 62, 77. Whiddon was elected to a fellowship in 1573.

them. Oliver Whiddon, son of a Devon knight and judge, was one such *generosus*.[168] The sojourner's undertaking, also set out in his oath, not to divulge College secrets learnt at table, and a record in the accounts of fellows and sojourners drinking wine together on Maundy Thursday 1544,[169] both hint at the gossipy, convivial atmosphere which was part of the relationship between the two groups and which transcended mere business dealings. In some cases a strong attachment developed between fellows and individual sojourners. When 'that most learned master and doctor Walter Wryght', former vice-chancellor, doctor of civil law, canon of Salisbury, Exeter, and Winchester, and a sojourner for many years, died in his College room in May 1561, his death and subsequent burial in the university church were specially noted in the College register. The fellows' respect and affection were evidently reciprocated, for in his will Wryght left the College a gilt cup worth £7 and £4 in money.[170] Sojourners such as Wryght were more than paying guests.

The College's undergraduates have left a fainter mark on the sources, and their identities and activities are correspondingly more difficult to assess. We have already seen that they are mentioned only incidentally in the fifteenth-century records, and the same largely holds true until the university matriculation registers begin in the late sixteenth century. Responsibility for undergraduates usually lay with the particular fellows, or sometimes sojourners, who acted as their tutors, sometimes paid the College for their rooms, and in turn collected their own payments for rooms and teaching fees from their charges. At Exeter, as at other Oxford and Cambridge colleges, their admission probably also lay with individual fellows and not with the whole fellowship; so much is implied by a later request to Sir William Petre that the Rector should have a veto in the admission of both sojourners and undergraduates.[171] The close links between tutors and pupils are suggested by the accounts, which often show, as they do more occasionally in the late fifteenth century, fellows renting rooms for their undergraduates. In 1517 Mr Thomas Vivian (fellow, 1511–20) paid 8d. for one term 'for the room in which his scholar Tankerd lodged'; in 1524 Mr Edmund Fletcher (1516–29) paid 16d. for a room for two scholars; while in 1526 Mr John Tucker (1521–6) paid 2s. for two scholars 'lying in college'.[172] Occasionally fellows from other colleges might rent rooms for their pupils, as Thomas Larke, fellow of New College, did in 1546. Larke was also responsible for meeting their kitchen expenses and for replacing the College keys which his scholars had lost, showing that the tutor's duties to the host

[168] Reg., 80, 87; Boase (2), 62, 77; J. H. Baker, 'John Whiddon', *ODNB*.   [169] RA, 261/3.
[170] Reg., 75; Boase (1), 42–3; *BRUO, 1501–40*, 641.
[171] Cobban, 'Decentralized Teaching', 197; below, 265.
[172] RA, 211/4, 217/2, 219/3; *BRUO, 1501–40*, 206–7, 578, 596.

college extended beyond payment for rooms.[173] Occasionally too an undergraduate might be found paying rent directly to the College, as 'Chapyn' did in 1519, when he paid 8d. 'for the old room in the corner next to Lincoln College'.[174] Chapyn was presumably among a small minority of undergraduates who had no College tutor to act for them. As these examples show, the usual room rent was 8d. a term: a charge which, like the rents for College property, and to the College's cost, failed to rise with the inflationary tide which set in from the 1520s.[175]

The number of undergraduates living in College cannot be accurately determined. It was certainly small: if the accounts can be relied on, perhaps no more than half a dozen in any term during the first half of the sixteenth century. In 1552, however, we have for the first time some more precise information, derived from the university census taken in that year which set out to record the names of scholars in all colleges and halls. The list for Exeter gives the names of twelve fellows (three masters, three bachelors, and six undergraduate fellows), six sojourners, and thirteen undergraduates, the latter group distinguished by their bare surnames, devoid of all titles.[176] Exeter's total compared with thirteen at Balliol and seventeen at University College, two comparable colleges which, with Exeter, were the smallest in the university. Magdalen, by contrast, had eighty-seven undergraduates and New College seventy-two, from a university total of 679.[177]

The census came at a time when undergraduate numbers were beginning to rise rapidly, moving towards the still greater expansion which characterized the period from 1560 onwards.[178] Partly as a consequence a new vocabulary evolved to describe a larger undergraduate body more evidently divided by wealth and status. Here an intricate tangle of related words has to be unknotted to provide a guide to social change. The Rector's accounts for the first part of the century invariably identify undergraduates simply as *scolarii* or *scolastici*. But in 1539, in Rector French's manifesto against the bachelors, we come across a new term for the first time: *battellarii* or batelers. French's statement of College rules and customs laid down that all fellows (*socii*) leading the scholastic life were to attend lectures and to take part in the appropriate academic exercises, and so too were the *battellarii*.[179] We have here a clear

[173] RA, 238/3/4; Boase (1), 37; *BRUO, 1501–40*, 342.   [174] RA, 213/4.
[175] 8d. was paid for an undergraduate's room both in 1519 and 1546: RA, 213/3, 238/2.
[176] Oxford University Archives, Hyp/A/5 (Reg. GG), fo. 75ᵛ, printed with some inaccuracies in *Register of the University of Oxford*, ed. Boase, xxiv. Boase includes several sojourners among those whom he calls 'subgraduati', a title not found in the manuscript. For comment, see McConica, 'Rise of the Undergraduate College', *HUO*, iii. 49, 57, and Stone, 'Size and Composition of the Oxford Student Body', 82–3.
[177] *Register*, ed. Boase, xxii–xxiv; Stone, 'Size and Composition of the Oxford Student Body', 82–3.
[178] Stone, 'Size and Composition of the Oxford Student Body', 6, 16–18, 82.
[179] Boase (1), 184; above, 207.

allusion to the two sorts of undergraduates living in College, those who were fellows and those—hardly more than lodgers—who were not. Both groups followed the same arts course and, so the manifesto states, were subject to the same rules. The equation of battelers with ordinary undergraduates is also clear from the manciple's assertion, made in 1557, that the College should take responsibility for the unpaid debts of the fellows (*socii*), the sojourners (*suggenarii*), and the undergraduates (*batillarii*)—the three groups living in College for whom the manciple provided.[180] Finally, another entry in the register, for 1562, lays down that fellows (*socii*), commoners (*commensales*), and battelers (*battillarii*) are all to settle their battels with the manciple within a month of the end of term.[181] '*Commensales*' later came to be applied to undergraduate commoners, as we shall see. But in this context it is clearly another word for the College's sojourners, and in fact throughout the sources *commensales* and *suggenarii* are used indifferently for the same group, though by the sixteenth century the latter word is the more usual. So here again we have the threefold division between fellows, sojourners, and battelers or ordinary undergraduates.

The word 'batteler' has given rise to a good deal of discussion, but at this stage in Exeter's history it probably signifies no more than those junior members of the College who paid for their board and lodging and were expected to settle their battels, or bills, with the manciple. Unlike the fellows, who received their commons free of charge but paid for 'extras', the battelers bore the full cost of their keep, with their tutors standing surety for payment. But we are about to enter a more complicated social world, which first becomes visible in Sir William Petre's new statutes of 1566 (and here we anticipate in order to carry forward the story of the College's undergraduates). The statutes make clear that at this time, and probably only *from* this time,[182] the College's ordinary undergraduates were divided into two groups, the *commensales*—a term confusingly shared with the sojourners and normally translated as 'commoners'—and the battelers. Three particular pieces of evidence point in this direction. First, Petre laid down that the dean, a new College officer, was to take specified fees from the *commensales* and *batellari* to whom he lectured. He would hardly be lecturing to *commensales* who were sojourners, senior figures who were mainly *magistri*, so here the word must refer to undergraduates. A little later we are told that in the dean's audience might be three categories of student: fellows of the College who were not graduates ('scholaribus huius collegii non graduatis'), *commensales*, and battelers—that is, the whole undergraduate body of the College, some of whom were fellows but most of whom, *commensales* and battelers, were not. Finally, the statutes state that expulsion might be the fate of any

[180] Boase (2), lxxvii; above, 205–6.   [181] Reg., 78; Boase (2), 72.
[182] McConica, 'Rise of the Undergraduate College', *HUO*, iii. 58.

commensalis or batteler who offended against College discipline, baulked at scholastic exercises, or was otherwise recalcitrant.[183] This sort of threat could hardly be held over the head of sojourner-*commensales*, who in any case would be far beyond undertaking scholastic exercises, so we can again conclude that both *commensales* (or commoners as we may now call them) and batelers were undergraduates.

What differentiated them? The usual view is that the division was social and economic, as we might expect. The undergraduate commoners were relatively wealthy men, often the sons of gentlemen, who paid for their commons and rooms, and could afford to do so. The batelers, on the other hand, were an inferior group, who paid in part for their board and lodging, but had to make up the balance by performing menial services around the College.[184] There is nothing in the Exeter evidence to confirm or deny this, but whenever the two groups are mentioned together the commoners always take precedence over the batelers, and the conventional view is almost certainly correct. That the division had an economic foundation is implied by the appearance, about the time of the Petrean statutes, of a third undergraduate group, the poor scholars. A university census of 1572 credits Exeter with some eighty undergraduates—a huge increase on the thirteen of twenty years previously—of whom nine are described as servitors and twelve as poor scholars.[185] The distinction between servitors and poor scholars is obscure, but both groups are likely to have belonged to an undergraduate category known at other Oxford colleges from about this time: those too poor to pay anything for board and lodging but who instead supported themselves by service, often the service of particular fellows.[186] The first known appearance of such a student comes from 1564, when one Chardener is recorded as the poor scholar of John Neale, the Rector.[187]

The full emergence of Exeter's undergraduate body from its fifteenth-century beginnings was thus an evolutionary process. The small group of undifferentiated batelers living in College in the mid sixteenth century had by the 1570s given way to a much larger and more hierarchically structured society of commoners, batelers, and poor scholars. This was the result of two connected developments, common to most colleges: the great expansion in undergraduate numbers from the 1550s onwards, and the increasing preponderance of the well-born, sons of the gentry, who could pay their way

---

[183] *Statutes*, 34, 35, 49.

[184] For discussion, see Emden, *An Oxford Hall*, 211; Russell, 'The Influx of Commoners', 723–4; Cobban, *The Medieval English Universities*, 306; McConica, 'Rise of the Undergraduate College', *HUO*, iii. 44 n. 6; Darwall-Smith, 196; L. W. B. Brockliss (ed.), *Magdalen College: A History* (Oxford, 2008), 186.

[185] *Register*, ed. Clark, II. ii. 32; Boase (2), xcvi–xcvii.

[186] Cf. Darwall-Smith, 138, 196; McConica, 'The Collegiate Society', *HUO*, iii. 668, 724.

[187] *Register*, ed. Clark, II. i. 287; Boase (2), 68.

through College and came to constitute the bulk of the commoners. Both developments may have owed something, perhaps much, to the successful efforts of the authorities, university and state, to force former town-dwelling undergraduates into colleges and halls in order to impose upon them both good order and religious conformity.[188] But it is doubtful if such a large-scale and general expansion can be wholly explained in these terms.

In Exeter's case expansion must have been particularly welcome, bringing as it did the prospect of a rise in income and contact with young men who might one day be well placed to serve the College. The College's recognition, at just this time, of some well-born sojourners as *generosi* is another sign of its growing interest in the status of its members, and probably for similar reasons. But status did not yet confer formal privilege. All these classes of undergraduates, commoners, battelers, and poor scholars, took the same oath on admission, swearing to defend the good fame of the College, to do nothing to its detriment, to observe the 'ordinary exercises of the College' (meaning presumably the prescribed academic studies), and to accept both its discipline and any penalties imposed for failings.[189] It was only in the early seventeenth century, when the gentleman commoners were first established as a rank above all other undergraduates, that wealth and status began to buy tangible privilege within the College. With this development a fourfold structure of undergraduate society was established which would persist until the late eighteenth century.[190]

We know unfortunately little about the origins, and still less the personalities, of the College's early undergraduates. Some of the names on the 1552 census list, such as Edgecombe and Coffin, suggest Devon roots; and although there was no regional limitation on undergraduate recruitment, as there was on the recruitment of fellows, it is very likely that the majority of the undergraduates came from the west country. This is borne out by the one source which provides any real insight into undergraduate identities. In August 1566 John Neale, then Rector, wrote to Sir William Petre to pass on the names of thirteen undergraduates whose proficiency and conduct made them eligible candidates, in Neale's view, for Sir William's new fellowships.[191] For each of them he provided a brief but invaluable verbal sketch, the whole constituting an undergraduate group portrait for which it is difficult to find parallels elsewhere in the university. Of those whom Neale named, five were lodged in other colleges and halls. Of the eight Exonians, three were from Devon, four from Cornwall, and one from Rutland, and six were said to be

---

[188] This is the argument of Russell, 'The Influx of Commoners', esp. 731–46. Cf. McConica, 'The Collegiate Society', *HUO*, iii. 724.

[189] DRO, MS Chanter 732; Boase (2), xcviii.

[190] Cf. J. Maddicott, 'College Servants', *Exeter College Association Register, 2006*, 31–4.

[191] ERO, D/DP Q13/1/1: list of names enclosed with John Neale's letter to Sir William Petre, 22 August 1565.

aged 19 or 20, and two 16 or 17. More interesting, however, is the information which Neale gave about the family background and status of some of his protégés. Henry Batsell, born in Devon, was 'poor and forward [precocious, advanced], now supplying a servant's room [place] in our college' (so presumably a poor scholar or servitor). John Symons, 'born in Devon by Exeter', was 'honest and tractable but a rich farmer's son having indeed many young children'. John Batte, 'a husband man's son, batteleth in our college'. John Ryman, from Cornwall, was 'a mean [middling] gentle man's son', and Nicholas Roscarrock, 'a good and worshipful man's son'—as indeed he was, scion of an ancient, wealthy, and armigerous Cornish family.[192]

In their social standing—poor scholar, sons of an ordinary farmer (husbandman), a rich farmer, a middling gentleman, and a wealthy one—these men were probably as representative a group of Exeter undergraduates as one could hope to find: a social microcosm of the whole College. Only students from the towns were perhaps missing. In other ways, however, they may have been less typical, for Neale clearly regarded them as a select and especially deserving group. John Batte and James Brooke, an outsider from St Mary's Hall, were 'like to make honest men and good scholars'. John Symons was 'an indifferent [moderate] scholar, meetly forward and studious'. George Benet and John Capet, both Cornish born, were 'both studious and desirous of learning... meetly apt [very intelligent] and always diligent'. Their subsequent careers largely bear out Neale's faith in their abilities. Three—John Capet, John Ryman, and Nicholas Roscarrock—left without taking a degree, a normal outcome for many undergraduates. But three—Kenelm Carter, from Rutland, Henry Batsell, and John Batte—went on to take the BA and the MA and to become fellows of the College, Carter by Sir William Petre's nomination. This is an important pointer to what we might not otherwise suspect: the recruitment of fellows from among the College's undergraduate intake. Two others among the eight, George Benet and John Symons, appear to have left the College after graduating as bachelors.[193] We shall meet some of this talented group again, for what many of them also proved to have in common was their catholicism: a religious faith shared by many of the College's west country undergraduates and a quality likely to commend these select few to Exeter's future catholic patron, whose benefactions will be discussed shortly.[194]

One other undergraduate lends himself to a fuller pen portrait. Tristram Farringdon was the son of John Farringdon, a minor member of the Devon

[192] *Nicholas Roscarrock's Lives of the Saints: Cornwall and Devon*, ed. N. Orme, DCRS, new ser., 35 (1992), 1–4; A. L. Rowse, *Tudor Cornwall* (London, 1941), 289, 368–9.
[193] Boase (2), 74, 75, 76; *Register*, ed. Boase, 261, 269, 273; *Nicholas Roscarrock's Lives*, ed. Orme, 3–4.
[194] Below, 294–5, 300, 302, 309.

gentry from the small parish, a few miles east of Exeter, which gave him his
name. We do not know when Tristram matriculated at Exeter, but we do
know that he died in July 1577, a victim of the devastating outbreak of typhus
which struck Oxford in that year, causing the College to disperse into the
countryside and killing two of its fellows, James Rainolds and John Simpson.
As Tristram also lay dying, 'sick and weak in body but of sound and perfect
memory', he made his will. Describing himself as 'gentleman', he left some of
his property to his cousin William and the rest to his father John, whose
portion included Tristram's seventeen books. Listed in the subsequent probate inventory, these were his most revealing (but not his most valuable)
possessions. They included works in Greek by Thucydides and Demos-
thenes, some of the Greek commentaries of Philoponus on Aristotle, Hermo-
genes on rhetoric, a set text for the arts course, in Greek and Latin, two
homilies of St John Chrysostom, also in Greek and Latin, another patristic
work by Athanasius, and—most valuable of all—a folio volume on Moses by
Philo Judaeus, the Hellenistic Jewish philosopher of the first century AD. His
other goods reflected his status as both *generosus* and undergraduate. Among
them was 'a cloak faced with velvet', valued at 50s., ten times more than his
copy of Philo; a gold ring set with turquoises, of equal value; and a satin
doublet, left to cousin William. Then there were the personal items in his
College room, among them a black gown faced with rabbit fur, probably his
academic gown; cushions, coverlets, blankets, and a bolster; a pewter basin
and chamber pot, an old cloak and an old cloak bag; and a pair of compasses,
useful perhaps for the geometry element in the arts course—the pathetic
detritus of a brief student life.[195]

Tristram Farringdon is an exemplar of some general trends, a few peculiar
to Exeter, others more universal. Son of a Devon gentleman, he came to
Exeter to study the arts course, like all undergraduates and as his books
indicate. But he clearly knew Greek as well as the Latin essential for arts,
and his books also point to the new humanist element in the sixteenth-century
syllabus. No doubt a dashing figure with his velvet-faced cloak and his satin
doublet, he represented the influx of the gentry and gentry style into the
Elizabethan university, and the education, both traditionally Aristotelian and
progressively classical, which its members expected to receive before they
returned home to a life of neighbourliness, estate management, and administrative service. Paradoxically, the consequences of his early death almost

---

[195] Family: *The Visitation of the County of Devon in the Year 1564*, ed. F. T. Colby (Exeter,
1881), 95. Typhus: Wood, *History*, ii. 188–92; Boase (2), lxxxviii; McConica, 'The Collegiate
Society', *HUO*, iii. 648; will and possessions: OUA, Hyp/A/5 (Reg. GG.), fo. 230ᵛ; Hyp/B/12;
Fehrenbach and Leedham-Green, *Private Libraries in Renaissance England*, v. 77–81; McConica,
'The Collegiate Society', 707 n. 7; Fletcher, 'Faculty of Arts', *HUO*, iii. 172.

certainly reveal more about Tristram and his aspirations than his survival would have done.

7. SETTING AND SOCIETY

In the sixteenth century Exeter's physical setting on its central site changed little. But what change there was continued the process of expansion which had been in train since the mid fourteenth century and brought the College a little nearer to its modern limits. It was at the south-east corner of the site, occupied today by the mound, the pond, and part of the Bodleian proscholium, that change was most evident. In the later middle ages this area had been occupied by two sets of schools (lecture rooms), the northern set belonging to Exeter, and the southern, in the angle between St Mildred's Lane (Brasenose Lane) and Schools Street (Radcliffe Square), belonging to Balliol. But in the mid sixteenth century this whole area was cleared of its buildings. Exeter's schools, owned by the College since 1333, were demolished in 1549, their timber and tiles carted off for use elsewhere, and the site rented out as a garden.[196] Balliol's schools, on the adjoining plot, were also demolished shortly afterwards, and the site laid out as another garden. This was rented to Exeter by Balliol from 1566 to 1572, when it came into the College's permanent possession by exchange for an Exeter tenement standing on the present main Balliol site in Broad Street.[197] The wall between the two gardens was then taken down, and it may have been about twenty years later that the present mound was constructed on the land where Balliol's schools had once stood.[198]

The demolition of these two sets of schools was a sign of the times. It marked the declining demand for lecturing facilities, itself a pointer both to falling numbers at the university and to the waning of the duty to lecture once imposed on all regent masters.[199] Just as the laying out of the main garden was a consequence of the Black Death, so its extension eastwards was a consequence of other external changes two centuries later. The result may have enhanced the College's attractions, but it also brought some loss of income. In the first decades of the century rent from the schools had brought in about 25s. a year, and latterly rather less; but the garden rent was worth only a little more than 2s. a year, adding marginally to Exeter's financial difficulties.[200] The College garden in general saw few changes at this time, with little activity

---

[196] RA, 241/3; Boase (2), lii n. 1; *Balliol Deeds*, ed. Salter, 156–7; Salter, *Survey*, i. 69–70.

[197] *Balliol Deeds*, ed. Salter, 156–7; Salter, *Survey*, i. 69, ii. 90, map NE II; Boase (1), 45.

[198] Mounds became fashionable in the middle years of Elizabeth, and the New College mound was begun in 1594: J. Buxton and P. Williams (eds.), *New College, Oxford, 1379–1979* (Oxford, 1979), 202. The Exeter mound is mentioned by Anthony Wood, c.1660: Bodleian MS Wood D. 2, 83.

[199] Above, 184–5, 207.

[200] Compare schools rent of £1 1s. in 1504, with a garden rent of 2s. 8d. in 1552: RA, 198, 245/1.

recorded on the accounts beyond the renewed cultivation of saffron in the 1520s, the planting of trees in 1533 (a year which saw a minor burst of spending on the garden), and the planting of apple trees in 1544.[201] Elsewhere in the College there was, as we have seen, little building besides the addition of some rooms in 1533 and the repairs which were a constant and expensive feature of College life. But although the site did not change much there was one minor but interesting alteration to the terminology used to describe it. In 1565 4d. was paid for cleaning the *quadrangulum*, the quadrangle, which presumably refers either to the area lying west–east between the chapel and the backs of the early properties fronting Somenor's Lane, or to the area between the hall and the chapel—each an open-ended rectangle rather than a true quadrangle.[202] It superseded the formerly used term *curia*, 'court', still used at Cambridge for what in Oxford is called a quadrangle. For the first time the College had a quadrangle: the word perhaps, if not the thing.

Within the College standards of comfort seem to have been rising, at least during the relatively prosperous early decades of the century. For example, glass appeared in windows. The Rector's room was glazed, apparently for the first time in 1505, and this was followed by further glazing operations in the rooms of four fellows and sojourners in 1505. Exeter was probably in the vanguard of Oxford colleges here.[203] But with the onset of rapid inflation from the 1530s any rise in living standards is likely to have been reversed. Even the extra cash decrements voted by the fellows as an addition to their commons could not keep up with accelerating food prices, and consumption almost certainly declined. The annual St Thomas's day feast came to an end after 1537, though this was a change dictated by prudence and religion, as we shall see, rather than by the need for economy;[204] and the feast was to some extent replaced by alternative festivities at Christmas, a few days before the date of the former feast. For the first time Christmas became a major event in the College year. The fellows' commons were sometimes augmented to pay for the celebrations—by 28s. in 1548, about as much as had previously been spent on the feast.[205] Delicacies were brought in for the table. In 1543 a conger eel was sent up from Devon (how was it preserved?), and in 1560 purchases were made of a special drink, *potus lupatus*, apples, and spices.[206] Pork and wild boar might sometimes be brought from Wittenham for the festivities.[207] Other minor celebrations punctuated the year. The short-lived custom of beer-drinking at the annual audit had long been abandoned but on three occasions in the year, on the eve of the Epiphany (5 January), St John the

---

[201] RA, 214/4, 215/4, 220/1, 227/2/3, 236/2.   [202] RA, 253/3.
[203] RA, 197/2, 200/1; Newman, 'New Building and Adaptation', *HUO*, iii. 629–30.
[204] Below, 231.
[205] RA, 241/2. Cf. RA, 239/2 for another Christmas 'augmentation'. For the comparable Christmas celebrations at Lincoln, more fully recorded than those at Exeter, see Green, 111–12.
[206] RA, 235/expenses 2, 250/2.   [207] RA, 242/2, 245/2.

Baptist's day (24 June), and the feast of St Peter ad Vincula (1 August), there were festive drinking sessions, *bibarii*, subsidized by the College to an agreed maximum of 4s.[208] On another occasion in 1553, but not at Christmas, two capons and a swan were delivered 'for the fellows' feast' by the maidservant of the Wittenham farmer.[209] When times were hard and food prices high, the little luxuries which the College's own lands could provide may have been all the more appreciated.

Food and drink were often shared with others in College hospitality. The entertainment of visitors did not differ greatly from the practices of earlier times, though the accounts give the impression, impossible to demonstrate statistically, that it may have happened rather less frequently and in more circumscribed ways. There is, for example, no record of the entertainment of the women guests who had sometimes appeared in College during the four-teenth and fifteenth centuries.[210] The general character of other guests remained much the same. Besides the bishops of Exeter, whose occasional appearances we have already noted, the Exeter cathedral clergy were some-times entertained to wine—the archdeacon of Exeter in 1513, the cathedral sub-dean in 1519, the chancellor of the bishop in 1527.[211] Former fellows were fairly frequent visitors, as they had always been. Dr Peter Carsley, canon of Exeter and for a short time vicar of Menheniot, was a particular favourite, occasionally given wine, the frequent recipient of gifts of gloves, and for some time the sojourner-tenant of a College room.[212] Some visitors were of more weight and influence. John Skewish, a Cornishman, one of Cardinal Wolsey's chief legal officers, and a man with important contacts among the nobility, was presented with gloves and entertained to wine on several occasions in the 1520s and 1530s, and may have resided for a time either in College or in Hart Hall;[213] while on two occasions in 1522 and 1523 the College entertained John Longland, a former sojourner, now bishop of Lincoln, and a future chancellor of the university.[214] The accounts suggest that the entertainment of all such guests declined markedly in the 1540s and 1550s, perhaps in response to the College's financial difficulties. But until then it followed along trad-itional lines.

Whatever other convivial and recreational activities the fellows may have enjoyed are largely hidden from view. But cultural pursuits were certainly among them. Music and drama, for example, played at least some part in the lives of some. A little beyond the end of our period James Rainolds, a fellow at the time of his death in 1577, owned 'a pair of virginals' worth 20s., and a lute worth 8s., while John Simpson, who died in the same year, possessed three

[208] Reg., 39; Boase (1), 37.   [209] RA, 245/3.   [210] Above, 152.
[211] RA, 207/4, 213/3, 220/2.   [212] RA, 197/2, 203/2/3, 208/1; above, 210.
[213] Boase (1), 32; *BRUO, 1501–40*, 517; P. Sherlock, 'John Skewys', *ODNB*.
[214] RA, 216/1/4; *BRUO*, ii. 1160.

lutes worth £3 and a 'luting book' worth 4s.[215] Music almost certainly accompanied the plays in which the College also participated. In Lent 1548 6s. 8d. was paid for 'the expenses of acting a comedy in public', and in Lent 1551 one Dolye received 5s. 3d. for painting 'what was needed for acting comedies'. The performances, similar to those laid on in other colleges, may have been a mark of humanist influence, providing as they did 'schooling in the arts of rhetoric'.[216] Or they may have been mere entertainment.

The social contacts of the fellows extended well beyond the College walls, to other colleges, the neighbourhood, and the town. Visits continued to be made to other colleges on their feast days, as they had been in the two preceding centuries, and in 1558 Trinity, a newcomer among the colleges, was added to the list.[217] Outside Oxford the College enjoyed long and friendly relations with some of its tenants. Its ties with one of them, Thomas Piers, were especially close. Piers, who lived just over the Thames at Hinksey in Berkshire, was the farmer of the Wittenham tithes for some twenty years from 1535 to the mid 1550s, and the father of John Piers, a future archbishop of York.[218] The College's dealings with Piers, like those with another Wittenham farmer, Eustace Young, 'Staci', in the late fourteenth century, went beyond mere business. His wife received regular gifts of money from the College, so regular as to suggest that she performed some service. Piers himself was sent clothing from time to time and was employed to distribute money to the Wittenham poor on the College's behalf.[219] During the mid century period his is the name which recurs more frequently in the accounts than any besides those of the fellows.

More extended and intricate were the College's relationships with the town. By the mid sixteenth century Exeter had accumulated a little archipelago of Oxford properties, though its value was not large. Its main components, most of them noted already, are listed in the two valuations of the College made in 1535 and 1546. They comprised a tenement in the parish of St Peter le Bailey, formerly Karol Hall, in the neighbourhood of the modern Westgate;[220] a house in Queen Street, in St Martin's parish;[221] a house on the present site of Balliol College, in St Mary Magdalen parish, exchanged in 1572 for Balliol's holding to the east of the College garden;[222] Peyntour's Hall the brewhouse in St Giles, on the site of St John's College, bought in 1478;[223] a

[215] J. Caldwell, 'Music in the Faculty of Arts', HUO, iii. 208 n. 5.
[216] RA, 240/2, 243/2; Boase (2), cxiii; McConica, 'The Collegiate Society', HUO, iii. 652. Note also McConica, 'The Collegiate Society', HUO, iii. 53, 209, 367, 398, 665.
[217] RA, 248/3.   [218] RA, 230/4, 247/2; C. Cross, 'John Piers', ODNB.
[219] RA, 238/1, 240/1, 242/2, 245/1/2, 246/2, etc.
[220] Valor, ii. 268–9; TNA, E 315/441, fo. 113ᵛ; Salter, Survey, ii. 129.
[221] Salter, Survey, ii. 117.   [222] Salter, Survey, ii. 190; above, 221.
[223] Salter, Survey, ii. 201–2; above, 168.

house, formerly Batayl Hall, in Magdalen Street;[224] a garden off Ship Street, the site of the former Ledenporch;[225] and—the most recent acquisition—the house in Cat Street, bought in 1531. Of these, only Batayl Hall and the Ledenporch garden, formerly a hall, had belonged to the College since the days of Stapeldon, and some properties were soon to be alienated. The Queen Street house had been sold by 1569, and the newly founded Jesus College bought a long lease on the Ledenporch garden before 1590.[226] On the whole, the century was one in which properties were shed rather than acquired.

Given its own place in Oxford and its properties in the town, the College could not but be involved with the town's administration. It paid a regular retaining fee to an agent to represent it in the mayor's court[227] and maintained friendly relations with the town's governing circle. The mayor and his colleagues (confratres) were entertained to wine in the Rector's room in 1520, and an alderman, Mr Fryer, was similarly treated in 1538.[228] For many years in the mid century the tenant of the College's most valuable Oxford property, the brewhouse and inn in St Giles, was Edmund Irish, city alderman, mayor in 1551, and, appropriately, a brewer by trade. In his will he asked the Rector and fellows to 'fetch me to the church the day of my burial', a request implying that he was more than just the College's valued tenant.[229] Relations between town and gown in the sixteenth century were not always smooth, and the privileges of the university were a fairly constant source of friction, particularly in the 1520s and 1530s.[230] But this never precluded friendly social ties between individual townsmen and the colleges, on whose presence the town economy was so dependent.

Over all colleges and their social connections in the sixteenth century hung a constant shadow: that of epidemic disease, usually bubonic plague but also the sweating sickness and influenza, all often covered by the generic term *pestis*. Oxford was an exceptionally unhealthy place at this time. Even when allowances have been made for the multiplication of records, plague appears to have been a far more frequent visitor to the town and university than it had been in the previous century. Between 1507 and 1557 it struck in some twenty-two years,[231] sometimes severely disrupting the work of the university (though probably none of these outbreaks was so severe as the typhus epidemic of 1577 which carried off Tristram Farringdon). In 1517 it was

---

[224] Salter, *Survey*, ii. 218.   [225] Salter, *Survey*, i. 33.   [226] Salter, *Survey*, ii. 118, i. 33.
[227] e.g. RA, 207/1.   [228] RA, 220/1, 231/3.
[229] RA, 229/2, etc.; *Register*, ed. Clark, II. i. 296–7, 324, 330; *Selections from the Records*, ed. Turner, 56, 160, 166, 174, 192–3, etc.; *VCH Oxfordshire*, iv. 155.
[230] Hammer, 'Oxford Town', *HUO*, iii. 86–94, 114–15; *VCH Oxfordshire*, i. 155.
[231] A list of plague years can be compiled from *Epistolae academicae*, ed. Mitchell, 3, 71, 83, 87, 98, 175, 178, 249; Wood, *History*, ii. 2, 6, 26, 57, 66, 74, 75, 138; and Green, 119–23. The sixteen epidemic years for the whole century, given in *VCH Oxfordshire*, iv. 76, is certainly too low a figure.

rumoured in London that some 400 Oxford students had died of plague, while in 1518 and 1519 further outbreaks caused the suspension of lectures and of the bachelors' determination exercises. The latter were suspended again in 1525.[232] The effect on the colleges was severe. Lincoln was struck in at least eleven years between 1507 and 1548, causing frequent deaths among the fellowship and, as in other colleges, precipitating flight into the country-side.[233] Before 1560 Exeter's accounts, less full than those of Lincoln, record epidemics only in 1518, 1538, 1544, and 1551; in all four years disease is mentioned only because it necessitated special dispensation to allow fellows to receive their commons when they had left for the country 'in time of plague'.[234] But there were almost certainly other years in which the College was afflicted. If Lincoln was struck so frequently, it seems unlikely that Exeter would have escaped more lightly; although, on the other hand, the absence of recorded deaths at Exeter, by contrast with the fatalities at Lincoln, may suggest that the College enjoyed rather better fortunes than its next-door neighbour.[235]

These recurrent plagues must have added greatly to the College's troubles. They are likely to have contributed to the fall-off in numbers which afflicted the university in the first half of the century. Wood was probably correct when he wrote that the 1545 plague 'prevented many coming to the univer-sity'.[236] Epidemic disease killed some, perhaps many, and deterred others. It disrupted college administration, removed fellows and undergraduates from their studies, and in lowering numbers, it also reduced income. Breeding fear and uncertainty, its psychological effects cannot be measured but are likely to have been profound. All these factors came to a head in the violent outbreak of 1563–4. This produced the greatest plague crisis which the College faced in the entire century; but, providing as it does the backdrop to Sir William Petre's re-endowment of the College, its discussion is best reserved for a later stage in the story.

8. THE COLLEGE AND THE REFORMATION

Greater even than the economic pressures bearing on the College in the mid sixteenth century were those resulting from religious change. Between 1530

---

[232] *VCH Oxfordshire*, iv. 76; *Epistolae academicae*, ed. Mitchell, 375; Wood, *History*, ii. 26.

[233] Green, 119–23.

[234] RA, 212/4, 231/3, 236/4; Boase (1), 31, 39; Boase (2), lxxxviii, 63.

[235] There was at least one plague death at Hart Hall in 1519: *Epistolae academicae*, ed. Mitchell, 375. The meeting of congregation at St Frideswide's (Christ Church) in 1533 rather than at St Mary's, probably because of the plague, and the transfer of other meetings from one part of Oxford to another, suggests that outbreaks of plague may sometimes have been very localized: see *Epistolae academicae*, ed. Mitchell, 334–5, 407.

[236] Wood, *History*, ii. 75.

and 1560 both religious doctrine and religious practice shifted frequently and in a wholly unprecedented way: from the regal catholicism of Henry VIII to the radical protestantism of Edward VI and thence to the restored catholicism of Mary and the protestant via media of her half-sister Elizabeth. The problems of allegiance which these shifts posed for all Oxford colleges sprang essentially from the imperative need of successive rulers of the English church to secure the university's support for their policies, whether by coercion, bullying, or persuasion. The university and its colleges were, as they had always been, the main nursery of priests and future bishops, and the country's chief reservoir of learned men, well equipped to use pen and pulpit to defend or attack the religion of the moment. They therefore possessed the means to promote the church's reformation, in whatever direction the crown might want to take it. For these reasons, and for the first time in their history, the intervention of the state became the main constraint on the colleges' freedom of action.

For most of this period Exeter was a particularly conservative college in a generally conservative university. In practice this meant an adherence, as far as possible, to traditional catholicism in the face both of royal claims to ecclesiastical supremacy and of the doctrinaire protestantism that followed. Later still, under Elizabeth, Exeter came to be marked out, even notorious, for the catholic sympathies of its fellows and undergraduates. The reasons are not far to seek. The College's members were largely recruited from the far southwest, one of the most catholic and conservative parts of England, and one distant from the centres of contemporary protestantism in London and along the counties of the east coast, exposed as they were (and as Devon and Cornwall were not) to the tides of reformed religion flowing in from Germany. Like so many other aspects of its development, Exeter's religious history was thus shaped by its local affiliations.

In the early stages of the Reformation the College's position can be made out only hazily and uncertainly, but what little we know of its members' opinions supports the position just set out. The College's first test came, as it did for most colleges, in the early 1530s, when Henry VIII was attempting to divorce his queen, Katherine of Aragon, in order to marry Anne Boleyn. In 1530 the king sought a verdict from the university on his marriage to Katherine, whose invalidity he wished it to declare, and in 1534 he sought from it a further declaration against the primacy of the pope in the English church. On the first occasion the king looked to the university's doctors of theology, de facto its most senior members, to give him an opinion. But there were objections to this procedure from the excluded and younger *magistri* in the arts faculty, though in the end it was the theologians who gave Henry the answer he wanted. The objections of the arts *magistri* were probably ones of substance as well as procedure and may well have sprung from their support for Katherine, which, if Anthony Wood is right, was widespread

throughout the university.[237] Exeter's opinion is open to speculation. But as
an all-arts College, with no doctors of theology, its fellows might have been
expected to side with the opposition. Two men associated with the College
certainly did so. According to William Forrest, a local priest present in
Oxford at this time, two of the leading opponents of any attempt to declare
Henry's marriage invalid were John Moreman and John Holyman. Moreman
had been a fellow of Exeter from 1510 to 1522 and was currently the College's
vicar of Menheniot, though in 1530 he still had a room in College and was
probably residing there. Holyman's links with Exeter were more tenuous: a
former fellow of New College, he had merely been a sojourner at Exeter a
few years earlier in 1525–6.[238]

Both men were similarly associated with opposition to Henry's plans
in 1534. Shortly before the king appealed to the university to rule against
papal headship of the English church, both Moreman and Holyman were
denounced to Thomas Cromwell, now the king's chief minister, as
'enemies to the king's cause'.[239] At this time Holyman was once again
residing in Exeter as a sojourner, an unlikely home for him had the
company and its views not been congenial. Moreman's links with his
old College are more obscure, but he remained as vicar of the College's
parish until 1559 and he remembered Exeter in his will. The evidence is
perhaps just sufficient to associate Exeter with opposition to the king's
divorce and to his declaration of independence from Rome. At any rate it
was not among the few colleges—All Souls, Balliol, Oriel, Brasenose, and
Lincoln—listed in 1534 as submitting to the removal of papal supremacy
from the English church.[240]

The following year, 1535, saw the first royal visitation of Oxford and
Cambridge, when visitors appointed and directed by Cromwell descended
both on the university and on its colleges and halls. The valuation of college
property, Exeter's included, which was to form part of the *Valor ecclesiasticus*,
immediately preceded this visitation, whose purpose was to secure sworn
assent to the royal supremacy and to promote the new learning in Latin and
Greek through the foundation of public lectureships. This was a more force-
ful assertion of state power in the affairs of the university than any yet seen.
Although there is a good deal of general evidence on the relations between the
colleges and their visitors, who were, for example, dined in at least five
colleges, the record for Exeter remains a blank. But all members of the

[237] *Epistolae academicae*, ed. Mitchell, xxiii. 269–80; Wood, *History*, ii. 40–9; C. Cross,
'Oxford and the Tudor State', *HUO*, iii. 124–6; J. M. Fletcher, 'The Faculty of Arts', *HUO*,
iii. 164; J. Loach, 'Reformation Controversies', *HUO*, iii. 364–5.
[238] *BRUO, 1501–40*, 295, 400; Wood, *History*, ii. 47–8; RA, 223/4; Loach, 'Reformation
Controversies', *HUO*, iii. 364–5.
[239] *L. and P.*, VII. 38.   [240] *L. and P.*, VII. 328.

university are known to have taken the oath acknowledging the king's
supremacy and the fellows of Exeter cannot have been an exception.[241]

The visitation of the universities was part of the wider visitation of the
country's religious houses which proved to be the prelude to the dissolution
of the monasteries, the smaller houses in 1536, the larger in 1538–9. The
dissolution had some material effects on Exeter, as we shall see, but it is likely
to have had a much larger impact on the religious susceptibilities and assump-
tions of the College's fellows. Prior to the dissolution Exeter had had friendly
contacts, part business, part social, with a large number of religious houses.
Their heads had sometimes been sojourners within the College, presumably
while they enjoyed a term or two's study leave at the university. To those
heads resident at different points in the previous century, we could add the
prior of Bruton in various terms between 1506 and 1513;[242] the prior of
Bodmin in 1515;[243] the abbot of St Augustine's, Bristol, in 1527;[244] and,
most recently, the prior of Launceston in 1535.[245] All these were west country
houses. Their heads must have been particularly welcome guests, since they
paid well for their rooms, the prior of Bruton as much as 23s. a year between
1511 and 1513. He and his *juniores*—perhaps young monks—were entertained
to wine in College in 1513 and, for so much money, may have enjoyed a suite
of rooms.[246]

With one house in particular the College had especially close ties. For much
of the 1520s the Rector and fellows were on notably friendly terms with the
great Benedictine abbey of Glastonbury in Somerset. A monk of Glastonbury
was entertained to wine in 1522,[247] and from then on exchanges were frequent. On several occasions presents of expensive gloves were sent to Richard
Whiting, abbot from 1525, and sometimes additionally to the prior, cellarer,
steward, 'and the rest of our friends there'.[248] In 1524 the Rector rode down
to Somerset to visit the abbot; letters were sent to him in 1525; and the abbot
in turn was given wine in College in 1528.[249] Two years earlier he had given
the Rector £2 as a contribution to building work on the College chapel.[250]
Although the relationship appears to have ceased in the 1530s, it had while it
lasted been the most intimate which the College had sustained with any
religious house.

The College's ties with Glastonbury seem to have been partly rooted in
business. In 1501 a Somerset knight, Sir John Byconyll, had endowed exhibitions of four or five marks each for scholars studying at Oxford. The
nomination of the scholars, ten in number, fell to the abbot of Glastonbury,

[241] F. D. Logan, 'The First Royal Visitation of the English Universities, 1535', *EHR*, 106
(1991), 861–78, esp. 871–3; Cross, 'Oxford and the Tudor State', *HUO*, iii. 127–9.
[242] RA, 200/3/4, 203/3, 204/1, 205/2, 207/4.
[243] RA, 209/4.   [244] RA, 220/2/4.   [245] RA, 230/1/3.   [246] RA, 207/4.
[247] RA, 215/2, 216/1.   [248] RA, 218/4, 219/2/4, 222/1.
[249] RA, 217/4, 218/4, 222/1.   [250] RA, 219/4.

where Sir John was buried, and the exhibitions, paid for by the abbot, came to be attached to Hart Hall, Exeter's dependency and later described by the seventeenth-century Oxford antiquary Brian Twyne as a 'colony' of Glastonbury. This connection almost certainly underlay the College's close ties with Glastonbury and its abbot. At the dissolution the right to nominate came to the crown, or more specifically to the officers of the exchequer. Although at least six of the ten scholars supported by the exchequer in 1546 appear to have been nominated before Glastonbury's dissolution in 1539, payments for them may well have lapsed in the years immediately following. This would explain an otherwise curious coincidence: the sharp drop in the annual rent paid to the College by the principal of Hart Hall at just this time. In 1538 the rent stood at £2 6s., but in 1539 it fell to £2 2s. 8d. and in 1540 to £1 16s., where it remained until 1551. If the Glastonbury income had ceased and not been renewed for some time, the loss to Hart Hall may have been of the order of 10 × 5 marks, or about £33 a year.[251] The effects of the dissolution on the monastic population of the university, often traversed,[252] may thus have touched even a secular College and contributed in a small way to Exeter's mid century financial difficulties.

The dissolution had other and more minor consequences, less material but perhaps equally jarring to contemporary susceptibilities. From its foundation the College had had regular financial dealings with local monastic houses, paying small ground rents to them for some of its holdings on the central site. To the nunnery of Godstow it paid 12s. annually for two of its original tenements along Somenor's Lane; to the priory of St Frideswide's, 6s. annually for the former halls along St Mildred's Lane, long since turned into a garden; and to Osney a similar small rent for its later acquisition, Peter Hall, on the corner of Turl Street and the Lane. But at the dissolution the revenues of these monastic houses, like those of all others, came into the king's hands, and the entries in the expenses section of the accounts were adjusted accordingly. The rent formerly payable to Osney was now noted as going to the lay grantee of the Osney property; 12s. was paid 'formerly to Godstow, now to the king'; while the 6s. rent was set down as 'formerly to Frideswide, now to the king's majesty' (6s. was still being paid annually to Christ Church, Frideswide's successor, in 1872).[253] As a result of the dissolution the state had intruded into the smallest interstices of College business.

Between 1536 and 1539 the whole nexus of the College's relationship with English monastic houses thus came to an end. A symbolic term to those relationships was set by the brutal execution of the College's former friend

---

[251] N. Orme, 'The Byconyll Exhibitions at Oxford, 1502–1664', *Oxoniensia*, 55 (1990), 115–20; Saul, 'Hart Hall', 337, 342; Wood, *History*, ii. 69; Wood, *Colleges*, i. 643; Boase (2), xxvii.
[252] e.g. J. McConica, 'Studies and Faculties', *HUO*, iii. 153.
[253] RA, 235/expenses 1, 239/4, 242/1; Boase (1), 32.

and benefactor Richard Whiting, abbot of Glastonbury, hanged, drawn, and quartered on Glastonbury Tor on 15 November 1539.[254] Nor was the domestic side of College life left unaffected by the events of these years. In 1538 the king had it proclaimed that Thomas Becket should no longer be venerated as a saint, his feast days no longer observed, his images and depictions removed from churches, and his name struck out from the ecclesiastical calendar.[255] This was awkward for the College, since Becket was one of the three patrons of the College chapel, together with the Virgin and St Peter. His image stood there,[256] and the College's annual feast on 29 December commemorated his martyrdom. The Chapel's dedication appears to have survived Becket's expunction from the record, but the feast failed to do so. In December 1537, when the cult of saints and their shrines was already under attack, the College celebrated, not 'the feast of St Thomas', the usual heading for feast expenditure in the accounts, but instead spent 41s. 8d. 'for a meal on the day of the lord Thomas (*pro refectione die domini Thome*)'.[257] Already demoted from sainthood, Thomas was soon to disappear completely. In the following year, when the usual celebrations should have been held, some six weeks after the king's proclamation, there was no feast. Although briefly revived in 1557, under catholic Mary, and in 1558,[258] it was effectively extinct after 1537. A long tradition going back to the 1330s had come to an end.

Other minor changes were associated with the suppression of Becket's name and cult. The accounts had customarily dated the end of the College's summer term to 'the Saturday before the Translation of St Thomas the Martyr', the feast celebrated on 7 July. But in 1539, in the summer term following the proclamation, prudence prevailed, and the term's ending was given more baldly in calendar form as 'the Saturday before 7 July'.[259] It was probably about the same time too that Becket's feast was deleted in red crayon in the College's copy of the Sarum Breviary, and the liturgy for its celebration similarly deleted from the text, in precise obedience to the proclamation.[260] The library book containing Becket's life and miracles, found a little later among a heap of waste paper, may have been discarded at the same time.[261]

---

[254] D. Knowles, *The Religious Orders in England*. III: *The Tudor Age* (Cambridge, 1959), 379–82. The last paragraph in Knowles's account is one of the most elegiac in all his works.

[255] *Tudor Royal Proclamations*. Vol. I: *The Early Tudors, 1485–1553*, ed. P. L. Hughes and J. F. Larkin (New Haven, 1964), 276.

[256] RA, 208/2.

[257] RA, 231/2. This curious anticipation of the king's later proclamation may perhaps be accounted for by the accounts having been written up a year later, after the proclamation. For a later instance, when this was certainly so, see below, 260–1.

[258] RA, 248/2, 249/2; below, 240.   [259] RA, 232/3.

[260] *Breviarium ad usum insignis ecclesiae Sarum*, ed. and printed C. Chevallon (Paris, 1531)—call no. 9M 15830 in Exeter College Library; Boase (2), lxxvii. For similar action at University College, see Darwall-Smith, 97.

[261] Watson, 133; above, 209.

More constructively, but again in accordance with the government's directions, the College provided an English bible for the church at Wittenham in
1538 at a cost of 7s. 6d.; for the royal injunction of that year had required
every parish to procure a copy and to display it in the church.[262] Nothing was
said about Gwinear or Menheniot, but for both churches it was probably the
dean and chapter of Exeter who were expected to provide.

The opinions of the majority of the College's fellows about the religious
changes of the 1530s are hardly likely to have been favourable. We should
remember, however, that it was at just this time, in 1539, that Rector French
launched his tirade against 'the insolence of the bachelors'—men whom we
have tentatively identified with a group of possible protestant sympathizers
among the younger fellows.[263] Tensions within the College, resulting from
the religious changes imposed from outside, may have contributed to the
difficulties of these years. But whatever divisions there may have been within
the College, and however strong the opposition to change, compliance with
the government's decrees was a tactical necessity.

After a few years of relative quiet, trouble threatened again in 1546. In what
it now had to fear Exeter was not unique. The act for the suppression of the
chantries, passed in the previous year, authorized the dissolution, not of the
chantries alone, but also of all colleges, including those at Oxford and Cambridge; and the colleges may have expected the worst when, in the early
months of 1546, the king ordered them to make a return of the valuation of
their property.[264] 'Arguably the very existence of the Oxbridge colleges was
never in greater danger than at this time.'[265] At Oxford the enquiry into
college wealth was carried through by Dr Richard Cox, dean of the short-
lived Osney cathedral, soon to be dean of its successor, Christ Church, and a
churchman high in Henry's favour, who was shortly to emerge as a protestant
zealot. An arrogant man, aptly described by Calvin as one with 'an immod-
erate fervour for meddling', Cox was a cleric whom few of the conservative
Oxford colleges had reason to regard as a friend.[266] His enquiries in the late
winter of 1546 left their mark on Exeter as on other colleges. When he visited
the College two capons and wine were provided for his dinner, and he
evidently went through the statutes and accounts to produce his valuation,
for whose writing the College had to pay. If the fellows had hoped that Cox's
dinner would produce an untemptingly low valuation, they were to be
disappointed, for the assessment of Exeter's annual income at just over £81

---

[262] RA, 232/1; R. Whiting, *The Reformation of the English Parish Church* (Cambridge, 2010), 90.

[263] Above, 189–90.

[264] Cross, 'Oxford and the Tudor State', *HUO*, iii. 133; Loach, 'Reformation Controversies', *HUO*, iii. 366.

[265] Darwall-Smith, 98.

[266] *L. and P.*, XXI. i. 116, 139–41; F. Heal, 'Richard Cox', *ODNB*.

was accurate enough.[267] But the threat passed, largely, it seems, because Henry was taken aback by the relative poverty of the colleges and took a stand against the nobles who wanted to lay greedy hands on them. When an amended Chantries Act came in 1547, the universities were specifically exempted from its terms.[268]

The relief was temporary. The Edwardian Reformation which followed Henry VIII's death in January 1547 was far more radical than the sum of the changes introduced by Henry, and it had a correspondingly deeper impact on the colleges.[269] It signified an attempt by the government of the young Edward VI, led at first by Protector Somerset and assisted by Archbishop Cranmer, to turn England into a protestant nation and, at a local level, Oxford into a protestant university. From 1547 the university and its colleges were subjected to more vigorous central regulation than ever before in order to establish a firm pattern of protestant doctrine, worship, and teaching. Since most of the university's members continued to be conservative and catholic in their inclinations, this was an uphill task. It mainly fell to Richard Cox, recently appointed dean of Christ Church and chancellor of the university, whose protestant energies now found a cause to pursue. The instruments of reform were twofold: the statutes, injunctions, and commissions which came from the government, and the decrees and further injunctions, in whose drafting Cox took a large part, which marked their local application. A central role was played by the royal visitation of 1549, in which Cox was again a leading figure and which resulted in new statutes for the university and in injunctions issued to every college. The intended outcome was the destruction of traditional catholicism and its replacement by a protestantism imported from Germany and Geneva. This entailed wholesale change: the cessation of prayers for the dead, the replacement of the Latin mass by the English communion service and of the catholic altar by the protestant communion table, and the removal of the material objects associated with unreformed worship—images, paintings, bells, vestments, organs, and relics. Upheaval was the order of the day.

These changes had multiple consequences for Exeter, as for all colleges, but two were especially important: the abolition of obits, or anniversary services, and the cessation of annual elections to the rectorship. The first of these followed from the second Chantries Act of 1547. While this had the reassuring effect of excluding the universities from its destructive provisions, so ensuring the colleges' continuance, it placed in jeopardy one of their

---

[267] RA, 238/2; Boase (2), lxxix n. 2; *L. and P.*, XXI. i. 139–41; TNA, E 315/441, fo. 113.
[268] Cross, 'Oxford and the Tudor State', *HUO*, iii. 133; Loach, 'Reformation Controversies', *HUO*, iii. 366.
[269] The best introduction is D. MacCulloch, *Tudor Church Militant: Edward VI and the Protestant Reformation* (London, 1999).

functions, since 'the act condemned the theology of purgatory and interces-
sory masses on which chantries and perpetual obits were based'.[270] At both
Exeter cathedral and Exeter College they were celebrated for the last time in
1548. In the winter term of that year the College remembered and prayed for
its past benefactors in the usual way: for Edmund Stafford, bishop of Exeter,
who had been second only to Stapeldon in his generosity; for Fulk Bourgchier, one of the donors of Menheniot; for Rector Palmer, builder of Palmer's
Tower; for Robert Lydford, fellow from 1365 to 1375 and a friend to the
college for many years; for Henry Webber, dean of Exeter from 1459, and
another generous friend; for Roger Keys, who had given to the library the
magnificent set of the works of Hugh of St Cher; and for Nicholas Gosse,
who, along with Stafford and Palmer, had been Exeter's leading patron of the
fifteenth century.[271] But by 1549 the obits for all these men had ceased. They
were specifically banned by the injunctions which Cox's visitors issued to all
colleges in that year.[272] There was a short-lived revival under Mary, and the
fellows did not suffer materially, since their payments for officiating at the
obits were continued.[273] Nevertheless the ending of obits signified a sharp
break with the past, and a compulsory act of oblivion which may have seemed
to fellows with strong religious sensibilities, probably the majority, like a
breach of faith with their predecessors. Vested in prayer and thanksgiving, a
large part of the College's collective memory had gone.[274]

The abolition of annual elections to the rectorship jarred in a different way.
The Rector at Edward VI's accession was William More, elected in October
1546 and re-elected in the following year. But in April 1548 the government
prohibited further elections to headships and fellowships at all colleges as part
of its attempts to secure a body of opinion favourable to reform within the
university.[275] Aware of this decree, the College wrote to Cox on 17 October
1548, shortly after the due date for the annual election, to ask for his advice.
Cox's response was immediate: More was to be continued in office 'until the
time you shall know farther from the king's majesty's council concerning the
same'.[276] His decision was confirmed and extended in the visitors' injunctions
for the College issued in the summer of 1549: More was now to hold the

[270] *Death and Memory*, ed. Orme and Lepine, 246.
[271] *Death and Memory*, ed. Orme and Lepine, 247; RA, 241/1. For these benefactors,
see above, 118, 121, 155–6, 164.
[272] The injunctions issued to Oriel were printed in *Johannis de Trokelowe annales Eduardi
II. Henrici Blaneforde chronica, et Eduardi II. Vita*, ed. T. Hearne (Oxford, 1729), 359–65. Those
for Exeter, identical to the Oriel set but for some *ad hominem* additions, appear as a separate
pamphlet bound into the front of the manuscript register, ECA, A. I. 5. For the prohibition of
prayers for the dead, see *Trokelowe annales*, ed. Hearne, 360, and Reg., Injunctions pamphlet, 2.
[273] e.g. RA, 245/1/2/3; below, 242, 289.
[274] For similar changes at Lincoln, see Green, 85–7.
[275] Wood, *History*, ii. 86–7; G. D. Duncan, 'Heads of Houses and Religious Change in Tudor
Oxford', *Oxoniensia*, 45 (1980), 227.
[276] Reg., 47, noted by Wood, *History*, ii. 87.

PLATE 15. Portrait of Sir William Petre, aged 61, painted in 1567.

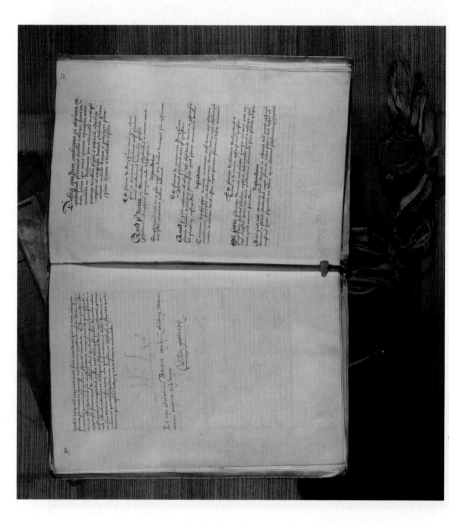

PLATE 16. The master copy of Petre's statutes, 1566, signed on its final page by William Alley, bishop of Exeter, and by Petre himself.

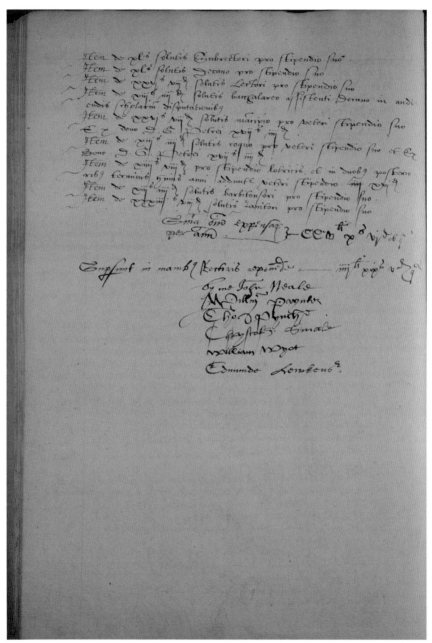

PLATE 17. The concluding section of the Rector's accounts, 1567–8, signed by Rector John Neale and five fellows.

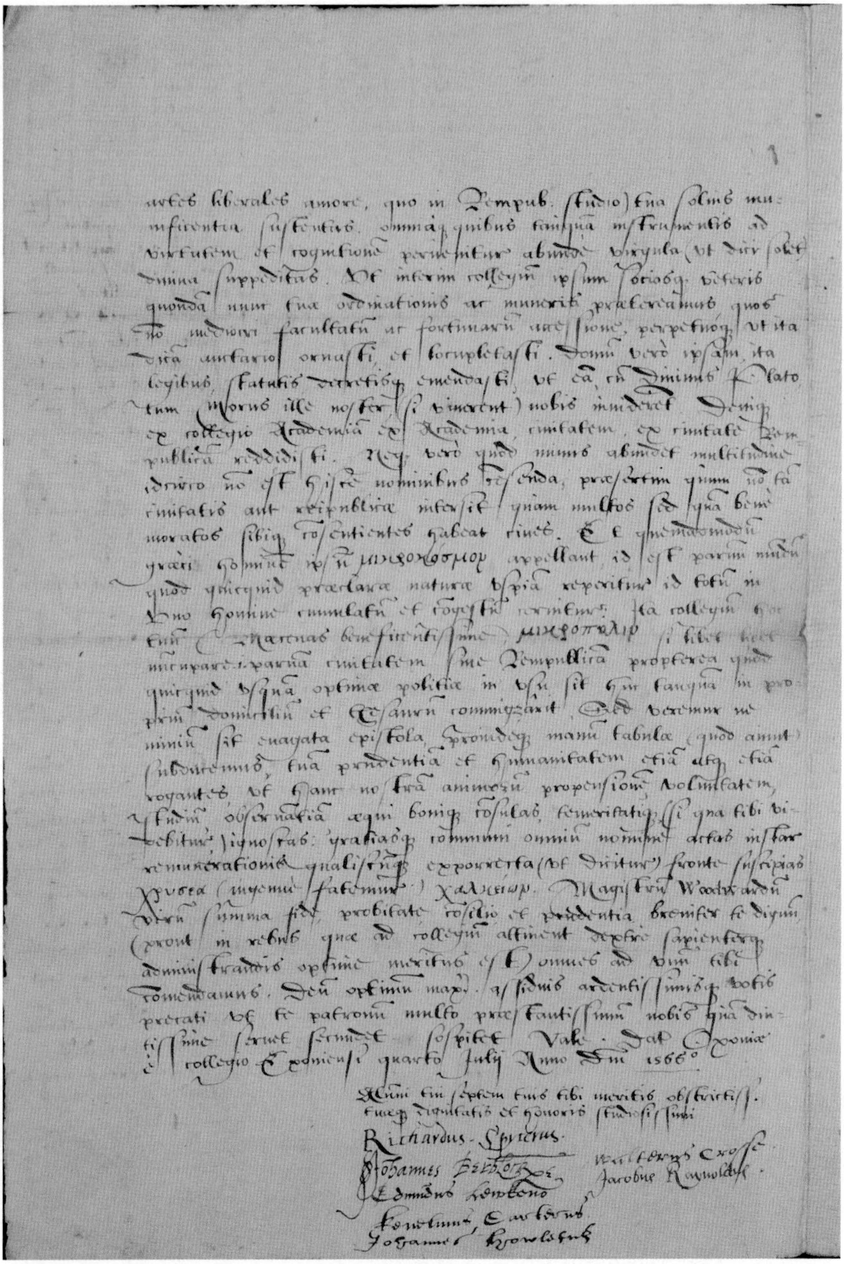

PLATE 18. Letter of thanks to Petre from his seven new fellows, 4 July 1566.

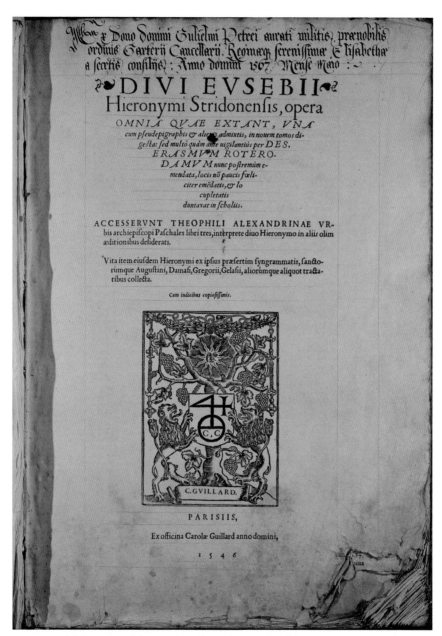

Ex Dono domini Gulielmi Petrei aurati militis, praenobilis ordinis Garterii Cancellarii. Reginaeq; serenissimae Elisabethae a secretis consiliis: Anno domini 1567, Mense Maio :-

DIVI EVSEBII

Hieronymi Stridonensis, opera

OMNIA QVAE EXTANT, VNA
cum pseudepigraphis & alienis admixtis, in nouem tomos di-
gesta: sed multò quàm ante uigilantiùs per DES.
ERASMVM ROTERO-
DAMVM nunc postremùm e-
mendata, locis nõ paucis foeli-
citer emẽdatis, & lo
cupletatis
duntaxat in scholiis.

ACCESSERVNT THEOPHILI ALEXANDRINAE VR-
bis archiepiscopi Paschales libri tres, interprete diuo Hieronymo in aliis olim
aeditionibus desiderati.

Vita item eiusdem Hieronymi ex ipsius praesertim syngrammatis, sancto-
rúmque Augustini, Damasi, Gregorii, Gelasii, aliorúmque aliquot tracta-
tibus collecta.

Cum indicibus copiosissimis.

C.C

C.GVILLARD.

PARISIIS,

Ex officina Carolæ Guillard anno domini,

1 5 4 6

PLATE 19. Title page of the works of Eusebius, edited by Erasmus, recording the book's gift from Petre.

PLATE 20. The remains of the sixteenth-century sundial on the inner face of Palmer's Tower.

PLATE 21. The first depiction of the College arms, 1574.

PLATE 22. The tomb of Sir William Petre and Lady Anne Petre, Ingatestone church, Essex.

rectorship, not merely for another year, but in perpetuity—and so were his successors.[277] The ruling was noted in the College register in October 1549, almost certainly by More himself, but with one significant difference. The injunctions had stated that the Rector could be removed from office for some grave offence. But the paraphrase which appeared in the register stated that his office was to be held for life unless he wished to give it up.[278] More clearly intended that there should be no grounds on which his rectorship could be challenged, and in fact he remained as Rector until Mary's accession.

More was plainly in favour with Cox, and, it is safe to assume, a committed protestant. We have already seen that his place among the 'insolent' young bachelors of 1539 may have owed something to his religious radicalism. While the government put its own men into some colleges, such as Magdalen and New College, and sought to manipulate elections at others, such as Oriel and University College, it clearly had confidence in More at Exeter.[279] But although More had initially been freely elected by the fellowship, as a protestant now given his head in a largely catholic College, he is unlikely to have been popular. At some stage Cox's letter in the register telling the College to continue him in office has been scored through with pen strokes and deliberately blotted with ink. More's exaltation was by no means Cox's only intervention at Exeter. In July 1547 he had imposed on the College as fellow one Maurice Ley, an Irishman, as part of a general scheme to strengthen the Irish church and despite the fact that Ley's Irish origins disqualified him.[280] In both cases the most offensive aspect of Cox's actions lay in his blatant overriding of the College's statutes, which provided for annual elections to the rectorship and for elections to fellowships only of men from prescribed English regions. By the injunctions of 1549 the statutes of all colleges were more explicitly circumscribed: they were to stand only as long as they were not in opposition to the king's decrees and until the king's majesty decided otherwise.[281]

Acting as the agent of the government, Cox had introduced changes which struck deep into the fabric of the College's corporate life; for the remembrance of the dead and a recognition of the statutes' authority had been an integral part of that life. These changes were accompanied by others which were similarly designed to embed protestant ideals in an otherwise unreceptive soil. The more important lay in the introduction of books and other texts intended both to record the government's religious decrees and to provide for

---

[277] Reg., Injunctions pamphlet, 9.
[278] Reg., 50; Boase (2), 61. The entries throughout the register for More's period as Rector, and only those entries, are in the same hand—presumably his.
[279] Duncan, 'Heads of Houses', 227–31.
[280] Reg., 42; Wood, *History*, ii. 96; Boase (2), lxxix, 65.
[281] *Trokelowe annales*, ed. Hearne, 364; Reg., Injunctions pamphlet, 7.

the public use of the English prayers and scriptures which were central to the protestant reformation. Between 1547 and 1552 Exeter, like other colleges, spent a good deal of money on equipping itself as a reformed institution. In 1547 the fellows bought Archbishop Cranmer's new Book of Homilies and a copy of the injunctions issued for the forthcoming visitation of the whole country by the king's commissioners. Both texts denounced many aspects of traditional catholicism, such as images, pictures, and bells, in the interests of reformed religion. All Souls, Merton, and probably all other colleges made similar purchases.[282] From this point onwards expenditure on books and texts features frequently in the accounts. In 1548 the College bought two books 'for administering communion of the Lord's body and blood', now required by royal proclamation. For the church at Wittenham it also bought a copy of Erasmus's *Paraphrases* in English, a rewriting of the Gospels, whose possession by all parish churches had been ordered by the 1547 injunctions.[283] This was followed in 1549 by 'two books of public prayers bought by the king's order' (meaning the 1549 prayer book), a New Testament for use in the College hall, new books for singing psalms in English, and copies of the new statutes issued for the university by the king's visitors and of the visitors' parallel injunctions issued to the colleges.[284] In 1550 the College acquired a book concerning the ordination of bishops, priests, and deacons, and copies of further royal injunctions, and in 1552 a book of public prayers—the revised prayer book of that year—and another book of psalms in English.[285] The fellows of Exeter now had the means, if not perhaps the inclination, to follow the path of reformed religion.

Most of these books were intended for use in the College chapel, and it was there that the changes brought about by government intervention were most visible. Some of the chapel's sacred fittings were discarded and sold. In 1549 a *labella*, part of a vestment, fetched 20s., and the much larger sum of £16 7s. 1d., nearly 13 per cent of that year's receipt, was raised from the sale of a cross, a pyx, and other silver ornaments. A further sale of chapel silver, bringing in £5 6s. 8d., followed in 1551, while in 1553 the organ pipes were sold for 5s.[286] By that time there had also been two sales of chapel books, now presumably redundant after the purchase of the new English prayer

[282] RA, 239/4; Boase (2), lxxviii; E. Duffy, *The Stripping of the Altars: Traditional Religion in England, c.1400–c.1580* (New Haven, 1992), 448–52; MacCulloch, *Tudor Church Militant*, 65–71; *VCH Oxfordshire*, iii. 177; J. M. Fletcher and C. A. Upton, 'Destruction, Repair and Removal: An Oxford College Chapel during the Reformation', *Oxoniensia*, 48 (1983), 1234. Exeter's copy of the 1547 Book of Homilies may be that still remaining in the College library: call no. 9M 13641.

[283] RA, 240/3, 241/1; Boase (2), lxxviii; Fletcher and Upton, 'Destruction, Repair and Removal', 123.

[284] RA, 241/3/4; Boase (2), lxxviii, lxxix n. 2.   [285] RA, 242/3, 245/1; Boase (2), lxxvii.

[286] RA, 241/4, 244/1, 245/3; Boase (2), lxxviii.

books and psalters.[287] The chapel was moving towards the condition of unadorned spareness which, for all churches, was part of the protestant ideal.

Yet it remains surprising that more was not done to bring the College into line with that ideal. By comparison with some college chapels, Exeter's escaped lightly. At All Souls the images were destroyed and their gold coverings sold, the vestments sold for just over £27, the choir whitewashed, and the altar replaced with a communion table.[288] At Merton too the altar gave way to a table, the walls were whitewashed, and the stained-glass windows painted over or covered.[289] At New College the images were destroyed and the stained glass only saved because the fellows pleaded that they were too poor to replace it with plain glass.[290] Little of this is recorded for Exeter; and although we are arguing from the silence of the accounts, they deal in such detail with the purchase of books and the comparatively few changes that *were* made in the chapel for us to suspect that if money had been raised from further sales or spent on destruction, then it would have been recorded. The absence of any mention of a communion table, central to the protestant rite, and the tardy sale of the organ pipes only in 1553, are particularly striking, since the provision of a table and the removal of organs had been demanded by the visitors' injunctions sent to all colleges in 1549. At New College the organ had gone before that year.[291] And had the college vestments been sold, rather than a small part of one of them (the *labella*), this would surely have been noted. For some survivals there is more positive evidence. The stained-glass depictions in the chapel windows inviting prayers for the souls of William Palmer and John Westlake, fifteenth-century Rectors, remained *in situ*, to be seen and recorded by Anthony Wood in the seventeenth century,[292] despite their assumption of the doctrine of purgatory anathematized by the protestant reformers. It looks as though the fellows may have done as little as possible to change the functions and fitments of the chapel, falling into line with reformist demands mainly in ways which would bring them profit at a time of acute financial difficulty, such as through sales of silver. They may have dragged their feet to some effect.

If this is so, it throws some light on that most difficult of problems, the general temper of the College in these years and the response of its individual fellows to the changes which the Edwardian Reformation forced on them. Exeter's west country connections helped to ensure that it remained a fundamentally catholic college in a catholic university: only at Christ Church, Magdalen, and Corpus were 'pockets of committed protestantism' likely to

---

[287] RA, 242/2, 243/1; Boase (2), lxxvii.   [288] *VCH Oxfordshire*, iii. 177–8.
[289] Fletcher and Upton, 'Destruction, Repair and Removal', 123–4.
[290] Buxton and Williams (eds.), *New College*, 47; *VCH Oxfordshire*, iii. 146.
[291] *Trokelowe annales*, ed. Hearne, 362; *VCH Oxfordshire*, iii. 146.
[292] Wood, *Colleges*, i. 116.

have been found.[293] The catholicism of the west country and the ethos of the College were linked, if only in a rather vicarious way, in the person of one man: John Moreman. We have already met Moreman as a former fellow (1510–22) and an Oxford opponent of the earlier Reformation changes of the 1530s. Still the College's vicar at Menheniot in the 1540s, he was arrested early in Edward VI's reign for preaching in favour of catholic practices, and imprisoned in the Tower. During the south-western rebellion of 1549, directed against religious change and against the new prayer book in particular, his release was demanded by the rebels. Their actions demonstrated the religious allegiances both of a man still closely associated with the College and of the College's main recruiting ground. On the accession of the catholic Mary, Moreman was released on the queen's orders, appointed as her chaplain, and a little later given a canonry at Westminster.[294]

But by Edward's reign Moreman's fellowship at Exeter was long in the past, and we have less evidence about the religious opinions of the College's contemporary fellows. Rector More was not entirely isolated in his protestantism. Latterly at least he had an ally in Richard Tremayne, a sojourner in 1550–1 and elected to his fellowship in March 1553, during More's last months. Shortly after Mary's accession Tremayne fled to the Continent, participating in conspiracies against the queen, but returning under Elizabeth to become treasurer of Exeter cathedral.[295] More had almost certainly preceded Tremayne in his precipitate departure from the College. After Mary's accession on 19 June 1553 he did not even stay to complete his rectorial year. Both the register's last entry for that year, made on 17 July, and the accounts for the autumn term, July to October, were drafted in a new hand.[296] More had gone.

More's successor as Rector, William Corindon, had been a fellow since 1543, and it is safe to assume that he favoured the catholic regime under which he had taken office. The purchase by William Grylls, another fellow, of the liturgical books discarded from the College chapel in 1550 seems to identify another catholic sympathizer.[297] The opinions of the remaining fellows are impossible to gauge with any certainty. But the departure of six from their fellowships in 1551, a quite exceptionally high number, may well be a mark both of the College's acute financial difficulties and of internal discontent with its governance, both that of Cox within the university and of More

[293] C. Cross, 'The English Universities, 1553–58', in E. Duffy and D. Loades (ed.), *The Church of Mary Tudor* (Aldershot, 2006), 62.
[294] *BRUO, 1501–40*, 400; C. S. Knighton, 'John Moreman', *ODNB*; J. Youings, 'The South-Western Rebellion of 1549', *Southern History*, 1 (1979), 99–122, esp. 115.
[295] Reg., 52; Bartlett, 'Edmund Tremayne'; Garrett, *The Marian Exiles*, 311–12; Cross, 'The English Universities', 63.
[296] Reg., 57; RA, 245/4; Boase (2), lxxix n. 3.   [297] RA, 242/2; Boase (2), lxxviii.

within the College.[298] The relatively limited changes in the chapel, the evident unpopularity of Rector More, and what little we know about the allegiances of the fellows, past and present, all suggest that the protestant practices signified by the purchases of prayers books, psalms, homilies, and injunctions had been only superficially imposed on a reluctant College.

After the upheavals of Edward's reign, the accession of Mary brought in a period of relative calm.[299] Mary was the university's friend and benefactor, viewing its students as men who by their preaching might 'instruct and confirm the rest of our subjects, both in the knowledge and fear of Almighty God, in their due obedience towards us, our laws, and all other their superiors, and in their charitable demeanour towards all men'.[300] The general sympathy of the university for a catholic restoration, the departure of Cox both from the chancellorship of the university and from the deanery of Christ Church, and the exodus of protestant scholars such as Tremayne to the Continent, all allowed the queen to rule with a light touch. Unlike her predecessor, she intervened very little in elections to headships and fellowships, since there was little need for her to do so.[301] Her friend and ally the papal legate, Cardinal Reginald Pole, held a legatine visitation of the university in 1556, but one much less disruptive than Cox's visitation of 1549. Indeed, its objectives—the promotion of learning, the enforcement of student discipline, and the uncovering of heresy—were probably viewed as generally beneficial.

For Exeter too this was a time of recovery and restoration. With the departure of William More, annual elections to the rectorship resumed. Any investigation of more material changes is hampered by the loss of accounts for two years, 1553–4 and 1556–7, but enough remains for us to see how the practices of the previous reign were abandoned or reversed. By 1554 the mass had been restored and obits were being celebrated once again. In the winter term of that year 10s. 6d. was spent on food and drink 'when the exequies of our founders were celebrated'; and, in another mark of the shortage of ordained *magistri* in College during these years, a priest from Brasenose was brought in to celebrate mass in 1557.[302] 1556 saw the refurbishment of the chapel, with the purchase of new books and the consecration of a new

[298] The six were: John Collyns, William Grylls, Robert Talkarn, Henry Reynolds, Robert Venner, and William Peryam: Boase (2), 63, 65, 66.

[299] For general accounts, see E. Russell, 'Marian Oxford and the Counter-Reformation', in C. M. Barron and C. Harper-Bill (eds.), *The Church in Pre-Reformation Society: Essays in Honour of F. R. H. Du Boulay* (Woodbridge, 1985), 212–27, and Cross, 'The English Universities', 56–76.

[300] Mary's letter of August 1553 to the two universities, cited in Russell, 'Marian Oxford', 214–15.

[301] Duncan, 'Heads of Houses', 232–4.

[302] RA, 246/1/2, 248/1; Wood, *History*, ii. 133; above, 187–8.

high altar.[303] Pole's visitation of the same year led one of the fellows, Henry Dotyn, to make an inventory of the College's goods by order of the visitors, who were probably especially anxious to know about the books in the College library. All colleges had to do the same.[304] Outside the College, the Rector and fellows helped to set right the consequences of Edwardian destruction in the church at Wittenham, where 6s. 8d. was spent on repairing and reconsecrating the bells, their use curtailed or prohibited by the injunctions of 1547, and 6d. on repairs to the windows, possibly damaged by protestant iconoclasts.[305] Nearer home, a reversion to a more distant past came in 1557 when 2s. was spent on wine 'on the day on which we celebrated the lord Thomas'.[306] Even now, Becket was deprived of his sainthood. But it must have looked as though the annual feast, in abeyance since 1537, was on its way back.

The character of the fellowship, so far as it can be judged, remained firmly catholic. Mary's reign saw the election of two fellows who were to end their days as catholic priests. John Neale, elected in 1556, Rector from 1560 to 1570, and a key figure in the College's negotiations with Sir William Petre which resulted in Exeter becoming still more strongly catholic, was deprived of his rectorship in 1570 and by 1578 was living as a catholic priest in Rome. A second fellow, Christopher Smale, also elected in 1556, was ordained abroad in 1578, and later participated in the catholic mission to England. Both men were born and educated in Cornwall, that catholic domain.[307] The migration of three fellows, Stephen Marks, Roger Crispin, and Roger Evans, to Trinity College in the same year was a mark of similar sympathies, for Trinity was an avowedly catholic institution, whose founder, Sir Thomas Pope, 'was in genuine sympathy with many of Mary's policies'.[308] Two of the three, Marks and Evans, were again from Cornwall, and Evans from Devon. These allegiances characterized the whole tone of the College during Mary's reign. When, in April 1554, Oxford's theologians met the protestant Archbishop Cranmer and Bishops Latimer and Ridley to dispute formally on transubstantiation, the Oxford party gathered in Exeter before moving off to the Divinity School for the disputation.[309] They would hardly have done so had the loyalties of the college not been securely catholic. We know nothing about the response of the fellows to the subsequent burning of these

[303] RA, 247/2; Boase (2), lxxviii.

[304] RA, 247/3; Boase (2), 68; Cross, 'Oxford and the Tudor State', HUO, iii. 146–7.

[305] RA, 247/3; Duffy, Stripping of the Altars, 451–2; Whiting, Reformation of the English Parish Church, 172–6.

[306] RA, 248/2.

[307] Boase (2), 68–9; Anstruther, 244, 319. For Neale's education, see above, 182; for his later career, below, 252–3, 260–8, 297.

[308] Hopkins, Trinity, 17–18, 22–3.

[309] Wood, History, ii. 125; Loach, 'Reformation Controversies', HUO, iii. 375.

protestant martyrs, which took place in 1555 and 1556 in the town ditch, about a hundred yards or so from the College gate. But they may well have viewed it as a positive step towards the full restoration of catholicism.[310]

With Elizabeth's accession in 1558, however, came a swing back towards a moderate form of protestantism; though the moderation was more on the queen's side than on that of many of her clerical subjects, newly returned from exile in the heady protestant milieu of the Swiss and German cities. The change in direction was registered by statute. By the Act of Supremacy an oath recognizing the queen as supreme governor of the church of England was to be imposed on all those taking orders or university degrees; while the Act of Uniformity brought back what was essentially the 1552 protestant prayer book. Both were passed in Elizabeth's first parliament in 1559 and both had a particular application to the universities. One of the primary objects of Elizabeth's government, as it had been of Edward's and to a lesser extent of Mary's, was to impose religious conformity on the universities. Oxford and Cambridge were not only the training grounds for the clergy, whose preaching and example gave them influence over the people at large, but also, and increasingly, for the state's servants, whose allegiance to the sovereign's religion was a vital buttress for royal authority. Within the universities the Elizabethan religious settlement was the means to a specific end.

Elizabeth's policy had from the start a much more direct effect on Oxford than Mary's. For a university said in 1559 to contain 'few gospellers...and many papists',[311] this was not surprising. Her policy's means to protestant reform was yet another visitation, taking place in the summer of 1559 and led once again by the egregious Dr Cox, one of the returned exiles. Its main purpose was to enforce the oath of supremacy, and its consequence was the expulsion of heads of houses and fellows who were either unwilling to take the oath or were otherwise recalcitrantly catholic. The resulting purge was on a large scale and continued beyond the period of the visitation. Three heads of houses were deprived in 1559 and another four were forced out in 1561. At New College six fellows were expelled in 1560 and another four resigned and went into exile. From Merton four were expelled for refusing the oath.[312] The number of catholics who left the university was almost certainly greater than the comparable protestant exodus at Mary's accession: perhaps two or three times greater.[313] Yet the government's campaign encountered intense and

[310] For Oxford's response to the burnings, see Cross, 'Oxford and the Tudor State', *HUO*, iii. 143–5.

[311] P. Williams, 'State, Church and University, 1558–1603', *HUO*, iii. 406; Russell, 'Marian Oxford', 221.

[312] Williams, 'State, Church', *HUO*, iii. 406–7, 410; Wood, *History*, ii. 146; Heal, 'Richard Cox'.

[313] Russell, 'Marian Oxford', 222.

partly successful resistance, and it was not until the late 1570s that protestantism could be said to have been established in Oxford.[314]

For such a strongly catholic college Exeter emerged remarkably unscathed from the visitation of 1559 and its long aftermath of expulsions and deprivations. The Rector at Elizabeth's accession, Robert Newton, had been elected under Mary in 1557 and left office in the usual way in October 1560.[315] He was succeeded by John Neale, whose catholic sympathies have already been noted but who survived as Rector until 1570, when he was ejected by a new group of protestant visitors.[316] Three fellows vacated their fellowships in 1559 by their absence from the College, and two of them, who appear to have held no subsequent benefices, may have gone overseas.[317] But no fellow is known to have refused the oath of supremacy and none was deprived by the visitors. Meanwhile men who, like Neale, were later to be known as committed catholics continued to be elected to fellowships: in 1561, Edward Risdon, one of the founders of Douai in 1568 and later a Jesuit priest; and in 1564 Raymond Westlake, another later exile at Douai.[318] Exeter's catholic loyalties in these years are hard to doubt; yet persecution passed the College by.

This is probably to be explained by the College's emollient willingness to conform. When Cox's visitors called in 1559 they were welcomed with wine, beer, cakes, and sweetmeats, and the College paid 18s. 8d. to cover some of the costs of their visitation.[319] Following the visitation, the chapel was refurbished and re-equipped in the approved protestant way. Purchases were made of the new 1559 prayer book, four psalters, and a communion table to replace the Marian altar.[320] In 1561 the Ten Commandments were set up, probably on a board in the chapel, in accordance with a government decree of that year, while two psalters were bought for singing in the chapel in 1565 and another three in 1566.[321] Obits ceased, this time for ever, though the former payments to fellows for their celebration were continued.[322] The December feast, briefly revived under Mary, was held once more in 1558, this time daringly noted in the accounts by its pre-Reformation name as 'the feast of St Thomas'[323]—another small sign that catholic habits had not been overlain

[314] Williams, 'State, Church', *HUO*, iii. 413.
[315] Boase (2), 65. Reg., 72, 75, makes clear that Newton left office in 1560 and not in 1559, as Boase states.
[316] Boase (2), 68; Williams, 'State, Church', *HUO*, iii. 411.
[317] Robert Elston, John Farrant, and Francis Banger: Boase (2), 68, 69, 70. Only Banger is known to have been beneficed.
[318] Boase (2), lxxxi, 71, 73.
[319] RA, 249/4; Boase (2), lxxix n. 2. The visitors were similarly entertained at Lincoln: Green, 93.
[320] RA, 249/4; Boase (2), lxxviii.
[321] RA, 250/2, 254/1/4; Boase (2), lxxviii; Whiting, *Reformation of the English Parish Church*, 132.
[322] e.g. RA, 251/1.   [323] RA, 249/2.

by protestant authority. But thereafter the feast, like the obits, was abandoned, and the Christmas festivities once again took its place.

Superficially—and it was only superficially—Exeter was a reformed and protestant College, obedient to the injunctions of government and visitors. Here it may not have been alone. 'Many there were that conformed', wrote Wood, under the year 1560, 'especially for a certain time till they saw how matters would be determined'. This tactical compliance was perhaps abetted by the visitors' reluctance, certainly evident at Corpus Christi and New College, to enforce the oath of supremacy for fear of emptying the colleges.[324] We should see the unheroic fellows of Exeter as 'church papists' *avant la lettre*, precursors of others well known in later Elizabethan England, whose outward willingness to conform disguised deeply held catholic beliefs.[325]

This was the College's religious situation when Sir William Petre appeared on the scene in 1564.

9. SURVIVAL, REPUTATION, AND ACHIEVEMENT

For all colleges the first thirty years of the sixteenth century were a time of relative ease and prosperity. The next thirty years were to be very different. The changes brought by the Reformation threatened the stability and security of all ecclesiastical property-holders, as the dissolution first of the monasteries and then of the chantries showed how easily institutions far older than most colleges could be swept away by a ruthless state. Had the governments of Henry VIII and Edward VI not been firm believers in the utility of learning, the colleges might well have met the same fate. As it was, they remained subject to an unprecedented degree of external intervention and regulation. Unprecedented too was the concurrent rise in prices, which raised college costs and lowered living standards. In conjunction with the new uncertainties now hanging over the clerical careers which had been the traditional outcome of an Oxford education, the price rise was probably responsible in part for the mid century fall-off in numbers evident from all the sources. The frequency of plague, more urban than rural in its incidence, provided a third deterrent to those who might otherwise have come up to Oxford. The ten or fifteen years on either side of 1550 were tangled in a knot of difficulties more intractable than any that the university had faced since the Black Death.

These problems faced all colleges, but Exeter was less well equipped than most to confront them. Its small income placed it among the three or four poorest colleges, the temporary prosperity brought by its acquisitions in the late fifteenth century now entirely offset by rising prices. Its regional affiliations both limited the area of its recruitment—a significant drawback in an

[324] Wood, *History*, ii. 143; Loach, 'Reformation Controversies', *HUO*, iii. 381.
[325] See A. Walsham, *Church Papists: Catholicism, Conformity and Confessional Polemic in Early Modern England* (Woodbridge, 1999).

era of falling student numbers—and gave rise to the catholic allegiances of most of the fellows, so making the demands of the protestant reformers especially repugnant. Other peculiar features of the College statutes, the stipulation that the Rector be elected annually and that the fellows study only the arts course, deprived it of consistent and unchallenged leadership and of the older and senior men who might have given the College both political weight and a broader intellectual base. Although a few fellows now went on to study for higher degrees, they formed a much smaller proportion of the whole fellowship than in other colleges such as Merton and University College, which had from the start been planned as largely or wholly graduate institutions. It was another consequence of its statutes that the College remained small: never more than fifteen fellows, including the Rector and chaplain, and sometimes fewer in the mid century years of hectic turnover in the fellowship. The few batteler undergraduates who resided in College hardly counted as more than peripheral members, though in the long term their presence sowed the seeds of a transformative development. Exeter was indeed what Rector Neale, in a letter of 1565 to Sir William Petre, poignantly termed 'our little college', *collegiolum nostrum*.[326]

The various difficulties arising both from external circumstances and from Exeter's peculiar features have been discussed separately in the course of this chapter. Yet it was their frequent conjunction that often accounted for their severity: economic, environmental, and religious pressures coincided in time. This is shown well enough by the events of the year 1551, perhaps the most wretched of the whole period. In that year two successive bad harvests in 1550 and 1551, together with the final phase of the massive coinage debasement begun in 1542, raised prices to new heights.[327] The withdrawal of £16 5s. from the reserves in the College chest during the single winter term of 1551 was a mark of the cash-flow problems which this caused and perhaps, and more seriously, of the College's penury. But a new sale of chapel silver in the same term, following on from the larger sale in 1549, probably owed less to the College's need for money, stark though that was, than to the exigencies of protestant reform, unimpeded by the College's unpopular protestant Rector, William More.[328] In the previous term a different sort of blight, an outbreak of the sweating sickness, had scattered the fellows and almost emptied the College.[329] It was perhaps no wonder that six fellows should have vacated their fellowships in this year: the worst in the protracted mid century crisis.

---

[326] Emmison, 280.

[327] C. J. Harrison, 'Grain Price Analysis and Harvest Qualities, 1465–1534', *Agricultural History Review*, 19 (1971), 149; C. E. Challis (ed.), *A New History of the Royal Mint* (Cambridge, 1992), 228–44; Phelps Brown and Hopkins, 'Seven Centuries of the Prices of Consumables', 183, 194.

[328] RA, 244/1; above, 236.   [329] RA, 243/4; Boase (2), lxxxviii n. 1.

It is difficult to know how far Exeter's peculiarities account for another important feature of its general history between 1500 and 1560: the College's lack of distinction and of distinguished men. Although not precisely a backwater, the College in this period contributed little either to scholarship and learning or to the management of the university or to the public life of the country. In the fourteenth and fifteenth centuries it had produced at least a few men who went on to become authors (John Trevisa, William Wey) and bishops (Walter Lyhert, John Arundel, Michael Tregury, John Halse). Between 1500 and 1560 it produced none. Its standing in the university seems to have been low. Anthony Wood, who was near enough to events to know more than we do, provided a list of university men who, in Mary's last year, 1557, 'were eminent for logical and philosophical disputations, performed in some houses of learning and sometimes in the public schools'. In New College there were 'many', two of whom Wood names. He names another three at Merton and two each at Oriel, All Souls, Balliol, Corpus, and Lincoln; while at Magdalen and Christ Church were 'men of no ground in disputations, though good rhetoricians'.[330] Exeter goes unmentioned; though since logic, philosophy, and rhetoric were basic to the arts course which the College's fellows followed it would not have been surprising to find some appearing on Wood's list.

A more objective measure of the College's place in the university is provided by figures for the holding of its highest offices. The highest office of all, the chancellorship, was now in the hands of external grandees, such as Archbishop Warham, but the commissary's post, soon to be known as the vice-chancellorship, was open to election by congregation, though no doubt subject to influence.[331] In our period commissaries were drawn for long stretches from the fellows of five colleges—Magdalen, New College, Merton, Lincoln, and Christ Church and its predecessor colleges, Cardinal College and King Henry VIII's College. Exeter provided only one commissary, Richard Duke, who held office in 1518–19: the same number as Oriel, but more than University College and Queen's, which provided none.[332] It was much the same story with the two proctorships. There were five years between 1500 and 1560 when Exeter proctors held office. Brasenose proctors held office for the same number of years, but University College only for two years, and Queen's and Balliol only for one; Trinity, a late arrival among the colleges, also provided one. By contrast, Magdalen provided proctors in twenty-one years, New College in seventeen, Oriel in sixteen, Merton in

[330] Wood, *History*, ii. 136–7.
[331] Cross, 'Oxford and the Tudor State', *HUO*, iii. 117–19; Williams, 'State, Church', *HUO*, iii. 401–2.
[332] The names and colleges of commissaries and proctors for each year are given in A. Wood, 'Fasti Oxonienses', in his *Athenae Oxonienses*, new edn., ed. P. Bliss, 4 vols. (London, 1813–20), ii. part 2, 3–158. For Duke, see *BRUO*, i. 602.

fifteen, All Souls in ten, Lincoln in nine, and Christ Church and its predecessor colleges in eight. Exeter was thus not quite at the bottom of the table for either office; but in neither case was it far off.

There seems to be a rough correlation here between wealth and public status. For whatever reason, it was the poorest colleges, Exeter, Balliol, and University College, which produced fewest office-holders, and the wealthiest, Magdalen and New College, which produced most. Part of the explanation is obvious: the wealthier colleges, with numerous fellows, had more men who were eligible for office than the poorer colleges which had relatively few fellows. But two other related factors perhaps do more to explain Exeter's particular position: the relatively low standing of its Rector, who was generally no more than a *magister* and whose office, alone among the headships of Oxford colleges, was subject to annual elections; and the paucity of its graduates holding higher degrees. The commissary's post was almost always held by a doctor of divinity, as the chancellor's had once been, and it is worth noting that Exeter's one commissary, Richard Duke, had obtained his doctorate in theology two years prior to his taking office. On the wider university stage, both ad hoc decision-making and the right to elect were becoming increasingly restricted to those senior figures whom Exeter lacked. We have already seen how Henry VIII had sought and obtained a decision on the validity of his marriage to Katherine of Aragon from a committee of theologians, to the deliberate exclusion of the young masters in the arts faculty. In 1541 Henry moved further in the same direction, ordering that in future the right to elect proctors should be confined to the chancellor, the commissary, the doctors, and the heads of colleges, while the proctors themselves were to be chosen from masters of at least eight years' standing.[333] In its increasingly frequent interventions in the affairs of the university the crown found it easier to deal with an institution organized along quasi-oligarchical lines than with the old quasi-democracy of regent masters. This oligarchical tendency was to become even more pronounced from 1564 onwards, under the chancellorship of the earl of Leicester.[334] But Exeter could never rank highly in this scheme of things, since it very rarely had doctors among its fellows and its masters were almost never of eight years' standing.

Particularly significant was the College's lack of theologians. The Reformation gave to academic theology a political prominence which it had not possessed since the days of Wyclif and made it a subject of public debate. But when it came to the theological disputations on which so much Reformation history turned, Exeter had nothing to contribute. Whatever its fellows may have talked about in private, they were publicly uninvolved, for example, in

[333] Cross, 'Oxford and the Tudor State', *HUO*, iii. 124–6, 132–3; Fletcher, 'The Faculty of Arts', *HUO*, iii. 164.
[334] Williams, 'Church, State', *HUO*, iii. 401–2, 426.

what has been called 'the great Eucharistic debate of the 1550s'. The conservative opponents of the protestant Peter Martyr in the preliminary controversies of 1549 were Richard Smith, a former fellow of Merton, William Tresham, a canon of Christ Church, and William Chedsey, fellow of Corpus. All three were doctors of divinity.[335] When the vice-chancellors and doctors of both Oxford and Cambridge met in Exeter in 1554, prior to their debate with Cranmer, Ridley, and Latimer on transubstantiation, eight of the eleven on the Oxford side were doctors of divinity and the remaining three all had theological qualifications. Of the doctors, two came from Christ Church, two from New College, and one each from Lincoln, Magdalen, Corpus, and Oriel. Four were heads of their houses. None came from Exeter.[336] When royal preferences and Reformation issues gave increasing authority to doctors, and especially to doctors of divinity, Bishop Stapeldon's statutes inevitably placed Exeter on the sidelines.

It was not primarily within the university, however, that Stapeldon had intended the fellows of his College to make their mark, but in the parishes. Their parochial achievements are much less easy to assess than their largely negative record within the university, and in placing so much emphasis on the latter we may be judging the College by inappropriate criteria. In the case of only two former fellows, John Moreman and John Dotyn, both of whom we have already met, can we reach any conclusions about the scope and impact of their local work.[337] Both came from Devon, Moreman from South Hole in the far north-west, Dotyn from Harbertonford, near Totnes, in the south. Both were among the few fellows to graduate as doctors and both combined learning with devotion to their parishioners in ways which would have won Stapeldon's approval. Moreman vacated his fellowship in 1522 and achieved his doctorate in theology in 1530; Dotyn vacated in 1539, when he was already a bachelor of medicine, and achieved his doctorate in medicine in 1559. Both spent most of their careers as parish priests (though with periods of further residence in Oxford), Moreman at Menheniot, Dotyn in a number of different and mainly west country parishes. We are relatively well informed about Moreman, 'the most distinguished parish priest of his time in Cornwall',[338] because he taught John Hooker, later the historian of Exeter (city), who wrote of him with affection: 'He was of a very honest and good nature, loving to all men and hurtful to none; and that he was the first in those days that taught his parishioners and people to say the Lord's Prayer, the Belief [i.e. the Creed] and the Commandments in the English tongue, and did teach

---

[335] S. L. Greenslade, 'The Faculty of Theology', *HUO*, iii. 318; Loach, 'Reformation Controversies', *HUO*, iii. 369–70; *BRUO, 1501–40*, 113–14, 524–5, 576–7.

[336] Wood, *History*, ii. 125.

[337] Above, 210–11, 228, 238. Unless otherwise stated the material in this paragraph derives from *BRUO, 1501–40*, 173, 400, and, for Moreman, from Knighton, 'John Moreman', *ODNB*.

[338] Rowse, *Tudor Cornwall*, 152.

and catechise them therein.'[339] He maintained his interests in theology, preparing, so Hooker says, a commentary on Paul's epistle to the Romans, which was never published; and in his will he left his ten-volume edition of the works of Augustine to the Rector of Exeter, on condition that it should be made available to any fellow studying theology. Throughout his long years in a parish, learning and pastoral work had evidently remained in harness together.

Dotyn too was both a learned man and a parish priest, commemorated, as we have seen, with a brass in the church of his final parish at Kingsdon in Somerset, where he died in 1561. In his will, made two years earlier, he had described himself as parson of Aveton Giffard in Devon—appropriately enough, Bishop Stapeldon's first parish. His own first parish had been Whitstone in Cornwall, to which he apparently went immediately after vacating Exeter's rectorship in 1539. But Bampton in Oxfordshire, a parish closely linked with both Exeter College and Exeter cathedral, was the focus of his interests and affections. It was at Bampton as well as at Kingsdon that he asked to be remembered with a memorial after his death. He was vicar there from 1543 to 1559, and Bampton and the College were the twin centres of his world, both mentioned repeatedly in his will.[340] The will included bequests to the poor of his various parishes: 10s. to those of Whitstone and Kingsdon and 20s. to those of Aveton Giffard, but 40s. to those of Bampton. He left his house in Bampton to the College on condition that the Rector and fellows gave 10s. a year to the prisoners in Oxford castle and 3s. 4d. to those in Bocardo, the town gaol. He also assigned to the College the unexpired term of his leasehold lands in Bampton, held from the chapter of Exeter, so that from the proceeds the College could provide 26s. 8d. a year 'towards the marriages of poor maidens in Bampton' and a further 13s. 4d. a year to Bampton's poor. The fellows of Exeter were also to have the joined chair from his Bampton house 'for their ease in the time that any shall be sick there'. Like Moreman, he must have undertaken some basic teaching, for he mentions incidentally that he had taught his kinsman, Andrew Dotyn, to write. And, again like Moreman, he left his academic books—medical rather than theological—to the College: where they remain.

Here were two men who led parallel lives. Leaving the College behind them, each had gone on to a higher degree and then to a lifetime of parochial work. If Hooker's warm memories of Moreman give a special insight into his pastoral activities at Menheniot, Dotyn's will, with its double bequest to the

[339] Hooker's 'Synopsis Chorographical of Devonshire', BL MS Harley 5827, fos. 45ᵛ–46, whence Prince, *Worthies of Devon*, 601. See also Orme, *Education in the West of England*, 102.
[340] TNA, PROB/11/45, fo. 211ᵛ. The will is excerpted in *BRUO, 1501–40*, 173, and more extensively in Blair, *The Medieval Clergy*, Bampton Research Paper 4, Appendix C, 16–17, where further details of Dotyn's life are given. His nephew Henry, also vicar of Bampton, was a fellow of Exeter from 1554 to 1560.

poor of Bampton and its provision for the marriages of the 'poor maidens' of the parish, suggests the same sort of charitable and Christian concerns. Fulfilling the Stapeldonian ideal of an educated and pastorally minded priesthood, both retained links with the College long after they had ceased to be fellows. Exeter's lack of standing in the sixteenth-century university is difficult to deny. But we should also remember that the College's primary purpose had always been to educate clergy for a life of service in the local church. Though exceptional in their learning, Moreman and Dotyn may also serve as exemplars of what must have been a numerous class of former fellows labouring in the parishes in ways unknown to us: men who 'lived faithfully a hidden life and rest in unvisited tombs'.

4

Sir William Petre and his Legacy,
1561–1592

1. THE CRISIS OF 1561–5

After the religious turmoil of the previous three decades, the years following the Elizabethan visitation of the university and its colleges in 1559 brought in a period of calm. Yet in other ways this was far from being a time of order and stability. For Exeter in particular it saw the greatest crisis in the College's history since the Black Death. As in that earlier period, bubonic plague was a major component of the crisis, but it was preceded and partly accompanied by another resulting from the College's effective insolvency. This had no close medieval precedent, and while it lasted it was even more serious than the more prolonged economic depression of the mid fifteenth century.[1] The consequences of this desperate situation brought the College as near to dissolution as it ever came. When Sir William Petre intervened, initially in 1564, more conclusively in 1566, it was hardly surprising that he was seen not just as a benefactor but almost as a saviour. The significance of his patronage cannot be properly appreciated until we know something of the recent dangers which had imperilled the College's existence and which were the prelude to his generosity.

Exeter's initial troubles had their roots, as so often, in the College's lack of money. By 1561, before either of the leading threats had materialized, it was already in financial difficulties. The accounts for 1561–2 showed deficits in each of the year's four terms and an end-of-year deficit of just over £67: by far the largest of the century. It is difficult to be precise about the causes, but heavy spending on College properties (including the building of a new boat for Clifton Ferry), arrears in payments from Gwinear, and a fall-off in room rents were all among them.[2] But the real crisis came in the autumn of 1562. Its

---

[1] Above, 135–8. The crisis of 1561–5 can be reconstructed only from the manuscript accounts and the College register. Some of the key entries in the register were printed in Boase (2), 72–3.
[2] RA, 251.

roots lay in that year's bad harvest, a national disaster which raised the price of corn to levels exceeded only once or twice since the start of the century.³ Unfortunately the accounts are missing for the year 1562–3, but we have enough information in the register to show how vulnerable Exeter was to this sort of unforeseeable blow. The first sign of trouble comes from an entry in the register for 17 October 1562, which states that three previously elected fellows, Henry Chichester (elected 22 October 1560), William Wyatt (13 October 1562), and Peter Randell (15 October 1562), could not yet be admitted to commons 'because the College is so severely afflicted by this calamity (*tempestas*), such is the dearth (*charitas*) of almost all things, that it cannot support them'. In fact Wyatt was not to be admitted until February 1564 and Randell not until April 1564, while Chichester resigned in July 1563 without ever having been admitted.⁴ The College was able to elect fellows, but it could not find the money to pay for their commons and allowances: the first time, so far as we know, that this had happened.

By the late winter of the following year, 1563, the College's position, already weak, had deteriorated still further, no doubt as the meagre grain supplies from the previous year's harvest dwindled and prices continued to rise. The high tide of the crisis came around Lent 1563, when the College reached the brink of dissolution. The register tells us that there was a complete dearth of grain and other foodstuffs. The College's treasury (*aerarium*, meaning the College chest) was drained dry, and its income, in arrears for many years, was insufficient to pay for the fellows' commons and allowances. For these reasons it was decided to permit any fellow to leave the College for a more extended period than the statutes sanctioned and to go into the country for up to two years, there to devote himself to study or teaching, until the College's resources again sufficed to provide for stipends, commons, and other perquisites. Compelled as they said by penury, the fellows judged that these arrangements did not run counter to the intentions of the statutes or the wishes of the founder. Any fellow who took advantage of this licence to stay away beyond the statutory period was to lose all his emoluments but to retain his room as a mark of his College membership.⁵ It was probably at this time too that the College pledged some of its silver to the cook in return for a loan, redeemed in 1564 for 36s. 8d., and other silver to one John Stasy for a further 26s. 8d.—reminiscent of an earlier and equally desperate humiliation in the rather similar circumstances of the 1370s, when a loan had been raised by pledging a bible to the College barber.⁶

³ W. G. Hoskins, 'Harvest Fluctuations and English Economic History, 1480–1619', *Agricultural History Review*, 12 (1964), 37, 39, 41; Harrison, 'Grain Price Analysis', 149; *Agrarian History*, iv. 628, 848.
⁴ Reg., 79; Boase (2), 71–2.   ⁵ Reg., 80; Boase (2), 72.
⁶ RA, 252/4, 253/4; above, 78.

Clearly famine and insolvency had brought not only a material crisis but also one of conscience: the statutes remained the College's lodestar and breaking them had to be justified to posterity in the register, though in the circumstances no one could have quarrelled with the decision to override the founder's directions. How many fellows took advantage of this decision by departing is less clear. Three were certainly present a few months later in July 1563, when two of them incepted in arts.[7] But in the main the College seems to have filled up with sojourners at this time. About fourteen had been in residence in October 1562, an unusually large number, and a further three joined them in the spring of 1563. As paying guests they may have been sought after and welcomed by a College oppressively short of money. Since two of the three newcomers were *generosi*, gentlemen, as the register took care to state, they perhaps had the means to maintain themselves which the body of the fellowship lacked.[8]

Within a few months of the fellows declaring the College insolvent, a worse danger than famine and high prices had appeared. The bubonic plague which ravaged London and the provinces in 1563–4 was 'probably the severest national outbreak...in this century'.[9] Beginning in the summer of 1563, it followed and partly coincided with the subsistence crisis which we have just noticed, in what was a fairly normal conjunction. Although vulnerability to plague does not appear to have been increased by lack of food, famine and plague, two of the four horsemen of the apocalypse, quite often rode together.[10] Plague certainly struck Exeter on the tail of the famine. Our first notice of it comes from an entry in the register for 14 October 1563. Early October was the usual time for the election of the Rector and the audit of the previous year's accounts. But in this year the register notes that the plague was then violently attacking (*eo tempestate ingruebat*) Oxford and many other places, and that in consequence only two fellows were then present in the College. So although the Rector was ready to present the accounts it was decided to defer their audit until the plague had abated and more fellows were present. As a result there was no election, and the accounts were held over until Christmas.[11] It may be no coincidence that, from this year of chaos, they have failed to survive.

The accounts for the next year, 1563–4, which do survive, show that numbers in residence remained low throughout the winter term, never rising above five and in most weeks no more than two or three. It was not until 4 February 1564 that the postponed election took place, the existing Rector,

---

[7] Reg., 81; Boase (2), 73, where the date is incorrectly given as July 1564.

[8] Reg., 79–80; Boase (2), 62.

[9] J. F. D. Shrewsbury, *A History of Bubonic Plague in the British Isles* (Cambridge, 1971), 200–3.

[10] P. Slack, *The Impact of Plague in Tudor and Stuart England* (London, 1985), 70–7, esp. 75; Bowen, 'Agricultural Prices', *Agrarian History*, iv. 633.

[11] Reg., 81; Boase (2), 72.

John Neale, was re-elected, and the accounts received, with the consent of all the fellows present—still no more than seven.[12] The plague, however, had by no means gone away. On 30 March it was decided by those fellows resident in College—by now increased to nine, but still well short of the total complement—that any fellow wishing to leave the College because of the renewed attack of the plague should have a weekly allowance of 14*d*. until the start of the following winter term in October. As a consequence, the old method of allocating commons, which took account of temporary periods of absence, was abandoned and each fellow, whether present or absent, was credited with 14*d*. a week:[13] another minor perturbation of administrative practice, among several more major ones, that the plague had brought.

But if the plague continued, there was at least some relief from the financial pressures which had borne down on the College for the past two years. The harvest of 1563 was good, lowering corn prices, and the College's income recovered, with payments at the agreed rates from Gwinear, Wittenham, and Menheniot, and an additional payment for arrears from Gwinear. The result was an end-of-year surplus in October 1564 of some £40. This was partly achieved at the expense of the College servants, who received no wages in the summer term.[14] With money in hand, the College could begin to make up for lost ground. William Wyatt and Peter Randell, elected to their fellowships in October 1562, were now finally admitted to commons in February and April 1564. Two new fellows, John Wylliams and Raymond Westlake, were elected in February and March 1564, the first such elections since 1562, and admitted to commons in the following October. Some of the silver pledged in return for a loan was redeemed in the course of the summer.[15] It may have seemed as though the bad times were coming to an end.

This would have been too optimistic a view, however, since the continuance of the plague prevented any thought of a full return to normality. It was prevalent enough during the summer of 1564 to cause the cancellation of the Act, the university's celebratory annual degree ceremony, which usually took place in June.[16] When the College reassembled in October only a very few fellows were present, and the election was postponed, as it had been in the previous October. The Rector himself, still John Neale, appears to have been among the absentees, for one of the fellows, Thomas Fortescue, received an extra allowance for his custody of the College. The register again cites the plague as the reason for these absences.[17] For most weeks in the winter term there were only three fellows in residence, and when the election for the

---

[12] Reg., 82; RA, 252/2.
[13] Reg., 83; RA, 252/3; Boase (2), 72–3. Boase's two entries dated 30 March 1564 and summer 1564 record the same arrangements.
[14] Hoskins, 'Harvest Fluctuations', 39, 41; Harrison, 'Grain Price Analysis', 149; RA, 252.
[15] Boase (2), 71, 73; RA, 252/4.   [16] Wood, *History*, ii. 154.
[17] RA, 253/1; Reg., 83.

rectorship eventually came to be held, on 9 January 1565, there were still no more than six in college. The register additionally tells us that the other elections which would normally have been held, for the bursars and the keepers and auditors of the College chests, did not take place because of the small number of fellows in the College.[18]

But although the plague may have lingered into 1565, as it did in some other parts of England, the signs are that by the spring of that year the outbreak was over. In March three fellows who had forfeited their fellowships after pro-longed absences during the plague—John Babbe, Christopher Smale, and Raymond Westlake—returned to the College and were re-elected. A fourth, Ralph Gittisham, followed in May. Numbers in College steadily rose: to between eight and eleven in the summer term of 1565 and to twelve or thirteen during the winter term.[19] By this time the long crisis which had begun in 1561 had come to an end.

The crisis had shown the extent to which the College was at the mercy of external events, unforeseen and unpreventable. The harvest failure of 1562 and the plague of 1563–5 were natural and national disasters. Even wealthy colleges, well stocked with fellows, could not have been expected to escape them. Exeter, with its small resources and its income often in arrears (as the register had ruefully noted), was very exposed, in the first place to any sharp rise in corn prices. This had been seen repeatedly in the mid sixteenth century, but never more so than in 1562–3, when complete penury threatened the College. Both disasters brought resourceful responses from the fellows: the postponement of admissions to the fellowship, the permission granted to fellows to absent themselves, in justified breach of the statutes, and the later provision of money allowances for those who did so. Yet they could not but be extremely disruptive. The postponement of the October election of a Rector in two successive years, the parallel postponement of the audit, and the decision to pass over the election of College officers, were, so far as we know, unprecedented. But above all it was perhaps the paucity of resident fellows throughout the period which did most to reduce the College to a shell. When there were only three or four fellows in College, as was the case for many months, the College's ordinary work could hardly go forward, nor could the programme of studies for fellows and undergraduates (the latter an invisible presence throughout the crisis) be continued in anything like its normal form. This is not a subject on which either the accounts or the register throws any light, but Wood makes an apt general comment about the effects of the plague, saying that it dispersed 'those that were remaining in the University to the damage of learning'. It was among several causes by

---

[18] RA, 253/2; Reg., 84.
[19] Shrewsbury, *History of Bubonic Plague*, 203; Boase (2), 69, 70, 73; RA, 253/4, 254/1.

which 'the schools, considering former times, were ... left empty and little of exercises performed in them'.[20] In these circumstances the College's primary function as a place of learning must also have been in abeyance. If there was anything to be thankful for, it was the complete absence of plague deaths among the fellows; for the twelve fellows listed in the register for October 1562 can all be traced through to 1565, though two had resigned to go elsewhere.[21] Here the liberal policy of encouraging dispersal outside Oxford may have paid off. Lives were saved; yet the double crisis of famine and plague cannot have been less than traumatic for all who lived through it.

It was during this crisis, in April 1564, with the College's finances recovering but the plague unabated, that Sir William Petre appeared on the scene.

2. SIR WILLIAM PETRE

After Stapeldon himself, Sir William Petre was the most significant figure in the early history of the College, enlarging its endowment, augmenting its fellowship, rewriting its statutes, and reforming its constitution. The background of the two men was not dissimilar. Like Stapeldon, Petre came from rural Devon. His father, John Petre, farmed at Torbryan, a village situated in the rich pastoral country of south Devon, between the moors and the sea. Tornewton, the successor of the Petre family house and probably incorporating its remains, still looks down on the deep green valley where the village lies. This was a more promising location than Stapeldon's home in the harsh claylands of north Devon, and it helped to place John Petre among the wealthier men of the neighbourhood. He was never more than a freeholder (and so not an esquire or a gentleman), but a prosperous one, whose money came from cattle and possibly from a sideline in tanning. Direct comparisons are impossible, but we should probably see the status and wealth of the Petres as rather above those of the Stapeldons. William Petre, seemingly John's second son, was born in 1505 or 1506, as we know from contemporary portraits still surviving at Exeter College and at Ingatestone in Essex, his later home, each dating from 1567 and giving his age as 61 (see Plate 15).[22] The local education which enabled this farmer's son to get to Oxford is as obscure as that of Stapeldon. We first hear of him at Oxford in 1519, when he was studying Roman and canon law.[23] Four years later, in 1523, he was elected to

[20] Wood, *History*, ii. 151.
[21] Reg., 79, 84. The two who resigned were Richard Braye and Edward Risdon: Boase (2), 70–1.
[22] Emmison, 1–3; C. S. Knighton, 'William Petre', *ODNB*. What follows largely derives from Emmison and Knighton. For the house at Tornewton, see Pevsner and Cherry, *Buildings of England: Devon*, 866.
[23] Petre's engagement with the law course in 1519 is nowhere directly stated, but he supplicated for the BCL on 14 December 1524 after 5½ years' study as a scholar of civil law, which puts his start in 1519: *BRUO, 1501–40*, 445, where Emden's '1542' should clearly read '1524'.

a fellowship at All Souls, where he remained until about 1535. Latterly, from 1530 to 1534, he was also principal of Peckwater Inn, one of the halls for legists, undergraduates reading law. In 1526 he gained his baccalaureate in both laws and in 1553 his doctorate in civil law.[24] So as a young man he would have become thoroughly familiar with Oxford and its colleges and halls: his base for some sixteen years and the stage for his considerable academic achievements.

Did Petre at any time study at Exeter? That he did so is first stated in a description of Oxford published in 1602 and written by Nicholas Fitzherbert, a prominent English catholic then living in Rome. Fitzherbert writes that Petre enriched (*auxit*) Exeter, remembering with gratitude the benefits which he had received from the College in his youth.[25] The author had very probably been an undergraduate at Exeter in the late 1560s, the period of Petre's benefactions, and might be expected to have known the truth of the matter.[26] Yet he was almost certainly mistaken. Had Petre been a fellow, he would undoubtedly have been listed in the accounts as receiving commons and allowances. Had he been an undergraduate, he might well have escaped notice, since, as we have seen, the names of undergraduates are recorded only haphazardly in the accounts and most go unmentioned. But Petre's birth in 1505 or 1506 implies that when he started reading law in 1519 he could not have been older than 14. He would have been unable to take the subject at Exeter, whose students were all arts men, and it is much more likely that at this early stage he was attached to one of the legists' halls, such as Peckwater Inn, before gaining his All Souls fellowship four years later. It is just conceivable that he spent a term or two on the arts course at Exeter before moving elsewhere to study law, but this remains no more than the barest possibility, since 14 was probably the statutory minimum age for undergraduate entry to the university. It was perhaps a mark of the 14-year-old Petre's precocity that most students were about 17 when they came up.[27] Nor is there any sign in the extensive documentation relating to Petre's later benefactions to Exeter that he had ever had any prior contacts with the College. At this stage of the story, therefore, the mystery of why Petre's charitable hand was extended to a College of which he had no previous personal knowledge or experience remains to be resolved.[28]

---

[24] Emmison, 3–4; *BRUO, 1501–40*, 445.

[25] 'Nicolai Fierberti Oxoniensis Academiae Descriptio', in *Elizabethan Oxford*, ed. C. Plummer, OHS, viii (1887), 14. That Petre studied at Exeter is stated as a fact in Boase (2), lxxxi, and Emmison, 3, but discountenanced by Emden, *BRUO, 1501–40*, 445, and Knighton, 'William Petre', *ODNB*. All four overlook Fitzherbert's statement.

[26] Wood, *Athenae*, ii. 119; Boase (2), xcvii; M. E. Williams, 'Nicholas Fitzherbert', *ODNB*. But for a more agnostic view of Fitzherbert's presence at Exeter, see *Register*, ed. Clark, II. iii. 7.

[27] Evans, 'Numbers, Origins', *HUO*, ii. 499–500.   [28] Below, 307–16.

After obtaining his Oxford doctorate in 1533, Petre entered the king's service and rose rapidly, thanks partly to the patronage of Thomas Cromwell, Henry VIII's leading minster. He may initially have come to Cromwell's notice in the late 1520s as the tutor to George Boleyn, son of Thomas Boleyn, earl of Wiltshire, and brother of Anne Boleyn. Beginning as a clerk in chancery, he was much occupied from 1535 onwards with the affairs of the church, first visiting and then dissolving monasteries. He thus played a major part in one of the decade's, and the century's, most sweeping exercises of state power. In 1536 he was made Cromwell's deputy in ecclesiastical causes, and in 1539 Cromwell appointed him to negotiate the king's projected marriage with Anne of Cleves. But for whatever reason he failed to take part in the subsequent embassy and so avoided implication in the débâcle of the Cleves marriage which followed: the first of several lucky, or dexterous, escapes from events which might have pulled him down. When Cromwell fell in 1540, largely as a result of his responsibility for the marriage, Petre managed to survive his patron's dismissal and execution—indeed, to do more. It was in the year of Cromwell's fall that he was first appointed to the king's council, and from this time onwards he held an established place near the centre of power. In 1544 he was named as one of the two principal secretaries of state and in the following year he was effectively in charge of the country's government during the king's absence in France. He had been knighted two years earlier in 1543.[29] On Henry's death he was reappointed as secretary by the young king Edward and he was a leading actor in the events of the reign, notably in securing the fall of Somerset, whom he had at first supported, in 1549.[30] As a diplomat and civil servant he made his mark in negotiating for the return of Boulogne to the French in 1553 and in preparing the way for the succession of Lady Jane Grey after Edward's early death.[31]

Despite Petre's close identification with Edward's protestant regime, he was taken up by the catholic Queen Mary after the failure of Queen Jane's brief reign. Made a councillor and secretary once again, he was one of the negotiators for Mary's unpopular marriage with Philip of Spain. He was close enough to Mary to serve as the effective leader of the parliamentary commons in her interest and to be named as one of her executors.[32] When Elizabeth succeeded in 1558, he continued to serve on the council and for a time acted once again as principal secretary, deputizing for William Cecil during Cecil's absence in Scotland. When he finally retired from the council in 1567, a year after his plans for Exeter had come to fruition, he had served on it for some twenty-seven years and under four monarchs.[33] Among other Tudor ministers only William Cecil had a comparable record of service.

---

[29] Emmison, 43–64. For his knighthood, see *BRUO, 1501–40*, 446.
[30] Emmison, 65, 75–82.   [31] Emmison, 87–9, 100–9.
[32] Emmison, 161, 166–8, 196–7, 209.   [33] Emmison, 227, 231–4, 261–2.

Petre's career was marked throughout by a consistent 'adroitness in high politics'.[34] No one so close to the centre of government survived so successfully over such a long period of religious upheavals, palace revolutions, and factional conflicts. At all points he maintained a reserve and an ability to conceal motives and feelings which partly accounts for his staying power but also makes his character exceptionally difficult to assess. The guarded, almost furtive, look which he wears in his portraits at Exeter and Ingatestone may have owed something to the constant pain and ill-health which he suffered in his later years;[35] but it may also be a reflection of the inner man. It would be easy to see him as another vicar of Bray, temporizing before the prevailing wind, and certainly not all his actions were honourable. His desertion of Somerset in 1549 can be justified in terms of Somerset's ineptness,[36] yet it was also an exercise in skin-saving. If he followed a consistent principle it was one of service to legitimate authority, whether catholic or protestant. His service was wanted by his employers because he was clever, shrewd, efficient, discreet, and trustworthy. These qualities were in particular demand for negotiations abroad, both for negotiations with France and, in the cases of both Anne of Cleves and Philip of Spain, for royal marriages. His expertise in the technical side of negotiations owed something to his Oxford doctorate in civil law, a training in which was often a qualification for diplomacy.[37] Here too he resembled Stapeldon, another Oxford lawyer and foreign negotiator whose academic training opened the way to a career in public life. But it also owed much to his personal diplomatic finesse and—another leading characteristic—to his incorruptibility. Unlike most sixteenth-century men of power, he seems to have consistently rejected the gifts, bribes, and douceurs often used to buy the favour of potential patrons.[38]

But Petre's honesty did not stand in the way of his becoming immensely rich. Already by 1540 he was reckoned to have an income of over £500 a year (at a time when Exeter's income was about £80 to £90).[39] A large part of this had come from his purchases of monastic lands. It was by purchase from the crown in 1539 that he acquired the Essex manor of Gynge Abbas, formerly held by the nuns of Barking, where he was later to build his great house of Ingatestone, near Chelmsford, still in the possession of his descendants. His marriage in 1533 to Gertrude Tyrell, daughter of an Essex knight, had already enabled him to put down roots in the county, and shortly after her death in 1541 he married another Essex woman, Anne Tyrell, a widow, daughter of a London merchant who had been the city's mayor, and her father's sole heir. From her he acquired other large holdings. London money went to the

---

[34] Knighton, 'William Petre'.   [35] Emmison, frontispiece, plate 2, 249–54.
[36] Emmison, 81, followed by Knighton, 'William Petre'.
[37] Barton, 'Faculty of Law', *HUO*, iii. 271.   [38] Emmison, 274–5, 295–6.
[39] Emmison, 25.

making of him, as it did for others rising towards the peerage.[40] Unlike
Stapeldon, whose family connections and office as bishop of Exeter had tied
him to the county of his birth, Petre had turned his back on Devon. Although
he came to hold very extensive lands there, again by purchase from the crown
of what had been monastic property, and although he had two brothers
remaining in the county (and himself retained a holding in ancestral Torbryan), he never returned to a shire too inconveniently distant from the main
scene of his activities in London. By the end of his life he had accumulated
nearly 20,000 acres in Essex and over 20,000 in the west country, including
some estates in Somerset and Dorset. In 1556 his gross income amounted to
just over £3,350, of which about £2,480 came from rents and agricultural sales.
Although he remained no more than a knight, a gross income of this size put
him on a level with the higher ranks of the aristocracy.[41] Unlike Stapeldon,
who had been cash rich but land poor, Petre was rich in both—and well
provided with the means to re-endow Exeter College. His determination to
defend these interests, and his ability to reconcile their defence with his
conscience, were both demonstrated in 1555, when he secured a bull from
Pope Paul IV confirming his property rights, including those in former
monastic lands: the only individual in Mary's reign to be so privileged.[42]

As relevant as Petre's wealth to his future dealings with Exeter was his
interest in learning. He maintained intermittent links with his alma mater
throughout his life. He sent three of his wards to Oxford in the 1550s, paying
for their education and maintenance, and he supported other poor scholars
there with whom he had no apparent ties, as Stapeldon had done before him.[43]
He was thought an appropriate person to appoint as one of Edward VI's
visitors for the university in 1549, though he did not act, and he may have
played a part in Mary's plans for Oxford's reform in 1553, but whether as
initiator or merely as Mary's secretary is not clear.[44] He was always an avid
bibliophile, receiving books from his friend Nicholas Wotton, ambassador in
Paris in 1553, pressing the works of various classical authors—Terence,
Aesop, Ovid, Livy—on his 9-year-old son John, and later passing on a
substantial collection of the Latin fathers to Exeter. From the titles of some
of the books purchased we can perhaps detect a particular interest in history
and orthodox catholic theology; though the books chosen for John also

[40] Emmison, 2–3, 22–4, 26; L. Stone, *The Crisis of the Aristocracy, 1558–1641* (Oxford, 1965), 628–9.
[41] Emmison, 266–73, 290; F. G. Emmison, *Elizabethan Life: Wills of Essex Gentry and Merchants* (Chelmsford, 1978), 32; Stone, *Crisis of the Aristocracy*, 138–40, 760. But 1556 was an unusually prosperous year. In 1564 Petre's gross income was c. £2,460 and in 1570 c. £2,700: Emmison, 273.
[42] Emmison, 185.   [43] Emmison, 304–5.
[44] Emmison, 72, 163; Russell, 'Marian Oxford', 214–16.

suggest a strong humanist bent.[45] In his later portrait at Ingatestone a clasped book rests on the table beside him. Besides state papers, only a single contribution is known to have come from his own pen, but one that, from Exeter's point of view, was overwhelmingly important: the new statutes for the College, drafted in 1565–6.

The most significant aspect of Petre's mental world is also the most resistant to analysis. The personal religious beliefs of a man closely identified with the very different ecclesiastical policies of four monarchs are inevitably difficult to ascertain. Closely involved with the dissolution of the monasteries, he was at no time linked with the anti-traditionalist protestant and evangelical elements at Henry's court. Yet under the protestant Edward VI he played a leading part in the prosecution of the catholic bishops Stephen Gardiner and Edmund Bonner, and in attempting to enforce religious conformity on the catholic Princess Mary.[46] But he fully supported Mary's policies as queen, while at the same time avoiding all association with the burning of protestants, whether in London or in Essex.[47] For thirty years he trimmed successfully if unheroically through every change of religious policy. Viewed by one contemporary as a seeker of 'moderation in all things',[48] he can easily be seen as a man of no particular religious convictions beyond those common to all Christians. It is only when he became the patron and benefactor of a distinctively catholic college from 1564 onwards that his true religious beliefs begin to be highlighted by the direction of his philanthropy.

3. REFOUNDING THE COLLEGE, 1564–6

In April 1564, when Exeter's finances were recovering but the plague was still troubling Oxford, the College was visited by a Mr John Woodward, an Oxford MA and a priest. He came to ask the fellows a simple question. If a certain person, whose identity was as yet concealed but whom Woodward described as a well-wisher to the College and to learning, should want to enrich and enhance the College with a larger income and rents and with seven new fellowships, would the fellows unanimously and willingly accept the offer? They replied instantly (if hardly surprisingly) that they would. There the matter rested until Christmas, when the College's still unknown patron asked for and was sent a copy of the College's statutes, followed a little later, and again at his request, by full details of the fellows' rooms, commons, stipends, decrements, and much else.[49] By the time the accounts for the year came to be written up, which must presumably have been after Christmas, the patron had revealed himself, for they note the April episode by recording a

---

[45] Emmison, 220–1; below, 291–2.   [46] Emmison, 112–22.   [47] Emmison, 186–96.
[48] Emmison, 78. Cf. 291–2.
[49] Reg., 83. This key episode, recorded only in the manuscript register, is unaccountably ignored by Boase.

charge of 14*d*. 'for wine and sugar at the reception of Mr Woodward when we talked over the design and wishes of Sir William Petre'.[50]

Petre's appearance on the Exeter stage was as mysterious as it was unexpected. We have seen that the College had almost certainly played no part in his education, nor, so far as is known, had he had any direct contacts with the Rector and fellows. The reasons for his choosing Exeter as the object of his charity, however, are not beyond conjecture (and conjectures will follow);[51] nor are those for his choosing to remain, initially at least, anonymous. Perhaps he was uncertain as to whether Exeter would accept his largesse, and wished to conceal his identity in case of a refusal. Perhaps, should this happen, he had another college in mind and would not wish it to be known that he had first made an offer elsewhere. John Woodward, whom he employed as his agent, was his trusted friend and domestic chaplain, though the fellows of Exeter were clearly unaware of this.[52] It is equally clear that, by the time of Woodward's visit to the College, Petre's plans for its refoundation, centred on the provision of new fellowships and the enlargement of the endowment to make this possible, were already fully formed, and that it needed only the fellows' assent to put them into motion.

Those plans took more than two years to come to fruition. It was only in June 1566 that the seven new fellows were admitted to the fellowships first spoken of in April 1564, and not until November 1566 that the new endowment was finally made over to the College. We can follow the process with exceptional clarity through the documents preserved among Petre's papers in the Essex Record Office and, to a lesser extent, through others in the College register. Petre's papers give particularly full coverage to the period between March 1565 and June 1566 which saw his most intensive engagement with the College's affairs.[53] They include twelve letters from the Rector and fellows to Petre, two in draft form from Petre to the Rector and fellows, and three exchanged between Petre and John Kennall, the university's vice-chancellor, who acted as the local go-between in Petre's dealings with the College, together with numerous memoranda, valuations, and accounts. Some letters are in English and some in Latin. Although Petre worked through agents and appears never to have visited the College in person, his many miscellaneous jottings and notes to himself, as well as his formal letters, bear witness to his

[50] RA, 252/3; Boase (2), lxxxi; Southern, *VCH Oxfordshire*, iii. 109.   [51] Below, 308–9.

[52] Emmison, 230, 278–9, 288–9, 291; below, 309. Woodward had been a fellow of Merton, obtaining his BA in 1546: B. C. Foley, 'John Woodward, Marian Priest, 1530?–1597/8?', *Essex Recusant*, 4/1 (1962), 13.

[53] ERO, Petre Papers, D/DP Q13/1/1/1: Letters, accounts, etc., re benefactions of Sir William Petre, knight, to Exeter College, Oxford—hereafter 'PP'. The dossier contains some forty-four documents. Since none have individual piece numbers, they are identified in what follows by their contemporary titles or by their opening words or by contemporary endorsements. Dates are cited when given. Spellings in English documents have been modernized. Some of these documents were used by Emmison in his account of Petre's benefaction: Emmison, 279–83.

involvement in every detail of his plans. The sharp eye of the practical and experienced civil servant, financial administrator, and diplomat rested closely on the work of the philanthropist and patron.

The fulfilment of Petre's plans rested on four parallel processes: the acquisition of funds for the College's re-endowment; the devising of a financial scheme for the support of his seven new fellows; the selection of the fellows themselves; and the drafting of new statutes to provide for the College's better governance, the better learning and instruction of its members, and the integration of the new fellows into its life. These were interlinked, for, as events were to show, Petre's provision of money for the College was dependent on the fellows' acceptance of his reforms and, in particular, their acceptance of his statutes. He was to be given a free hand to remodel the College as he thought best.

His first concern was financial; how much would it cost to endow the seven new fellowships which lay at the centre of his scheme? The answer came in a letter from John Kennall written on 13 March 1565, the first in the surviving series.[54] Kennall wrote that he had conferred 'sundry times' with the Rector and fellows, who were most happy that he had undertaken to augment 'their small and poor company'. They were entirely willing to accept the new fellows into their fellowship on his terms. But, continued Kennall, the seven new fellows could not be supported on £50 a year—evidently the sum which Petre had proposed to make available—since every fellow cost £7 5s. a year to support (most of it presumably for commons, decrements, and allowances). In addition, the provision of rooms would cost another £5 a year, resulting altogether in a loss of £3 15s. to the College. Better perhaps to endow six fellowships, as this would leave the College with 30s. in hand. He emphasized its plight: 'the College is poor and not able to bear their ordinary already [sic] charges.' This situation he blamed on the meagre allowance of 12d. a week for commons and, in consequence, the substantial additional outlay on decrements. The ultimate cause, therefore, was the high price of food—as we have seen, a crucial factor throughout the mid century period. He promised to provide Petre with a full account of the College's financial state, following this up a week later with a valuation of its income and expenditure.[55] The customary revenues of the College from Gwinear, Wittenham, room rents, etc., were assessed at £90 gross, against which the main charges lay in the general expenses of the fellowship, ranging from commons and decrements, at 95s. per fellow per year, to 12d. for 'coals for the hall'. Total charges amounted to £108 15s. a year, excluding servants' wages. In a covering letter Kennall wrote that his enclosure would show Petre 'the estate of Exeter College as much as

    [54] PP, 'Mr doctor Kennall touching Exeter College', 13 March 1565.
    [55] PP, 'The rents and revenues... in primis'. This document is badly damaged, with many of the figures missing.

I can understand the same, by what means they do bear the charges sur-
mounting their revenues'.[56] But the figures had shown that those charges
were not to be borne. Petre had at least been given a clear-eyed view of the
College's difficulties and the scale of the rescue needed.

Kennall had brought out, both in his own words and in the figures which
he had supplied, the extent of Exeter's poverty. The Rector and fellows' sense
almost of elation at what they might expect from Petre by way of a remedy
was evident in the letter which they wrote to him on 8 April 1565—their first
formal communication with their benefactor.[57] Written in Latin, in a beautiful
calligraphic humanist hand, and couched in the effusively deferential language
which characterized all their correspondence with Petre, it was intended not
only to express their gratitude but also to impress their patron with their
learning and their love of learning. Of all God's gifts, Petre was told, none
shone more brightly than learning and the liberal arts. They went on to
compare Petre, the immediate provider of these goods, with Maecenas, the
wealthy patron of the Roman poets under Augustus, citing Horace as one of
Maecenas's protégés, but praising Petre as one who, unlike the Roman poets
with their pagan stories, worked instead to the glory of Christ. They rejoiced
that he was prepared to enrich *nostrum collegiolum*, 'our little college', and
ended by offering him the gift of a pair of gloves, the traditional way of
showing honour and respect to a benefactor. 'Farewell, shining light and
protector of good learning' were their final words. They marked the address
on their letter 'With speed'.

This flowery missive was followed in early May by a burst of more
businesslike activity. On 4 May Petre wrote to the Rector and fellows to
acknowledge their letter agreeing 'to receive such order as by me may be
thought good' (a letter which does not survive), and to say that he was sending
'certain articles' for their perusal and response.[58] In a parallel letter to Kennall,
sent with the articles, he asked his friend to lay the articles before the Rector
and fellows, from whom he would gladly receive a speedy answer.[59] The
articles themselves constituted an outline statement of Petre's plans and of
what he expected from the College.[60] Bishop Stapeldon's statutes, he wrote,
were 'in many parts imperfect'. In consequence the Rector and fellows were
to make a submission under their seal agreeing 'to receive, perform and obey

[56] PP, 'Doctor Kennall touching Exeter College', 20 March 1565.
[57] PP, 'Ornatissimo viro D. Gulielmo Petro', 8 April 1565.
[58] PP, 'Copy of my letters to the rector and fellows of Exeter College in Oxford', 4 May 1564.
[59] PP, 'After my most hearty commendations, where I have heretofore put you to some pains . . .',
4 May 1565.
[60] PP, 'Articles to be showed to the rector and scholars of Exeter College wherein their answer
is required'. The articles exist in two copies, identical but in different hands, both drafts. Petre's
preliminary notes for these articles also survive: 'Exeter College. To make a submission and to
grant . . .'.

such orders as may be made by me and my heirs', with the advice and consent of the bishop of Exeter, for their revision and enlargement. They were also to agree to accept his seven new fellows as full members of their fellowship, together with such statutes as he might make for the ordering of the new fellows. They would receive a schedule showing the lands which he proposed to confer on them and which, once the leases fell in, would be worth more than £100 a year, 'as I am informed'. The Rector's period of office was to be extended, as in other colleges, to give him the authority to govern the College, and to that end he was to receive a larger income. It was also intended to ask the queen for a charter of incorporation which would confirm them in all their present possessions. Finally, if they could think of any further articles profitable for them, which might be included in the charter, or if they took against any of the articles sent to them, they were to let him know speedily. 'Nothing is meant but to have the College so established as may be to God's glory, their own profit, and surety for continuance.'

The points set out in these articles were ones central to Petre's scheme: the revision of the statutes, the establishment of the seven new fellows, the provision of an additional landed endowment, and the extension of the Rector's term of office to bring Exeter into line with other colleges. If the tone was peremptory, Petre was none the less willing to take the College's own views into account and to enlarge the scale of his prospective generosity. Kennall's first letter to him had spoken of a mere £50 for the support of the new fellows, but the sum now held out to the College was more than £100, which would leave a considerable surplus beyond the monies set aside for Petre's fellows. Submission to Petre's orders, in any case for the College's benefit, was surely a price worth paying.

That submission was made, exactly as Petre had desired, in formal letters sent out on 18 May by Rector Neale under the College seal.[61] Neale noted, in words which echoed Petre's, that Stapeldon had left the College statutes 'imperfect in parts'. Now Petre, 'fervent for God's glory, the honour of the nation, and the increase of good learning', intended to enrich the College with new lands, etc., but needed their consent in order to carry through his plans. They submitted to him, agreeing to his reform and enlargement of the statutes, his nomination of seven new fellows, who were to be full members of the College, and to whatever new rules he might make both for his fellows and for the management of the proceeds of the new endowment. The submission and its dispatch were duly recorded in the College register.[62]

The next stage in Petre's planning passed the College by, but was essential to what he had in mind: the acquisition of the properties which were to provide for the new endowment. On 28 May 1565 Queen Elizabeth granted

---

[61] PP, 'Omnibus Christi fidelibus ad quos hoc presens scriptum pervenerit...', 8 May 1565.
[62] Reg., 85.

Petre various lands and rents in five Oxfordshire parishes, for which Petre paid £1,376 11s. 4½d. This was a very large sum, equivalent to about 55 per cent of Petre's annual income, which had stood at £2,458 in 1564, and it demonstrates the scale both of Petre's generosity and of his commitment to the College. From the properties came a gross annual income of nearly £53 under the current leases, but more might be expected when the leases fell in, as Petre had noted in the articles sent to the college earlier in the month. Within the next few years other properties would be added to those enumerated in the queen's grant.[63] None was yet made over to the College, but all were for the moment held in reserve until the new fellows had been nominated and the revised statutes accepted by the College.

It was to the statutes that Petre now bent his mind. In a letter which compared their benefactor not only to Maecenas, as before, but also to Minerva, the Roman goddess of wisdom and of arts and sciences, the Rector and fellows wrote on 2 July to say that they had sent him their statutes and, at his request, those of Trinity College (founded only a few years earlier in 1555), together with a summary of the latter.[64] His work, they said, would benefit not only their successors, but also the whole nation (*patria*) and the commonwealth (*respublica*) itself. Their letter, elaborately written in Latin and again in a fine italic hand, was intended, like their earlier letter of 8 April, less to convey information than to gratify and impress, and so to maintain Petre's goodwill.

It was probably at the same time, or very shortly afterwards, that the College forwarded to Petre a paper headed 'What we think worthy to be redressed': points set down clearly with an eye to their incorporation in the future statutes.[65] The concerns of the fellows were essentially internal and domestic, and they throw a good deal of light on their preoccupations at a crucial moment in the College's history. It is perhaps surprising that the list should have been headed by a request that no one should bring hawks or hounds into College. This and the second request, that no woman of ill repute should be 'feasted' within the house, suggest that undergraduate misbehaviour ranked high among the College's problems. Much was designed to define and enhance the powers of the Rector, at that time still John Neale, who almost certainly drafted the paper. The Rector was to have a veto on the admission of battelers and sojourners, his permission was to be required when bachelors or scholars (meaning undergraduate fellows) wished to leave the town, and his office was to have 'a longer continuance'. This last was in line with Petre's already expressed wish. No fellow was to leave the College for another house without the consent of the Rector and 'certain fellows', nor

[63] *CPR, 1563–66*, 251–2; Emmison, 273, 283; below, 283–4.
[64] PP, 'A honorabili viro domino Gulielmo Petri...', 2 July 1565.
[65] PP, 'What we think worthy to be redressed.'

were probationer fellows to have a vote in elections. Bachelors were to be obliged to attend lectures in natural philosophy, and undergraduates in logic. Then followed a series of questions, mostly concerned with the fellows' studies. Would the new scholars be permitted to stay beyond the eight years after their regency which was all that the current statutes allowed? How many days absence a year were they to be allowed? Should all those going on to higher degrees study theology, as was usually the case, or would the study of civil law and medicine also be permitted? Finally, should any fellow be allowed to appoint servants and to admit fellows to commons in the Rector's absence without his consent?

Discipline, governance, and academic studies: the College's paper reveals that these were the subjects uppermost in the fellows' minds as the new statutes moved into the foreground of their relations with Petre. On 16 July Petre replied to the letter which they had sent earlier in the month with a letter of his own, whose subject matter hints that he may also have had before him their list of points 'worthy to be redressed' By contrast with the ornate and deferential Latin letter of the Rector and fellows, Petre's reply was written in English, down-to-earth in its substance, and distinctly *de haut en bas* in tone. After acknowledging the receipt of extracts from the Exeter and Trinity statutes he continued:

Your travail in these matters do well declare to me your good wills to have your statutes reduced directly to such order as may be most to God's honour, increase of learning, maintenance of honest manners and conversation, and preservation of such lands as is or shall be hereafter bestowed upon you. If you continue to walk this way with due respect to God, assure yourselves God will assist all your doings and from time to time succour and provide for you. And the more you bend your endeavours this way, the more comfort shall I have to do that I have determined...[66]

He went on to say that he thought it very necessary for the Rector's office 'to be made perpetual' (that is, held for life), and that he was very willing to provide for a sub-rector. This is the first we hear of this important office, evidently proposed to him by the fellows and soon to be fully established in Petre's statutes. If they wanted one of the new fellows to study law, that would be acceptable to him. The new fellows were to be subject to the College's ordinary statutes, though he might wish to make some special ordinances for them (as he was later to do). He would write to Mr Huckle (his agent) to ask him to pass on to them £6 13s. 4d, due from the tenants of his recently purchased lands in Oxfordshire, to be disbursed by the Rector with the consent of a majority of the eight senior fellows. If any of the fellows were going to the west country that summer, it would be useful to inform the

---

[66] PP, 'After my right hearty commendations...', 15 July 1565. This passage is given in Emmison, 281.

bishop of Exeter of what had been done, so that Petre could move towards a final agreement with him when they met at the next parliament (and the consent of the bishop as visitor would, of course, be necessary for the promulgation of any new statutes). He was sending other proposals to them, including a draft of the charter for incorporation, for their comments. 'There must be', he concluded, 'some good discipline for order and good education of youth. All I desire is that God may be well known and served. And thus I bid you hasty farewell.'

Petre's letter has been cited at length because it illustrates so effectively both his aspirations and his working methods. His spiritual ends in reforming the College come through clearly: they were the service of God through the promotion of learning and the education and disciplining of the young. Although his opening words may seem almost minatory in tone, he was prepared to consult the Rector and fellows, to submit his plans for their approval, and to take note of their opinions. That he should have thought it necessary to specify the precise means for deciding on the dispersal of his first gift of money shows his remarkable but characteristic attention to detail. The Rector and fellows replied almost immediately to his suggestions with some of their own. In a further letter of 24 July 1565 they thanked him for sending then the draft charter of incorporation but disclaimed any expertise in such matters, which they were prepared to leave to his judgement, making only one minor proposal for the charter's amendment.[67] But it might be for their future benefit, they suggested, if one, two, or more of the fellows were allowed to study civil law, or if two or more took the law course and another studied medicine. They were clearly reluctant to see their higher studies confined to theology: perhaps reflecting their desire for a more directly vocational education which we have already surmised to have been influencing their choice of careers, at a time when the traditional progression from fellowship to benefice was declining in popularity. They also wished to know what allowances in the way of commons and stipends should be granted to a fellow who left the College for a set period in order to teach. They may well have had in mind here the recent absences brought about by the plague. They ended, with their now customary deferential flourish, 'Farewell, shining light of learning and singular patron'.

Petre's response to these points is known only in the context of the later statutes. Meanwhile Rector Neale supplemented the College's response to Petre's letter of 16 July by writing his own reply on 22 August.[68] After alluding to the lease of Kidlington, the most valuable of the Oxfordshire properties which Petre proposed to give to the College, Neale added that he

[67] PP, 'A honorabili viro domino Gulielmo Peter militi aurato...', 24 July 1565.
[68] PP, 'Right honourable my most hearty commendations promised as my bounden duty considered...', 22 August 1565.

was enclosing the names and particulars of those scholars 'most meet and worthy of help', for which Petre had evidently asked in casting around for promising young men to fill his seven new fellowships. Neale's enclosure names and sets out the credentials—'their countries [counties], their aptness, their conversation, their poverties, ages, and of what house they be'—of thirteen men, some of them already discussed in relation to the undergraduate body, and to be discussed again when we look at the new fellows.[69] He went on to raise the question of his old school at Week St Mary in Cornwall, 'always a ready (and now a needful) nursery for Exeter College', which, he said, had been dissolved 'because Jesus mass was there weekly sung or said'. We have again already mentioned this school in relation to the educational background of the College's fellows.[70] Neale's purpose in raising this apparently irrelevant side-issue was to ask Petre to use his influence for the school's revival. He ended by saying that he was going into his country a few weeks before Michaelmas and would inform the bishop of Exeter of what was being done—as Petre had asked in his last letter.

For the next few months the question of the new statutes and the new fellows hung fire. But in the interim came an unanticipated moment of danger. In the autumn of 1565 deep divisions within the fellowship meant that the usual October election of the Rector could not be carried through. There were at least three candidates for the post; some malcontents laid their 'complaints and calumnies' before the bishop of Exeter; and it was feared that Petre would withdraw his support from the College. Eventually, after several weeks of dissension, Neale was re-elected as Rector, but only 'with the assent of many', as the register noted, and not unanimously.[71] By this time the College had received the £6 13s. 4d. promised earlier by Petre and handed over on 23 October;[72] and when, on 4 November, the Rector and fellows wrote to thank 'our most munificent and most eminent Maecenas' for his gift, they went out of their way to stress their newfound (but perhaps fragile) unity. 'We are all one body', they wrote, and all were labouring hard to forward his work.[73] On 9 December they wrote at greater length to emphasize that, despite their recent dissensions, they were now united once again.[74] The bishop of Exeter, showing particular kindness, had composed their quarrels, and they begged Petre to continue his beneficent work. Their valediction 'from our poor and indigent college' made no bones about the need for it. Whether there was ever a real threat that Petre might abort his plans for the College is impossible to say. But the fellows had certainly feared that their quarrels might once again leave them stranded in poverty.

---

[69] PP, 'The names of the scholars fittest for us'; above, 218–19; below, 294–5.
[70] Above, 182.
[71] Reg., 86–7.   [72] PP, 'Anno domini 1565. Octobris 23. Received...'
[73] PP, 'Accepimus (vir nobilissime) munus tuum et gratuitum...', 4 November 1565.
[74] PP, 'Quamvis nuperrime ad tuam dignitatem scripserimus...', 9 December 1565.

One other major act remained to be carried through before the establishment of the new order. On 22 March the queen issued a charter of incorporation in favour of the College.[75] The charter and the new statutes which followed shortly afterward were the twin keystones of the reformed College. The charter's drafting, like that of the statutes, was undoubtedly Petre's work: he had earlier sent a preliminary text to the fellows for their approval, a summary of the contents survives in his own hand, and a copy of the final text also exists among his papers.[76] But its promulgation depended, of course, on the favour of the queen. Like the queen's grant of land to Petre for the College's benefit, the publication of the charter under the royal seal showed Exeter's good fortune in having for its benefactor a man who was not only wealthy but also an experienced lawyer and a privy councillor who had the queen's ear. If Petre was the College's patron, the queen was his.

The charter's terms were all that the College could have wished for. In it the queen noted Petre's 'good, pious, laudable and devout intention' in seeking to reform the College; confirmed its establishment as a body comprising a Rector and twenty-one fellows (so taking account of the new fellows yet to be nominated); decreed that the College should be called Exeter College (so removing any lingering doubts about its former status as Stapeldon Hall); authorized the bishop of Exeter, with the advice and consent of Petre, to make new statutes (although in fact and in practice the position of the two parties was the reverse of that stated in the charter); laid down that Petre's statutes and ordinances were to regulate the governance of the College and to be inviolably observed; confirmed the Rector and fellows in possession of all their lands and other rights, and of all the liberties and franchises held by the university of Oxford; and licensed the College to acquire, and Petre to grant, further lands, etc., to the annual value of £100 net. The sum which the charter cites here provides one of the best instances of Petre's regard for College opinion, for his draft charter sent to the College had set the value of lands to be acquired at 100 marks, to which the Rector and fellows had diffidently responded that this was perhaps too little.[77] The increase of one-third in the final text of the charter shows that the point had been taken.

The general effect of the charter was to ground the College's current standing on royal authority and to authorize Petre to go forward with his plans, notably the new statutes which were to govern the College, and the new endowment which would soon be conferred on it. If it confirmed the College as a corporate legal entity, able to sue and be sued, its chief benefit lay

[75] The charter is printed in *Statutes*, 13–19. The original is in the College archives: ECA, L. I. 4.
[76] PP, 'After my right hearty commendations...', 16 July 1565; 'Where there is and hath of long time continued within the university of Oxford...'; 'The copy of Queen Elizabeth's letters patent for incorporating Sir William Petre's scholars...'.
[77] PP, 'Where there is and hath of long time continued within the university of Oxford...'; 'A honorabili viro domino Gulielmo Peter...', 24 July 1565.

elsewhere and in its whole rather than in the sum of its parts. In his articles sent to the College in May 1565 Petre had spoken of his concern 'to see the college so established as may be to ... their due profit and surety for continuance'—and it was this 'surety for continuance' that the charter conclusively provided. It secured the future existence of the College; and at a time when, only twenty years earlier, the Oxford colleges had been threatened with the fate of the monasteries and chantries, when the queen's heir was the catholic Mary Queen of Scots, and when yet another reversal in religion was by no means inconceivable, future security was one of the greatest blessings that any benefactor could confer.

With the issuing of the charter and the conclusion of Petre's work on the statutes it remained only to initiate the new order ceremonially and solemnly. The occasion for that came at midsummer 1566. Shortly after Pentecost, 2 June, the College received the new statutes, signed by the bishop of Exeter and Sir William Petre.[78] At the end of the month, on 29 June, the queen's charter of incorporation was read aloud by the Rector, John Neale, before a large gathering in the chapel and in the presence of John Woodward, whose visit to the College in April 1564 had initiated the whole process and who was now presumably acting again as Petre's representative. Next day the seven new fellows nominated by Petre, 'by whose labour, wealth and favour all things were carried through', were formally admitted to the fellowship. Finally, on 2 July all the fellows, both those of the old foundation and the new, were sworn to observe the new statutes, and on 4 July the seven new fellows wrote a gushing letter to Petre, which each signed, thanking him for his bounty (see Plate 18).[79] At some later point the names of the new fellows were entered in the register, in order of seniority, by Petre himself, followed by his signature.[80] This brought to a close the most momentous series of events since the College's foundation.

4. THE NEW STATUTES

Petre's statutes, delivered to the College in June 1566, governed its general working until they were superseded by the later statutes of 1856. A few of their innovations—the office of sub-rector is the prime example—have survived into modern times. Although they preserved some of the essentials of Stapeldon's statutes, such as the regional limitations on the recruitment of

---

[78] Reg., 88. This is probably the signed copy of the statutes, preserved in a contemporary wooden case, which survives in the College archives: ECA, A. I. 2. See Plate 16.

[79] These details appear as an addendum on Petre's copy of the charter: PP, 'The copy of Queen Elizabeth's letters patent for incorporating Sir William Petre's scholars...'. The accounts show that the new fellows received their commons from 30 June: RA, 254/4. For the letter of thanks, see PP, 'Domino Gulielmo Petraeo Georgiani ordinis militii inclytissimo...'. 4 July 1566.

[80] Reg., 88–9. Since Petre himself never visited the College, the register must have been sent to him, probably at his London house in Aldersgate Street, for him to enter the names and to sign.

fellows on the old foundation, they largely reflected Petre's aims, principles, and cast of mind, just as Stapeldon's statutes had reflected his. Still more personal to Petre was the supplement to the statutes which he drafted under his own name and without that of the bishop of Exeter, who was the nominal originator of the statutes themselves. Probably issued at the same time as the statutes but separate from them, Petre's supplement chiefly provided directions for the distribution of the income arising from his new endowment. But it also added to much that had already been set down in the statutes about such matters as teaching arrangements and the management of the College's lands. Statutes and supplement need to be taken together to provide a full guide to Petre's intentions and the projected future of the College.[81]

The new statutes comprised a long document: some thirty-one pages of Latin in their nineteenth-century edition, compared with a mere eight pages for Stapeldon's statutes. This contrast is to be explained not only by the more complex situation of the sixteenth-century College, which had, for example, to accommodate non-fellow undergraduates unknown in Stapeldon's day, but also by the degree of precision and foresight which characterized Petre's approach. The trained lawyer and administrator was concerned to provide for every possible circumstance and eventuality, and to leave no loose ends. But for all their length and elaborateness, the statutes lend themselves to a simple fourfold division under the headings of government and structure, teaching and learning, financial management, and discipline. This is the broad classification adopted in the following discussion.

The keystone of the College's government remained the Rector. The most important innovation here lay in the statutes' provision for the life tenure of all future Rectors, superseding the old system of annual elections. Although the extension of the Rector's period of office had been given a high priority in the earlier correspondence between Petre and the College, the statutes introduced this fundamental change almost glancingly and without emphasis ('ordinamus . . . ut in hoc Collegio . . . sit perpetuo unus Rector et duodecim Scholares . . . '), though it is confirmed by their later assumption that vacancies in the post will arise only from the death, departure, or removal of the previous Rector.[82] In overturning one of the central tenets of Stapeldon's earlier statutes, the new rule thus brought the position of Exeter's head firmly into line with that of other heads of houses.

Petre's other objective regarding the Rector, set out in his articles of May 1565, was 'to make his authority such as he may be able to rule', and this was

---

[81] The statutes are printed in *The Statutes of Exeter College, Oxford* (London, 1855), probably from the College's master copy, ECA, A. I. 2. The supplement is printed in Boase (1), liv–lvii, from the same manuscript, but under a heading ('Decretum domini Gulielmi Petrei de suis possessionibus') which is not present in the manuscript and which must be Boase's invention.

[82] *Statutes*, 22, 23.

certainly followed through in the statutes. The Rector was to be a paragon of moral integrity, learning, and practical expertise. Aged at least 30, not a bishop, and preferably reading for the baccalaureate in theology, but at least a *magister*, he was to be of strict morals, chaste life, and unblemished reputation, learned and devout, and skilled and experienced in matters relating to profits, rents, buildings, and leases: a man of virtue, a scholar, and a man of business. In many respects his powers were those of Stapeldon's Rector—to appoint servants, to allocate rooms, to manage the College finances, and to account at the annual audit. But he was also to have an additional general oversight of the whole College and its members—fellows, officers, sojourners, and undergraduates. He was to enforce the statutes, to punish delinquents, to maintain the College's cause in lawsuits, and to have charge in his room of the College chest containing the College seal, money, statutes, and silver plate.[83] Although it was assumed that he would often be away on business, he might if he wished have a teaching role by moderating in theological disputations.[84] For all this he was to be handsomely rewarded. The statutes gave him no more than the customary allowances of 12*d.* a week for commons (plus decrements) and an additional 20*s.* a year, the same stipend as Stapeldon had prescribed for the Rector. But Petre's supplement to the statutes went much further, assigning the Rector and his successors the vicarage of Kidlington and everything that pertained to it.[85] The Rector of Exeter thus became ex officio the vicar of Kidlington, as he was to remain until the late nineteenth century. For this position he was obliged to pay the College £7 6*s.* a year. But since a separate assessment of the vicarage among Petre's papers put its net value at £29 0*s.* 8*d.*, the Rector's profit amounted to nearly £22, or about a quarter of the College's annual income before the re-endowment. Petre had earlier matched his intention to enhance the Rector's authority with a complementary undertaking 'to enlarge his living'.[86] This had now been amply fulfilled.

Beneath the Rector, but sharing with him in the government of the College, were the fellows, the fourteen on the old foundation (including the chaplain) now to be joined by the seven on the new. The regional qualifications for membership of the first group remained the same: twelve were to come from the four archdeaconries of Devon and Cornwall and two from the diocese of Salisbury. In a piece of misremembered College history, the statutes incorrectly ascribed the founding of the Salisbury fellowships to Edmund Stafford, bishop of Exeter, in the early fifteenth century, when they were actually a

---

[83] *Statutes*, 22–3, 26–7, 45–6; PP, 'Articles to be shewed to the rector and scholars of Exeter College wherein their answer is required'.

[84] *Statutes*, 36.   [85] *Statutes*, 39–40; Boase (1), liv–lv.

[86] PP, 'Com. Oxon.'; 'Articles to be shewed to the rector and scholars of Exeter College wherein their answer is required'; below, 286–7.

consequence of the College's appropriation of the church of Wittenham in 1355. The seven new fellows were to come from the counties where Petre held land, which included Devon, Somerset, Dorset, and Oxfordshire, as well as Essex. Other moral and academic qualifications for a fellowship were taken over directly from Stapeldon's statutes: those elected were to be the more fit to make progress, the more virtuous in character, and the more impoverished in their means. In their academic standing they were to be 'at least sophists', and in age—this not prescribed by Stapeldon—at least 16.[87] Their upward steps were clearly defined in the statutes. Incoming fellows were first elected as probationers, and during their probationary year they were barred from taking part in College business or voting in elections. At the end of that year their merits were assessed and their rejection or admission as 'perpetual fellows' decided.[88] The academic course to be followed by those admitted was again set out in the statutes. Each was to take the BA within five years of admission as a probationer and the MA within a further four or at most five years, and then to progress first to the baccalaureate in theology and eventually to the doctorate.[89] During this time they were to receive the customary allowances of 12d. a week for commons and a stipend of 10s. a year. Petre's supplement, however, made additional and more generous provision, discriminating especially in favour of his new fellows, each of whom was to receive 22d. a week in commons and 26s. 8d. a year in stipend. It may have been in order to mollify any ill feelings provoked by such favouritism that the supplement also conceded additional allowances to fellows on the old foundation: 13s. 6d. to each *magister*, 10s. to each bachelor, and 6s. 8d. to each undergraduate fellow.[90] All fellows had a part to play in the government of the College. They were obliged to be present at elections, under penalty of expulsion from the College if they failed to appear for the election of a Rector, and the Rector was obliged to consult them on all important College business, such as the requested departure of fellows to other colleges, entry into major litigation, and the leasing of lands.[91] Most of these matters required the consent of a majority of the fellows. Although Petre had enlarged the Rector's authority, the College remained, as it had always been, a kind of constitutional monarchy.

The statutes thus changed the position of Exeter's fellows in some significant ways. Perhaps most significant was their assumption that a fellowship would henceforth be held for life and no longer for a limited period of years. Like the Rector's life tenure, that of the fellows is specifically if inconspicuously provided for in the statutes, and is further implied in their several references to 'perpetual fellows'[92] and in the provision for the long years of

---

[87] *Statutes*, 28–9. For the Salisbury fellows, see above, 74–5.   [88] *Statutes*, 29–31.
[89] *Statutes*, 38–9.   [90] *Statutes*, 39–40; Boase (1), liv–lv.
[91] *Statutes*, 24, 27, 31, 33–4, 45.   [92] e.g. *Statutes*, 31, 32.

study needed for higher degrees in theology enjoined on all fellows after their inception as masters. Higher degrees were in themselves an important innovation. Given no place in Stapeldon's statutes, they had been licensed in Pope Innocent VII's amendments to the statutes, but they had never become popular.[93] Now higher qualifications in theology were seen as the normal and culminating phase of the academic *cursus honorum*: a reflection of Petre's religious ends in refounding the College. Higher degrees in other subjects received a very limited recognition when, in his supplement, Petre stated that he would permit one of his fellows (but by implication none on the old foundation) to study either civil law or medicine at a foreign university for four years.[94] Yet it must have been assumed that only a limited number of fellows would want to stay on for a higher degree in theology. The statutes indicated a second and more normal career path when they stipulated that a fellow's acceptance of a benefice worth 10 marks a year, or acquisition of an income to that value, would necessitate his resignation. A living was, as it had always been, a likely berth for many graduates. Resignation would also follow, the statutes said, from a fellow's marriage: an event inconceivable in Stapeldon's day, but licensed for priests in 1549 and again in 1559, though priestly marriages were not yet widespread.[95] It is not known how many fellows, if any, gave up their fellowships for marriage at this time.

Behind the Rector and fellows stood the bishop of Exeter as visitor of the College and wearer of Elijah's mantle. The bishop's role had dwindled since the days of Stapeldon and his immediate successors. Petre's statutes continued to give him a wide if vague remit: he was to see that the statutes were fully observed, teaching and virtue nurtured, the College promoted in its temporal and spiritual possessions, and its rights, liberties, and privileges defended and protected. But in place of the bishop's annual visitation prescribed in Stapeldon's statutes, the bishop of the new statutes was to visit the College only once in five years, though he might be called in at any time by the Rector and senior fellows if the need arose for his guidance or disciplinary powers.[96] Since the new statutes also laid down that the accounts should be audited annually by the College officers and senior fellows,[97] the bishop had lost the formal justification for annual visits prescribed in the old statutes. That he was now to be no more than a very occasional presence reflected his declining function in the College since the late fifteenth century. Although the current bishop, William Alley, had resolved the fellows' disputes in 1565, he had not otherwise (so far as can be seen) shown much interest in the College. He was the nominal instigator of the statutes, made only with Petre's advice and

---

[93] Above, 96–8, 212.   [94] Boase (1), lvi.
[95] *Statutes*, 42–3; E. J. Carlson, 'Clerical Marriage and the English Reformation', *Jnl. of British Studies*, 31 (1992), 3–5, 12–13.
[96] *Statutes*, 46–7.   [97] *Statutes*, 25.

consent, and on the master copy of the statutes in the College archives his signature precedes that of Petre (see Plate 16). But Petre's direction to the Rector and fellows, in his letter of 16 July 1565, that if any one of them was about to go to the west country he should tell the bishop what was happening suggests a fairly casual attitude to Stapeldon's successor.[98] Nor do copies of any letters to the bishop survive among Petre's papers, as they surely would have done had they been in correspondence about the statutes. So the statutes both reflect and confirm the limited part which the bishop now played in the College's affairs, and in that sense they helped to establish the College as a body now more independent of external authority.

Petre's regulations for the College's government overlapped with those for teaching and learning: the second of our four topics. The overlap came in his statutory establishment of 'a little hierarchy of college officers':[99] sub-rector, dean, lector, and teaching assistant. The leading officer, the sub-rector, has proved more permanent than all the rest. As his title suggests, the sub-rector was the Rector's deputy, his appointment necessitated, the statute explained, by the frequent absences of the Rector on College business and by his many other preoccupations. He was to be elected annually by the Rector and the five senior fellows, and he was to be at least a *magister* and preferably one who had gone on to study theology (the statute does not make this obligatory). As well as being in general charge of the College during the Rector's absences, living in, and presiding in hall, he had an important teaching role as the moderator in theological disputations. For his labours Petre's supplement to the statutes awarded him a stipend of 40s. a year.[100]

The other new officers took on a larger share of the teaching. The dean in effect supervised the basic arts course followed by the College's bachelors and undergraduates, both fellows and non-fellows. He presided over the bachelors' disputations in logic and philosophy, lectured on logic on certain days to the undergraduates, and heard their daily disputations on logic. For this he was to receive 8d. a quarter from every commoner and batteler (i.e. all non-fellow undergraduates). Petre's supplement also gave him the same 40s. stipend received by the sub-rector.[101] It was in the supplement, and almost as an afterthought, that a third officer, the lector or lecturer, appeared. His task was to lecture during the term on Cicero, Livy, Quintilian, and other Latin authors prescribed by the Rector and fellows, and on four days a week in the long vacation to give further lectures on arithmetic, geometry, and astronomy, the main subjects of the quadrivium. Between them, the dean and lector thus covered most of the seven liberal arts comprising the traditional arts course. The lector was to receive a stipend of 26s. 8d., and both he and the dean were to be elected annually, in the same way as the sub-rector. Finally,

[98] Above, 266–7; Emmison, 281. [99] Southern, *VCH Oxfordshire*, iii. 110.
[100] *Statutes*, 35–6; Boase (1), lv. [101] *Statutes*, 36–7; Boase (1), lv.

the most junior member of the teaching hierarchy was to be a bachelor appointed by the Rector to act as the dean's assistant, hearing disputations and exercises in logic, and receiving in exchange 13s. 4d. a year.[102]

These men, all fellows of the College, were responsible for a teaching system which the statutes set out in prescriptive detail. Throughout the academic year all the College's bachelors and regent masters were to dispute twice weekly on three questions concerning logic, natural philosophy, and metaphysics, and put to them in writing. In Lent the *quaestiones* were to be on moral philosophy. The disputations were normally to last for two hours, and those absent without reasonable cause approved by the Rector and dean were to lose their commons for a month. For those studying theology there were to be disputations once a week in full term in the chapel, provided that there were four theologians present in College. Absence was again to be punished by loss of commons. If the majority of the theologians went into the country in time of plague, then the disputations were to be held there, and the same applied to all other disputations and lectures. Petre may have envisaged the use of the vicarage at Kidlington for this purpose, since his supplement reserved the vicarage as a refuge for the fellows when Oxford was afflicted by plague. The daily lectures on logic by the dean or his bachelor assistant were to be given in hall from 6 a.m. to 7 a.m.; disputations on logic were to be held from 10 a.m. to 11 a.m. and from 6 p.m. to 7 p.m.; while the exercises known as 'repetitions' were to be held from 3 p.m. to 4 p.m. three times a week.[103] It was a full and rigorous timetable.

These statutes were intended to give a primacy to teaching and learning in the life of the College which Petre deemed to have been previously lacking. Justifying the appointment of the sub-rector, he wrote that 'hitherto there have been no officers in this college for the better ordering of the young fellows (*scholares*) or the greater progress of sound learning'.[104] His achievement in the statutes was to establish a new framework for the College as a teaching institution, catering in a newly defined and regulated way both for beginners taking the arts course and advanced students taking theology. The emphasis on logic and the other liberal arts indicates that at Exeter, as in the university generally, 'the medieval curriculum had by no means been abandoned'.[105] But it was now leavened by the statutes' provision for lectures on classical authors: with Livy and Cicero, a place was found for history and civic humanism. The largely oral nature of teaching, still general throughout the university, made for a heavy burden on the teachers and necessitated the appointment of the 'teaching staff' for which Petre so creatively provided. Undergraduates would still have had their individual tutors, unmentioned by the statutes, but most of the group teaching was now supplied by the new

---

[102] Boase (1), lv.   [103] *Statutes*, 37–8; Boase (1), lv.   [104] Boase (1), lv.
[105] Fletcher, 'Faculty of Arts', *HUO*, iii. 173–5.

College officers. The arts syllabus was viewed only as a preliminary to the study of theology, at least for the fellows. Non-fellow undergraduates would not progress beyond the MA—if indeed, given the numbers who seem to have left without taking any degree, they ever reached that exalted status.

The statutes initiated one further set of changes which affected both College government and College teaching. They amended and defined with new precision the main dates and stages in the College year. This was particularly important with regard to elections. Formerly, elections to fellowships had taken place throughout the year, as fellowships were vacated and possible candidates for election came into view. Admission to commons followed some time afterwards, as we have seen, but that might be a matter of days, weeks, or even months. These arrangements were now changed. Under the new statutes all elections to fellowships were to take place annually on 30 June, when the Rector or sub-rector would declare to the fellows assembled in the chapel the number of places to be filled. This had the advantage of bringing forward the names of potential candidates in what would nowadays be called a 'gathered field', and of allowing comparisons to be made between them. For those elected, admission to commons was to follow within ten days. On the same day, 30 June, the College officers, sub-rector, dean, and lector, were also to be elected for the coming year.[106] These changes had the effect of concentrating business on the midsummer meeting of the fellowship, from this time onwards the high point in the College's administrative year. They also marked the silent abolition of the former main meeting of the year in early October for the election of the Rector, now no longer an annual event, and for the election of other College officers, the bursars and the keepers of the chests, who go unmentioned in Petre's statutes. An autumn date, 2 November, was, however, still retained for the Rector's presentation of the accounts. The further stipulation in the statutes that the accounts were now to be kept in book form, and no longer on the increasingly archaic rolls in use since the 1350s or before, was another mark of Petre's modernizing programme. The final account roll, for 1565–6, records the acquisition of a book for keeping the accounts, and the first account in the book itself runs from 2 November 1566, as the statutes prescribe.[107] The weary historian who has struggled with some 250 separate rolls will view this as the blessed end of an era.

The same spirit of practical efficiency and orderliness was equally evident in the rules laid down in the statutes for the financial management of the College and its possessions: the third of our four topics. In April 1564, at the start of his engagement with the College, Petre had asked for full documentary

[106] *Statutes*, 28–9, 35; Boase (1), lv.
[107] *Statutes*, 21; RA, 254/3; ECA, A. II. 9, Rector's Accounts, 1566–1639, fo. 1r.

information on the College's finances.[108] From this he may well have seen how the College's acute financial difficulties during the mid century period, and up to the time of his own intervention, had been partly caused by the lax management of its resources: arrears had been allowed to accumulate, long leases had been tolerated and granted to fellows on favourable terms, even as prices rose, and little attempt had been made to maximize income. These failings the statutes set out to rectify. The stress which they laid on the professional skills required in the Rector—a man with the aptitude and experience to handle matters relating to profits, rents, buildings, and leases— was one mark of this businesslike approach. But much more specific was the chapter in the statutes headed 'The granting out of lands (*De terris dimittendis*)'.[109] This laid down rigorous conditions for the leasing not only of the College's lands but also of its tithes and other resources. There were to be no reversionary leases, promising entry after the expiry of the current lease. No land was to be leased for more than twenty years and no tithes for more than ten years. Neither the Rector nor any fellow was to be granted the lease of any College lands or tithes. When leases were renewed, reasonable entry fines might be imposed. Covenants were to be inserted in all leases binding the lessees to a series of obligations: rents were to be paid, on pain of terminating the lease; all repairs were to be the responsibility of the lessee, including those to the chancels of appropriated churches; and the lessee was also to take responsibility for the sowing, planting, and conservation of fruits and trees. The precise enumeration of these latter—oaks, elms, chestnuts, walnuts, apple and pear trees—wafts a breath of country air through a formal document. In all these matters the Rector was to act only with the consent of the fellows. The means to supervision of properties was provided by the final chapter of the statutes, which laid down that every third year the Rector and another fellow should make a progress around the College's properties within forty miles of Oxford in order to check on their state and to see what repairs were needed, reporting to the fellows on their return.[110]

In making these regulations, the re-endowment of the College must have been in the forefront of Petre's mind. The College would soon have a much larger estate to administer than it had ever previously possessed, and the bulk of it lay close at hand. Petre's purchase of lands in Oxfordshire for the College's benefit marked a deliberate attempt to provide it with holdings whose proximity would make them easy to supervise. The establishment and perpetuation of the seven new fellowships for which most of the new endowment was to provide depended wholly on the endowment's efficient management, and this the statutes sought to ensure. In other smaller ways, money might also be saved. When the bishop made his visitation the statutes

---

[108] Reg., 83.   [109] Above, 194–5, 197–8; *Statutes*, 22, 44–5.   [110] *Statutes*, 51–2.

stipulated that his entertainment and expenses should amount to no more than 40s. and, when his deputy acted for him, to no more than 20s. or two meals.[111] Such Gladstonian penny-pinching might make its own minor contribution to the College's well-being.

If the novel enlargement of the College's estate required new regulations, the problem of discipline, our fourth and final topic, was an older one. Rector French's manifesto of 1539 against 'the insolence of the bachelors' had already shown the threats which the unruly young were seen to pose to their elders and betters. Since then the rapid growth of the undergraduate body had magnified the problem. In Rector French's day the College housed seven fellows who were bachelors, one who was an undergraduate, and perhaps half a dozen other undergraduates. By 1572 there were some eighty undergraduates.[112] But it was not on them alone that the statutes sought to impose norms for social conduct. Some were directed solely at the fellows, some at the undergraduates, and some at both. Here we must remember once again that if most undergraduates were mere commoners and batelers, *commensales* and *batellarii*, who were not on the foundation, a small minority were fellows, *scholares* in the language of the statutes. For all these groups the statutes had a common purpose in the preservation of hierarchy, decorum, and order.

Respect for hierarchy was writ large throughout the statutes, but it was chiefly found in the regulations for dress and for dining in hall, and in the privileges offered to one group but denied to another.[113] No undergraduate fellow or bachelor should leave his head covered while eating with the Rector (presumably *magistri* were permitted to keep their hats on); nor should an undergraduate fellow have his head covered in the presence of a *magister* (in this case bachelors were presumably permitted to keep their hats on). During meals in hall silence was to be maintained while the Bible was read aloud, and when the reading was finished all talking, whether by fellows, sojourners, or undergraduates, was to be in Latin or Greek. Undergraduates, however, were to speak Latin or Greek wherever they went in College. In hall, sojourners and undergraduates were to sit apart from the fellows unless they were *magistri* or bidden to sit with the Rector and senior fellows. Undergraduate fellows, commoners, and batelers were barred from entering the buttery (was it feared that they would get at the drink?), while bachelors might do so only if permitted by the Rector or sub-rector. Much was made of matters of decorum. Fellows must wear black shoes—the statute noted that this had been laid down by Stapeldon—and sober clothes, and, in chapel, surplices and dress appropriate to their academic standing.

More revealing of social life within the College were the rules governing what might be called leisure activities. Fellows must abstain from cards, dice,

---

[111] *Statutes*, 47.   [112] Above, 215, 217.   [113] *Statutes*, 40–2.

and other games, but were permitted to play at cards for moderate stakes at
All Saints, Christmas, and Candlemas, provided that they did so publicly and
in hall. Rowdiness, high spirits, acts of bravado, and the importing into
College of the pastimes of the countryside—the particular prerogatives of
the undergraduates—were all met with disapproval and prohibition. No guns
or cross-bows were to be brought into College; nor were hunting dogs,
greyhounds, ferrets, rabbits, or hawks.[114] No strangers were to be admitted
to the College without the permission of the Rector and fellows; and the
fellows should especially beware of admitting drunks, prostitutes, and other
undesirables.[115] The gates of the College were to be bolted at 9 p.m., or 9.15
p.m. at the latest, and no one, fellow, sojourner, or undergraduate, was to
spend the night outside College without the permission of the Rector or sub-
rector (a rule which survived into modern times). Nor was anyone to climb
the walls of the College—clearly an allusion to climbing in at night, and the
first reference to an undergraduate late-entry system commonplace until the
late twentieth century. This was evidently viewed as an especially heinous
offence. Most misdemeanours were punished by a day's or at most a week's
loss of commons, but the penalty for climbing the wall was a month's loss
and, for a second offence, expulsion from the College. Expulsion was also the
punishment prescribed for commoners and battelers who refused to work or
were otherwise refractory, and who failed to mend their ways.[116]

From the statutes it would be easy to forget that the College had another
function besides the promotion of teaching and learning, the management of
estates, and the maintenance of an orderly life. It was also, and perhaps
primarily, seen by Petre as a religious institution. Yet beyond a short section
on the chaplain and his duties, and the requirement that the Rector and
fellows should attend chapel on Sundays and feast days, the statutes have
little to say about religious observances. Petre's supplement to the statutes is,
however, more expansive about the religious life of the College, and more
revealing about his personal religion: a subject central to his intentions for the
College and reserved for later discussion.[117]

It would be a mistake to see Petre's statutes as *sui generis*, the product of his
own unaided reflections on how a college should be ordered. Unlike those
other contemporary benefactors, Sir Thomas Pope, who founded Trinity, and
Sir Thomas White, who founded St John's, Petre was not a founder but a
refounder. In his plans for Exeter he did not start with a *tabula rasa* but with
a College already two hundred and fifty years old and already equipped with
its founder's statutes, to which some respect was due. Hence Exeter's basic
structures—a Rector, a chaplain, eleven other fellows from Devon and

[114] *Statutes*, 41.   [115] *Statutes*, 51.   [116] *Statutes*, 44, 51.
[117] *Statutes*, 34; below, 307–12, 316.

Cornwall, a predominantly arts syllabus—were all left in place. Petre's was in part a modernizing venture, intended to bring Exeter into line with other colleges and to loosen the College from the archaic grip of Stapeldon's statutes but not to erase them. His most significant innovation was the institution of the life rectorship and the concentration of executive power in the Rector's hands: measures which enlarged the authority of the Rector and gave him a position comparable to other heads of houses, in a university where heads were increasingly coming to dominate their colleges and to be the leaders with whom governments preferred to deal.

The extension of the Rector's term was only one of the points on which Petre's statutes embodied the wishes of the fellows. In the paper which they had submitted to their benefactor in July 1565 they had asked for much else besides 'a longer continuance' of the Rector's office: no hawks or hounds in College, no loose women, no transfer of fellows to other colleges without the consent of the Rector and fellows, no votes for probationers in elections, the compulsory attendance of bachelors and undergraduate fellows at lectures and disputations, the need for the Rector's consent when members of these two groups sought leave of absence, and the possibility of studying civil law and medicine as well as theology. All these desiderata were accepted by Petre in his statutes or in his supplement, often in expanded form, and the new regulations were all the more authoritative for resting in part on the expressed wishes of the fellows.

Most of the statutes, however, did not emerge from the wishes of the fellowship but from the statutes of other colleges. All sixteenth-century college statutes embodied a large element of common form: for example, in providing, as in Exeter's case, for weekly disputations in theology, to be moderated by some senior figure.[118] Other rules, against keeping dogs and hawks, against playing cards, against speaking English rather than Latin or Greek within the college, to name only a few further examples, were similarly common to many colleges.[119] In Exeter's case the recent statutes of Trinity provided a particular model. Sir Thomas Pope, Trinity's founder, was also Petre's friend, though not a particularly close one, and Petre had consulted the Trinity statutes, apparently on the recommendation of the fellows, in drafting his own.[120] Some of his statutes were taken over almost word for word from those of Trinity. The reasons which the statutes gave for appointing a sub-rector as deputy head (the Rector's frequent absences, etc.) followed very closely those given by Trinity's statutes for appointing a vice-president; while

[118] Greenslade, 'Faculty of Theology', *HUO*, iii. 309.
[119] Dogs, hawks, cards: 'Statutes of Brasenose College', *SCO*, ii. 27; 'Statutes of Corpus Christi College', *SCO*, ii. 68; 'Statutes of St John's College', *SCO*, iii. 65–6. Latin and Greek: 'Statutes of Brasenose', 24; 'Statutes of St John's', 56; *Statutes of Trinity College, Oxford* (London, 1855), 28.
[120] Emmison, 69, 177, 281–2; Reg, 85; above, 265–6.

the chapter in the Trinity statutes on the letting of lands (no reversionary leases, etc.) was reproduced almost word for word in Petre's statutes.[121] This shows no more than that all colleges faced common problems and sought common solutions.

Yet there were substantial differences. Elaborate though Petre's statutes were, they were succinct by comparison with those of Pope, which were about twice as long. Petre had very little to say about domestic matters, while Pope went into minute detail about such subjects as sleeping arrangements and servants' duties entirely ignored by Petre. Like Trinity, Exeter was to have a dean and a lector (two lectors in Trinity's case). But Trinity's dean was largely concerned with discipline and Exeter's with teaching.[122] Disciplinary matters were left largely to the Rector or, in his absence, the sub-rector. This instance points to one of the two ways in which Exeter's statutes seem to be distinctive. They invest very considerable power in the hands of the Rector, for whom the sub-rector was a deputy rather than an adjunct. The Rector's powers were especially wide-ranging in financial matters. Unlike Trinity and St John's, where in each college two bursars had charge of the College's finances, Petre's statutes made no mention of bursars. They certainly survived, but it looks as if their already very limited duties may have been circumscribed still further by the elevation of the Rector, who was left in full command of finances and accounts.[123]

A second individual feature of Exeter's statutes is more difficult to explain. Almost all sixteenth-century college statutes stipulated that fellows should take holy orders at some specified stage in their College careers, usually within a period of years after incepting as *magistri*. This provision is found in the statutes of Brasenose, Corpus Christi, St John's, Trinity, and—the college whose statutes followed next after those of Exeter—Jesus. At Brasenose, Corpus Christi, and St John's it was additionally laid down that the head of the house must also be a priest.[124] Petre's statutes made no such provisions. Although some preliminary notes which he made on the qualities needed in his new fellows had specified that they should 'determine their minds to the study of divinity and to be of the clergy',[125] the second of these requirements found no place in the statutes, nor was anything said about the need for the Rector to take orders. It was enough for him to be 'devoted to divine worship (*cultui divino deditus*)',[126] and more space was given to his business credentials than to his religious qualifications. The statutes also made the curious stipulation,

---

[121] *Statutes*, 35, 44–5; *Statutes of Trinity*, 13, 64–5.

[122] *Statutes*, 36–7; *Statutes of Trinity*, 14–15.

[123] *Statutes of Trinity*, 15–16; 'Statutes of St John's', 25; above, 203. For Exeter bursars in the 1590s, see Boase (2), xciii, xcv n. 1.

[124] 'Statutes of Brasenose', 2, 31; 'Statutes of Corpus Christi', 2, 62; 'Statutes of St John's', 13, 59; *Statutes of Trinity*, 47; 'Statutes of Jesus College', *SCO*, iii. 68.

[125] Emmison, 282.   [126] *Statutes*, 22.

apparently unique to Exeter, that he should not be a bishop. It was almost as though, for whatever reason, Petre wished to circumvent the question of priestly orders. This is a point to which we shall return.

Petre's letter of 16 July 1565 to the College had set out his opinions on the purposes of his prospective statutes. They were to be 'reduced directly to such order as may be to God's honour, increase of learning, maintenance of honest manners and conversation, and preservation of such lands as is or shall be hereafter bestowed on you'.[127] To these ends he drew on the fellows' recommendations, the statutes of other colleges, and his own deductions as to what was needed. Perhaps his youthful experiences at All Souls, a college which he still remembered with charitable affection, also helped to shape his thinking.[128] The result was a code designed to promote sound religion and good learning under a powerful Rector and to bring Exeter into the modern age. But what Petre may have understood by sound religion remains to be determined.

5. THE NEW ENDOWMENT

The new endowment which Petre conferred on Exeter between 1566 and 1568 more than doubled its income. But, rather surprisingly, it did not greatly increase the level of its corporate prosperity, though it certainly left individual fellows better provided for. At the core of the endowment were the properties granted by Queen Elizabeth to Petre on 28 May 1565, before the College had been set up with Petre's new statutes and new fellows. They comprised four Oxfordshire rectories—Kidlington, Yarnton, South Newington, and Merton—together with smaller properties in Thrupp, near Kidlington, and Little Tew, both also in Oxfordshire. The value of the four rectories lay in the lands and other rights attached to them, so essentially this was a landed estate. Reckoned to produce an annual net income of nearly £53, it had cost Petre £1,376 11s. 4½d. as the purchase price paid to the queen.[129]

For the next eighteen months these properties remained in Petre's hands. They were formally granted to Exeter only on 8 November 1566, after the College's acceptance of the new statutes and the admission of the seven new fellows in the previous June. To the bundle of properties bought from the queen Petre now added others: lands in Garsington, which he had purchased in 1563, and a rent charge in Kiddington, both again in Oxfordshire, plus further minor holdings in Tintinhull and Montacute, in distant Somerset. The whole assemblage was now given a current value of just under £99. It was, however, bestowed only conditionally. In the concluding section of the grant Petre laid down that the College's continuing possession of its new endowment was dependent on its full enforcement of the statutes and of certain

---

[127] Emmison, 281. [128] Emmison, 278–9.
[129] CPR, 1563–66, 251–2; ECA, A. II. 1, fos. 24ᵛ–36 (transcript); Boase (2), lxxxv–lxxxvi.

other articles. Failure here, and continuing failure to reform after due warn-
ing, would result in the reversion of the endowment to Petre and his heirs
until the College found surety for its future observance of statutes and
articles.[130] The articles themselves, set out in the form of an indentured
agreement with the College dated on the same day as the grant, embodied
all the main items in Petre's earlier supplement to the statutes, already discussed. Like the supplement, the articles set out the financial provisions for
the support of the new fellows and for that of the existing fellows on the old
foundation: the sums which the new fellows were to receive for commons and
allowances, the stipends payable to the new College officers, and so on. These
two documents, the conditional grant and the complementary articles, made it
absolutely clear that Petre's money was intended primarily to support his
seven new fellows. Only when their needs had been met was any surplus to be
made available for the College's general use. This surplus, Petre reckoned,
would amount to £11 8s. 1¼d. a year.[131] Should revenues decline, those set
aside for the support of the new fellows were to be as far as possible protected,
leaving the deficit to fall on the surplus earmarked for general purposes and
then on the revenues for the support of the fellows on the old foundation.
Precise and carefully thought out, Petre's plans and calculations testified once
again to his financial acumen and to his priorities for the College.

These proceedings on 8 November 1566 were followed some eighteen
months later by a third transaction which completed the endowment. On
18 May 1568 the queen granted to Exeter three further properties: two mills
and adjoining land in Kidlington, a tenement in South Newington, where the
College already held the rectory, and another tenement in Oxford, near
Balliol College. She did so at the suit of Sir William Petre, who had paid her
£116 for the three holdings. They were reckoned to be worth £5 2s. a year.[132]
Petre's total expenditure on the College endowment, comprising his two
purchases from the crown, was thus nearly £1,500—probably rather more if
the properties at Garsington and in Somerset, bought for unknown sums, are
added to the account. It had always been Petre's intention to add further
fellowships to the original seven when funds permitted, and the purpose of
this new purchase was to endow one such additional fellowship. It went to
Ralph Sherwin, who was admitted to the College as the eighth Petrean fellow
on 10 July 1568.[133] The full tally of new fellows was now complete.

The properties which Petre intended for his College were chosen with care
and with an eye to their easy management. With the exception of Tintinhull

    [130] ECA, M. III. 4 (original); A. II. 1, fos. 5ᵛ–12ʳ (transcript); Boase (2), lxxxvi–lxxxviii
(translation).
    [131] ECA, K. I. 6 (original); A. II. 1, fos. 5ᵛ–12ʳ (transcript); Boase (1), liv–lvii; Boase (2),
lxxxvii–lxxxviii.
    [132] CPR, 1566–69, 210; ECA, O. I (original); A. II. 1, fos. 17ʳ–24ᵛ (transcript).
    [133] Statutes, 22; Reg., 94; Boase (2), 76.

and Montacute, all were in Oxfordshire and none far from Oxford itself. Even the most distant, South Newington, towards the north of the county, was no more than about twenty miles from the College. All could be visited without difficulty on the triennial progresses of the Rector and fellows which Petre had envisaged in the statutes. This gave them a clear advantage over the Cornish properties at Gwinear and Menheniot: expensive to visit, difficult to supervise. The most valuable properties were the four Oxfordshire rectories, where the College acted as impropriator, drawing from a single tenant in each place a fixed rent which the tenant largely derived from the profits of glebe land and tithes. The rectories, like most of Exeter's other rural properties, were in effect tenanted farms, needing little direct attention and leaving the tenant responsible, so the statutes had decreed, for all repairs and running costs. In several cases the high status of particular tenants suggests that a property must either have been sub-let or managed by a bailiff. This was clearly true, for example, at Kidlington, where the successive tenants of the rectory between 1566 and 1573 were Richard Taverner and Thomas Fraunces, the first a protestant controversialist, prolific author, firebrand preacher, and in 1569 high sheriff of Oxfordshire, and the second the university's former regius professor of medicine.[134] Neither was a son of the soil, nor is either likely to have resided at Kidlington.

Most of the properties which came to the College were former monastic estates. The rectories of South Newington, Merton, and Yarnton, for example, had all been held by the Benedictine abbey of Eynsham, and Kidlington by the Augustinian house of Osney.[135] Their acquisition by Petre bore witness to the great dispersal of monastic land which had followed the dissolution, and it was the vigorous post-dissolution land market which partly made possible Exeter's re-endowment. The standard price for monastic property in the 1560s was usually 30 years' purchase (i.e. thirty times the annual yield);[136] so Petre's purchases of the main block of rectories, etc., in 1565 for c. £1,377, to produce an income of c. £53 (26 years' purchase), and of the three minor properties in 1568 for c. £116, to produce an income of £5 (23 years' purchase), was a good deal less than the going rate, and indeed something of a bargain. The explanation for such favourable terms may well lie in Petre's close relationship with the queen: in which case it was a relationship from which Exeter was the direct and considerable beneficiary.

The annual yield of these properties at the time of their purchase represented much less than their potential yield. When the College received its new

[134] PP, 'Com. Oxon.'; ECA, M. III. 4; *BRUO, 1501–40*, 215–16, 557–8.

[135] *VCH Oxfordshire*, v. 299–30 (Merton), xi. 155 (South Newington), xii. 206 (Kidlington), 484 (Yarnton).

[136] H. J. Habbakuk, 'The Market for Monastic Property, 1539–1603', *Economic History Review*, 2nd ser., 10 (1957–8), 362, 366.

lands from Petre in 1566 and 1568 it took over with them an existing set of lessees whose rents had been fixed earlier, when their leases had been drawn up. The eventual termination of the lease would allow the negotiation of new terms with the incoming tenant, and these would be likely to include the payment of both an entry fine and an enhanced rent. At Tintinhull, for example, the College's tenant, one Tooker, was paying a £2 rent in 1566–7, but also a further £5 as the first instalment of a £20 entry fine, fully paid off by 1571.[137] At South Newington there was a change of tenant soon after Petre's acquisition of the property, to the College's great advantage. In 1565 the tenant of the rectory was George Gyfforde, who was paying £8 a year. But by 1568 the rectory was in the hands of a Mr Palmer, who was paying £42 a year.[138] Such a steep rise might follow the termination of a lease held for many years at a rent which had become increasingly outdated as prices rose sharply during the mid century period. This was seemingly true of the rectory at Merton, where Richard Gunter, tenant until 1566 or shortly before, had taken on a ninety-nine-year lease from the monks of Eynsham in 1530.[139] In all these arrangements there was much scope for profitable adjustments when leases fell in. It is easy to see why their negotiation was given such attention in the statutes, which required the Rector to obtain the consent of the fellows in all matters concerning leases. On their terms the prosperity of the College largely depended.

Of all the properties which Petre gave to Exeter, Kidlington had a special place in his thoughts and plans. Here the College acquired not only the rectory farm, tenanted by Richard Taverner for a rent of £20 a year, but also the vicarage, an adjacent but separate estate with its own sources of income from glebe and tithe. Both holdings are vividly described in a survey made for Petre about 1565: the only one of his properties to warrant such a survey.[140] Concerning the rectory, we are told that 'the mansion house is much in decay and so is the barn, which barn is a very great one' (probably the consequence of having a non-resident tenant). The rectory has its sheep-houses, stables and garners, and its fields sweeping down to the river Cher-well—I look out on them as I write—providing pasture, meadow, and arable for 30 cows and 180 sheep, and for growing wheat, barley, rye, oats, peas, and beans. The vicarage estate was similarly productive, and worth just over £29 a year, most of it from the profits of the glebe (£10) and the tithe of wool and lambs (£14). The total annual yield of Kidlington was thus just over £49, making it the most valuable of all the College properties. But its peculiarity lay, as we have seen, in Petre's ruling that the vicarage and the bulk of its revenues—all but an annual £7 6s. payable to the College—should be held by

---

[137] ECA, A. II. 9, fos. 2ᵛ, 25.   [138] CPR, 1563–66, 210; ECA, A. II. 9, fo. 8ᵛ.
[139] VCH Oxfordshire, v. 230; ECA, M. IV. 6; CPR, 1563–66, 252; Boase (2), lxxvi, 330, 334.
[140] PP, 'Com. Oxon.'

the Rector of Exeter in order to enhance his standing and authority. The Rector was to provide a suitable vicar to look after the parish church and its people. The vicarage itself—'the house with some cost might be made a very handsome one'—was to be available as a refuge for the fellows when Oxford was stricken by plague.[141] Only five miles from the centre of Oxford, it was well suited for this purpose. More firmly anchored to the College, and especially to its Rector, than any of its other properties, Kidlington might almost be regarded as Exeter's annexe.

Petre's gifts to the College had an immediate effect on its income. In 1564–5, the last complete year of the old regime, income amounted to just over £80. In 1566–7, the first year of the new, it had risen to £244 18s. 7d.[142] Over the next six years the new endowment brought in between £75 and £130 a year. Its proceeds averaged £112 a year out of a total average receipt of £201, so providing some 51 per cent of total revenues. Petre had reckoned that his main gifts, excluding the three minor properties granted in 1568, would bring the College £98 19s. 3¼d. a year, so he was not so far out.[143] By contrast, Gwinear, Wittenham, and Menheniot, the core of the old endowment, brought in a lesser but steady £73 2s. 4d. a year, or about 36 per cent of the total. Remarkably, and unusually, payments from the older properties at no point fell into arrears between 1566 and 1572, suggesting a new spirit of efficiency in the collection of revenues. The remaining contributions to income came mainly, and as always, from Oxford properties, room rents, occasional sales, and minor gifts. With the exception of Kidlington, where in any case a large proportion of the revenue was reserved for the Rector, the most valuable property was the rectory of South Newington, at £42 a year, usually followed by Little Tew, at £8 to £9 a year.

Despite the massive increase in the College's income brought by Petre's gifts, there was no general improvement in its finances, at least in the short term. Between 1566 and 1574 the accounts show surpluses in four years and deficits in the remaining four. The surpluses ranged from £1 10s. 6d. to £8 8s. 7d., and the deficits from £8 9s. 1d. to £34 12s. 1d. How can we explain this apparently surprising situation? An analysis of a particular account gives us some partial answers. The account for 1568–9 records receipts of £207 0s. 7d., expenses of £219 4s. 7d., and a debit balance of £9 1s.[144] By far the largest set of

[141] Boase (1), liv–lv.
[142] RA, 253/4; ECA, A. II. 9, fo. 2ᵛ. The following figures and calculations derive from the accounts, A. II. 9.
[143] ECA, A. II. 1, fos. 5ᵛ–12ʳ; Boase (1), lvi; PP, 'This indenture made the eighth day of November...'. Petre had earlier estimated the annual value of his gifts to be £90 19s. 3¼d.: Boase (1), lvi.
[144] ECA, A. II. 9, fos. 14–19. Note that these figures do not balance. Those for receipts and expenses should produce a debit balance of £12 4s., not the stated debit balance of £9 10s. In none of these eight accounts does the final balance accurately reflect the recorded figures for receipts and expenses, even to the extent that what ought, from the receipts/expenses figures, to be a

items on the debit side of the account comprised what might be called establishment charges: recurrent running costs which could not be avoided. Chief among these was spending on commons, decrements, and other small charges for provisions, which totalled £95 18s. 5d. In the same general category came cash stipends and allowances (£18 11s. for fellows on the old foundation, £22 15s. 6d. for those on the new), stipends for College officers (£6), servants' wages (£6 18s. 4d.), clothing allowances for fellows on the old foundation (£9 6s. 3d.), and a small general payment to fellows in continuation of what their predecessors had once received for obit services (£1 13s.). Altogether these establishment charges came to £161 2s., leaving just under £46 for extraordinary and incidental expenses—entertainment of guests, gifts to friends of the College, travel on College business, etc. Of the ten items in this category charged at more than one pound, six related to building and repairs. The three largest payments comprised one of £4 12s. 4d. paid each year to All Souls by Petre's direction,[145] another of £3 1s. 8d. for coal for the hall, and a third of £3 8s. 5d. for nails. As this last item suggests, building expenses in these years continued to be the heavy drain on the College's resources that they had always been. The largest extraordinary item on the account for 1570–1 was a payment of £8 18s. 6d. to tilers for two months' work in re-roofing the College, and for 1572–3, £25 14s. 3d. to stonemasons building the boundary wall—probably the great wall which now divides the garden from Radcliffe Square and Brasenose Lane.[146]

The essential reason for the failure of Petre's endowment to lift the College's fortunes to any great degree lay in the heavy costs of the Petrean fellows, supported as they were by very generous allowances. The new fellows absorbed the bulk of Petre's new money, as of course he had intended. Once the College's establishment charges had been met, the new endowment, large though it was, left a sum insufficient to ensure that the College's other expenses could be settled and the College kept in credit. In an era of continuing price rises, the sum of just over £11 which Petre had reckoned that his endowment would contribute to the general uses of the College could not entirely obviate the sort of financial problems which had faced it before Petre's appearance. The financial position of the individual fellows, on the other hand, improved. As we have seen, the vicarage of Kidlington provided the Rector with a handsome income of nearly £21 a year; all on the old

deficit, is recorded as a surplus (e.g. in the account for 1566–7). Yet the final figure stated for the balance must be correct, since any surplus cash arising from a surplus balance is recorded as having been paid into the College chest in the following year, and any debit balance is recorded as a debt to the Rector, again paid in the following year. The money, or its lack, was real enough. Unless the arithmetic of the accountant was exceptionally poor, we can only conclude that the final balance took into account monies either received or paid out but not recorded in the body of the account.

[145] Boase (1), lvi.   [146] ECA, A. II. 9, fos. 27ʳ, 40ʳ. Cf. Boase (2), xcix, for the wall.

foundation drew additional cash allowances, according to their status as masters, bachelors, or undergraduates; and the four new College officers, including the bachelor teaching assistant, received additional stipends. The wages of the College servants were also raised on Petre's directions, because, as he said, they were 'poorer than is just'.[147] It was a mark of his humanity that he should have considered the interests of the College cook, the porter, and the barber among others, as well as the fellows.

Much less equitable was Petre's invidious treatment of the two groups of fellows, those on the old foundation and those on the new. This was to cause problems. Although those on the old foundation certainly benefited from Petre's arrangements, their gains were far outstripped by those on the new. 'Old' fellows received an annual cash allowance of 10s., as laid down in Stapeldon's statutes, plus a further 6s. 8d. as a customary payment for obits; new fellows received a single annual cash allowance of 26s. 8d. 'Old' fellows received the customary 12d. a week for commons; new fellows, 22d. a week, supplemented for both by decrements. 'Old' fellows received a clothing allowance of about 12s. a year; new fellows, 26s. 8d.[148] Altogether the income of the Petrean fellows exceeded that of their colleagues on the old foundation by some 65 per cent. Petre's favour for his new fellows, obvious throughout his arrangements, had resulted in gross disparities between the two groups. These disparities clearly rankled, and immediately after Sir William's death in 1572 those on the old foundation took the matter up with his son, John Petre. A large payment of £8 18s. to William Paynter, sub-rector and one of the 'old' fellows, 'on college business for producing equality (*pro aequalitate facienda*)', followed by a further payment to the Rector and Paynter for their expenses in journeying to Ingatestone, probably marked the start of the negotiations.[149] These were successful. In 1573 John Petre, noting how easily discord might spring from inequality (as it almost certainly had done), equalized the allowances. In future every fellow in each category was to receive 26s. 8d. for stipend and the same sum for clothing, making a total allowance of £2 13s. 4d. Commons were also to be equalized. To make this possible John Petre and his mother Anne, Sir William's widow, offered to provide an annual cash sum of £15 6s. 8d.[150] In 1573–4 the accounts for the first time record the new allowance against the name of each fellow.[151] By the same decree Petre amended his father's licence for one fellow on the new foundation to study abroad by giving the same permission to two fellows, one of whom might

---

[147] Boase (1), liv–lvi. The payments stipulated in this text, Petre's supplement to the statutes, for College officers, etc., are recorded as payments in the accounts.

[148] *Statutes*, 39–40; Boase (1), liv–lvi.   [149] ECA, A. II. 9, fos. 37ᵛ, 38ʳ.

[150] ECA, A. I. 2; A. II. 9, fo. 36ʳ (payment of £40 by Lady Petre and John Petre for equalizing stipends).

[151] ECA, A. II. 9, fo. 42ʳ.

be on the old foundation. So in all material respects by 1574 the two groups of fellows were on a par.

John Petre's sensible and generous amendment of his father's arrangements established all Exeter's fellows in modest and comparable prosperity. But it did little for the corporate prosperity of the College. In 1573–4, the first year of the new scheme, the accounts showed a deficit of just over £34, and in 1574–5 a further deficit of just over £26.[152] Nor, in the longer term, did the Petrean endowment do much to promote the College in the 'league table' of College wealth. When the queen visited Oxford in 1592 the Colleges were taxed on their rental income in order to pay for her visit. Exeter's income was assessed at £200, about the right order of magnitude. This placed the College above Lincoln (£130), University College, and Balliol (each £100), and on a level with Trinity and Oriel, but below nine other colleges, headed by Christ Church, Magdalen, and New College.[153] The College's relative position had hardly changed since the start of the century.

But a caveat hangs over all these figures and the deductions concerning the College's no more than modest level of prosperity to which they seem to point. They take no account of monies brought in by undergraduate commoners and battelers. The problem of the financially invisible undergraduate is not a new one,[154] but at this time it is a particularly vexatious one. In all colleges undergraduate numbers were now rising rapidly—Exeter had some eighty in 1572[155]—and we might expect their fees and charges for board and lodgings to have made a large collective contribution to the College's wealth. At St John's in 1569 income from commoners exceeded that from land rents, while at Balliol in the 1580s room rents from undergraduates were so lucrative that they enabled the fellows to increase their own allowances for commons.[156] It is inconceivable that Exeter did not profit in the same way. Yet this is hardly deducible from the accounts, which almost invariably fail to record any income from undergraduates. Even the infrequent payments by fellows for the rooms of their scholars, found occasionally in earlier accounts, have disappeared.

Only very exceptionally is our darkness lightened. We learn from the statutes, as well as from earlier evidence, that fellows were responsible for seeing that the debts of those whom they tutored (*quem tuitionem susceperunt*) were paid to the manciple, Rector, and others at the end of each term, and there are just two helpful complementary statements in the accounts. That for 1574–5 notes at its conclusion that £32 in monies from commoners (*commensales*), net of all charges, has been paid to the Rector, while that for

[152] ECA, A. II. 9, fos. 45ᵛ, 49ᵛ.
[153] *Registrum annalium Collegii Mertoniensis, 1567–1603*, ed. J. M. Fletcher, OHS, new ser., xxiv (1974), 287. See also G. D. Duncan, 'The Property of Balliol College', *HUO*, iii. 559.
[154] Above, 160–3.   [155] *Register*, ed. Clark, II. ii. 32–3; Boase (2), xcvi–xcvii.
[156] McConica, 'Rise of the Undergraduate College', *HUO*, iii. 47, 58.

1576–7 mentions a similar payment of £28 10s. o½d., again paid to the Rector. In both cases these sums are set against College expenses in order to reduce the overall deficit; though the deficit was not wiped out but merely diminished.[157] So it would seem that undergraduates made payments to the College via the Rector, but that this income was kept apart and entered in the accounts only very occasionally.

We are still less well informed about the income accruing to fellows from teaching fees paid by undergraduates. Given the rising numbers of undergraduates, we can say only that for fellows who acted as tutors fee income is likely to have been considerable. The fellows' allowances payable under the decrees of the two Petres, father and son, are likely to represent only minimum figures for income. We know that Petre's statutes allowed the dean to take a fee of 8d. a quarter from each undergraduate attending his lectures, but we know nothing of any private arrangements between tutors and pupils. The sum of the financial evidence suggests that moderate private affluence may have existed within a college of straitened corporate means.

The new landed endowment which Petre conferred on his College was by far his greatest benefaction but it was not his only one. He made two gifts of money to the College—£14 in 1566–7, £20 in 1567–8—and left it £40 in his will, made in April 1571.[158] But more important, both for the contemporary academic purposes of the College and for our views of Petre's motives, were his gifts of printed books. As we have seen, Petre himself was a noted bibliophile, the possessor of a large library and a frequent purchaser of books from Paris,[159] and in May 1567 he presented to the College what was clearly a carefully chosen selection. The College paid for them to be brought up from London[160] and they still remain in the College library. There were eight of these books, bound in nineteen volumes and constituting an almost exclusively theological collection: recent editions of the two greatest Latin fathers, Augustine (in eight volumes, printed at Basle in 1543) and Jerome (in four volumes, printed at Paris in 1546); the works of Eusebius, edited by Erasmus; the Commentary on Daniel, by Theoderet, bishop of Cyrrhus (c.393–457); a Latin bible; a concordance to the New Testament, by Johannes Benedictus; the Lives of the Saints, by Lippomanus, bishop of Bergamo (1500–59); and a volume of Aquinas.[161] Each bears a contemporary ex dono

[157] Statutes, 42; ECA, A. II. 9, fos. 50ᵛ, 60ʳ; above, 205.

[158] ECA, A. II. 9, fos, 1ᵛ, 2ʳ, 8ʳ; Emmison, 285.

[159] Emmison, 72, 220–2; above, 259–60. Petre's gifts of books are briefly noticed in Boase (2), clxv–clxvii; Ker, 'Oxford College Libraries', 418; and Ker, 'The Provision of Books', HUO, iii. 450.

[160] A. II. 9, fo. 4ᵛ.

[161] Now Exeter College Library 9K 1543 (Augustine), 9F 1546.2 (Jerome), 9K 1549 (Eusebius), 9I 1562.3 (Theoderet), 9I 1557.4 (Bible), 9F 1562.5 (Concordance), 9L 1565 (Lippomanus), 9I 1555.3 (Aquinas).

inscription inserted by the College and recording its accession in May 1567 (see Plate 19). In addition, the Augustine is signed by Petre and so probably came from his personal library, while the Latin bible is signed by John Woodward, his chaplain and agent in everything to do with Exeter College. The Augustine and Jerome were splendidly and ornately bound by the famous Wotton binder, the Parisian bookbinder who worked for the Kentish squire Thomas Wotton in the mid sixteenth century; others were bound by the College.[162]

Petre's choice of books reflected his wish to see theological learning placed at the centre of the College's intellectual life. He was now providing the fellows with the means to follow through his statutory stipulation that they should study theology after taking the MA. There was one other book, less pedagogical and more personal, whose association with Petre cannot be proved but which would now be placed above all his other gifts in value and interest. The Bohun Psalter, the College's greatest treasure, was written and illuminated in the fourteenth century for Humphrey de Bohun (1342–73), earl of Hereford and Essex.[163] A de luxe manuscript of the highest quality, it had passed by about 1500 into the possession of the Tudors. It is signed both by Elizabeth of York, Henry VII's queen, and by Queen Katherine of Aragon, first wife of Henry VIII: 'This boke ys myn Katherina the qwene'. The only firm reason to see it as a gift from Petre is a fly-leaf inscription in an eighteenth-century hand, which records that it was 'Given to the library by Sir William Petre'. Although there is no earlier record of its presence in the College, it seems overwhelmingly likely that Petre was indeed the donor. It has usually been supposed that it was a gift to him from Queen Elizabeth, but a much more probable source is Elizabeth's predecessor, Queen Mary. As a personal possession of Katherine of Aragon, it is likely to have been passed on to Katherine's daughter Mary, and this catholic descent may explain why the feasts of St Thomas Becket and the popes have not been erased from the calendar,[164] as they surely would have been had the Psalter passed into Henry VIII's library. Of all the Tudor monarchs, it was Mary to whom Petre was closest. As princess, she had stood as godmother to his daughter Catherine, and in his will he bequeathed to his daughter-in-law a gold and diamond ring 'given me by the queen of good memory, Queen Mary'.[165] It would have been entirely appropriate if Mary had given him the Bohun Psalter, containing part of the liturgy of the pre-Reformation church, as a token of their common religious sympathies. It survives as a tangible link between the College, its greatest benefactor, and the dynasty which made his fortune.

---

[162] ECA, A. II. 9, fo. 4ᵛ. For the College's Wotton bindings, see *Fine Bindings 1500–1700 from Oxford Libraries: Catalogue of an Exhibition*, Bodleian Library (Oxford, 1968), 30–7.
[163] For the Bohun Psalter, see Watson, 78–82.
[164] Watson, 79.   [165] Emmison, 54 n., 160–2, 209, 289.

In various small ways the College did what it could to reciprocate Petre's generosity. Honour, deference, respect, and hospitality were the currency in which it expressed its gratitude not only to him but to his family. Parts of the College became a monument to the new connection. In 1566–7 Petre's shield of arms was set in glass in one of the hall windows: perhaps the same set of arms later removed from the College and now to be found in the south-east window of Kidlington parish church.[166] It may have been at this time too that the same arms, with accompanying verses, were set up on the College sundial, probably the same dial whose remains can still be seen on the south face of Palmer's Tower (see Plate 20).[167] In the following year the College paid £3 6s. 8d. for the portrait of Petre which now hangs in the hall (see Plate 15). Brought from London at a cost of 2s. 8d., it was later curtained with a piece of green silk costing 6s. 8d.[168] Other social and business contacts, together with the giving of gloves, the traditional way of honouring a superior, remained as expressions of a continuingly close relationship. In 1568–9 gloves were sent to Sir William, his wife, his son, and to Mr Woodward.[169] In the following year gloves were again sent to John Petre and his new wife Mary, the daughter of another Essex landowner, Sir Edmund Waldegrave, on the occasion of their wedding, while William Paynter, the sub-rector, and John Bereblock, one of the Petrean fellows, rode to see Petre on College business.[170] In 1572, in the immediate aftermath of Sir William's death, there was an extraordinary burst of activity on the College's part, as the Rector and fellows sought the favour of their new patron, and in particular his amelioration of the inequalities between the two groups of fellows. The Rector and sub-rector paid a visit to Ingatestone; gloves were presented to Woodward on no fewer than six occasions; other gloves were sent to John Petre (twice), his wife (twice), and his mother (twice); three pairs of gloves were given to a servant of the deceased Sir William; and Woodward's expenses were paid when he came to stay at the College.[171] Woodward emerges, more clearly than ever, as the essential go-between, linking the College first with Sir William Petre and latterly with the whole Petre family. We shall see the possible significance of this when we look more closely at catholic Exeter. For the moment we merely note the College's anxious desire to maintain its standing with a family whose fortune had been the making of its own good fortune.

---

[166] ECA, A. II. 9, fo. 3ᵛ; E. A. Greening Lamborn, *The Armorial Glass of the Oxford Diocese, 1250–1850* (Oxford, 1949), 139, plate 51.

[167] Reg., 141; below, 314.   [168] ECA, A. II. 9, fos. 9ᵛ, 32ʳ.

[169] ECA, A. II. 9, fo. 16ᵛ.

[170] ECA, A. II. 9, fo. 22ᵛ; A. C. Edwards, *John Petre: Essays on the Life and Background of John, 1st Lord Petre, 1549–1613* (London, 1973), 17.

[171] ECA, A. II. 9, fos. 37ᵛ–39ᵛ.

6. THE NEW FELLOWS: CATHOLIC EXETER

The seven new fellows nominated by Petre in June 1566 were a varied group possessing some strong characteristics in common. At the time of their nomination they spanned the academic hierarchy. Two were MAs (Richard Spicer and John Bereblock); three were BAs (Edmund Lewknor, Kenelm Carter, and John Howlett); and two were still undergraduates (Walter Crosse and James Rainolds). Ralph Sherwin, who joined them in 1568, was also an undergraduate.[172] Their geographical origins varied widely. Only Rainolds, son of a prosperous Devon farmer, and very probably a commoner or batteler at Exeter before he caught Petre's eye, and Spicer, also a Devonian, came from 'Stapeldon country'. Bereblock was born near Rochester in Kent; Sherwin was from Derbyshire, and Lewknor from Sussex; and by an improbable coincidence both Carter and Howlett came from Rutland.[173] The Petrean nominations thus broke out of the regional boundaries which had circumscribed Exeter's recruiting since the fourteenth century. In widening the range of local voices to be heard in hall and chapel, they made for a more cosmopolitan College.

The immediate academic origins of the first Petrean fellows were equally diverse. Lewknor had graduated with a BA from St John's College, Cambridge, in 1563; Bereblock had been one of the founding fellows of St John's College, Oxford, the choice of the founder, Sir Thomas White; Spicer had already held a fellowship at Exeter, which he had vacated in 1561 before spending a year as probationer fellow at Merton.[174] The two men whose background we know most about are Carter and Howlett, because they were among those whose names and brief biographies were forwarded to Petre by Rector Neale in 1565 in recommendation for his new fellowships. Carter was 'xix or xx years of age, studious, very honest and quiet, fatherless and almost friendless, apt [intelligent] and well entered [advanced] in learning already, for these ii years abiding and relieved [supported] in our house. Very well liked of us all.' Howlett was recommended in similar terms: 'xviii years of age, very honest, very quiet, sober and tractable, marvellous poor and toward [making good progress in learning], studious, and a pretty scholar. For one year lay in our college, relieved partly with us and partly at Magdalen College. Now a postmaster in Merton College.'[175] These miniatures of two young scholars, both poor and both keen to learn, point to the sort of qualifications sought

---

[172] The Petrean fellows are listed in order of seniority, and in Petre's hand, in Reg., 89. For Sherwin, see Boase (2), 76.

[173] Boase (2), 69, 74, 75; Anstruther, 210; PP, 'The names of the scholars fittest for us'; M. E. Williams, 'Ralph Sherwin', *ODNB*; M. Feingold, 'John Rainolds [Reynolds]', *ODNB*.

[174] Boase (2), 69, 74–5; A. Hegarty, *A Biographical Register of St John's College, Oxford, 1555–1660*, OHS, new ser., xliii (2011), 12–13.

[175] PP, 'The names of the scholars fittest for us.'

in potential fellows and, in the case of Howlett and some of the other Petrean fellows, to the range of their preceding experiences in other colleges.

Few of these men held their fellowships for very long. Crosse resigned within months of his nomination and was replaced by Richard Bristow, originally from Worcestershire but more recently graduating from Christ Church; while Spicer resigned on the grounds of ill health in 1567 and was replaced by Thomas Fortescue, a former fellow of Exeter, who himself lasted no more than two years. Bereblock, Howlett, and Bristow went abroad in 1570 and never returned. Of the original seven, only Lewknor, Rainolds, and Carter held their fellowships for more than ten years, Lewknor resigning in 1577, Rainolds dying in post in 1577, and Carter resigning in 1583.[176] None stayed the course long enough to take the higher degree in theology which Petre had prescribed as the ultimate aim for fellows on both the old and the new foundations.

If these men thus varied greatly in background, they were alike in their intellectual abilities. It must be significant that for five years, from 1566 to 1571, the two main teaching posts in the College, those of dean and lector, were held exclusively by Petrean fellows. Petre himself nominated Bereblock as the first dean and Spicer as the first lector, but thereafter the two officers appear to have been freely elected by the fellowship: a common recognition perhaps of the quality of the Petrean intake. The senior post of sub-rector, on the other hand, always remained with a fellow from the old foundation until 1577, when Lewknor was elected.[177] Other more piecemeal evidence shows the variety of talents which the Petrean fellows contributed to the College. Bristow, the most intellectually distinguished, became 'noted in the university for his acute parts', and was one of those chosen to dispute publicly before the queen during her visit to Oxford in 1566. He later became a ferocious catholic polemicist and was partly responsible for the Douai-Rheims Bible, the English translation of the Vulgate.[178] Sherwin was the star performer at the Act, the university's annual celebratory degree-giving ceremony, in 1574, 'being then accounted an acute philosopher and an excellent Grecian and Hebritian' (and mastery of Hebrew was not a common accomplishment).[179] Rainolds's intellectual interests were suggested by the very large library of more than 360 books, ranging from humanist texts to religion and medicine, which he left at his death in 1577.[180] But perhaps the most unusual talent was that of Bereblock, a scholar famous also as a draughtsman and calligrapher, who produced the earliest known drawings of Oxford and its colleges for the queen's

---

[176] Boase (2), 69, 74–5.
[177] Annual elections to College offices are entered in the register: Reg., 89, 92, 94, 95, 98, 101, 116.
[178] Wood, *Athenae*, i. 482; P. E. B. Harris, 'Richard Bristow', *ODNB*.
[179] Wood, *Athenae*, i. 478; Williams, 'Ralph Sherwin'.
[180] Fehrenbach and Leedham-Green, *Private Libraries in Renaissance England*, v. 104–37.

visit. His drawing of Palmer's Tower, the hall, and the chapel, reproduced in Plate 12 and on the dust-jacket of this book, is a permanent memorial to the Petrean fellow possessing the most exceptional gift. Bereblock's election as proctor in 1569, the first Exeter proctor for many years, was an indication of his wider standing in the university.[181]

If Petre's object in endowing his new fellowships was partly 'increase of learning', as he himself stated,[182] he had chosen well. The nomination of such luminaries as Bristow and Sherwin redeemed the College from academic mediocrity and raised its reputation in the university. Within a few years, however, Petre's fellows had begun to give the College a different and much less favourable reputation. It derived from their strong and public catholic loyalties, at a time when catholicism was coming to be increasingly identified with treason, threats to the throne, and a challenge to the whole basis of the Elizabethan regime.

Supported by the Petrean endowment, the new fellows would have felt at home in Exeter. We have already seen how Exeter's ancestral links with the religiously conservative west country had made it a particularly catholic college in a generally catholic university. Oxford's prominence as a bastion and repository of old catholic allegiances had not been expunged by the expulsions, deprivations, and voluntary departures which had followed the royal visitation of 1559.[183] Since then, and partly in consequence, the university's catholicism had begun to seed outwards as catholic émigré students found a refuge on the Continent, first at Louvain and then from 1568 at Douai. The English college at Douai, founded by the Lancashire catholic, Oriel graduate, and future cardinal, William Allen, functioned both as a catholic Oxford in exile and a seminary—'a forcing ground for missionary storm troopers in the fight against Elizabethan Protestantism'. The temporary move of the college to Rheims between 1578 and 1593 marked a change of location but not one of purpose.[184] Yet the steady drift of Oxford's catholic zealots to the Continent by no means drained the university of like-minded sympathizers: until the 1580s there were always replenishments. By that time both seminary priests and Jesuits, often Oxonian in origin, were returning to England to prepare the ground for what they hoped would be the reconversion of their country to Roman Catholicism.

Exeter's position as a catholic stronghold intensified during these years, waning only with the general decline of Oxford catholicism from c.1580. It owed this position partly to the successful dissimulation which had preserved

[181] Durning, *Queen Elizabeth's Book*, 17–21; Hegarty, *Biographical Register of St John's College*, 12–13; Wood, *Athenae*, ii. 183.

[182] Emmison, 281.   [183] Above, 227, 237–8, 240–3.

[184] E. Duffy, 'William Allen', *ODNB*; A. C. Southern, *Elizabethan Recusant Prose, 1559–82* (London, 1950), 25–30; J. Bossy, 'The Character of Elizabethan Catholicism', *Past and Present*, 21 (1962), 44–7.

Exeter's catholic fellows through the 1559 visitation and left the College unscathed by resignations or deprivations. But much too was owed to the leadership and convictions of John Neale, Rector from 1560 to 1570. Neale had seen the College through some crucial episodes in its corporate life: the financial crisis of 1562–3, the plague which followed, the long train of negotiations with Petre, and the College's reconstitution in 1566 which was their culmination. By then he had already shown his catholic proclivities by pleading with Petre for the restoration of his old school at Week St Mary in Cornwall, dissolved under Edward VI 'because Jesus mass was there weekly sung or said'.[185] Under Neale, the College's catholicism became flagrant, so much so that in 1570 it was singled out for a royal visitation, headed by the vice-chancellor. The visitors' actions were drastic. William Wyatt, the sub-rector, was imprisoned from early January until late March, first in Oxford castle, then in Bocardo, the town prison, because he refused to inform against the College's papists. In October it was Neale's turn. Absent from the College for a lengthy period, he was repeatedly summoned to appear before the visitors. Failing to do so, he was deprived of his rectorship and expelled from the university. About the same time the visitors ordered the College to remove the unprotestant image of Christ which adorned the window of his room.[186] When next heard of, he was imprisoned in the Marshalsea. Released in 1577, he crossed immediately to Douai and went thence to Rome, where he was ordained into the catholic priesthood. We have a description of him when he said his first mass in 1579: 'about 50 years of age, tall and slender in body, a brownish grey beard, lean and slender faced, little eyes, and fast of speech'— the only surviving record of the appearance of any of Exeter's Rectors before the age of portraits. From Rome he journeyed first to Rheims and then to England, where he was again imprisoned and then banished in 1585. He probably died abroad, and a long way from the start of his catholic voyage at Week St Mary.[187]

Among the fellows on the old foundation, Neale was not alone in following this course. His near contemporary and fellow Cornishman, Christopher Smale, resigned his fellowship in 1575, crossed to Douai, was ordained there in 1579, and went on to obtain a doctorate in canon law from the university of Paris.[188] Thomas Hole, from Devon, elected in 1568, was given leave to study at Paris, but was at Douai in 1577 and never returned to his fellowship.[189] John Cory, from Cornwall, elected in 1573, was given

[185] PP, 'Right honourable, my most humble commendations...'; above, 267–8.
[186] Reg., 96, 100; Wood, History, ii. 168–9; ECA, A. II. 9, fo. 23.
[187] J. H. Pollen, 'Official Lists of Prisoners for Religion from 1562 to 1580', Miscellanea, I, CRS, i (1905); Anstruther, 244.
[188] T. F. Knox, The First and Second Diaries of the English College, Douay (London, 1878), 9, 145, 148, 150; Boase (2), 69; Anstruther, 319.
[189] Douay Diaries, 122; Boase (2), 76.

leave to study abroad in 1575 and had been ordained at Douai by the time he finally vacated his fellowship in 1578. Later a Jesuit, he subsequently flitted to and fro between England and the Continent.[190] These defections, all in the late 1570s, do much to explain the descent of another royal commission on the College in 1578.[191] There were others. Raymond Westlake, from Devon, fellow from 1564, resigned his fellowship in 1580 and was at Douai two years later.[192] The west country origins both of Neale and of these four are striking; none of the fellows from the diocese of Salisbury is known to have been among the Douai exiles. But these were the most committed of Exeter's catholics, largely known to us because the start of each self-imposed exile is recorded in the contemporary diaries kept by the English college at Douai. Other catholics, the church papists who stayed at home and outwardly conformed, may well have gone undetected. That the sub-rector was called on to identify them in 1570 suggests that their numbers may have been high and their sympathies concealed.

This was the milieu in which the Petrean fellows were now located. Almost all of them shared the general catholic sympathies of the College. If their backgrounds and origins were diverse, their catholicism was a factor which they had in common, both with each other and with the fellows on the old foundation. Yet they also formed a discrete group, marked out by their exceptional zeal for their faith. Their course was in most cases similar to that of the old-foundation catholics, but followed a more extreme trajectory. Of the ten Petrean fellows appointed between 1566 and 1568, five can be securely identified as 'public' catholics (Bereblock, Lewknor, Howlett, Bristow, and Sherwin), and two (Carter and Rainolds) as catholics of the church papist sort. Of the five, Bereblock went abroad in 1570 and by 1575 was living as a religious exile in Bologna, after obtaining papal licence for ordination as a priest.[193] Lewknor resigned his fellowship in 1577, moved to Rheims (where he was later professor), and was ordained in the following year.[194] Howlett left the College in 1570, travelled to Douai, and was received as a Jesuit in 1571, later becoming professor of scholastic theology at Vilna in Lithuania, dying there in 1589.[195] Bristow, the most gifted of the five, went to Douai in 1570 and, after taking a leading part in the translation of the Douai-Rheims Bible, returned to England in 1581, where he died in prison.[196] Sherwin, the last of the five, vacated his fellowship in 1575, crossed to Douai, was ordained priest, and went on to become a leading member of the English college in Rome. After travelling back to England with Edmund Campion in 1580, he

[190] *Douay Diaries*, 8, 276; Boase (2), 77; Anstruther, 95–6.
[191] For this commission, see below, 304–6.   [192] *Douay Diaries*, 184; Boase (2), 73.
[193] Anstruther, 65; Hegarty, *Biographical Register of St John's College*, 12–13.
[194] Boase (2), 74–5; Anstruther, 210.
[195] Boase (2), 75; G. M. Murphy, 'John Howlett', *ODNB*.
[196] Boase (2), 75; Anstruther, 52–3; Harris, 'Richard Bristow'.

was captured, tried, and then hanged, drawn, and quartered in 1581. Canonized by Pope Paul VI in 1970 as one of the Forty English Martyrs, he remains the College's only saint.[197]

For most of these men their time at Exeter, in most cases only a few years, was no more than an early passage of intellectual training, in English careers which were often cut short by imprisonment, execution, or permanent exile. But despite the brevity of their fellowships, their proselytizing catholicism soon led to their being recognized within the College as a distinct coterie, and to their later opponents a notorious one. This first became clear in 1583, when a protestant counter-movement emerged within the College. Despite Exeter's strongly catholic tradition, it had probably never lacked a small minority of protestant fellows. College protestantism is perhaps traceable as far back as the episode of the 'insolent bachelors' in 1539 and had become more apparent under Edward VI, when both the Rector, William More, and at least one of the fellows, Richard Tremayne, had been committed protestants. It may be too that protestant dissatisfaction with Neale's catholic rule lay behind both the contested election of 1565, when Neale's continuing headship of the College had been questioned and Petre's benefaction placed in jeopardy, and his subsequent re-election only by a majority and not unanimously.[198] But it was not until a good many years later that the protestants in College found a public voice. In doing so they moved the Petrean fellows and their legacy into the forefront of controversy.

The College protestants broke cover in a letter of 27 May 1583 sent to Sir Francis Walsingham, the queen's principal secretary and himself a strong protestant. Now among the Elizabethan state papers, it was signed by Reginald Bellott, a fellow since 1575, and six other fellows. Their petition was directed against the activities of Sir John Petre, Sir William's son and heir, knighted in 1575, and their main target was Sir John's unstatutory and unjustifiable interference in College affairs, to be discussed later. But a powerful weapon in their armoury, and one designed to appeal to Walsingham's particular susceptibilities, was the aggressive catholicism of the former Petrean fellows. Emphasizing the patronage of the two Petres, Bellott and his colleagues wrote: 'So may we well doubt of the corruption that will grow thereof, both in our college and in the church generally by the example of these bad members, Bereblock, Bristow, Sherwin, Howlett and others that have been Sir W. Petre his scholars, whereof divers have become priests, Jesuits and notorious seminary men and never yet any minister in the true church of God.' In an accompanying submission they added to their list the names of Lewknor and of Arthur Stratford, a Petrean fellow appointed by Sir John in 1577 and later ordained as a catholic priest in Rome. In sixteen or

[197] Boase (2), 76; Anstruther, 311–13; Williams, 'Ralph Sherwin'.
[198] Above, 189–90, 234–5, 238, 268.

seventeen years the Petrean fellows had produced no ministers, 'but there have been many notorious papists, Bristow, Bereblock, Lewknor, Sherwin, Howlett, Stratford, and of those suspected beside, let the university speak generally'.[199]

The unnamed 'others' alluded to by Bellott and his allies very probably included a further two of the original seven Petrean fellows: Kenelm Carter and James Rainolds. Carter was particularly close to Sir John Petre, who apparently tried to extend the term of his fellowship and in 1583, after Carter had resigned his fellowship, appointed him as tutor to his son William. Since Sir John was staunchly catholic (but circumspectly so), he would hardly have offered the post to Carter had he not been catholic too. In his case against Petre, Bellott accused him of favouring 'such as have been most suspected among us'—for example, Carter, 'his son's schoolmaster, under whom many popish scholars have prospered'.[200] The catholicism of James Rainolds is more difficult to be sure about, but the evidence for it is strong if circumstantial. His father was a catholic; his uncle, Thomas, Warden of Merton, lost his post in 1559 for his refusal to conform in religion, and died in prison; two of his brothers, Edmund and Jerome, both fellows of Corpus, were catholic, and Edmund's religion partly accounted for his expulsion from Corpus in 1566; William, another brother, after a youthful fling as a protestant zealot, crossed to Douai and was ordained as a catholic priest; while John, President of Corpus, and the most distinguished of the brothers, moved in the reverse direction, from cradle catholic to later protestant.[201] James Rainolds, fellow of Exeter, is the only one of this brilliant family, six of whose members became fellows of Oxford colleges, whose religious position is obscure. But in such a family nest of catholics it seems highly unlikely that he would have been the only cuckoo, and it is safe to assume that he, like Carter, was a committed but conforming catholic: the fifth of the original seven Petrean fellows to have rejected the protestantism of Elizabethan England.

It was not only among the fellows that Exeter's catholics were to be found, but also among the undergraduates, whose rapidly rising numbers matched the general trend throughout the university. A university listing of College members in 1572 names about eighty undergraduates, a massive increase on the thirteen of 1552.[202] Exeter's undergraduates, however, were distinguished from those of other colleges by the high proportion of catholics which they included. Although the list unfortunately provides only surnames and not Christian names, there are among them those of some well-known catholic,

[199] TNA, SP 12/160, fos. 116ʳ, 117ᵛ.

[200] TNA, SP 12/160, fo. 118; Edwards, *John Petre*, 27, 30; N. Briggs, 'William, 2nd Lord Petre (1575–1637)', *Essex Recusant*, 10/2 (1968), 2.

[201] Feingold, 'John Rainolds'; Williams, 'State, Church', *HUO*, iii. 406, 410; Wood, *History*, ii. 228.

[202] *Register*, ed. Clark, II. ii. 32–3; above, 290.

and later recusant, families, such as Bawden, Coningsby, Abington, and Throgmorton.[203] Many came from the west country, especially Cornwall, and to a large extent the catholicism of the undergraduates had the same regional origins as that of the fellows. Nicholas Roscarrock, for example, whom we have already met as one of the young men commended by Neale to Petre for a fellowship, came from a Cornish family of conforming catholics. Leaving the College without a degree in 1568, he became a more active catholic from the 1570s, moving temporarily to Douai and then to Rome. In 1580, now regarded by the government as 'a dangerous papist', he moved into close association with another Exeter catholic, Ralph Sherwin. After returning to England, he was imprisoned in the Tower, where he was racked, before being released in 1586. He went on to write the 'Lives of the Saints', perhaps the most substantial and scholarly work ever to come from the pen of an Exeter author.[204]

But by no means all Exeter's catholic undergraduates hailed from the west country. There were no regional restrictions on the recruitment of under-graduates, as there were for the fellows, and some of those whose catholicism later brought them a modest fame (or infamy) came from other parts of England. Two such men were Nicholas Fitzherbert and John Gerard, both from Derbyshire. Fitzherbert, probably an undergraduate between about 1568 and 1572, was later resident in the household of William Allen, founder of Douai, whose life he went on to write, and spent some years in Rome, where he was regarded as a possible future bishop for the English catholics. Gerard, briefly at Exeter in 1575–6, later became a Jesuit, took part in the mission to England, was arrested and tortured, but escaped from the Tower, and died many years later in Rome in 1637.[205] It was clearly Exeter's repu-tation as a catholic college which drew these men and others like them to a society where men from Devon and Cornwall are still likely to have been in the majority. For all catholic families with aspiring sons, the College exercised a natural attraction.

In moulding and encouraging catholicism among Exeter's undergraduates, two influences were particularly important: those of the catholic gentry who often sent them there and of the tutors who taught them. Predictably and usually, but not invariably, the undergraduate's initial sponsor was his father. Gerard, for example, was the second son of a catholic knight, Sir Thomas Gerard, who had been imprisoned in the Tower early in Elizabeth's reign and who ensured that his son spent his early years at home under a catholic

[203] *Nicholas Roscarrock's Lives of the Saints*, ed. Orme, 5; below, 303–4.
[204] *Nicholas Roscarrock's Lives of the Saints*, ed. Orme, 3–23.
[205] Williams, 'Nicholas Fitzherbert'; T. M. McCoog, 'John Gerard', *ODNB*. For Fitzherbert, see also above, 256.

tutor.[206] Nicholas Roscarrock, from a similar background, was in the words of Rector Neale 'a good and worshipful man's son', whose father's standing in Cornwall was shown by his having held office as sheriff and JP.[207] Both men formed part of the great influx of sons of the gentry which has been seen to characterize late sixteenth-century Oxford. But gentry patrons might also be drawn from outside the family. The catholic John Cornelius, almost certainly an Exeter undergraduate before he was elected to a fellowship in 1575, went on to join the English college in Rome, to become a Jesuit, and to take part in the mission to England in 1583. Captured in Dorset in 1594, he was hanged, drawn, and quartered at Dorchester in the same year. Originally from a humble family of Irish immigrants in Cornwall, Cornelius had been given his start in life by Sir John Arundell of Lanherne, the doyen of the Cornish catholics, who had sent him to Exeter and later sheltered him in London during his missionary years.[208] It was from the households and families of the catholic gentry that the College's most prominent catholics often emerged; but no doubt there were many others who conformed and remained concealed.

The influence of tutors is harder to detect, but it was certainly believed by the authorities that it was there, that it worked to the detriment of true religion, and that it was pernicious. All this was illustrated in 1577, when the privy council ordered the bishops to make a return of the names of recusants in their dioceses. Coming to his entry for Exeter College, the bishop of Oxford named three fellows or former fellows, Sherwin, Cory, and Hole, all then abroad and all 'reputed to be of a very corrupt religion'. He went on to add that there were four 'young gentlemen', two Plowdens, a Catesby, and a Savage, 'that never came to the church'; so the sons of the gentry were prominent as usual. Catesby and Savage 'are Mr Carter's scholars, fellow of the same college', while the two Plowdens had until recently been 'scholars to Mr Raynolds, that died this summer'.[209] Kenelm Carter and James Rainolds, the two longest serving of the original Petrean fellows, were thus linked with recusant pupils, three of them, Catesby and the two Plowdens, from well-known catholic families. A similar relationship helped to shape the life of the later Jesuit John Gerard. In his autobiography he wrote that when he went to Oxford (in 1575) his tutor was Edmund Lewknor, whom we know to have been another of the Petrean fellows: 'a good and learned man and a catholic in

    [206] McCoog, 'John Gerard'; *John Gerard: The Autobiography of an Elizabethan*, trans. P. Caraman, 2nd edn. (London, 1956), 1.
    [207] PP, 'The names of the scholars fittest for us'; *Nicholas Roscarrock's Lives of the Saints*, ed. Orme, 4.
    [208] T. M. McCoog, 'John Cornelius', *ODNB*; Anstruther, 88–9; Rowse, *Tudor Cornwall*, 332–3, 342–5, 356–8, 361–7.
    [209] P. Ryan, 'Diocesan Returns of Recusants for England and Wales, 1577', *Miscellanea, XII*, CRS, xxii (1921), 2, 100.

sympathy and conviction'. Lewknor later resigned his fellowship, leaving Oxford with his young charge and wanting 'to become a catholic and lead a catholic life'. For several years he served as Latin tutor in the Gerard house-hold before leaving for the English college at Rheims.[210] Such relationships— and there were probably many similar ones within the small community of the College's catholic fellows and their catholic pupils—are likely to have consolidated and strengthened the religious convictions of both parties.

More than most colleges, and more perhaps than any other institution except the Inns of Court, Exeter thus linked the two centres of resilient catholicism in mid Elizabethan England: the catholicism of the gentry house-hold, often but not invariably of a quietist, church papist sort, and the more active and aggressive catholicism, founded on rejection of the royal suprem-acy and looking to the reconversion of England, found in the university.[211] Reginald Bellott and his fellow opponents of Sir John Petre went some way to identify the linkage and its malign effects when they drew Walsingham's attention to the evil influence of the Petrean fellows 'in respect of the corrup-tion of our youth, whereof there are so many lamentable examples'.[212] They were probably right to single out Sir William Petre's nominees from Exeter's other catholic fellows, for the intellectual leadership of the first group and, as deans and lectors, their early monopoly of the College's two main teaching posts gave them more opportunities than most to influence the young. It was, after all, Carter and Rainolds alone, two Petrean catholics, who had been identified in 1577 as suspect tutors with suspect pupils on their books.

By this time the longstanding concern of Elizabeth's government with Oxford's catholicism was coming to focus on Exeter College in particular. After *Regnans in excelsis*, Pope Pius V's bull of 1570 freeing the queen's subjects from their allegiance, the government increasingly saw all catholics, including those at the university, as potential plotters and subversives. Nor were their fears entirely unfounded. Edward Abington, for example, an Exeter undergraduate in 1572, was later to be one of those who, in 1586 and under the leadership of Anthony Babington, plotted the queen's assassination and her replacement by Mary Queen of Scots. Sir Thomas Gerard, father of the catholic undergraduate John Gerard, was also marginally involved in the plot and had already been imprisoned in 1571 for his part in the earlier Ridolfi plot, which had also aimed to put Mary on the throne.[213] Even catholics whose religion took a more quietist turn might become spreaders of sedition once they had left the university. Nicholas Bawden, yet another catholic undergraduate from Cornwall, matriculated at Exeter in 1575, but, like his

[210] Anstruther, 210; *John Gerard*, trans. Caraman, 1.
[211] Cf. Bossy, 'The Character of Elizabethan Catholicism', 39–44.
[212] TNA, SP 12/160, fo. 117v.
[213] *Register*, ed. Clark, II. ii. 33; P. Williams, 'Anthony Babington', *ODNB*.

compatriot Roscarrock, left without taking a degree. Back home in Cornwall, and making use of his College education, he converted to catholicism John Hambly, a yeoman from Bawden's village of St Mabyn: a conversion which led Hambly first to give up going to church and eventually to his departure for Rheims, his ordination abroad, his return to England as a missionary priest in 1585, and his execution at Salisbury in 1587.[214] Catholics came to Exeter; but they also returned to their localities with their faith fortified, and well equipped to infect others, as the government would have seen it. The outward ripples of Exeter's catholicism had few natural boundaries.

During this period of rising tension Exeter's reputation as the most catholic college in the university placed it at the centre of the government's apprehensions. The ousting of Rector Neale in 1570 had made no perceptible difference to its catholic complexion. The 1577 return of recusants had revealed catholics at only four colleges—All Souls, Balliol, Queen's, and Exeter—but Exeter stood out as the most prominent of these, with five fellows named and five other members of the College also under suspicion.[215] Many must have gone undetected. Another contemporary source notes 'that in Exeter College, Oxon., of eighty were found but four obedient subjects: all the rest secret or open Roman affectionaries and especially one Savage of that house, a most earnest defender of the pope's bull and excommunication [of the queen]'.[216] Clearly the eighty must have accounted for the bulk of the undergraduate body. Equally catholic, but perhaps less conspicuously so, was Exeter's dependency at Hart Hall. Under its principal, Philip Randell, a fellow of Exeter and a man 'very much suspected', it gained a justifiable reputation as a home for catholics. It was there, for example, that Alexander Briant, a future catholic missionary priest and one of the Forty English Martyrs, studied in 1574 under his catholic tutor Richard Holtby, himself a future Jesuit.[217]

In 1578 the authorities finally took action. A fierce letter from the privy council to the bishop of Exeter denounced the fellows of Exeter as 'very evil and obstinately affected against the present state of religion established in the realm', and the College as 'a great receptacle of divers other persons of very evil disposition, which is very dangerous to be suffered in this time of government'. The council went on to appoint a powerful commission, headed by the vice-chancellor and including six other doctors, who were to visit the College, expel any members found wanting (and this presumably included undergraduates as well as fellows), and reform abuses.[218] When the

[214] 'The Confession of John Hambly, Priest and Martyr, 18 August 1586', *Miscellanea, VII*, CRS, ix (1911), 168; Anstruther, 144; *Register*, ed. Clark, II. ii. 63; Rowse, *Tudor Cornwall*, 355, 358–60.
[215] Ryan, 'Diocesan Returns', 100; Williams, 'State, Church', *HUO*, iii. 413.
[216] J. Strype, *Annals of the Reformation*, new edn. (Oxford, 1824), II. ii. 96–7.
[217] Ryan, 'Diocesan Returns', 100–1; T. Cooper, 'Alexander Briant', *ODNB*.
[218] *Acts of the Privy Council*, new ser., x, 1577–78, 221.

commissioners came to the College on 2 August they were treated hand-somely: wine and beer, apples and pears, sweetmeats 'and other delicacies', were all brought in for their enjoyment. In the event the measures taken by the visitors were limited. John Cornelius, the Cornish catholic elected to a fellowship in 1575, was dismissed and soon afterwards made his way to Rheims; Kenelm Carter and Nicholas Cliff, also fellows, were temporarily suspended; and Carter was replaced as sub-rector by Reginald Bellott, whose subsequent denunciation of the Petrean fellows confirmed his prot-estant credentials. In an action reminiscent of those of the Edwardian commissioners thirty years earlier, the new commissioners ordered the College chapel, where they sat, to be stripped of its screen and rood loft, which had evidently escaped the earlier purges of chapel furnishings; and this was done. They left behind them ordinances and decrees which have unfortunately failed to survive.[219] Writing to Sir John Thynne on 2 Octo-ber, Sir Henry Neville, a prominent Berkshire landowner, MP, and ortho-dox churchman, passed on the news of the recent visitation of the College, 'and never a protestant found in it'. Worse still, only four of its members were 'indifferent', while the rest 'denied the queen to be supreme governor': in effect, a rejection of the oath of supremacy and a blatant declaration of papistical loyalties, too close to treason for the College's comfort.[220]

The most significant reaction to Exeter's hubris followed after the com-missioners' departure, though it was very probably initiated by them. In the same month as Neville's letter, Thomas Glasier replaced Robert Newton as Rector. Newton had been a fellow since 1548, Rector from 1557 to 1560, and Neale's successor as Rector again in 1570. Although he had shown no obvious catholic tendencies, an invitation in 1555 from Sir Thomas Pope, the catholic founder of catholic Trinity College, to become one of Trinity's founding fellows, which Newton first accepted and then declined, had shown where his sympathies lay.[221] He had evidently run Exeter on too loose a rein, to the advantage of its catholics, to find favour with the authorities, and on 4 October 1578 he resigned and left the College. It is unlikely that he did so willingly. On the same day Glasier was admitted to a Petrean fellowship, on the orders of Sir John Petre and in place of Arthur Stratford, one of the catholic Petrean fellows, who may have been a late casualty of the visitation, possibly forced out to create a place for Glasier. Less than three weeks later, on 21 October, Glasier was unanimously elected as Rector (so the College register says) and immediately sworn in.[222] Glasier was a highly respectable figure. A graduate of Christ Church, university proctor in 1570, and doctor of

[219] Reg., 2, 122–3; ECA, A. II. 9, fos. 64–5; Boase (2), 78, xcv.
[220] Longleat House, Thynne Papers, Vol. IV, fo. 192^r; M. Riordan, 'Privy Chamber of Henry VIII', *ODNB*.
[221] Boase (2), 65; Hopkins, *Trinity*, 21–2.   [222] Reg., 122–3.

civil law, he was clearly seen as the man to return the College to the protestant fold. That he was fully in tune with at least one aspect of liberal protestant thinking was shown by his marriage to the daughter of an Oxford alderman in 1579. He thus became the first married Rector of the College.[223]

The manner of Glasier's election, however, caused a scandal. He had in effect been intruded into office by Sir John Petre, acting no doubt on directions from the government. Under the statutes the Rector had to be chosen from among the fellows, and Petre's powers of nomination gave him the opportunity to place his man in the fellowship as a necessary preliminary to his election to the Rectorship. Much was made of these questionable tactics in the appeal of Reginald Bellott and his friends in 1583. Writing to Walsingham, they accused Sir John of having acted ultra vires in permitting two of his probationary fellows to have a voice in Glasier's election to the rectorship, when the statutes specifically excluded probationers from voting in elections. In so doing, Petre had helped to secure the election of a man 'to all us not a month before a mere stranger'.[224] Sir John's behaviour was the real nub of Bellott's grievance: one can sense the indignation in his voice. But to those behind Glasier's election, who may well have included Walsingham himself, the disgruntlement of a few fellows was a small price to pay for a safely protestant college.

The commission of 1578 and the election of Thomas Glasier did indeed mark the beginning of the end for catholicism at Exeter. The succession of catholics among the fellows faded, and in the 1580s there is no record of any who took refuge on the Continent, sought ordination to the catholic priesthood, or joined the Jesuits—in strong contrast to the 1570s. The stricter regulation of undergraduates may have helped to turn the university and the College in a more firmly protestant direction: from 1580 all were bound on oath to recognize the royal supremacy and from 1581 to subscribe in addition to the Thirty-Nine Articles. At the same time tutors suspected of 'popery' were banned from retaining pupils unless they were able to purge themselves from the charge.[225] In Exeter's case the *coup de grâce* to any lingering traces of catholicism was given by the election of Thomas Holland in 1592. Holland was a much weightier figure than Glasier. A former chaplain-fellow of Balliol, doctor of theology, regius professor of theology from 1589, and a first-rate scholar, he was one of those later chosen to translate for what became the Authorized Version of the Bible. He was also, and more significantly, a loyal evangelical protestant and an enemy to catholicism, whose 'common farewell to the fellows of his College when he took any

---

[223] Boase (2), 80; Hammer, 'Oxford Town', *HUO*, iii. 113; Newman, 'New Building and Adaptation', *HUO*, iii. 627.
[224] TNA, SP 12/160, fo. 117.
[225] *SA*, 421–2; McConica, 'Rise of the Undergraduate College', *HUO*, iii. 50–1.

longer journey was this...I commend you to the love of God and to the hatred of all popery and superstition'.[226] It was Holland who set the College on the protestant-Calvinist course which was to characterize its development in the early seventeenth century.

Holland's election was as equivocal as that of Glasier and was managed in an almost precisely similar way. Glasier died on 9 March 1592. Almost immediately, on 24 March, Holland was nominated to a Petrean fellowship by Sir John Petre, with a peremptory and highhanded demand that he be exempted from the usual probationary year. On the same day the fellows met to elect a new Rector in place of Glasier. There was an internal candidate, Nicholas Mercer, but the election was put on hold by the reception of a superbly imperious letter from the queen with her 'express recommendation' that Holland, 'a grave, wise and very learned man', be elected. Objections to Holland, she said (and some had clearly been voiced), were 'merely frivolous'. The queen was hardly to be denied. In the case of Glasier's election, queen and council had concealed their hand. In the case of Holland's, it was plainly and forcefully displayed. The result was that Mercer's claim was dismissed and on 24 April Holland was elected as Rector.[227] There was a certain irony in the fact that a committed catholic, Sir John Petre, had been the instrument by which two protestant rectors came to be elected, and a further irony in the opposition of the protestant Reginald Bellott to Petre's nomination of one of those protestant rectors. But it was through these convolutions that a new chapter began in the College's history.

7. THE RELIGION OF THE PETRES

One final question remains: how far was Exeter's role as the university's leading catholic college between 1566 and 1578 shaped by the religious convictions of the two Petres, Sir William and Sir John? About Sir William's personal religion historians have sometimes been reluctant to speculate. 'Nothing he said, nothing others said of him, justifies any categorical statement as to his faith,' writes his biographer.[228] Given Petre's dutiful service to four monarchs with very different religious views, and throughout the period of the Reformation, the difficulty of coming to any conclusions about his religious convictions is obvious.

Yet if we take as our guide, not his role in politics, but rather the known allegiances of his immediate family, the religion of this paterfamilias comes sharply into focus. The only contemporary comment comes from the memoirs of Robert Persons, the Jesuit leader and companion of Edmund Campion, who had been in Oxford from 1564 to 1574, for most of the time as

---

[226] Boase (2), 83; J. A. Lowe, 'Thomas Holland', *ODNB*; R. Kilbie, *A Sermon Preached in Maries Church in Oxford March 26. 1612 at the funeral of Thomas Holland* (Oxford, 1613), 18.
[227] Reg., 157–8, where the queen's letter is transcribed verbatim.   [228] Emmison, 291.

chaplain-fellow of Balliol, and who should therefore have been well informed. Writing of Petre's actions under Edward VI, Persons noted his prosecution of the catholic bishops, 'notwithstanding in heart he was an earnest Catholic'.[229] All that we know about the religion of his wife, his children, and their spouses bears this out. Petre's second wife Anne, whom he married in 1542, declared in her will, made shortly before her death in 1582, that she had lived and would die 'a true member and in the unity of the Catholic Church'.[230] In 1570, within their lifetimes, their son John married Mary, daughter of Sir Edward Waldegrave, a prominent Essex catholic who had died in the Tower in 1561 after refusing to accept the Elizabethan religious settlement.[231] Both John's mother and his wife, 'the old Lady Peters' and 'the young Lady Peters', were denounced as papists by a government agent about 1580 and were presented for recusancy in 1581.[232] John himself became the model of a church papist, conforming outwardly, but inwardly dissenting. In a classic statement of the church papist's position, he advised one of his mother's servants 'to go to the church for fashion sake, and in respect to avoid the danger of the law, yet to keep mine own conscience', and not to participate in prayers or communion.[233] In 1561 John's elder sister Catherine married John Talbot of Grafton in Worcestershire, by 1581 'a noted recusant', imprisoned in the Tower in that year and then released into the care of his brother-in-law, Sir John Petre.[234] Catherine's half-sister Dorothy, the child of Sir William's first marriage, and with her husband Nicholas Wadham the founder of Wadham College, was also in her later life suspected of being a recusant and a harbourer of catholic priests.[235]

At the centre of this web of catholic family connections, Sir William Petre himself can hardly have been anything other than catholic in his convictions. His own marriage and the marriages arranged for his children point only in this direction. If Petre's catholicism is acknowledged, a good deal becomes clear about his relations with Exeter College, his reasons for selecting the College as the object of his philanthropy, and his choice of fellows for his new foundation. It is highly likely that Exeter was chosen because by 1564 it was known to be the most catholic College in the university. The survival of its catholic fellows through the royal visitation of 1559 provided a hospitable base for the reception of others. As we have seen, at least seven of the ten

[229] 'The Memoirs of Father Robert Persons', *Miscellanea, II*, CRS, ii (1906), 53; V. Houliston, 'Robert Persons', *ODNB*.
[230] Emmison, 26, 292.
[231] Emmison, 288; A. Weikel, 'Sir Edward Waldegrave', *ODNB*.
[232] D. Mateer, 'William Byrd, John Petre and Oxford Bodleian MS Mus. Sch. E. 423', *Royal Musical Association Research Chronicle*, 29 (1996), 30–1.
[233] Mateer, 'William Byrd, John Petre', 30; Walsham, *Church Papists*, 82.
[234] Emmison, 287; C. S. L. Davies, 'A Woman in the Public Sphere: Dorothy Wadham and the Foundation of Wadham College, Oxford', *EHR*, 118 (2003), 886–7.
[235] Davies, 'A Woman in the Public Sphere', 888–9.

Petrean fellows appointed between 1566 and 1568 are known to have been catholics, and in most cases fervent catholics, who later sought sanctuary and training abroad in the furtherance of their faith. They had surely been nominated by Petre, not only on the stated grounds of their intellectual abilities but on the unstated premise of their known catholicism and the catholicism of their families.

This suggestion is supported by the important and revealing part played in this process by Petre's agents. Chief among them was John Woodward, who opened Petre's negotiations with Exeter in 1564 and from first to last represented him in his dealings with the College. It was Woodward, for example, who was the leading witness to Petre's main conveyance of property to the College in November 1566 and who was the most regular recipient of treats from the College—food, drink, and gifts of gloves.[236] Rector of Ingatestone from 1555 to 1566, Woodward was also Petre's domestic chaplain and tutor to the young John Petre. These were household positions often used to shelter catholics; the catholic and former Petrean fellow Kenelm Carter, later tutor to John Petre's son William, was another case in point. In his will Sir William left Woodward a legacy of £40, a very substantial sum, and the same as that left to the College.[237] Petre's death allowed Woodward to declare his allegiance more openly. By 1577 he had crossed to Douai, and in 1580 and at some later date he was at Rouen, on the first occasion in company with Ralph Sherwin and on the second with John Neale, both former catholic fellows of Exeter. There he was paid some attention by Elizabeth's spies.[238] Woodward's closeness to Petre, his undoubted catholicism, and his leading role in Petre's relations with Exeter, all suggest that he may have played a larger part in choosing the new fellows than the records reveal. Ralph Sherwin was his nephew, and it was to Woodward, his 'dearest uncle', that Sherwin wrote from the Tower on the eve of his execution.[239] If Sherwin was recommended for a fellowship by Woodward, as seems very likely, Woodward may have acted as patron and recommender to other Petrean fellows. At the least we can say that his frequent comings and goings between Ingatestone, London, and Oxford formed one substantial thread in the skein of connections between a catholic benefactor and his catholic college.

Two other threads in that skein may have been important. We have already seen that John Neale's recommendation of Kenelm Carter and John Howlett secured their nomination to two of the original seven Petrean fellowships— catholic students put forward by a catholic Rector. The parallel role played by

---

[236] ECA, M. III. 4; above, 293.
[237] Emmison, 230, 288–9, 291; Foley, 'John Woodward, Marian Priest', 13–15; Mateer, 'William Byrd, John Petre', 22; Bossy, 'The English Catholic Community', 40; above, 300.
[238] Douay Diaries, 121, 362; Foley, 'John Woodward, Marian Priest', 14–15.
[239] B. C. Foley, 'II. John Woodward', Essex Recusant, 4/3 (1962), 92–3.

Dr John Kennall is less clear but not unlikely. Vice-chancellor in 1566, a civil lawyer, like Petre, and very probably a Cornishman, like many of the fellows of Exeter, Kennall had acted as Petre's Oxford contact during the early stages of his dealings with Exeter, reporting on the College's financial state and passing on Petre's directions. Kennall was a reluctant protestant, whose desire to hold on to his many livings had led him to go against his conscience in taking the oath of supremacy in 1559, but who apparently died a catholic in 1592. He was certainly instrumental in drawing Petre's attention to Exeter's poverty and perhaps also to the strength of the College's catholicism: two characteristics likely to appeal to a benevolent catholic patron.[240]

Petre's links with Woodward, Neale, and Kennall help to explain how he was able to identify suitable catholics for nomination to his fellowships. If we were venturesome, we might go further to suggest that his intentions went beyond the mere provision of fellowships for co-religionists. After an initial training at Exeter his fellows may have been expected to go abroad and to seek ordination as catholic priests. One or two pieces of evidence point firmly in this direction. In the supplement to his statutes Petre had laid down that one of his fellows might travel overseas in order to study civil law or medicine at a foreign university for up to four years, during which time he was to be supported from the Petrean endowment.[241] Several of the early Petrean fellows took advantage of this offer to move abroad for purposes very different from those ostensibly envisaged by Petre. In March 1570 John Howlett was given permission by Petre, in instructions conveyed by Woodward, to travel abroad 'for the increase of his learning'. In the next year he is found studying theology at Douai, and in 1574 he was received as a Jesuit.[242] John Bereblock followed the same course: permitted to study abroad by Petre in September 1570, he next surfaces at Bologna in 1578, where he was awaiting ordination.[243] So it was too with Richard Bristow, given permission by Petre to study abroad in September 1570, ordained at Brussels in 1573, and found at Douai later that year.[244] All three had required Petre's specific permission to travel abroad; none ever returned to the College. It seems very likely that Petre was using his statutory provisions for study abroad in order to give these men the opportunity to train for the priesthood. We might go further and speculate that the clause in Petre's supplement permitting travel abroad, a privilege initially confined to the Petrean fellows alone and by implication barring study of the two stated subjects at an English university, had been inserted with just this purpose in mind. Here we may recall not

---

[240] BRUO, 1501-40, 328; Orme, 'The Cornish at Oxford', 70; 'Memoirs of Father Robert Persons', 61; Davies, 'A Woman in the Public Sphere', 887; above, 261-3.

[241] Boase (1), lvi.   [242] Reg., 97; Douay Diaries, 4, 24; Murphy, 'John Howlett'.

[243] Reg., 99; Anstruther, 34.

[244] Reg., 99; Anstruther, 52; Harris, 'Richard Bristow'. Both Anstruther and Harris are incorrect in stating that Bristow left Exeter in 1568 rather than 1570.

only Petre's firm direction in his statutes that the Rector should not be a bishop, but also the statutes' equally anomalous omission of the need for either the Rector or the fellows to take holy orders: a stipulation found in one form or another in the statutes of most of the sixteenth-century colleges. When Bellott and his party referred to the catholic careers of the Petrean fellows 'and never yet any minister in the true church of God', repeating their allegation later,[245] they may have been unwittingly alluding to Petre's deliberate intention to turn aside from the provision of any such protestant ministers.

If Sir William Petre saw his new fellowships, and the endowment which supported them, as offering clever catholics the means to a university education and further progression into the catholic priesthood, his son was much more cautious. Of the five Petrean fellows appointed by Sir John Petre between his father's death in 1572 and the royal visitation of 1578, only one, Arthur Stratford, left his fellowship for Douai, while at least three of those elected on the old foundation, Cory, Cornelius, and Thomas Bruning, were probable or certain catholics.[246] It is striking that when Bellott and his friends accused Sir John Petre of highhanded interference in College affairs and in elections in particular, the names of the catholic 'bad members' among the fellows whom they cited—Bereblock, Howlett, Bristow, Sherwin, Lewknor, and Stratford—were, with the exception of Stratford, all Sir William's appointments and not Sir John's. When Bellott's petition against Sir John came before Walsingham and the privy council, his case was dismissed and Sir John was exonerated.[247] This would hardly have happened had Sir John been open to the charge of promoting catholics.

Catholic though he was, Sir John Petre was very anxious to give no cause for offence and to do nothing which might submit his conduct to public scrutiny. No more than a major landowner, he was not the national figure and trusted servant of the crown that his father had been; and had he become notorious as a supporter of catholics he could not have expected the protection which came from office and public service. One of Sir John's servants said that he was 'very timorous in respect of the law',[248] and this timorousness does much to explain his withdrawal from his father's policies of fostering catholicism at Exeter. It was a line of conduct capped by his willingness to nominate first Thomas Glasier and then Thomas Holland, both committed protestants, to Petrean fellowships, with a view to their immediate election to the rectorship of the College. In the first case he was almost certainly under

[245] TNA, SP 12/160, fos. 116^r, 117^v; above, 282–3.
[246] Boase (2), 77–9; Ryan, 'Diocesan Returns', 100.
[247] TNA, SP 12/160, fos. 116, 117^v; Reg., 140–1.
[248] Anon., 'The Religious Beliefs of the Petres under Elizabeth I', *Essex Recusant*, 3/2 (1961), 64. Cf. Mateer, 'William Byrd, John Petre', 29.

pressure from the government and in the second undoubtedly so. That a catholic patron should have done so much by his appointments to close down Exeter's position as a catholic college was to a degree paradoxical. Sir William Petre's nomination to fellowships built up catholicism at Exeter; his son's nominations largely brought it to an end.

8. SIR WILLIAM PETRE: ACHIEVEMENTS AND MOTIVES

Sir William Petre left an ambiguous legacy to his favoured College. By his commitment and generosity Exeter was reformed, enlarged, and enriched. But by his religious principles the College's catholic reputation was reinforced at a time when catholicism was coming to be increasingly identified with sedition, and by the powers of patronage which he conferred on his son it was opened up to external exploitation in ways which the father had never intended. He was a benefactor whose liberality had some unforeseen consequences and could not be regarded as having been wholly beneficial.

Petre's greatest achievement lay in the charter of incorporation which he obtained for the College from the queen, and the remodelled statutes which followed shortly afterwards. The charter gave the College security and guaranteed its continuance; no small blessing after the great financial crisis of 1562–3 which had threatened its dissolution. The new statutes established the College on a firmer basis, sweeping away many of the outmoded features of Stapeldon's statutes, never fully revised in 250 years. The life tenure and the vicarage of Kidlington which they conferred on the Rector gave the head of the College a new authority, with an income to match. The creation of the offices of dean and lector provided for the teaching of undergraduates, College residents unknown in Stapeldon's day (except for a very few fellow-undergraduates), but now probably an important source of income; while the books which the lector was to expound recognized the growing role of humanistic learning within the university. The new office of sub-rector, and the statutes governing conduct within the College, laid down a new framework for discipline, all the more necessary at a time when undergraduate numbers were rising rapidly. The derivation of the Petrean fellows from the counties in which Petre held land usefully widened the area of the College's recruitment and made it less exclusively a west country College (though it was an incidental irony that the first generation of Petrean fellows, few of them from the conservative and catholic west, made the College more catholic rather than less). In all these ways renewal amounted to modernization. It is unlikely that either internal initiatives or mere evolution would ever have produced the same results. It took an external benefactor, wealthy, powerfully connected, and practised and skilled in business and administration, to bring them about.

These constitutional changes formed a more important part of Petre's legacy than his new endowment. Large and welcome though this was, most of it was earmarked for special purposes. Petre's primary object in providing it was to support his eight new fellows. What remained to the College when all fellowship costs had been met, including small additional allowances for fellows on the old foundation and larger ones for those on the new, was in the nature of left-overs: a mere £11 8s. 1¼d. a year, according to Petre's own calculations.[249] In terms of its corporate income, Exeter remained one of the poorest colleges. Writing to Walsingham in 1583, Bellott asserted that it was 'not meet that Sir John, the son of a benefactor, should require more than any founder in either university', adding ungraciously 'whereas he [William Petre] gave less than hundred pound by the year, but many founders gave v. or x. hundred pounds and some twenty'.[250] He exaggerated the generosity of other founders and slightly underestimated that of Petre. But it was true that Petre's endowment of just over £100 a year could not compare with that of a William of Wykeham in the fourteenth century (£600 p.a. for New College) or even with that of a contemporary founder such as Sir Thomas Pope in Petre's own day (c. £226 p.a. for Trinity).[251] Nor did Petre's endowment stimulate other gifts and legacies: potential benefactors were perhaps deterred by the College's reputation for disloyalty, reflected in the succession of seminary priests and Jesuits which it produced. It was only in the early seventeenth century, when, under the protestant Rector Prideaux, the number of undergraduates burgeoned, the College's international reputation rose, and Prideaux was able to attract some large benefactions, that Exeter could be said to have become even moderately wealthy.

The priority accorded to Petre's new fellows clearly caused tensions within the College. The Petrean fellows were nominated and did not have to undergo the rigours of election; their larger allowances put them above their colleagues on the old foundation; and to them alone was given the opportunity to study abroad, on a continuing income provided by Petre. Some of these anomalies were ended after William Petre's death by the generosity of his son John, who, as we have seen, equalized allowances and offered the opportunity of foreign study to the whole fellowship. That in the first case he had acted only after agitation from the 'old' fellows hints at the discontents produced by Sir William's provisions. And Sir John Petre exacted a price for his own and his father's bounty. If Bellott and his supporters spoke the truth—and their accusations are too circumstantial to be dismissed—Sir John had asserted his authority in a number of unwarrantable and offensive ways. He had claimed to be able to nominate fellows at any time of the year, rather than on the specific midsummer date prescribed in his father's statutes, and to exempt the Petrean fellows from the usual probationary year; he had taken hundred-pound bonds from some of his fellows in order to secure their resignation

[249] Boase (1), lvi; above, 284.   [250] TNA, SP 12/160, fo. 117ᵛ.
[251] VCH Oxfordshire, iii. 155; Hopkins, Trinity, 28.

when he called on them to resign, with the object of influencing their votes at fellowship elections; and he had extended the right to nominate future Petrean fellows to his own heirs, although his father had limited that right to himself and his son, after whose death the right of election was to revert to the College.[252] This last accusation is vouched for by Sir John's own decree, entered in the College's book of statutes, by which he acted in precisely the way alleged by Bellott: he conferred on his heirs male the right to nominate, on the factually correct but thoroughly disingenuous grounds that his father had given him the right to amend the statutes. This piece of highhandedness stored up troubles for the future. They came to a head in 1613, when William Petre, Sir John's eldest son, claimed the right to nominate, and the College had to go to law to defeat him.[253]

It would be wrong to think that, even in their justifiable grievances, Bellott and the six other signatories of his letter represented all fifteen fellows on the old foundation. By most fellows Sir William's generosity was recognized, and his name and memory venerated. His portrait, with its green silk curtain, hung in the hall; his arms were set in the hall windows and on the College sundial, where verses adjoined them; and in 1591–2 the College helped to pay for the repainting of his tomb effigy at Ingatestone (see Plate 22).[254] All that he had done for the College justified these commemorative gestures. Yet it remained true that his work was not seen by the whole fellowship as an unalloyed good. The privy council's dismissive reply to Bellott's submission made the extraordinary charge that Sir William's arms on the College sundial had been defaced and the accompanying verses erased.[255] It was almost certainly Petre's catholic nominations which had elicited this violent response from the College's protestants. Petre's legacy was thus in part one of wrangling, dissent, and ill-will, which lasted beyond his own death. The long-term benefits of his generosity were seen in the steady succession of Petrean fellows, paid for from his endowment, which lasted until the Petrean fellowships were finally wound up by the Reform Commission of 1855.[256] But in the immediate aftermath of his sometimes controversial reforms, the College's eventual gains over the centuries could hardly have been foreseen.

In one of his letters to the College in 1565 Petre had written that he intended to order his new statutes 'as may be most to God's honour, increase of learning, maintenance of honest manners and conversation, and preservation

[252] TNA, SP 12/60, fos. 117–18.
[253] ECA, A. I. 2; Boase (2), cviii. For William Petre's conveyance of powers only to his immediate heir, both to nominate to fellowships and to amend the statutes, see his supplement to the statutes: Boase (1), liv, lvii.
[254] Above, 293; ECA, A. II. 9, fo. 134ᵛ.   [255] Reg., 140–1.
[256] Boase (2), clxxii. The last Petrean fellow was Joseph Chitty, elected in 1852, and later a justice of the high court: Boase (2), 190; J. M. Rigg, 'Joseph Chitty', ODNB.

of such lands as is or shall be hereafter bestowed upon you'.[257] We may take this to be a statement not only about the statutes but about Petre's broader motives in founding the College. His interest in learning and his piety, evident from his words, are well attested by his other activities. The first was seen in his early career as a fellow of All Souls, his book-collecting activities, his detailed regulations for the education and teaching of fellows and undergraduates at Exeter, and in the selection of books in theology and history which he presented to the College. His piety was shown in some of his own reflections. In a letter of 1551 to Cecil about the many who were 'angling' for office in the church, he wrote:

We who talk much of Christ and His Holy Word have, I fear me, used a much contrary way; for we leave fishing for men and fish again in the tempestuous seas of this world for gain and wicked mammon.[258]

It was a more material sign of his piety that he was exceptionally attendant to his charitable obligations, entertaining his tenants on a lavish scale, finding a place at his Christmas table for both the local and the travelling poor, giving generously to those among his servants who were in distress or about to marry, and founding an almshouse for the poor on his manor of Ingatestone.[259] The hospitality which he offered may have been rooted in a particular catholic sensibility,[260] but it was also part of a larger awareness of a more broadly Christian duty. Seen in this light, we do not need to seek an ulterior motive for his promotion of catholics at Exeter. It was rather part and parcel of a wider resolve to advance what he regarded as true religion and what he wrote of as 'God's honour'.

The refoundation of Exeter College was thus the fulfilment of a divinely imposed obligation, already manifested by Petre in many more minor ways. It was another strand 'in the umbilical cord that had joined religion and philanthropy since biblical times'.[261] But, in the same way as most catholic acts of charity, it was also in part salvific, intended, like the foundation of a monastery or a chantry in earlier times, to plead for the donor's salvation—and here we might note that those two other contemporary founders of Oxford colleges, Sir Thomas Pope at Trinity and Sir Thomas White at St John's, were both catholics. When he established his new fellows at Exeter and set up his endowment, Petre was old and ailing, and on the verge of retirement from public affairs.[262] He may well have had

---

[257] Emmison, 281.
[258] Emmison, 96. For the original passage, see Knighton, 'William Petre'.
[259] F. Heal, *Hospitality in Early Modern England* (Oxford, 1990), 75–7; Emmison, 276–8.
[260] Heal, *Hospitality*, 169–73.
[261] M. Feingold, 'Philanthropy, Pomp and Patronage: Historical Reflections upon the Endowment of Culture', *Daedalus*, 116 (1987), 160.
[262] Emmison, 249–56, 261–3.

on his conscience his own appropriation of former monastic lands (and it was largely monastic lands that he returned to Exeter). But perhaps a more pressing sense of guilt stemmed from the various religious tergiversations which had characterized his whole political life. He had shifted with the prevailing winds and had served the crown well; how well had he served the God whom he would shortly meet? We may reasonably believe that his greatest act of charity, the refoundation of Exeter College, was intended as one of expiation, to promote religion and learning in general and the true catholic church in particular. When, in the supplement to his statutes, he asked for the daily prayers of the College, he instructed the Rector and fellows to request God's grace for himself and his family 'that, freed from all offences and not deprived of temporal aid, they may rejoice in your eternal blessedness in the heavens'.[263] It was to Petre's hopes of eternal blessedness, as it had been to Stapeldon's, that the College owed so much.

---

[263] Boase (2), lvi.

5

Conclusion

Continuity and Change

Like all Oxford colleges, Exeter was set on course by its founder's aims and wishes. They were embodied in Bishop Stapeldon's statutes, which governed the College's life and work until they were superseded by Sir William Petre's, almost exactly 250 years later. The statutes determined that Exeter would be an arts-only College, its Rector holding office for a single year, its fellows recruited from the west country, limited to thirteen in number (fifteen after the addition of the two Salisbury fellows in 1355) and receiving fixed commons and allowances, and the whole under the general if distant supervision of Stapeldon's successors, the bishops of Exeter. These leading features of the College's corporate life were subject to some later modification, especially after the statutes' grip had been loosened by Pope Innocent VII in 1405. Stapeldon Hall gradually gave way to Exeter College, some fellows went beyond the basic arts course to read theology, and a few even to study law and medicine, and the allowances for commons were raised. But there was no sharp break with the past, and respect for the statutes remained a guiding principle. The Rector travelled to Exeter to consult the bishop about them in 1556; and when, during the great dearth of 1563, penury compelled the fellows to sanction absences from the College beyond the statutorily permitted term, they voiced their belief that this did not run counter to the spirit of the statutes, nor to their founder's assumed wishes.[1] Even during a crisis, Stapeldon's statutes remained the point of reference against which the actions of the Rector and fellows had to be measured and judged.

There was another, more human, sort of continuity by which the College was sustained. It was one which mitigated the consequences for continuity of the fellows' youthfulness and of the relative brevity of their time at Exeter. It is easy to forget how young most of them were during this early period of the

[1] Above, 203, 251–2.

College's history. Even during the fifteenth century, when fellowships might occasionally be held for fifteen or sixteen years, there can have been very few who were beyond their early thirties, and the average ten-year duration of a fellowship meant that most would have left at the age of only 26 or 27. A fellow's time at Exeter was a brief interval in what was often a much longer life; it provided the means to a career but it did not in itself constitute one. This fairly rapid throughput of fellows detracted from the continuous life of the College. Yet its effects were offset throughout by the contacts which the College maintained with its old members, sometimes extending for many years beyond the termination of their fellowships. Robert Lydford, for example, fellow from 1365 to 1375, and then rector of Lockinge in Berkshire, paid frequent visits to the College until his death in 1412, attended the St Thomas's day feast in 1407, was himself visited at his rectory by the fellows, and made use of medicines sent to him by the College in his ailing old age.[2] Like many other former fellows, he by no means lost contact with his alma mater, nor it with him. With the advent of the sojourners from the early fifteenth century, including alumni now resident in College again for a period of months or even years, some of these irregular contacts were institutionalized and put on a more solid basis.

Old members were important to the College partly because they provided the steady stream of benefactions on which a poor college such as Exeter was necessarily dependent. Lydford himself gave the College 40s. towards the building of a new room, and in his will bequeathed it £12 and a copper pot. From the time of the building of the library in 1383, almost all the College's major building works were largely financed from such donations and legacies rather than from corporate revenues. But links with old members, often via their entertainment in College or by the visits of the fellows to the south-western counties where many had gone on to live and work, must also have served in more concealed ways to sustain the continuity of the College—by, for example, maintaining the flow of anecdotal reminiscence which has always helped to bridge the gap between the generations in Oxford colleges, and by providing the College with a living repository of its history and traditions. When Rector French set down the College customs in 1539, in an attempt to counter 'the insolence of the bachelors', he drew upon the memories of former fellows now 80 years old (so he said) and handed down from still earlier times.[3] Some at least retained their place in the College's own memory, particularly if they had been benefactors, through the obits and other anniversary services which were regularly celebrated for them in the College chapel and which represented a sort of contractual relationship between the living and the dead.

---

[2] Boase (1), 12–13.   [3] Boase (1), 182; Boase (2), lxxiii; above, 188.

The College was thus a community extended in time both by its statutes, by the links between past and present members, and by corporate prayer. In the sixteenth century, however, these and other continuities came under threat and to some extent decayed. Their solvent was the Reformation. External upheavals in the church and internal regulation by the state combined to disrupt the life of the College and its connections with its past. Its very existence was placed in jeopardy in 1545, when the first Chantries Act made the College's dissolution a real possibility. But in the main the breakdown was insidious rather than abrupt, a process rather than an event. Stapeldon's statutes, the backbone of College governance, were not overthrown, but they were overridden by the Edwardian reformers when, in the 1540s, and for the first time in the College's history, elections to the rectorship and to fellowships were determined by external authority.[4] Along with the maintenance of the statutes, the most notable example of continuity had been the regular flow of Exeter graduates into benefices, particularly into those of Devon and Cornwall, maintained since the days of Stapeldon. But this now slowed and dwindled as clerical careers lost their attraction and law and medicine emerged as alternative career paths. In conjunction with rising prices, the College's precarious and uncertain future caused donations too to decline. Very short periods of tenure, often less than four years for the fellows of the 1540s and 1550s, impaired the preservation and transmission of oral traditions, while other more material traditions, most notably the St Thomas's feast, disappeared for ever. The cessation of obits struck a similar blow at the College's past, for their loss carried with it what had been a persisting way of remembering the names and achievements of former fellows and friends. The concurrent liturgical moves from Latin to English in prayers and scriptures, and the stripping of the chapel's catholic furnishings, completed the attempted transformation of the College's religious life.

The Reformation thus brought a partial erasure of Exeter's past and of its collective memory. How much was then known of that past is not clear. The College had no written history beyond what was embodied in its deeds, charters, and statutes; and the occasional errors in one or two of the statements made in Petre's statutes, presumably derived from College sources, suggest that by this time confusion surrounded some crucial episodes in its early development. So, for example, Petre could claim that it was because Stapeldon had been 'prevented by death' that his statutes had been left defective (when they had actually been completed and issued ten years before his death), and that the two Salisbury fellowships had been founded by Edmund Stafford, bishop of Exeter, in 1404 (when they actually resulted

----

[4] Above, 234-5.

from the appropriation of Wittenham in 1355).[5] It was almost certainly to initiate a record of the College's past, partly dependent as its preservation had been on an oral tradition now rapidly waning, that in 1574 Robert Newton, then Rector, and William Wyatt, the sub-rector, compiled the first College benefactors' book, listing benefactors from the times of Stapeldon, together with the names and dates of the fellows, again from the beginning (see Plate 5). In pursuit of this project, they searched the early charters and account rolls, and it was probably they who added to each roll the name of that year's Rector as a sort of archival aid.[6] Their attempts to record and conserve the College's fading history were a minor and more local expression of the much more powerful drive by contemporary Tudor antiquarians and topographers to set down the wider history of their country, and to preserve its relics and antiquities, while this was still possible and in the face of the overwhelming destructiveness brought by the Reformation. If men such as William Lambarde and William Camden were 'bridging a gap between past and present', so too in their own small way were Robert Newton and William Wyatt.[7] They showed an awareness of what was in process of being lost.

A much more substantial change than this miniature example of reactionary innovation, and a more transformative one, lay in the burgeoning presence of undergraduates in the sixteenth-century College. This was an organic development, whose origins lay in the early fifteenth century. There had always been a few undergraduates among the fellows, men on the foundation who drew their commons and allowances from the College, along with their seniors, the bachelors and the *magistri*. But from the second half of the sixteenth century these fellow-undergraduates came to be heavily outnumbered by their unprivileged counterparts, men who paid their way through the College in cash or service. The effects of this rapid expansion in undergraduate numbers elicited no contemporary comment, but are not hard to deduce. We have only to glance at the long inventory of silver plate given to the College by former undergraduates in the seventeenth century to realize the potential for material enrichment which their coming presented.[8] Among them, the *generosi*, sons of the gentry, proved to be especially worth cultivating for their future influence and for the professional skills which they might wield on the College's behalf. It was as an old member and rising lawyer (and Charles I's future attorney general) that William Noye, a Cornish-born *generosus* who had matriculated at Exeter in 1593, gave his services gratis in the court of common pleas in 1614 when the College defeated

[5] PP, 'Articles to be shewed to the Rector and scholars of Exeter college', 4 May 1565; *Statutes*, 21.
[6] ECA, C. II. 11.
[7] Cf. R. W. Southern, 'Aspects of the European Tradition of Historical Writing: 4. The Sense of the Past', *Transactions of the Royal Historical Society*, 5th ser., 23 (1973), 256–63.
[8] Boase (2), 276–83.

William Petre's attempts to nominate to his grandfather's fellowships.[9] These were tangible benefits—and there were others. The education of all such undergraduates, now divided into a hierarchy of commoners, batteiers, and poor scholars which was itself an indication of their rising numbers and wide social range, necessarily meant an expansion in the teaching role of the fellows. Although the growing undergraduate presence introduced (or at least magnified) problems of discipline, evident from the rules laid down in Petre's statutes (no guns in College, etc.), it was in other ways wholly positive. By enlarging the College's functions as a teaching institution, it brought new money both to the College and to individual fellows, while it also extended and thickened Exeter's external contacts, as Noye's example shows. It thus created a broad relationship with an important sector of lay society which had been lacking in the College's earlier days, when its teaching function had been largely confined to the instruction of junior fellows by their seniors. In wider social terms, the College was now providing an education, based both on the mental training promoted by the traditional study of Aristotelian logic and on the newer and more humane study of the classics, which was generally desired. It was seen to provide a practical grounding for future careers, not only in the church but—at opposite ends of the spectrum of status—for school teachers (who often emerged from the class of servitors and poor scholars) and for the gentry governors of the counties.[10] These developments, common though they were to all colleges, enlarged Exeter's role in society to a degree unknown in the middle ages.

The process of change was capped and extended by Sir William Petre's statutes. They marked a distinctive stage in the protracted withering of the medieval College. Although they left in place some of the key features of Stapeldon's statutes, such as the west country recruitment of fellows on the old foundation and the financial responsibilities of the Rector, some of the least satisfactory features of the old statutes were silently done away with. In particular, the replacement of annual Rectors by others holding office for life gave the Rector the authority which he had previously lacked. In conjunction with the Rector's large income from Kidlington, life tenure made the post attractive to distinguished men. It must be doubtful if Thomas Holland, doctor of theology, regius professor of divinity, and Rector from 1592, would have accepted office on the old terms. The simultaneous enlargement of the fellowship from fifteen to twenty-three, the approximate doubling of the endowment, and the charter of incorporation which Petre obtained from the queen, all gave the College both a new status and a new security (though without greatly increasing its surplus income). Equally important were the formal arrangements for

---

[9] *Register*, ed. Clark, II. ii. 195; Boase (2), cviii.
[10] Cf. Stone, 'Size and Composition of the Oxford Student Body', 9–10, 18–28.

undergraduate teaching made through the establishment of new College offices for dean, lector, and graduate teaching assistant. They represented an acknowledgement of the College's corporate responsibilities towards undergraduates, beyond the mere provision of private tuition by the fellows, on which the statutes are silent; and they adapted the College to take account of the social forces which were now amending its form and function.

Petre's reputation as Exeter's second founder is thus well deserved. If Stapeldon was the innovator, Petre was the modernizer. But in one central way his changes were reactionary and produced the opposite effect to that which he had perhaps intended. His appointment of fervent catholics to his new fellowships, most of whom soon went abroad to train as seminary priests or Jesuits, confirmed and strengthened Exeter's reputation as a late bastion of catholicism within the university; while the catholicism of those Petrean fellows who stayed at home, notably Kenelm Carter and James Rainolds, impressed itself on a generation of undergraduate pupils. It was these features of the College, embodied most hubristically in 1578 in the denial by most of its members of the queen's position as supreme governor of the church, which provoked the intervention of the authorities in the same year.[11] With the intrusion of Thomas Glasier as Rector, and still more conclusively with that of the protestant zealot Thomas Holland in 1592, catholic Exeter had come to an end, and so in a sense had the College's 'middle ages'. The way was opened for a new phase in Exeter's development. It was under Rector Holland that John Prideaux, a poor scholar from Devon, matriculated in 1596 and, as Holland's learned and protestant protégé, was elected to a fellowship in 1601; and it was under Prideaux's own long rectorship from 1612 to 1642 that the College was transformed, its site replanned, its hall and chapel rebuilt, its finances fortified by generous benefactions, its undergraduate numbers greatly increased, and its reputation established for the scholarship and learning which reflected Prideaux's own qualities.[12]

None of this could have been foreseen by Petre. Yet his own religious convictions, very different in their confessional stance from those of Holland and Prideaux, had played a large part in bringing this new and respectably protestant college into being. In the case of the appointments of both Glasier and Holland, his catholic son and heir John Petre was the instrument of protestant change. From these developments, full of paradox and involved irony, came a College transformed, and well equipped, as Stapeldon's had been in his day, to meet the needs of the society in which it found itself. 'A state which is without some means of change', wrote Edmund Burke, 'is without the means of its own conservation.' So too with colleges.

---

[11] Above, 304–5.
[12] There is no adequate account of Prideaux's rectorship. But see VCH Oxfordshire, iii. 110, 116–17, and A. Hegarty, 'John Prideaux', ODNB.

Bibliography

MANUSCRIPT SOURCES

Bodleian Library, Oxford
MS Wood D. 2   Anthony Wood's notes on Oxford colleges

British Library, London
MS Harley 5827   Hooker's 'Synopsis Chorographical of Devonshire'

Cornwall Record Office, Truro
Arundel of Lanherne and Trenrice MSS   Stapeldon Deeds

Devon Record Office, Exeter
Chanter Catalogue 12, Parts 1 and 2   Exeter Bishops' Registers, 1456–1504
Chanter Catalogue 13–18   Exeter Bishops' Registers, 1505–70
MS Chanter 732   Exeter College statutes and memoranda

Essex Record Office, Chelmsford
D/DP Q13/1/1   Petre Papers: Sir William Petre's benefactions to Exeter College

Exeter College Archives
A. I. 2   Sir William Petre's Statutes and other Petrean Decrees
A. I. 5   College Register, 1539–1619
A. II. 1   Book of Evidences
A. II. 9   Rectors' Accounts, 1566–1639
C. II. 11   Benefactors' Book
E. V. 2   Library Papers
E. V. 5   Chapel Papers
F. IV. 1   Statutes
K. I. 6   Sir William Petre's Indenture with the College, 1568
L. I. 4   College History Documents
L. II. 9   Bull of Pope Gregory XII
L. III. 10   Members' Personal Affairs
L. V. 3, 4, 7   Early Halls Documents
M. II. 3, 4   Benson Documents
M. II. 7   Clifton Ferry Documents
M. III. 3   Gwinear Documents

M. III. 4   Kidlington Documents
M. IV. 5   Menheniot Documents
N. II. 4, 5   Long Wittenham Documents
RA, 1–254   Rectors' Accounts, 1354–1566

Exeter Cathedral, Dean and Chapter Archives
1176, 1177, 1190, 1191   Documents relating to the appropriation
                                                  of Menheniot, 1478–9
1487, 1496, 1497, 1498, 1946, 2142   Gwinear Documents
  2922, 3498/4
3625   Stapeldon's Statutes for Stapeldon Hall
3777   Dean and Chapter Accounts, 1377–85

Longleat House, Longleat, Warminster, Wilts.
Thynne Papers, Vol. IV, 1573–80   Letter from Sir Henry Neville to
                                                  Sir John Thynne, 2 October 1578

National Archives, Kew
C 1/1217/62   Early Chancery Proceedings
JUST 1/181, 184, 1273   Eyre Rolls
PROB 11/10, 25, 45   Wills
SC 8/14/664, 37/1811, 73/3624, 81/4001   Ancient Petitions
E 315/441   Exchequer, Court of Augmentations,
                                                  Survey of University of Oxford, 1546
SP 12/160   State Papers Domestic, April–May 1583

Oxford University Archives
Hyp/A/5 (Reg. GG)   Chancellor's Register, 1545–1661
Hyp/B/12   Probate Inventories

PRINTED SOURCES

Accounts of the Executors of Richard Bishop of London 1303, and of the Executors of Thomas Bitton Bishop of Exeter 1310, ed. W. H. Hale and H. T. Ellacombe, Camden Soc. (London, 1874).

The Accounts of the Fabric of Exeter Cathedral, 1279–1353. Part 1: *1279–1326*, ed. A. M. Erskine, DCRS, 24 (1981).

Account Rolls of University College, Oxford. Vol. I: *1381/2–1470/1*, ed. R. H. Darwall-Smith, OHS, new ser., xxxix (1999).

Acts of the Privy Council, new ser., x, 1577–8.

'Annales Paulini', in *Chronicles of the Reigns of Edward I and Edward II*, ed. W. Stubbs, 2 vols., RS (London, 1882–3).

The Black Death, trans. and ed. R. Horrox (Manchester, 1994).

Boase, C. W., *Register of the Rectors and Fellows, Scholars, Exhibitioners and Bible Clerks of Exeter College, Oxford* (Oxford, 1879).

——*Registrum Collegii Exoniensis: Register of the Rectors, Fellows and other Members on the Foundation of Exeter College, Oxford*, new edn., OHS, xxvii (1894).

Breviarium ad usum insignis ecclesiae Sarum, ed. and printed C. Chevallon (Paris, 1531).

Brodrick, G. C., *Memorials of Merton College*, OHS, iv (1885).

The Brut, ed. F. D. Brie, vol. I, Early English Text Soc., 131 (1906).

Calendar of Charter Rolls, 1257–1300, HMSO (London, 1906).

Calendar of Entries in the Papal Registers relating to Great Britain and Ireland: Papal Letters. Vol. VI: *1404–15*, ed. J. A. Twemlow, HMSO (London, 1904).

Calendar of Fine Rolls, 1307–19, HMSO (London, 1912).

Calendar of Inquisitions Post Mortem. Vol. II: *Edward I*, HMSO (London, 1906).

Calendar of Memoranda Rolls, 1326–1327, HMSO (London, 1968).

Calendar of Patent Rolls, 1272–81, 1292–1301, 1452–61, 1563–66, 1566–69, HMSO (London, 1895–1964).

A Calendar of the Registers of Llanthony by Gloucester, 1457–66, 1501–25, ed. J. Rhodes, Gloucestershire Record Ser., 15 (2002).

Chronicon de Lanercost, ed. J. Stevenson (Edinburgh, 1839).

'The Confession of John Hambly, Priest and Martyr, 18 August 1586', *Miscellanea, VII*, CRS, ix (1911).

The Cornish Lands of the Arundells of Lanherne, Fourteenth to Sixteenth Centuries, ed. H. S. A. Fox and O. J. Padel, DCRS, 41 (2000).

Councils and Synods. II: *A.D. 1205–1313*, ed. F. M. Powicke and C. R. Cheney, 2 vols. (Oxford, 1964).

Croniques de London, ed. G. J. Aungier, Camden Soc. (London, 1844).

Death and Memory in Medieval Exeter, ed. D. Lepine and N. Orme, DCRS, 47 (2003).

Documents of the Baronial Movement of Reform and Rebellion, 1258–1267, ed. R. F. Treharne and I. J. Sanders (Oxford, 1973).

The Early Rolls of Merton College, ed. J. R. L. Highfield (Oxford, 1964).

Emden, A. B., *A Biographical Register of the University of Oxford to A. D. 1500*, 3 vols. (Oxford, 1957–9).

——*A Biographical Register of the University of Oxford, A.D. 1501 to 1540* (Oxford, 1974).

Emmison, F. G., *Elizabethan Life: Wills of Essex Gentry and Merchants* (Chelmsford, 1978).

Epistolae academicae, 1508–1596, ed. W. T. Mitchell, OHS, new ser., xxvi (1980).

Exeter Freemen, ed. M. M. Rowe and A. M. Jackson, DCRS, Extra Ser., 1 (1973).

Fehrenbach, R. J., and Leedham-Green, E. S., *Private Libraries in Renaissance England*. Vol. III: *PLRE 67–86* (New York, 1994).

Flores Historiarum, ed. H. R. Luard., 3 vols., RS (London, 1890).

Hegarty, A., *A Biographical Register of St John's College, Oxford, 1555–60*, OHS, new ser., xliii (2011).

Historical Manuscripts Commission, *Report on Manuscripts in Various Collections*, Vol. IV (Dublin, 1907).

Johannis de Trokelowe annales Eduardi II. Henrici Blaneforde chronica, et Eduardi II. Vita, ed. T. Hearne (Oxford, 1729).

John Gerard. The Autobiography of an Elizabethan, trans. P. Caraman, 2nd edn. (London, 1956).

John Lydford's Book, ed. D. M. Owen, DCRS, 20 (1975).

Kilbie, R., *A Sermon Preached in Maries Church in Oxford March 26. 1612 at the funerall of Thomas Holland* (Oxford, 1613).

Knox, T. F., *The First and Second Diaries of the English College, Douay* (London, 1878).

Le Neve, *Fasti Ecclesiae Anglicanae, 1300–1541. IX: Exeter Diocese*, comp. J. M. Horn (London, 1964).

Letters and Papers, Foreign and Domestic, of the Reign of Henry VIII, ed. J. S. Brewer, J. Gairdner, and R. H. Brodie (London, 1862–1932).

'The Memoirs of Father Robert Persons', *Miscellanea, II*, CRS, ii (1906).

Munimenta academica, ed. H. Anstey, 2 vols., RS (London, 1868).

Newington Longeville Charters, ed. H. E. Salter, Oxfordshire Record Soc. (1921).

Nicholas Roscarrock's Lives of the Saints: Cornwall and Devon, ed. N. Orme, DCRS, new ser., 35 (1992).

'Nicolai Fierberti Oxoniensis academiae descriptio', in *Elizabethan Oxford*, ed. C. Plummer, *OHS*, viii (1887).

Oliver, G., *Monasticon Diocesis Exoniensis* (Exeter, 1856).

The Oxford Deeds of Balliol College, ed. H. E. Salter (Oxford, 1913).

Parliamentary Writs and Writs of Military Summons, ed. F. Palgrave, Record Comm., 2 vols. in 4 (London, 1827–34).

The Parliament Rolls of Medieval England, 1275–1504. Vol. III: *Edward II, 1307–1327*, ed. S. Phillips (Woodbridge, 2005).

Place Names of Devon, ed. J. E. B. Gover, A. Mawer, and F. M. Stenton, 2 vols. (Cambridge, 1931–2).

Queen Elizabeth's Book of Oxford, ed. L. Durning (Oxford, 2006).

The Red Book of the Exchequer, ed. H. Hall, 3 vols., RS (London, 1896).

The Register of Congregation, 1448–1463, ed. W. A. Pantin and W. T. Mitchell, OHS, new ser., xxii (1972).

Register of Congregation, 1505–17, ed. W. T. Mitchell, 2 vols., OHS, new ser., xxxvii–xxxviii (1998).

The Register of Edmund Lacy, Bishop of Exeter, 1420–1455, ed. G. R. Dunstan, 5 vols., DCRS, new ser., 7, 10, 13, 16, 18 (1963–72).

The Register of Edmund Stafford (AD. 1395–1419): An Index and Abstract of its Contents, ed. F. C. Hingeston-Randolph (London, 1886).

The Register of John de Grandisson, Bishop of Exeter (AD. 1327–1369), ed. F. C. Hingeston-Randolph, 3 vols. (London, 1894–9).

The Register of Thomas de Brantyngham, Bishop of Exeter (AD. 1370–1394), ed. F. C. Hingeston-Randolph, 2 vols. (London, 1901–6).

Register of the University of Oxford. Vol. I: *1449–63, 1505–71*, ed. C. W. Boase, OHS, I (1885).

Register of the University of Oxford. Vol. II, parts 1–4: *1571–1622*, ed. A. Clark, OHS, x–xii, xiv (1887–9).

The Register of Walter Bronescombe (A.D. 1257–80) and Peter Quivil (AD. 1280–91), ed. F. C. Hingeston-Randolph (London, 1889).

The Register of Walter de Stapeldon, Bishop of Exeter (AD. 1307–1326), ed. F. C. Hingeston-Randolph (London, 1892).

The Registers of Roger Martival, Bishop of Salisbury, 1315–1330, ed. K. Edwards, C. R. Elrington, and S. Reynolds, 4 vols., Canterbury and York Soc. (1959–72).

Registrum annalium Collegii Mertoniensis, 1567–1603, ed. J. M. Fletcher, OHS, new ser., xxiv (1974).

Registrum Cancellarii Oxoniensis, 1434–1469, ed. H. E. Salter, 2 vols., OHS, xciii–xciv (1932).

Ryan, P., 'Diocesan Returns of Recusants for England and Wales, 1577', *Miscellanea, XII*, CRS, xxii (1921).

Salter, H. E., and Pantin, W. A., *Survey of Oxford*, 2 vols., OHS, new ser., xiv, xx (Oxford, 1960–9).

Selections from the Records of the City of Oxford, 1509–1583, ed. W. H. Turner (Oxford, 1880).

Shadwell, C. L., and Salter, H. E., *Oriel College Records* (Oxford, 1926).

Snappe's Formulary and Other Records, ed. H. E. Salter, OHS, lxxx (1924).

Statuta Antiqua Universitatis Oxoniensis, ed. S. Gibson (Oxford, 1931).

The Statutes of Exeter College, Oxford (London, 1855).

Statutes of the Colleges of Oxford, 3 vols. (London, 1853).

Statutes of Trinity College, Oxford (London, 1855).

Taxatio Ecclesiastica Papae Nicholai IV, Record Comm. (London, 1802).

Thomas of Walsingham, *Historia Anglicana*, ed. H. T. Riley, 2 vols., RS (London, 1863–4).

Thomson, R. M., *A Descriptive Catalogue of the Medieval Manuscripts of Merton College, Oxford* (Woodbridge, 2009).

Thorold Rogers, J. E., *A History of Agriculture and Prices in England.* Vol. I: *1259–1400* (Oxford, 1866).

Valor ecclesiasticus. Vol. II, Record Comm. (London, 1814).

The Visitations of the County of Oxford, 1566, 1574, 1634, ed. W. H. Turner, Harleian Soc., 5 (London, 1871).

The Visitation of the County of Devon in the Year 1564, ed. F. T. Colby (Exeter, 1881).

Vita Edwardi Secundi, ed. and trans. W. R. Childs (Oxford, 2005).

Vivian, J. L., *The Visitations of the County of Devon: Comprising the Heralds' Visitations of 1531, 1564 and 1620* (Exeter, 1889–95).

Watson, A. G., *A Descriptive Catalogue of the Medieval Manuscripts of Exeter College, Oxford* (Oxford, 2000).

William of Worcester, *Itineraries*, ed. J. H. Harvey (Oxford, 1969).

SECONDARY SOURCES

Anon., 'The Religious Beliefs of the Petres under Elizabeth I', *Essex Recusant*, 3/2 (1961).

Anstruther, G., *The Seminary Priests*. Vol. I: *Elizabethan* (Durham, 1968).

Aston, T. H., 'Oxford's Medieval Alumni', *Past and Present*, 74 (1977).

——and Faith, R., 'The Endowments of the University and Colleges to *circa* 1548', in *HUO*, i.

Aylmer, G. E., 'The Economics and Finances of the Colleges and University, *c.*1530–1640', in *HUO*, iii.

Baker, J. H., 'John Whiddon', *ODNB*.

Bartlett, K. R., 'Edmund Tremayne', *ODNB*.

Barton, J. L. 'The Study of Civil Law before 1380', in *HUO*, i.

——'The Faculty of Law', in *HUO*, iii.

Bindoff, S. T., *The House of Commons, 1509–1558*, 3 vols. (London, 1982).

Blair, J., *The Medieval Clergy of Bampton*, Bampton Research Paper 4 (Oxford, 1991).

Bolton, J. L., *Money in the Medieval English Economy, 973–1489* (Manchester, 2012).

Bossy, J., 'The Character of Elizabethan Catholicism', *Past and Present*, 21 (1962).

Bowden, P., 'Agricultural Prices, Farm Profits and Rents', in *Agrarian History*, iv.

Boyle, L. E., 'Canon Law before 1380', in *HUO*, i.

——'The Constitution "Cum ex eo" of Boniface VIII', in his *Pastoral Care, Clerical Education and Canon Law, 1200–1400* (London, 1981).

Brigden, S., 'Youth and the English Reformation', *Past and Present*, 95 (1982).

Briggs, N., 'William, 2nd Lord Petre (1575–1637)', *Essex Recusant*, 10/2 (1968).

Britton, C. E., *A Meteorological Chronology to AD. 1450* (London, 1937).

Brockliss, L. W. (ed.), *Magdalen College: A History* (Oxford, 2008).

Buck, M., *Politics, Finance and the Church in the Reign of Edward II: Walter Stapeldon, Treasurer of England* (Cambridge, 1983).

——'The Reform of the Exchequer, 1316–1326', *EHR*, 108 (1983).

Butcher, A. F., 'The Economy of Exeter College, 1400–1500', *Oxoniensia*, 44 (1979).

Buxton, J., and Williams, P. (eds.), *New College, Oxford, 1379–1979* (Oxford, 1979).

Caldwell, J., 'Music in the Faculty of Arts', in *HUO*, iii.

Carlson, E. J., 'Clerical Marriage and the English Reformation', *Jnl. of British Studies*, 31 (1992).

Catto, J. I., 'Citizens, Scholars and Masters', in *HUO*, i.

——'Theology and Theologians, 1220–1330', in *HUO*, i.

——'Wyclif and Wycliffism at Oxford, 1356–1430', in *HUO*, ii.

——'Conclusion: Scholars and Studies in Renaissance Oxford', in *HUO*, iii.

——'Robert Rygge', *ODNB*.

——'A Radical Preacher's Handbook, *c.*1383', *EHR*, 115 (2000).

——'The Triumph of the Hall in Fifteenth-Century Oxford', in R. Evans (ed.), *Lordship and Learning: Studies in Memory of Trevor Aston* (Woodbridge, 2004).

Challis, C. E. (ed.), *A New History of the Royal Mint* (Cambridge, 1992).

Chaplais, P., *English Diplomatic Practice in the Middle Ages* (London, 2003).

Cheney, C. R., *Hubert Walter* (London, 1967).

Cherry, B., and Pevsner, N., *The Buildings of England: Devon*, 2nd edn. (London, 1989).

Chope, R. P., *The Book of Hartland* (Torquay, 1940).

Cobban, A. B., 'Colleges and Halls, 1380–1500', in *HUO*, ii.

——*The King's Hall within the University of Cambridge in the Later Middle Ages* (Cambridge, 1969).

——'Decentralized Teaching in the Medieval English Universities', *History of Education*, 5 (1976).

——*The Medieval English Universities: Oxford and Cambridge to c.1500* (Aldershot, 1988).

——'John Arundel, the Tutorial System, and the Cost of Undergraduate Living in the Medieval English Universities', *Bulletin of the John Rylands University Library*, 77 (1995).

——*English University Life in the Middle Ages* (London, 1999).

Connor, A. B., *Memorial Brasses in Somerset*, reprint (Bath, 1970).

Cooper, T., 'Alexander Briant', *ODNB*.

Courtenay, W. J., 'Theology and Theologians from Ockham to Wyclif', in *HUO*, ii.

Courtney, W. P., rev. J. R. Maddicott, 'Charles William Boase', *ODNB*.

Crook, J. M., *Brasenose: The Biography of an Oxford College* (Oxford, 2008).

Cross, C., 'The English Universities, 1553–58', in E. Duffy and D. Loades (eds.), *The Church of Mary Tudor* (Aldershot, 2006).

——'Oxford and the Tudor State from the Accession of Henry VIII to the Death of Mary', in *HUO*, iii.

——'John Piers', *ODNB*.

Cuttino, G. P., *English Diplomatic Administration, 1259–1339*, 2nd edn. (Oxford, 1971).

Darwall-Smith, R., *A History of University College, Oxford* (Oxford, 2008).

Davies, C. S. L., 'A Woman in the Public Sphere: Dorothy Wadham and the Foundation of Wadham College, Oxford', *EHR*, 118 (2003).

Duffy, E, *The Stripping of the Altars: Traditional Religion in England, c.1400–c.1580* (New Haven, 1992).

——'William Allen', *ODNB*.

Dunbabin, J., 'Careers and Vocations', in *HUO*, i.

Duncan, G. D., 'Heads of Houses and Religious Change in Tudor Oxford', *Oxoniensia*, 45 (1980).

——'Public Lectures and Professorial Chairs', in *HUO*, iii.

——'The Property of Balliol College, c.1500–1640', in *HUO*, iii.

Edwards, A. C., *John Petre: Essays on the Life and Background of John, 1st Lord Petre, 1549–1613* (London, 1973).

Edwards, K., 'Bishops and Learning in the Reign of Edward II', *Church Quarterly Review*, 138 (1944).

Emden, A. B., *An Oxford Hall in Medieval Times* (Oxford, 1927).

——'The Remuneration of the Medieval Proctors of the University of Oxford', *Oxoniensia*, 26–7 (1961–2).

Emmison, F. G., *Tudor Secretary: Sir William Petre at Court and Home* (London, 1961).

Evans, T. A. R., 'The Number, Origins and Careers of Scholars', in *HUO*, ii.

——and Faith, R. J., 'College Estates and University Finances, 1350–1500', in *HUO*, ii.

Exeter Cathedral: A Celebration, ed. M. Swanton (Exeter, 1991).

Farmer, D. L., 'Prices and Wages, 1350–1500', in *Agrarian History*, iii.

Feingold, M., 'John Rainolds [Reynolds]', *ODNB*.

——'Philanthropy, Pomp and Patronage: Historical Reflections upon the Endowment of Culture', *Daedalus*, 116 (1987).

Fletcher, J. M., 'The Faculty of Arts', in *HUO*, i.

——'Developments in the Faculty of Arts, 1370–1520', in *HUO*, ii.

——'The Faculty of Arts', in *HUO*, iii.

——'The Organisation of the Supply of Food and Drink to the Medieval Oxford Colleges', in A. Romano (ed.), *Università in Europa: Le isitutione universitarie dal Medio Evo ai nostri giorni: strutture, organizzazione, funzionamento* (Rubbetino, 1995).

——and Upton, C. A., 'Destruction, Repair and Removal: An Oxford College Chapel during the Reformation', *Oxoniensia*, 48 (1983).

————'Expenses at Admission and Determination in Fifteenth-Century Oxford: New Evidence', *EHR*, 100 (1985).

Foley, B. C., 'John Woodward, Marian Priest, 1530?–1597/8?', *Essex Recusant*, 4/1 (1962).

——'II: John Woodward', *Essex Recusant*, 4/3 (1962).

Fowler, D. C., 'John Trevisa and the English Bible', *Modern Philology*, 58 (1960).

Fox, H., 'Medieval Farming and Rural Settlement', in R. Kain and W. Ravenhill, *Historical Atlas of South-West England* (Exeter, 1999).

——'Taxation and Settlement in Rural Devon', *Thirteenth Century England*, 10 (2005).

——'The Occupation of the Land: Devon and Cornwall', in *Agrarian History*, ii.

Fryde, E. B., 'The Deposits of Hugh Despenser the Younger with Italian Bankers', in his *Studies in Medieval Trade and Finance* (London, 1983).

Fryde, N. B., *The Tyranny and Fall of Edward II, 1321–26* (Cambridge, 1979).

Garrett, C. H., *The Marian Exiles* (Cambridge, 1938).

Gee, E. A., 'Oxford Masons, 1370–1530', *Archaeological Jnl.*, 109 (1952).

Gillam, S., *The Divinity School and Duke Humfrey's Library at Oxford* (Oxford, 1988).

Gorski, R., *The Fourteenth-Century Sheriff* (Woodbridge, 2003).

Green, V. H. H., *The Commonwealth of Lincoln College, 1427–1977* (Oxford, 1979).

Greenslade, S. L., 'The Faculty of Theology', in *HUO*, iii.

Habbakuk, H. J., 'The Market for Monastic Property, 1539–1603', *Economic History Review*, 2nd ser., 10 (1957–8).

Hackett, M. B., 'The University as a Corporate Body', in *HUO*, i.

Hamilton, J. A., rev. D. Ibbetson, 'William Peryam', *ODNB*.

Hammer, C. I., Jr., 'Oxford Town and Oxford University', in *HUO*, iii.

Harris, P. E. B., 'Richard Bristow', *ODNB*.

Harrison, C. J., 'Grain Price Analysis and Harvest Qualities, 1465–1534', *Agricultural History Review*, 19 (1971).

Harvey, J. H., 'Architecture in Oxford, 1300–1500', in *HUO*, ii.

Hatcher, J., *Rural Economy and Society in the Duchy of Cornwall, 1300–1500* (Cambridge, 1970).

——'The Great Slump of the Mid-Fifteenth Century', in R. Britnell and J. Hatcher (eds.), *Progress and Problems in Medieval England: Essays in Honour of Edward Miller* (Cambridge, 1996).

Hayes, R. C. E., 'John Hals', *ODNB*.

Heal, F., 'Richard Cox', *ODNB*.

——*Hospitality in Early Modern England* (Oxford, 1990).

Hegarty, A., 'John Prideaux', *ODNB*.

Henderson, C., 'The 109 Ancient Parishes of the Western Hundreds of Cornwall', *JRIC*, new ser., ii, pt. 4 (1956).

Highfield, J. R. L., 'The Early Colleges', in *HUO*, i.

Hodgkin, R. H., *Six Centuries of an Oxford College: A History of the Queen's College, 1340–1940* (Oxford, 1949).

Hopkins, C., *Trinity: 450 Years of an Oxford College Community* (Oxford, 2005).

Horrox, R., 'Peter Courtenay', *ODNB*.

Hoskins, W. G., *Devon* (London, 1954).

——'Harvest Fluctuations and English Economic History, 1480–1619', *Agricultural History Review*, 12 (1964).

Houliston, V., 'Robert Persons', *ODNB*.

Hudson, A., *The Premature Reformation* (Oxford, 1988).

——'Wyclif's Books', in L. Clark, M. Jurkowski, and C. Richmond, *Image, Text and Church, 1380–1600: Essays for Margaret Aston* (Toronto, 2009).

——'Wycliffites (active c.1370–1420)', *ODNB*.

Jones, J., *Balliol College: A History*, 2nd edn. (Oxford, 1997).

Jones, M., *The Family of Dinan in England in the Middle Ages* (Dinan, 1987).

Keen, M., *England in the Later Middle Ages*, 2nd edn. (London, 2003).

Kelly, J. N. D., *The Oxford Dictionary of Popes* (Oxford, 1986).

Ker, N. R., 'Oxford College Libraries before 1500', in his *Books, Collectors and Libraries: Studies in the Medieval Heritage*, ed. A. G. Watson (London, 1964).

Ker, N. R., 'The Provision of Books', in *HUO*, iii.

—— 'Oxford College Libraries in the Sixteenth Century', in his *Books, Collectors and Libraries: Studies in the Medieval Heritage*, ed. A. G. Watson (London, 1964).

—— 'Chaining from a Staple on the Back Cover', in his *Books, Collectors and Libraries: Studies in the Medieval Heritage*, ed. A. G. Watson (London, 1964).

Kingsford, C. L., 'Historical Notes on Medieval London Houses', *London Topographical Record*, 10 (1916).

Knighton, C. S., 'John Moreman', *ODNB*.

—— 'William Petre', *ODNB*.

Knowles, D., *The Religious Orders in England*. III: *The Tudor Age* (Cambridge, 1959).

Lamborn, E. A. G., *The Armorial Glass of the Oxford Diocese, 1250–1850* (Oxford, 1949).

Lawrence, C. H., 'The University in Church and State', in *HUO*, i.

Lepine, D. N., 'The Origins and Careers of the Canons of Exeter Cathedral, 1300–1455', in C. Harper-Bill (ed.), *Religious Belief and Ecclesiastical Careers in Later Medieval England* (Woodbridge, 1991).

—— 'Cathedrals and Charity: Almsgiving at English Secular Cathedrals in the Later Middle Ages', *EHR*, 126 (2011).

Lewis, G., 'The Faculty of Medicine', in *HUO*, iii.

Lewry, P. O., 'Grammar, Logic and Rhetoric, 1220–1320', in *HUO*, i.

Little, A. G., and Easterling, R. C., *The Franciscans and Dominicans of Exeter* (Exeter, 1927).

Loach, J., 'Reformation Controversies', in *HUO*, iii.

Logan, F. D., 'The First Royal Visitation of the English Universities, 1535', *EHR*, 106 (1991).

Lowe, J. A., 'Thomas Holland', *ODNB*.

MacCaffrey, W. T., *Exeter, 1540–1640* (Cambridge, Mass., 1958).

McConica, J., 'Humanism and Aristotle in Tudor Oxford', *EHR*, 94 (1979).

—— 'The Rise of the Undergraduate College', in *HUO*, iii.

—— 'Studies and Faculties: Introduction', in *HUO*, iii.

—— 'Elizabethan Oxford: The Collegiate Society', in *HUO*, iii.

McCoog, T. M., 'John Cornelius', *ODNB*.

—— 'John Gerard', *ODNB*.

MacCulloch, D., *Tudor Church Militant: Edward VI and the Protestant Reformation* (London, 1999).

Maddicott, J., 'College Servants', *Exeter College Association Register*, 2006.

Magrath, J. R., *The Queen's College*, 2 vols. (Oxford, 1921).

Martin, G. H., and Highfield, J. R. L., *A History of Merton College* (Oxford, 1997).

Mateer, D., 'William Byrd, John Petre and Oxford Bodleian MS Mus. Sch. E. 423', *Royal Musical Association Research Chronicle*, 29 (1996).

Murphy, G. M., 'John Howlett', *ODNB*.

Newman, J., 'The Physical Setting: New Building and Adaptation', in *HUO*, iii.

O'Day, R., 'The Reformation of the Ministry, 1558–1642', in R. O'Day and F. Heal, *Continuity and Change: Personnel and Administration of the Church in England, 1500–1642* (Leicester, 1976).

Oliver, G., *Lives of the Bishops of Exeter* (Exeter, 1861).

Orme, N., *Education in the West of England, 1066–1548* (Exeter, 1976).

—— 'The Church of Crediton from St Boniface to the Reformation', in T. Reuter (ed.), *The Greatest Englishman: Essays on St Boniface and the Church at Crediton* (Exeter, 1980).

—— 'The Byconyll Exhibitions at Oxford, 1502–1664', *Oxoniensia*, 55 (1990).

—— 'The Charnel Chapel of Exeter Cathedral', in F. Kelly (ed.), *Medieval Art and Architecture at Exeter Cathedral* (London, 1991).

—— 'William Elyot, a Fifteenth Century Registrar, and his Books', *Archives*, 26 (2001).

—— *Medieval Schools from Roman Britain to Renaissance England* (New Haven, 2006).

—— *Exeter Cathedral: The First Thousand Years, 400–1500* (Exeter, 2009).

—— 'The Cornish at Oxford', *JRIC* (2010).

—— 'Hugh Oldham', *ODNB*.

—— 'Thomas Bitton', *ODNB*.

Ormrod, W. M., 'Agenda for Legislation, 1322–c.1340', *EHR*, 105 (1990).

—— *Edward III* (New Haven, 2011).

—— and Lindley, P. G., *The Black Death in England* (Stamford, 1996).

Outhwaite, R. B., *Inflation in Tudor and Stuart England* (London, 1969).

Page, M., 'The Ownership of Advowsons in Thirteenth-Century Cornwall', *Devon and Cornwall Notes and Queries*, 37 (1992–6).

Pantin, W. A., *Oxford Life in Oxford Archives* (Oxford, 1972).

Parkes, M. B., 'The Provision of Books', in *HUO*, ii.

Phelps Brown, E. H., and Hopkins, S. V., 'Seven Centuries of Building Wages', in E. M. Carus-Wilson (ed.), *Essays in Economic History*, Vol. II (London, 1962).

———— 'Seven Centuries of the Prices of Consumables Compared with Builders' Wage Rates', in E. M. Carus-Wilson (ed.), *Essays in Economic History*, Vol. II (London, 1962).

Phillips, J. R. S., *Aymer de Valence, Earl of Pembroke, 1307–1324* (Oxford, 1972).

Postles, D., *The Surnames of Devon* (Oxford, 1995).

Powicke, F. M., *The Medieval Books of Merton College, Oxford* (Oxford, 1931).

Prestwich, M., *Plantagenet England, 1225–1360* (Oxford, 2005).

Prince, J., *Danmonii orientales illustres: The Worthies of Devon*, new edn. (London, 1810).

Rigg, J. M., 'Joseph Chitty', *ODNB*.

Riordan, M., 'Privy Chamber of Henry VIII', *ODNB*.

Roskell, J. S., Clarke, L., and Rawcliffe, C., *The History of Parliament: The House of Commons, 1386–1421*, 4 vols. (Stroud, 1992).

Rowse, A. L., *Tudor Cornwall* (London, 1941).

Russell, E., 'The Influx of Commoners into the University of Oxford before 1581: An Optical Illusion?', *EHR*, 92 (1977).

——'Marian Oxford and the Counter Reformation', in C. M. Barron and C. Harper-Bill (eds.), *The Church in Pre-Reformation Society: Essays in Honour of F. R. H. Du Boulay* (Woodbridge, 1985).

Salter, H. E., *Medieval Oxford*, OHS, c (1936).

Saul, N., 'The Pre-history of an Oxford College: Hart Hall and its Neighbours in the Middle Ages', *Oxoniensia*, 54 (1989).

——*English Church Monuments in the Middle Ages* (Oxford, 2009).

Seymour, D., *Torre Abbey* (Exeter, 1977).

Shaw, C. C., *A History of the Parish of Aveton Giffard* (Kingsbridge, c.1966).

Sherlock, P., 'John Skewys', *ODNB*.

Sherwood, J., and Pevsner, N., *The Buildings of England: Oxfordshire* (Harmondsworth, 1974).

Shrewsbury, J. F. D., *A History of Bubonic Plague in the British Isles* (Cambridge, 1971).

Slack, P., *The Impact of Plague in Tudor and Stuart England* (London, 1985).

Smith, D. M., *Guide to Bishops' Registers of England and Wales* (London, 1981).

Southern, A. C., *Elizabethan Recusant Prose, 1559–1582* (London, 1950).

Southern, R. W., 'Aspects of the European Tradition of Historical Writing: 4. The Sense of the Past', *Transactions of the Royal Historical Society*, 5th ser., 23 (1973).

Spufford, P., *Money and its Use in Medieval Europe* (Cambridge, 1988).

Steggle, M., 'Thomas Fortescue', *ODNB*.

Stevenson, W. H., and Salter, H. E., *The Early History of St John's College, Oxford*, OHS, new ser., I (1939).

Stone, L., *The Crisis of the Aristocracy, 1558–1641* (Oxford, 1965).

——'The Size and Composition of the Oxford Student Body, 1580–1910', in L. Stone (ed.), *The University and Society. Vol. I: Oxford and Cambridge from the 14th to the Early 19th Century* (London, 1974).

Strype, J., *Annals of the Reformation*, Vol II, part ii (Oxford, 1824).

Swanson, R. N., 'Universities, Graduates and Benefices in Later Medieval England', *Past and Present*, 106 (1985).

Taylor, T., 'Bevile of Drennick and Woolston', *JRIC*, 17 (1907–8).

Thomson, R., 'William Reed, Bishop of Chichester (d. 1385)—Bibliophile?', in G. H. Brown and L. E. Voigts (eds.), *The Study of Medieval Manuscripts: Festschrift in Honor of Richard W. Pfaff* (Tempe, Ariz., 2010).

Victoria County History of Oxfordshire. Vol. III: The University of Oxford, ed. H. E. Salter and M. D. Lobel (Oxford, 1954).

Victoria County History of Oxfordshire. Vol. IV: The City of Oxford, ed. A. Crossley (Oxford, 1979).

Walsham, A., *Church Papists: Catholicism, Conformity and Confessional Polemic in Early Modern England* (Woodbridge, 1999).

Watson, A. G., 'The Post-Medieval Library', in *Unarmed Soldiery: Studies in the Early History of All Souls College, Oxford* (Oxford, 1996).

Weisheipl, J. A., 'Curriculum of the Faculty of Arts at Oxford in the Early Fourteenth Century', *Mediaeval Studies*, 25 (1964).

——'Ockham and the Mertonians', in *HUO*, i.

Whiting, R., *The Reformation of the English Parish Church* (Cambridge, 2010).

Williams, M. E., 'Nicholas Fitzherbert', *ODNB*.

——'Ralph Sherwin', *ODNB*.

Williams, P., 'Elizabethan Oxford: State, Church and University', *HUO*, iii.

——'Anthony Babington', *ODNB*.

Wood, A., *The History and Antiquities of the Colleges and Halls in the University of Oxford*, ed. J. Gutch, 2 vols. (Oxford, 1786–90).

——*The History and Antiquities of the University of Oxford now first published in English by John Gutch*, 3 vols. (Oxford, 1792–6).

——*Athenae Oxonienses*, 3rd edn., with additions by P. Bliss, 4 vols. (London, 1813–20).

——*Survey of the Antiquities of the City of Oxford*. Vol. I: *The City and Suburbs*, ed. A. Clark, OHS, xv (1889).

Wood, S., *English Monasteries and their Patrons in the Thirteenth Century* (Oxford, 1955).

Woolfson, J., 'Richard Croke', *ODNB*.

Youings, J., 'The South-Western Rebellion of 1549', *Southern History*, 1 (1979).

Index

Place-names are identified by reference to the pre-1974 counties. 'Books and authors' are listed under that heading. Authors contemporary with the period under discussion also appear separately. The following abbreviations are used: abp (archbishop); bp (bishop); F (fellow); R (Rector); S (sojourner/senior boarder); U (undergraduate); WP (Sir William Petre); WS (Walter de Stapeldon). Fellows' dates are given in the form '1359–61' when the years of both election/admission and of demission are known; 'c.1359–61', when the fellow was in post in the first year, the particular year of admission is uncertain, but the year of demission is known; and 'c.1359–c.1361', when the fellow is known to have been in post during that period, but the particular years of both election/admission and demission are uncertain. In some sequences of undifferentiated page numbers, the main sources of information are indicated in **bold**.